In the Shadows of Glories Past

The title of this volume implies two things: the greatness of the scientific tradition that Muslims had lost, and the power of the West, in whose threatening shadow reformers now labored to modernize in order to defend themselves against those very powers they were taking as models. Copernicus and Darwin were the names that dominated the debate on science, whose arguments and rebuttals were published mainly in the religious and secular journals in Cairo and Beirut from the 1870s. Analysis and interpretation of this literature shows the hope that Arab reformers had of duplicating the Japanese success, followed by the despair when success was denied.

A cultural malaise festered from generations of despair, defeat and foreign occupation, and this feeling transmogrified after 1967 to a psychosis in a significant number of secular writers, educators and religious reformers. The great debate on assimilating science was turned inward where defensive mechanisms of denial spun out perversions of science: the Quran becoming a thesaurus of science; and a more extreme derivative of that, something called "Islamic Science," arising as an alternate science that was to be in harmony with the Quran, Shari'a and Muslim belief.

This volume reveals the undermining effect of European imperialism on western-oriented religious reformers and secular intellectuals, for whom science and political reform went together, and concludes with a chapter on the state of science in contemporary Muslim societies and the efforts to institutionalize science (before the upheavals of 2011) so as to bring to life an authentic and indigenous culture that would sustain scientific study and research as autonomous pursuits.

John W. Livingston is Associate Professor of History at the William Paterson University of New Jersey, USA.

Cover images: Muhammad Abdus Salam (left side of the 3 images), Pakistani, Nobel Prize winner, 1979, in particle physics; died 1996. Image from the portrait collection of St. John's College, Cambridge University, UK. Ahmed Zewail (middle image), Egyptian, Nobel winner, 1999, in chemistry; died 2016. Image from the portrait collection of the American Chemical Society, Philadelphia. Maryam Mirkhani, Iranian (right image), Field's Medal winner in pure mathematics, 2014; died 2017.

In the Shadows of Glories Past

Jihad for Modern Science in Muslim Societies, 1850 to the Arab Spring

John W. Livingston

LONDON AND NEW YORK

First published 2018
by Routledge
2 Park Square, Milton Park, Abingdon, Oxon OX14 4RN

and by Routledge
711 Third Avenue, New York, NY 10017

Routledge is an imprint of the Taylor & Francis Group, an informa business

© 2018 John W. Livingston

The right of John W. Livingston to be identified as author of this work has been asserted by him in accordance with sections 77 and 78 of the Copyright, Designs and Patents Act 1988.

All rights reserved. No part of this book may be reprinted or reproduced or utilised in any form or by any electronic, mechanical, or other means, now known or hereafter invented, including photocopying and recording, or in any information storage or retrieval system, without permission in writing from the publishers.

Trademark notice: Product or corporate names may be trademarks or registered trademarks, and are used only for identification and explanation without intent to infringe.

British Library Cataloguing-in-Publication Data
A catalogue record for this book is available from the British Library

Library of Congress Cataloging-in-Publication Data
Names: Livingston, John W. (John William), 1932– author.
Title: In the shadows of glories past : jihad for modern science in Muslim societies, 1850 to the Arab Spring / John W. Livingston.
Description: New York : Routledge, 2017. | Includes index.
Identifiers: LCCN 2017019730 | ISBN 9781472447340 (hardback : alk. paper) | ISBN 9781315101491 (ebook)
Subjects: LCSH: Islamic modernism. | Islamic renewal. | Science—Islamic countries—History. | Islam and science—History.
Classification: LCC BP166.14.M63 L58 2017 | DDC 297.2/65—dc23
LC record available at https://lccn.loc.gov/2017019730

ISBN: 978-1-4724-4734-0 (hbk)
ISBN: 978-1-315-10149-1 (ebk)

Typeset in Times New Roman
by Apex CoVantage, LLC

 Printed in the United Kingdom by Henry Ling Limited

I dedicate this book to my long deceased professor and friend, Martin Dickson. Martin was a professor of Persian language and Iranian history, specializing in the Safavid period and Islamic mysticism, at Princeton University, from 1958 to 1991, the year of his death. He was a mentor and inspiration in learning and life, to me and to many other of his students and those who were fortunate enough to become his friend. His memory lives on, carried by his former students who now teach in universities across the country. Like the mystical poets he studied, and emulated, Martin had a knack of turning the prism to see the universe revealed in unexpected lights. It was my good fortune, my best fortune I should say, to have had him as a friend. With him always in mind, I wrote this book.

Contents

List of figures ix
Acknowledgements x

PART I
Copernicus, Darwin and Islamic intellectual reform in Muslim societies during the last half of the 19th century 1

1 The Ottomans: Absolutist state reformers versus Young Ottoman constitutionalists 3

2 Post Muhammad Ali reform in Egypt: Khedive Ismail and Ali Mubarak's *Dar al-Ulum* and *Rawdat al-Madaris* 36

3 Beirut: the American College and the popularization of science 59

4 *Muqtataf*, *Rawdat al-Madaris* and the Fikri treatise on a moving earth 79

5 Darwin between *Muqtataf* and the American evangelists 114

6 From Copernicus to Darwin 133

7 Shibli Shumayyil's Darwin: a theory for everything progressive 147

8 Scientific Interpretation: Shaykh Husayn al-Jisr and Darwin 175

9 Darwin between Sayyid Ahmad Khan's *Natcheriyya* and Jamal al-Din al-Afghani's refutation 190

10 Muhammad Abduh 210

11 Abduh's legacy 226

PART II
Science, society and government in the modern Muslim world   251

12	Overview of the 20th century	253
13	Darwin at the center of debate	262
14	Inverse appropriation: science by Quran	314
15	Scientific Interpretation	334
16	Scientific Interpretation and evolution	351
17	The place of Al-Azhar and the ulema	371
18	Science and the contemporary state	389
	Epilogue	429
	Index	439

Figures

3.1	Cover of the journal *al-Muqtataf*	77
4.1	The phases of the moon as it orbits the earth	82
4.2	The motion of the moon in the course of a lunar year as it orbits the sun	83
4.3	A diagram representing the Ptolemaic system (right); a hybrid model of the solar system by Shaykh Nasif al-Yaziji (left)	85
4.4	A diagram representing the Copernican system (right); a diagram representing the peculiar system of Tycho Brahe (left)	86
4.5 a and b	Roemer speed of light	88

Acknowledgements

In addition to Martin Dickson, to whom this book is dedicated, I would like to thank William Paterson University for two decades of financial assistance in my research for this book; and also the library, whose interlibrary loan librarians were able to locate and provide me with hard-to-find, centuries-old books in Arabic and Ottoman Turkish.

I should also like to thank the American Philosophical Society for a research grant I was awarded, which helped cover expenses for a year in the National Library of Egypt and the library of the American University at Cairo. I also wish to thank Dr. John McClain, formerly in the Department of Physics at the American University of Beirut, who meticulously went over every sentence I wrote, correcting grammar, punctuation, word choice and errors in the science. Professor George Robb of the History Department of William Paterson University is as well to be thanked for the time and effort he graciously put into reading the book and giving critical and insightful recommendations in organization and in deleting what could be deleted and what could be written in shorter form.

Lastly, I would like to thank Melissa Williams for her uncanny ability to put into type a most messy, illegible, hand-written copy covered with crossed-out lines, a dozen arrows stretching across the scrawl-crowded page indicating where to insert a wild artistry of words within bubbles that might have won a prize in a Jackson Pollack imitation contest. How she did it is a mystery, and I am forever indebted to her for it.

Part I
Copernicus, Darwin and Islamic intellectual reform in Muslim societies during the last half of the 19th century

1 The Ottomans

Absolutist state reformers versus Young Ottoman constitutionalists

Before Sultan Mahmud II's long, eventful and traumatic reign, an elite circle of ministers and reformers were convinced that in order to survive, the empire had to change drastically by adopting innovations from the West. By the end of his reign, the circle of reformist believers had widened to embrace a large section of literate society. That something had to be done and done quickly, and that the West had the answers, was no longer whispered by a few at the head of government who were living in perpetual fear of accusations by conservatives of treason and heresy one moment and Western demands, threats and ultimatums the next. Europe was not the only threat. The dire weakness of the empire, having suffered the humiliating loss of Greece, and then defeat and loss of Syria at the hands of the governor in Egypt, had made what had been unthinkable during the century following the Tulip Period very thinkable and acceptable, even inevitable, and so between the late 1830s and mid-century, the West as a model to be followed had become generally accepted.[1] Once the Janissaries had been crushed, respected members of the high ulema emerged from the veil of fear to publicly advocate innovative change and an active pursuit of reason in human affairs and social organization, rather than passively relying on God's will. Fatalism, they now agreed, had been disastrous for both religion and empire.

This activist thesis offended the more conservative ulema, men whose outlooks had been expressed 50 years earlier by the historian Vasif's condemnation of the French for rejecting God's absolute control of natural and human events by believing that superiority in means of waging war, not God, determined the victor. The conservatives had managed to muffle the voice of the activist theologians, but by the end of the 1830s such words as reason, human choice and free will were gaining currency, and in the 1840s and 1850s, words and concepts such as freedom, rights, liberty, the people and the nation were given Ottoman equivalents and brought into the common language. In the following decade, as the legacy of the Enlightenment and French Revolution was finding a place in Ottoman political parlance, words for republic, constitution and revolution found their way into the dictionaries.

The catastrophic events that befell the Ottomans at the end of Sultan Mahmud's life set the stage for an even more intensive program of modernization. In 1839, Ibrahim Pasha's Egyptian army inflicted a crushing defeat on the reformed army of the Ottomans in Anatolia, leaving the road to Istanbul open. Then the new navy Mahmud had put so much care into building absconded to Alexandria to serve Muhammad Ali. Mercifully, Mahmud, whose undeserving end was incommensurate with his reforming effort, died in his sickbed before news of these untoward events reached him. What he knew of Ottoman misfortunes was bad enough for the dying man. For his having achieved what he did, which in context is considerable – setting the government on a sound course of reorganization, destroying the Janissaries, building a new army and navy, instituting military schools and an educational system, and founding a commendable engineering school and medical school – for all that, no worse ending to a life dedicated to renewal could be imagined than the military disasters of 1839. It is not often that a country's fleet sails off to join the enemy.

As the British were busily assembling a European coalition to prevent Muhammad Ali from taking over the empire, the new sultan, abd al-Majid, issued a proclamation in the Rose Chamber of the royal palace. The document, known as the Royal Rescript of the Rose Chamber, or *Hatti Sharif-i Gulhane*, expressed, among other intents of modernization, the sultan's decision to establish a more equitable legal basis for the religious minorities of the empire. This officially initiated a new program of reform, the *Tanzimat*. (The word is an Arabic feminine plural meaning the act of organizing and putting things in order, and it derives from the same verbal root as *nizam*, as in Selim's New Order, Nizam-I Jadid.) If such cultural movements could be quantified, the *Tanzimat* was a program of change whose social impact was greater than Selim's *Nizam* raised to the third power.

Before the *Tanzimat*, modernization had been limited to government education, administration, industry and the military. Now it would reach right into religious law, the social heart of Muslim culture, affecting practically every facet of Ottoman life. Western cynics regarded the part about establishing equality between Christians and Muslims as a polite but insincere payoff to Britain and her allies for saving the dynasty from Muhammad Ali. The confluence of events that produced the Rose Chamber document might suggest that something of the sort may indeed have been in abd al-Majid's thoughts, but there is no way of surely knowing what cunning insincerity, duplicity and hypocrisy the proclamations of rulers in any society conceal. In terms of Ottoman political tradition and religious law, the Rose Chamber Proclamation was as momentous as were the Tennis Court Oath and the Declaration of the Rights of Man in revolutionary France.

The men who led the *Tanzimat* had been reared in Mahmud's schools, had learned languages, served in European embassies and been appointed to high offices owing to their knowledge of the West. Their language skills, which allowed them to monopolize communications with the West, gave them extraordinary influence as the empire was drawn into the web of international diplomacy. The art of diplomacy, of making alliances and playing one nation against another, was to be a defensive weapon against Western aggression, and the best players in this high-stakes political game of international balance and alliance were the men of languages and European experience. Inexpendable, they were able to marginalize the traditional elites. The small corps of more or less Westernized bureaucrats, whose holy trinity was secularism, efficiency and progress, set out to remake the empire, from inside out, in the image they had captured of the West during their days of embassy service, but minus the parliaments and elections and energy-wasting frictions of political parties. Deep-rooted reform was to be made whatever the price and made quickly and efficiently. What had to go in the old empire would go, without debate.

To the reformers themselves, the *Tanzimat* meant the salvation of empire, but to those who cherished tradition and Ottoman culture, the *Tanzimat* reformers were unthinking, insensitive, autocratic butchers: raw, uncultured and arrogant modernizers who were chopping off and discarding sinews, nerves and limbs of what enriched Ottoman life and made it a civilized society. By tearing society from its roots, they were ripping the heart and soul out of the culture, condemning Ottomans to political suicide, to limping in humiliation behind Europe, beggar's hand outstretched. European diplomacy's contemptuous name for the empire – Sick Man of Europe – made the point.

The *Tanzimat's* invasive reforms introduced a broad range of European legal codes: criminal, penal, property, commercial, maritime and tax.[2] Translated and enacted into Ottoman law practically overnight, and without much tailoring to fit Ottoman contours, whole codes were imported and transplanted like so many tulip bulbs. Many Ottomans were shocked. Some were determined to resist this outage of mindless reform. The great majority of Ottomans gave a dismissive shrug as daily life continued its customary rhythms: *la plus ca change* (some things did change). Those who drove this force-draft Westernization took to wearing trousers, smoking jackets and cravats, topped by the now popular tasseled fez. Desks and chairs replaced the customary divans.

Opponents of the *Tanzimat*, from radical conservative to moderate reformist, saw nothing but senseless uprooting and destruction. Their civilization was being reduced to a barren wasteland of meaningless imports that did nothing but confuse and contradict what people understood and lived by. The mismatch the reformers made of their new style clothing, another example of their aping what they only superficially understood, added contempt to disgust.

Europeans joined the local opposition. "Orientals imitating their civilized betters and getting it all wrong," they scoffed. The *Tanzimat* reformers got it from both sides, amused contempt from the West and, from their Ottoman critics, the accusation of cultural betrayal for trading their dignity for foreign frills and institutions as ill-fitting in Ottoman society as the Western clothes the reformers wore like trained monkeys. Whether the *Tanzimat* hastened or postponed the end of the Ottoman Empire is a matter of debate, but it is without question that the movement's twin drives of modernization and secularization led to the birth of the republic that rose from the ashes of the empire.

The reformers had little sympathy and less patience for the ulema and their institutions and cherished traditions. They hacked away at what had survived Sultan Mahmud's attack on the economic foundations of their power, wielding the sword of secularist reform and progress with Jacobin fervor. But as much as they wanted to, the one thing *Tanzimat* reformers dared not touch was Islamic law as it related to personal status and the family, marriage, polygamy, separation, divorce, inheritance and custody of children. The farthest they went was to pare down the Shari'a to this essential core, which was organized by a *Tanzimat* religious scholar into a digest called the *Majalla*, one of the *Tanzimat's* prize accomplishments.[3]

Modeling their innovations on those European institutions that were part and parcel a product of 19th century Western liberalism, the *Tanzimat* leaders were anything but liberals. They stood for the sultan's absolutist rule. Nobody was above the sultan. No institution, constitution, assembly or opposition party could challenge or abrogate the sultan's orders that issued from the centralized government of his ministerial reformers. No commercial and industrialist class existed with leverage enough to contest absolutism in the name of liberalism. Industrialization, institutions of capitalist investment and entrepreneurship were alien to the Ottomans – to all Muslim societies. The soil of free enterprise and free trade from which liberalism had sprouted in 19th century Europe, and had grown powerful enough to shape the state to serve its own interests, did not exist yet in the east. Like Peter the Great in Russia, the *Tanzimat* reformers built from the top down, without the institutional foundations of parliament, constitution, representative government, rights of man and such that could put into debate the goals and methods of modernization, secularization and progress. Reforms that were considered liberal in the European context were in the context of the *Tanzimat* autocratic. Western liberalism was turned on its head: absolutist monarchy fighting for a progressive secular state.

The only serious collective opposition to this reformist dictatorship was a diverse, loosely connected society of individuals called "Young Ottomans." More of a collection of protesting writers than an organized movement, they adopted the political ideas of Western liberalism, of constitutional and parliamentarian government as their own in their fight against autocracy and its radically secularizing New Order. But they were not against secularization itself or the separation of religion from politics. They were against the rampant displacement of cultural authenticity by foreign transplants. But as far as the necessity of deep reform was concerned, these liberal essayists and pamphleteers did not disagree with the men of the *Tanzimat*.

The career line of the reformers normally began in the Language School. This was the early training ground of both those who would serve the *Tanzimat* and those who would fight it as Young Ottomans. The reformer's career followed a pattern: from the Language School to the Translation Bureau, followed by several years of foreign service in a European embassy at a middling level. For the men who joined the *Tanzimat*, their career course would continue in government through an ascending sequence up the diplomatic ranks to ambassador, advisor to the sultan, to pasha, and for three of the reformers, grand vizirates. Language and knowledge of Europe were essential, but so too were intelligence and devotion to the sultan and the cause of reform. Others whose careers had started in the Language School and Bureau of Translation and who had then been sent to serve as embassy functionaries in Europe returned with ideas different from those who served the *Tanzimat*. These young men read the literature of Europe, imbibed the liberal culture, studied the political institutions, read Voltaire, Rousseau, Condorcet, Montesquieu and Locke and came back filled with liberal ideas that they wanted to institutionalize in their homeland: constitution, parliament, representative government, liberal education and science – humanist ideas informed by the essentials of Ottoman culture and Muslim civilization. Islam was essential not purely because it was God's given religion to man but because it was the vital center of culture and social cohesion.

Many of these young men did not have to go to Europe for their ideas. The Translation Bureau was itself a school of liberal learning, doing much at many different levels to broaden minds and render them receptive to the science, social philosophy and organizational techniques of the West. As it was meant to be, the Bureau was a rich breeding ground for Ottoman modernization. The Bureau's service in this regard was evident as early as its first translator and director, Yahya Efendi, a liberal-minded Greek convert to Islam. Yahya went from being director of the Translation Bureau to instructor in the Engineering School, where he made Turkish translations of Italian and French texts on science and technology. Hoja Ishak Efendi, author of the compendium on the mathematical sciences, was director of the Translation Bureau after Yahya Efendi, whom he later followed to the Engineering School. Another who began in the Translation Bureau and rose to make a name for himself in the cause of liberal reform was Mustafa Sami (d. 1855). The liberalism he acquired through his years in Europe did not, however, diminish his support of the *Tanzimat* reformers, as happened later with the writers who became known as Young Ottomans. Mustafa Sami traveled extensively in Europe in the 1830s. He served on the secretarial staff of the Ottoman Embassies in Vienna and Paris. Based on that, without yet having learned a European language or penetrating European cultural and institutional life very deeply, he wrote a short treatise, about 40 pages, on his thoughts and experience regarding Europe: *Avrupa Risalesi*.[4]

In several ways his book is reminiscent of both Mehmet Chelebi's (Yirmisekiz) treatise on his impressions and experiences in France in 1722 and Shaykh Tahtawi's on his experiences in Paris a century later. Mustafa Sami's book was published in Istanbul only a few years after Tahtawi's in Cairo. The striking similarities in the three accounts reveal what in Europe most impressed Muslim travelers. All three commented on fashions in dress, literacy, status of women, education, museums and science, which they saw as a major factor in Europe's strength. Mustafa Sami added religious freedom to Shaykh Tahtawi's political and intellectual freedom. Yirmisekiz, Tahtawi and Mustafa Sami understood the relationship between science and Europe's advance in civilization and power. The last two essayists recognized Europe's expansion of thought and enrichment of life as a process of civilization, where knowledge was not only handed down generation by generation but also expanded. Mustafa Sami saw how in their museums Europeans preserved and extolled the past and how important it was for them. But so too was the future, and each generation made its contribution to the next so it could enjoy a richer civilization. Museums, so abundant and cherished in Europe, preserved the memory of the past, while the application of experience, accumulated by successive generations, connected the past to the future and made progress in science possible. The sooner Muslims adopted science, the sooner they would be independent of European help.

Mustafa Sami was no less exuberant than Shaykh Tahtawi about museums, observatories, educational institutions and simplicity of literary language. Both were much impressed by the orderliness, literacy, cleanliness and opulence of European cities – of which, as foreign guests, they would have seen only the more privileged sections. Echoing Shaykh Tahtawi, Mustafa Sami commented in surprise on the extent of literacy: it seemed to him everyone was able to read, even porters, shepherds, peasants and women. In writing of Western science, Mustafa Sami uses the word *fen* (Arabic *fann*; plural *funun*) instead of the usual word *ilm* for science. Other Ottoman writers will follow his usage. The choice of words was important, since the ulema strictly reserved the word *ilm* for the religious sciences. Referring to the modern sciences by a name associated with art, craft and mechanical technique was an attempt to dissociate them from the religious matrix conveyed by *ilm* and avoid ruffling the ulema's sensitivities the way that Greek science and philosophy had in an earlier age. Calling the modern sciences *funun*, however, did not spare Mustafa Sami from the ulema's sharpest criticism for having gone "frank," to the extent he was even castigated by some as having become in Europe a heretic and unbeliever.[5] In spite of his association with the *Tanzimat* autocrats, Young Ottoman liberals coming a decade and two later would find in Mustafa Sami an inspiring model.

Sadik Rifat (d. 1856), another reformist writer and diplomat whose career began in the Translation and Language Bureaus, was in Europe during several of the same years as Mustafa Sami. Sadik learned German and French, started his career as a low-level embassy official and ascended the diplomatic hierarchy to become ambassador in Vienna in 1837. He wrote two books on Europe and reform that conveyed to Ottoman readers many of the same sentiments and responses found in Sami's and Tahtawi's, books but his commentaries on certain facets of European culture showed him to be more penetrating. He was the first Ottoman writer to analyze the conceptual essentials of what it was that made Westerners so different from Muslims. Westerners thought differently. Their basic assumptions were different. What they wrote or said about politics or society could not be grasped until the underlying assumptions were understood. What Europeans did would not make sense until it was understood how they thought. Their understanding of how nature worked was different and so too their thought processes. The European way of thinking had to be mastered before European science, inventions and institutions could be successfully adopted. Otherwise, adoption would be reduced to hollow imitation. His study of European languages taught him that language should be expressed simply and clearly for direct communication of thoughts. Here he is at one with Tahtawi. Eloquence, complexity, convoluted sentences, poetic phrases and literary allusions all wrapped in the pleasant sensations of sounds when certain words are cleverly strung together like a necklace of pearls serve only to cloud meaning and defeat the intent of language, which is to communicate thought as directly as possible.

Mustafa Sami and Sadik Rifat were pioneering explorers of Europe and, like Tahtawi in Egypt, found no great following in their admiration of the people, cities and institutions about which they wrote. Sadik's implication that *Tanzimat* reformers did not understand what they were doing because they had not mastered the basic assumptions and thought patterns of Europeans made him few friends among them, while his admiration of European civilization, which could be taken to imply an inferiority of Islamic civilization and its religious core, earned him some resentment among the ulema. Grounds for resentment abounded. Sadik criticized Muslims for their docile willingness to be tyrannized by custom and tradition and for their fear of authority and acceptance of arbitrary authority, which he contrasted to the Western concepts of rights and freedom, and the role of reason in organizing European life and pursuing goals. Western governments, whose operations were guided by a system of established laws and rights, existed in idea and reality for the general welfare of the citizens, unlike Muslim governments, which existed for their own sake and enrichment.[6] Europe's advance over Islamic civilization was directly related to this reversal in concepts. Science flourished in a society of rights and freedom. Cultivation of the sciences made for civilization and progress. The organizing power of the Western mind to create new sciences and technologies was the same that gave rise to new social, political and economic institutions. If the Ottomans were to adopt these institutions, it was vital that the way of thinking that produced them be clearly understood and assimilated.

This would not be easy. Underlying assumptions that gave rise to Western institutions were not always explicitly expressed by the institutions. But if these underlying assumptions were not accepted heart and soul, the adopted institutions would be meaningless. As an example of what he meant, he cited Sultan Mahmud's offer of a prize for the best refutation of ibn Rushd's Aristotelian logic of cause and effect as operating in nature and that supported al-Ghazali's Ash'arite position. A member of the ulema won the prize and his work became the arbiter in any argument between atomism's non-causality or occasionalism (that God directly creates and commands phenomenal existence, at every instant) and a system of natural philosophy based on cause and effect. A strange philosophical position for a reforming advocate of modern science and medicine to take, Sadik remarked. But again, by the mid-19th century, the old parading with the new was everywhere to be seen. For all of Mahmud's modernizing reforms, the sultan was as metaphysically stuck in the past as his contradictory contemporary in Egypt, Shaykh Tahtawi. Both wanted the products of science but stripped of the underlying principles and modes of thinking that made science possible.

As with Egypt's ulema and al-Azhar, a number of Ottoman religious scholars flourished as outspoken advocates of reform, while the religious institution itself remained passively antagonistic. A small cadre of "enlightened ulema" arose through exposure to a world of learning outside the traditional confines of the madrasa system of textual memorization and unquestioned acceptance of the authoritative sources. Some religious scholars, whose minds had expanded too far beyond the narrow vision of orthodoxy to remain any longer contained by traditional belief, left the ulema and religious studies altogether. Five in particular of those enlightened ulema who remained were important contributors to the reform movement. (Mulla Mehmad Esad, who it will be recalled led educational reform during Sultan Mahmud's reign, would make it six.) Bereketzade Ismail Hakki, a moderate religious scholar, openly espoused a parliament. His outspoken pursuit of this got him exiled, but even in exile he carried on his work of reform.[7] The second was Kamil Efendi. A member of the ulema, he accompanied to Paris, as his moral guardian, a young Bey from a noble Ottoman family who was to study in the Ottoman school there. It was another case of the religious guardian who got the education.

Kamil Efendi utilized his time studying French, in the course of which he became fascinated with the idea of secular law. It seems that the idea that law could be manufactured, that it could be the product of human endeavor rather than of divine will, had never occurred to him: one could take on the role of God and make law. His mind opened to a new world of possibilities. Exploring it in depth, he applied to the University of Paris law school and was accepted. When he received his law degree, he returned to Istanbul and was appointed to a high position in the Imperial Customs Bureau. Kamil Efendi was exceptional not only as a member of the ulema who studied secular law in a European university, but also in that he studied completely on his own, independent of the government.

The third, Shanizade (1826), was a founding member and head of the Beshiktash Scientific Society. The Society was not one that would attract anyone whose mind had been molded by dogma and tradition. Founded in the 1830s and named after the quarter of Istanbul where it met, the Society brought men together who had an interest in the West and its science, literature, politics and history, similar to the literary salons of 18th century Paris, upon which the Beshiktash Scientific Society was modeled. It was one of the first significant attempts outside of officialdom to bring minds together to reflect on the problem of the West and Ottoman reform.[8] Composed of secular intellectuals and several ulema scholars, the society met at a seaside villa to discuss causes of the empire's weakness, Europe's power, the right paths of reform, science, education and politics and Voltaire and other Enlightenment writers. Almost as unusual as a member of the ulema like Kamil Efendi earning a law degree in Paris was the scholar of the ulema who served as the Beshiktashi Society's lecturer on philosophy. Instruction was, on occasion, offered by anyone well-versed in a book or a science. In addition to being a meeting place for companionship and solace of kindred minds in an unraveling world, the Society aimed to widen the small circle of Ottomans who knew and looked positively on modern science and Western knowledge in general.

Shanizade, who wrote and spoke French perfectly, supported assimilation of Western science as an essential element of the transformation the Ottomans would have to make in order to survive. His knowledge of religion, medicine, physics, mathematics, astronomy, poetry, music, painting, history and European political institutions so impressed his associates that they considered him a walking encyclopedia. He must have had considerable medical training, since he wrote a modern textbook on anatomy and was for a time Sultan Mahmud's personal physician. Any French-speaking Ottoman cleric who rose so high and was known to be a fount of Western knowledge would have no end of enemies within conservative circles of the court and ulema. No less than Muhammad Ali in Egypt, Sultan Mahmud was suspicious of any group outside government and his control, especially one that met to discuss dangerous things like politics and ideas. It took only a little fanning of the flames of rumor alleging the Beshiktash Science Society to be involved in revolutionary activity for the sultan to bring it to an end. Shanizade was fortunate to only be exiled.

The fate of the Beshiktash Society helps answer why an autonomous scientific culture failed to grow in either the Ottoman Empire or Egypt. Rather than it being simply because of hostility on the part of the ulema, the reasons for the hard time science had in blooming can be found in the fear, insecurity and suspicion of autocratic government that rejected as a political threat any seed planted in society by private initiative.[9]

Carrying on Shanizade's spirit into the next generation was Arif Hikmet Bey, a leading religious scholar who joined the government's effort to reform. Arif Bey became a member of the Imperial Academy of Arts and Sciences that the *Tanzimat* reformers founded in the 1850s to prepare textbooks for a projected Ottoman University. From there he ascended to the highest religious office of Shaykh al-Islam, which he held during the 1860s. By then, religious resistance had weakened as a serious factor in the empire's drive to reform, though the ulema continued to be the populist spokesman for the preponderant part of the community.

For pure devotion to science, it is Hoja Tahsin who must be regarded as the most remarkable of these men who joined their religious devotion to educational reform. Tahsin was sent to Paris to study natural science by the first of the three *Tanzimat* grand viziers, Mustafa Rashid Pasha – a former slave of Sultan Mahmud who shared with his Egyptian contemporary Ali Pasha Mubarak the hope of creating a religious leadership consisting of ulema learned in the sciences as a means of coopting the ulema as an institution to support science education. If the career of Hoja Tahsin is in any way emblematic of the effort, the Ottoman ulema proved more receptive than its Egyptian counterpart.

Hoja Tahsin Efendi sailed to France where he lived a total of 12 years, 1857–1869. Like Tahtawi 30 years earlier and Kamil Efendi more recently, he was to act as a spiritual guide to keep students who had been sent by the government to study in Paris from wasting themselves in the city's cafés, taverns and brothels. In this case, it was the spiritual guide, a middle-aged man of 47, who ventured out beyond the walls of the Ottoman school after his students were supposedly in their beds fast asleep. While learning French and studying science, Hoja Tahsin took to exploring French life, reading French literature and imbibing Parisian culture, enough to critically appreciate French politics. In Paris, he came into contact with the Young Ottomans who were there in either forced or voluntary exile for their opposition to what they saw as the ruthless destruction of Ottoman society and culture by the dictatorial *Tanzimat* reformers, the very people for whom Hoja Tahsin was working. Befriending several of the Young Ottomans, Tahsin seems to have easily assimilated their liberal ideas. By the end of 12 years in Paris, he was completely transformed.

On the lighter side, he doffed his imam's robe and turban for a straw hat and trousers and frequented café's, one in particular that was a favorite of celebrities. His fellow Ottomans mockingly called him Mosyo (Monsieur) Tahsin and more bitingly, Gyavur (Kafir) Tahsin.[10]

His study of cosmography, astronomy, mechanics, physics, mathematics, chemistry and geology and the evolutionists Lamarck, Darwin, Hollbach and Buchner, seemed to give no problem to his religious beliefs, not outwardly at least. While his study of science convinced him that the Ottomans could not survive without it, his life in Paris and association with the Young Ottomans convinced him that constitutional reforms were equally necessary. Tahsin underwent a long internal voyage from *mullah* to liberal constitutionalist. His transformation having made him into a secularist advocate of separation between religion and politics, he had little regard for his fellow religious colleagues who failed to take up the call of reform. Knowing nothing of the modern world and worldly affairs, or even of their duties as protectors of religion, they were in his eyes more destructive than protective.

The *Tanzimat* vizier's sending of Tahsin to Paris to study science was a new development in the Ottoman approach to modernity. Previously, the Ottoman grasp at Western coattails had been in the form of translations, of schools designed by and run by Europeans. Tahsin Hoja's career initiated a new direction: a member of the ulema commissioned by the state to study the exact sciences and return to disseminate his acquired knowledge as a teacher in the new *Dar al-Funun*. The concept was sound, and it would have reaped more profound effects had many more been sent, and of a younger age, considering the subjects they were to master.

Like Sadik Rifat, Tahsin learned in Europe that the surest way to change society was to change the way people thought. Change began with one's self. Before one could change others, he had to go through the process of change himself. Ottomans had to go through what Tahsin went through. They could not all go to Paris as he had, but the experience could be delivered through writing. Thought processes had to change in step with the assimilation of science. Accordingly, his first book was on modern psychology, his second on the fundamentals of modern astronomy: the science of the mind opening the door to the science of the stars. A Turkish translation of Volney's *Loi Naturelle* was attributed to him. His work on astronomy, *Esas-i Ilm-i Heyet Mir'at as-Sima* (*The Foundations of Astronomy: Mirror of Heaven*) was Tahsin's most important literary contribution introducing the empire to the new science. A survey of astronomy since Copernicus and Kepler, the book unequivocally accepted the sun-centered system, reproducing Ishak Hoja's section on Cartesian vortices whirling the planets around the sun, as well as Laplace's nebular theory of the earth's formation.

The *Dar al-Funun* that the *Tanzimat* reformers built in Istanbul at the end of the 1860s was to instruct young Ottomans in science and technology. Hoja Tahsin was brought from Paris in 1869 to be its first director. A member of the ulema who knew science and enjoyed teaching it, he was seen as the ideal man for the task. His scientific studies and literary accomplishments made him just what the *Tanzimat* grand vizier Rashid Pasha had hoped he would become when sending Tahsin to Paris as a young religious scholar. Hoja Tahsin did not disappoint expectations. As director, he attempted to fascinate the students in science by presenting lively demonstrations. By keeping his students up with the continuing discoveries in physics, astronomy and chemistry that were being made in Europe, he showed them how it was a never-ending search. Even as director, he enjoyed lecturing and performing novel experiments in class to help the students understand not just the principles of science, but what was meant by natural law.

However appreciated Hoja Tahsin may have been by his students and the grand vizier, within the corridors and offices of *Dar al-Funun* the director was sorely resented. The European teachers did not take to a religious scholar at the head of the new scientific and technical institute. His knowledge of science and success in teaching it were resented. His popularity with the students proved he was unfit for the post. Nor did many in the ulema appreciate one of their own going off to Europe and returning religiously poisoned by alien secular learning, the virtues of which he publicly praised and drilled into the young minds of Muslims. Animosity welled up against him. Discrediting gossip and rumors were spread about him. His public lectures were disrupted by protestors claiming he denied God's power over nature. A visiting religious scholar of some renown, Jamal al-Din al-Afghani, whose tumultuous life will be taken up later, opposed Tahsin's ideas during an official public ceremony in which Tahsin spoke on natural science and technology. The attack opened the way for religious extremists to cut short the lecture and end the ceremony.

Hoja Tahsin lasted less than a year as director. An experiment he performed in his physics class gave his opponents what they needed. To demonstrate the existence of a vacuum and its effect, he put a pigeon under a glass bell and began to evacuate it by means of a small mechanical hand pump. The pigeon went limp and died in full view of the astonished class. News of the mysterious murder soon reached members of the ulema who were hostile to him. They accused him of magic and heresy. His scientific colleagues at *Dar al-Funun* failed to come to his defense. With some of the ulema still able to raise public emotions, and the government wanting no problems with religion, Hoja Tahsin was dismissed from his post. The following year the university was closed down to the dismay of many and delight of others.

Not only did the affair show the vast chasm of mind that existed among the ulema and within Ottoman society, it revealed that, without the ulema's general support, modern education was going to have more than a hard time taking root in Muslim society. Support by a handful of liberal ulema who had been abroad was not going to be enough. As long as an activist and highly vocal faction of the ulema was able to exert public pressure on the state's efforts to modernize education, success required the support of the religious institution as a whole, and this was highly unlikely to happen. The ulema was not becoming more receptive as reforms progressed, but more unreceptive. By the 1860s, its ranks had been depleted of its more intelligent members as the result of a generation of intense secular reform. A religious career had lost much of its shine. Bright young men no longer looked to the madrasa as the way to a promising future. The more that reforms progressed, the more it was that madrasa students were drawn from the nether levels of society. The more conservative the ulema became as an institution, the firmer became the wall of religious resistance, as seen by the example of the telegraph that was being set up in the 1860s that terrified members of the ulema. The distance between the poles supporting the wires, and how close they could come to a mosque, were subjects of religious and governmental debate. Some reacted out of fear that the wires conveyed some form of magic or satanic evil and that they attracted lightning. Some government officials joined the ulema in opposing the telegraph.[11] Samuel Morse praised Sultan abd al-Majid as the first ruler to appreciate the importance of his invention. A demonstration of how it worked was given by Samuel Morse in the sultan's summer palace on the Bosphorus. The sultan was ecstatic: the telegraph could unite the empire by electrifying communication across its far provinces. He was so excited about it that he had the demonstration repeated for some of his ministers. This time the demonstration failed. It was later discovered that a pasha had secretly cut the wires that ran through an adjoining room. The pashas did not want the newfangled wires reporting to Istanbul what they were up to in the provinces.[12] In such little ways did members of reformist government and the ulema, each for their own reasons, deflate the pressure of reform.

Secularism and industrialization were not changing society rapidly enough to deprive the religious institution of its popular social base. By the mid-1860s, secularization of education in the *Tanzimat* secondary schools had been completed and enough students had gone through the medical and engineering school curriculums to challenge the traditional madrasa education, bringing anew into heated argument the old conflict between science and religion, the very thing the *Tanzimat* pashas and religious scholars like Hoja Tahsin hoped to avoid or resolve.[13] As long as the custodians of orthodoxy were on the defensive, there was little hope of their joining the reformers, and there was no way they would not be on the defensive while facing the advance of a system of education that was based on teaching a non-religious curriculum. Although many of the higher ulema sided as individuals with the sultan's reforms, the ulema as a religious class and an institution, following the ulema of long ago that had taken an unfriendly position regarding the rational sciences ever since their rise in the 8th century, now saw religion fighting to hold what social place was left to it and its hallowed traditions. Fighting to preserve their teaching positions and careers in the madrasas and mosques, the collective attitude of the ulema was not about to change. Only a clutch of individuals of the ulema changed: men like Hoja Tahsin.

An active and creative scholar who had studied long in Europe and continued to be a professional member of the ulema, Hoja Tahsin was sadly disappointed in his mission to bring modern science to the ulema and bridge the intellectual fissure. After he had been forcibly retired from academic channels dedicated to promoting modern science, he is reported to have become a one-man institution in pursuit of his mission. He continued speaking and writing; he taught classes for free, and in his library, he surrounded himself with scientific books and equipment, which he demonstrated to anyone interested. His home was described as a museum of science and he was a walking encyclopedia. He had his own microscope, his own telescope and all the equipment of science in between. Being especially keen on astronomy, he built his own observatory and was in the 1870s and 1880s the most important source of modern science in the empire. In particular, he opened Ottomans to new ideas in astronomy and geology: to the vastness of space and the age of the earth with its epochal formations. At the same time, he held to his religion, believing, as he said, along with many other reformists, the Quran and Hadith contained nothing contradictory to science.

There was, however, he admitted, one inescapable problem between them. If one accepted the materialist foundation of a science that strictly demanded the universe to be understood in its own autonomous terms of force, mass, motion and measurement, where did that leave religion in terms of creation and the end of time? Tahsin knew too much about the common terrain that had been fiercely claimed and fought over by medieval theology and modern cosmology, and he was too honest to enter the fray frivolously or opt out on the easy dichotomy of heart and mind. To some things there were simply no answers. But he never gave up trying. Toward the end of his life, Tahsin was living in a room cluttered with scientific instruments and continuing to carry on in his efforts to establish the essentials of Muslim belief on naturalistic foundations.

A convincing work on that conundrum was well needed. Science study and religious education continued to be contrary bedfellows. The contrariness permeated society. Secular secondary schools of the *Tanzimat* sat incongruously next to the traditional religious schools. Some schools employed both religious teachers and secular, giving courses in religion and science. Young students would be introduced to geography and science, encouraged to enjoy knowledge of the world and given morally uplifting stories of the prophets of the world's religions from a simply written book called *Useful Knowledge* (*Malumat-i Nafia*) by Jevdet (Cevdet) Pasha, one of the leading *Tanzimat* reformers and codifier of the Majella. Then in the subject that followed, the same students would read a traditional moralistic book of the 16th century which taught that playing, talking a lot, laughing, singing or listening to music were horrible sins, that the enemy of religion was "love of the world, deadlier in its destruction than that which a pack of hungry wolves can bring to a flock of sheep."[14] The result was such a jumble of confusion in their young minds that, for many of them, it threatened the possibility of clear thinking throughout the rest of their lives.

The confusion was already to be seen in the life, actions and thought of the most exceptional of these exceptional men of religion, who perceived science to be at the heart of survival of Muslim civilization and the Ottoman Empire. In application of action to perception, the most extraordinary of them was Ali Suavi. While his contemporary Hoja Tahsin was peacefully studying and teaching the exact sciences as a path to change, Ali was preaching, writing and fomenting it by violent action outside of government. Ali Suavi was not devoted to science in the way Tahsin was. He was not a student of it. He did not translate it. What he did was write of its necessity for survival. He identified science with civilization in answer to the *Tanzimat*'s godless secularism and political tyranny that was dooming Islam and the Empire.

Ali Suavi's thought and action defy categorization: religious conservative, defender of Shari'a law, fiery orator, disciple of change, advocate of Western science, constitutionalist, free speech journalist, leader of violent revolt and, ultimately, martyr. He fit uncomfortably in the Young Ottoman Society, of which he was a founding member. Unlike the other writers of the constitutionalist Young Ottomans, Ali Suavi came from a poorer class of society. But it was not for that reason that the other Young Ottomans were ill at ease with him. It was his strange, unpredictable character, his odd mix of religious and revolutionary ideas, his zeal, his clerical garb that he never doffed, his acceptance of change through violence and above all, his inelegant style of writing: hurried, passionate, unpolished, un-Ottoman. Quite as the word "Ottoman" conveyed the image of dignified refinement, a style of life, culture, education, dress, manners, so too did "Young Ottoman" convey this – and something more: a studied cosmopolitanism, knowledge of languages, of the West, of its institutions, culture and ideas, to which the Young Ottomans wanted to marry high Ottoman culture and religion, even though, except for Ali Suavi, the Young Ottomans were not particularly religious. Being Ottoman simply conveyed a certain tradition of culture and civilization that was sanctified by religion. Being an Ottoman implied a religious belief but did not require being religious.

Founded in the mid-1860s during a picnic in the countryside outside Istanbul, the Young Ottoman Society brought together a loosely related group of educated young men, teachers, essayists, pamphleteers, poets, dramatists, journalists, government critics and former officials. What made them a society was a broad range of reformist values they shared that had been acquired through various channels of Ottoman contact with Europe: the Language and Translation Schools, student missions, independent travel and foreign service in the permanent embassies in Paris, London, Berlin and Vienna. Political exile, both forced and voluntary, was a special form of Young Ottoman foreign travel, rich in its importation of ideas that the *Tanzimat* government would have preferred to remain in Europe. Sharing with many others the resentment that arose against the forced-draft secular reforms imported from Europe and imposed from the top down by the *Tanzimat* ministers, these Young Ottomans wrote critically on issues related to religion, culture, politics, civilization, government, science, progress, literature and history, all within what might be considered a liberal humanist framework informed by the cultural authenticity of their Ottoman traditions. As the Beshiktash Scientific Society reflected the advanced ideas of the Ottoman intelligentsia of the generation 1820–1840, so too did the Young Ottoman Society reflect them for the generation from mid-century to Ali Suavi's failed revolt against Sultan abd al-Hamid's despotism in 1878, putting an end to the otherwise literary and peaceful mission of the Young Ottomans.

Young they generally were, but the point of their calling themselves such was not their age but their mission to bring the Ottomans, reborn as it were, into the modern world through reform that would not sever the people from their culture, history and religion, and it was this that signified the Ottoman in their labeled identity. As Muslim humanists, they searched for and propagandized a way of reform that would lead to cultural revitalization and progress without sacrificing the vital roots that gave life and meaning to Ottoman culture and identity to its people.

Informed by the literature, science and political institutions of France and England, this small, oppositional intelligentsia of reformist writers set themselves to answer the question of how to preserve the essence of Ottoman civilization and, at the same time, adopt the liberal institutions, constitutions and humanist values of secular Western society. What was the complex algebra that allowed institutional transfers from one civilization to another without causing spiritual death or cultural transmogrification but rendering the receiving civilization stronger than it had been before? The importations of the *Tanzimat* reformers, according to their Young Ottoman critics, were causing confusion and absurdity. They were creating a two-headed monster, one Islamic, the other Western, neither of which recognized the other, their forced cohabitation bearing an abominable abortion, a Babel of desolation in a cultural wasteland. What was happening was in fact evident enough in the growing social and institutional confusion: even voices from within the *Tanzimat* establishment arose to join the Young Ottoman chorus in questioning where the empire was headed.

By the early 1860s, Arif Hikmat and others of the higher ulema who had initially tolerated the European transplants, or had held their silence, at last began to speak out, claiming that the sultan's reforming ministers were casting out the good with the bad and filling the vacuum with borrowings whose alien roots had no place in Ottoman culture. The borrowings would wither and die, leaving the social fabric in tatters. The *Tanzimat* reformers were creating a desert where there had been a culture. The Ottoman heritage was being destroyed, reform by reform, innovation by innovation and import by import. They were demoralizing and impoverishing the people. Money was being wasted on imitation of a lavish European lifestyle. Morals were being corrupted by European music and dancing. Muslim women were immodestly dressing like Europeans. The concessions that the *Tanzimat* reformers had granted to European companies, delivering the country's wealth into their hands, were eating away at the Ottoman patrimony, worse than even the Capitulations that put Ottomans at a commercial disadvantage and that the European creditors held between their teeth like snarling dogs with a juicy bone they never tired gnawing on and would never let go.

The ulema and Young Ottoman critics pointed out that the Royal Rescript of 1856 (issued by the sultan as the European delegates were assembling to draw up a peace ending the Crimean War in which Britain and France had joined to defend the Ottomans against Russian aggression) reaffirmed the equality of Christians with Muslims but without removing the special Capitulatory privileges that Europeans enjoyed at Ottoman's expense or without revoking the special privileges that European powers had forced the Ottomans to grant the empire's Christians. What good, Shaykh al-Islam Arif Hikmat and other critics asked, was coming from the reforms or from being so close to Europe? Mt. Lebanon had been delivered to an autonomous administration under French protectorship in 1860. That same year, after half a century of Ottoman military reform, a revolt in tiny Montenegro was able to get the best of Ottoman troops in battle. What kind of pitiful reform was that? The *Tanzimat* method of reform had rendered the government incapable of defending anything but itself in power, leaving the empire at the mercy of those who, while pretending to be the empire's protectors and supporters of reform, in reality coveted its lands and only waited for the chance to divide them. The *Tanzimat* government would soon be ruling a corpse. The sultan's reformers were building the empire's coffin.

Defeat on the battlefield, loss of provinces and continuing economic decline made the charges difficult to answer.

It was becoming evident by the 1860s that the price of *Tanzimat* modernization was breaking the Ottomans, or at least was not helping in holding back the Europeans. The Ottomans paid what was asked without protest as the Europeans built and profited. To pay for the telegraphic link between Istanbul and London, for the roads and railways, the factories and harbors, all built by European firms, the Ottomans had to borrow from European lenders at cutthroat rates. By using their own engineers and staff, Europeans were guaranteeing continuing Ottoman dependence on Europe. Everything was European, European firms, European engineers and managers, European plans, European technological imports and European banks. All that the Ottomans got out of it were the bills and bankruptcy – the unfortunate result of an absolutist government following misdirected policies of willful reformers who faced no correcting resistance. Sultan Mahmud's annihilation of the Janissaries and all sources of resistance had produced an arbitrary absolutist despotism which, in the hands of the *Tanzimat* reformers, prohibited debate and monopolized decision-making, all in the illusory name of efficiency, progress and military defense.

Growing disillusionment with the *Tanzimat* was vented in an accusatory lament against government and reform that was coming from all directions. Members of the ulema joined Young Ottomans in calling for liberal reform, in particular for a representative assembly to check dictatorialism, fiscal irresponsibility and wasteful, socially destructive projects. It was what drove Ali Suavi, the graduate of religious studies and ulema scholar, to align himself with poets, essayists and former officials of the Language and Translation section who had served in Ottoman Embassies in European capitals, men of a more advantaged background that he might otherwise never have known or had little to do with.

Coming from a pious family of modest means, Ali Suavi was more a voice of the common people calling for social justice and egalitarian democracy than a proponent of the moderate parliamentarianism of his Young Ottoman associates who were at times affiliated with state bureaucracy and who fully accepted the idea of an elitist leadership under a constitutional sultanate. Where Ali Suavi called for justice and equality based on God's Shari'a law of Islam, the other Young Ottomans called for assemblies and parliaments that would provide laws made on the rational human level. His forced marriage of popular political action on the street level to the Young Ottoman journalism calling for a peaceful program of reform grounded in Ottoman institutions carried Ali Suavi way beyond the limits of opposition accepted by the other Young Ottomans. Revolution, violence, assassination and martyrdom, these were not prescriptive medicines the Young

Ottomans endorsed to save the empire. His violent death in 1878 during a muddled attempt to strike against despotism by assassinating Sultan abd al-Hamid II was a fitting end to an enigmatic life dedicated to reviving the long-gone ruling spirit of a once-glorious empire in its death throes. Preceding the empire to the grave by a generation, Ali Suavi took with him his oddly compounded spirit of religious absolutism and Young Ottoman humanism that somehow sustained him through the decades of turmoil and stress that were tearing the empire and society apart, as much as himself. His life, a journey of adventurous desperation to save what could not be saved in the meaninglessness of a world falling apart, was given meaning in the absolutist's dream of martyrdom. The road he traveled is worth examining.

Ali Suavi made the Hajj pilgrimage to Mecca before completing his religious studies. His entering religious study was at the guiding hand of his pious father, a merchant making a middling living selling paper. It was from his father, he said, that he received early in life his strong principles on social justice and Shari'a law.[15] Upon completing his studies he became a member of the ulema and was given a secondary school teaching position in the provinces, first in Bursa, followed by Plovdiv in modern Bulgaria.

It was a time when nothing seemed to be going right for the empire. The *Tanzimat's* advancing secularization was doing nothing in defense against Europe's advancing influence in the upper reaches of Ottoman society and its military inroads in the frontier provinces. Europe was taking over the empire from the inside and out. In Plovdiv, he had come to share many Young Ottoman ideas on the necessity of change. This was bizarre for a religious scholar so married to Shari'a law. But justice was justice, whether it came from God or parliament, and so he blasted his criticism of government and his call for constitutional reform from all three barrels at his disposal: the mosque, the classroom and a Young Ottoman journal for which he wrote. When Ali was not teaching school, he was preaching in the mosque, giving him two audiences for his ideas on justice and reform. His political activism first emerged in his Friday mosque sermons denouncing tyranny and the secular government's unbridled policy of importing everything Western that was destroying religion and the soul of the empire. A modified version of this he delivered in the classroom.

He became associated with several leading Young Ottomans, most importantly Namik Kemal and Ziya Pasha, with whom he collaborated in editing and writing for their journal, *Muhbir* (Arabic: *Mukhbir*; *Informer*). His fiery oratory in the mosque and his articles in the journal won him a popular following among both those whose allegiance was to religion and Shari'a on the one side and those who supported a Western style constitution limiting the sultan's authority on the other. The intemperate criticism of government policy that he unleashed in his journal articles was enough for the *Tanzimat* grand vizier to order his dismissal as a teacher and his exile to the far provinces, along with his associates Namik Kemal and Ziya Pasha. Ali Suavi was sent to the distant Black Sea coast where he was free to preach his fire to the wind and waves. His more sophisticated and literary Young Ottoman colleagues were from then on a bit leery of his emotional diatribes: not only were they too dangerous but they were too overly laden with raw religious passion.

Ali was a misfit in a society of young rebels who themselves felt they fit nowhere in their half-fused worlds of East and West. The Young Ottomans defied definition. They were more a band of young educated discontents, critics of the political and cultural condition, than they were a closely-knit society with a focused outlook on means and goals, being as diverse in their ideas from one another as those of the *philosophes* of the Enlightenment, whom they resembled in many ways, particularly in their advocacy of progress through science and opposition to autocracy. They all found inspiration in John Locke. And though their ideas did not package easily into a unified movement defined by an ideology or bound by a singular vision, they did collectively broadcast the destructive effects that the *Tanzimat*'s authoritative and uncritical imposition of foreign institutions, laws and customs were having on Ottoman society. Thoughtless imitation of Western institutions and law codes could not grow in Ottoman soil. Reform by dictatorship from the top was another form of political tyranny. Reform should come from a consensus that took into account the cultural ethos of the people. Their first priority was a representative government that would implement a program of reform coming from the will of the people, not an irresponsible absolutist tyranny that put the people in a stupor.

"What is this ignominiousness that has befallen us?" Ali Suavi wrote in 1868 during another period of exile, this one in London:

> What is this inability to stir ourselves, what is this sleepiness, what is this effeminateness? Why should it be that the Franks who are not congenitally smarter than we should hold their government to account for state expenditures while we contribute our dues and then do nothing but stupidly stare?[16]

The *Tanzimat* innovators, he went on, were a pack of mindless bureaucrats inured to the abuses of power, ruthlessly crushing the foundations of Ottoman society with their importations. Wielding the sword of state, they hacked down Ottoman cultural and institutional life, replacing what they destroyed with wholesale European importations that they understood not.

In place of *Tanzimat* wreckage that passed as reform, the Young Ottomans advocated an evolution of representative and constitutional government through political reform as a first step to engaging the Ottoman public in the work of reform. Reform could only work by opening the political process. Minds, too, had to be opened for change to be made and roots to grow and this had to begin by abolishing autocratic power.

Autocratic power aside, the Young Ottomans had much in common with the *Tanzimat* reformers. Both believed in the Ottoman state, caliphate and sultanate; both were familiar with the West; both were Westernized in a fashion and dressed accordingly, spoke European languages, had lived in Europe, and wanted changes in their society that were inspired by Europe. Most of the Young Ottomans came from the same social origins and had the same early education as the *Tanzimat* people; they began their careers in the same Translation Bureau and Language School as had the *Tanzimat* reformers. Several Young Ottomans were intellectually nurtured in those private literary associations whose origins went back to the Tulip Period, small groups of people getting together in someone's house, a café or a teahouse. The most influential of these associations was the Beshiktash Scientific Society that was mentioned earlier. Though denied a long life, the Beshiktash Society started something in nurturing an intellectual inquisitiveness about science, philosophy and Western civilization, indicative of a general rise in intellectual curiosity in the middle and upper strata of Istanbul. Several of the society's members rose to high positions. In unwitting emulation of the defunct Beshiktash Society, individuals in and out of government are reported to have met quietly together, if not secretly, in the great homes of the wealthy. Every owner of a large mansion is said to have tried to have at least one learned man in residence to instruct the guests and members of the household in modern knowledge and political affairs of the West. The intellectual heat generated by these salons appears to have been more in the nature of philosophical discourse than it was politically motivated criticism against the sultan's policies. Instead of a manifesto of rebellion, an Armenian member of one of those salons in 1850 made a Turkish translation of a history of Greek philosophy to introduce his Ottoman peers to contemporary Western philosophy, perhaps in answer to Sultan Mahmud's literary debate between ibn Rushd's natural philosophy and al-Ash'ari's theology of nature and miracle. Since a Christian could get away with doing what would be considered heretical for a Muslim, having a knowledgeable Christian come around for a chat with the guests had its advantages. It was not long before Muslims themselves followed the Armenian into the dangerous waters of philosophy.[17]

One of the earliest Muslims to do so was a young man from a family of strong religious tradition. He is famous enough in Ottoman history to be known simply as Munif. Munif went straight from his religious schooling in Istanbul and Cairo, where he attended al-Azhar, to the Translation Bureau, which by then, 1852, offered a more promising career to a young man than straight religious studies. With an eye to his son's future, Munif's father, himself a member of the ulema, may have come to the conclusion through experience that a career in the ulema was rapidly becoming a dead end. From the Translation Bureau, Munif was appointed second secretary to the Ottoman Embassy in Berlin, where he remained for several years. Thanks to Mahmud's Translation Bureau and the permanent embassies, Munif's transformation from religious student to intellectual reformer and literary innovator was complete by 1859, the year he published his Turkish translation of selections of philosophical dialogues taken from the writings of Voltaire, Fenelon and Fontenelle. Intended to introduce ideas of the Enlightenment to the Ottoman public, his translation was vehemently attacked as atheistic, an indication of how conservative the ulema were becoming during the last half of the 19th century, as the brighter and more privileged students were being drawn away from the madrasas for the new careers opening up in the reformist government. Modernist initiatives were consistently being challenged by the narrowing ulema. About 20 years after Munif's condemnation for his book of philosophy, the renowned reformist grand vizier, Midhat Pasha, who himself had been a member of the Beshiktash Society, was attacked for merely using the term "Islamic Philosophy," the ulema claiming it was a contradiction in terms since there could be no philosophy in a society formed around a religion of law and revelation.

Munif was not easily intimidated. Coming from an influential family, he had friends in high places, one of whom was the last of the two *Tanzimat* rulers, Sultan abd al-Aziz. Not only did the sultan shield Munif from the ulema's accusations of heresy, but he permitted him to assemble a society of philosophically minded Ottomans and publish a new journal, *The Journal of Science* (*Mejmua-i Funun*). An offspring of the Beshiktash Scientific Society, Munif's was formally called the Ottoman Scientific Society (Jami'at-i Ilmiyye-i Osmaniye).[18] The aim of Munif's journal, as in so many others that were to appear in Turkish and Arabic in the 1860s and after, was to attract enough students to science so that in a generation or two it would become an integral part of Muslim learning. The life of Munif's society and journal was brief, three years (1861–1864), but it came to an end for reasons other than those that ended the Beshiktash Society and sent Shanizade into exile. Economics, not politics, downed the journal. Subscriptions were low and neither state support nor private subsidy came to the rescue. Two generations of 19th century reform had failed to produce the critical mass of readers needed to sustain an independent popular scientific journal. The deadweight of poverty and illiteracy that burdened Ottoman society was too great to sustain privately run literary journals without some form of external support, and the practice of state or private subsidy of intellectual enterprise had not yet caught on.

In his private support of the Young Ottoman journal *Muhbir*, the Egyptian prince Mustafa Fazil Pasha was the exception to the rule. Though from Egypt and the Muhammad Ali dynasty, he served as a high functionary in the sultan's bureaucracy and was in every way an Ottoman – and a Young Ottoman constitutionalist: a royal foot in each camp. One of the six founding members who in 1865 formed the Young Ottoman Society, Mustafa Fazil funded the liberal journal from his private fortune, without which the Young Ottoman's place in 19th century Ottoman intellectual and literary history would have been significantly diminished.

Here was another innovation from the West: critical journalism struggling to be free. The government took over a year to close *Muhbir* down and send its principal writers, Namik Kemal, Shinasi, Ziya Pasha and Ali Suavi, to official posts far from Istanbul and from each other, from Cyprus to the Black Sea. The government treated the Young Ottoman editors and writers gently. They were part of the Ottoman family, young men from comfortable circumstances with connections, who had been educated in state schools and who had perhaps served as state officials. Like men of the *Tanzimat*, they were students of language whose knowledge of French had gained them a ticket to the Translation Bureau, that training ground of *Tanzimat* absolutists and liberal constitutionalists. Whatever the argument between them, it was still one Ottoman family and that called for civility among its members. It was in fact this lack of civility on the part of Ali Suavi, a wild stallion of religious passion that refused bit, saddle and stirrup, that so troubled Young Ottomans like Ziya, Namik Kemal and Shinasi, whose style of protest was kept within the unwritten boundaries of provocation with self-restraint. The difference was a matter of social background – and the accidental encounter of life as experience and opportunity. Shinasi, for example, got his start for a career through his fortuitous acquaintance with a French training officer in Ottoman service that he happened to meet when serving in the artillery corps.

The chance encounter became a friendship that opened Shinasi to the West and the beginning of a new life. Having learned French from his friend, he applied to the Translation Bureau and was accepted. After a few years in translation, he requested the government to fund a tour of study for him in Paris. This was generously granted by the *Tanzimat* reformers, and from 1848 to 1853, he was in Paris studying public finance and literature while at the same time writing poetry and drama. After imbibing the culture of Paris and the literature of France for five years he returned to Istanbul and founded the biweekly *Tasvir-i Efkar* (*The Image of Thoughts*), in which he published articles on modern science, education, literature, European intellectual advances, and a Turkish translation he made of Buffon's evolutionist *Histoire Naturelle*. Darwin had not yet published his *Origin of Species*.

Shinasi introduced a simple, clear and straightforward style of expression that marked a break with the bombastic style universally favored by Ottoman writers. He came to be considered the founder of the modern school of Ottoman literature, his style of writing attracting far more adherents than did the ideas expressed in his writing. As the government-sponsored study tour had turned him into an anti-*Tanzimat* constitutionalist, his political writing now obliged him to flee his former absolutist benefactors and return to Paris. Better self-exile in Paris than a punitive government position on the far shores of the Black Sea or Plovdiv. In the mid-1860s, he was with the Ottoman community in Parisian exile, writing for political reform and having his pamphlets smuggled into Istanbul. Because the *Tanzimat* reformers were in need of men who knew the West, the wayward son managed to get back into the good graces of the Ottoman family and return to Istanbul and a government position. However, unable to restrain his criticism, which was far from advocating forceful resistance, he returned to voluntary exile. Exile was a constant feature of Young Ottoman life. Like naughty school children sent to the back of the room, they came and went from exile to government position, and then back to exile, only to return again. Once they had at last learned their lesson, they were welcome back into state service with open arms. They were too valuable for prison.

The most well-known of the Young Ottomans, Namik Kemal, was another of those constitutionalist pamphleteers who started his career in that breeding ground of reformism, the Translation Bureau. Born in 1840 into an old and well-established Istanbul family – his father had been a court astronomer, his grandfather a pasha in government service – Namik went through the government *rushdiyye* school system of Sultan Mahmud, then on to a secular higher education, coming of age at the height of the *Tanzimat* in the 1860s with his early belief that religion was an essential foundation of civilization still intact. Learning French as an employee in the Translation Bureau, he became a mid-level official in several Ottoman embassies in Europe. His writings make it apparent that his discovery of Europe was a positive and enriching experience, and that his admiration of Europe's civilization did not lessen his devotion to his own, as was the case with some Ottomans who spent years in Europe, becoming, as a *Tanzimat* Pasha had put it, more syphilized than civilized. His youth, combined with his outcry against the *Tanzimat*'s ministerial crew of cultural wreckage, drew him to other like-minded young critics, leading to the Young Ottoman Society, of which he was one of the founding members and a leading writer for *Muhbir*.[19]

Namik believed, or at least claimed to believe, that he saw in his reading of early Islamic history the embryo of the liberal philosophy and political institutions that arose in Europe. Here was a theme that would often recur in the Turkish and Arabic reformist literature of the 19th and 20th centuries: Because Muslim leaders and institutions had failed to develop politically, the embryo was lost and forgotten, the impressive beginning Muslims had made in science, medicine and philosophy going down the drain of political and religious tyranny. In quest of a political vocabulary to express the new ideas that Namik Kemal became familiar with in Europe, he searched into the mother language, Arabic, and came up with Ottomanized equivalents for patriotism, fatherland, citizen, freedom, rights, liberty, constitution and representative assembly: explosive neologisms that terrorized the sultan and his ministers. To show that the *Tanzimat* people were all wrong with their bulk importations of Western institutions and law codes, he worked the sources of early Islamic history and religion to show how they offered a clear path to modern civilization; that the ideas of Locke, Montesquieu and Rousseau were there, imbedded in the Quran and early authorities, proving that the true Islamic polity was constitutionally governed by the voice of the people, not by the whims of absolutist rulers.

Mustafa Fazil's bankrolling of *Muhbir* allowed these ideas and criticism of government to flow unimpeded into Ottoman literate society. When the government lost patience, Mustafa Fazil was politely asked to stop his financial support and the leading Young Ottomans were simply transferred to other positions outside of the capital, not exactly exiled, nor even fined, not even watched – within months, with Mustafa Fazil's help, Namik Kemal, Ziya, Shinasi and Ali Suavi had slipped away from their respective outposts without difficulty. Making their way to Italy by different routes, and from there to Paris and London, they resumed publication of *Muhbir*, copies of which were smuggled into Istanbul and other major cities of the empire. This lasted a year.

Taking full advantage of his position as chief editor, Ali Suavi launched a series of extreme attacks against the government, its false promises, its superficial reforms, its unelected and unrepresentative ruling bodies, its cowardly bending to European intervention in Ottoman internal affairs. He called for the establishment of a national representative body, the elimination of all foreign influence in domestic affairs and a system of reform, institutionally organized and modeled on Ottoman and Islamic precedents. These were essential elements in the Young Ottoman program, but Ali Suavi voiced them in such bellicose terms that he further alienated his colleagues. The attacks were too strong for Mustafa

Fazil and the other Young Ottomans who identified with the state and the ruling institution. They desired no more than a moderating constitution and a curb to the *Tanzimat*'s Europeanizing secularization of society, not a revolution led by a proletarian imam.

Mustafa Fazil was unnerved. He was, after all, a ranking prince in the house founded by Muhammad Ali and a friend and officer of Sultan abd al-Aziz. Deeming *Muhbir* to be now too tarnished by Ali Suavi's radicalism, he requested Namik and Ziya to give up *Muhbir* and begin anew with a change of name. The new journal would be called *Hurriyet*: *Freedom*. It first appeared in mid-1868, under the editorship of Ziya, who had risen to the high status of pasha before turning into a Young Ottoman. But now even Ziya's criticism of government was too much for Mustafa Fazil, who had made his amends with the sultan. An Egyptian prince close to the sultan and in Ottoman service, while at the same time being a member of the opposition and funding its journal, was an anomaly too fragile to last. Funding was gradually withdrawn and *Hurriyet* suffered an early demise as it followed *Muhbir* to the grave.[20]

By 1870, Namik Kemal was back in Istanbul with Mustafa Fazil. Several other Young Ottomans remained in Paris and joined the socialist Commune of the French Revolutionary Republic following the fall of Louis Napoleon. Ziya Pasha fell into limbo. Namik Kemal, enjoying the patronage of Mustafa Fazil, resumed his reformist journalism in Istanbul. It was not long before he overstepped the line of public criticism of government policy that was tolerated by the ministerial pashas and their conservative bureaucracy and was requested to leave. It was a purely Ottoman form of voluntary exile. Again, he was having his articles smuggled into Istanbul from Paris and London, and again, he was allowed to return and resume writing. This brought him a short period of not uncomfortable lockup in the Ministry of Police followed by a longer one, more than 2 ½ years, in Cyprus under house arrest. This was as far as the government went in punishing their recalcitrant children who, even under house arrest, were able to write and smuggle out their poems, plays and pamphlets.

After the closing of *Hurriyet* in 1868, Ali Suavi, who had by now been totally rejected by Mustafa Fazil, Namik Kemal, Shinasi and Ziya Pasha, remained in Paris and London. In London, he took a young English bride, Mary. He was not yet 30. Photos of him around that time show a virile, handsome man of dark piercing eyes, long mustache, turban, clerical robe and sternly focused as he sat writing an article for his press. Even in Europe he wore his religious garb. No Tahsin straw hat for this Hoja abroad. Religion and its formal dress were too much a part of him for that. But the rebel in him opened him to the West. For all his devotion to *Din ve Devlet*, he could put aside religion and empire enough to give in to his admiration of the West and those political and educational institutions he wanted to reinvent as Islamic and Ottoman. Mary was a pleasurable part of his discovery of the West: not a philosophical idea or political institution but a warm woman with a beating heart, an offering to the passion he put into everything that he did, a comforting helpmate in his sacred quest to change his world and help him pick up English on the quick.

He and Mary left London for Paris where he began his own small journal, a monthly lithograph of 21 pages in the beginning, then lengthening to 25 the next year. Meaning to bring modern natural science under the umbrella of the Islamic sciences, he called it *Ulum Gazetisi, Journal of The Sciences*, dropping Munif's *funun* that was now normally used to designate the natural sciences. For the religious revolutionary and secularist modernizer, *Ulum* covered all knowledge, sacred and profane. His *Ulum Gazetisi* was a one-man operation run on a shoestring budget and containing articles on a broad range of topics: science, religion, philosophy, economics, education, history and culture, all written by Ali Suavi who, thinking to be another Tahsin Hoja, fancied himself encyclopedic. His writing continued to be as erratic and jagged in style as it was radically politicized. Straining to convince instead of inform, it proved ineffective as a source enlightening the public on modern science in the way Munif's *Mejmua-i Funun* did 20 years earlier. Hammering the Ottomans for not learning to do things for themselves rather than always relying on Europe, *Ulum Gazetisi* continued the same intemperate criticisms that Ali Suavi had broadcast in *Muhbir*. More seriously, he now sanctified violent resistance against unjust government. *Ulum* lasted almost three years, until 1871, by which time it was down to 11 pages.

Then, 1876 was a tumultuous year. In the rush to modernize, the *Tanzimat* governments had borrowed so heavily at high rates of interest from European banks and financiers that it was becoming more difficult every year to meet the interest payments. Loans were made to pay the interest on earlier loans, each time at a higher rate of interest. Interest payments were devouring the government's revenues, leaving little to run the country and pay salaries. As did the Egyptians, the Ottomans paid a high price for their European railroads, dams, telegraph lines, generating plants, armaments and warships. Europeans did the planning, engineering, construction and financing, while Muslim governments paid through the nose and watched. The Ottomans holding responsible positions, some of them graduate engineers, watched while the peasants did the low-level labor, and the country slid into bankruptcy – exactly what Ali Suavi was railing against in *Muhbir* and *Ulum* several years earlier.

The first loan was made in 1854. Borrowing was easy and addictive. Once the door of living on credit was open, Ottoman leaders found it impossible to close. By 1875, the public debt was 200 million English pounds. The annual interest came to 12 million, more than half the national income. When the European financial institutions refused further credit, the Ottomans defaulted. Since protecting the nation's wealthy trumped capitalist theory in the higher councils of Europe, laissez faire economics was not a viable government option when it involved foreign loans and money owed to Europe's wealthy financiers and empire builders. The wealthy were national assets; their wealth had to be protected. They were too big to fail. Besides, the lenders were friends and close associates of the men leading government. National honor demanded that the loans be repaid in full, with interest. A European-controlled Ottoman Debt Commission was established in 1881. Much the same had happened in Egypt and Iran several years earlier.

The crisis of irresponsible financial oversight was worsened by the vagaries of nature. Drought had ravaged the agricultural sector in 1873, floods in 1874. The added burden of increased taxation to meet the interest payments on the loans drove the peasants off the land and into the urban slums. Protests of Christian peasants under Muslim landowners in Bosnia and Herzegovina, who refused to pay higher taxes, led to insurrection and war in the Balkans.

Fired up by pan-Slavic nationalism and the promise of Russian support, Serbia and Montenegro attacked Ottoman forces in Bosnia and Herzegovina. The cost of defense was the straw that broke the back of Ottoman finances. In October of 1875, the sultan informed his European creditors that he could not pay the full interest on the debt. Germany, Russia and Austria aligned to pressure abd al-Aziz to enforce earlier reforms regarding the Christians under Ottoman rule. The Europeans rulers introduced a raft of new reforms to alleviate the condition of the Christian peasants in Bosnia and Herzegovina. This was the price they demanded for helping the Ottomans out of their financial troubles. Otherwise, there was little the powers could do to end the insurrection. The sultan had no choice but to accept what was tantamount to an ultimatum. The treasury was empty, and the revolt was deteriorating into a series of Christian–Muslim massacres. To reject the European demand would only provide the pretext for European occupation of Bosnia and Herzegovina. The sultan also knew that accepting it would be seen by the conservative opposition as surrender and a price would have to be paid. Cries of betrayal and heresy were bound to fill the streets. The call for the sultan's head would come next. But the European offer could not be refused.

The sultan accepted and was deposed by a council of ministers and ulema. With him went the last of the *Tanzimat* grand viziers. A week later the former sultan was found dead, his wrists slit by scissors. Though few doubted abd al-Aziz was murdered, his death was officially declared a suicide. An autopsy was not allowed. His successor reigned only three months. Declared mentally unbalanced, Murad V was deposed.[21] The prince of the Ottoman family who succeeded him had been using words such as liberty, fatherland, constitution, representative assembly, icons of Young Ottoman neologisms, which raised liberal hopes when he became sultan. It looked as if the new sultan was serious about a constitutional assembly when a Grand Council of Notables was assembled at the official residence of the Shakyh al-Islam to discuss constitutional reform. Through the gloom of insolvency and European intervention, the promise of a new dawn brightened the Ottoman horizon. Reformers headed for the capital. From his exile in Cyprus, Namik Kemal arrived. Young Ottoman political ideas looked about to triumph. In Paris, Ali Suavi wrote to the new sultan for permission to return.

Abd al-Hamid II was known to be cunning, untrustworthy and pathologically suspicious. Haunted by the horror of abd al-Aziz's fate, he lived up to his reputation. He was reputed never to sleep two successive nights in the same place and to have ordered that Ottoman warships sailing the Bosphoros be stripped of all ammunition lest their guns be directed at the palace. Considering his obsessive suspicions, it was odd that he and his advisors would accede to Ali Suavi's petition to return from his Paris exile. Probably the maverick *mullah's* menacing rhetoric had faded during the five years since his journal folded. Memory could have evaporated in the heat of events since 1875. His English wife may have made him look less prone to violence, but within two years of his return, the rebel cleric would die fighting for the betrayed promise of a constitution and his dream of an egalitarian Muslim state, where science and religion coexisted in peaceful harmony and the wrong-minded thinking of al-Ash'ari and al-Ghazali was purged to oblivion.

Not only was the severe critic allowed back, he was incredibly given a plum position as director of the prestigious Galata Saray Lyceum. Good connections, but primarily his criticism of certain reformist officials opposed to abd al-Hamid's succession, had much to do with the appointment. Ali Suavi also had good credentials and experience to recommend him. He knew English and French. He had lived eight years in London and Paris and had intimate knowledge of the West, its learning and civilization. His wife Mary gave him another dimension of intimacy with Western culture. Topping all that, he was a member of the ulema. He gave religious credence to science and secular change. But it was not a fortunate appointment.

The Galata Saray Lyceum had been founded by the third of the *Tanzimat* grand viziers, Fuad Pasha, in 1868. Built as a preparatory school next to the Galata Saray Hospital and Medical School, the Lyceum was patterned after the French lycee and followed more or less the same curriculum. A strictly secular school, it had a mixed faculty of French and Turkish instructors. Having as a new director a long-exiled member of the ulema whose only in depth form of study was religion did not sit well with the secular faculty. His turban and clerical robe were jarring contradictions to the mission of the school. A Muslim cleric having a young English wife was another contradiction hard to swallow. His settling Mary in the headmaster's chambers rubbed against the secular faculty's sense of decorum.

Who was this cleric who wrote on the necessity of intense school instruction in mathematics, physics, chemistry and the disciplines that prepared students for industry and engineering, but who in the same stroke of the pen wanted Muslim rule under Shari'a law, as if there had been no New Order of Selim, no Mahmud, no *Tanzimat*? The turban invading the sacred halls of their secular fortress of learning baffled the faculty. Ali Suavi's peremptory management style was a more serious problem. Accustomed to the freewheeling independence of an editor and writer of his own journal, he was too used to running his own show to manage a high caliber school and faculty effectively. He was difficult to work with. Writing on everything, but nothing in depth, he was mistakenly, and infuriatingly, convinced of his encyclopedic breadth. Conflict could not but abound. The faculty wanted him out. Within months he was dismissed.

This may have bitten deeply into his self-respect, but he could pass it off as just more of the same institutional weakness, injustice and corruption that were destroying the empire. In any case, something on a far larger scale than the personal affront he suffered was biting into him: the adverse turn of political events between 1876 and 1878 that was destroying the empire. He had preached and written in promotion of violent resistance to injustice and tyranny for over a decade, and now the time had come for him to put his words in action. Abd al-Hamid II had abrogated the constitution and the two-chamber Assembly of Deputies. The crushed hopes of liberals were worsened by terrifying news coming from the Balkans and Bulgaria. In the summer of 1876, troubles simmering in the Balkans spread to Bulgaria, where Christian peasants rose up against the Ottoman authorities, killing a hundred of them. This led to religious strife and what Western reporters and diplomats called the "Bulgarian massacres," the Turkish slaughter of Christians, forgetting to mention the Christian slaughter of Turks that had set it off, and so reinforcing the late 19th century Western image of Ottomans as cruel, fanatical Turks. Predictably, the armies of Austria and Russia intervened. Taking advantage of the invasion, the armies of Serbia and Montenegro advanced further into Bosnia and Herzegovina. Then Romania, allied with Russia, went to war against the Ottomans. Sofia was occupied, followed by Edirne (Adrianople). The Russians were, meanwhile, advancing into the Caucasus along the Black Sea. When the western prong of the Russian pincer reached the village of San Stefano, not far from Istanbul, the Ottomans, drained of blood and treasure, sued for peace.

The Sultan's reluctant agreement to the treaty that was drawn up by Russia and Austria required that the Ottomans surrender their authority in the Balkan provinces to the victors. Awakened from her splendid isolation, Britain, under Prime Minister Benjamin Disraeli, sent the fleet to restore the balance of power. Rather than risk a general European war, Russia and Austria agreed to an international conference. The conference was held in Berlin, the capital of the recently created German Empire, and hosted by the empire's architect, Iron Chancellor Count Otto von Bismarck. But it was Benjamin Disraeli who was the architect of the treaty that was signed in Berlin in 1878. For the Ottomans who, though invited to participate, were passive spectators at the conference, it was not much less disastrous than the Treaty of San Stefano. Romania went from autonomy under Ottoman suzerainty to complete independence, as did Serbia and Montenegro. A new state called Bulgaria was created and placed under Russian tutelage. Novi Bazar was lost to Austria. Russia annexed territory along the Black Sea. In the rush to despoil the dying empire, Britain took Cyprus, while Greece claimed Crete. France laid claim to Tunis; Italy claimed Albania and Libya. If the Treaty of Versailles 40 years later was the funeral ceremony for Ottoman existence, the Treaty of Berlin was its last supper. The guests ate well and between courses contemplated the leftovers they might next feast upon at the next banquet.

Conditions in Istanbul were volcanic. The loss of territory that had for centuries been Ottoman was a bitterly felt amputation. The loss of Crete, where so many Muslims lived, was particularly painful because it was given to the Greeks, who for centuries had been Ottoman subjects. Defeated soldiers straggled into the capital, ragged, weary and hungry. Rioting filled the streets in protest to the sultan's acceptance of such a humiliating treaty. The truncated empire, sunk in insolvency by mindless borrowing from Western financial institutions, its religious minorities placed under Western protection, was now being wholly delivered to European control. Abd al-Hamid was labeled a traitor to Islam and Empire, a toady of the West.

In a desperate attempt to save the decaying empire from what he feared would be its grave, Ali Suavi took to arms. Leading a small band of 30 defeated and angry soldiers recently arrived in the capital from the front against the Russians, he went on a suicidal mission to assassinate or dethrone abd al-Hamid and return Murad V to the sultanate. The plan was poorly thought out, badly executed and easily thwarted. Amidst the riotous fear and tumult engulfing the unprotected city, Ali Suavi, in turban and cloak, rifle in hand, led the charge of his bedraggled, miniscule and lightly armed force against the palace where the sultan had sequestered himself in fright. The well-armed palace guard made quick work of it. Ali Suavi was wounded and publicly hanged. With him went the last of the Young Ottomans.

In the throes of the life and death crisis threatening the diminishing empire, the legacy of the Young Ottomans and the *Tanzimat* was transformed into a more extreme society of young ideologues devoted to saving the remnants of empire from tyranny within and from Europe without. In place of Ottomanism and Islam, a tougher ideology was adopted: nationalism. This European particularist, secularist and divisive strain of modern identity transmogrified the intellectual heirs of the Young Ottomans, who now called themselves Young Turks: strident soldiers of secular nationalism. The curtain call of the old Muslim empire's end was at hand.

Ali Suavi himself had been bitten by the nationalist bug. In his later writing it becomes the Turks, not the Ottomans, who will save the empire. Turks. Turks everywhere. Turks in Central Asia, Turks in Anatolia, a pan-Turkish union against the West, but most immediately against Russia. Ziya Gokalp, Turkish nationalism's chief ideologue, would in the next generation develop Ali Suavi's fragmentary and emergent ideas into a full blown radical fantasy dressed up as historical anthropology that ennobled the Turks as the origin and progenitors of language, science and civilization, like a tribal sun radiating its light through the universe, bestowing it upon less fortunate peoples over the ages.

It did not take long after the Ottoman Empire's new ideologues discovered that it was being Turkish that made for greatness that the empire's rulers started running the show as a purely Turkish enterprise. Then, the Arabs, who after the Ottoman losses suffered at the Treaty of Berlin were now the majority in the empire, came to realize that they were Arabs, not Ottomans, bound in a common brotherhood of Islam, and they too began to romanticize their own mythology of racial superiority, driving another fault line into the cratering empire. If Turks insisted on being Turks, Arabs would be Arabs, and through the racial cracks between them the dying spirit of Ottomanism drained away. The four centuries of Arab–Turkish brotherhood bound in Islam and protected by the great Ottoman Empire of sultan and caliph was reaching its end. The brief constitutional period had been the last spark of Ottoman enthusiasm. Arab and Turkish provincial delegates had assembled in Istanbul arm in arm as Ottoman brothers in Islam to set the ship of empire on its constitutional course, but the sun had too quickly set on the golden dawn of this new day that the Young Ottomans had campaigned and written so hard to deliver.

In alliance with the discontented ulema and their students, Sultan abd al-Hamid was able to turn the constitutional government out, send the delegates packing back to the provinces, abrogate the constitution and initiate his 33-year long period of despotism. Islam would be the constitution, pan-Islam the foreign policy. As Muslims, the people had already voted by virtue of their membership in God's blessed community, and they had already been issued their constitution in the Quran and Shari'a, with the ulema their representative assembly. Hamidian despotism succumbed in 1908 to a secularist government headed by leaders of a semi-secret organization, the Committee of Union and Progress. The CUP had been organized by a group of Westernized activists whose ideas came from the Young Ottomans, but stripped of the Islamic cultural and institutional grounding in which the Young Ottomans claimed their ideas were rooted. The European virus of secular nationalism that informed the CUP killed Ottomanism, from whose decaying chrysalis was born the Young Turks. The work of a generation of Young Ottoman constitutionalist opposition to the despotism of the secularist *Tanzimat* was taken over by a generation of Young Turk nationalist–secularist opposition to al-Hamid's pan-Islamic, anti-constitutional despotism.

Carried away by nationalism, the Young Turk government cut away the political and religious roots that for four centuries had bound all Muslims: Turk, Arab, Kurd, Circassian, Bosnian and Albanian, all brothers in the great empire of Islam whose sultan–caliph was thought equally by all to be their God-given ruler. The Ottoman identity came crashing to an end. The harsh policy of Turkish nationalism enforced by the Young Turk government alienated leaders of the major ethnic group left in the empire before the outbreak of World War I: the Arabs. It was not a welcome adjustment for the great majority of Arabs and Turks. Four centuries of Muslim marriage between them had brought comfort, security and familiarity. Especially for the Arabs, this divorce meant facing the world alone, a world filled with lusting predators driven to possess and exploit. Severed from the empire and the sultan–caliph protector, Arab lands would be easy prey.

In the last throes of imperial existence, a dictatorial triumvirate of Young Turks took the Ottomans into World War I on the side of Germany. Germany's enemies, France, Russia and Britain, had devoured great chunks of the empire. Germany had taken nothing and a German victory over the colonial empires would restore the lost lands to the Ottomans. The Young Turk gamble cost them what was left of the empire. The end of the war left the empire under occupation and its occupiers planning its partition as spoils to the victors. The empire was over. All that remained was the secret horse trading of the winners and their drawing of new borders.

Following the deposition of Sultan abd al-Hamid, the Committee of Union and Progress government provided organization, planning, focus and ideology for continuing secularization, taking up where the *Tanzimat* reformers had left off a generation earlier. Mustafa Kemal, who had been a member of the Committee of Union and Progress as a young military officer in Salonika and an ardent admirer of Young Ottoman literature, particularly that of Namik Kemal, was one of the very few Ottoman generals to emerge from World War I as a genuine hero. His army's defeat of the Greek invasion of Anatolia in 1922 turned the political death of the Turks into life, as Kemal's new Turkey rose from the imperial ashes of the Ottomans, resurrected in the principles of republican progressive secularism.

Mustafa Kemal was the product of a century's cumulative experience in Ottoman modernization. His long march had been prepared by generations of reform and came with a ruthless and decisive rejection of sultanate, caliphate and the civilization that had been informed by Islam for over a millennium. It brought to reality the mother of nightmares that Tahtawi, the Young Ottomans and every Muslim feared who contemplated the fate of Islam and Muslim civilization ruled by intemperate rulers who tore the culture apart to meet the challenge of Western power. A century of attempted reform, from the Tulip Period to the New Order, followed by Mahmud's innovations, the *Tanzimat* and a generation of liberal writers and activists, imparted a momentum that at last overcame the well-intentioned resistance of vested tradition, whose strength was the will to survive in a familiar world, a world of one's own, informed by a moral way presumed to be drawn from infallible authority.

A world of one's own it was not to be. The catastrophic war of 1914–1918 set the final stage for the departure of the old and familiar. The transition from sultanate to secular republic was informed by two centuries of movers – Damad Ibrahim Pasha, Yirmisekiz, Ibrahim Muteferrika, Raghib Pasha, Khalil Hamid, Selim III, Mahmud II, Hoja Ishak Efendi, Mustafa Sami, Sadik Rifat, Hoja Tahsin, Shanizade, Shinasi, Ali Suavi, Namik Kemal, the *Tanzimat* reformers, the Young Turk nationalists and Mustafa Kemal – who cumulatively, building one on the other, created the momentum for change in a world where the old institutions no longer seemed to work.

The 19th century had been a losing battle for the traditionalists, and equally losing for the reformers when it came to saving the empire. Mahmud's reforms and the *Tanzimat* made it clear that no synthesis of mutual compromise would be reached between secular reform and tradition. No Young Ottoman constitutionalist coup d'etat saved the day. Secularism was the order of the day, and nationalism had the last word, as Islam was squeezed ever more narrowly to the margins, for better or for worse. By the last decade of the century, Western education was being offered to females. In 1900, a secular Ottoman University was founded with four faculties, literature, mathematics, the physical sciences and religion, the poor fourth. The Hamidian period, though politically repressive, witnessed a rush in building Westernized schools to meet the demands of student population. Wherever there was space in Istanbul a school was built, whether over the courtyard of a mosque or in the corner of a graveyard.[22] The war merely provided a speedy culmination to a historical movement of change two centuries in the making. Half a century before Mustafa Kemal abolished the caliphate, Ali Suavi had written that the caliphate was no more than an office created in a moment of political crisis and in no way was it condoned by the Prophet nor supported by the Quran. It was a political invention having nothing to do with religion.

With this historical tumult as political background to Ottoman intellectual progress, what in the way of scientific assimilation was accomplished during this last half century of Ottoman existence? As for the Young Ottomans, they did nothing in the way of scientific work. They praised it, encouraged Ottomans to study it, wrote of it superficially, wrapped it in religion, but never translated anything of it or started a school to teach it. Theirs was another mission. But the message in the mission, at work with the reforms of the *Tanzimat*, leavened the cultural soil that made possible the first glimmer of modern scientific endeavor, even as the empire was wracked by defeat, bankruptcy, European fiscal control and imminent collapse. In the midst of the turmoil and insecurity, scientific assimilation continued quietly in the capital, at an unhurried pace, and is seen in the works of two men toward the end of Ottoman times.

Vidinli Husayn Tawfik Pasha (1832–1901) wrote a book on a new field of linear algebra called quaternions, equations involving a real number and three complex numbers. Published in English in 1882, the book signaled a quiver of genuine creative scientific life at last emerging from generations of reforms and military engineering institutes. Husayn Tawfik was born in Vidin, Bulgaria, went through primary (*rushdiye*) education there, and then went to Istanbul, where he entered the *Muhendishane-i Berri-i Humayun*, (Imperial School of Military Engineering). From there he entered the *Mekteb-i Harbiye* (War Academy), where he studied mathematics under an Ottoman mathematician, Tahir Pasha, who was a mathematics graduate of Cambridge University (1859).

Significantly, less than a decade after Tahir Pasha's graduation, a journal of scientific studies was being published in Istanbul, *Mebahis-i Ilmiyye*, founded in 1866, to which Husayn Tawfik greatly contributed. Upon Tahir Pasha's death, Husayn Tawfik was given his former mentor's position at the War Academy, by which time his mathematical expertise is reputed to have reached the level of his peers teaching in European universities. He gave courses in calculus, advanced algebra, analytical geometry and astronomy.

Mathematics had to share time with Husayn Tawfik's other professional functions, military and civil. As a graduate of the Military Staff College, he had a career as staff officer before him and never left it, advancing up the ranks to captain, major and colonel, to the very top as marshal. This meant being assigned periodically to military missions abroad. One was to the United States in order to inspect new weaponry developed during the Civil War; another was to Prussia. Posted in Paris as military attaché from 1870 to 1872, he advanced his mathematics at the University of Paris and College de France. In Paris, he met up with Namik Kemal and Ali Suavi and the other Young Ottoman exiles, whose views he generally shared but not enough for him to compromise his military career or trade his pursuit of mathematics for political pamphleteering.

The prestige Husayn Tawfik gained from his book on quarternions made him irresistible to government. It was a costly loss to the nascent scientific community, for he could not resist the attractive remuneration and status of high government office, and he cut short his scientific career. He was appointed to several high positions, the highest coming in 1889 as Minister of Commerce and Public Works. He was by then, however, approaching 60, with his innovative years in mathematics long over, though he could have beneficially served the state as a teacher informing the young minds of another generation working to nurture a scientific culture. Before going into government service, he published several specialized books on linear algebra, one on modern astronomy – this more of a general college textbook on the subject than a specialized study – and a number of professional articles in *Mebahis-i Ilmiyye*, the aforementioned science journal founded in 1866. One of the articles he published in 1867 was in reaction to one that appeared in the previous issue, which argued that the earth was stationary. Incredibly, the debate on that old subject was still going on, not only in the Ottoman Empire, but everywhere in Islamdom. It would not be until 1876 that the idea of a moving earth burst into the science journals of Cairo.

A second sign that a nascent Ottoman scientific culture was coming out of the work of reform was Salih Zaki Bey (1864–1921). It was he who introduced modern physics and mathematics to the Ottoman secondary school curriculum. From a dirt poor family and orphaned at 10, Salih Zaki assiduously studied his way through primary and secondary school and gained a position in the postal and telegraph service. Seen to be a bright young man with a keen scientific mind, he was sent by the government to study electrical engineering at the Polytechnique in Paris. He remained there for four years. Upon returning to Istanbul, he taught physics and chemistry at what was later to become the University of Ankara. In 1910, he was made director of the Galata Saray Lyceum. Going to the grave with the empire, Salih Zaki Bey was, after Vidinli Husayn Tawfik, the last of the scientists to be considered Ottoman.

The ground prepared by over a century and a half of reforms and new schools, of work done by Bonneval and de Tott, of *Tanzimat* innovation and Young Ottoman contention was finally bringing forth the green tendrils of a scientific culture. It had taken a long time to prepare the soil, plant the seeds and see evidence of their having taken root. It would also take a long time in the life of the Republic that replaced the Empire for those roots to grow and support an indigenous national community of scientists creatively contributing to the global society of science.

Notes

1 Mardin, *Genesis of Young Ottoman Thought*, Princeton University Press, Princeton, NJ, 1962, p. 171.
2 For a brief, concise overview of the legal dimension of Tanzimat reforms see Omer Turan, "Legal Adjustments of the Tanzimat and 'Mecelle'," in *Academie Bulgare des Sciences: Institut d'Etudes balkaniques*, Sofia, issues 1–2, 1999.
3 Omer Turan, "Legal Adjustments, of the Tanzimat and 'Mecelle'".
4 For a penetrating modern Turkish inside interpretation of Mustafa Sami's reformist significance see: *Turkiye Diyanet Vakfi Ansiklopedisi*, Istanbul, vol 31, 2006, p. 356.
5 Niyazi Berkes, *The Development of Secularization in Turkey*, McGill University Press, Montreal, 1994, p. 130.
6 Berkes, *Development of Secularization in Turkey*, p. 131.
7 While in exile he translated into Turkish the Arabic reformist treatise of Khayr al-Din Pasha, *Reforms Necessary to Muslim States*, a treatise that was highly appreciated even by the *Tanzimat* reformers who exiled him. Khayr al-Din, a Tunisian, became Ottoman grand vizier for a few years. Mardin, *Genesis of Young Ottoman Thought: A Study in the Modernization of Turkish Political Ideas*, Princeton University Press, Princeton, NJ, 1962, pp. 385–395.
8 Mardin, *Genesis of Young Ottoman Thought*, p. 229.
9 Exceptions to this government tyranny of independent thought in collectively organized groups occurred in Beirut, which because of its large Christian minority that

offered French religious orders and American evangelists a rich field to harvest souls through missionary education, escaped close Ottoman control and gave rise to a number of autonomous, foreign educational institutions, whose influence in propagating scientific interest extended throughout the Arab world, as will be seen.
10 Omer Faruk Akun, "Hoca Tahsin," in *Turkiye Diyanet Vakfi Islam Ansiklopedesi*, Istanbul, 1990, p. 200.
11 R. Davison, *Essays in Ottoman Turkish History*, University of Texas Press, Austin, 1990, pp. 138–139; Rudolph Peters, "Religious Attitudes Toward Modernization in Ottoman Empire: A 19th Century Pious Text on Steamships, Factories and the Telegraph," *Die Welt des Islams*, vol 26, 1986, pp. 76–105.
12 For a detailed study of the financing, construction and difficulties of the Ottoman telegraph system see Yakup Bektas, "The Sultan's Messenger: Cultural Construction of Ottoman Telegraphy, 1847–1880," *Society for the History of Technology*, 41, October 2000, pp. 669–696.
13 Ekmeleddin Ihsanoglu, *History of the Ottoman State, Society and Civilization*, vol. 2, Research Center for Islamic History and Culture, Istanbul, 2001–2002, p. 444.
14 Berkes, *Development of Secularization in Turkey*, pp. 174–176 note 29.
15 Mardin, *Genesis of Young Ottoman Thought*, pp. 360–361.
16 Mardin, *Genesis of Young Ottoman Thought*, p. 370.
17 Mardin, *Genesis of Young Ottoman Thought*, pp. 229–251.
18 In spite of the title of his journal, Munif used *fann* and *funun* for science and sciences, since by the 1860's Mustafa Sami's usage had become a permanent fixture in Ottoman vocabulary, the more precise *'ilm* and *'ulum* being reserved, as previously mentioned, for the religious sciences, which was a step toward resolving the epistemological rivalry, as well as confusion. Davison, *Essays in Ottoman Turkish History, 1774–1923: The Impact of The West*, University of Texas Press, Austin, 1990, p. 140.
19 Davison, *Essays in Ottoman Turkish History*, p. 174.
20 Khedive Ismail, because of a spat he was having with the *Tanzimat* grand vizier Ali Pasha, came to the rescue of the Young Ottomans and kept *Hurriyet* and its attack on Ali Pasha's government going a year longer, but the journal was reduced to existing on sufferance as a polemical instrument rather than elucidating a program of scientific education and democratic reform dressed in the sacred robes of Islam and venerable Ottoman tradition. Mardin, *Genesis of Young Ottoman Thought*, pp. 52–53.
21 Letters of Sultan abd al-Hamid that have only recently surfaced indicate that abd al-Aziz was murdered out of fear that his successor, Murad V, was mad and would be deposed, and that there would be a call to restore abd al-Aziz. Murad may have acted strangely the day of his enthronement (vomiting, throwing himself into a pool, shouting that his guards intended to kill him), but the eery way abd al-Aziz suddenly departed would have adversely affected all the Ottoman princes who were close to the throne. Abd al-Hamid II, Murad's successor, was justifiably paranoid for the whole of his long reign.
22 Davison, *Essays in Ottoman Turkish History*, pp. 166–174.

2 Post Muhammad Ali reform in Egypt

Khedive Ismail and Ali Mubarak's *Dar al-Ulum* and *Rawdat al-Madaris*

Following the death of Muhammad Ali just before mid-century, reform limped on in Egypt without any defining purpose. His adopted son Ibrahim Pasha had died the year before, and with him went much of the will to reform. Ibrahim is reported to have entertained plans of reform that went beyond industry, administration and the military, to have in fact even considered investing in social progress by bettering the living conditions of the people. Advised by the Armenian Egyptian Nubar Pasha, he is said to have planned to send groups of 10- to 12-year-old boys to study in Europe for 10 to 15 years so that when returning they would be as familiar with the cultural and psychological mindset of Europe and its methods of social improvement as with its analytical and scientific thinking and innovative technology.[1] A few hundred boys sent yearly for a decade may have made a difference. Economically, the support was there to sustain energetic reform. Production of cash crops increased 12-fold between 1832 and 1872, "generating a surplus that might have been converted into a self-sustaining industrial expansion."[2]

Unfortunately for the cause of reform, the political substance of focused leadership and the strength of will were lacking. Muhammad Ali's next two successors were not keen on reform. Abbas was rightly suspicious of European intentions. He suspected European honesty. He had seen how little his father's reforms had gotten him: his navy sent to the bottom of Navarino Bay in 1821 by a coalition of European powers, his factories emasculated by Britain in 1833, his army pushed out of Syria and reduced to insignificance by the same power in 1840. The new ruler feared and mistrusted the West. He feared the growing number of Europeans coming into the country and the influence they exerted. He detested the imposition of their capitulatory privileges that put them beyond the law, and despised their arrogance and rapacity in milking the country under the guise of helping it. By nature conservative, Abbas had no desire to associate with Europeans the way Muhammad Ali and Ibrahim had. Hence, their innovations were either ended or left to die in neglect. Abbas closed 55 of the 63 secondary schools and the several engineering schools Muhammad Ali had opened during his reign.[3] The student missions were ended and contracts with individual Europeans and European companies left to expire. Ali Mubarak, one of the most successful and well known of the Bulaq Engineering School's graduates and its last director, wrote the school's obituary, lamenting that after a brief existence of 20 years it was snuffed out before it had a chance to achieve its purpose, as if it had never been.[4] Hard to start, easy to end, impossible to revive, the abu Za'bal Medical School had much the same obituary, though it wasn't formally closed until 1855, a year after Abbas's death. Syziphus left the boulder at the foot of the mountain and walked away.

Muhammad Ali had never invested enough in the schools to make the difference he wanted, but they were nonetheless a start that could have been pushed forward. Egypt now went into a stall, or even worse, a relative reverse as the West continued progressing, with Japan, its success a shaming embarrassment to Muslim countries, rapidly catching up. The conservative shaykhs of al-Azhar who had Abbas's ear conspired to get the leading reformer, Shaykh Tahtawi, exiled, as mild and guardedly conservative as the now middle-aged Tahtawi was.

Sa'id, who succeeded Abbas in 1854, was more friendly to Europeans and their entrepreneurs in Egypt, but he lacked the energy and vision to pursue change. It was Sa'id who closed abu Za'bal, dispersing the students and physicians among the army units fighting with the Ottomans against the Russians in Crimea. As regrettable as the closure was for the cause of reform, it was not a great loss in itself, considering the condition it had fallen into. The graduate physicians of the school received ridiculously low pay, little respect and, as an added insult, no vacation time. Controlled and employed by the state, they were treated as state property, to be used as the ruling elite so desired. As state possessions, Egyptian physicians were expected to treat without payment everyone above them in government service. Even had the physicians been able to take up private practice, they might not have bettered themselves, since anyone who could afford a physician went to one of the many European ones making a comfortable and profitable living for themselves in Egypt. Late in Sa'id's rule an attempt was made to reopen the medical school under Dr. Antoine Barthelemy Clot's (known as Clot Bey) direction. Clot Bey had instituted western medicine in Egypt during the time of Muhammad Ali, and built and organized the teaching hospital at abu Za'bal. The effort to reopen the hospital, which had fallen into ruin after Muhammad Ali and Clot Bey had left the scene, fared poorly. Clot had returned from France specifically to revive abu Za'bal, but the level of medical training had by then fallen so low, the school having been eviscerated by corrupt hospital and school administrators in search of easy pay and impressive sounding but meaningless positions, that he gave up and returned to France. Closed again in 1862, the school had by then little but a skeleton faculty, few students and depleted equipment, most of it having been plundered over the years.

With the passing of Muhammad Ali and Sultan Mahmud, the parallel trajectories that reform had followed in Egypt and the Ottoman Empire during their regimes came to an end. Thereafter, the respective paths of reform in the two countries began to diverge. No activists pushing hard for reform emerged in Egypt comparable to those in the Ottoman Empire, men such as Mustafa Sami, Rifat Sadik, Hoja Tahsin, Ali Suavi, Shanizade and the Young Ottomans, not to mention the ministerial bulldozers of the *Tanzimat*. Egypt had to wait until the 20th century for that. The reason for the lag might in part be explained by Egyptian provincialism and conservatism, the country's isolation prior to Muhammad Ali and also the timeless patterns of agricultural life reinforced by traditional religion and the patriarchal nature of family and society, reinforced again by millennia of autocracy. Other factors tended to resist change, especially political change. Muhammad Ali's stern methods of controlling modernization as a state monopoly effectively muted all open criticism and opposition to government and its policies. Consequently, education in Egypt between 1848 and 1863 made little advance worth mentioning, aside from the primary and secondary schools founded by European religious missions to educate Copts, Greek Orthodox, Armenians and the children of Europeans residing in Egypt. This was to change with the third successor in the Muhammad Ali dynasty: Ismail (1863–1879).

Muhammad Ali had wanted to create a modern economy that translated into military power. Ismail wanted the trappings of modern civilization that could pass Egypt off as Europe's southern sister, a perhaps noticeably less prosperous sibling but one nonetheless a recognizable member of the civilized family of Europe. Fancying himself an Enlightened Monarch, Ismail brought modern civilization to his country as far and as fast as it could be delivered by money on hand and money borrowed from Europe. A disastrous mix of overblown royal pretension, unrealistic goals and fiscal irresponsibility led to, in sequence over a few years, bankruptcy, militarism, political collapse and finally foreign occupation. It was a high price for a railroad, a telegraph, a canal and a capital city that Ismail so proudly refurbished: Italianate plazas and villas, leafy Parisian boulevards lined with cafes, restaurants, chic boutiques, a grand opera house to rival Milan's. Ismail's profligacy became legendary, with himself becoming an easy mark for every European swindler, huckster, charlatan, loan shark and jackanape with a passport and the price of passage to Egypt. The sharpsters swarmed to Egypt like jackals to a ripe cadaver. But it was the powerful financial houses of Paris and London that made the big killings. They gladly loaned Ismail what he wanted, at a royal interest rate. Much was wasted. He paid a fortune to the Ottoman sultan for a title, khedive, derived from khoda, an old Ottomanized Persian word meaning lord, but the title put him a head above the run-of-the-mill pashas and provincial governors of the empire. Except for the sultan, Khedive Ismail was almost a king – enough of one at least to hobnob with the European aristocracy. This cost another fortune: paying his way into the charmed circle of European royalty with his kingly excursions to European capitals and expensive gifts showered upon those glittering rulers he wished to emulate. In the end, Ismail delivered his country to Europe's imperial debt collectors and ultimately to the British army. The disastrous end of Muhammad Ali's expansive policies had taught the newly minted Khedive that it was not rivalry but cooperation with the European maritime powers that was the best insurance policy for regime longevity. That turned out to be only half a lesson. As culpable as a Middle Eastern potentate's military expansion was in European eyes, his defaulting on debts to European financiers and banks was no less a punishable offense. Muhammad Ali had refused to borrow for his projects. His sons and successors Abbas and Sa'id had kept the loan sharks at arm's length. Ismail could not resist them. His aspiration to make Egypt a part of Europe had made it a possession.

By 1869, the seventh year of his reign and the year the Suez Canal opened, European debts on loans were mounting. Europe was inundating Egypt. As many as 100,000 Europeans were residing in the country, and they lived like princes. The capitulations that protected them were sorely resented by Egyptians who had to suffer the superiority that their European guests arrogated for themselves as they took over the country. The capitulations made a mockery of the Khedive's so-called absolute power. In the words of a sympathetic British historian of the Egyptian press:

> Though according to the custom of the land the Khedive is regarded as an absolute ruler in the valley of the Nile, yet seventeen consuls dispute his authority in many cases, on the ground that the Capitulations, which were framed for the protection of their lives and property and those of Christian residents, confer authority to render these residents inviolable in all their acts and enterprises. A greater abuse is not to be found in the habitable globe, and anything more grossly unfair to Egypt than the conduct of many consuls in virtue of the protection afforded by the Capitulations cannot be imagined. It is scarcely necessary to add that the representatives of the nations which are the most insignificant in Europe are the most exacting and tyrannical in Egypt. The minor States count upon the greater making common cause with them in the event of dispute or attack.[5]

By the end of Ismail's reign in 1879, Europeans had opened about 130 private schools, in which European teachers taught Egyptian students the language, literature and history of the European motherland.[6] French and English teachers who were imported to staff the government's new secular schools battled over which of the two European languages the lectures would be in.[7] Arabic was becoming secondary in the Europeanized secular world Ismail was transporting to Cairo and Alexandria. The Suez Canal zone, where Europeans running it resided, grew into a lush garden of transplanted European villas. The better sections of Cairo were taken over by Europeans. Leafy suburbs, off-limits to Egyptians, were built specially for the privileged foreigners, Egypt's new Mamluks, with all the familiar conveniences sprouting up to make them feel at home: pharmacies, boutiques, hair salons, restaurants, cafes, brasseries, patisseries. Afternoon teas and drinks at Shepherd's, the Cecil, Pastroudis or Groppi's were part of the daily routine, as were tailors catering to their sartorial tastes, and a plush Italianate opera house done in red velvet and gold to please their aesthetics.

Tourist steamboats plied the Nile, and wealthy Europeans sailed their private yachts to winter in sunny Egypt and luxuriate in splendid hotels built just for them along the river in Luxor and Aswan. By 1870, Egypt was well-connected to Europe in terms of trade, tourism and technology. In addition to the Suez Canal, there was the telegraph and Mediterranean cable. The steamers that transported entrepreneurs and tourists from the ports of western Europe to Alexandria formed another umbilical cord tying Ismail's Egypt to the Europe he wanted his country to become, which really meant transforming parts of Cairo and Alexandria to pass for Paris on the Nile. Emulating that "sphinx without a riddle" Louis Napoleon, the Khedive's grand contemporary in the theatrics of royal pomp and state building, Ismail graced Cairo with broad tree-lined boulevards, public plazas, gardens, parks, paved gas-lit streets, sewers, bridges, a geographic society, the splendid opera house and a railroad that ran the length of the country, Alexandria to Aswan. French became the language of culture of the westernized Egyptian. The well-to-do elite took to dressing European and drinking cognac and scotch. Ismail spoke French fluently, much better than Arabic, a language he barely knew, which could be said for his successors down to King Farouk and the end of the dynasty in 1952. In cuisine, language, furnishings, architecture and lifestyle, Alexandria became a Mediterranean melange of Greek, French and Italian influences. Italian and French Catholic mission schools educated generations of well-to-do Egyptians who looked to Europe for high civilization, while, with a sense of shame and self-contempt, they regarded their own country to be backward, as they were repeatedly being told by their European schoolteachers, whose grimaces at the sound of Egyptian dialect branded humiliation deep into their souls.

Khedive Ismail resumed the student missions to Europe, to France mainly, but for reasons other than those that Muhammad Ali had sent them there. The Khedive aspired to no modern military or industry that would incur British or French hostility. Student missions to Europe for advanced specialized training were for agricultural development in building barrages, canals and pumping stations, and for development of municipal facilities in order to Europeanize the cities for the greater glory of Ismail, who, mistakenly as it turned out, believed that joining Europe was Egypt's best defense. Muhammad Ali had restricted native Egyptian students to the study of language, translation and medicine, with some exceptions. Under Ismail, native Egyptians were able to study science and technology, since the Turko–Circassian Egyptian elite of Muhammad Ali's creation was beginning to Egyptianize and native Egyptians were concomitantly entering the lower and mid-level ranks of the officer corps, state bureaucracy and land owning class. By the time of the British occupation in 1882, the Turko–Circassians were well on the way to losing their status as a privileged caste. The assimilative process was complete by the end of the century.

Several attempts of varying success at scientific and technical acculturation marked Ismail's 17-year tenure. In 1865 an Arabic medical journal was founded by the Egyptian physician Ali al-Baqli, who had studied medicine in Paris. The journal, *Yusu' al-Tibb*, or *The Queen Bee of Medicine*, was a private effort to revive and expand public medical interest as a step in resuscitating the defunct abu Za'bal Medical School. Assisted by other French-trained Egyptian physicians, Baqli began a scientific venture that was essentially Egyptian, not state-promoted and governed and not ruled over by Clot Bey or any other European. Although intended for a general reading public, the journal nonetheless turned out to be overly technical for a non-professional readership. The selections, mainly translations of groundbreaking articles in European medical journals, were too specialized for the general Egyptian reader, of which there were not all that many to begin with. Since the journal was a private endeavor and depended on a readership large enough to keep it going, it lasted only a few years. *Yusu' al-Tibb* was years ahead of its time. More concerned about serious medicine than running a successful journal, its founders were too professionally set to settle for watered-down articles designed to cater to a lower-level readership. While the journal's birth indicated that some professionally trained Egyptians wanted to develop medical studies, its demise proved that institutional development was still dependent on government. But government lacked the will to support even its own projects.[8]

In 1868, just as the journal was going down, Khedive Ismail, in one of those sporadic reformist urges from the top that never seemed to last, founded a society with the intention of generating public interest in science. It translated and published modern scientific texts along with classical Arabic works. The idea was a resuscitation of Clot Bey's: to inseminate modern European science with Arabic classical science, so that offspring, like parent, had a Muslim birth certificate, one as legitimate as the other. The historical bridge was to be reinforced by public readings and discussions. The society had its own press, which printed 1,000 copies of each publication, giving an idea of the size of the Arabic reading public interested in science.

The same year that the science society was begun, Ismail opened a new engineering school, the *Madrasat al-Muhandishane*. This replaced the *Bulaq Muhandishane* that had been closed down by Abbas. Thanks to those students of Muhammad Ali's time who had gone through the Bulaq School and received specialized instruction in Europe, Egypt had a small but competent pool of trained men, from whom were selected the new school's director, department heads, instructors and supporting staff. Two secondary schools, one in Cairo, the other in Alexandria, were also opened to prepare students to enter the new engineering school. In the mid-1860s the School of Administration and Languages was opened, which in 1886 became Egypt's first law school. A House of Science (*Dar al-Ulum*) was opened in 1872 under the directorship of Ali Mubarak, who by then had reached the rank of pasha, marking a native Egyptian breakthrough. That same year, the School of Medicine, which had not been exactly closed down but existed unfunded in a state closer to death than limbo for a quarter century, was given new life and expanded. Three years later the Geographical Society was founded and housed in a beautiful neo-classical building in the Garden City section along the Nile. The society had a library and published a journal that reported on geographical discoveries, bringing the outside world that much closer to the maturing westernized intelligentsia that had been more than half a century in embryo.

One of the two secondary schools founded by Ismail he named after himself, the Khedival School. Ismail also founded several technical schools in the late 1860s: the *Madrasat al-Funun wa'l Sina'a* (School of Crafts and Industry); a school for railroad engineers; a telegraphy school; a steamship school; an agricultural school; and a school for the deaf and blind. Just after Ismail's removal in 1879 but still belonging to the stream of institutions he founded, the Egyptian Scientific Institute was created, which was an indigenous version of Bonaparte's *Institut d'Egypte*. In some ways, Ismail's reign was the realization of the French

Expedition's grand projects led by Bonaparte three generations earlier: the canal, the industrial projects, the learned societies, the opera, the support of science, popularity of the French language. Ismail went one further. In 1873, under his wife's patronage, the Arab world's first school for girls was opened.

The first independent, non-governmental newspaper was founded in the late 1860s. The readership was there, but the paper was too independent, too political, too critically outspoken and too soon closed. Several other newspapers that were founded later took care not to be too confrontational and lasted longer. The most successful of these was *al-Ahram* (*The Pyramids*), founded in 1875 by two Lebanese Christian immigrant brothers. Founded in Alexandria as a weekly reporting on political and economic current events, literature, innovations in technology and discoveries in science, *al-Ahram* was significant in its role of opening the world to Egyptians. It continues until today, though degraded to a mouthpiece of the totalitarian government with the military takeover in 1952.

Egyptians who had been students during Muhammad Ali's time were by the last years of Ismail's rule beginning to feel confident enough to write in their fields of expertise. The first director of the new engineering school, Ismail Mustafa (d. 1885), known as al-Falaki (The Astronomer), had gone through the Bulaq School, studied in Paris and written a treatise on astronomy. Another trained astronomer, also with the sobriquet al-Falaki, became the second director. This was Mahmud Hamdi al-Falaki, who as a young man in the 1830s had been considered an outstanding student of science and engineering by his peers at Muhammad Ali's Citadel Engineering School. Upon completing his studies in 1834, he taught at the Citadel School and was later sent to France, where he studied science and astronomy for nine years. When Khedive Ismail opened his *Madrasat al-Muhandishane*, Mahmud Hamdi was made director of the new institute's observatory, whose origins went back to the observatory that the French of Bonaparte's day had constructed in Azbakiyya 68 years earlier. As a student of science and author of mathematical and astronomical texts for students, Mahmud Hamdi al-Falaki became a paramount figure in publicly advocating the study of science in Egypt. But there were not enough voices like his to make a difference in either public response or government funding.

Hamdi wrote his astronomy and mathematics in French rather than Arabic, putting it beyond the reach of those students who did not know the language, though he may have written in French to give distance between al-Azhar and his implicit acceptance of a sun-centered system, since the shaykhs were not expected to read anything in a foreign language. During his long residency in Europe he published several articles in various academic journals based on research he had done on calendrical studies and the earth's magnetic field. He continued this work in Egypt as director of the royal observatory. Mahmud Hamdi made the country's first astronomical and topographical map. He also produced geographical and meteorological studies, making him an attractive ornament to adorn Khedive Ismail's government. Who could resist the prestige and the pay of a government ministry? The example of Mahmud Hamdi's scientific training being lost to government service was typical. As it had others, ministerial appointment took him away from a career as scientist and teacher that could have prepared a dozen graduate students to participate in the cultivation of an indigenous scientific community. Government was not seriously focused on creating one, and the very few men who had the experience to begin the creative process were naturally flattered when offered government positions that offered high status and a means to modest wealth.

Amin Sami was another whose career began as a student in Muhammad Ali's Bulaq Engineering School, blossomed under Ismail and ended up in government. Like the other important figures, he received advanced study in Paris. As a teacher of mathematics and topography in the Egyptian city of Beni Suwayf he served in a small way to engender a scientific interest among students outside of the capital. His great contribution was authoring the monumental *Taqwim al-Nil*, a multi-volume encyclopedia devoted to the Nile, its flow, methods of measurement, topography and engineering works employed to control and utilize the river for agriculture. Considered a literary and scientific fundament of Egypt's intellectual revival, the massive work has given Amin Sami a name of enduring fame in Egypt, overshadowing the contributions of Mahmud Hamdi, as well as those of other important men who flourished under Ismail, such as the physican al-Baqli.

Al-Baqli had barely reached his twenties when he was sent to Paris in 1832 to study surgery. Having excelled, he was employed in the Qasr al-Ayni Hospital, where after achieving a distinguished reputation he was left to languish with the medical school and hospitals during the stagnant years of Abbas and Sa'id. When Ismail came to power he appointed Baqli director of the revived medical school, which then experienced its greatest period. Baqli encouraged research and was able to persuade Ismail to import modern equipment to support it: a remarkable achievement since all evidence depicts Muslim rulers resenting having to pay for the modern science they claimed to want. It was Baqli who founded the medical journal mentioned earlier, The Queen Bee of Medicine. Baqli also convinced Ismail to provide funds for expanding the medical school's clinical and research facilities and for sending more medical students to France for advanced study and training. The school's growth and the bright future that Baqli's guidance had brought to it were cut short when Ismail was forced to declare bankruptcy. Ibrahim Mustafa, Mahmud Hamdi, Amin Sami and Ali Mubarak formed the intellectual nexus between Muhammad Ali's and Khedive Ismail's reforms, bridging the 15-year hiatus of the reigns of Abbas and Sa'id. Ismail's profligacy, however, brought on an even more severe hiatus, this in the form of bankruptcy followed by foreign occupation.

The lack of funding, planning and continuity was the bane of Egypt's infant scientific community. Absent these, science failed to grow to maturity as a self-sustaining institution rooted in a supportive society. Scientific institutions in Egypt were always in embryo, never quite reaching full term, then atrophying in neglect, neither dying nor living, but cast in a dust-laden limbo. Science and technology, the double helix of modernization, never came to stand on their own legs. A religious establishment that was passively but not totally unfriendly to science, and a fiscally irresponsible and autocratic government without serious policies regarding science and education, made for soil too ungiving for the tender shoots of science to flourish. What can be said of a positive nature is that during the final third of the 19th century, with Ismail's reign at the heart of it, an embryonic westernized intelligentsia whose bloodstream emanated from Muhammad Ali's innovations in education was forming in Cairo and Alexandria, comparable to the one that arose in Istanbul during the second third of the century. What Shaykh Tahtawi's career intellectually personified for Muhammad Ali's reforms, Ali Mubarak did for those of Khedive Ismail.

Between the resumption of state reforms under Khedive Ismail in the 1860s and the British occupation in 1882, Mubarak's name became emblematic of the Egyptian Awakening, tied to Shaykhs Attar's and Tahtawi's before him and Muhammad Abduh's after him. Ali Mubarak was devoted to advancing the work initiated by Shaykh Tahtawi in positing an Islamic basis for modern science. The two reformers, and other supporters of science who would follow, took it as a fundamental truth of Egyptian and Muslim life that without al-Azhar's active support the chances of a scientific culture blossoming in the bosom of society were slim. If Muslims were ever to accept new ways of understanding the world and nature, and engage in scientific study, it would require al-Azhar's blessing. For a millennium al-Azhar had dominated intellectual life in Egypt. Awe of the institution was fixed deep in the national psyche: al-Azhar was the indispensible voice adjudicating on tradition and innovation. Even an outsider like Bonaparte knew that for Egypt to be won, the shaykhs of al-Azhar had to be won. Like politics like science.

The unquestioned maxim was that Egyptians followed authority. But if this were true, as it certainly was believed to be in the writings of Tahtawi, Mubarak and their followers, one might then ask how could science, whose double-edged sword in its epistemological rebellion against the stated truth of authority was the critical, doubting, probing question, ever blossom? Reformers avoided the question by devoting much print to the axiom that science and religion had everything in common, that they were mutually supportive, or that they belonged to absolutely divorced realms of consciousness and had nothing in common, one a realm of the mind, the other of the heart. Many reformers argued both cases on different pages of the same treatise without admitting to contradiction.

Tradition seemed to constrict the reformers as much as the reformers perceived it to constrict the audience they were trying to reach. The binds of tradition acted on different levels. Ali Mubarak's secular education and long years in Europe had severed those village roots of traditionalism that had never let loose of Tahtawi. They both appreciated the importance of science, but Mubarak was able to disregard the strands of speculative theology that had choked off natural philosophy from the main body of Sunni Islam and that even now stood as a barrier against the encroachment of modern science, encumbered as it was with its mathematical metaphysics of natural law. As implied in his treatise *Ilm al-Din* (*The Science of Religion*), science and religion either had nothing to do with each other or were mutually affirmative. In either case, they could coexist peacefully, free of restraint, enmity and contradiction. They could be cozy bed fellows without compromise having to be made by one or the other. Ali Mubarak's two paramount institutional achievements in preparing the ground for a scientific culture are based on that bipolar premise. Those achievements are seen in his *Dar al-Ulum* (House of Science), and the student journal he assisted in editing, *Rawdat al-Madaris* (*Garden of Schools*).

His career prospered in government service during Ismail's reign, and as a high official he was able to give action to the modern ideas he had acquired during his many years in Europe. In addition to *Dar al-Ulum* and the student journal, he created the Khedival Library, which became the basis of the present Egyptian National Library, *Dar al-Kutub*. The library had annexes for special collections of scientific books, display rooms for scientific equipment and chemicals that were made available for students to use in familiarizing themselves with the experimental method.[9] In 1867 the Khedive appointed him Deputy Minister of Education and sent him to Paris to study the French school system.[10] In the early 1870s he rose to director of the *Diwan al-Madaris* (Ministry of Schools), and set himself an ambitious agenda of reorganization that began right where formative education began: at the village level.

He knew from his own experience, reinforced by what he had learned in studying the French system, that without a sound primary and secondary system of education, any project of education at the higher levels was condemned to failure. Teaching subjects at one level that should have been taught at the previous level was not a system but a waste of teaching expertise, student potential and state treasure. Ali Mubarak also recognized that student health was as basic to education as was a coherent system, and this too began in the village. Village clinics had to be set up as adjuncts of the primary school with programs in place to ensure a student's health. Also, if the deadening tradition of memorization of the Quran, the sum total of primary education as it then existed, was to be broken, primary schoolteachers had to be as competently trained in general science as they were in religion.

Implementing Mubarak's plans would have cost far more than anything Khedive Ismail was prepared to provide or could provide, for Egypt was already sliding down the slippery slope of foreign loans and into the bottomless pit of interest payments that ended in bankruptcy. Only two new primary schools, one in Cairo, the other in Alexandria, were opened, in addition to the girls' school funded by Ismail's wife. The idea of education for girls had been in Shaykh Tahtawi's head ever since his residence in Paris, where to his amazement he had seen women who could read and write, and who could discourse intelligently with men, a discovery that brought him to the conclusion that literate mothers were the earliest, best and least expensive institution guaranteeing literate children.

Dar al-Ulum

With the Khedive's blessing, Mubarak founded his *Dar al-Ulum*. The name evoked the memory of high intellectual efflorescence symbolized by the Abbasid *Bayt al-Hikma* (House of Wisdom) in ninth century Baghdad and the Fatimid *Dar al-Ulum* in 11th century Cairo. Founded in 1872, Ali Mubarak's *Dar al-Ulum* was historically closer to Bonaparte's *Institut d'Egypte* than it was to its classical Muslim forerunners. It was quite likely an inspirational offspring of both the memory of the *Institut d'Egypte* and the academic institutions Ali Mubarak saw during his many years in France, but the name he chose tied it to the great days of Muslim science. In immediate practical terms, *Dar al-Ulum* was to be a training college for primary and secondary teachers, and in the long term, a modern institute where all knowledge from sources east and west were studied under one roof: where students and teachers of the religious and modern sciences sat, studied, discussed, argued and learned together. That was the idea. Though it fell short of Mubarak's hopes, it was nonetheless the embryo of the country's first university, whose official founding had to wait until the early 1920s.

Mubarak was provided with funds to import some of the latest scientific equipment from Europe for *Dar al-Ulum's* laboratories and exhibition halls. Several European scientists were hired at handsome salaries and made directors of the departments of physics, engineering and construction. These were complemented by Egyptians who had achieved a degree of scientific accomplishment, among them Ismail Falaki Pasha, who lectured in modern astronomy, and Ahmad Mansur Efendi, who lectured in physics. Both of them were scientific luminaries who, like Ali Mubarak, were former religious students who had begun their scientific studies in Muhammad Ali's new schools and survived. *Dar al-Ulum* achieved precedence over its closest competitor, the Giza Engineering School, whose leading teachers Mubarak borrowed for his own institution.[11] The school was intended to bring together the two worlds of religion and science. It was hoped that by educating a choice selection of young religious shaykhs and Azhar students in the sciences, a future generation of religious leaders would work out a modus vivendi of peaceful coexistence between the two worlds, where toleration and respect replaced passivity, suspicion, fear and hostility. To this end, he requested the rector of al-Azhar to send him ten of the seminary's brightest students. As the student body of *Dar al-Ulum* was only 50 in all, the religious contingent constituted 20 percent. Mubarak also arranged to borrow some of al-Azhar's best teachers. Muhammad Ali had also taken Azhar students for his secular schools and used its shaykhs as teachers, but without any thought regarding intellectual cohesion. Ali Mubarak's scheme was of another category of pragmatism; rather than aiming to build factories and a world class military, he was attempting to create a generation of open-minded students. As he conceived it, *Dar al-Ulum* would bring science and religion into a shared environment where exposure would induce an intellectual osmosis. The ten religious students were to be seeds planted in al-Azhar. Every year more would be added. The seeds would blossom and multiply. *Dar al-Ulum* would be the catalyst that inwardly transformed al-Azhar from a medieval seminary to a modern university.

As a teacher training college, *Dar al-Ulum's* other seminal goal was to provide a harmonious academic environment in preparing advanced religious students to be primary and secondary schoolteachers competent in teaching science and mathematics, as well as religion. A teacher of religion teaching science would signal compatibility.[12] The academic format was left deliberately unstructured.

By minimizing structure and requirements and maximizing freedom of choice in courses, Mubarak hoped to spare the Azharites any sense of being pushed into the shadows of heresy. Accordingly, students chose the courses they wanted. For the first three years of the school's existence there was no set syllabus or curriculum and nothing to prevent religious students from taking only religious courses. At the end of the academic year the students had three days of exams.

Dar al-Ulum duplicated many of al-Azhar's courses – *tafsir*, Hadith, Shari'a law, Arabic literature and calligraphy. The secular offerings included astronomy, physics, chemistry, geology, mathematics and mechanics. Turkish, French and English languages were also offered. In the event of the worse-case scenario where students failed to cross over to explore the knowledge on the other side of the intellectual frontier, Mubarak and his *Dar al-Ulum* associates hoped that at least by placing ten religious students in close proximity to 40 secular students there would be some interchange of thought, if not by active intellectual interest then at least by passive curiosity. To relax the defensive posture of the Azhari students and shaykhs, the natural sciences were not called western. They were "the sciences al-Azhar had lost." *Dar al-Ulum* would retrieve them. Unfortunately, but typically, the historical record lacks comment from the religious side of the experiment.[13]

Mubarak's *Dar al-Ulum* was the first institute in which religious subjects and modern science were taught side by side. Classes and lectures were held in the main lecture hall of the Khedival Library. Shaykh Husayn al-Marsafi lectured on Arabic literature on Sunday and Wednesday mornings from 8 to 10; Tuesday mornings it was Ismail Bey al-Falaki, director of the Engineering School, on astronomy; and Saturday and Tuesday mornings, Shaykh abd al-Rahman al-Badrawi on Islamic jurisprudence (*fiqh*). Saturday mornings, Ahmad Mansur Efendi of the Engineering School taught physics and performed experiments for the audience. Sundays, Tuesdays, Wednesdays and Thursdays, various French professors lectured in French on history, engineering construction, steam engine technology and physics, their lectures then being translated into Arabic for the students and anyone else who wished to hear.

Ali Mubarak recorded no instances of friction. This could mean that either the religious students did not venture into the sciences that al-Azhar had lost or they kept their objections to them to themselves. The probable points of friction would have been in astronomy and geology, where one presented an earth in motion and the other an earth in formation over millions of years. The theory of evolution – or public discussion of it – had not yet penetrated the Muslim world. It was decided that offering astronomy and geology together would produce too much of a shock to traditional sensitivities, and so geology was pulled and not introduced until 1888, by which time the theory of heliocentricity had been published, argued and accepted – more or less, depending on who was asked. Responses regarding acquiescence or rejection depended on the place and the person queried. Almost everything related to the problems that modern science was presumed to present to religion and that might be considered to have been resolved in Muslim society has to be qualified as more or less. This is especially so regarding the controversy over Darwin, which continues today in full swing. Regarding Copernicus, Arabs writing on science and religion still to this day feel themselves obliged to prove to their readers that to believe in a moving earth is not only in accordance with Islam but is alluded to in the Quran.

When geology was finally introduced at *Dar al-Ulum*, the curriculum had to be balanced by adding another course in Islamic jurisprudence.

Designed to be both a laboratory incubator for stretching the religious mind to the realm of science, and an institute for advancing the study of science and technology, *Dar al-Ulum* and its lectures were open to the public. It would be difficult to assess how much more successful *Dar al-Ulum* was as an incubator than its forerunner of generations earlier, the French *Institut d'Egypte*. An Egyptian historian of *Dar al-Ulum* claims that the ten Azhar students who attended it went on to become teachers and contributed to the formation of a nucleus of scientific learning during the next generation.[14] Whatever the dimensions were of that nucleus before the end of the century, it did not include any members of al-Azhar who were currently registered as such. Regarding *Dar al-Ulum*'s success in producing enlightened shaykhs to teach in the village *makatib* elementary schools whose students were to be taught to accept science and religion as being different but not contradictory, Shaykh Muhammad Abduh's benighted village schooling, followed by his lonely experience as a religious reformer arguing the case of science during the last two decades of the 19th century, would indicate that not much progress was made on that score either. What with the prestige of their education and their taste of life in the city, neither the Azhar shaykhs nor their students who responded to Ali Mubarak's call were of a mind to return to the quiet rural villages of their origins to suffer the boredom and penury of an elementary schoolteacher's life.

The number of religious figures associated with *Dar al-Ulum* who embraced science was small, too small for any but the most exceptionally courageous shaykhs to strike a positive public position on the subject of Islam and science. Muhammad Abduh would be the principal exception. An earlier exception, one that might be taken as typical of those rare shaykhs of the 19th century who accepted modern science, was Hasan al-Tawil. A teacher of religion at al-Azhar and *Dar al-Ulum*, he was described by his contemporaries as a philosophical Sufi who became "expert in the modern arts." Since mathematics was one of the modern arts that he is said to have mastered, science presumably was included among his interests.[15] Shaykh Tawil's knowledge of the modern arts apparently presented no problem to his Sufi-oriented faith, but unlike the philosophical Sufi of the previous century, the Turkish Ibrahim Hakki of Erzerum, Hasan al-Tawil did not produce an Arabic *Marifetname* on the legitimate cohabitation of these two worlds of knowledge.

In words reminiscent of Tahtawi's earlier complaints, and of those more forceful expressions of regret that would come later from Shaykh Abduh, Ali Mubarak guardedly alluded to his frustration with the ulema's lack of response. "The peak of Egypt's happiness and power," he declaimed, "came when the country had sultans and an enlightened ulema who valued knowledge, but when ignorant and coarse rulers and ulema took their place, Egyptians and all Muslims became backward."[16] Mubarak recognized, as did all Egyptian reformist thinkers before and after him, as did Bonaparte as well, that without the active support of the ulema no leaders, however energetically disposed to reform they might be, could move the country. The ulema, heart and conscience of the Muslim community, had to be the vanguard if change was to be something more than just a theatrical appearance of motion acted out by a government spinning in place and going nowhere in tune to the endless chorus of its leaders' hollow words singing in praise of themselves.

A product of the Khedive's funding and Ali Mubarak's vision, *Dar al-Ulum* was Egypt's first independent effort to institutionalize a scientific community. After Ali Mubarak moved on to become a government minister *Dar al-Ulum* lost sight of its purpose and drifted directionlessly into the 20th century, becoming another vestige of a promising beginning that failed to take root and flourish. Once again, the ruler had snatched away a quality product of the state's system of advanced education who could have been better employed. In 1874, two years after the school's founding, Ali Mubarak was appointed Director of Engineering in the Ministry of Public Works, in which capacity Khedive Ismail awarded him one of the country's highest medals. The following year Egypt fell into bankruptcy. With European comptrollers in charge of Egyptian revenues to make sure European creditors were paid, the already meager funds allotted to education were all the more diminished. The education budget had risen from 6,000 Egyptian pounds during Sa'id's reign to a peak of 75,000 during Ismail's, but then plummeted to 20,000 with bankruptcy.[17]

Shortly after Egypt's finances fell under French and British control, the country fell under British occupation. With an eye to Egypt's strategic location and the Suez Canal as a vital link in the empire's communication with India, Britain's government felt obliged to save Egypt from itself by protecting the investments of its international financiers. For the British pro-consuls, whose first duty was to pay off European creditors and put Egypt's finances in order, Egypt was a country of peasants best served by remaining true to its agricultural destiny. Egypt had no need of science. To the new rulers, an educated Egyptian was a useless rarity, a flightless bird, an anomaly, an oxymoron. Planting, irrigating and harvesting were all an Egyptian had to know about science and nature. And so, soon after the British had settled in and Lord Cromer had set up a shadow government composed of pliant Egyptians, pro-consul Cromer dismissed Ali Mubarak as Minister of Education, deeming him unsuitable for the position.

British rule was no boon to education. After 20 years under foreign occupation, Egypt had no more than three secondary schools graduating a total of fewer than 100 students a year.[18] The British were there to collect the debt, secure Suez and keep Egypt firmly under the imperial thumb. Advancement of education and scientific literacy was not on the agenda of British interests. Half-educated peasants were only capable of making trouble, while the semi-westernized urban Egyptians, with their perverse and superficial smattering of education, were a sleazy, brutish, hopelessly corrupt tribe of louts, from whom the British nobly took it upon themselves to protect the downtrodden peasantry, salt of the earth of the real Egypt. Trying to educate such a greedy self-serving lot would have been a waste of resources. Glacial progress in generating a scientific culture before the occupation would remain glacial during it. For all his severity and faults, Muhammad Ali began to be missed.

Rawdat al-Madaris

Like all Egyptian advocates of science study, Ali Mubarak directed himself more to generating an interest in science than he did to writing on scientific subjects or adding to the scientific literature available in Arabic. Laying the structural groundwork for a scientific culture and writing treatises to encourage students to take up science were considered more urgent than translating an important book of science or writing about science on a popular level to introduce it to the reading public, as Cornelius Van Dyck and Butrus Bustani were doing in Arabic in Beirut, as we shall see. Ali Mubarak did this to a limited extent early in his career, when he composed a few scientific treatises in a popular vein, such as his little treatise on geography, *Recent Truths on the Description of the Seas* (*Haqaiq al-Akhbar fi Awsaf al-Buhar*), and his *On the Characteristics of Numbers* (*Khawass al-A'dad*), a Pythogorean reflection on numerical correspondences existing in man, nature and the heavens, based on the number seven.[19] In it Mubarak repeats Tahtawi's claim of the Egyptian origins of Greek science through Pythagoras: a transmission that argued for Egypt's legitimate parenthood of modern science in that its origin of origins was Egyptian.[20]

He also wrote a forerunner of Amin Sami's *Taqwim al-Nil*, entitled *On the Organization of Egypt's Nile* (*Nakhbat al-fikr fi Tadbir Nil Misr*), which gives the height of the rising Nile year by year from 642 to 1880. His major work was not in science but a history of Egypt in 20 volumes, *Khitat al-Tawfiqiyya*, published in 1888 and named after Tawfiq, who succeeded Ismail in 1879. Inspired by both medieval Egyptian scholarship and the monumental publication by Bonaparte's *Institut d'Egypte* of the *Description d'Egypt*, Mubarak's *Khitat* is an expression of the idea of the continuity and unity, or rather complementarity, of Muslim and western knowledge that he was striving to foster among Egyptians. A more concise expression of this is found in his early treatise, *The Science of Religion*, in which religion and natural philosophy are shown to be separate sciences, each residing in its own sphere of knowledge, the one moral and spiritual, the other rational and physical, but with each complementing the other. The treatise is in the form of a fictional dialogue, a literary device often used by reformers hoping not only to render their narrative in a lively manner but also thinking that their innovative ideas or arguments would be less offensive to religious or political authorities if fictionalized. Discourse on problematic political and scientific ideas was also cast in the form of having come in a dream, a flimsy veil reformers hoped would protect them from the state censors.

In Ali Mubarak's little story, a traditional Azharite theologian who has never been out of Egypt travels to London. The shaykh is so astonished by the civilization he sees there that he is compelled to seek the causes that gave rise to its cultural, institutional and organizational splendors. Upon discovering that the underlying dynamism is belief in progress and expanding scientific knowledge, he understands that this is precisely what true Islam is all about. The story is a slim modernized version of the medieval philosophical romance *Hayy ibn Yaqzan* by the Andalusian ibn Tufayl: awareness of the world and inner reflection on nature and on the heavens expand consciousness to higher realms of reality and the ultimate discovery of true religion. Mubarak's fiction does not delve too deeply into the subject. By sticking to broad generalities he avoids the specific points that Tahtawi identified as irresolvable contradictions between modern science and religion. Mubarak realized the dangers that threatened anyone writing openly on the thorny specifics of Muslim occasionalism and scientific causality, and he was not that philosophically or argumentatively inclined as to get involved in medieval dialectics. That was a battle best left to the Azharites. Mubarak's little opus is a hopeful reconciliation of religion and science but without the theology. The shaykh in the story simply realizes in the end that the thought and the action underlying western civilization were essentially the same that produced the greatness of classical Islamic civilization, and that by their taking from the West, Muslims would be doing no more than reclaiming "the sciences al-Azhar lost."

Closely associated with Ali Mubarak's *Dar al-Ulum* was the student journal *Rawdat al-Madaris*. Published under the auspices of the Ministry of Schools (*Diwan al-Madaris*), which Ali Mubarak directed, *Rawdat* was the Arab world's first academic journal of science and technology.[21] The journal was not just that. By juxtaposing religious, scientific and technical articles, it was a subliminal version of *Dar al-Ulum* in its purpose of insinuating religious acceptance of science and its encouragement of Muslims to study it. Applying the same method of legitimacy by association that brought Azharites and science teachers together in *Dar al-Ulum*, the journal featured articles on the Quran, religion and Muslim history alongside the scientific articles and lectures given at *Dar al-Ulum*. The first issue of *Rawdat* appeared on April 17, 1870. Its appearance was a watershed of sorts in Egyptian education and intellectual history. Intended for students at the secondary and advanced levels, *Rawdat* was not dependent on a public readership to keep it going. It would have had little appeal to the general reading public as its articles on science and industrial technology were often demanding. It lasted all of seven years and no doubt would have continued had Ismail not fallen into bankruptcy and the country's finances into European receivership.

Rawdat had three primary goals: to kindle an interest in science among secondary school students, to convince them that such an interest had no problem with their religion and to instruct them in the principles of practical science and processes of industrial technology.[22] The journal was edited by Ali Mubarak, who was assisted by Shaykh Tahtawi until his death in 1873, and also by Tahtawi's liberal-minded son, Ali Fahmi Bey, who was the editorial workhorse keeping the journal running as long as it did. The format of juxtaposing sections on science and religion would seem to have been Ali Mubarak's idea, though the objective of doing so was shared by all three editors and the authors who contributed to the journal. It is fascinating how the articles alternate from physics to stories of the Prophet to industrial electrolysis to classical Arabic literature. The interleaving of the classical Islamic with the secular modern served to suggest a congenial cohabitation in place of the intellectual divorce that had arisen between science and religion, or as it was often put, the struggle between modern and traditional that was splitting the Egyptian mind.

The editors of *Rawdat* were a complementary troika of as many generations of reform: Tahtawi, once a young pioneer but now the old traditional shaykh held by the past; Ali Mubarak Pasha, former Azharite student but now the middle-aged military officer and engineer who, thoroughly secularized, had lived for years in France; and young Ali Fahmi, the shaykh's son who had freed himself from his father's immersion in tradition and exemplified how religion and science could comfortably inhabit the same mind. Collectively spanning the 19th century, their careers represent the generational stages of progress Egyptians made, one building on the other, but each having to fight the same battles over again as if, deceptively, reformers often seemed to be running on a treadmill. The journal Tahtawi, Mubarak and Ali Fahmi edited is a measure of the intellectual transition that a section of Egyptian society, both secular and religious, had in fact traversed during the century between the French invasion in 1798 and the British occupation in 1882.

An issue appeared every other week, a copy of which was given free to each secondary school student – a remarkable advance considering the wretched days of Muhammad Ali, when even students in the specialized schools had no reading material. In terms of numbers, the journal was a modest endeavor. Three hundred copies of each issue were printed the first few years of the journal's existence, rising to 700 during its last several years, the rise owing to public sales and the journal's inexpensiveness. The numbers give an idea of how few secondary school students there were, even in the 1870s, in a country of four million, where mass illiteracy dragged on like a great boulder chained to the rear of a struggling carriage up to its axles in mud. Unlike in Japan at the time, whose rulers were waging a vigorous campaign to eradicate illiteracy, Muslim rulers appeared sublimely content to live with that boulder, as if it were a condition of life willed by God.

Copies of *Rawdat* could be purchased at a minimal price by engineering students or by anyone with an interest in science and industry, or in mathematics and mathematical puzzles. The technical articles were on a level that could have profited first- and second-year university engineering students in a mid-level university in the United States. A good deal of chemistry was presented. Chemical and electrical engineering processes were described and provided with helpful diagrams. Each issue contained around 100 pages, including diagrams and technical drawings.

Well known over the Arab world, Shaykh Tahtawi's name as director and editor supplied the journal's religious credentials and gave it prestige.[23] The shaykh did little editing. He was old, and his time was taken up by his duties as director of the Ministry of Schools's Translation Section, but he accepted to act as an editor because he believed in what Ali Mubarak wanted to achieve through the journal. His contribution was the religious articles. He studiously avoided those issues of religious dialectics that had given him pause in accepting the epistemological principles of science at the beginning of his reformist literary career. What had disturbed him concerning western science was now, on the authority of his editorial name, implicitly assumed to be acceptable. *Rawdat* avoided anything of the metaphysics of science that might trouble a religious soul. There were no attempts at either reworking theology or reducing science to orthodox terms. The philosophical tangle of causal relations, determinism and occasionalism had no place in the journal. Darwin's theory was not broached, nor was it anywhere else in Arabic literature until midway through the year of the journal's demise in 1876. The earth was referred to as moving without comment, as if it were a commonly accepted fact, though at the time it indeed was not. Even Tahtawi himself appeared no longer to accept it. The shakyh's last major work was published in serial form in *Rawdat*, a traditional history of the Prophet and the Hejaz, and was still running when he died in 1873, the journal's fourth year of publication. Tahtawi died serving as an official in the Ministry of Schools under Ali Mubarak Pasha, ironically in the kind of political environment he had despaired would be Egypt's future, where religion was reduced from the raison d'etre of an Islamic state to a tolerated appendix of a secular one.

Tahtawi's son, Ali Fahmi, a teacher of composition in the School of Administration and Languages, had none of his father's problems with modern science. Ali Fahmi represents the mindset of a cadre of Egyptian teachers in the engineering and medical schools who, having come of age by the 1870s, could write competently and informatively on science, technology and medicine. Owing to the endeavors of these three editors and the journal's scientific contributors, a scientific and technical Arabic lexicography had come into existence by the time the journal expired.

The astronomer Ismail Falaki, the first director of Khedive Ismail's resuscitated engineering school, was on *Rawdat's* editorial board and contributed astronomy articles. His successor, Mahmud Falaki, was also an astronomy contributor. Ahmad Naddah, another teacher at the engineering school, contributed articles on physics, chemistry and medicine. Their writing style was simple and direct, as were the journal's literary articles. Pretentious flourishes, rare words, rhymed prose, layered meanings and complex phraseology were avoided. Since most of *Rawdat's* contributors were teachers at *Dar al-Ulum* and the engineering school, the style of Arabic was patterned on the language and texts in which they studied science and technology. The Arabic translations of scientific texts reflected the simple and direct style of the language from which the translations had been made, usually French, and this of course was true for translations into Turkish as well: Hoja Ishak's *Compendium of the Mathematical Sciences* was a revolutionary piece of clear and straightforward writing of Ottoman Turkish for the 1830s. The objective was to inform with clarity and brevity, not impress with virtuosity of language, and in this *Rawdat* marked a significant advance in the evolution of what has come to be called Modern Literary Arabic.[24]

Anyone perusing an issue of *Rawdat al-Madaris* without knowing what the editors were up to would be perplexed when encountering the seemingly desultory juxtaposition of absolutely unrelated articles that followed one after the other: Hanafi jurisprudence, chemistry, the life of the Prophet, industry, the Quran, astronomy, Abbasid poetry, physics, Sufism, mathematics, Shari'a law, electromagnetism, Hadith, metallurgy, Muslim historical heroes, mechanics. An issue always opened with a religious article, followed by, say, an analytic description of commercially extracting sulfur from iron sulfide, accompanied by schematic diagrams of machines and apparatus and the relevant chemical equations. The reader might then be treated to a critique of Jahiz's (ninth century) literary ability, and after that presented with a mathematical puzzle. Secondary students were encouraged to send in their solutions to the puzzle, and the names of those who submitted correct solutions were mentioned in the succeeding issue. Solutions usually involved a combination of second and third degree algebraic equations and analytic geometry; there were always several students who sent in correct solutions. To lighten things up, Ali Mubarak assigned an Azharite scholar to contribute funny stories, jokes, riddles, puzzles, enigmas and happenings beyond belief.[25] Now and then some mild sex was thrown in for comic relief. One story, "The Return of the Shaykh to His Youth," which today can be seen as a futuristic vision of the coming of Viagra, was about a condition that would have most likely aroused the prurient interest of the journal's editors far more than any of its young readers.[26]

As the journal continued through its less than a decade of existence, the articles on chemistry, astronomy, physics and industrial chemical processes took up more and more of its space. Lengthy articles on conic sections, solid geometry and cubic equations by Mikhail abd al-Sayyid, a mathematics teacher at the Syrian Protestant College in Beirut that had been founded in 1866, began to appear in the fifth year of *Rawdat's* publication. By its final years, the journal was predominantly scientific with articles on hydrolysis, electrolysis, the physics of gases, heat, light, gravity and sound. Authors referred to the concept of natural law in their articles without apology. The general law (*al-qanun al- 'amm*) of the conservation of energy governed transformations from one form of it to another. That nature had its own set of physical laws was explicitly stated in 1876 by Ahmad Mansur, a physics and chemistry teacher at the Khedival Engineering School. The four acoustic laws were given as examples. Frequency relates directly to the length of the vibrating string and inversely as the square root of its diameter. Inverse square relationships governing the dynamics of heat, radiation, light, electricity and gravity were introduced as laws. "The intensity of radiated heat varies inversely as the square of the distance and this law (*qanun*) can be proved by intuitive reason and experiment."[27] The experiment demonstrating the theory was described.

Ahmad Mansur wrote one of *Rawdat's* finest treatises on chemistry. It appeared serially during the last two years of the journal's existence. Written in rhymed prose (an exception to the journal's norm) and titled *al-Lali' al-Saniyya fi Qawa'id al-Kimawiyya* (*The Shining Pearls of Chemical Principles*), the treatise is an introduction to the basics of chemistry as they were known in the middle of the 19th century, from the work of Lavoisier to Berthollet – the same Berthollet who accompanied Bonaparte to Egypt and entertained the shaykhs with exploding bottles and electric shocks. Now what the Egyptians were getting was electrical valence, atomic weight, molecular weight, equivalent weight, combining weights, the tripartite division of acids, bases and salts, oxidation, reduction and double displacement reactions. Ahmad Mansur also introduced the young reader to the Arabic version of the European system of chemical symbols that Lavoisier was creating, until the Jacobin guillotine put an end to it. In the Arabic system, those elements whose existence had been known in the Islamic alchemical tradition were given symbols based on their names in Arabic: h (*hadid*) for iron, kb (*kibrit*) for sulfur, rs (*rasas*) for lead. Those elements that had been unknown by Muslim chemists were given symbols based on their French names: cl for chlorine, fl for fluorine, yd for hydrogen, az (*azout* in French) for nitrogen.

It was of course taken as axiomatic that modern science was rooted in earlier Muslim accomplishments. A glance at the advances Muslims made in descriptive and analytic geometry, algebra and trigonometry made this clear as day. The science writers of *Rawdat* also included modern chemistry as one of those sciences originating in Muslim achievements. The extraction of hydrogen and oxygen from respectively water and iron oxide was asserted to be based on medieval Muslim alchemy. Regarding biology, evolution theory was cautiously adumbrated: germ theory and cell formation were claimed to be alluded to in the Quran, which reveals life to have begun with the *'alaq* or clot of blood. An alternate view accounting for the beginning of life based on Greek mythology was given, as if to say a range of possibilities explaining the origin of life was out there in the world of science, evolution being among them.

Each issue of *Rawdat* reserved a place for handy household hints in practical chemistry: how to prepare chemicals that removed stains from clothes and unpleasant odors from bodies. Packets of powdered charcoal sewn into underwear diminishes the noxious odors of flatulence. The chemistry of tobacco was reviewed to show its harms and warn against its use, as was the chemistry of musk and amber in relation to compounding cosmetics to make the body fragrant. The fat and brains of sheep compounded with Peruvian balsam, American carrot and walnut oil produced an exotic formulation guaranteed to prevent baldness.

The journal listed newly translated scientific texts in Arabic and Turkish that were on sale at the Khedival Library for secondary school or specialist students, or anyone who was interested. Salih Majdi, contributor to *Rawdat* and first biographer of Shaykh Tahtawi, translated a book on algebraic applications of geometry. A book on descriptive geometry was translated by Ahmad Najib, another contributor to *Rawdat*.[28] By the seventh and final year of its life, *Rawdat* had collectively published in its scientific articles the equivalent of a sizeable general textbook in each of physics, chemistry, astronomy, mathematics and industrial engineering. Any secondary level student entering advanced specialization would have been well served by the journal. Had something similar been available to the students in Muhammad Ali's schools, the course of Egypt's modernization would have been a happier story. As it was, the approximate equivalent of the comprehensive scientific text that Ottoman students had with Hoja Ishak's *Compendium* in the 1830s was not available to Egyptian students until 40 years later, this time delivered piecemeal in journal form over several years, with subjects in science interspersed with articles about religion, as it was designed to be.

Copernican theory

Before *Rawdat* closed down, the editors published a treatise of great importance on the history of Muslim assimilation of Copernican theory. The treatise was the culmination of a long series of articles on astronomy that began in the fourth issue of the first year of publication.[29] Many articles of the series were written by Ismail al-Falaki, director of the Khedival Observatory; by the conclusion of the series, Ismail al-Falaki's contributions amounted to a textbook. The articles were published as appendices in *Rawdat* and collectively known as *Bahjat al-Matalib fi 'Ilm al-Kawakib* (*The Delight in Seeking Knowledge of the Heavenly Bodies*). Yet in all of his many articles, Ismail al-Falaki avoided mentioning one of the most important fundamentals of modern astronomy, that the earth orbited the sun. Such was editorial caution. Uncertain as to what the religious temper would be if the idea of a moving earth were to be published in a school text that was partly religious, the editors ushered it in on the coattails of Muslim precedents, like an orphan whose parentage is at last revealed through a little historical research.

The first issue contained a piece on the history of the solar months, one on the zodiac and another on the precession of the equinoxes based on the work of the tenth-century astronomer abu Ma'shar. The system of solar months used in the West was shown to be of Muslim origin. Astronomers like abu Ma'shar, Battani and Ulug Bey were declared to have moved science forward from its Ptolemaic stage to what would become modern astronomy. (Paradoxically, while the science writers of *Rawdat* were linking modern astronomy to Muslim antecedents in preparing the way to introduce the heliocentric system, Shaykh Tahtawi, their chief editor, was at the time defending Ptolemy over Copernicus. Contradictions like this give pause to the historian inclined to make an interpretative judgment or draw a general conclusion regarding Muslim acceptance of modern science.) Not until 1875, when Mahmud al-Falaki had replaced Ismail as director of the observatory and was writing for *Rawdat*, and Shaykh Tahtawi had been dead two years, was the heliocentric theory at last referred to, though only by implication. In an article analyzing the transit of Venus across the ecliptic, Mahmud al-Falaki described the phenomenon in words that clearly implied, without expressly stating, that earth orbited the sun. The cautious editors went a step closer to Copernicus in a later issue of that year when another astronomical treatise began to appear in serial form.

Discussing the constellations and star names, and giving values for the brightness of certain stars as a function of their distance from the earth, the author was in fact saying that the old astronomy, according to which all the stars were fixed in a sphere, the so-called starry firmament that turned daily around the earth at the center, was wrong. The stars were not equidistant from the earth. There was no spherical firmament, only a myriad of stars clustered and scattered through an immense universe. Ahmad Mansur, the chemistry and physics teacher, was writing in the same issues about the principles of falling bodies and forces of attraction, leading up to Newton. Toward the end of 1875 the journal announced that the Ministry of Schools had decided to introduce a new course called cosmography. It was to be taught in the final year of the four-year *tajhiziyya* curriculum.[30] The course was described as covering a variety of astronomical subjects, one of which was the motion of the stars and the two motions of the earth (*dawran al-ard*). Also to be included in the course were subjects related to planetary orbits, the principles of a spherical earth, diurnal and relative motion, universal gravitation, apparent motion of the sun, motion of the earth around the sun and solar axial rotation. The course description is the first explicit and positively expressed reference to the heliocentric theory in Egypt since Tahtawi's airing of it in his Paris book and his *Kashf al-Buhar* in the early 1830s.

Rawdat was not in fact the first Arabic journal to introduce the theory of a moving earth. The first was in 1872 in Beirut, with Butrus Bustani's *al-Jinan* (*The Garden*). *Jinan's* readership was generally limited to Syrian Christians in and around Beirut, Tripoli and Damascus. An article in *Jinan* would in all likelihood not have come to al-Azhar's attention, and even if it had, the ulema in Egypt would have taken no issue with the ideas of a Christian in Syria, heretical though they may have appeared. In any case, by the mid-1870s, the idea of a moving earth was apparently neither heretical nor shocking to the Azharites. Otherwise, the course description of the new cosmography course in *Rawdat*, which was as much a religious journal as it was a scientific one, and one the venerable shaykhs often read and contributed to, would have elicited some objection. There was none. Silence signaled al-Azhar's passive acceptance of Copernicanism. The religious protest the heliocentric theory provoked came not from Muslim religious authorities in Egypt, but from Christians in Syria.

In 1876, in Beirut, a new popular scientific journal, *al-Muqtataf* (*Choice Selections*), edited by two young Syrian Christians, Ya'qub Sarruf and Faris Nimr, came out with a series of articles on the new astronomy. The religious controversy that the series aroused within the Christian community of Syria and Mt. Lebanon came to the notice of the editors of *Rawdat* and high officials in the Egyptian Ministry of Schools. The controversy in Syria, a tempest in a Christian teapot, gave Egyptian reformers in the government a pretext to clear the air and publish a treatise in *Rawdat* that openly and in a public literary forum defended Copernicanism and modern science.

While several Christian theologians in Syria were beating the drums of protest against the heresy of a moving earth, the Azharites, a body sublimely at rest, remained true to their institutional inertia, passively letting the controversy roll over them like a wave over an immovable boulder. Where no problem is seen, no problem exists. So, it was left to the Egyptian government's Ministry of Schools's journal, *Rawdat al-Madaris*, to answer the boisterous Christian clergy of Syria in defense of astronomical freedom.

Notes

1 Ahmad Izzat, *Ta'rikh ta'lim fi 'asr Muhammad Ali*, Maktabat-al-Nahda al-Misriyya, Cairo, 1938, pp. 48–50.
2 Patrick O'Brien, "Long Term Growth of Agricultural Production in Egypt, 1821–1962," in *Political and Social Change in Modern Egypt*, edited by P.J. Holt, Oxford University Press, Oxford, p. 179.
3 Zaki Salih and Mahmud Mursi, *al-Bu'athat al-ilmiyya fi qarn al-tasi' 'ashar*, Cairo, 1959, p. 63.
4 *Khitat al-Tawfiqiyya*, Bulaq Press (20 vols.), Cairo, 1888, ix, p. 41.
5 Rae W. Fraser, "The Egyptian Newspaper Press," in *The Nineteenth Century*, vol 32, Henry S. King and Co., London, 1892, pp. 213–223. See also Jacques Tajir, *Harakat*

al-Tarjama bi Misr khilal qarn al-tasi 'ashar, Cairo, 1945, p. 93. A good account of Ismail's profligacy and the fierce practices of European financiers, particularly in regard to the building of the Suez Canal, is David Landes, *Bankers and Pashas*: *International Finance and Economic Imperialism in Egypt*, Harvard University Press, Cambridge, MA, 1980.

6 Heyworth-Dunne, "Printing and Translations under Muhammad Ali of Egypt: The Foundation of Modern Arabic," *Journal of the Royal Asiatic Society*, vol 3 (July 1940), p. 349.
7 Jaques Tajir, *Harakat al-tarjama*, Cairo, pp. 85–86.
8 Muhammad abd al-Ghani Hasan and abd al-Aziz al-Dussuqi, *Rawdat al-Madaris*, Cairo, 1945, p. 32. And more recently on *Rawdat al-Madaris*, Terri Deyoung, *Mahmud Sami al- Barudi*, Syracuse University Press, Syracuse, 2015, pp. 186–192.
9 Muhammad abd al-Jawwad, *Taqwim Dar al-Ulum*, Cairo, 1950, p. 5.
10 Ali Mubarak, *Hayati* (*My Life*), Maktabat al-Adab, Cairo, 1989, p. 43.
11 al-Jawwad, *Taqwim*, pp. 5–7.
12 Muhammad abd al-Ghani Hasan and abd al-Aziz al-Dusuqi, *Rawdat al-Madaris*, 1945, p. 26; for *Dar al-Ulum's* funding, organization, staff, al-Azhar shaykhs and students who attended, and purpose of the institute, see Lois Aroian, *The Nationalization of Arabic and Islamic Education: Dar al-Ulum and al-Azhar*, American University in Cairo, Cairo, 1983.
13 Mubarak, *Hayati*, p. 46.
14 Samir Muhammad Taha, *Ali Basha Mubarak wa atharuhu fi al-hayah al-fikriyya wa'l-siyasiya fi misr fi'l-qarn al-tasi ashar*, Maktabat Said Rafat, Cairo, 1985, pp. 146–150.
15 *Taqwim al-Nil*, Diamond Issue of *Dar al-Ulum*, 1872–1947.
16 Husayn Fawzi al-Najjar, *Ali Mubarak, abu Ta'lim* (Father of Education), Cairo, 1987, p. 122.
17 Ghani and Dusuqi, *Rawdat al-Madaris*, p. 28.
18 Donald M. Reid, *Cairo University and the Making of Modern Egypt*, Cambridge University Press, Cambridge, 1990, p. 18.
19 Yusuf Ilyas Sarkis, *Mu'jam al-Matbu'at al-'Arabiyya wa'l Mu'arraba*, vol 2 (columns 1368–1369), Cairo, 1928.
20 Fawzi al-Najjar, *Ali Mubarak, abu Ta'lim*, pp. 118–119.
21 For Ali Mubarak and his relationship with Rawdat al-Madaris see Samir Muhammad Taha, *Ali Basha Muybarak*, pp. 120 ff.
22 Ghani and Dusuqi, *Rawdat al-Madaris*, pp. 14–15.
23 Samir Taha, *Ali Basha Mubarak*, p. 123; Dusuqi, *Rawdat al- Madaris*, p. 14.
24 Anwar Abdel Malek, *Ideologie et Renaissance Nationale, L' Egypte Moderne*, L'Harmattan, Paris, 1969, pp. 176–177.
25 See *Rawdat al-Madaris*, Wazirat al-Ta'lim al-Misriyya (Egyptian Ministry of Education), Cairo, 1870, issue 1, p. 6 for examples.
26 *Rawdat al-Madaris*, 1876, issue 19.
27 *Rawdat al-Madaris*, 1876, issue 13, p. 261.
28 *Rawdat al-Madaris*, Year 6, 1875, issue 3, p. 14.
29 *Rawdat al-Madaris*, 1870, issue 4, p. 74.
30 *Rawdat al-Madaris*, 1875, issue 4, p. 24.

3 Beirut

The American College and the popularization of science

In the second half of the 19th century Beirut joined Istanbul and Cairo as a city of major importance in the Muslim world's growth of scientific awareness. In this instance it was not Muslims who came directly into contact with western science, but Arab Christians inspired by a few exceptional American teachers and missionaries. The large Christian communities in Mt. Lebanon and Syria were strong attractions to western missionary workers.

The Americans had been preceded centuries earlier by French missionaries in the Levant. Mainly Jesuit, these missionaries had arrived in the wake of French merchants pursuing commercial interests in the port of Beirut in the 17th century. The Maronite community was the missionaries' chief target. So long as the French missionaries, and later the American evangelists, restricted their activity to the Christian communities, the Ottoman authorities and local Muslim leaders left them to their work: Christians converting Christians to Christianity.

The French connection with the Maronites of Mt. Lebanon went back to the Crusades, when the Maronite clergy accepted the Latin rite and papal authority. In 1584, a Maronite College was founded in Rome with an enrollment of 20 students selected from the villages of Mt. Lebanon. Graduates went on to teach Arabic and Syriac at the University of Paris, or they returned to the mountains to teach in Maronite and Jesuit secondary schools. In the 17th century, Capuchin, Franciscan, Carmelite and Jesuit missionaries from France set up schools in Christian areas of Syria and Mt. Lebanon. One of the schools that would play an important part in the Arab intellectual revival in Beirut and Mt. Lebanon was Ayn Waraqa. It began as a Maronite seminary in the 17th century, was turned into a secondary school by French-educated Lebanese Jesuits in 1789 and in the 1820s became a European style college preparatory school. Another school of importance was at Ayn Turah. In 1656, the French Jesuits had been given land there; some 80 years later a Maronite priest who had studied in the Maronite College in Rome built a high school on it. The Maronite school then turned Jesuit when the founder joined the order.

The brightest graduates of these secondary schools were sent to study in the Maronite College in Rome. A number of them distinguished themselves. Yusuf Sam'ani (d. 1768), an eight-year-old child when he went to study in Rome, became director of the Vatican Library. Sam'ani expanded the library's collection of Arabic, Syriac and Hebrew manuscripts to make it one of the finest collections in the world. A Lebanese Maronite held the chair of Arabic and Syriac at the Vatican's Sapienza College. Another, Mikha'il Ghaziri, became head librarian in the Escorial in Madrid. Known by the Spanish form of his name, Casiri, he catalogued the Escorial's 8,000 Arabic manuscripts in the two volumes they are listed in until today. Mikha'il Ghaziri was named after his native mountain village, Ghazir. This is where in the 1840s French Jesuits founded a high school. They founded another in the village of Zagharta around the same time. The schools of Zagharta, Ghazir, Ayn Waraqa and Ayn Turah, to name only the best known, taught French, history, mathematics, modern science and the works of Thomas Aquinas.

On the commercial side of the Franco–Maronite connection, members of influential Maronite families were appointed by the French government as consuls in Syria. One was given a title of nobility and made a prince by Louis XIV, after which the ennobled family held the office of French consul in Beirut as a hereditary right. Religious, educational and commercial ties had by the mid-19th century formed a powerful Franco–Maronite bond. French became a second, if not first, language for many educated Maronites. Paraphrasing a venerated 20th century Lebanese historian of Mt. Lebanon, Philip Hitti, these Catholic educational missions created the knife's edge that opened and cracked the hard Maronite shell of traditional conservative thinking.

The shell was further cracked by American missionary schools. The Boston Board of Commissioners for Foreign Missions made its first foray into the Ottoman Empire in 1820. Arriving initially in Malta, the evangelists sailed on to establish a mission in Izmir. With this their base, other missions advanced southwards to the Syrian cities that contained sizeable Christian communities. The first American missionary reached Beirut in 1823. With its large Greek Orthodox population waiting to be saved, the city, though quite small at the time, was soon to become a chief center of American evangelism.

It was not long after the arrival of these first Americans that the region entered a period of turbulent change. Muhammad Ali's army had seized Syria and Mt. Lebanon from Sultan Mahmud in compensation for the Egyptian fleet that went to the bottom of Navarino Bay in 1826 (Sultan Mahmud having reneged on his agreement to cede Crete to Muhammad Ali for Egyptian help in putting down the Greek revolt.) The ruler of Mt. Lebanon in the north, Amir Bashir, a former Druze prince who became a Maronite for geo-political reasons, allied himself with the Egyptians when Ibrahim Pasha was pushing the Ottomans northwards across the Taurus Mountains and into Anatolia. The alliance between the Maronites under Amir Bashir and the Egyptian army of occupation under Ibrahim Pasha opened Beirut, Mt. Lebanon and south Syria to international trade and the outer world. American evangelical missions were welcomed with open arms. In 1835, Eli Smith and other American missionaries opened a secondary school, Beirut High School for Boys, which taught English, math, geography, astronomy, natural and moral philosophy and logic.

Modern astronomy caused some head shaking among the students. Eli Smith commented in a letter to the *Missionary Herald* in March 1835, how, after completing a series of lectures on modern astronomy, the students were initially reserved toward the idea of a moving earth.[1] Smith thought it was the first time Copernican astronomy had been taught in the country. The subject aroused much talk in the city. There was no public consensus one way or the other on the strange idea of a moving earth, but the subject awakened a lively interest in science. By 1837, the missionaries were conducting well-attended public scientific experiments in pneumatics and electricity, arousing considerably more curiosity about the wonders of science in the Beirut populace. But excitement of science brought no converts to Protestant evangelism: neither from the public audience nor from the student body, which failed to grow. Instead of sending students to the American school, Amir Bashir sent young Maronites to study in Muhammad Ali's new specialized schools. For dearth of converts and students, the school closed in 1842.

By the end of the Egyptian occupation in 1840, Beirut, a city of only 8,000 at the time, had become home to a hundred European families, which included physicians, merchants, naturalists, teachers and missionaries.[2] The city was rapidly opening up to the outside world. Practically every day one or more British ships docked in Beirut harbor. Greeks and Italians opened hotels and restaurants. European-style shops and living quarters sprang up, transforming sections of the city in the same way certain quarters of Istanbul, Cairo and Alexandria were becoming Europeanized enclaves. In 1834 the Lazarite order of French monks founded a secondary school in Ayn Turah. The year after, an American missionary, William Tomsom, opened the Beirut School of Girls. American evangelists set up a printing press in 1843, and a few years later, in answer to the Jesuit school the French had built in 1843 in the Maronite village of Ghazir in the hills above the coastal town of Juniyya, they established a secondary school in the Greek Orthodox mountain village of Abayh, overlooking Beirut.[3] With the Maronites so tightly bound to the French, the Americans focused their interest on the Greek Orthodox community.

In 1850, the missionary Daniel Bliss, founder of what would eventually become the American University of Beirut, rode a donkey over the mountains from Damascus, and upon reaching Beirut began ministering to the Christians there, hoping to rejuvenate their faith through the Protestant interpretation of scripture and the American evangelist example of living it. A Franco–American academic rivalry sprang up in Beirut and the mountains above it. In response to the American Protestant press established in 1843, the French Jesuits founded the "Catholic Press" in 1853. In 1866, Reverend Daniel Bliss founded his American College, shortly renamed Syrian Protestant College (SPC). In 1875, the French responded with a new Jesuit college, St. Joseph. The American College specialized in medicine and science, St. Joseph in law, with a faculty of medicine being added in 1883. The secondary schools that the two western rivals had built – Ayn Waraqa, Ayn Turah, Ghazir, Zagharta and Abayh – prepared students for higher studies at Syrian Protestant College or St. Joseph, or in France where some Maronites went to continue their studies. The Americans, with an eye more to religion and conversion than high science and research, did not follow the French lead by sending their exceptional science or medical students to the U.S. for doctoral degrees. The Americans were there to save souls, not create scientists.

The secondary schools that the French and Americans built, staffed, financed and supplied were better able to prepare students for university study than those founded in Cairo or Istanbul, where funding, organization, instruction, equipment and reading material were in short supply. The same can be said in comparing Syrian Protestant College and St. Joseph to the specialized schools in Cairo and Istanbul. Entry was voluntary in the schools of the American evangelists and French Jesuits; and the students did not come from the lower levels of society, though some, rich in the spirit of learning, were relatively poor in regard to the cost of tuition. The goal of the schools in Cairo and Istanbul was to produce servants of the state and officers trained in modern military science, while in Beirut it was to produce firm believers in one or another interpretation of Christianity, with the medicine, science, law, history and literature that came with it being the reward for joining the flock. Since the educational institutions that the missionaries established were autonomous, science instruction was free of the narrow and distorting emphasis that state and military requirements imposed on science instruction in Cairo and Istanbul. A number of SPC graduates became leaders in midwifing modern science in the Arab world and, on a more general level, in the Arab intellectual revival that took place during the six decades between 1860 and the imposition of Anglo–French mandates over the Fertile Crescent following World War I.

Butrus Bustani (d. 1883) was one of the earliest of these promising young men. A product of both French and American education, he graduated from the Jesuit Ayn Waraqa school, where he learned French, Latin, Syriac, Arabic and canon law. Then in 1840, having just turned 20, he had the fortune of meeting the American physician, naturalist and missionary Cornelius Van Dyck (d. 1895) in Beirut. Bustani learned Hebrew, Greek and English from Reverend Van Dyck and other American missionaries and biblical scholars. The science he learned came particularly from Van Dyck.

Cornelius Van Dyck was the most extraordinary of a great many extraordinary American missionaries who descended on the Middle East in a fervor of evangelical revivalism that had gripped New York, New England and Pennsylvania in the 1830s and 1840s. He was born in 1818 in Kinderhook, Columbia County, New York, of Dutch parentage. His father was a physician–farmer who taught his son some chemistry and medicine, enough to enable Cornelius to go straight from high school to medical school. He was 21 when he graduated from Philadelphia's prestigious Jefferson Medical College. A year later, caught up by the missionary fever sweeping like a hot summer wind through the northeast of the country, he was in Syria, where, falling in love with the people and terrain of Mt. Lebanon and coastal Syria, he found his true home. He would spend the rest of his life there. He studied theology under his fellow American missionaries, who were all ordained ministers, and, without losing his open-minded humanism and dedication to science, he became one himself.

From his friend Butrus Bustani he learned Arabic in exchange for his giving Bustani lessons in English and science. Having perfected his speaking, reading and writing ability in Arabic, Cornelius went on to compose, in clear and simple Arabic, books and many articles on algebra, chemistry, physics, astronomy, mathematics, medicine and the history of classical Muslim science. Many of his books on mathematics and modern science were used as student texts when the American College opened in 1866.

Cornelius became fluent in classical and colloquial Arabic and could have passed as a local shaykh, dressed, as he did when administering medical care in the mountains, like a Maronite villager: tassled red tarbush, tight vest with laced buttons of silver thread, waist-high open jacket, voluminous pantaloons, crimson waistband and leather slippers turned up at the toes. With his flawless dialect he was assumed to be a Maronite, which on one occasion almost cost him his life. When riding his donkey from mountain village to village on his medical rounds, he unwittingly entered a Druze village, where he was immediately surrounded by armed men and accosted as an intruder from the nearby Maronite community, with whom the Druze had been trading massacres since the Egyptian evacuation of Syria and Lebanon in 1841. The Arabic dialect Van Dyck had learned from Bustani had something suspiciously Maronite about it, and the more he tried to convince the Druze villagers he was an American doctor from Kinderhook, the more they were convinced he was a Maronite spy preparing a plan of attack on their village. According to Van Dyck's account of the episode, he was saved from being strung up when a former patient who happened by to see what all the fuss was about attested to the American physician being what he claimed.[4]

If Cornelius Van Dyck had a Syrian counterpart it was his young friend Butrus Bustani. Bustani was impressed by the small colony of American missionary teachers, tall, lean men of unbending moral stamina, educated men who were dedicated to a mission, who had braved the seas and traveled from a distant world, a new world with exotic sounding cities – Boston, New York, Philadelphia, Kinderhook – to preach the Christian Gospel to Syrian Christians who were in fact born in the very same place as were their savior and their religion. By proximity, the Syrians saw themselves truer Christians and closer to Christ than these people from the other side of the world with the westernized version of their religion they brought with them. Their certainty of preaching the True Gospel was amusing to the eastern Christians, but it wasn't long before the targeted proselytes realized that these strange Christians from distant lands had brought something more than religion with them. The more Butrus came to know them, the more impressed he became, especially by Cornelius Van Dyck, who, not yet 30, was only a year or two older than Butrus and was already a practicing physician who had left his home to heal and educate a people a world away. Butrus was impressed enough to leave his Maronite religion to accept their evangelist version of Christianity and spend his life working with them.

The missionary-educators were especially proud of their science program. "It is, we suppose," in the words of Eli Smith, "the only institution in Syria where the true principles of science are taught." In 1846–1847, Butrus and Cornelius built the American Protestant School in Abayh. It taught modern science and, following the closure of the missionary Beirut School for Boys, was probably the only secondary level school to do so in the 1840s and 1850s.[5] They also created at that time (1847) the Syrian Society of Arts and Sciences (also known as the Arab Learned

Society) in association with another American missionary and two Lebanese Christians, the poets and writers Ibrahim Yaziji and Nasif Yaziji. The society had a small library of around 750 books in different languages, most of them in Arabic, 17 of which were on astronomy and mathematics. Meetings were monthly and included discussions on specific topics: the principle of natural law, the benefits of science, women in science, female education, botanical studies of the region. As seen from the subjects discussed, the purpose of the society was to create a scientific interest in the community couched in liberal humanism, and a pretty advanced one at that. Female education would not be a subject of serious literary discussion in Beirut until the late 1870s, and not in Egypt until the very end of the century.

The Learned Society's discussions were always in Arabic. The American missionaries had taken to the language with that same religious zeal exhibited by young Mormons today who in short time master the language of their destined country of mission work. The founders of the Society would all become teachers at the new American College in the 1860s and would form the nucleus of the college's humanists, as opposed to the stern biblical conservatism of the evangelicals who founded it. The Syrian Society of Arts and Sciences, similar in longevity to those forming in Istanbul at the time, lasted only five years. It was succeeded in 1857 by the Syrian Scientific Society, which was also centered in Beirut. Its membership of 150 indicates a growing interest in science. Whereas the former society was composed of American and Arab Christians, the Syrian Scientific Society included Muslims.[6] No records have survived of the Society's meetings and lectures, but it can be presumed they were in substance not much different from those of the Society of Arts and Sciences, and that natural law, modern astronomy and female education were topics of lively debate.

The British began contributing to the growing intellectual scene in a small way around 1860, when a branch of the British YMCA opened a secondary school in Beirut, called *Shams al-Barr*. Several future Lebanese literary luminaries graduated from it before going on to the American College, among them Ya'qub Sarruf and Faris Nimr, the future editors of *al-Muqtataf*, a popular scientific journal that would become the first and most famous of its kind in the Arab world for half a century. Jurji Zaydan, creator of the modern Arabic novel, was another of the British school's graduates. The high standards of *Shams al-Barr's* English, mathematics and science instruction made it an unofficial preparatory school for students planning to study science or medicine at the American College when it opened in 1866.

Tiny Beirut had by then already begun to manifest the intellectual fruits of its Franco–American missionary activity. In 1858, Butrus Bustani and his Protestant correligionist Khalid al-Khouri founded and edited Beirut's and Syria's first journal, *Hadiqat al-Akhbar* (*Garden of News*), a commercial, historical and scientific weekly review that opened a literary window to the western world. Two years later another opened. This was Bustani's newspaper, *The Syrian Bugle*. Bustani also opened a secondary school, the first in Syria and Mt. Lebanon to be founded by a local. The name he gave his school is significant: *al-Wataniyya*, the National

School. The thought that Mt. Lebanon and Syria formed a nation apart was just beginning to occupy the minds of some western-educated Syrian Christians.

Bustani founded his school in the Christian village of Abayh, the same village in which he had helped Van Dyck and the Protestant missionaries build their secondary school some 17 years earlier. Probably what happened was that Bustani took the missionary school over and renamed it, since two secondary schools in a small village would have been redundant. Bustani moved the school to Beirut in 1863 and renamed it *al-Jinan* (*The Garden*). Three years later the school became an annex of the American College that Daniel Bliss founded right next to Bustani's school. The building in Abayh that had housed Bustani's original school was shortly taken over by the British and used to house an Arabic language training center that was operated by British Military Intelligence and was referred to by the locals as the British Spy School, a name that has stuck.

In 1870, by which time Bustani was teaching at the American College, he began publishing a periodical of science, history and literature that bore the same name he had given his secondary school in Beirut: *al-Jinan*. By some coincidence, this was the year Egypt's first scientific journal was founded, *Rawdat al-Madaris*. Both *Rawdat al-Madaris* and *al-Jinan* were founded with an identical purpose and with synonymous names to express it, *Rawdat* and *Jinan* being Arabic synonyms meaning garden. The names were meant to convey the image of a garden of knowledge in which young minds blossomed. To complete the image, "Bustani" means gardener, but the cultivating aspect of his patronym may have been purely coincidental in regard to his choice of name for school and journal.

While teaching at the American College and running his journal, Bustani still found time to publish a two-volume encyclopedia on ancient and modern knowledge, *al-Muhit* (*The Encompassing Ocean*), which would remain the Arab world's only encyclopedia for more than half a century. The last two decades of Bustani's intellectual career fold into the origins and early history of the American College.

Reverend Bliss hadn't been long off his donkey, having arrived in Beirut, before he was told by the local Protestant community that what would really draw the eastern Christians to the American evangelical calling would be something more than moral preaching and singing hymns. The Syrians fancied they were pretty good at that and had been for several millennia. Why didn't the Americans bring them something they needed? Say a medical clinic or hospital, something that would improve the health of the body as preaching and hymns did the soul. A hospital would bless the community with something of practical importance and value in daily life. Even the Jesuits had not thought of that. Being convinced that a medical clinic was an excellent idea, Dr. Bliss sailed back to New York. In 1861 the Board of Missionaries in New York and Boston agreed to fund the creation of an institute of higher learning that would teach medicine, the Arabic language and Arabic literature.[7] It was the language and literature part that determined Bliss's choice of where in Beirut to locate the new college. It would be in the same place Butrus Bustani had built his school, in the western part of the city, where the headlands jutted into the blue sea: Ras Beirut.

Bustani figured prominently in the American evangelist community. His association with Americans went back to the early 1840s: he and Cornelius Van Dyck had exchanged language lessons; Bustani had collaborated with the American evangelists in making a new Arabic translation of the Bible from its original sources. His school would feed students to the new American College, which, in order to get on its feet, would need a ready source of medically and scientifically inclined students. The spectacular beauty of the setting seemed not to impress Reverend Bliss. He described the land he bought for the campus as a dumping ground for offal.

When the College opened its doors in 1866 it offered only language and literature to an unpromising student enrollment of 16. Among those 16 were two of the most exceptional men to graduate from the school that has now been in existence for a century and a half. These were Ya'qub Sarruf and Faris Nimr, who, a few years after their graduation, would found *al-Muqtataf*, the Arab world's uncontested leading scientific journal until well into the 20th century.

During the first year of the college's existence there were only two American teachers, the president, Reverend Daniel Bliss, and his associate, Reverend David Dodge. The following academic year the American faculty was slightly expanded in order to staff a new medical department. This gave the students a choice between a literary and a medical degree. As all instruction was in Arabic, the American faculty was obliged to master the language. Better the Americans learn Arabic, the evangelist founders figured, than the students master English and be lured from religion to the high paying opportunities that would be open to them in Ottoman service or in the foreign consulates as translators. Graduates were expected to become pastors and evangelical teachers in their Christian community, not make a good living.[8]

For the first several years of its existence the American College was housed in rented buildings, at least one of which the Bustani family owned. When the medical faculty was about to come into operation Reverend Bliss negotiated an agreement with the nearby Prussian Hospital that belonged to the German branch of the Order of St. John. The agreement allowed the faculty and students of the American College to use the hospital's teaching and clinical facilities. The College struggled to survive year to year. By 1870, the possibility of survival started to look more promising. The College had close to a hundred students, and President Bliss had completed the purchase and payment of the large piece of land on the bluff of Ras Beirut overlooking the Mediterranean, that aforementioned plot he referred to as a garbage dump. Everything was going well for the college. The campus and student body were expanding, and so too the faculty. Cornelius Van Dyck was hired to teach natural science, along with several other missionary-physician scientists residing in Beirut, among them a Scotsman and an Englishman, all of whom, as missionaries, knew Arabic. Bustani taught Arabic and in collaboration with Cornelius Van Dyck wrote Arabic textbooks in the physical sciences and mathematics. The completion of the astronomical observatory in 1877 introduced another weapon of science in the arsenal of evangelical conversion. It was a landmark achievement. In his Annual Report, Bliss wrote of his hope that the observatory would "prove useful in the direct education of students and in attracting the attention of natives to the superiority of western knowledge, thus helping to dispel ancient deep-rooted superstitions."[9] President Bliss could by then feel assured that the American College was on its way to becoming a permanent fixture in the Christian community of Beirut, owing to the school's being adequately funded by evangelicals in America as to the hard work, dedication and perfection of Arabic of its teachers and administrators that made the high moral tone of President Bliss appear genuine to the Beiruti community, in spite of the paternalistic tone coming from his unquestionable convictions of doing God's work and therefore always being right.

The stern, god-fearing, patriarchal authoritarianism with which Daniel Bliss ran the College fit well in the cultural landscape. In a political context, it would have been called tyrannical. Even Muhammad Ali, Clot Bey, abd al-Hamid II and the Jesuits might have learned something from the reverend president's sense of absolute power and demand for obedience. His plumb line of moral rectitude, particularly in regard to carnal weakness, drinking and the mention of Darwin, tolerated not the least deviation from the absolute straight and narrow as measured by himself. If challenged, he could be merciless, even to the extent of expelling students, firing faculty and closing down the school to destroy his enemies, like Samson bringing down the pillars. If his stony visage and wintry demeanor were not intimidating enough, his known use of corporal punishment was convincing back-up.

Bliss did not scruple to inflict bodily pain on students when he felt the occasion warranted it, which he often felt it did. Nothing excited his ire so much as the sins of the flesh. He was known to be patient in cases of minor irregularities, but "when a student endangered the morality of others," he wrote in his *Reminiscences*, "we isolated him as in the case of smallpox or plague." Once when informed by a professor that "a certain student had vile books in his possession, illustrated by obscene pictures," President Bliss marched into the student's room and demanded that he open his trunk. "He did so, and I saw that the report of the professor was correct. I told him he could send for his trunk, but that he must go immediately from the College. I had my cane in my hand and used it not as a staff but as a rod. I kept in touch with him as far as the Medical Gate, out of which he went, not saying a word, not even thanking me for accompanying him thus far."[10] Clot Bey's 30 days in the stockade were in comparison a mercy.

It is hard to imagine that the Lebanese literary revival pioneered by Butrus Bustani, Ibrahim Yaziji, Ya'qub Sarruf, Faris Nimr and Jurji Zaydan would have come when it did and in the shape it did without the French and their Jesuit schools preparing the way, and without the Syrian Protestant College with its Americans like Cornelius Van Dyck, Eli Smith, Daniel Bliss and David Dodge. Bustani had been teaching at the American College four years before his periodical *al-Jinan* appeared in 1870. Printed on the college's Missionary Press, Bustani's journal can be considered at least partially an enterprise of the American College and the liberal humanist members of its faculty. The journal's articles on science were the fruit of Bustani's studies with Van Dyck and the student textbooks they wrote together. Encyclopedic in content, the journal contained articles on classical Arabic and western science, history, literature, politics, industry and commerce, everything that Butrus and his son Salim, who was co-editor, considered to be contributions made to high civilization in Islamdom and the West. *Al-Jinan* was the workhorse from which would come Bustani's universal dictionary (*Da'irat al-Ma'arif*) and encyclopedia (*Muhit al-Muhit*, literally, *Ocean of the Ocean*.) *Al-Jinan* included reviews of past history and current events in America and Europe, of China to a lesser degree, and increasingly of Japan, which was astonishing the world with its quick mastery of technology.

The journal's science articles were not usually written in the same pedagogic detail and depth as those in the Egyptian *Rawdat al-Madaris*. The science in *Jinan* came in brief form, typified by the one-page chemical review of elemental carbon and carbon-based acids that Dr. Cornelius Van Dyck wrote for the first issue. Bustani's journal was principally literary, political and economic, with a focus on Europe, the Arabs and reform in the Ottoman Empire and Egypt. Pronouncements for the necessity of reform were always poking out between the lines. Reform was in fact what the journal was all about, and the editors were outspoken in their criticism of government's failure to enforce the reforms it had legislated. *Jinan's* Egyptian counterpart, *Rawdat al-Madaris*, funded, operated and printed as it was by the government, could never be critical. *Jinan* on the other hand did not shrink from depicting Egyptian and Ottoman officials as lazy, incompetent, parsimonious and corrupt – quite opposite, the editor stated pointedly, of the Japanese. Not that any of *Jinan's* editors had ever met a Japanese or even knew anyone who had, but this did not stop them from praising the Japanese to the high heavens, as it was not the Japanese they were praising but the Ottoman and Egyptian governments they were shaming.

A *Jinan* article of 1872 featured Japan as a model of expeditious transformation, reporting that the Mikado had just built five schools to teach the modern sciences and languages, each with an enrollment of between 1,500 and 2,000 students, altogether around 8,000 young Japanese sent to study science, technology and language by a single stroke of the ruler's pen. In Japan the ruler's word was respected as holy law. No one thought of disregarding it. Officials in Japan were appointed to enforce the ruler's reforms, while in the Ottoman Empire and Egypt the reforms were merely political fanfare without enforcement, as if just declaring them was enough of a mental breakthrough, and writing them down worthy of a long and deserved vacation. And even before a new law ever got to be promulgated, *Jinan's* critique went on, the people of the Ottoman Empire and Egypt had already figured out a hundred ways to get around it. Not that it took much to get around a law, since the only laws that were enforced were those that brought treasure straight into the pockets of government officials. Compared to the advanced nations of the West, the Japanese had not too long ago been in the same wretched boat as the Muslims, but now the Japanese were sailing forth, while the latter were drowning. Reforms had no chance of taking root in Ottoman society as they did in Japan, where the men put in charge of enforcing the Mikado's reforms were men who had lived in Europe and America and so were closely familiar with the mind and spirit of western people and their institutions. Japanese reformers knew how to go about designing and implementing reforms so they would accomplish what they were supposed to. To his people, the Mikado stood as a shining example of reform. One of the five new schools he had ordered to be built was housed in the emperor's largest imperial palace, which he had donated for the common good. Japan was astonishing the world with its reformist spirit and the rapid progress born of that spirit.[11]

By praising Japanese reform, the editors of *Jinan* revealed what they considered to be another grave defect in Ottoman and Egyptian reform: the overwhelming poverty and illiteracy that Muslim governments tolerated in mindless neglect. Focusing on military modernization while tolerating illiteracy undermined reform in every way. In two or three years Japan had been able to do more than Egypt and the Ottomans had done in 50. The Mikado had recently brought 23 French and ten English officers to Japan to modernize the military, and the progress was remarkable. Muhammad Ali had started this a half century earlier, but the illiteracy and poverty in Egypt canceled out the effort. The difference was that in Japan the Mikado appointed a council to study the problem of poverty. One of the results of the study was that girls who had been sold by their impoverished families were now put into government schools. Many of these girls were even sent to schools in America. Measures to reduce poverty through education were a vital part of Japan's reformist policy. Self-reliance was the key to success. The Japanese took responsibility in building roads, railroads, dams, communications and whatever had to be done. They learned from westerners, and once they had learned they sent the westerners back home and carried on the work themselves. They did not have the westerners do all the work for them as did the Egyptian and Ottoman governments, which had no sense of shame or dignity. Such was the gist of Bustani's critique.

The same theme was revisited a year and a half later by Bustani's son, Salim. While Japan continues to surge ahead, the Ottomans and Egyptians are left behind in backwardness, poverty and illiteracy. Stagnation is accepted as a normal condition of life. Few people read, and no one bothers to study science. Few books on science are to be seen in the bookstalls in Beirut or any other Arab city. Salim Bustani asks how can the public learn anything about the world and modern knowledge without books. He laments that it wasn't just the dearth of modern books that kept the public ignorant. It was also the nature of modern science itself, so alien to the cultural mentality of the public that the subject put people off. Remaining ignorant of modern science, they persisted in their belief in the science of antiquity. And even the old science was known only by a few, who in any case were worse than the most ignorant because they refuted modern science in defense of the old, arrogantly thinking that they knew what they did not. They rejected that which gave benefit for that which gave nothing. People still believed in the influences of the heavenly bodies on earthly affairs and feared the heavens. They lacked the patience and determination to study something not immediately understood.[12]

The younger Bustani complains bitterly of governmental and private lethargy and the sorry lack of initiative from any part of society. The government does nothing to increase the student population. No new schools are being built. By the same token, private investment in education is as bad as the government's record. Not even industrial or agricultural schools are being built. The same old outmoded methods of construction are being used that were used hundreds of years ago. There are no pulleys or modern technical devices for lifting heavy loads in constructing buildings and ships; modern technical methods of digging are unknown. Modern hydraulics and irrigation, laying pipes, machines for pumping water and lifting, the modern technology of dressing iron, manufacturing textiles and dyeing: all are unknown and unseen in the Middle East, as if they and the technical and scientific knowledge of chemistry, physics, mechanics and electricity that are necessary for these processes did not exist.

Anyone reading *Jinan's* criticisms, and those that were soon to come from other journals, would have had a hard time believing that the more than half century of reform in Egypt and the Ottoman Empire had been done seriously. On that same note, anyone reading the critical literature in Arabic today would have a hard time believing that modernizing reforms began two centuries ago. Salim Bustani's continuing critique offers an explanation for their lack of progress. Government and bureaucracy, rife with suspicion, corruption and graft, had prevented the entrepreneurial spirit from arising, except on the rarest of occasions, so rare as to be culturally meaningless. All that people did was write about the great accomplishments of the past in hopes of kindling an awakening in the reader. Such a piddling effort was at least a beginning to some kind of mental motion, but it was too small a beginning to lead to anything.

Political critique shared space with science. *Al-Jinan* was the first Arabic literary journal to publish a review of the heliocentric system since Tahtawi's *Kashf al-Buhar* saw the light of day in Cairo some 40 years earlier. It was not that the idea of the system did not exist in the minds of some tutored Middle Easterners, but what had been apparently accepted by an elite of educated Ottomans and Egyptians studying physics, mechanics and astronomy in the new secular schools since the 1820s, and by Syrian Christians in the American College since 1866, had gone unmentioned in the public domain, where modern astronomy, as late as the 1870s, remained a dark secret. Nothing of Copernicanism was published in Egypt's *Rawdat al-Madaris* until 1875, but five years before that, in 1870, the same year as *Jinan's* founding, the dark secret was coming to light. This started in Syria, not only with Bustani's *al-Jinan*, but also with a small book by another Syrian Christian, Fransis Marrash (1836–1873), whose book was published in Aleppo. As its name implies, *Nature's Testimony to the Existence of God and Divine Law* (*Shahadat al-Tabi'a fi Wujud Allah wa'l Shari'a*), the author's argument is that modern science proves the existence of God.[13]

Fransis Marrash came from a Christian Malikite family of considerable standing in nothern Syria. His father hired an English physician residing in Aleppo to teach Fransis medicine and then sent him to Paris to complete his studies, which he did between 1866 and 1870. During his five years in Paris, Marrash became influenced by the works of Catholic theologians who were at the time producing a modern version of the medieval argument that the beauty and perfection of nature's products and processes were proof that a super-human intelligence designed and created the cosmos. In his book, Marrash describes Galileo's and Newton's laws as being written across nature like geometrical figures sketched in the sand of an abandoned beach, proving to anyone coming upon the beach that someone had been there. Natural law pointed to an invisible architect who was apparent through his creation. "The precision of the delicate balance in the masses and distances of the planets orbiting the sun is a sign of God's hand." Following the format of William Paley's *Natural Theology* fairly closely, Marrash proves God's existence through self-revelation in nature's perfect laws and organization. He then proceeds to the necessity of God's revealing Himself through scripture in order to give man a moral law to cage the tiger of his free will.[14] From the architecture of the heavens, Marrash proceeds to the biological levels of life: plant, animal and human, in that order. The structuring of these living organisms was part of the grand design. His medical training is evident in his description of human physiology and anatomy. In spite of his biological study and years in Paris, he has nothing to say about Darwin or evolution. Marrash's version of Intelligent Design had no room for Darwin. Copernican theory and the Newtonian universe, however, gave no problem to divine structuring.

Marrash took ill and died at 37, three years after the publication of his little treatise. His acceptance of a moving earth aroused no more reaction in Syria than had Tahtawi's 40 years earlier in Egypt. A public reaction would not come until the concept of a moving earth was publicized in the Arabic journals in the mid-1870s. Marrash's treatise did, however, influence several Muslim shaykhs who either read it or heard of it: most notably Husayn al-Jisr of Syrian Tripoli and Shaykh Tantawi Jawhar of Egypt, both of them ardent promoters of Intelligent Design and the belief that Quranic revelation is a repository of natural science, subjects that will be taken up in later chapters.

Public tranquility over heavenly motion was first disturbed in 1872 by an article of Salim Bustani's in *Jinan*, entitled "*al-Falak*": Astronomy. The author approached his subject with great delicacy, step by measured step, as one about to expose a most dreadful secret. The first third of Salim's article is taken up by a long introduction, as bland as it is innocuous, about the well-known relationship between survival and knowledge, that those who don't learn end up either extinct or slaves, for knowledge was power over nature and people. Knowledge of geography was necessary for trade and commerce; commerce produced wealth and wealth power, a principle accepted since the time of ibn Khaldun. As commerce depends on ships and navigation, so do these depend on geometry and trigonometry, essentials of proper ship construction and navigation, along with algebra and other branches of mathematics that are necessary for business keeping accounts – and above all, astronomy for navigation. Astronomy explains many things. Just as the science of optics explains to us that the sky is blue because of the scattering of the sun's rays in the atmosphere, astronomy too is a source of truth about things not immediately apparent, such as gravitational attraction and the identity between the attraction of heavenly bodies and freely falling objects on earth. The force of attraction depends on distance, and such is the vastness of God's creation that it takes eight minutes for light from the sun to reach earth. It takes three and a half years for light from the nearest star to reach earth, and hundreds of years from distant stars. Finally, as a reflection of God's power and glory, the author, after this long elliptical approach, divulges that the earth revolves around the sun. And with that, promising to take up the subject at a later time, he abruptly returns to where he left off in his discussion of celestial mechanics and gravity.

It would seem that as Tahtawi had done 40 years earlier, Salim Bustani felt himself obliged to test the water before leaping in. It would also seem that he received several sharp letters of rebuttal, but far more in support, enough in any case that in the very next issue he expanded his discussion of the heliocentric universe and Newtonian mechanics, in the course of which he declared that those who opposed modern astronomy and its mathematical physics were ignorant. "No one can be blamed for studying this since it is knowledge which has been discovered about the true way the universe works." What up to this point had been a purely scientific excursus, now devolved into a religious defense against

> so-called religious scholars who are in reality ignorant people filled with empty pride thinking they know things, but about which they know nothing. Even the most learned of the ulema are ignorant. They pride themselves and their ancestors for their old knowledge, but they are a source of shame to us rather than a source of pride. We should forget what we know of past knowledge, for it is wrong. It is no secret that we believe more of what is ignorance than is truth. Knowledge is endless: one discovery opens the door to a new multitude of questions of which we are ignorant . . . And so each discovery manifests God's power . . . Every discovery reveals God's qualities in their entirety and wholeness. His creation of new worlds is not a denial of His grace, care and providence for man, but a reaffirmation in a light all the more powerful and glorious.[15]

Salim Bustani was addressing specifically the Christian ulema here, but his complaint, like his father's, was directed generally against both Muslims and Christians who, as he described them, contentedly wallowed in lethargy and ignorance by their disinterest and negation of science, while the West, and newcomer Japan, raced forward into the future, leaving the Arabs behind to dream their comforting dreams of the past. Going theological, Salim cites a well-known verse of the Quran, that God creates nothing in vain, and interprets it to show that science is a religious pursuit and should be pursued as zealously as religion, the way westerners and Japanese study science. The vastness of space with its multitudinous planets and stars makes obvious the presence of a mighty God. But then why would God have created all those distant stars and new planets that are being discovered through modern telescopes? To what purpose, unless life and consciousness exist on those distant and many planets? These, Salim answers, are questions that only someone devoid of wisdom in God's creation would ask. "Many Christian ulema say the spirits of the departed understand the purpose of these creations and that is their happiness in heaven: to understand what they had not understood on earth as corporeal bodies. This heavenly knowledge is the soul's reward for a good life on earth."

Salim Bustani's argument would be for generations the essential model upon which would be based the ensuing Arab discourse on modern astronomy, physics and religion, both Muslim and Christian. Anyone speaking for science was obliged to pay respect to divine creation and the promise of salvation and rewards in paradise. This was the price of getting a hearing, for publishing without repercussions. The Quran's rich imagery would provide Muslims with a limitless palimpsest to write science over verses of revelation, whatever the science. Christian spokesmen, limited to the Gospels, had less to work with, but the pattern was the same. God created the universe, whose structure, motions and vastness are revealed by science and whose purpose is revealed by religion and the knowledge that comes with the promise of eternal life. Modern astronomy would have to be delivered from the womb of scripture. Evolution would have a harder time of it.

It was not until more than a year later, mid-1874, that Salim returned to the subject of modern astronomy and an earth in motion with his *"Dawran al-Ard"* ("The Two Motions of Earth"). In it he explains what was most perplexing to people: how the earth moves without it being apparent. "When observing motion it is vital for the observer to know if he is on a fixed or moving stage. The earth moves and takes with it the atmosphere . . . so we feel nothing of its motion . . . The earth is like a ship sailing a smooth sea in the silence of night. When we are on a moving wagon or ship and throw a ball up, the ball will travel with us and fall back into our hands, if there is no wind, for everything on earth moves as a system."[16] About the same time that Salim's article appeared, his father's mentor, colleague and longtime friend, Cornelius Van Dyck, published his Arabic college text on modern astronomy, *Usul 'Ilm al-Hay'a (The Principles of Astronomy)*. His purpose in writing it was to give students at the American College a comprehensive text on astronomy that they could read and understand without the language getting in the way. Van Dyck's book may have had something to do with the timing of Salim's article on the moving earth. The small literate society of Arab readers with an interest in modern astronomy and science would be more likely to go to an inexpensive journal than a book to satisfy their interest. The journals had a wider circulation and reached other Arab countries. According to Salim Bustani, copies of Van Dyck's astronomy textbook were available in the bookstalls for those very few Beirutis who might have been interested in the subject, but it was not Cornelius Van Dyck's or Fransis Marrash's books that disseminated the revolutionary ideas of modern astronomy in Arab society. It was the journals of *Rawdat*, *Jinan* and, most important of all, *Muqtataf*, founded in 1876, that were the primary sources introducing the general principles of modern astronomy to the Arab reading public.

Salim Bustani kept *al-Jinan* in operation until three years after his father's death, in 1883. What made Salim decide to end it after 17 years of successful operation, the longest run yet of a non-governmental publication anywhere in the Muslim world, was the Hamidian poisoning of the free atmosphere Beirut had enjoyed ever since Ibrahim Pasha pushed the Ottomans out in 1828. In the 1880s, once the cloud of Sultan abd al-Hamid's fear-ridden government of censorship, repression, secret police and surveillance had settled heavily over Syria, and the American evangelicals administering SPC came down no less severely on academic freedom over the issue of Darwin's theory of evolution, a great many of the intellectual lights that had shone in Beirut moved themselves to Cairo, where the British were now running things. But much happened in Beirut between the mid-1870s and the Syro–Lebanese exodus to British Egypt a decade later.

The sun of 1876 shone brightly over Beirut. The first volumes of Butrus Bustani's 11-volume encyclopedia appeared in 1876. It was also the year of the first issue of the journal *al-Muqtataf*. The American College was doing fine, the medical school was growing and excellent chemistry and biology professors had been recruited from America. An agreement had been reached for American College medical students who had completed four years of course work to train for a year in the German Hospital, formerly the Prussian Hospital that had been renamed after the unification of Germany in 1871. Additional land had been purchased for the campus, College Hall had been built and the bell clock successfully hoisted up almost 100 feet and installed in its tower. Things were looking up on other horizons as well. The new Sultan abd al-Hamid II had, so it seemed at the time, taken on Young Ottoman ideas and proclaimed a constitution. The formation of a representative assembly had been announced, and there were to be elections for parliamentary government. Egypt had gone bankrupt under Khedive Ismail, but it was a rich country and would soon recover and no doubt go constitutional along with the rest of the empire. With government going liberal, the energies of the people would be released. Soon Muslims would be following the Japanese example. From the top of the American College's new clock tower overlooking the shimmering sea, 1876 proclaimed a new dawn. And it was the turning Earth orbiting the sun bringing it.

In the third volume of his encyclopedia, which came out in late 1876, Butrus picked up on the theme of heliocentrism where his son had left it in *al-Jinan*. It appears under the entry entitled *Ard*: Earth. "First the Semitic ancestry of the word: *Ard* in Arabic, Eretz in Hebrew, becoming Erd in German and Earth in English – the third most distant planet from the sun whose motion is a subject of study."[17] Bustani then reviews the history of astronomy in terms of the place of the earth among the planets according to the systems used by the ancient Egyptians, Mesopotamians, Israelites, Indians, classical Greeks, the Hellenistic Ptolemaic astronomers, followed by the Arabs (Muslim astronomy being called Arabic), whose refinements of the Ptolemaic system led up to Copernicus and modern astronomy. When the Franks came on the scene and further developed Arab astronomy, two systems emerged, the first of which is (in Bustani's terms) the "astronomy of the majority," where the earth is at the center of creation with the sun orbiting it in accordance with scripture, and the second of which is the "astronomy of the minority," the astronomy of modern science.

Biblical accounts, Bustani warns, must be taken figuratively and metaphorically, since scripture describes natural phenomena as they are perceived, not as they are. In order to debunk the Bible-based majority astronomy, Bustani describes the extremities of mythic imagination to which cosmologists of this school went in giving divine structure to the earth-centered universe. Pillars are supposed to support the earth and the sea it rests on. Cosmographers, for all the fine astronomy that was achieved in Islamic civilization, went far beyond what was explicitly stated in the Bible and the Quran. The cosmologist Tha'alabi, for example, has an account of a surrounding sea with a divine bull sent from heaven standing above it and balanced on a sturdy emerald and a brilliant ruby 500 years long (sic), with the earth fixed between its two horns. The ruby and emerald give stability. The bull breathes in and out once a day, causing the tides to rise and fall. Because of the tides, greater stability was required, and so God created a great whale and rested the whole structure of emerald, ruby, bull and earth on its back. The seven earths and heavens related in the Quran come from this. The first earth is inhabited by people, the second by the barren wind that destroyed the people of 'Ad mentioned in the Quran, the third by the Stone of Hell, the fourth by burning sulfur, the fifth and sixth respectively by the serpents and scorpions of hell. On the seventh resides Iblis, the devil, and his troops.

Butrus Bustani goes into the details of how this fantastic structure came to be conceived. An even more intricate and fantastical version of Tha'alabi's cosmography was presented two years later in *Muqtataf*,[18] and was published for the same reason Bustani dug it up: to tie the mythic to the scriptural and help the reader decide which of the two systems, biblical or scientific, was the more credible. To show that true Muslim scientific thinkers were far more rational and indeed very close to reality (and that therefore the new astronomy was really not that strange at all but in fact just a small step from what was considered by Muslims to be heavenly reality) Bustani introduces the more rational version of the earth and the surrounding cosmos presented by the medieval Islamic cosmologist Qazwini. In his *Marvels of Creation* (*Aja'ib al-Makhluqat*), Qazwini describes the earth as a simple spherical body resting at the center of the universe. Because of its mass and density, the earth draws everything to it and keeps everything held firmly to its surface, while the earth itself is held fixed in place by the interactive quality of the planets and the all-encompassing firmament. A system of forces of attraction acting from every side and direction holds everything in the cosmos in balanced motion around the earth. A study of eclipses, of the phases of the moon and of the surface convexity of bodies of water proves the earth's sphericity. It is an elegantly structured and rational universe. To emphasize the rational version of cosmogony, Bustani then turns from Qazwimi to the 13th century Egyptian historian ibn al-Athir's *Tuhfa al-Aja'ib* (*The Precious Gift of Marvels*) and the discoveries made by astronomers during the Caliph Ma'mun's time: Muslim astronomy is the model of reason. Bustani's article is a clever juxtaposition of fable and science that is intended to stitch Muslim astronomy to the modern version, for when compared to the fantasy of an earth that is supported and fixed in position by giant turtles, elephants and huffing bulls balanced on rubies and emeralds on the back of a whale, the rational astronomy described by Qazwini, ibn al-Athir and Ma'mun's astronomers makes Muslim and modern astronomy look almost like clones, the genetic transfer being the Latin translations of Arabic science, as Bustani points out in so many words.

Bustani's encyclopedic article goes on. The later discoveries of Nicolas of Cusa, Giordano Bruno, Copernicus, Brahe and Galileo produced a struggle in Europe between those who believed in the old astronomy, which was Muslim astronomy, and the new, which had been evolving ever since Copernicus. The geocentrists were the majority. The heliocentrists were the minority. The struggle between them was framed by three issues: the earth's position, its geological formation and its age. Because of the majority's resistance to accept or tolerate the science of the minority, Bruno was burned at the stake and Galileo forced to recant and then put under house arrest. Bustani implies that Arab and Muslim acceptance of the new astronomy would be no more than going back to a time during the golden age of Arabo–Muslim creativity when these ideas had been discussed, as expressed by the words of Bustani himself: "Those ideas that had been discussed freely among the Arabs for a short time during the Middle Ages were severely repressed in Europe once westerners had mastered Arab science, and it was a long time before opposition against the new ideas would be overcome."

Putting the finishing touch to his presentation of proofs that supported the theory of a turning earth, Bustani describes the pendulum experiments of Huyghens, Newton and Foucault. A pendulum suspended freely from a great enough height would in the course of 24 hours knock over 24 blocks of wood that were equidistantly spaced from one another in the form of a circle whose center was vertically below the pendulum's suspension point. Pendulum experiments recently carried out by the French at various places on the earth's surface – Africa, Europe, Caribbean, Atlantic islands – demonstrated that the earth bulged at the equator and was flattened at the poles, a consequence of the earth's spinning, as Newton had explained. Because of the earth's bulge and the law of universal gravitation, an object placed between the equator and a pole would weigh less than the same object if placed at a pole. The closer to the equator that the object was placed, the less it would weigh, since the distance between the object's center of mass and the earth's center would be increased. The object would weigh more at the poles, where the distance was less. By measuring the difference in the period of a pendulum placed at different latitudes on the earth's surface, one can show conclusively that not only was the earth shaped oblately, but that it rotated around a polar axis. To put the issue of a moving earth to rest once and for all, Butrus Bustani amassed all the scientific evidence there was, from pendulums to telescopes, and in a closely reasoned 27-page article of early 1876 he laid bare the physical laws (*nawamis*) that governed planetary motion around the sun. Butrus left no stone in the garden of astronomy unturned. His article was a tour de force. But there was more.

In regard to the three problems that he stated as confronting the biblical astronomy of the majority and the new astronomy of the minority, there was still another problem he included in the list. This one was quite different from the problems related to the earth's position, motion and age. It was a question that did not relate purely to astronomy. It was more of a philosophical problem related to cosmology. It was the one that delivered Bruno to the Vatican and the stake: that man was not the center of existence on a stationary earth at the center of the universe. The

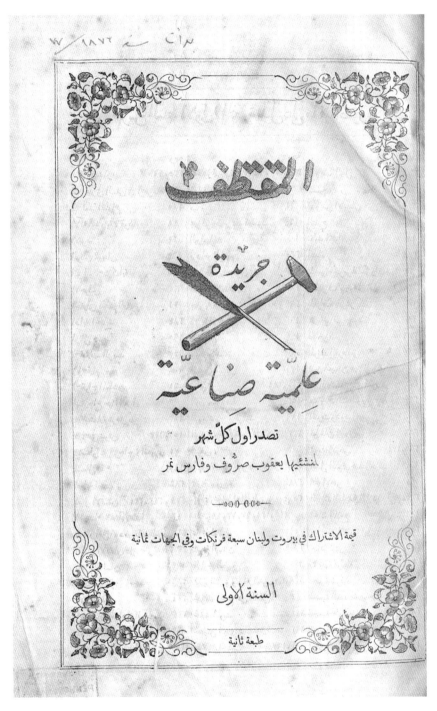

Figure 3.1 Cover of the journal *al-Muqtataf*

earth moved, the universe was infinite, and in that star-filled infinity how many other earths were there that supported intelligent life? What Bustani had in mind was not infinity but geological ages and formations, and man's place therein. He had Darwin on his mind.

The theory of evolution had been exercising the minds of some Middle Eastern thinkers at least since the early 1860s. Bustani no doubt learned of Darwin from Cornelius Van Dyck, whose young son William, a botanist and also a professor at the American College, was soon to have a correspondence with Darwin over the variation in species of wild Syrian dogs. The last letter Darwin wrote just before his death in 1882 was to William Van Dyck in Beirut on the subject of his study of wild Syrian dogs.

Bustani did not go into the problem of man's position at the center of creation. The position of the earth was problem enough. He left to others the problem of man's place, once the proper place of the earth had been fixed in the cultural mind.

Notes

1 Marwa Elshakry, "The Gospel of Science and American Evangelism in Late Ottoman Beirut," *Past and Present*, issue 196 (August 2007), pp. 183–184.
2 Philip Hitti, *Lebanon in History*, Macmillan, London, 1962, p. 426.
3 Kamal al-Yaziji, *Shaykh Ibrahim al-Hourani*, Beirut, 1963, pp. 29–31.
4 Lutfi Sa'di, George Sarton and W. T. Van Dyck, "Al-Hakim Cornelius Van Dyck," *Isis*, vol XXVII, issue 1 (May 1937), pp. 20–45.
5 Elshakry, "The Gospel of Science," pp. 187–188.
6 Adel Ziadat, *Science in The Arab World: The Impact of Darwinism, 1860–1930*, Palgrave Macmillan, London, 1936, r p. 11, citing Jurji Zaydani, *Tarikh Adab al-lugha al-arabiyyah*, Hilal, vol 4, pp. 80–81.
7 For a recent brief account of the origins of the American College in Beirut see Elshakry, "The Gospel of Science," pp. 192–198.
8 Olivier Meier, *Al-Muqtataf et le debat sur le Darwinisme: Beirut 1876–1885*, Dossiers du CEDEC (Centre d'Etudeset Documentation Economiques, Juridiques et Sociales), Cairo, 1996, p. 19.
9 Cited by Elshakry, "The Gospel of Science," p. 190.
10 John Munro, *A Mutual Concern: The Story of the American University of Beirut*, Caravan, New York, 1977, p. 27.
11 *al-Jinan*, edited by Butrus Bustani, Beirut, vol III (1872), pp. 221–222.
12 *al-Jinan*, vol V (1874), pp. 517–521.
13 For Marrash and his works see Marwa Elshakry, *Darwin's Legacies in the Arab East: Science, Religion and Politics, 1870–1914*, Princeton PhD dissertation, 2003, pp. 186–201. This has recently been published as *Reading Darwin in Arabic, 1860–1950*, University of Chicago Press, Chicago, 2014.
14 Fransis Marrash al-Halabi, *Shahadat al-tabi'iyya fi wujud allah wa'l shari'ah* (*Nature's proof of god's and divine law's existence*), Paris, 1892, pp. 8–9, 13.
15 *al-Jinan*, vol III (1872), pp. 518–523.
16 *l al-Jinan*, vol V (1874), pp. 517–521.
17 *Da'irat al-Ma'arif*, edited by Butrus Bustani, Beirut, vol III, 1878, p. 108.
18 *al-Jinan*, Vol III, 1878, pp. 1–4. Ya'qub Sarruf believed Tha'alabi's story originated in Indian sources, where a giant turtle supports four elephants, which in turn hold up a hemispherical earth.

4 *Muqtataf, Rawdat al-Madaris* and the Fikri treatise on a moving earth

Muqtataf was a commercial and intellectual success. It had to be to survive. No government ministry subsidized it. Within the Arab world it immediately became what could be likened to an international journal, its issues finding their way from Beirut to Damascus, Aleppo, Cairo, Alexandria, Baghdad, Basra, Najaf and Mosul. Letters to the editors came from as far afield as Tunis. Its popularized science, biographical sketches and announcements of new discoveries and technological inventions had a much broader appeal to both Muslims and non-Muslims of the Arab reading public than *Rawdat al-Madaris* could ever have had as an academic journal laced with religion and meant for Egyptian students. *Muqtataf's* format was no less appealing than the substance of its articles, which came uniformly written in a simple, direct prose style. The journal was a model of clarity and organization, its print neat and clear, its text more accessible because of spacing and the innovative use of commas, periods, question marks, paragraphs, headers and even on occasion diacritical marks to indicate a passive verb. Where *Rawdat* might have broken an article off in the middle of a thought, to be continued in the next issue, *Muqtataf's* articles tended to be short, sweet and complete. Installments of articles published in series ended at a point that made the piece complete in terms of the idea being developed.

In a society where more than 90 percent were illiterate, even in the last quarter of the 19th century, those who could read were reasonably educated, which permitted the editors to maintain an intelligent level of discourse that reached the professional readers without losing the more general ones. Not being an academic journal, it was free of *Rawdat's* solutions for cubic equations, algebraic puzzles, double displacement chemical equations and descriptions of chemical and mechanical engineering processes. *Muqtataf's* emblem was a drawing of a feather pen and an awl above the name of the journal, the former standing for the work of mind, the latter for the technical application of the products of mind: science and technology. Two versions were given for the origin of the journal's name: that it came from an American magazine called the *Eclectic* that published popular articles on science and technology selected from other publications, which was much what the editors of *Muqtataf* did; and that the name was suggested by Dr. Cornelius Van Dyck.[1] Perhaps Van Dyck had the *Eclectic* in mind. It was he more than anyone who had encouraged young Sarruf and Nimr, science graduates of the

American College who had been hired as Arabic instructors, to go for their dream of founding a scientific journal, the likes of which, as they hoped, the Arab world had never seen. Butrus Bustani was another of their former teachers who must have inspired and encouraged them. Cornelius Van Dyck, however, was the only one who the two founders mentioned by name in the article they wrote regarding the origins of their journal, which appeared in *Muqtataf's* 20th anniversary volume.

The avowed purpose of *Muqtataf* was stated in terms that were almost identical to *Rawdat's*: to revitalize science in society, especially in the youth, so that Arabs could regain their lost place among the ranks of high civilization and take pride not only in their past heritage but in their present contributions. Those were not empty words in the 1870s. They expressed the hope for a bright future that the intelligentsia and political leaders believed to be within their grasp through learning, government reorganization and modern education. Once re-initiated in the sciences, the Arabs would again make their contribution and rejoin the caravan of civilization. In spite of all the implied and overt criticisms of government and society that the editors put in the journal, it was a time of hope, and *Muqtataf* was a child of that hope. Not until some years later, when it was obvious that the Japanese had accomplished what Muslims had not, did the hope start to fade and the tone become bitter and accusatory.

In advance notices that advertised the introduction of the new journal, the editors pledged to avoid all religious and political issues that didn't impinge directly on science. Criticizing society was to be fair game, though in the early years it was mostly implied. Almost every issue had a brief article or notice on famous women of the world who had been or were scientists, artists, musicians or writers. Women who had defied family and social tradition by refusing marriage and who ventured out on their own to pursue their dreams were favorites. Wealthy individuals, professional societies and companies that gave scholarships to deserving students and endowed university chairs for the study of particular branches of science were praised as pillars of a healthy society.[2] Often the criticism was stated directly: women should be liberated and educated; the wealthy should support worthy students, endow scholarships and found societies for the advancement of science. Cornelius Van Dyck reported on a new physics book of around 300 pages written in Arabic by an American woman who taught in a Syrian secondary school that had adopted her book as the student text for that subject. Dr. Van Dyck recommended that her book be adopted by all secondary schools, as it was well written and organized, covered magnetism, optics, heat and electricity, and was the cheapest and best book in Arabic on modern science. The implication was obvious. American women were doing more to introduce young Arabs to science than the Arabs themselves were doing.

The journal offered practical advice on hygiene and personal care: how to get rid of lice, freckles, pimples, bad breath, body odor. Technical questions were answered: how to gild metal surfaces by electrolysis; how to make wine, beer, brandy, champagne; how to produce opium. A European company had developed chemically treated underpants that absorbed foul odors, a windfall for those suffering from flatulence.

The unity of science and religion was a running theme. Kepler saw the geometry of the solar system as a symphony of cosmic harmony so perfect and beautiful that it was nothing less than God having set his heavenly creation to music. Galileo was a devout believer in God and a faithful follower of the Catholic Church but fell victim to the religious ignorance of others in authority and was forced to recant what he knew to be true. Newton spent more time studying the Bible than nature. Roemer's determination of the speed of light and other astronomical discoveries showed the earth to be but a drop in the ocean of space "which manifests God's power, may He be praised."[3]

In their praise of science and its benefits, the editors went beyond anything that had been written before in Arabic. Writing in 1877 on Oersted, Faraday, Maxwell and the history of electricity and electromagnetism, the editors conclude that had it not been for these scientists and their discoveries, there would be no telegraph, no power-driven machines that make for modern communications and industry, and mankind would be no better off than wild animals.

The first issue of *Muqtataf* hit the streets of Beirut in early May 1876. The several hundred copies slowly spread through the Arab world, transmitted hand to hand, city to city, country to country, eventually reaching North Africa and Iraq. Around 500 copies of each issue were printed between 1876 and 1885 – enough to satisfy Syria's reading public out of a population of 2.7 million. The journal was an immediate success in Beirut and Cairo.

Sarruf and Nimr constantly reviewed science and technology publications from Europe and America to inform themselves and their readers of any new discoveries. They wrote articles on atomic physics, wave theory of light and electricity, spectroscopy and its use in determining the chemical composition of sun and stars, the discoveries of uranium and plutonium, Marie Curie's discovery of radium and polonium, J. J. Thomson's discovery of electrons, Rutherford's discovery of alpha particles and gamma rays, and the inventions of light bulbs and telephones. Scientific books that would be of interest to Arabs were publicized.

Some readers loved what they read and eagerly awaited the next issue. Some detested it for religious reasons, considering it heretical or close to it, especially for the articles on astronomy, and would read no more of it. Some sent indignant letters to the editors accusing them of spreading ideas that were not only false but against religion. The journal's popularity (notoriety for some) made it a magnet of public response, attracting and repulsing with more or less equal magnitudes of emotional intensity. For this reason, public emotion over the idea of a moving earth did not erupt from the weighty treatment of Copernicanism found in Bustani's encyclopedia published earlier that year, nor from the articles in his journal *Jinan* dating back to the early 1870s. It was from the brief articles of a column or two in *Muqtataf* that brought the subject to a public boil.

The journal's first astronomical article was in fact on the moon, not the earth, but it referred to earthly motion. Appearing on the seventh page of the first issue and entitled "The Moon," the article begins by describing the phases of the moon as it rises and sets during its monthly orbit around the earth, and then states that the daily rising and setting of the sun is only an appearance, not a reality, in that it is not the sun moving but the earth, which rotates on its axis while orbiting the sun.

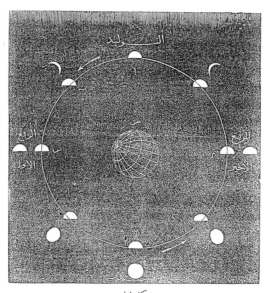

Figure 4.1 The phases of the moon as it orbits the earth

The first article on modern astronomy that implied, and expressed in the midst of the text, that the earth orbited the sun and rotated on its polar axis came in the first issue and was on lunar motion. In explaining the orbit of the moon around the earth, the editor writing the article incidentally mentions the earth's motion around the sun. This was the first public expression in the Arab world that the Ptolemaic system is wrong and the Copernican system is the right one (meaning Kepler's system, but Copernican to keep it simple in terms of circles; the complexity of Kepler's ellipses would come later). Lunar motion, which was perfectly known and accepted, was a wedge for opening the delicate truth of earthly motion, and just as the editors feared, it caused a big enough religious furor and controversy, on the part of the Christian community, that the Ottoman authorities had to intervene before the European powers used it as another pretext to intervene themselves and cut out another chunk of Ottoman territory or claim European supervision over it (coastal Syria, including Beirut) just as they had in 1860.

The first article shows the phases of the moon as it orbits the earth, seen at the center in the diagram, with the sun shown as rays at the top of the diagram, the phases being explained by the interposition of the moon between earth and sun (at the upper half of the diagram), and the interposition of earth between moon and sun (lower half of the diagram).

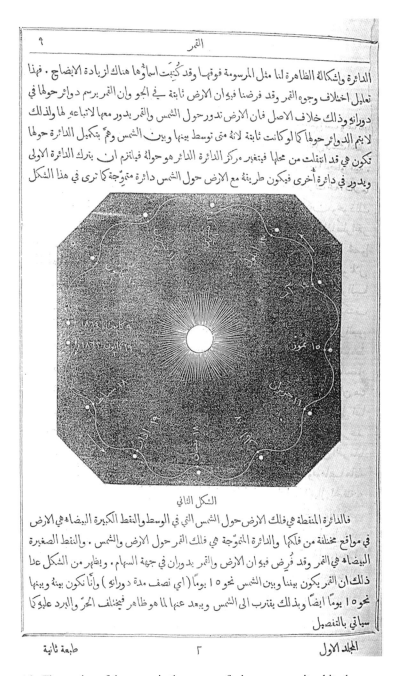

Figure 4.2 The motion of the moon in the course of a lunar year as it orbits the sun

The diagram shows the motion of the moon in the course of a lunar year as it orbits the sun, seen at the center of the diagram. The earth is seen as a small dot whose yearly solar orbit is traced out in the diagram as a broken circle of dashes. The track of the moon is seen as wavy because of the combined motions of moon and earth. It is in describing this diagram that the editor casually writes, "It is supposed in the diagram that the earth and the moon orbit in the direction of the arrows."

In the following issue a month later, its young co-founder, Ya'qub Sarruf, who edited and wrote most of the scientific pieces those early years, goes on to describe the moon as a barren, waterless, lifeless planet of valleys, mountains, craters and deserts. In the third issue, a general review of the solar system was presented. The editors were approaching the subject in cautious stages, in the same careful manner that the editors of *Rawdat al-Madaris* had approached the subject in Cairo the previous year. Entitled "The Solar System," the article repeats in greater detail the Newtonian principles alluded to in the previous lunar articles, and explains briefly how the heliocentric system replaced the Ptolemaic system through the work of Copernicus.

The next issue contained an even more detailed exposition. The sun, Sarruf wrote, provided the material that formed the orbiting planets and so was the mother planet who kept her children running around her by the mutual force of gravitational attraction that they exerted on each other, though the children ran not in circles, but ellipses, with mother sun fixed at one of the two focal points. The closer the earth approached the sun, the faster it went; the further away, the slower. For those readers who desired a more detailed account of the earth's motions and planetary astronomy, Sarruf referred them to the astronomy text written recently in Arabic by the American woman who directed the Syrian School for Girls in Damascus. This was Sarruf's two birds with one stone: boosting both modern astronomy and women as scientists.

By mid-summer, protesting letters were storming into *Muqtataf*'s editorial room, some letters even questioning the earth's being spherical.

As might be expected, some of the younger generation, who presumably had been studying something of modern science in the secular high schools established by the *Tanzimat* reformers, welcomed the new journal.[4] With each new issue the circulation increased, as did the letters of solar discontent. Sarruf met the protests head on. In the sixth issue he wrote, in an article entitled "The Orbiting Earth," that so many questions had been received concerning the subject that the editors felt obliged to forego the queries received on industry and crafts and devote the space to the letters questioning modern astronomy. Sarruf would not burden the readers with mathematical proofs. That was not necessary to prove that the earth rotated on its axis and circled the sun. There were many other natural laws that demonstrated "as clear as dawn and without any doubt the truth that the earth moves, a natural fact evident to anyone who has eyes to see or a mind to think, a truth agreed upon by scientists from East and West."

Sarruf reproduced many of the proofs Bustani used in his own long article on the solar system. Gravitational theory was explained: a man falling off a house was subject to the same force that held the moon to the earth and the earth to the sun in their heavenly orbits. Recent telescopic and spectroscopic discoveries, he added, confirmed gravitational theory and revealed stars beyond number and many other planets, some of which could be like earth. All of these millions of heavenly bodies clustered in galaxies, like the earth's Milky Way, turned about a common center. Given the immense number of bodies and mind boggling distances between the stars and earth as determined by spectroscopy, it was

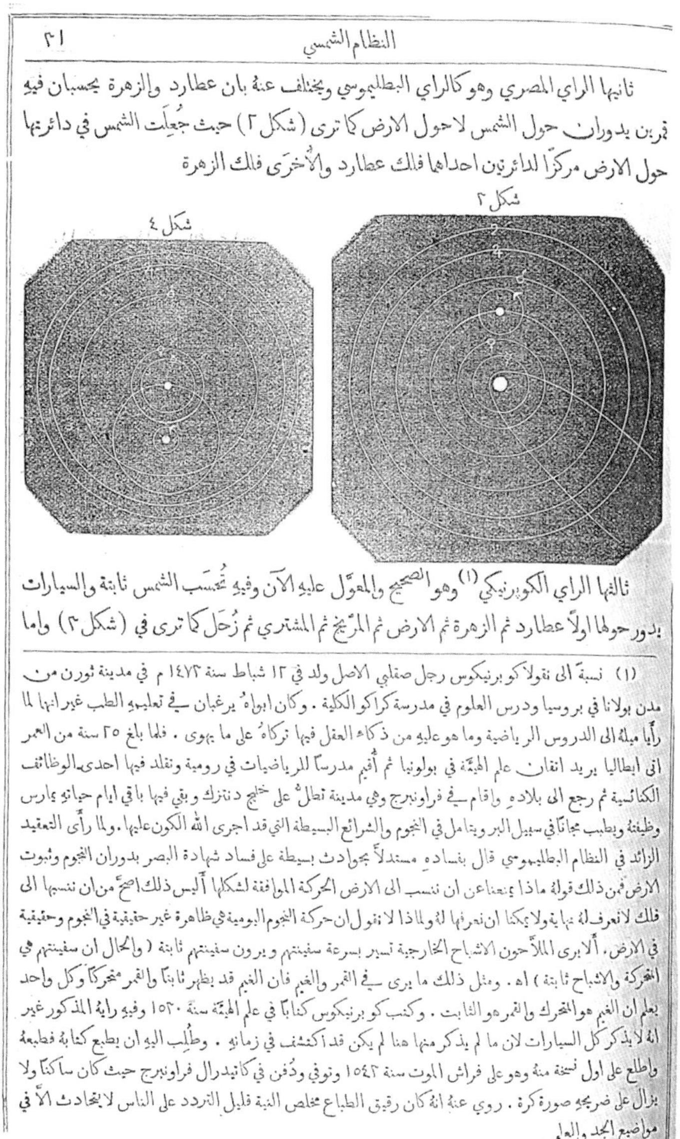

النظام الشمسي

ثانيها الرأي المصري وهو كالرأي البطلميوسي ويختلف عنه بأن عطارد والزهرة يحسبان فيه قرين بدورانٍ حول الشمس لاحول الأرض كما ترى (شكل ٣) حيث جُعلَت الشمس في دائرتها حول الأرض مركزًا للدائرتين احداها فلك عطارد والأخرى فلك الزهرة

شكل ٣

شكل ٤

ثالثها الرأي الكوبرنيكي(١) وهو الصحيح والمعوّل عليه الآن وفيه تُحسَب الشمس ثابتة والسيارات بدور حولها أولاً عطارد ثم الزهرة ثم الأرض ثم المريخ ثم المشتري ثم زحل كما ترى في (شكل ٤) وأما

(١) نسبةً الى نقولاً كوبرنيكوس رجل صقلابي الأصل ولد في ١٢ شباط سنة ١٤٧٣ م في مدينة ثورن من مدن بولاندا في بروسيا ودرس العلوم في مدرسة كراكو الكلية. وكان أبواه يرغبان في تعليمه الطب غير أنها لما رأيا ميله الى الدروس الرياضية وما هو عليه من ذكاء العقل فيها تركاه على ما يهوى. فلما بلغ ٢٥ سنة من العمر اتى ايطاليا بريد انفاذ علم الهيئة في بولونيا ثم أقيم مدرسًا للرياضيات في رومية وتقلد فيها إحدى الوظائف الكهنوتية ثم رجع الى بلاده وأقام في فراونبرج وهي مدينة تطل على خليج دنزك وبقي فيها باقي أيام حياته يمارس وظيفته ويطبب مجانًا في سبيل البر ويتأمل في النجوم والشرائع البسيطة التي قد أجرى الله الكون عليها. ولما رأى التعقيد الزائد في النظام البطلميوسي قال بفساده مستدلًا بحجج ذات بساطة على فساد شهادة البصر بدوران النجوم وبثبوت الأرض من ذلك قوله بأنه لا يمتنع ان نسبب ماذا يمتنع أن ننسب الى الأرض الحركة الموافقة لشكلها ألبس ذلك اصح من أن ننسبها الى فلك لا نعرف له نهاية ولا يمكنا ان نعرف لماذا لا ننول في حركة النجوم اليومية ظاهرة غير حقيقية فالنجوم في حقيقتها وحقيقة في الأرض. ألا يرى الملاحون الأشباح الخارجية تسير بسرعة سفينتهم ويرون سفينتهم ثابتة (والحال ان سفينتهم هي المتحركة والأشباح ثابتة) اهـ. ومثل ذلك ما يرى في الغيم والغيم. فان الغيم قد يظهر ثابتًا والغيم متحركًا وكل واحد يعلم ان الغيم هو المتحرك والغيم هو الثابت. وكتب كوبرنيكوس كتابًا في علم الهيئة سنة ١٥٣٠ وفيه رأيه المذكور غير أنه لم يذكر فيه كل السيارات لأن ما لم يذكرها هنا لم يكن قد اكتشف في زمانه. وطلب اليه ان يطبع كتابه فطبعه واطلع على أول نسخة منه وهو على فراش الموت سنة ١٥٤٣ وتوفي ودفن في كاتدرال فراونبرج حيث كان ساكنًا ولا يزال على ضريحه صورة كرة. روي عنه أنه كان رقيق الطباع مخلص النية قليل التردد على الناس لا يحادث الا في مواضع المجد والعلم.

Figure 4.3 A diagram representing the Ptolemaic system (right); a hybrid model of the solar system by Shaykh Nasif al-Yaziji (left)

The first diagram (going from right to left) represents the Ptolemaic system, described in the text above as clear and simple at first look, but then, upon closer scrutiny, obscure, muddled and overly complex; yet, for all that, Ptolemy's models were accepted by all as representing the reality of the world system until the 15th century of the Christian era.

The second diagram comes from (*al-marhum*: recently deceased) Shaykh Nasif al-Yaziji in his *Maqamat al-Falaki*. Earth is at the center with the moon orbiting it. Mercury and Venus orbit the sun, which in turn orbits earth, as do Mars, Jupiter and Saturn. Nasif al-Yaziji, who died in 1871, was a Lebanese Christian literary scholar associated with the Arab intellectual revival promoted by the American evangelical missionaries of Beirut. He must have taken Tycho Brahe's compromise hybrid system and modeled a hybrid of his own, which was at least a step closer to the Copernican system.

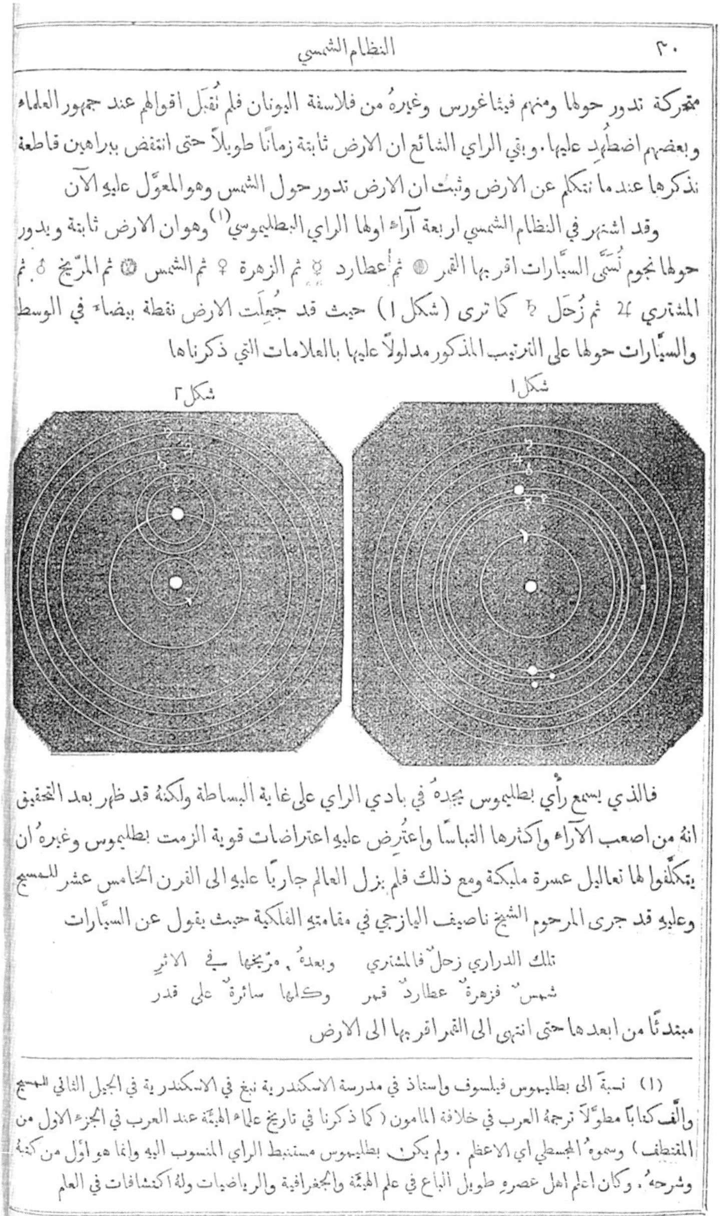

النظام الشمسي

متحركة تدور حولها ومنهم فيثاغورس وغيرهُ من فلاسفة اليونان فلم تُقبَل أقوالهم عند جمهور العلماء وبعضهم اضطُهِد عليها. وبقي الرأي الشائع ان الارض ثابتة زمانًا طويلاً حتى انتقض ببراهين قاطعة نذكرها عندما نتكلم عن الارض وثبتَ ان الارض تدور حول الشمس وهو المعوّل عليه الآن

وقد اشتُهِر في النظام الشمسي اربعة آراء اولها الرأي البطليموسي(1) وهوان الارض ثابتة وبدور حولها نجوم تُسمّى السيّارات اقربها القمر ۞ ثم عُطارد ۞ ثم الزهرة ۞ ثم الشمس ۞ ثم المرّيخ ۞ ثم المشتري ♃ ثم زُحَل ♄ كما ترى (شكل ۱) حيث قد جُعِلَت الارض نقطة بيضاء في الوسط والسيّارات حولها على الترتيب المذكور مدلولاً عليها بالعلامات التي ذكرناها

شكل ۲   شكل ۱

فالذي يسمع رأي بطليموس يجدهُ في بادئ الرأي على غاية البساطة ولكنهُ قد ظهر بعد التحقيق انهُ من اصعب الآراء واكثرها التباسًا واعتُرِض عليه اعتراضات قوية الزمت بطليموس وغيرهُ ان يتكلّفوا لها تعاليل عسِرة ملبِكة ومع ذلك فلم يزل العالم جاريًا عليه الى القرن الخامس عشر للمسيح وعليه قد جرى المرحوم الشيخ ناصيف اليازجي في مقامته الفلكية حيث يقول عن السيّارات

تلك الدراري زحلٌ فالمشتري   وبعدهُ مرّيخها في الاثرِ
شمسٌ فزهرةٌ عطاردٌ قمر   وكلّها سائرةٌ على قدرِ

مبتدئًا من ابعدها حتى انتهى الى القمر اقربها الى الارض

(۱) نسبةً الى بطليموس فيلسوف واستاذ في مدرسة الاسكندرية نبغ في الاسكندرية في الجبل الثاني للمسيح والّف كتابًا مطوّلاً ترجمهُ العرب في خلافة المامون (كما ذكرنا في تاريخ علماء الهيئة عند العرب في الجزء الاول من المقتطف) وسمّوهُ المجسطي اي الاعظم . ولم يكن بطليموس مستنبط الرأي المنسوب اليه وانما هو اوّل من كتبهُ وشرحهُ . وكان اعلم اهل عصره طويل الباع في علم الهيئة والجغرافية والرياضيات ولهُ اكتشافات في العلم

Figure 4.4 A diagram representing the Copernican system (right); a diagram representing the peculiar system of Tycho Brahe (left)

The first diagram (going from right to left) represents the Copernican system, "the correct one," with the sun at the center and all the planets orbiting it, including earth, placed between Venus and Mars.

The second diagram represents the peculiar system of the equally peculiar Tycho Brahe, where earth is at the center and the sun orbits it, with Mercury and Venus orbiting the sun along with the three outer planets. The difference between the Egyptian system (refer to Nasif Yaziji) and Tycho's is that in the Egyptian system the outer planets orbit earth.

patently absurd to think that all these bodies orbited the earth, which was no more than a single body in an immense galaxy in a universe composed of innumerable immense galaxies. Why would God sacrifice the great economy of motion for a system that required the stars to travel many billions of billions of miles in a second when the surface of the earth had only to travel a little more than a quarter of a mile a second on its axis.[5]

The physics of the pendulum experiment commonly used to prove that the earth spins on its axis is described in some detail in the same piece. Another proof comes from spectroscopy. Because of the earth's movement, the light rays we see coming from the sun and stars do not give the true positions of the luminous bodies. By the time their light reaches earth, earth has moved some distance away from the point where it was when the observed light started its stellar journey. What is seen are apparent positions.

> Translated to the science of spectroscopy we have another proof of earthly motion. There are others, but because of their complexity and the limitations of space in the journal, and in consideration of the scientific level of *Muqtataf*'s general reading public, let what we have presented suffice.[6]

Muqtataf's article on the Dane Ole Roemer's measurement of the speed of light, in the year 1676, demonstrated the point, and more. Observing over many years that the eclipse of Jupiter's satellite Juno varied by about 11 minutes when earth was closest to Jupiter and when it was furthest, Roemer concluded the difference was due to the added distance the light of the sun had to travel, namely, the diameter of the earth's orbit around the sun. By dividing the 11 minutes into the distance of the earth's solar orbit, Roemer obtained an approximate figure for the speed of light, proving once and for all that it was not infinite.

In the eighth issue of the first year (December 1876), the editors at last addressed themselves to the hostile criticisms attacking the journal's acceptance of a moving earth that had been pouring in from one end of the Arab world to the other during the last half year. These criticisms and the editorial replies provide a valuable source in the record of public discourse related to the new science that was for the first time being presented to society at large outside the walls of the state schools. *Muqtataf*'s response came in an article called "The Natural Sciences." Written mainly by Sarruf, it bristled with impatience at the mental opacity of some of the criticisms. Sarruf and his co-founder colleague, Faris Nimr, were barely 25, had lived their young lives in academic environments and may have been taken aback at the naivete of some readers. To those who were troubled by what appeared to be scriptural contradictions to modern science, and there were many who were bothered, Sarruf wrote:

> If the excellences of the sciences were determined only by the benefits they bestow, there would be no need to establish proof of their necessity. Nor would it be necessary to repeatedly urge acceptance of the intellectual expedients required to make science one's own. The innumerable benefits given by the physical sciences are in no need of witnesses testifying on behalf of

سرعة مسير النور

اذا وقفنا على شاطىء البحر ونظرنا الى بارجة تطلق مدافعها رأينا أولاً نور البارود ثم سمعنا صوت المدفع عنها. وكلما ابعدنا عن البارجة تأخّر صوت المدفع عن سماعنا وأما ظهور نور البارود فلا يتأخّر. وسبب ذلك واضح فان نور البارود يصل الينا حالاً فنراهُ وقت اطلاق المدفع وأما الصوت فابطأ جدًّا من النور ولذلك يتأخّر وصولهُ الينا فنسمعهُ بعد ما نرى النور. وقبل أن القدماء كانوا يزعمون النور لا يحتاج في سيره الى زمان أعظم سرعتهِ غيران ذلك قد تغيّر الآن وقد توصل الناس الى تعيين ابعاد لا يقطعها النور الا بعد مضي ايام واجيالٍ حتى لو لاقى العالم وهو بشكلٍ التعب من مشقة السفر

وأوّل من عيّن سرعة النور العلّامة رومر وهو برصد اقمار المشتري في الجيل السابع عشر. فلا يخفى على من يطالع ما ذكرناهُ عن المشتري في هذا الجزء ان لهُ اربعة اقمار تدور حولهُ في مدات معينة وتنخسف كلما مرّت في ظلهِ. فالقمر الأوّل من اقماره يدور حولهُ بـ ٤٢ ساعة و ٢٨ دقيقة فاذا عبر الآن في ظلهِ وجب ان يعود ويعبر فيه ايضاً بعد ٤٢ ساعة و ٢٨ دقيقة. غير انهُ اذا كانت الارض قريبة الى المشتري اعظم القرب بتقدم وقت انخساف قمره نحو ثماني دقائق وربع عن المدة المذكورة آنفاً واذا كانت الارض بعيدة عن المشتري اعظم البعد يتأخّر وقت انخساف قمرهِ نحو ثماني دقائق وربع عن المدة المذكورة آنفاً فتكون جملة الدقائق ست عشرة ونصف (½ ١٦ دقيقة) ولزيادة الايضاح وضعنا هذا الشكل السهل الفهم على من يمعن النظر فيه

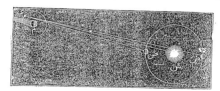

لنفرض ان الحرف ش بدل على صورة الشمس وان الدائرة التي حولها هي دائرة الارض حول س. وان الحرف ض بدل على صورة الارض وان الارض تدور حول الشمس من ض الى ضَ يجع الى ضَ ضَ وهلم جرًّا. ولنفرض ايضاً ان الحرف م بدل على صورة المشتري وظلهِ الممتد وراءه ه ذ ب لهُ. وان الحرف ي بدل على صورة قمر المشتري دائرًا حولهُ في الدائرة المرسومة. فمي

Figure 4.5 a and b Roemer speed of light

Roemer computed the speed of light by observing the difference in time, over many years of observation, between the time of the eclipse of the satellite Io as it orbited Jupiter when it was nearest to earth and when it was furthest away. Dividing the distance of the earth's solar orbit by the difference in time between the occurrence of the two eclipses, Roemer found a close approximation of the speed of light, resolving once and for all the question of whether the speed of light was finite or infinite. The depiction of Roemer's method of computation was *al-Muqtataf*'s earliest illustration of modern astronomy. The diagram shows positions of the earth when closest and furthest from Jupiter's satellite Juno, as the earth orbits the sun (lower right in part a of the diagram), and of Juno at the corresponding times of their being eclipsed by Jupiter (upper left in part a of the diagram).

Part b of the figure shows a clear version of the diagram in the article, where E1 and J1 represent an observation of Juno's eclipse when earth is closest to Jupiter; E2 and J2 when earth is furthest. The difference in time between the two observations divided into the distance of the earth's orbit around the sun gives the speed of light.

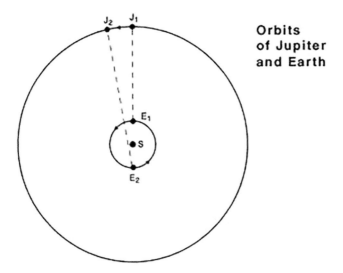

Figure 4.5 a and b (Continued)

their virtue. But there are those who say the natural sciences are harmful and misleading, that they lead to disbelief and moral corruption by casting doubt on revelation, and even go so far as to deny the benefits of science. Others, admitting the benefits of science, claim that science nonetheless casts doubt on religion. And there are those who claim that natural science is true and beneficial and then conclude that revelation is wrong and should be rejected.

Then there are the rest who say science, the child of radiant mind, confirms scripture and is a hidden treasure to be mined for the goodness of life it can provide. These latter are no doubt correct. We do not bother to consider the worthless opinion of those who fear and deny the natural sciences and their benefits. In fact, what motivates study of the natural sciences is their kinship to revelation as manifestations of God's greatness, power and benevolent grace . . .

God invites people to study his creation to understand His greatness through wisdom. This is beyond the understanding of ignorant people . . . Revelation is truth delivered, passively received and either actively or passively obeyed. Science is truth that is actively and mentally strived after . . . Science has unequivocally shown that the earth rotates and moves around the sun. Scripture has it the opposite way because scripture's aim is to instruct people in their duties and so uses phrases and figures of speech appropriate to that aim and to the level of understanding of people at that time . . . The uninstructed masses and their religious scholars call science unbelief because, as they say, it contradicts revelation, but the contradiction is in them who confuse and misinterpret revelation. They are just as mistaken as those who believe science and reject religion. Unduly swayed by one, they reject the other. . . . Only those who have things in their proper order in the two separate realms of truth and reality know that science is not only a treasure of beneficial gifts but as well an affirmation of revelation.[7]

Sarruf replied impatiently to those critics who, in his words, knew what was written thousands of years ago but nothing of modern science. They never took the time to understand what science was based on but spoke as if they did. These were the so-called educated of his society "who should know better but who refuse to learn for themselves and so become a curse on society, leaders of stagnation." Bleating with the herd, they claim the physical sciences to be wrong and against scripture. Their avoidance of responsibility and rejection of knowledge were beyond belief.

Sarruf held the Arab Christian and Muslim ulema responsible for the wretched condition of ignorance that was suffocating Arab society. They were proud of their ancient scientists but afraid of the modern ones: "What would ibn Sina say if he were with us today to hear most of us crying out in fear 'we seek refuge in God from the evil of scientists and their knowledge!' And how would Qazwini feel if he heard us say about a scientist of animal life 'Verily this naturalist is an unbeliever!' And what would al-Battani and al-Tusi and al-Naysaburi say were they to learn that astronomy had become among us a pursuit in the past tense after they had worked so hard in the present tense to create a foundation for it in the Arab community?" With this, Ya'qub Sarruf joined Salim Bustani in that miniscule club of angry young men not afraid to publicly protest the timidity, ignorance, greed and ineptitude of religious and political leadership in their dark world.

The sharpness of the public rebuke directed against political and religious leadership in the Syro–Lebanese region of the empire is striking when compared to what went for criticism at this time in Egypt. In Beirut, the reformist critics were independent academics and journalists who, as Christians associated with the American evangelical community, enjoyed a special place in relation to Ottoman authority. In Cairo, they were the Khedive's servants, and as Muslims had no particular guarantees or immunity protecting them from government grievance. Hence the temperate tone of Shaykh Tahtawi, his son Ali Fahim and Ali Mubarak, who all refrained from criticisms that would reflect poorly on the government and perhaps cut short both their positions in government, and with it their careers.

Of the many critical letters sent to *Muqtataf*, the editors published in full one that they considered to be not only typical but coming from high enough authority to warrant a respectable reply. Gabriel Jabbara was Archimandrite of Antakya, ancient Antioch in northern Syria, and was residing in Beirut when *Muqtataf* began publication. His long letter mustered all the arguments of the literalist defenders of scripture against a moving earth. For young Sarruf and Nimr, the old Archimandrite made a choice target: a high ranking member of the eastern church, supposedly educated, whose simple faith and literal reading of the Bible assured him beyond any doubt that the earth was not only stationary but was flat and surrounded by the ocean. For proof that the scientists were wrong, he referred the editors to verses in Genesis, Isaiah, Job and other books of scripture. As for all the so-called proofs of a moving earth, the Archimandrite wrote that they did no more than reveal the ignorance of scientists who were so blinded by arrogance and greed for fame that they dared slander the holy books.

The editors did not reply at once, but they assured Archimandrite Jabbara and *Muqtataf's* readers that a reply would soon appear. They may have delayed their answer to let interest build in order to increase sales, and it did build. The controversy had everything going for it: modern science's challenge denying a flat earth that was encircled by an ocean, a perception that was still accepted by many of the literate but scientifically ignorant population; the novelty of a moving earth, still only accepted by the scientifically aware, a fraction of a percent of the population; and the old challenge of science to religion that all scriptural monotheisms were destined to address.

The Archimandrite's letter was the challenge that the voice of uninformed religion presented to a half century of secular education. *Muqtataf's* readers eagerly awaited the reply. Interest was further broadened by a recently established newspaper in Egypt. *Wadi al-Nil* (*The Nile Valley*) was publicizing *Muqtataf* and excerpting some of its articles. One of them included the Archimandrite's letter. This drew Egyptians into the confrontation. Political leaders and the rising but still miniscule modernizing class in Egypt had invested enough of themselves in modern education that they could ill afford not to take interest or feel involved in the altercation going on in Beirut. Thoughtful scholars of all religions who were committed to traditional belief, but who nonetheless respected the accomplishments of science, offered little public guidance. The learned few of the ulema who may have known something of science, and to whom the believers turned, held their silence. Just how little the ulema intellects had contributed to a dialogue of conciliation is shown by the fact that the issue came to a head through two young Christian graduates of the American College in Beirut and a scientifically ignorant Christian priest from Antakya who for the moment became the guiding light of religious truth.[8]

Officials in the Egyptian Ministry of Schools and editors of *Rawdat* had been reading *Muqtataf* and its articles on modern astronomy. Archimandrite Jabbar's letter worried them. It wouldn't be long before ranting fatwas would be springing up from the populist depths of the Syrian Muslim ulema in emulation of their Christian counterparts. Then it would be the Egyptian ulema not wanting to be outdone by the Syrian guardians of the faith. Egyptian Muslims would be writing letters of protest to *Wadi al-Nil*, *Muqtataf's* Nile-side cousin. Ali Mubarak and his editorial and ministerial associates feared that the Azharites would be forced out of their comfortable cocoon of silence to bombard the public with their own inflammatory fatwas demanding action to save Islam. If the Azharites were to get fired up against Copernicanism, the whole body of scientific thought associated with it would be branded heretical, undermining everything Mubarak, the Ministry of Schools and Education, *Rawdat-al-Madaris* and *Dar al-Ulum* had been striving to achieve.

Mubarak pressed the government to act. Something had to be said or written to answer the Archimandrite before ignorance passing for religion won the day. Egypt had to join *Muqtataf* in the fight for modern science.

Responsibly, the voice that spoke for religion should have come from a leading shaykh, but none was found either audacious enough or astronomically knowledgeable enough to formulate a convincing response to counter the conservative undertow of traditionalism that was supported and inflamed by the rank and file of an angry ulema vehemently opposed to the West in all its forms. Ando so it therefore fell by default to the government to make the statement.[9] Once having decided that pre-emptive action was necessary and that it would have to come from a ministry, Ali Mubarak made contact with the editors of *Muqtataf*. Letters were then exchanged between them and the editors of *Rawdat al-Madaris*, and out of the exchange a collaborative effort to answer the Christian literalists in Syria began to take shape.[10]

The Fikri treatise

The question was how should a statement in defense of modern astronomy be framed to answer religious objections to it? And who would write it? It was agreed that the general approach should be to legitimize science by showing that anything in traditional religion that went counter to modern astronomy was a matter of either misunderstanding or misinterpretation: a balanced statement legitimizing but not authorizing or advocating Copernicus over Ptolemy was called for. It would leave the believer free to choose. In other words, the statement would be similar to Ali Mubarak's fictional *The Science of Religion*, in which the traditionalist shaykh in London discovers that modern science and modern civilization not only do not oppose religious belief but embody the true ideals of Islam.

Details on how cooperation between the Egyptians and *Muqtataf's* editors was worked out are found in Sarruf's synopsis of the episode that appeared months later in *Muqtataf* under the title "The Natural Sciences and Religious Texts." According to this, Riyad Pasha, Egyptian Minister of Education under Khedive Ismail, initiated the plan.[11] Riyad Pasha contacted *Muqtataf's* Cairo agent, a Greek named Galiyanish Efendi Philipidis. Philipidis then put Riyad Pasha in contact with Sarruf and Nimr. Between them it was agreed that a rebuttal to the Archimandrite would appear in *Rawdat al-Madaris* as soon as possible. A rebuttal appearing in a journal that presumably spoke for both Islam and the Egyptian government would bear more heft on the religious side than if appearing in a purely secular organ such as *Muqtataf*, which, in addition to being secular, was founded and edited by Syrian Christians educated in an American evangelical college.

Consultation between top officials of the Ministry of Schools and the editors of *Rawdat* led to Riyad Pasha assigning Ali Mubarak's deputy minister of schools to write a treatise reconciling scriptural references to astronomical phenomena with astronomy. The deputy minister assigned to respond to the brouhaha in Beirut was Abdallah Fikri Pasha, a 43-year-old government official of secular education, little of it in science, who had absolutely no religious authority or standing.

Rawdat al-Madaris, an academic journal as religious as it was scientific, was the right vehicle to convey the message, but a secular government official was not its ideal chauffeur, considering what the message was intended to accomplish and to whom it was directed. A respected shaykh with prestige and enough knowledge to compose a treatise on religion and modern astronomy would have been a more fitting spokesperson for the issue of principles in modern science agreeing or not agreeing with religion. No such shaykh willing to take on the task stood up, if one existed. Even if Shaykh Tahtawi had still been alive, he may not have accepted to write the article, since just before his death in 1873, in a bizarre reversal of mind, he had written in favor of Ptolemy over Copernicus, a sign of just how hesitant and fragile the 19th century intellectual revival was. Islam's ranks of religious scholars lacked the al-Ghazali of the day needed to speak out on behalf of science. And so it was Abdallah Fikri Pasha, who came forth to contribute the latest version of the millennial literary effort in Islamdom devoted to reconciling religion and natural philosophy, a man who was no more nor less authorized to speak on behalf of religion than had been al-Kindi, al-Farabi, al-Biruni or ibn Sina in their own time. With more than a touch of history's often curious irony, it was Egyptian secular Muslims who assumed the position of defending modern science against protesting Syrian Christians, whose Syriac ancestors had undertaken the original translation movement that brought Greek science into Arabic and spearheaded a scientific renaissance. What a difference a millennium makes.

Born eight years after Tahtawi had left for Paris, and like him a country lad of traditional religious upbringing, Abdallah Fikri was another product of Muhammad Ali's reforms who rose from humble origins upward through the ranks of government service. His history is a social study in the evolution of a family from its rural and religious roots to its place of prestige and status in an urban and secular setting, as Egyptian society underwent its successive transformations from Bonaparte's invasion to the reign of Khedive Ismail. Abdallah's grandfather on his father's side had been an Azhari shaykh. His father had also graduated from al-Azhar, but as a child he had witnessed Bonaparte's invasion and reorganization of Egypt, and then as a young man he had lived through Muhammad Ali's reforms; so that upon graduating from al-Azhar, he left the religious career that had been destined for him and entered Muhammad Ali's Citadel Engineering School. Like Ali Mubarak before him, he was one of the few native Egyptians who before the 1850s made it into an engineering school and the officer ranks of the military. Considered an outstanding mathematician, he made something of a name for himself among army engineering circles, and, after serving in Muhammad Ali's Hejaz and Greek campaigns, rose to the rank of colonel. Soon after, he became chief inspector of the engineering schools in Giza and Buhayra. His son Abdallah was born in Mecca at the time that the Egyptian army was fighting the puritanical Wahhabi reformers in Arabia. Influenced by both the scholarly religious temperament of his grandfather and the active secular career of his father, Abdallah Fikri followed a middle course between educator-shaykh and soldier-engineer to become a secular educator.[12] Rather than entering a madrasa or al-Azhar, he went to the state primary and secondary schools. Then, oddly reversing direction and the usual course of education, he entered al-Azhar. The unusual change may have been owing to family tradition coming late into play, as suggested by his son and biographer, Amin Fikri.[13]

Through his father's connections, Abdallah was given a responsible position in the Translation School. Gaining responsible positions through family connections had always been a problem hampering the efficacy of reform. Abdallah had received no oversees academic training. He may have not even graduated from a specialized *khususiyya* school. Unschooled in any European language, a rarity in the Translation School, he translated Turkish books into Arabic. His translations included nothing of reformist significance. Had he translated Hoja Ishak Efendi's *Compendium of the Mathematical Sciences for Teachers* from Turkish into Arabic he would indeed have had done something significant, but Abdallah was strictly a literary person. He had a general interest in science but never applied himself to the effort of learning any branch of it in depth. His expertise in Arabic literature and exposition earned him a position under Ali Mubarak, who was at the time busy collecting the books from all over Egypt that became the Khedival Library, and later the nucleus of the present Egyptian National Library, *Dar al-Kutub*.

Abdallah's facility with Arabic made him the choice to answer Archmandrite Jabbar. Officials in the Ministry of Schools and the editors of and scientific contributors to *Rawdat al-Madaris* guided him in the astronomy. (Also employed in the Ministry of Schools at the time, and involved in a minor way with Ali Mubarak, Ali Fahim, Abdallah Fikri and the treatise to be written in *Rawdat*, was Shaykh Muhammad Abduh, who several years later would aspire to reconcile science and religion.)

Given the somewhat cumbersome title of "On the Comparison of Certain Astronomical Researches with What Comes in the Holy Texts" (*fi muqarana ba'd mabahith al-hay'at bi'l-warid fi'l nusus al-shar'iyya*), the treatise was pitched as a special feature, and published in an appendix of the fifth issue of the seventh and final year of *Rawdat al-Madaris*, 15 Rabi'a al-Awwal, 1293: August 16, 1876. A 24-page dialogue of questions and answers, Abdallah Fikri's treatise is essentially an expansion of the same theme with the same questions as Ali Mubarak's *The Science of Religion*, upon which the treatise appears to have been modeled, but with its focus on astronomy. Compared to the cosmology course described in *Rawdat* two years earlier, or to the science that had been appearing recently in *Jinan*, *Muqtataf* and the Bustani encyclopedia, Fikri's tract was anything but groundbreaking in presenting an informative discourse on substantive science and its underlying principles. The job of the Egyptian Ministry of Education was to reconcile and not ruffle the feathers of the cantankerous Christian conservative clergy of Syria any more than they had been ruffled. What came out of it was an Egyptian version of Galileo's *Two World Systems* that was more Aquinas in synthesis than Galilean in analysis and would never have offended Cardinal Barberini and the Aristotelians. Accordingly, the pill of reconciliation delivered by Fikri's treatise was so sweetly layered over and washed out of substance that the reader could not be sure if it was the warming comfort of religion or the cold abstraction of science that was being swallowed.

Following the path set by *Muqtataf's* early articles, Fikri's treatise begins with a narrative in which lunar and solar evidence is presented along with other arguments abstracted from medieval Muslim astronomers to show that the earth is a sphere and not flat. This introduction is meant not merely to set what is to be the treatise's rudimentary level of scientific discourse, but to show that the earth is irrefutably spherical even though scripture describes it in places as flat. By analogy, even if scripture indicates that the earth is stationary, the opposite can be true: if it is round, it can roll. Fikri explains that science and religion express themselves on completely different levels. Scripture is meant to hit people loudly, immediately, directly and where they most feel it, in their hearts. Science, on the other hand, speaks to them quietly, slowly, dispassionately, abstractly. Fikri likens science to cherry picking: "The sciences are like fruits on a tree: pick the fruit, leave the twigs for fires." One must pick the true from the false.

Fikri's cherry picking, however, is not in the orchard of science but in the verses of the Quran whose variances with science require an allegorical or figurative interpretation. Quranic verses that convey the idea of a flat earth are not to be taken literally. Fikri cites al-Ghazali's dictum to the effect that to go headlong against proven science in defending religion is to do religion great harm. An obviously wrong defense casts doubt on what is being defended: "The enemy of the intelligent is better than the friend of the ignorant." Such are those ignorant but pious people who take eclipses as portents of life and death rather than a simple astronomical fact of the spherical bodies of the moon and earth totally or partially blocking out the light of the sun. There is nothing in the religious texts that denies a spherical earth. The earth appears flat because of its size, which explains why the word *daha*, flat, is used in the Quran to describe the earth's shape. It is used to express what people feel and think. It relates to human feelings and sensations of the heart, not to abstract astronomy. People who relate the word to earthly shape in an astronomical sense take the word out of its Quranic context. In this case, Fikri insists, the meaning of the word has to be rendered figuratively. What is essential in Quranic meaning here is not the geometrical shape of the earth but the truth that God created the earth. Once that is accepted it is irrelevant if God created it flat, spherical, octagonal or hexagonal. It is the same with the number and levels of heavens mentioned in the Quran. Their number is of no more consequence to true belief than the number of "layers in an onion or seeds in a pomegranate," for the universe is to be understood as an act of God and no more.

So, too, for the new astronomy's proofs of a moving earth that appear to contradict certain verses of the Quran and Prophetic Traditions. When transposing scripture from its spiritual context to the reality of astronomy, such passages require allegorical renderings. The Quran's seven levels of heaven would have to refer, in a scientific context, to the multitude of suns in the vast universe discovered by modern astronomers. In the vastness of space, stars at varying distances from earth radiate different intensities of light, and so the stars have been categorized into six intensities of light that are visible to the naked eye, the seventh being visible only by telescope. There is no starry firmament: only stars scattered through immense space.

In the dialogue between the shaykh and the astronomer that follows this introductory narrative, the shaykh brings up other Quranic verses steeped in mythopoetic imagery of the heavens, which, though beautifully expressed, are rationally incomprehensible. Using a mix of allegorical interpretation and what the interpreter calls analysis, the astronomer explains the meaning of the verses in the light of modern science but at the same time bows respectfully to venerable authority by referring to the medieval masters of Quranic interpretation, Baydawi and Fakhr al-Din al-Razi, as if to say the perspicacity of these recognized authorities of Quranic interpretation, pillars of traditionalist Islam, perceived the true meaning of these verses without their having known those secrets of the heavens that have only recently been discovered by modern astronomers. Here Fikri attempts to cast modern science in the glow of traditional authority.

He introduces another approach by having his shaykh ask what the Quran means when it speaks of rain from heaven, of thunder and lightning and of other meteorologic phenomena that filled people either with fear and awe of God's power or with thankfulness for the bounty and beauty that God provided through His creation of nature. This gives the astronomer the opportunity to explain the earth's hydraulic circulatory system, evaporation, condensation, crystallization, electric charge, discharge and acoustics, but all with careful reference to medieval authorities whose power of mind enabled them to see the secrets of modern science revealed in the Quran. Though natural phenomena have nothing to do with belief, the Quran nonetheless reveals them, making them easy to accept. The implication is that the believer doesn't have to accept the phenomena but he would be wrong to reject them. Modern science is present in the Quran, subliminally, an extra layer of truth revealed, a spin-off to be accepted or neglected; and, even though unrelated to belief and the essential message of the Quran, never to be denied.

The astronomer's depth of insight and interpretive power overwhelms the shaykh. He sees the man of science as a living example of wisdom and religious belief residing in harmony in the same soul and mind. The shaykh's acceptance of earth's sphericity and the meaning of the Quran's meteorological allusions opens the way to the next hurdle, earth's motion. The Quran clearly depicts the sun as moving. How is it that the earth moves also? The astronomer replies that it is true, the Quran has the sun moving, and so the sun does: around its own axis, as recently discovered by telescopic astronomy. This reveals why the sun spots are only periodically visible. The Quran prefigured the telescopic discovery by more than a thousand years, showing God's creative wisdom in revealing divine truths. But, the shaykh protests, the Quran states that the sun "runs" (*tajri*), not rotates (*tadur*). The astronomer is ready with another scientific revelation: "The sun does move, and takes with it as it does its planets and their moons. The sun turns around something that up to this time is undefined, some star in the Pleiades (*Thurayya*) so greatly distant that the sun's motion is almost like a straight line; but over an immense period of time the sun's trajectory is an orbit, just like the general motion that prevails in the heavens for all bodies."

The shaykh is overwhelmed by the astronomer's knowledge. Nonetheless, the astronomer's advice to use allegorical interpretation whenever Quranic verses defy reason or spiritual understanding is still difficult for the shaykh to accept: how can allegorical interpretation be controlled? It could be used to find all sorts of meanings in a scriptural passage that was not absolutely clear.

The astronomer could not agree more. Al-Ghazali had made the same point. That is why, he explains, astronomy relies on analysis. Proper analysis is more trustworthy. It brings the meaning to the surface in the light of modern science, while allegory explains it away. Allegory was fine for explaining certain Quranic passages in the light of the old astronomy, but that was because the old astronomy was wrong. This is why any analysis presupposing Ptolemaic astronomy would result in contradiction if applied to those Quranic verses bearing on heavenly phenomena. In the old astronomy with its nested spheres accounting for planetary motion, the Seven Heavens of the Quran had to be interpreted as being tangential at points, since this was the case with the spheres. But now with the new astronomy having swept away all those false constructions of nested concentric spheres, the tangential points that never stood up under scriptural analysis are done away with. The great distances between heavenly bodies agree with the Quran. The Quran confirms what we now know to be true in astronomy.

This puts the learned shaykh into a reflective silence. Seeing him on the knife's edge between doubt and acceptance, the astronomer cites several Quranic verses having to do with the astronomy of a moving earth and, applying his method of analysis, interprets them to show how deeply the Quran has penetrated the secrets of nature and laid them out for those who have eyes to see and minds to think. "And seeing the mountains you reckon them fixed, and yet they pass as the passing of clouds." The point the Quran makes is obvious: motion is relative and what we think to be fixed and stationary can be in motion, such as the earth we stand on. "God made that which renders perfection in all things." What could this mean other than that science and scripture exist in perfection, and therefore are in complete compatibility?

This elicits one last question from the shaykh, who at this point is obviously struggling within himself to resolve his traditional beliefs with this new understanding of scripture. The question he poses is based on a hypothetical case. Suppose there is something in astronomy that openly contradicts a point in the holy texts that is strictly forbidden – something that cannot be interpreted by allegory or analysis but must be accepted literally? The astronomer replies he doesn't do hypothetical cases. Hypothetical cases belong in the fuzzy dream world of make believe anything goes, of fantasy and absurdity in a "what if?" world that is as mixed up as the undeveloped mind of a child.

The shaykh appears to be on the verge of accepting this but cannot quite let go: "But still, just supposing?" he insists. The astronomer concedes that if there is any contradiction, the point in astronomy would have to be reviewed and decided in accordance with rational judgment. This has brought the astronomer to the point reached by Aquinas six centuries earlier.

There still remains the traditionalist problem of accepting innovation: *bid'a*. To help the shaykh climb over the stumbling block of accepting something reputed to be new, the horror of betraying *taqlid* for *bid'a*, the astronomer explains that what is called the new astronomy is in fact the old astronomy, going back to Pythagoras. Ptolemy is the new astronomy; Pythagoras, as revived by Copernicus, is the old and true. Ptolemy is *bid'a*, Copernicus *taqlid*. Thus, Islam and modern science are one in God's wisdom of revelation and universal creation.

The treatise concludes with a brief review of Newtonian inertia and gravity to explain to the uninitiated how it is that one doesn't sense the earth's swift motion. A wishful postscript makes an appeal for the creation of a scientific institute composed of experienced and insightful scholars to be chosen from among the ulema's brightest in order to end the misunderstanding between astronomy and religion – in other words, a refurbished version of Ali Mubarak's *Dar al-Ulum* that was founded four years earlier. Abdallah Fikri's vision of the institute is a dream palace of modernization. Attached to the imagined institute would be a board of scientifically trained religious scholars who would review books on science and religion that had been submitted for publication. The board would point out any misconceptions or errors, thereby preventing any slander against bonafide books of science. Such a board would maintain harmony between religion and science. The members of the institute would also teach science to promote the country's progress and prosperity in order for it to reach its full civilized potential, and would facilitate the development of Arabic as a language of science so it could replace the foreign languages that were then being used to teach science, as well as find good Arabic words to replace the foreign words being used to express scientific terms. "Because of a lack of consensus on Arabic words to mean a certain thing, foreign words continue to dominate, in spite of Arabic's richness of vocabulary." Modern Arabs were still in search of their Hunayn ibn Ishaq. The treatise ends with a pious postscript penned by Tahtawi's son, Ali Fahim, invoking God's blessing and a prayer that this marvelous treatise will bring accord between the religious scholar and the astronomer.

Fikri's was the first piece of Arabic writing of significant length and focus devoted specifically to proving the agreement between modern science and religion through Quranic interpretation. Egyptians could read the treatise in *Rawdat al-Madaris* or in the gazette *Wadi al-Nil*, which reprinted it. *Wadi al-Nil* was also available in some Syrian cities, where, as it was reported, there was such a rush to read Fikri's treatise that copies of the gazette quickly ran out. Fikri's treatise was the most significant piece of writing to appear in *Rawdat's* seven-year history that was meant to advance science in the public mind. In pushing an uncomfortable scientific idea from confinement in the silent shadows of the classroom to the light of public discussion, Fikri's treatise performed for Copernican theory what *Muqtataf's* articles would begin to do a few years later for Darwinian evolution. Sarruf wrote of the treatise, "No writer can deny that Abdallah Fikri's study was one of the strongest guiding factors in introducing the modern sciences into modern Arabic thought." A recent Arab historian regarded its publication as the decisive event in the battle between secularists who supported western science and those religious conservatives who believed Khedive Ismail and his men to be far too pro-western and who wanted a return to the days of Abbas Pasha.[14]

The sweeping statement may not be altogether a fair reflection of the collective intellectual composition that followed the treatise's publication. Pockets of religious opposition to the idea of a moving earth and western science continued, and still do. Few if any shaykhly spokesmen for the public conscience, those lanterns of right belief, took to their pens or pulpits to confirm credence in the theory. It also has to be remembered that the treatise was written by a reformist of secondary stature, a deputy minister employed by and speaking for a secular government. The treatise, cogently argued as it may have been, in fact expressed nothing more than the government's policy on scientific belief. The quiet, passive rift between science and religion continued, on and below the surface. Any shaykh who found the treatise convincing, such as Muhammad Abduh, who in a small way was involved in the idea of Fikri writing it, was already in the reformist camp. The epistemological rift remained, though for the most part in silence, particularly on the religious side in Egypt, where the resistance was passive and leaden, weighted by a ponderous institutional lethargy of immobility that by default left the difficult role of speaking for religion to secularist modernizers. A decade and more after publication of the treatise, a few shaykhs would speak up, Muhammad Abduh at the lead; and in the early decades of the 20th century a few more reformist shaykhs, inspired by Abduh, would speak up even more forcefully, but only to be silenced and driven out as heretics and apostates – not for espousing science, but for arguments that included it and went beyond: reinterpretation of Shari'a law, the Quran, the sources of jurisprudence, the historical origins of the caliphate.

Fikri's treatise was if anything a sign pointing to the fulfillment of what Tahtawi had so feared: that the silence and passive rejectionism of al-Azhar's leaders would open the way to secular government's usurpation of religion's authority in deciding what Islam was and was not, what it accepted and what it rejected. By their silence, the ulema were sacrificing the sphere of influence they could salvage as active participants in the modern state, and sparing themselves from being driven to the margins of society as a minor department of state, government appointees paid to carry out orders and confirm the religious legitimacy of secular rulers and their legislation. This would mean the withering of both the ulema and true Islam as a living religion.

Abdallah Fikri's treatise began a tradition in the literature of religious modernization that continues until today throughout Islamic countries. After the traumatic Arab defeat of 1967, that tradition was twisted into a form as assertive and aggressive as it was extreme in its absolutist claims of the Quran as an all-embracing encyclopedia of science, past, present and future. Fikri's article was also *Rawdat al-Madaris's* crowning achievement. The academic journal ended the following year when government bankruptcy made it a victim of budgetary cutbacks. The journal went down the drain of Khedive Ismail's financial irresponsibility, but not without having made its mark in Egyptian intellectual history. During its seven years of publication it achieved something in awakening Egyptians to science and assimilating it into the secular culture, and to some small extent into the religious culture. By equating nature's operations to God's *sunna*, it loosened the theological strictures denying causality and natural law, and fostered at least marginal acceptance of the compatibility of science and religion. Since none of the shaykhs of al-Azhar made any public statement regarding Fikri's treatise, or even commented on the course in cosmology that was to be given in the secondary schools, reviewed in *Rawdat* the year before, it might be concluded by the ensuing silence that the heliocentric theory presented no problem to them. Though with al-Azhar's shaykhs, that silence could have just as easily been double-edged. It left no way of knowing absolutely if the idea had been accepted by the religious authorities, or by that sector of literate society that took religion seriously and looked to al-Azhar for guidance in those confusing times of reform and innovation, when the fork in the intellectual road had dug deep in the public mind. Even *Muqtataf's* continuing articles on the subject suggest a considerable degree of public uncertainty. Arab writers continued to write on the subject as if the heliocentric system still needed proving.

Another feature of the Fikri treatise deserves noting. The conflict of ideas out of which it was born represents one of the rare instances of collaboration between reformers in two different regions of the Ottoman Empire engaged in the common effort to promote science.

The Fikri treatise marked *Rawdat's* signing off. The journal had been designed for Muslim secondary students in Egypt, and so only small numbers of copies were printed, in the hundreds. The science and technology in each issue were balanced with religion and Muslim history. *Muqtataf* on the other hand was purely secular, printed in the thousands, had a circulation that reached across the Arab world and enjoyed an audience that crossed the communal borders of Christian, Jewish and Muslim. Had it not been for the controversy that *Muqtataf* aroused, a provocation owing purely to the journal's popularity, *Rawdat's* final volume may not have been graced with what can be considered the single most important document in the long debate in the Arab world between science and religion over the system of a sun-centered universe.

The Fikri treatise didn't settle the issue by any means as far as the public was concerned, not even with those who read *Muqtataf*. In 1879, a letter from a reader in Tunis asked how it was that the earth could move without it being sensed. The question gave the editors the opportunity of once again reviewing Newtonian mechanics. The exercise became a periodic recurrence. Even as *Muqtataf* was broaching scientific ideas that were far more provocative to scriptural belief than a moving earth (geological ages, biological change in species, descent of man) the journal was forced – by the letters it received from a public that seemed impervious to learning last year's lessons and moving on – to revisit over and over again the arguments for a moving earth.

Six years after Abdallah Fikri's treatise appeared, the British occupied Egypt and had Abdallah Fikri Pasha appointed Minister of Education and Ali Fahim his deputy minister. Ali Mubarak, whom the British pro-consul disliked for personal reasons, was retired. Shaykh Muhammad Abduh, who had supported the Egyptian military government that occasioned the British occupation, sought exile in

Beirut, then Paris, where he and his enigmatic and charismatic mentor, Jamal al-Din al-Afghani, published their vanguard Arabic journal, the *Indissoluble Bond* (*al-'Urwa al-Wuthqa*) that called for religious and political reform to reverse the western tide that was washing over the whole of Islamdom, from Egypt to Morocco, and from the Ottoman Empire to Central Asia, India and Indonesia.

As the tide was washing over, *Muqtataf* stood at the vanguard of the secular call for reform, publishing its scientific articles on astronomy, physics and medicine, its biographical sketches of great scientists, inventors and women, and its editorials on the compatibility of science and religion, issue by issue, year by year, forging in Arab society a popular consciousness of the value of science.

A natural heavenly event, recorded and witnessed in Beirut, may have given popularity to the journal and credence in the science it was promoting there more than did the articles themselves on science.

In February 1877, *Muqtataf* announced the coming of a total eclipse of a full moon and gave the precise day and time of its occurrence. The lunar eclipse would last 96 minutes. The journal's popularity guaranteed that word of the heavenly event spread quickly. The astronomically ignorant of the Beirut populace were confused. How could the journal know such a thing? Only God, Master and Commander of the Heavens, could know this. People became apprehensive as the day approached. Faculty and students inside the walls of the American College remained calm. They were familiar with the astronomy behind the coming event. According to a report by a College administrator, pandemonium reigned outside the College gates: "Deep darkness came down on the land and the superstitious population with common consent set themselves to frighten it away. Copper kettles and drums were beaten, guns fired and rockets sent off as shouts filled the air, while the muezzins ascended the minarets and screamed 'There is no God but Allah,' and the devout Musselman chanted prayers for protection. Amidst the furore came shouts of 'Allah curse the Russians!' [the event took place during the Russo–Turkish war of 1876–1878] as though the eclipse were a Russian invention for the overthrow of the Turks . . . Superstition, ignorance of God and ignorance of his works keep these poor people in bondage of fear and terror."[15] The upshot was that many people in Beirut who had doubted *Muqtataf*'s credibility now believed.

That the journal had a decisive effect on the course of Arab society's embrace of science would be a risky assertion. In terms of scientific institutions and creativity, that long awaited embrace is still to come, but not for the lack of trying by the small community of reformist writers and government officials who embodied the 19th century intellectual renaissance: the *Nahda*. Decades of inconsistency, of confused planning and undefined national goals, and of underfunded educational initiatives, doomed any chance Egypt, and the Sunni Arab world that followed Egypt's lead, ever had of emulating the Japanese experience. Muhammad Ali had wanted an industrial-military complex of the first order; Ismail had wanted civilization's trappings and goodies that he could buy off the shelf, with manuals of operating instructions in French and English.

The Khedive's purchases in the name of civilization drained financial support for the Ministry of Schools and ended what could reasonably be considered the beginning of an educational efflorescence, especially when compared to the long drought that had preceded it during the reigns of Abbas Pasha and Sa'id Pasha. Muhammad Ali's bete noire had been British concern over India; Ismail's was the Suez Canal and the seductive powers of British and French financiers who all too liberally responded to the Khedive's requests for loans. By the early 1870s, with the treasury emptying quickly and the ship of state heading rudderless and rapidly down the Niagara of insolvency, the Khedive was reduced to making loans at increasingly cutthroat rates simply to pay off the interest on previous loans. In 1875, to meet one of those payments, Ismail sold to the Disraeli-led British government, for exactly the amount of the pending interest payment coming due in a day or two, all of the Canal Company shares that the French entrepreneur De Lesseps had forced his predecessor Sa'id Pasha to buy at an exorbitant price years earlier. In a double twist of irony, the country that had right from the beginning fought the canal's construction tooth and nail, in spite of being itself the world's leading maritime power, first ended up using it the most, and then, by pure serendipity, owning the controlling shares – and this after having refused to buy a single share when the Suez Company was being formed by the French in the 1850s.

When Ismail had nothing left for his next interest payment and was forced to default, an Anglo–French Debt Commission took over Egypt's bankrupt financial system in order to make sure the high finance capitalists of Europe would get their money back. Repayment of the debt to the European creditors was the commission's first and only priority. Egyptian revenues were collected and directed toward that end, leaving only enough to pay the civil servants and keep the country running. Funds for education and for continuing *Rawdat al-Madaris* fell victim to the new comptroller's budgetary axe. The Khedive's high style of royal splendor was also crimped. When Ismail attempted to use the Egyptian army to rid himself of the financial handcuffs the Debt Commission had clapped on him, the British had Sultan abd al-Hamid depose the recalcitrant Khedive, who in 1879 left Egypt in humiliation for a life of exile, obscurity and luxury in the Europe of which he so much wanted Egypt to become a part. The medical school and other institutions he had fostered fell once again into decline.

In reaction to a reassertion of Egyptian financial independence by the military, which had taken over the government and was strengthening Alexandria's coastal fortifications, the British warned the military government of Colonel Ahmad Urabi to tear down the defensive walls, then issued an ultimatum; and then invaded: an imperial pattern to be followed again and again in the West's manner of dealing with recalcitrant Middle East rulers who failed to respect western interests. Egypt's new foreign rulers, unlike the French 85 years earlier, had no interest in guiding Egypt to modern learning. In the British pro-consul's eyes, Egypt was an agricultural country that was in no need of higher education, beyond what it took to supply the administration with literate clerks and English-speaking officials prepared to act in accordance with what served British interests: security of the Suez Canal, political stability and servicing the foreign debt. Paying the Egyptian debt being the first concern of the country's new rulers, the British pro-consuls of Egypt put an even lower priority on education than had the Egyptian government.[16] Within a decade, the medical school was down to 27 students. Conditions during the final two decades of the 19th century were far less favorable to the development of a scientific culture than they were at any time since the expulsion of the French revolutionary army at the beginning of the century.

Ali Mubarak, the man whose public service in promoting scientific and technical studies at all levels in Egypt's educational system earned him the title of Father of Egyptian Education, had reached the end of his career with the British now controlling the levers of power. He was most unceremoniously dismissed from office by the first British lord and High Commissioner, Lord Milner, who claimed him to be incompetent, which meant he was not sufficiently submissive to the wishes of the foreign rulers. With occupation came the imperialist ruler's arrogance of assumed superiority, draining Egyptians of their self-assurance and confidence as surely as Ismail's loans drained the treasury of its reserves. The British occupation brought another bankruptcy to Egypt: that of the spirit.

Several of Ismail's achievements survived. There were of course the new secular professions in teaching, journalism, medicine and law. And though demoralized by political failure and foreign occupation and the sense of incompetence and inferiority that the new rulers incessantly drilled into the educated urbanites with whom they came into contact, outdoing even the Mamluks, Ottomans and Muhammad Ali's legion of Turko–Circassians, Egyptians continued to carry on. Some progress continued to be made. There was for example the Arabic taxonomy of scientific, technical and medical vocabulary that came into being. M. Gaignon, the French director of Ismail's School of Adminstration and Languages, which itself would survive to become the School of Law, did much to bring this work together in a hefty tri-lingual Arabic, French and English technical dictionary, which was evidence of the generational process of assimilation that took place from roughly 1840 to Ismail's exile in 1879.

This endeavor continued and was of great importance in that forging an indigenous language for science, technology and medicine was a preparatory step in Egypt's appropriating the new knowledge. Expressed in equivalents of the native idiom, the foreign concepts lost some of their alien provenance. On the other hand, that the man who composed the dictionary was a Frenchman reveals a less optimistic side of Egypt's interaction with western science. Egyptians had not yet achieved the degree of self-reliance that it took to sustain a creative scientific or medical tradition. The inconstancy of effort, imprecision of goals and vagaries of fiscal support undermined the projects of Muhammad Ali and Ismail, and made of the Egyptian Awakening of the 19th century exactly that: an awakening to the modern world and an attempt to join it, but one that moved too slowly to catch the train. While Egypt was being drained of its mental energies in a nationalist frenzy to rid itself of its second European master within 84 years, Japan, at one time during the 19th century far behind Egypt in the race to modernization, was readying itself to humiliate Russia.

Darwin

Not long after the publication of the Fikri treatise in *Rawdat al-Madaris*, *Muqtataf* was publishing other scientific ideas that made the conservative blood boil. The creation of the earth was explained in an article of 1879: "How the Earth Was Formed from The Sun."[17] The article was based on Laplace's nebular hypothesis. Instead of the universe having come from nothing out of the formless void and given shape by God's hand, it came from minute bits of incalculably hot matter scattered in space. The scattered particles were contained in the gravitational field of a rotating nebula that contracted through gravity and thickened into a fiery cloud that after eons contracted further, growing hotter, and at a critical temperature radiated white heat, thus forming the sun. Other suns and stars formed in the same way from other nebulae. All matter in the universe was in motion, orbiting around a body or a point and turning on itself. The turning of the great bulk of white heat, the sun, generated an outward centrifugal force acting against an inward gravitational force, and, in accordance with the natural laws of physics, outer chunks of matter separated from the sun and were hurled off, chunk after chunk flying into space, until a balance of forces was reached where the rotational momentum of each of these chunks of hot matter equaled the gravitational pull acting on each one, at which point they began orbiting the center of the body they came from, the sun, each at its own orbital speed as determined by the laws of nature. Such was the origin of the earth and the other planets of the solar system. Over the eons as the planets cooled off, a cold crust formed over a molten core. Geologists have been so far unsuccessful in determining the age of the earth. The implication is that the biblical account of creation is no more than an ancient myth.

One can imagine the deluge of literalist indignation this one brought the editors. Young Sarruf and Nimr did not avoid controversy. Indignation and controversy brought the issues into public debate and generated interest in the journal. Hot tempers sold issues, and the editors kept them hot. *Muqtataf* played the cool voice of reason, claiming to plant seeds of knowledge that would grow into wisdom and freedom, in answer to accusations of it being the seductive whisper of Satan spewing seeds of falsity that led to heresy and disbelief.

The article on the solar origin of the earth was followed a few issues later by a piece on Jupiter and the story of Galileo's telescopic discovery of four of the planet's satellites, which ends with the deliberately provocative question: Is there life on Jupiter? In reporting earlier on the discovery of two new satellites of Jupiter, Sarruf questioned another theological conceit: "Some people claim God made everything to serve a purpose but what possibly could be the purpose of these two moons that have never been seen or known of before? If the sun and the earth's moon were created to light our planet, as some claim, then I would like to know the use of these two moons that have been concealed from man since creation."[18]

In their dedication to sell science, it was inevitable that the editors would depart from their founding pledge to keep the journal free of religious subjects. Encroachment was unavoidable. Science and religion claimed too much common ground to be kept apart. Every so often *Muqtataf* put out an article that penetrated deeper into territory claimed by theology. In its second year of publication the journal posed the question of life having come into existence spontaneously, as if from nothing, such as maggots found on the surface of cheese or meat that were thought to be born from nothing but putrefaction: life coming from dead matter. The question of spontaneous generation was at the time an evolutionary speculation very much alive in Europe. In reference to *Muqtataf's* question, the editors referred to the 12th century Andalusian thinker ibn Tufayl and his philosophical romance about a nature child being born in a primeval organic stew. The doctrine of man being the center of God's creation was questioned by implication when Sarruf suggested ibn Tufayl's *Hayy ibn Yaqzan* anticipated Darwin's theory of evolution, a statement as exaggerated as it was inflammatory in its assumption, but the sin of exaggeration was worth the chance to be provocative in the cause of promoting discussion. It was a recurring question. "What do people think to themselves when seeing how small the earth is compared to the sun and other planets," Sarruf asked at the conclusion of an article reviewing contemporary telescopic and spectroscopic discoveries. "And all these stars and the sun amount to nothing compared to all the stars scattered in space . . . And the earth amounts to nothing compared to the smallest sun of the thousands of suns scattered in space. Man compared to space is a drop in the ocean and he dares be so proud as to consider himself the *Sayyid al-Makhluqat* [Master of Creation]."[19] This was in 1900, by which time *Muqtataf* had weathered 25 years of controversy and was confident in its role as chief challenger of untested beliefs.

In the early years, the editors exhibited a bit more caution. In 1879 *Muqtataf* advanced the idea espoused by *Rawdat* a few years earlier, that nature acted in accordance with laws that collectively patterned the ways in which nature acted. The undeviating laws could be called a *sunna*: God's divine plan for nature, a natural *sunna*. The term was charged with religious and legal meaning for Muslims. Translated to nature, *sunna* was God's natural law. From God's oneness of wisdom came two sets of laws, the laws of God's justice in Quran and Hadith, and the law of nature.[20] In the early decades of *Muqtataf*, reference to "God's will" was sometimes interjected in scientific discourse on natural law. Divine will was code for natural law. Discussing Newton's law of inertia Sarruf wrote that a body in motion encountering no resistance will remain in rectilinear motion – and with a bow to Muslim theology added "for as long as God wills," rather than the usual "until acted upon by an external force."[21]

To what extent was *Muqtataf* successful in creating an Arab interest in science? This can be partly answered by saying that however small the awakening to science was in Arab society by the time World War I came around, *Muqtataf's* share in achieving it was far greater than any other literary source's. Outside of Egypt there were no other sources in the Arabic-speaking regions worth mentioning, and even in Egypt – where Sarruf and Nimr were soon to transfer their operations – *Muqtataf* was the recognized literary leader in opening modern science to the Arab reading public. The journal was praised by its Egyptian readers as soon as they received copies from Beirut. So well received was *Muqtataf* and so warm the relations between its editors and the editors of *Rawadat al-Madaris* that when relations soured between the young liberal editors of *Muqtataf* and the much older and narrowly conservative American evangelical administrators of Syrian Protestant College the journal relocated in Cairo, where it prospered for almost another seven decades, until the country was taken over in 1952 by a decidedly unliberal regime. Hamidian style repression, reborn in the form of Nassarist military government, caught up to the journal and ended it.

Other Arabic-speaking regions did not offer the same open-armed embrace of the new journal as it found in Egypt, which had been opening to the world little by little during a half century of reform. In an intellectual backwater like Iraq, *Muqtataf* received a completely different kind of greeting. Muslims in Baghdad, Basra and Mosul who came into contact with a copy reacted either negatively or hostilely, while Christians and Jews, whenever they were able to find a copy, were positively impressed. The source for this report of *Muqtataf's* reception comes from an Iraqi Christian writing 50 years after the journal's founding. His account was based on what he was told by another Iraqi Christian, al-Shammas Fransis Augustin Jibran, a Chaldean who was educated by Carmelite missionaries and who was in Baghdad when the first issue of *Muqtataf* arrived in late 1876, meaning it took almost half a year for a copy to reach Baghdad from Beirut.[22] As it regards the positiveness of Jews and Christians and the divided reception among Muslims, the account should be considered with a grain of salt. It does however throw light on the intellectual conditions of what a millennium earlier had been the heartland of the classical period of the Muslim scientific and literary renaissance, and four millennia before that the cradle of civilization. Jibran's account is worth reviewing.

Some years after having graduated from the French Carmelite missionary school, Fransis Augustin Jibran, who was considered among the region's most learned men, opened a Christian school in Baghdad, similar to what Butrus Bustani had done in Lebanon after he had graduated from the French Jesuit school of Ayn Waraqa. Some Muslims and Jews attended Jibran's school. The opening year was 1874. Two years later, the first copies of *Muqtataf* reached Baghdad, the first four issues coming all at once in a bunch. Jibran was the first to get them. He read them in order, and after he had finished with one he would loan it to the leading scholars of the Sunni and Shi'i communities, one after the other in that order, and lastly to a Jewish scholar who was head of a Jewish school. According to the account, only the Jew reacted positively.

The Sunni scholar, Shaykh al-Alousi, is reported to have reacted with hostility, declaring on behalf of the Sunni community: "Our ignorance is better than the misleading science that corrupts our ideas and those of our ancestors." A better example would be hard to find of al-Ghazali's caveat on how ignorance of the exact sciences undermines religion. The Shi'i reaction was no different. As far as Muslim Iraq was concerned, Copernicus, natural law and all of *Muqtataf's* stories about the wonders of science and technology were heresy. Students in the Christian community reportedly accepted the journal as the most direct way to become educated in modern civilization, responding in a way similar to the way Christians from Beirut and Mt. Lebanon accepted French and American education as a path to a career and modern civilization. Since Christians and Jews were small minorities, *Muqtataf* remained essentially foreign to Iraq.

Jibran's reported account of how *Muqtataf* gained acceptance is revealing and plausible. A few Muslim students, probably the brightest of them, early teenagers, eventually became curious about the journal they saw being read so avidly by their teacher and a few of their fellow students. Curiosity matured to interest when Jibran let them read a few copies. The straightforward style of Arabic and attention-grabbing stories were like nothing they had ever read before. They passed the copies on to other Muslim students, but secretly for they feared the consequences if ever it got out to their elders what kind of heresy they were reading. This continued for some time. Eventually the Muslim students became more open about it, and the more open they became, the more the circle of young Muslims reading the journal widened, until at length the number of Sunni students in the school who advocated the journal equaled those Sunnis who considered it heretical. With time, the Sunnis who were avidly reading the single worn-out copy that was being passed around from community to community and reader to reader became sufficient in boldness and number to pool their meager resources in order to buy a copy of their own through Jibran, who gave them their copies as they arrived from Beirut. The Sunni students were nonetheless fearful of what they were doing and would tear up each issue once it had been passed around.

Boldness built on boldness, numbers on numbers. As more and more Sunni students joined the reading club, their fear lessened and no longer did they destroy their copy, becoming as open in reading *Muqtataf* as the Christian students. Then the same pattern occurred outside the school in the Sunni community at large, thoughts of heresy giving way to fearful secrecy, and finally to fearless openness. At this point, those who opposed the journal kept their feelings to themselves. Those who were reading it could now read it openly without any problem. So after having been divisive among the students and their Sunni community, *Muqtataf* became unifying, bringing more and more people together as they became familiar with the new learning they found in it. More than anything else, however, it was Egypt's wholehearted embrace of it that decided the Sunni community's acceptance, especially when the journal transferred to Egypt in 1885, where it was no longer associated with the American evangelists and their Protestant College in Beirut. When the Egyptian ministers extolled *Muqtataf* for its educational value and gave it their blessing, and the Egyptian Muslims sanctified it by accepting and reading it, the numbers of Sunnis reading it in Baghdad, Basra and Mosul increased. So, in regard to the Sunnis in the cities of Mesopotamia, *Muqtataf* first spread among the educated in high positions and then to those beneath them. Acceptance came in a three-stage process: agitation (*hayyaja*), followed by division (*farraqa*), concluding with unity (*wahhada*).

The Shi'i community meanwhile continued in hostility and rejection during these years, 1876–1890. Fear and indecision paralyzed them all, preventing any of the Shi'i from moving on to the second stage. With the Sunni community having accepted it and the Shi'i not, religious authorities in Iran took up the matter and made the decision on behalf of the Iraqi Shi'i community. A fatwa was issued permitting the Shi'i of Iraq to read the journal. The decision had to come from the ayatollahs of Iran. This is how *Muqtataf* came to Iraq and came at last to be accepted by all. "But you could count on your fingers the number who actually bought it to learn science." Such is the reported account given by Shammas Fransis Augustin Jibran as recalled a half century later.

It could be tempting to conclude from this account that the Shi'i community of Iraq was scientifically at absolute zero as late as the 1920s. This does not seem to be the case. In 1911 an Iraqi physician whose name suggests he was Shi'i, Hibbat al-Din al-Shahrastani, wrote a book called *Astronomy and Islam* that was reviewed by *Muqtataf* and described as having soundly demonstrated the concordance between the Quran and Newtonian science.[23] At the same time, an Iraqi Shi'i physician whose name indicates his family origns were in Isfahan wrote a critical two-volume work on Darwin's theory of evolution, *Naqd Falsafat Darwin*, the first undertaking of its kind in Arabic or any Islamic language. The author accepted evolution on the whole, but with the provision it was God's hand guiding natural selection and the development of species. Five years after that, Hibbat al-Din al-Shahrastani wrote another book, *The Sciences and Religion*, and in the Shi'i holy city of Najaf he founded a journal, *'Ilm* (*Science*). His books found little fame, and his journal was short-lived, but they, with Isfahani's critique on Darwin, indicate that the backwater provincial cities of what would become the main urban centers of Iraq after World War I were slowly moving through intellectual territory that Istanbul, Cairo and Beirut had traversed several decades earlier. Isfahani's critical study of Darwin's *Origin of Species* would indicate some Iraqi Shi'ites had advanced as far as anyone in Istanbul, Beirut or Cairo, at least on that particular issue.

In Egypt, it had been older men in high government positions who led the way for their religiously ensconced society's acceptance of science. In Lebanon, the movement had been spearheaded by American and Syrian Christians, Cornelius Van Dyck, Butrus Bustani and graduates of the American Protestant College. In Iraq it had been a French Carmelite-educated Chaldean Christian, Fransis Augustin Jibran and his high school students, first Christians and Jews, and then a miniscule group of Sunnis. In all three countries, *Muqtataf* had been a compelling literary wedge opening religious society to the secular science of the West. After 1876, *Muqtataf* was the tie that bound the different movements promoting science as they developed in their different cities throughout the Arab regions.

Jurji Zaydan

An example of the influence *Muqtataf* was capable of exerting on a young mind is found in the memoirs of a man who claimed his life was given meaning the moment his eyes fell on the journal. *Muqtataf* was an inspiration. It opened the door to his becoming one of the Arab world's great writers, recognized to this day as the "Father of the Modern Arab Novel." As soon as Jurji Zaydan started reading *Muqtataf* – he was not quite 16, the journal was just into its second year – his interest in science was sparked. Writing many years later, he clearly recalls the wonder and excitement that welled up in him when reading in those first issues about the science behind solar and lunar eclipses, thunder and lightning, cloud formations and rain. The knowledge of nature he gained gave him the thrill of understanding in reality what for most people around him was shrouded in mystery, superstition and fear. But his newly awakened interest caused a problem. He records that in the Lebanon of his youth there were no books available to quench the thirst for knowledge of nature that *Muqtataf* had aroused. He found one in Arabic in one of the city's few bookshops, and remembered its name after all those years – *Kitab al 'Arus al-Badi'a*, a book on the wonders of nature.[24] Unfortunately, it was so expensive it might as well not have existed. All he could learn of science came from *Muqtataf*.

Young Jurji wanted desperately to study science at the new college that had just opened a decade earlier, but coming from a poor family and obliged to work in a restaurant, his prospects of entering the Syrian Protestant College looked dim. The restaurant happened to be in Ras Beirut, near SPC, and the proximity of one to the other made his becoming a student of science look to be a short journey, however distant it was for the money. Possibly he could work and study at the same time. Would he earn enough to pay his fees? Would he have time to study? And if he was able, how would he ever support himself with a degree in science? Jurji reasoned that if he studied medicine, he would also be studying science, and as a physician he would have a supporting career to continue his study of science. As for making a living through science, that was unthinkable. No one could make a living on that. Medicine would be his springboard and mainstay to doing science. And with those thoughts buoying his hopeful heart, the 17-year-old set himself to it.

His earnings from the restaurant enabled him to hire a science tutor for the summer in order to prepare him for the entrance exam. His tutor, a former student of Ya'qub Sarruf, took Jurji through two years of course work in algebra, geometry and physics in two months. The tutor also arranged for him to have an interview with Sarruf. The idea of meeting Ya'qub Sarruf was overwhelming. Jurji was sure that the founder and editor of *Muqtataf* was the most respected man in Beirut and the whole of Syria and Mt. Lebanon. Meeting Sarruf, who at the time was himself only 27 or 28, was a high point in young Jurji's life. The meeting went well, Sarruf was impressed and Jurji Zaydan entered the American College as a first-year student in science.

Zaydan's memoirs portray the emotional side of his entry into the world of science. Knowledge of mathematics and physics gave him a sense of power and confidence. It prepared him to think and judge independently, to analyze and search into interacting forces and interrelated causes. Knowledge of science broke the "mold of traditions." Previously, he had always followed tradition. He had never thought, said or done anything that he had not heard said or seen done. The self-knowledge of having independent judgment, of being able to compare, contrast, analyze and decide on his own, was empowering. Studying science made him feel as if a blindfold had been taken from his eyes. The power to think for himself was like breaking iron chains that had bound him all his life. Knowledge was freedom.[25]

To pay his tuition he and his younger brother opened a little corner lunch shop down the street from the college. This was breaking custom in the most realistic sense. Students did not work their way through college or medical school by labor or gainful enterprise. A broad chasm divided privileged students from those who worked at menial jobs. His fellow students came from reasonably well-off families. Jurji's memoirs give no hint that his preparing and serving food to them diminished his status or gave him any problem. He may have found in his ability to work and pay his own way a different kind of liberation. However humble it was, he owned a business. But the little lunch shop failed to pay its way. During his first year in preparatory medical school he was obliged to take on various menial jobs. For three years he was able to support himself while doing courses in chemistry, botany, anatomy and Latin. In 1881 he entered medical school.

His favorite subject was chemistry. The science changed his way of looking at the world. He writes of loving chemistry for its beauty, elegance and usefulness. Great gains were being made in it in Europe at the time. Mendeljef had a few years earlier published his periodic table. Newly discovered elements were filling the table's blank spaces year by year. Jurji found it exciting. Science was discovery. Another reason for his love of chemistry was his admiration of the man who taught it, Dr. Edwin Lewis. The American professor's knowledge, his sense of organization and independence of thought, his fairness of mind and effortless style of teaching, and above all, his warm and gentle character, demanding but not stern compared to the American evangelicals who were all unsmiling and rigid, had won the admiration of all the science and medical students.

What Jurji was especially keen on in his study of chemistry was the analytical part of it, what is today called qualitative and quantitative analysis. He loved it for itself and out of his great respect for Dr. Lewis who taught the course. His greatest pleasure was qualitative analysis and the challenge of being the first student in the laboratory class to isolate and determine the unknown element or compound in the test tube that each student was given to analyze. Analytical chemistry was filled with mysteries to be solved by simple logical procedures, like life and knowledge in general: to turn the unknown into the known, step by logical step through the maze of possibilities until by elimination only one possibility remained, as if by magic, but magic by logic. Could life be mapped out as scientifically as the logic in a chemical flow chart, infallibly leading, step by step, try by try, from the unknown to the known? The triumph of being the first in the class to identify the unknown was as much a proof of his intelligence as it was a tribute to Dr. Lewis, who appeared to Jurji as having reached the highest level possible in scientific knowledge and excellence of life and character.

Anatomy was another favorite. But there were no human bones and skeletons for the students to study first hand because of the popular revulsion of handling and dissecting corpses. Even medical students were horrified at dead bodies. They thought it was unnatural and spooky to study the dead. It was irreverent. Jurji had no such problems with corpses. Thinking to help out the anatomy class, he and a like-minded student hired a couple of poor but strong men, and together, lanterns in hand, they went in the dead of night to the Ras Beirut graveyard and randomly dug up a corpse. In their fear and excitement, they neglected to return the dirt to the grave. When the empty grave was discovered the next morning everyone immediately suspected the medical students. The whole of Ras Beirut was in commotion. Something had to be done. People could not just go around digging up bodies, especially such respected ones. Complaints were made to the school authorities that one of their medical students had exhumed the body of a respected member of the Zaydan family. Jurji was aghast that it was a relative he had unknowingly dug up. The bright side was that since the exhumed body was a relative of his, he wouldn't be one of the suspects.

At the end of Jurji's second year of medical school, Dr. Edwin Lewis gave a commencement address in which he referred to Darwin as a careful researcher whose method of drawing conclusions demonstrated science at is best, regardless if his theory was right or wrong. This led to an episode that ended both Dr. Lewis's position at the college and Jurji's career in science and medicine.

Notes

1 Marwa Elshakry, "The Gospel of Science and American Evangelism in Late Ottoman Beirut," *Past and Present*, issue 196 (August 2007), pp. 199–201.
2 Typical was what appeared in 1887:

> Hardly a newspaper from Europe comes to us without the announcement of a prize or gift by someone wealthy in order to advance the sciences and spread knowledge. A 500,000 franc gift by an individual was recently announced in France. The money is to be used over a three-year period to award the year's best work in physics, chemistry, mathematics, zoology, botany.
>
> (*Muqtataf*, vol 12, p. 374)

3 *Muqtataf*, vol. I, issue 3, 1876.
4 A. Hourani, *Arabic Thought in the Liberal Age*, Cambridge University Press, Cambridge, 1983, p. 247; *Kitab al-Dhahabi fi Yubil: 50th Anniversary Volume of Muqtataf*, 1926.
5 *Muqtataf*, vol I, issue 6, 1876, pp. 137–142.
6 *Muqtataf*, vol I, issue 7, 1876, p. 19.
7 *Muqataf*, vol I, issue 8, 1876, pp. 22, 169.
8 Opposition to modern science, and technology too, came from lower level members of the ulema issuing fatwas condemning as heretical the steamships, railways, telegraph, electricity and modern innovations from the West, typifying the angry rejectionist mood of Muslims in the middle and lower stratas of society. In medieval times it was believed the devil could take hold of man's reason and pervert him; now the devil came in the guise of material comforts bestowed by science and the technology that disrupted religiously authenticated traditional life and in its place forced an immoral secularist materialism down the throats of the believers.
9 Egypt had enough problems at the moment. The country had gone bankrupt, French and British comptrollers had taken over the finances and the Khedive wanted at all costs to avoid having a medieval theological squabble empty his mission of transforming Egypt into a civilized member of the European family, to which goal he had emptied his treasury.

10 With the benefit of hindsight, it should be noted that the threat of a conservative Muslim reaction to the Copernican issue stewing in Beirut may have been over-estimated by the Egyptian government. The Muslim ulema in Beirut and Damascus were happy to leave the fighting to the Christians. The Christian controversy over Darwin that broke out in Beirut six years later also failed to exercise Syrian Muslims. Muslims did not involve themselves in the religious disputes exciting Christians. Copernicus and Darwin were Christian affairs, so let the Christians thrash out their own problems. And as long as Muslims made no issue out of them, al-Azhar's ulema were not about to stick their noses in Syrian Christian affairs and make judgments on things that did not concern them and they knew little about. But in as much as there was no way Ali Mubarak or anyone could have known this, fear was free to run wild, and this made the possibility all the more likely in the governmental mind.

11 Elshakry, "The Gospel of Science" and "Darwin's Legacy in the East" (Princeton doctoral dissertation), pp. 204–205. Both works cover the same ground; the dissertation is richer in detail but changes nothing in the author's study of the history of the impact of Darwin on Arab writers.

12 For a general account of his life, Muhammad abd al-Ghani Hassan, *Abdallah Fikri*, Cairo, 1965.

13 It seems that after graduating from al-Azhar, though sources disagree on this, he resumed his secular education by attending and graduating from a specialized school. This would make Abdallah's Azhari interlude all the more unusual. Apparently he was being pulled by the divergent careers respectively followed by his father and grandfather. Abdallah was not quite sure which way to go and alternated from secular to religious and back again. He ultimately followed the path of his father into government service, and of his grandfather as teacher. Amin Fikri, *al-Athar al-Fikriyya*, Cairo, 1898, p. 4.

14 abd al-Ghani Hasan, *Abdallah Fikri*, Cairo, 1965, pp. 202–203.

15 Elshakry, "Darwi's Legacy in the East" (Princeton doctoral dissertation), pp. 202–203. And Elshakry, "The Gospel of Science."

16 Typical of the critical views regarding British financial policy in Egypt was that reported in a French newspaper in Egypt, *Le Bosphore*, December 14, 1891: "All the nations of Europe have experienced, suffered from, and cursed fiscal exactions which characterized ancient Rome, while in Egypt, at the present day, similar exactions impress an indelible stamp upon the acts which the all-powerful English perform or suggest . . . In this respect the English have put Egypt back to the period which was the rudest in her history . . . Everything for the purse of which the English hold the strings. Such is the formula which represents the policy of noble England in Egypt." Cited in R. Fraser, "The Egyptian Newspaper Press," *The Nineteenth Century*, vol 32 (1892), p. 217.

17 *Muqtataf*, vol 4, 1879, p. 61.

18 *Muqtataf*, vol 2, 1877, p. 114.

19 *Muqtataf*, "The Moving Stars and Their Distances," vol 25 (April 1, 1900).

20 Natural law as divinely legislated *sunna* is given in the example of a projectile fired from a cannon. Two forces act on the projectile: gravity and the exploding gases propelling it upward at an angle. The resolution of the two forces takes the curve of a parabola: God's *sunna* in patterning the behavior of projectiles that could not but obey the laws set by the Master in ordering His House. *Muqtataf*, vol 4, 1879, pp. 122–123.

21 *Muqtataf*, vol 2, 1877, pp. 153–155.

22 *Al-Kitab al-Dhahabi li-Yubil al-Muqtataf al-Khamsiyyin* (Jubilee anniversary volume) 1926, vol 50, p. 129.

23 *Muqtataf*, vol 38, January 1911, p. 93.

24 This was an 1873 textbook on elementary natural science by As'ad Ibrahim al-Shadudi, *Kitab al-'Arus al-Badi'a fi'ilm al-Tabi'a* (Book of the Marvelous Bride of Natural Science), 1826–1906, Syrian Protestant College Press, n.d. Al-Shadudi, a math and

science instructor and House Tutor at SPC in 1871 and 1872, was 40 when the college was founded, and so, unlike Sarruf and Nimr, had acquired his knowledge of science the way Butrus Bustani had, through his association with people like Cornelius Van Dyck. His book was a general science college text of some 500 pages, a very much abbreviated Arabic version of Ishak Efendi's *Compendium of Mathematical Sciences*, and was very popular in Beirut. Al-Shadudi also wrote a treatise on natural philosophy, *Khulasat al-Hisab*, published in Cairo in 1882. But in neither of these works is there any mention of the Copernican system. For Zaydan, see Thomas Phillip, *Jurji Zaydan, His Life and Thought*, Oriental Institute Press, Beirut, 1979; and Elshakry, "The Gospel of Science," p. 197.

25 J. Zaydan, *Mudhakaati* (*Autobiography*), al-Hilal Press, Cairo, n.d., p. 53.

5 Darwin between *Muqtataf* and the American evangelists

The earliest mention of Darwin and evolution in Arabic print coincided with the publication of Fikri's treatise defending Copernicus. No sooner had one headline problem between science and religion been publicly aired and more or less settled than an even more prickly one came bursting forth. Seventeen years after the *Origin of Species* had been published in England, Butrus Bustani wrote a sketchy review of less than two columns on Darwin and the basic ideas of evolution in the seventh volume of his *Encyclopedia* under the caption "Darwin." He writes of Darwin's education and journey on the *Beagle*, the books he wrote, honors he received, and adds a few lines on his recently published *Descent of Man* and principle of natural selection, which he says aroused a storm of opposition, "the like of which was never before seen in this era." In the minds of Roman Catholic authorities and American Protestant evangelicals, the very mention of Darwin's name was as if Satan had entered the room. The world of science looked upon Darwin's theory differently. Bustani's entry in his *Encyclopedia* informs the reader that Darwin

> attempted in his book to relate the differences in the species spread over the globe to an abiding progress resulting from physiological relationships instead of to a creating cause for each species. Some accepted his theory, others denied and abrogated it with religious arguments. . . . He claimed in his *Origin of Species* that the origin of man lay in the realm of animal life, that man was not created human but developed to his present state after having had a tail and hair like an animal. The men of religion opposed his claim with scripture from the Holy Bible. In 1864 the Royal Society awarded him the Copley Medal and he was elected as a member to many scientific societies in England and all over Europe.[1]

Though Bustani's knowledge of natural selection was faulty, he was obviously not one who thought of Darwin as satanic. Darwin emphatically denied any idea of "progress" in the evolution of species through natural selection, and avoided the subject of human evolution in his *Origin of Species*. Bustani's imprecision is understandable. Darwin's ideas came eastwards in garbled bits and pieces. The *Origin of Species* had not even begun to be translated into Arabic until the early decades of the 20th century, and not until the second half of the century did the whole of the work become at last available in Arabic.

Defending the wall of hostility that denied the science of evolution and forbade even the mention of it was the evangelical community of American missionaries, in whose bosom Bustani lived and worked. With the exception of the physician and scientist Cornelius Van Dyck, the community regarded Darwin as the devil incarnate. Bustani, who converted from Greek Orthodoxy to Protestantism under the caring tutelage of the American evangelicals, was printing his *Encyclopedia* and *Jinan* on their missionary press. That he mentioned Darwin outside the frame of his satanic wickedness, and presented his theory as neutrally as he did, was in the eyes of the American evangelicals practically a declaration of atheism. Bustani did not return to the subject. Nor did his outspoken son Salim, who edited the journal during the two years it existed after 1876. Not even the name Darwin was printed in *Jinan*. But it was in *Muqtataf*.

As with heliocentrism, Bustani broke the ice on evolution, and the editors of *Muqtataf* cast their hooks in. Egypt's *Rawdat al-Madaris* played no parallel part in making evolution a subject of public debate as it had heliocentrism, since the journal had ceased to exist. Had it continued, natural selection may well have been a subject the editors of *Rawdat* would have stayed clear of, considering the ire it was causing in Syria and Mt. Lebanon. For the last quarter of the 19th century and into the 20th, only *Muqtataf's* editors and contributors, and two or three Syro–Lebanese Christian writers who had been associated with SPC, dared touch Darwin. Not too dissimilar from the case of heliocentrism, it would not be until Muslim Egyptian writers took up the subject and wrote approvingly of evolution that Darwinism could be said to have gained some degree of conditional acceptance, but this was not until the early decades of the 20th century, and even then the issue was far from being settled, just as it remains to be in many social sectors of the Muslim world.

Muqtataf first broached the subject in November 1876, in the form of a letter to the editors that was printed in full. This was at the same time Bustani's *Encyclopedia* article came out, but the letter in *Muqtataf*, written by a Christian named Rizq Allah Barbiri, did not mention the encyclopedia or anything about Darwin or natural selection. He spoke of evolution and the spontaneous origin of life from pure matter as being contrary to the Bible, the only source for knowledge of the subject.[2] What piece of writing the author of the letter was reacting against is unclear. A second letter from Barbiri conveying the same biblical anti-evolutionary thesis was printed in the next issue. This time Barbiri went into some detail about materialism and evolution and how they contradicted the account of creation in Genesis and so could not be right.[3]

In serving as a stalking horse to introduce sensitive scientific subjects, Barbiri's letters were to evolution what the Archimandrite Jabbar's letter was to heliocentrism, but on this issue Egypt's Minister of Education chose to remain silent. Even at SPC few people knew anything about Darwin's theory, other than the caricature that man originated from monkeys. When *Jinan* closed down, *Muqtataf* was left on its own to brave the hazards that came with publicizing such a religiously delicate question as man, monkeys and evolution. Slowly and carefully, the journal proceeded to bring Darwin to light.

A short piece entitled "Man" (*al-Insan*) by a Christian physician, Bishara Zilzal, gingerly opened discussion of evolution on a scientific level in the ninth issue of 1877. The two-and-a-half-page essay is a non-committal review of the range of ideas and theories on man's origins and existence from antiquity to modern times.[4] Some modern scientists, he wrote, claim that man should not be considered something apart from other animals, that man is an animal. Carl Linne (d. 1778), the Swedish naturalist also known as Linnaeus, the Latinized form of his name, categorized man as homo-sapiens, a primate that derived from an earlier form along with three other species of primates, the chimpanzee, orangutan and gibbon. Bishara Zilzal claimed this to be grotesquely wrong. It led to heresy, disbelief in God and denial of the highest blessed attribute of man, the eternal soul that bestows the power of speech and reason. Even many scientists believed man to be a special form of life, though they admitted to the organic, anatomical and structural similarities between man and some breast-feeding animals categorized as mammalian. In the words of Bishara Zilzal in the same article, "al-Insan":

> Concerning what is man, great thinkers like Plato, Aristotle, Galen, and Qazwini have differed in their theories on the relationships among body, soul, mind and spirit that define man. But only God knows these things, for the origin and essence of man belong to the divine realm.

In other words, these questions are better left to God. The author has opened up a subject in a scientific journal that occupies the minds and researches of great scientists, and then says at the end it is better left to God. Who was fooled? In the context of the essay, "only God knows" is a pious disclaimer meant to ward off attacks of heresy for even discussing such a thing, but it is also code for the fact that the subject is a valid one that scientists are studying. Answers await further research. Science goes on. And so did *Muqtataf*.

In the next month's issue, Dr. Zilzal again goes into the evolution of man as a thinking animal. Man's thinking makes him a unique animal with animal characteristics of self-defense, protection, aggression, feelings of kinship and mating. His real evolution came with his mastery of his emotions and instincts as he became civilized. He evolved with evolving civilization. Climate and geographical conditions influenced his behavior, an instance of nature conditioning human evolution. Geography and climate were factors in the evolution of white, brown, yellow, red and black peoples. While some anthropologists claim that intelligence, or the power of reason, is what separates man from animals, others say it is not, that some higher animals, such as the higher primates, have brains that are similar to man's, just as they share certain anatomical structures. This brings Zilzal to the essential question of where did man come from. He begins by asking if man is now what he was in the beginning when first becoming man? Or did he come from an earlier animal form and evolve over time, subject to environmental conditions; or in other words, evolve from a form of earlier monkey, a common ancestor of monkey and man, as some naturalists claim? The author denies man evolved from a former species, but not in the same admonishing tone he affected in rejecting the theory of evolution in the first article. He then proceeds to the holy scriptures: the Bible tells the story of how man came about. First the male species, then the female, and God created man in the best of all possible forms. If man evolved from earlier forms, then where are the intermediate forms? Where is an intermediate form between an animal who talks and thinks and one who doesn't? Dodging between negation, and being non-commital, Zilzal has introduced some provocative questions.

In the first of these two brief articles, Dr. Zilzal introduced the question of man's origin, and in the second he accepted much of the theoretical territory that goes with Darwin's *Origin of Species*, that is, the geological epochs, the vast stretches of time required for natural selection and the lapidary imprints and fossils of earlier forms of life. He then admits that the question is open to possible answers since it falls under the laws of science (*nawamis al- 'ilm*). So much for the biblical version's monopoly on creation.

In a following article Zilzal explains how it is that science and the Bible agree. The principles of modern geology can be accepted as long as it is maintained that God created man, the special case in God's creation. This, Dr. Zilzal claims, does not take anything away from science. Layers of geological formations make it clear that earlier forms of life existed. The earth evolved during four geological ages, each age with its own particular species of animals. Species multiplied with each age. Man, the last to enter creation, became lord of earth. God gave man kingship over all the animals on land and in the sea and sky. In his fourth article of that year he writes on the dispersion of man over the globe, from Asia to Europe, across Sinai to Africa, across the Bering Strait to the western hemisphere, and by sailing vessels to the islands and archipelagos of the world, until the human species was found everywhere as a result of the hundreds of thousands of years of wandering and sailing. Scientific and historical accounts of this dispersion are congruent with the biblical account of man being created at one time and place and then dispersing.[5]

Within a year of the publication of Bustani's slim item on Darwin in the seventh volume of his 1876 *Encyclopedia*, *Muqtataf* had introduced the literate Arab public to evolution theory and the question of man's origin from earlier animal forms. Prudence required denial of human evolution from an animal antecedent at this stage, but everything else was taken by the journal as comfortably within the limits of religious belief. The responses to Barbiri and articles by Zilzal were openers. The waters of tolerance being cautiously tested and found safe, Sarruf and Nimr sailed forth. In 1878 and for the next four years – until a crisis over Darwin temporarily closed the American College – *Muqtataf* put out an article of varying length on evolution practically every other issue. By 1879, evolution was being discussed without any of the former biblical reservations. An article of that year boldly asked: Does life in all its species originate from an autonomy of nature acting by its own laws of nature and through its own powers, or from a Creator who designed the form of each species and put it in a particular seed or germinal state to develop? The question implied acceptance of evolution in one form or another. *Muqtataf's* editors claimed to take no side, as they repeatedly said, but just asking the questions they did was provocative enough. The provocations kept coming, one following the next in small probing advances. In the calculus of introducing evolution, progress was the summation of infinitesimals cast in questions. But however small the steps and however veiled they were in their innocence of simply posing questions, the editors must have been feeling much heat from the American evangelists for even suggesting their readers think about the origin of life in terms other than biblical. It was, after all, the evangelical SPC press that was printing the journal.

They raised the subject of evolution again the next year with 'The Origins of Life and the Perplexity of Scientists,' in which the journal attempted to establish a religiously correct position without surrendering the challenge:

> Most people believe that life originated from an intelligent creator. It is our belief that this is correct . . . It has been disproven that worms coming from spoiling meat is an example of life giving rise to itself. But the scientific controversy over life's origins continues . . . now centering on bacteria, one faction led by Tyndall believing they come from invisible microbes, other scientists believing that bacteria are created of themselves, spontaneously. Experiments have concluded that heat kills bacteria and their microbic progenitors, if indeed they exist, suggesting Tyndall may be right, life cannot be born of itself. This would support a materialist position on the origin of life.

The views of John Tyndall (d.1893), who disproved the idea of spontaneous generation by proving germ-free air prevents food decay, and of Thomas Huxley (d. 1895), Darwin's most forward defender, were then presented without any reference to Darwin or evolution. The purpose of the article was simply to air the possibility of life forms coming from the power of nature.

Public introduction to the idea of evolution was incrementally advanced in the coming issue when the editors published a letter sent to them by Shibli Shumayyil, an 1871 SPC medical graduate who had gone to France to study on his own for two years, 1875–1876, and returned to the Middle East as a radicalized socialist, atheist and materialist. Shumayyil's letter commented on the experimental method used by Tyndall in proving the air was filled with microbes and spores that accounted for the decay of food and disproved the idea of spontaneous generation. In other words, the generation of life had a material basis as far as science was concerned. Something could not come from nothing.

Shumayyil had graduated from SPC a year behind Sarruf and Nimr and was their close friend and *Muqtataf's* devil's advocate for pushing evolution theory. In Paris, Shumayyil had adopted a materialist and socially revolutionary set of ideas that speciously claimed to be scientifically based on Darwin's theory of natural selection. Unfortunately for the cause of natural selection, Shibli Shumayyil would for half a century be the Middle East's most fervent and uncompromising prophet of evolution, preaching its pseudo-scientific social, economic and political spin-offs, which the editors of *Muqtataf*, assuming the neutral position of referees, would print, while disclaiming responsibility for the man's outrageous views.

Shibli and the editors played off against each other, but their readers could hardly have doubted the true position of *Muqtataf* on the issue. A brief entry on evolution in 1880 is an early example. The editors interjected that the theory of natural selection could pose problems to those devout believers who took the meaning of scripture in a literal sense. This then was immediately followed by a response from Shibli Shumayyil bluntly stating that life originated in a primal stew of organic matter and evolved to its present state in all its life forms, and that this origin of species had no more to do with religion than the diurnal motions of the earth:

> God is believed to be everywhere yet people say "Our Father who art in heaven." The words of belief and scripture cannot be applied to science. The religious belief of a blue dome over a motionless earth has been replaced by vast space and a moving earth but this does not affect the words of Moses and Christ. As with other scientific discoveries, religion first rejects and then at last accepts. So will be the case of evolution.

At this point the editorial claim to neutrality was inserted:

> We only report what scientists have concluded without our having any objective in the matter or having anything invested in it, neither a date nor a camel. As for religion, we believe faith came before eye witnesses, no matter what Zayd may say or Ubayd may claim, or anyone else. If what they say agrees with our faith, we accept it; if not, we reject it. That does not need to be expressed, but we express it in defense of the suspicions of those who can only suspect the worst in people.

This would then be followed by an article that brought more evidence supporting and explaining natural selection, only to end with a pious disclaimer. The exculpatory tone in the articles that appeared in late 1880 hints at the dark cloud that had been for some time gathering over the American College, polluting the evangelical atmosphere with the name of Darwin.

A few months into 1881, Shibli Shumayyil, true to his trouble-loving nature, threw oil on the fire with an article, "Life and the Origin of Living Bodies," in which he submits the biblical story of creation to scientific analysis and offers Darwin's account as a more reliable version. Refusing to back away from the heat, Sarruf and Nimr, whose careers as teachers at SPC depended on the good graces of its American evangelical administration, bravely published it. In the article, Shumayyil, for the moment uncharacteristically restraining his radical materialism, does not outright reject a Creator. Darwin's theory, he writes, does not deny God. It simply explains nature in its own terms. The biblical account makes creation a direct act; Darwin's theory of evolution takes nature through an indirect route over ages for it to have reached the state of species found in it today: "Man can only know why the creator did it one way and not the other by knowing the creator's mind and that is impossible." A year later the storm broke.

Edwin Lewis

The young American professor of chemistry and biology, Edwin Lewis, a doctoral graduate of Harvard, was chosen to give the commencement address for the class of 1882. Darwin died in April of that year, and many Christians were the happier for it, but Darwin's ideas obstinately refused to be buried with him. Many in the academic community revered Darwin's name and his works, not only Shibli Sumayyil, Ya'qub Sarruf and Faris Nimr, but others teaching science and medicine at SPC. In commemoration of the great scientist, the editors of *Muqtataf* ran an obituary in the May issue, extolling Darwin as "the most learned man of his age." This was followed by an article in the June issue that went into the principles of natural selection in some detail.[6] Either they were very courageous or the editors may not have been fully aware of the obsessional, even pathological, depth of hostility the American president and his evangelical administrators harbored for Darwin.

Professor Edwin Lewis was apparently not fully aware. Hired in 1870, he must have come to appreciate by 1882 the general prevailing evangelical conservatism at the college, though there had been signs that the conservative grip of the evangelicals was loosening. The presence of Edwin Lewis was one of them. After 15 years in existence, the American College was beginning to emerge from the cocoon of its missionary origins. The student body had been expanding since the school's founding and was becoming more sophisticated, some of its graduates already contributing to the literary renaissance that had been in progress. Integral to this growing maturity, which was a reflection of the general transformation that Beirut society was undergoing, were changes in the intellectual complexion of the faculty. Religious study had been the primary intent and purpose of the school's founders, but the pressure of student demand was pushing religion to the side for science and medicine. This meant recruiting teachers outside the missionary spirit and intellectual framework of American evangelism. At some point in the mid to late 1870s the faculty became constitutionally schizophrenic, split as it was between liberals and conservatives, or as a historian of the college has described it, Hebraist versus humanist, the former being conservative, authoritarian and scriptural literalists, the latter being liberal interpreters whose Protestant faith had no problem with science or evolution.[7] That is to say, the college was host to an American version of the same mental cleavage that had been splitting Middle Eastern society since the beginning of the reforms in the early part of the century.

With respect to the students, Professors Edwin Lewis and Cornelius Van Dyck were two of the most highly respected and popular science professors on the medical faculty. As did Van Dyck 30 years before, Lewis learned to speak, read and write Arabic fluently. Because the lectures were in Arabic, the teachers had to know the language, and their knowing it so well fostered an ease of communication and intimacy of understanding between the American teachers and their students that would otherwise have been impossible. It did not take long for the popular Edwin Lewis to acquire an unsavory reputation among the evangelist administrators: his intellectual attitude and social behavior rubbed against the fundamentalist missionary spirit. One of the more spirited of the new breed who had come aboard, Lewis was too well-liked and respected by the students, and his credentials and research too good, for him to be fired without good cause. Lewis's independence of mind and the discomfort he caused President Bliss and his close associates were too vague for a case to be made that could be used to be rid of him. This was soon to change.

His first sin was to serve wine at a dinner he hosted for some of the faculty and administrators. The incident was duly recorded and made out to be a grave breach of college morals. President Daniel Bliss and another founding father, Dr. David Dodge, exchanged letters in condemnation of Lewis's libertine behavior and decided that new teachers would henceforth be obliged to sign an evangelical 'Declaration of Principles' forbidding intemperate conduct, which included the serving and drinking of wine.

Considering the negative light in which Lewis was seen by Bliss, Dodge and several other powerful evangelical administrators, it is curious that he was chosen to give the commencement address. Perhaps it was a rotating obligation of the senior faculty and it came his turn, or because of his popularity with the medical students who by now formed the most important part of the college. Whatever the reasons, the administration accepted that Edwin Lewis give the July 19th commencement address for the class of 1882.

The title Lewis gave his address was "Knowledge, Science and Wisdom" (*Ma'rifa*, *'Ilm wa Hikma*.). He wrote and delivered it in classical Arabic. The theme of his address was that active, creative thought exists in three interrelated dimensions. Science "occurs in the mind when it is affected by the reflection of images which stir it from its unawareness into action. When the mind considers such images, it searches for their truth and investigates their cause in order to put them together in one specific system and then place them under specified classifications. When this takes place in the mind, its causes prevail over its effects. Knowledge is inferior to science as it is attained merely by paying attention, while science results from the use of thought and attention . . . Science searches in nature for the cause of events, and places them in their correct context."

As examples of correct scientific methodology, Lewis referred to the geology of Charles Lyell and the biology of the recently deceased Charles Darwin. Darwin had died two months earlier and been interred in Westminster Abbey next to Newton. Their theories, Edwin Lewis was careful to emphasize, were not true theories or tested science, but rather hypotheses that awaited proof or disproof. Their methods of research, their careful and precise ways of collecting and categorizing data and their systematic thinking in translating raw data into working hypotheses were models of scientific excellence, however right or wrong the hypotheses. Continuing research based on those models would bear out the correctness or falsity of their ideas. However it turned out, the methods of research used by Lyell and Darwin would be the same methods that proved them right or wrong. Wisdom, on the other hand, transcended science:

> Through science man may know something about the existence of God – the Cause of all Causes – but he fails to apprehend who and what God is. Through science man is able to know something about himself, and about the means by which he was created or evolved, but he is unable to know the origin of what makes man a man, or the origin of the strong desire inherent in him to know the state whither he is proceeding. No telescope will show us God; no microscope will show us the soul of man, and no chemistry will disclose the secret of life or the secret of man.

A fair reading of his address could hardly support that Lewis was being antagonistic to religion or the "Hebraists," but his mention of the name Darwin in a positive sense was the sin that put the administrators' noose around his neck. If by using Darwin as an example of research excellence Lewis had been trying to tell the administration something about academic freedom, he may as well have been talking into the wind. The minutes of the Board of Trustees meeting held shortly after the commencement address reveals the discontent Lewis caused the administrators: "Neither the Board of Managers, the Faculty, nor the Board of Trustees, would be willing to have anything that favors what is called 'Darwinism' talked of or taught in the College." What made it worse was that the address was a huge success with the students. Writing in *Muqtataf*, a student reporter who had attended the ceremony describes the address as a rare success in the history of commencement exercises. Bursts of enthusiastic applause interrupted the address, and at the end of it the speaker was surrounded by a crowd of congratulatory students and faculty, "and when the ceremony was over, literary men complimented him for having shown that beyond science is wisdom, which is the fear of God." Emphasizing fear of God was not Lewis's intention, but the writer of the account, Yusuf Hayek, may have hoped it to be, since, as he goes on to report, some of the American missionaries were visibly upset at hearing the names of Lyell and Darwin in the Chapel where commencement exercises had been held.[8]

Following the commencement address, Sarruf and Nimr, thinking to support Lewis in face of the administration's campaign of whispers that was poisoning the campus air, revisited natural selection in their journal's mid-July issue, this time pointedly drawing on arguments of leading western scholars that claimed the principle to be in no way contrary to religion or scripture.[9] This did nothing to assuage the fury of Bliss and Dodge. Dr. Lewis had strayed too far beyond the tolerable limits of proper Christian behavior and thought. Allowing him to stay was as out of the question as forgiving him. To the evangelists it appeared that by holding Darwin and Lyell up as models of scientific research Dr. Lewis was attacking them personally, openly challenging what was very clearly known to be their firm beliefs. Claiming science to be a road to wisdom and understanding God, as the American missionaries saw it, was tantamount to questioning the monopoly of scripture as the source of divine wisdom. The American founders had come to convert, not produce godless scientists and physicians. Students could go to the French for that.

The evangelists had grown up in an urban American society that accepted science alongside a religion of biblical literalism. To preserve belief in scripture's infallibility, the letter of scripture had been obliged to make accommodation for heliocentric theory, which by the mid-19th century gave no problem to educated evangelists or the Roman Church. To dismiss Copernicus, Galileo, Descartes and Newton would have been unthinkable. But Lyell and the evolution of earth through geological ages, and Darwin and the evolution of living forms and man from primitive ancestors, these were horses of another color. The evolutionary hypothesis was unproven, dangerous to belief and morals, and could no more be tolerated in the college community as an idea worthy of discussion than could the presence of those who would even tentatively allude to its credibility in any way, shape or form.

An entry in President Bliss's daybook that was made the same day of the commencement address indicates his unbending intent to be rid of Lewis. Curiously, no entry in the President's daybook mentions anything about the article in *Muqtataf* or Shibli Shumayyil's outspoken support of evolution. It wasn't that the editors were convincing in their declaration of neutrality, or that Americans on the faculty were held to a stricter standard of orthodoxy, but that a cancer in a leading faculty member was most lethal to the college community. The young Arab Darwinists would be taught their lesson once Edwin Lewis had been properly disposed of.

Daniel Bliss, David Dodge, Henry Jessup and Alfred Post, all of whom have beautiful old buildings named after them on the campus of today's American University of Beirut, came to a decision over the summer break to have Edwin Lewis summarily dismissed from his position. Aware of what Bliss and his supporters were up to, and that President Bliss would need authorization from the New York Board of Evangelical Missions to dismiss him, Lewis made an English translation of his address and sent it for review to the Union Theological Seminary in New York. The Seminary's decision would be decisive. Lewis failed to include the Arabic original. When the readers at the Theological Seminary informed Bliss of their having found nothing heretical in the Lewis commencement address, it seemed the affair was over and that Bliss and company had been thwarted. But Reverend Bliss was determined. Whatever the merits of the case for Lewis, however nasty the issue became, Lewis would have to go, and any means would justify that necessary and moral end. It had now also become a matter of saving face as well as morality.

Bliss wrote back to the Director of the Union Theological Seminary that what they had received from Dr. Lewis was a watered-down translation of his original address in Arabic. Bliss then skipped to issues that had nothing to do with the address and insisted Lewis was a bad influence whose teachings would corrupt the students, offend the religious beliefs of their parents and do a grave disservice to the College. A series of exchanges ensued in which Bliss kept up the attack on Lewis's intemperate and immoral character, until he had at last worn down the opposition in New York and was given the authority to dismiss Dr. Lewis.[10] When the new academic year began in October, President Bliss informed Lewis that he was being terminated. Lewis appears to have accepted the decision without protest and agreed for the sake of appearance to resign his post at the end of the fall semester. He had in fact already decided on his own that the intellectual ambience was too incongenial for him to remain at the College and do his work with any sense of satisfaction.

A number of faculty members, the "humanists," resented the high handed way the administrators were treating Lewis, a sentiment that was shared by a large part of the student body. When word that Lewis had agreed to resign became known, student tempers rose, and they continued to rise through the months of the fall semester. Sarruf and Nimr, who had been indignant of the administration from the start of the affair, reproduced the whole of Lewis's commencement address in the August issue of *Muqtataf*, leaving the public to judge whether it was irreligious or not. Cornelius Van Dyck, his son William and two other professors came out in support of Lewis. William Van Dyck had recently joined the faculty, adding to the numbers of those humanists loosening the evangelical fist gripping the college.

A staunch advocate of evolution, William Van Dyck had received his medical degree in the United States in 1878 and two years later joined his father in Beirut as a professor of medicine. He arrived with an armload of books on evolution by Darwin and others, which, to the dumbfounded horror and fury of the American evangelicals, he freely loaned out to interested medical and science students. In fact, the younger Van Dyck had been in correspondence with Darwin. Weeks before the great scientist's death William had sent him a book on the varieties of Syrian dogs based on natural selection that he had written during the year or so since his taking up teaching and research duties at SPC. One of the last things Darwin had written was a letter to William Van Dyck praising him for his work.

As the fall semester progressed and the administration refused to back off on forcing Lewis out, the students supporting Lewis became more demonstrative. By the beginning of November the campus atmosphere was explosive. In 1963, Shafiq Jeha, an employee of the American University of Beirut, discovered a box in the college archives that contained 40 letters from David Dodge to President Bliss on the subject of Edwin Lewis. Based on these letters, Jeha wrote a book on the episode,[11] which revealed there was more to the mounting student discontent over administrative policy than Edwin Lewis and evolution. Trouble had been brewing since 1880 when it was decided by the administrators to change the language of instruction from Arabic to English and demote Sarruf and Nimr, the former of the two being transferred from teaching science to teaching Arabic. New science teachers, preferably religious ones whose minds were not polluted with ideas of Darwin and natural selection, were to be hired from the United States for the science and medical faculties. They would not have to learn Arabic. Everything now was to be in English. The demotions would seem to have been the punishment meted out to the editors for the articles on Darwin that had been appearing in *Muqtataf* since the journal's founding, though nothing in the administration's correspondence substantiates this.

The abrupt decision to change the language of instruction was of extreme importance to the students. The medical students had been up in arms ever since the decision. Top science and medical students who were hoping to find positions in the College's expanding faculties saw themselves being put at a disadvantage. With the lectures being in English it would be difficult for them to compete with American candidates. There was no reason for the change. Arab students had had no need to learn English. They were not leaving their homeland for England or America. As for reading material and lectures, Cornelius Van Dyck's books had provided them with scientific texts in Arabic, and the American professors knew classical Arabic better than the students did, and colloquial almost as well. With instruction being in English, the new professors wouldn't have to know Arabic. If they didn't have to learn it they wouldn't. They wouldn't get to know the people and the culture. The college would no longer be so comfortably integrated in the Beirut and Syrian community. It would become more American and enclosed in itself, a little island of America floating in its own world, disconnected from the real world it was in. The Americans were going to do what the arrogant French were doing, forcing everyone to learn their language – hitting them over the head with the superiority of French civilization! One of the reasons for the warm feelings the indigenous people had for the Americans was their charm in speaking classical and colloquial Arabic.[12]

Another problem affecting the American College was that physicians had to stand for an imperial Ottoman state medical exam before being accredited to practice. The problem here was that the exam could be taken only in Turkish, Arabic or French. Not English. Medically, English was a dead language in the Ottoman Empire. With SPC switching to English, students would be learning medicine in one language and examined in another. It wasn't fair. Most of the medical students knew neither Turkish nor French. Their discontent over the language change poured into their grievance over the administration's treatment of Lewis, making the autumn semester of 1882 one of the most critical in the history of the American College, until 1967 and after.

Student discontent did not overly worry the administration. American evangelicals knew how to deal with recalcitrant youngsters. But it became an entirely different matter when support for Lewis came from the heart of Beirut's Protestant community, particularly in the voice of Shaykh Ibrahim al-Hourani. Shaykh Hourani, scholar, essayist, poet, religion teacher, evangelical theologian, instructor of logic, mathematics and Arabic at SPC, and leader of the Angelic Church in Beirut, was the most authoritative figure in that community.[13] To ignore his voice was to ignore the Arab Protestant community of Beirut, the very flock that the American evangelicals were there to shepherd. Hourani was also a highly respected official of the American Protestant mission and SPC. On top of that, he was the chief editor of the *Evangelical Weekly*, *al-Nashrat al-Usbu'iyyah*, printed by the Protestant Press at SPC. By association, the *Evangelical Weekly* was considered as much a publication of the American College as the Protestant community.

Hourani agreed with other Protestant authorities in Britain, America and elsewhere that evolution theory did not negate scripture. Shaykh Hourani attended

SPC's commencement program in July, and a few weeks later, as soon as it became clear that an altercation was brewing, he came out in support of Lewis, praising his address as an informative lesson in the harmony of science and scripture.[14] Going far beyond what Lewis had said in his address, Shaykh Hourani wrote in his *Evangelical Weekly* that nothing in the principles of natural selection refuted religion.[15]

With Shaykh Hourani throwing his hat in the ring, the affair was threatening to degenerate into a conflict within the evangelical community: Arab Protestants supporting Darwin and Lewis were pitted against the three American administrators and their "Hebraist" followers, led at the time by the American Director of the School of Protestant Theology in Beirut, James Denis. Sarruf, Nimr and Shibli Shumayyil, aligned with Hourani, tried to maintain a peaceful dialogue by putting out articles in *Muqtataf* on the theme that science, and evolution as a branch of it, had no bearing on scripture, neither confirming nor denying it.

Following Shaykh Hourani's defense of Lewis and Darwin in a September issue of the *Evangelical Weekly*, Reverend James Denis countered in a November issue of the *Evangelical Weekly*. In classical Arabic, Reverend Denis wrote of how he deplored having to discuss Darwin openly since it exposed Syrian youth to vile and irreligious views that might seduce the weak-minded of them. Being that the so-called scientist Charles Darwin was devoid of truth and that his ideas were doubted by most leading scientists, he was as a person not worth consideration and his books should never be read for fear that the naïve reader might lose faith in the Holy Spirit, Christ and religion.[16]

At the same time, the editors of *Muqtataf* published a letter by a former student of Professor Lewis, Yusuf Hayak, the same who had written favorably in *Muqtataf* of the commencement address in July and who by October was residing in Alexandria, to whose shores the Christian tempest in Beirut had reached. Once again he wrote in defense of his former professor, praising him to be one of the College's finest professors: rather than being attacked, Dr. Lewis should be honored.

With all the support that was coming his way, Lewis agreed to write something in his own defense. In the December issue of *Muqtataf* he wrote a brief reply to the charges Reverend Denis had made against him by asking, "What difference would it make had God endowed His holy spirit to one original form of life at one time or to many forms one at a time?" He professed himself to be a believing Christian, a follower of the Gospels, just as Darwin had been. One could be a scientist and believe in the Gospels.[17]

By December, with Lewis's resignation only weeks away from coming into effect, the campus was being torn apart. Students supporting Lewis, mostly medical students but also upperclassmen of the Literary Department acting on behalf of freedom of expression, signaled their opposition to the administration by refusing to attend religious services in the Chapel. Chapel was a compulsory ceremonial exercise of great importance to the missionaries, one that continued into the 1950s. Not attending Chapel sent a strong message of rebellion to the administration. The mounting crisis split the faculty. Cornelius Van Dyck, his son William and Dr. Wortabet resigned. The resignation of Cornelius Van Dyck, now a distinguished scholar of 64 and of all the Americans in Beirut the most respected and well-liked by the local populace, was a powerful blow to the administration. Highly admired and respected by the locals for his ability in mastering Arabic and Arab culture, for his knowledge, dignity, kindness, humanity and love for his adopted country, Van Dyck struck a sympathetic chord in all of the Arabs who knew him. In fact, the Beirut populace thought him to be the founder of the American college, which was popularly known as Van Dyck College, a misnomer that could not have pleased President Daniel Bliss. Before resigning, Cornelius tried to persuade Bliss to reconsider his firing of Lewis. Bliss and his top administrators refused to buckle. On the contrary, to show their determination, they punished a group of medical students thought to be the leading troublemakers by suspending them from classes for a month. This made the decision for Van Dyck and the others to resign, putting the College's administration in a particularly bad light among the Beirutis of both the Christian and Muslim communities.

Tensions were now at the breaking point. A campus scrap broke out between students in the Literary Department and the Medical School. The literature faction thought that stopping classes and possibly causing the closure of the College was too high a price to pay for defending a professor in the Medical Department. Indeed, closure was becoming a distinct possibility. The administration blamed the trouble on a group of malcontents in the Medical School and was threatening to suspend or even end the school's operations. With closure looming ever more threateningly, the majority of students studying Arabic literature who had little interest in Lewis or science, and who did not have to stand for a qualifying exam in French or Ottoman Turkish to validate their Arabic literature degree, accepted the decisions of the administration.

What was happening at SPC went beyond the crisis of a professor being dismissed for his liberal thinking and acting. The disharmony tearing the College apart was a reflection of the changes taking place in the Arab and Muslim world, where the authority of old was being challenged. SPC appeared to be following in the pattern of the larger society around it, whose influences and problems became part of the College as much as the people from that society were a part of it. Reverend Bliss was ruling SPC the way Sultan abd al-Hamid was ruling the empire. On whatever level in whatever institution, repression was authority's answer to perceived resistance, however expressed. Whether constitutionalism or evolution, authority was being challenged and knew only to answer it with a determined show of force, the standard currency of a fearful authority facing a current of change that it could neither appreciate nor understand. President Bliss's liberal use of his cane to march pornography-reading students across the campus grounds and out the gate in defense of moral purity was on its level little different from the bull whips and instruments of torture liberally used by the sultan's agents to preserve the crumbling empire.

Both sides carried the crisis to the brink. A student protest took place in the Chapel led by 50 science and medical students. President Bliss responded predictably. Classes were suspended and the college closed. Stunned, the medical students organized a strike committee to negotiate with the administration. Elected to the head of it was Jurji Zaydan, by now a second-year medical student. His memoirs confirm that as much as the administration's treatment of Dr. Lewis angered the medical students, their protest and strike were motivated as much by the decision taken by the Ottoman government to institute the medical examination administered by the state board of physicians, to be given in Turkish or French, in distant Istanbul. The students' concerns were reflected in a letter submitted by Jurji on behalf of the strike committee to President Bliss. It began with a review of the unjust treatment Dr. Lewis had received and requested that he be reinstated. The letter then turned to the other injustice, the state medical exam in Istanbul, and requested the administration to have it canceled. The President responded. Supported by Dodge and Post, Bliss adamantly refused to have Lewis reinstated or even allow him to teach until the end of the academic year. As for the second appeal, there was little that the Syrian Protestant College could do to change an order from the sultan's government. That ended negotiations.

The College remained closed. For a while President Bliss himself wasn't sure if its doors would ever be reopened. However, by the end of the second week of closure, the will of the strike committee was wavering. The anger of the Literary Department students, as well as those science and medical students who thought more of the time, money and effort invested in their education at SPC than they did of the unjust treatment of Dr. Lewis, drained the determination to carry on. The leaders of the strike committee felt themselves to be abandoned, as did their supporters outside the College. The editors of *Muqtataf*, who had been the most active in defending Lewis, while profiting from the crisis to advance public awareness of Darwin's principles but standing to lose a great deal if the College closed down, had in the meanwhile decided to back off and let the matter rest before it destroyed what mattered to them most, the continuation of the school; for if the Medical School went, the heart and soul of the sciences would go with it. The College would turn into a meaningless seminary for American-trained evangelists pouring out more religion in a society besotted with it. The striking students in support of Lewis had lost.

Sensing the mood, the administration announced the resumption of classes, but not without punishing the troublemakers. Students involved in the strike were given a month's suspension, at the end of which they each had to sign a Pledge of Obedience, a student version of the Declaration of Principles that had been forced on the faculty a few months earlier in order to enforce a code of behavior congruent with evangelist orthodoxy.[18] Several medical students refused to sign and left the college and medicine for other careers. One of them, Jurji Zaydan, pursued a literary career in Egypt and became one of the foremost deans of modern Arabic literature. Of the several professors who resigned over the Lewis Affair, as it came to be called, only Dr. Wortabet returned. Cornelius and William Van Dyck did not.

The American College began the spring semester of 1883 without three of its leading science professors. As reported by *Muqtataf*, it was a sad conclusion for a college that for almost two decades had contributed to the future of Syria and the Arab world by infusing the sciences into the minds of young men:

> It has sown the seeds of the sciences in the minds of the students and nurtured ethics and high qualities in their souls. . . But now, with the passage of time, and after having long praised the college for all it has done, we

must regretfully report the heavy damage it has suffered with the resignation of three of its teachers, one of them being the renowned Dr. Cornelius Van Dyck, professor of pathology and director of the observatory. Dr. Edwin Lewis, professor of chemistry and physics, has also resigned, and William Van Dyck. The three of them depart like a sun and two moons.

The Van Dycks remained in their beloved Lebanon as private educators. Lewis returned to his native country to find a position at Wabash College, where he pursued a distinguished career.[19] To the extent that Bliss, Dodge and Post would have liked to clear the College of all the "liberal humanists," the Lewis–Darwin Affair could be said to have ended in a complete victory for the "Hebraists," a victory they wanted even if it meant ending the college. According to personal correspondence, they would have gone that far.[20]

The restrictive atmosphere at the American College proved to be too much for men of liberal spirit. A few years after the departure of Lewis and the Van Dycks, Sarruf and Nimr left for Cairo and took their journal with them. Following soon behind them to Cairo came Jurji Zaydan and Farah Antun, another key figure in the Arab literary renaissance. This Egypt-bound exodus of Syro–Lebanese Christian writers was not entirely due to the denouement of the Edwin Lewis Affair, though that sharply influenced the thinking of some who left. There was also that other level of repression at work, Sultan abd al-Hamid's iron grip crushing the constitutionalist movement and his policy of press censorship that went along with it, the effect of which was to snuff out the possibilities of creative literary careers in Syria.

The Lewis Affair reflects poorly on President Bliss. It seems, in retrospect, it could have been easily avoided. Allowing free discussion of Darwin's theory as a tentative hypothesis as it might relate to religion seems never to have crossed the evangelical mind. Bliss's depth of feeling against Darwin, or against being challenged on the issue, or perhaps any issue, was so profound that in order to punish those who stood against him he would even have ended the school he had done so much to build and expand. What explains his harsh stand? Highly respected Syrian theologians as learned as he, Shaykh Ibrahim al-Hourani being one, could embrace modern science and evolution according to Intelligent Design without compromising their belief. So could many reverends in Britain.

One interpretation explaining Bliss's action is that he harbored some fear of modern science, not fear that it was wrong but fear it might pose more of a challenge to himself than his faith could bear. Related to this was his fear that Muslims, who were beginning to send their sons to the college in larger numbers, would be offended no less than himself by a free discussion of Darwin.[21] The only Muslim involvement in the 1882 episode came in the form of letters from a group of notables in Beirut and Damascus who warmly supported Cornelius Van Dyck when they heard he had resigned from the College. The irony is that the Americans were more offended by the idea of evolution than the Muslims. As for the conservative Muslim ulema, whose general mentality and regard of science was similar to that of Dr. Bliss's, their means of dealing with science and evolution, perhaps the wisest means of all for those of the pious who are ignorant of science, was simply to ignore it as having nothing to do with religion, while hoping science would adopt the same attitude in regard to religion.

Between the hammer of Hamidian repression and the anvil of American evangelical intolerance, the young intelligentsia blossoming at the American College headed to Egypt for deliverance. Sarruf and Nimr remained with SPC for two more years, and for many months shied away from writing on evolution. It may have have been their return to the subject in 1884 that did them in once and for all with the American administrators. Both Sarruf and Nimr had been promised promotions from instructors to assistant professors. The general rule was that Americans were the professors and locals the instructors. This was because no local had as yet earned a doctoral degree. Unlike the French in Beirut, the Americans gave no encouragement to promising graduates to go abroad for doctoral study, and so Sarruf and Nimr would have been the first locals to rise from the instructor level. The promotions were to come into effect at the beginning of the 1885 academic year. But in the spring of 1884, the administration informed Sarruf and Nimr that their promotions would not be forthcoming. Rather than being promoted, they were to be discharged at the end of the current semester. Their treatment by the administration was as brusque as Edwin Lewis's.

The abrupt reversal must have been shattering. Yet even at that bitter moment of having been so summarily discharged from the college that they loved and praised and had worked for, Sarruf and Nimr were able to think of it as something greater than the people who ran it. Reporting on the commencement exercise that took place in June 1884, the month they left for Egypt, they could graciously write that the American College had "sown the seeds of the sciences in the minds of the students and nurtured ethics and high qualities in their souls."[22]

With their careers at SPC over, Hamidian repression was enough to convince them to leave for Cairo. It was the same for Shibli Shumayyil. After the end of the brief constitutional period in 1877, the abrasive edge of Hamidian government became intolerably intrusive for those who believed in freedom of expression. Some of the young men from the Beirut intelligentsia were joining secret societies that looked toward a change in Syria's status in the Ottoman Empire. Working for SPC had provided a softening buffer from that abrasive edge, until the administration revealed itself to be just as abrasive. Cairo and Alexandria looked to be healthier places politically and intellectually than Beirut under the Hamidian regime.

Syria's and SPC's loss was Egypt's gain. Egypt's literary and intellectual revival that had been slowly and timorously growing through state action was leavened by the more intrepid and experimental humanist individualism of the Syro–Lebanese arrivals, a number of whom emulated Sarruf and Nimr by starting up journals and newspapers in Cairo and Alexandria, and writing books, with Zaydan in the lead, pouring out a steady stream of enthralling historical romance in the new style of clear literary Arabic that *Muqtataf* had inspired in him. His novels earned him a high pedestal in the pantheon of modern Arabic literature. The main characters in Jurji's stories were heroic figures in Arab history who were great because of their virtues as Arabs, the implication being that if Islam was a religion of high virtue and morality, it was because of the character of those who had founded and spread the religion. Zaydan's secular portrayals of Arab heroism and genius was to become a fundament in the ideology of Arab nationalism.

In Cairo, he the founded periodical, *al-Hilal* (*The Crescent*). Primarily a literary journal, it contributed to the public discussion of science, religion and social issues. In its first issue, Zaydan listed 30 leading topics whose discussion would help clear the way toward modernization. One of them was, "Does the study of science lead to unbelief?" Others were, "Should women demand the same rights as men?" and "Are women capable of the same work as men?" The answers in his essays that followed were foregone conclusions. *Hilal* stood with *Muqtataf* as one of the twin pillars of secular Arab journalism calling for Arabs to make science their own as they had in the past. Religion, Zaydan repeatedly stressed in his *Hilal*, echoing the editors of *Muqtataf*, had nothing to fear since science and scientific discovery were based on things such as social morality, which in turn was based on justice, honesty, self-reliance, tolerance, mutual respect, public mindedness and social responsibility. Of such parents was born the scientific spirit.[23]

In 1890, with Sarruf and Nimr now famous and *Muqtataf* going strong everywhere in the Arab world, Bliss and Dodge, who must have undergone some mellowing, offered their earliest graduates and former instructors honorary doctorates. The two editors courteously accepted the honor but claimed to be too busy to come to Beirut to attend the ceremony. William Van Dyck stood in for them. His father Cornelius had died in his leafy villa in Ras Beirut the year before, having lived 50 marvelous years there, a model of the best kind of man from a faraway country. A decade later, Sarruf and Nimr were awarded honorary doctorates of philosophy by New York University. This time they found time to attend the ceremony and traveled to the country that had given theirs a college.

Not long after their deaths in the 1920s, life-size white alabaster busts of Sarruf and Nimr were placed just inside the main gate of the College, which by then had been renamed the American University of Beirut. There their busts stood for the rest of the 20th century, facing College Hall surmounted by the Bell Tower. At the turn of the millennium, the two busts suddenly disappeared from their commanding position at the main entrance off Bliss Street. If one diligently searches, the busts will be found guarding the now-defunct observatory that Cornelius Van Dyck operated and held his astronomy classes in, with its domed stone structure perched at the neglected edge of the headland and hidden in the hanging shade of the banyan trees, where the campus slopes lushly down to the sea.

Notes

1 *Da'irat al-Ma'arif*, edited by Butrus Bustani, Beirut, vol 7, 1882, pp. 547–548.
2 *Muqtataf*, vol 1, 1876, pp. 231–232.
3 *Muqtataf*, vol 1, 1876, pp. 242–244.
4 Bishara Zilzal, "al-Insan," *Muqtataf*, vol 2, 1877, pt 9, pp. 202–205.
5 *Muqtataf*, vol 2, 1877, pp. 273–275.
6 Ya'qub Saruf and Faris Nimr, *Muqtataf*, vol 7, June 1882, pp. 2–6.
7 John Munro, *A Mutal Concern: The Story of the American University of Beirut*, Caravan Books, Delmar, NY, 1977, p. 26 ff.

8. Munro, *A Critical Concern*, p. 31; *Muqtataf*, vol 7, July 9, 1882.
9. Ya'qub Saruf and Faris Nimr, *Muqtataf*, vol 7, 1882, pp. 65–72; 121–129.
10. Olivier Meier, *Al-Muqtataf et le debat sur le Darwinisme: Beirut 1876–1885*, Dossiers du CEDEC (Centre d'Etudeset Documentation Economiques, Juridiques et Sociales), Cairo, 1996, pp. 28–29.
11. Shafiq Jeha, *Darwin wa'l Azma 1882 bi'l Da'irat al-Tibbiyya* (Darwin and the 1882 Crisis at the Faculty of Medicine), American University of Beirut Press,1991, Beirut. A translation of this by Sally Kaya in 2004 was published by the AUB Press, Beirut.
12. This must sound strange today when the world takes for granted that every Beiruti and Lebanese knows French and English, while Americans, knowing no foreign languages and having little interest to learn, demand that everybody in the world should know English.
13. Marwa Elshakry, *Darwin's Legacies in the Arab East: Science, Religion and Politics, 1870–1914*, Princeton PhD dissertation, 2003, p. 163.
14. Kamal al-Yaziji, *al-Shaykh Ibrahim al-Hourani*, Beirut, 1963, p. 47; Jeha, *Darwin wa'l Azma*, pp. 65–66.
15. "al-'Alim Darwin" (The Scientist Darwin), *al-Nashrat al-Usbu'iyyah*, issue 36 (September 1882), Beirut, pp. 397–398.
16. "Al-Madhhab Darwin," *al-Nashrat al-Usbu'iyyah*, section 8, vol 4 (November 1882), p. 233; Jeha, pp. 66–67. Considering the present deplorable condition of American relations with the Arab world, one can only admire those Americans of more than a century ago who, whatever their intellectual stance on evolution, thrashed out their theological and scientific differences in classical Arabic.
17. "*Radd Lewis 'ala Denis*" (Lewis Response to Denis), *Muqtataf* (December 1882), pp. 287–290.
18. Jeha, p. 137; Meier, pp. 28–29.
19. *Muqtataf*, vol 9, 1884, p. 183.
20. Jeha, p. 124; D. Leavitt, "Darwinism," *The Muslim World*, vol 71, no 2, 1981, p. 93, quoting a letter of December 18, 1882, written by the wife of Daniel Bliss, Abbey, to her sons.
21. Leavitt, *Darwinism*.
22. *Muqtataf* (1884), p. 701.
23. *Hilal*, vol I (September 1892), pp. 26–27.

6   From Copernicus to Darwin

The general acceptance of heliocentrism was a symbolic victory of sorts for that small literate elite who were appealing to government, ulema and the public to invest in science education at all levels. *Muqtataf* and *Madaris* spoke to the public, and out of the effort came Abdallah Fikri's treatise, but there was no government action for a crash program in science education on the primary, secondary and university levels, no increase in the school budget, nor any program to send a hundred students to the West for doctoral study. Egypt still did not have what could be considered a university. Al-Azhar was a purely religious institution, and even there the shaykhs failed to back the government by issuing a fatwa embracing modern science and the new astronomy. Some of the ulema had inherited the medieval Hanbali animosity toward the rational sciences; others wondered what it all had to do with obeying God. Even as heliocentrism was being pulled through the half-open window of semi-official religio-cultural acceptance, a much larger challenge coming from Europe's continuing progress in science was looming over the horizon, namely Darwin. The West was not standing still for the rest of the world to catch up. Abdallah Fikri's treatise may have settled Muslim accounts to a large extent with 17th and 18th century science, but Darwin opened a new one as the river of discovery flowed through the 19th century, its current growing ever swifter. Seeing it rush on, more and more Middle Eastern reformers joined the chorus bemoaning the paralysis of their society and their governments that were leaving Muslims as mute observers at the margins of civilization.

If any century before the 20th could be called the Age of Science in Western Civilization it was the 19th. This was not simply in terms of discovery, but the magnitude with which society took to science, the numbers who became professional scientists or were amateur practitioners of it, and who religiously believed in it as a way to medical and material salvation. Since the impact of science on society was delivered through technology, perhaps it would be safer to say it was the transforming technical application of science that so impressed social consciousness with the seemingly limitless power of science that made it possible for the middle and upper levels of society in the 19th century to believe science, medicine and engineering were going to remake the world, rid society of its ills, eradicate squalor, disease and back breaking labor, and banish the world's darkness with the electric light. Galvani's research in electricity led to the telegraph,

Faraday's in electromagnetism to the dynamo, Edison's to the light bulb. The wave of optimism mounted with each discovery and invention. Discovery, machine and amenity became the holy trinity of capitalist liberalism marching in affluent defense of the consumerist creed.

The march was impressive. Research based on the foundations laid by Newton, Lavoisier and Dalton gave rise to an integrated structure of the inherent principles governing physics and chemistry. The 17th century Scientific Revolution had centered on astronomy and gravity; the 19th century revolution on physics and chemistry, and their underlying forces of electricity and magnetism. Electromagnetism, light, heat, radiation and all forms of energy were reduced to matter in motion. Nineteenth century biology also came to be interpreted as matter in motion: organic matter subject to variations that in relation to the surrounding natural conditions led to the evolution of new forms. The construct of matter in motion was by its critics often called materialism or materialistic. In the socio-economic realm of western life the critics of liberal consumerism applied the same term as a lifestyle. Materialism's disenthronement of the spiritual had been centuries in the making of science and economics. In the 19th century the usurpation crystallized so clearly that social philosophies parodying the naturalist's natural selection and survival of the fittest were propounded and believed by thinkers of sound mind. A word should be said about that science, and the spurious dogmas spawned from it by non-scientists, in order to appreciate not just the challenge presented by western progress, but as well the harsh critique that religious spokesmen in the Islamic world pronounced on the West and its intellectual exports, once the content and implications of western knowledge with its science-insinuated social and economic philosophies became clear to them. Otherwise, it would be difficult to appreciate what Middle Eastern modernizers found themselves up against, faced as they were from the outside by a West light years ahead of them, and from the inside by religious critics who found modern science to be threatening and reprehensible. The critique focused on Darwin's theory of evolution, and included what was seen to be the materialist basis of secular western science and life. As interpreted by the spokesmen of Islam, this perceived materialism left no place for anything that could not be weighed, measured, observed, sensed, detected, quantified and, if possible, neatly mathematized. Even light, symbol of the soul's journey to divine truth, was matter that could be captured, analyzed and measured. What precisely was the materialist basis of this 19th century science from which social philosophers borrowed so heavily, and, as it reflected on science, so detrimentally? The problem bears critically on Islam's confrontation with western science. We return to Isaac Newton and light.

In addition to his prism experiments and discovery of the spectral composition of white light, his experiments on the colored rings in a thin film of air between a lens and a smooth glass plate convinced him that light had defined physical properties, which meant, as he understood physics, it was composed of discrete, immutable particles, later to be called photons. Newton's particle theory of light was half the story. Interference patterns produced by other experiments indicated light was propagated in waves. A century after Newton, the experiments of two scientists who advanced the wave theory, Thomas Young in England and Augustin Fresnel in France, determined more precise values for the speed and wave length of light and showed it was composed of oscillating waves vibrating perpendicularly to the axis of propagation. Wave theory was developed further in England by James Maxwell, who determined the speed of electromagnetic waves, which he found to be identical to the speed of light, establishing electromagnetism to be a form of light and light to travel in waves. This presented a problem. The waves, like the force of gravity or electromagnetism that acted over a distance, had to travel through something that transmitted the waves, some subtle medium for the waves to propagate themselves, since it defied reason and the mechanical theory of physics that light or gravitational force could travel in a vacuum. Waves had to be transmitted by a material substance. Hence, the hypothetical ether, that ethereal substance that pervaded the universe so that waves and forces could be transmitted in the same way water propagated waves in the sea or air transmitted sound. If sound could not travel in a vacuum how would light?

The theory of the ether stood until A. A. Michelson built his interferometer, an ingenious construction of mirrors and lenses designed to split a beam of light and direct the two beams in perpendicular directions and then reunite them. One of the two beams would travel in the direction of the earth moving through space against the presumed stationary ether, the other at a right angle to the first. The light beam traveling in the direction of the earth would have a speed equal to the speed of light plus the speed of the earth. The perpendicular beam would simply move at the speed of light. Once they were reunited the difference in speed between the beams could be detected by the interference rings that the reunited beam would project on a screen. Interference rings are produced when light waves that are out of phase are united and projected on a screen. Being out of phase, the troughs and crests of the two waves coincide in such a way that when the crest of one wave meets the trough of the other, the waves cancel themselves out, producing a dark ring on the screen. Those crests and troughs that are not canceled out appear bright on the screen. The presence of alternating bright and dark rings indicates interference. Careful measurement of the numbers and widths of the rings can be used to determine the speed of the two beams after their having been split by Michelson's interferometer. By subtracting the speed of the beam that was reflected in a perpendicular direction from the speed of the beam traveling in the direction of the earth's motion, the speed of the earth's motion with respect to the stationary ether could be computed. Known as the Michelson–Morley experiment – Edward Morley was his assistant – it surprisingly detected no interference. The paradoxical conclusion was that light traveled at the same rate in both the direction of the earth's motion and in a direction perpendicular to it. It was the same when a beam was split and then split again to travel opposite the beam going in the direction of the earth, and then rejoined and projected on a screen. No interference patterns. Apparently the motion of the earth had no effect on the speed of light. The speed of light was always the same. No one could figure that out. The paradox wasn't resolved until the beginning of the 20th century when Einstein formulated his theory of relativity.

By passing a beam of light through a prism Newton discovered the spectrum and resolved the mystery of the rainbow. The color spectrum was to have a future in science as brilliant and awe-inspiring as the rainbow. Spectroscopy, combining optics, chemistry and astronomy into a science of its own, became a powerful tool in analyzing the composition of heavenly bodies and their distances and speeds relative to the earth. The spectrum was being analyzed in the early 19th century by Wollaston in England and Fraunhofer in Germany. Black bands found in the spectrum fascinated them. What did they signify? Building on their studies, the astronomer Sir John Herschel discovered that the colors of the spectrum could be used to detect the presence of metallic elements. The physicist Jean Foucault in France then discovered that the black bands in the spectrum could be stripped away from the light that was producing them by passing the light through the light produced by a voltaic arc, electrochemical light as it were. The conclusion was that light of a particular frequency could absorb energy from another light, a component of which had the same frequency of vibration, allowing the two to coincide as one. One light in contact with another could absorb any light in the spectrum that had the same frequency, or rate of vibration. This in effect transferred that "color" of light in its spectrum from the one light to the other – essentially an energy transfer effected through one set of vibrations that perfectly coincided with another vibrating in unison. The color corresponding to that frequency was removed from its companions who were all vibrating together but to their own particular color frequency in their collective spectrum. Red absorbs red, blue absorbs blue. Spectrum analysis made it possible to detect elements in heavenly bodies through the light they emitted. Analysis of the sun's spectrum in 1878 revealed that a dark line was present in the green band that did not coincide with any known line in earthly spectra. This meant that the sun contained an element unknown on earth. The element was discovered in 1895 and named helium after Helios, God of the sun. Spectroscopy indicated that the earth, moon and planets originated from the sun, and that the sun and stars of the universe probably originated from a common source.

Based on the work of Lagrange and Laplace in expanding Newtonian calculus as applied to motion, the German mathematician–astronomer Carl Gauss had during the first half of the century developed a technique to apply differential equations to electric phenomena. By mid-century George Riemann was investigating a non-Euclidean system of geometry that went beyond what could be comprehended by the senses to pure mathematical conceptions of space. This was the beginning. Mathematics, to be followed by the science of particle physics in the next century, was beginning its transcending journey beyond the ordinary, that world of three dimensions that made good sense and could be described and spoken about in words used to describe the making of a cake, without having to resort to a mathematics that related to nothing one could see, envision or even imagine, like infinity and the infinitesimal, or dimensions more than three or four, and multiple universes. Riemann's work was advanced by Helmholtz and Whitehead during the second half of the 19th century, by which time the essential mathematical methods of operations that Einstein would need to express his theory of relativity had been formulated. In 1905, with the publication of Einstein's paper on the theory, the West embarked on a new Scientific Revolution, some half century after the beginning of its second Industrial Revolution. Between them another revolution had occurred, the biological. Even with biology and Darwin aside, the 19th century was in every way a momentous progression of discovery and unification of separate branches of natural knowledge, of which a cursory review presents a daunting challenge. Perhaps the task has been put to words as tersely, succinctly and comprehensively as it can be by the English historian of the period's science, William Dampier:

> Dalton's atomic theory, the reduction of the phenomena of electricity and magnetism to mathematical laws, the concordance with experiment of the wave theory of light, the revelation by spectrum analysis of the composition of sun and stars, the explanation of the constitution of all the host of organic compounds by structural formulae, the production of new compounds and even of new elements, and the method of predicting their existence even before their discovery – all these and other triumphs gave an overwhelming sense of growing power both in the interpretation of nature and in the control of natural forces.[1]

The study of electricity and magnetism had a firm foundation in the creative experimentation of 18th century professional and amateur scientists. In the middle of that century experimenters fastened tall metal rods atop their houses to draw sparks from thunderclouds. One overzealous amateur in St. Petersburg got himself electrocuted. Around the same time, Joseph Priestly and Henry Cavendish found that Newton's inverse square law also related the attractive and repellent force of magnetism and electricity to the inverse of the square of the distance between the positive and negative poles. Benjamin Franklin demonstrated the identity between electricity and lightning through his experiments and described how electricity could be used for fusing and cutting metals. Before the century was out, electrical machines were being built; the first electrical condenser was constructed. Known as the Leyden jar for its having been made in that Dutch city, the jar was coated inside and out with a foil of tin that contained the electricity charged onto its inner surface.

Simple machines were being constructed in the 17th century that sent sparks leaping through space from one conductor to another. Such contraptions, built at first more for their novelty and amusement than for basic research, had delivered shocks to members of the Ottoman ambassadorial delegation visiting Vienna in the middle of the 18th century, and half a century later to the shaykhs of al-Azhar visiting the French *Institut d'Egypte*, neither being much amused by this European frivolity. The study of electricity, as discovery piled on discovery in a progression of critical experiments, required standardization and definitions of a new nomenclature that were provided by the names of the experimental pioneers: Volta, Ampere, Joule, Oersted, Coulombe and Ohm, the last of whom formulated the fundamental relationship that the flow of current is directly proportional to electromotive force and inversely to the resistance of the conducting wire. In the very early 19th century, Volta discovered that an electric current was produced by stacking a zinc disk over a copper disk with a brine-soaked piece of paper between the disks. The more the number of alternating metallic disks piled on, the greater was the electrical potential, later to be called voltage, and the higher was the current, to be called amperes, flowing through the stack of disks, which came to be called a cell or a pile. By arranging so many of the piles in series, one had a battery. Volta's invention of the battery was the critical event that eventually brought electricity and chemistry together. News of his discovery quickly reached England, where, in 1800, electrochemistry was born when a brass wire connected to the terminals of a voltaic cell was immersed in water. The current passing along the wire produced hydrogen gas at the zinc terminal. When a platinum-gold wire was connected to the terminals, in addition to hydrogen gas forming at the zinc terminal, oxygen gas was produced at the copper terminal. The volumes of the two gases collected at the terminals were always two of hydrogen to one of oxygen. Obviously, the two gases combined in a two to one ration to form water. Electrochemistry and electrolysis were then applied to other compounds.

   The self-taught Michael Faraday (1791–1867) gave electrochemistry its Greek-derived nomenclature: electron, electrode, anode, cathode, ion, electrolysis, and its law that relates the strength of current and time of flow to the quantity of elements, in proportion to their combining weights, liberated at the terminals. Faraday was father to both electrolysis and electromagnetism. During his experimentation with electricity in the very early 19th century he noticed the magnetic needle of a nearby compass oddly moving in its case. Suspecting some action taking place between the electric current and the magnetic needle, he observed that passing a coil of copper wire back and forth near the poles of a magnet produced an electric current in the coil. He theorized that the magnet produced a "field" of force in the space around the magnet that induced a current in the wires of the coil by their "cutting" the lines of force in the magnetic field. Iron filings spread over paper that was underneath a magnet produced a clear image of the lines of force composing the field. He then demonstrated the converse, that a magnetic field can be produced by a current. Electricity and magnetism were faces of the same physical force.

   Later in the century the Scottish physicist James Maxwell would give mathematical formulations to Faraday's basic discoveries and make a fundamental discovery of his own, that light was an electromagnetic wave traveling through space at 30 billion centimeters a second. Here the study of light and electromagnetism converged into new branches of scientific exploration, namely field physics and wave theory. Chemistry, electricity, magnetism and light were all folding into each other as forms of an underlying physical reality of energy and matter. Faraday's conceptualization of an electromagnetic field of force presented the German physicist Hermann von Helmholtz a point of departure in reasoning out a new branch of science called "field physics." If elements are atomistic, as it had been earlier reasoned out by Dalton working in chemistry, Helmholtz concluded electricity must be too, since each atom of an element (that is, charged atom of

From Copernicus to Darwin 139

an element, or ion as it is called, from Greek "I go," referring to the charged atom going to an electrolytic terminal) deposited at the terminal is carried there by an atom of electricity. The relationship Helmholtz drew between an electron as an atom of electricity and an electrically charged atom of an element provided the basis for modern electronic and atomic physics. Hermann von Helmholtz also reasoned out another basic law of science, the law of conservation of energy, that all forms of it, mechanical, heat, electrical and chemical, could be used to do work by exerting force and could be transferred from one form to the other and back again without loss, as long as such things as heat of friction and wire resistance were accounted for.

The science of heat, like those of the other forms of energy, was given a composite name coined from two Greek words. In particular, thermodynamics was the science of heat as available energy that could be put to work. Heat, in the form of steam, the driving force of the Industrial Revolution, was early in being analyzed and formulated into a mathematical science, thanks to the steam engine. With the development of thermodynamics came a new order of mathematical standardization of measurement and conceptual definition: temperature, graduated thermometers that measured it, caloric heat, latent heat of vaporization and condensation, steam tables, measurement of heat flow, radiation, conduction, convection – and entropy, that gloomy mathematical index of heat unavailable for work in a system. In any working system there is always a decrease in universal order, that is, a net increase in entropy, meaning a step closer to total disorder through diminishing order, or diminishing energy available for work, since no process is perfectly reversible. Entropy is always on the rise. Philosophically, entropy posits a determinist understanding of the universe as an ordered system that like all systems is irreversible and running down through energy loss and increasing disorder. One day the universe will become cold and dead.

Theories of Helmholtz and Joule, who between 1840 and 1850 mathematized the flow of heat and its relationship to temperature and work, provided the paradigm theorizers of electricity would follow. Electricity was a fluid, a stream of electrons flowing from one energy level to another. As heat flowed from a higher temperature to a lower, electric particles, electrons, flowed from a high level of charge to a lower. Between these paradigms and Newton's inverse square law relating force to mass and distance, scientists had several well defined patterns with which to ponder the mysteries of electrical phenomena. But it was through chemistry that scientists came to understand the underlying physical reality of electricity.

The birth of modern chemistry in the 19th century, as in electricity, was prepared by the seminal experiments and discoveries of 18th century scientists, Boyle, Priestley, Cavendish and Lavoisier. Their laboratory work collectively produced and isolated carbon dioxide, hydrogen, oxygen and chorine gas, and, a tremendous surprise to all, demonstrated water to be composed of two gases. A system of relating the two sides of a chemical reaction, that is, the state of reactants before the reaction and the state after, was established by Lavoisier, who also initiated the modern system of a chemical nomenclature and symbols. The experiments of John Dalton (d. 1844) at the beginning of the 19th century opened the way to a conceptualization of matter that revolutionized chemistry no less than Galileo, Kepler and Newton had astronomy and physics. The chemical combination of discrete quantities, or proportions, of elements suggested to Dalton that matter consisted of miniscule lumps bound together by a force of attraction. Oxygen combines with hydrogen to form water in a proportion of one to eight, with respect to weight. The proportions were later called combining weights. The Greek word "atom," that which cannot be broken, was revived from the materialist philosophy of Democritus and Epicurus in order to accommodate the materialist understanding of this lumpish combination of elements. A system of notation for the elements was then worked out in terms of relative mass, or atomic weight, that is, the units or multiples of units in which they combine. The close parallel between the affinity of an element to unite with another element, or chemical affinity as it was termed, and electric polarity of negative and positive charge, led to the discovery of the correspondence between chemistry and electricity. The chemical elements had valence, or potential electronic charge, metals being assigned by convention a positive charge, non-metals a negative charge, with inert elements being neutral. The marriage of chemistry and electricity in electrochemistry gave rise to electrolysis, which by the middle of the century had become an important process in the chemical and metals industries.

Measuring the volumes of two gases that chemically combine with each other, oxygen and hydrogen for example, led Gay-Lussac to the discovery that gases always combine in volumetric units. Avogadro came to understand the meaning of this, that every gas has a certain number of atoms per unit volume, so that equal volumes of gases contain a number of atoms that are in a similar ratio to each other, as in valence in relation to all the elements. By the middle of the century a formulation had been found relating the rate of chemical reaction and equilibrium points of reversible reactions to molecular concentrations and temperature of the reactants. Not long after, in Russia, Mendeljef produced his periodic table, an ascending order of the elements based on their atomic weight and graphically arranged in rows of eight in such a way that all the elements in a particular column could be distinguished as a group sharing similar characteristics in terms of their valence, of their degree of reactivity and of being metallic, non-metallic or inert. Each element was given an atomic number. Blank spaces in the table provided a hypothesis for undiscovered elements and their probable properties. This was in 1869, the year the Suez Canal was opened and imperial Britain sharpened its sights on Egypt as a stage on the way to India, and seven years before Beirut and Cairo collaborated in their public declaration of the earth moving around the sun, the former event indicating how the Middle East was being drawn into the network of imperial global interests, the latter how desperately behind Muslims were falling.

Organic chemistry mushroomed during the first half of the century to become a separate branch of science. The manufacture of organic chemicals and their many uses added to the expansion of the chemical industry, already growing owing to the many applications of electrolysis. Ammonia, urea, ethyl alcohol, glucose and fructose were industrially synthesized. An immense industry in hydrocarbon production developed beginning in 1865 with the German chemist Kekula's brilliant conceptualization of benzene's six carbon atoms being bonded in a closed hexagon – the imaginative shift from a linear to a closed configuration being as revolutionary in organic chemistry as was the Copernican shift in astronomy. During the last half of the century a large number of organic chemicals found in living matter were isolated and synthesized, leading to the bold assertion of materialist philosophers, and even some scientists themselves, that science could explain the beginning of the universe and everything in it, including life itself. Such unbounded enthusiasm for science, going back to the turn of the century, gave rise to the popular image of the fiendish scientist at work in his hidden laboratory, surrounded by bubbling distillations and bolts of electricity, where like a demented god he synthesized the monster that once given life could not be controlled.

With the chemical industry and the new Bessemer and Open Hearth processes, and electricity taking the place of steam as a source of machine-driving power, a second Industrial Revolution was in the making: generators, turbines, electricity, synthetic chemicals and steel replacing steam pumps, spinning jennys, textiles and iron. While the West was racing into the new age, the Middle East was struggling with the challenge of the old, still buying antiquated steam engines from England.

In 1831, the year Tahtawi returned from Paris having glimpsed a transformed western civilization with its heady science, Charles Darwin set off as ship's naturalist on *HMS Beagle's* charting expedition to Patagonia, Tierra del Fuego and the Galapagos Islands. His observations and mountains of data collected during the five-year journey were finally put together around a set of integrating principles and published almost a quarter century after his return, crowning the biological revolution that had been building for half a century before the *Beagle* set sail. Two of the three basic principles that constitute Darwin's evolutionary theory were by 1830 generally accepted by scientific circles and the much larger circle of aspiring amateurs from whom arose the professionals. One was that organic nature possessed the mechanism to change itself; another was that the earth had existed long enough for that mechanism, acting as it does very slowly over hundreds and thousands of generations, to have effected those great changes that to the naturalist are quite apparent; the third principle was Darwin's original contribution and brought the other two together in a grand unifying theory of biology that made sense of his great mountain of data: the principle of natural selection.

For a century before Darwin's voyage, a legion of amateur and professional naturalists had been busily at work collecting specimens of every kind, observing lakes, mountains, caves, exposed strata of rock, flora, fauna, minerals, marine life and insects, and digging into mud, clay and mountain to unearth bones of extinct animals. Caught up in the passion of scientific investigation, they collected everything that could be carried and made detailed sketches and descriptions of what couldn't. Specimens were preserved in alcohol, later in formaldehyde, as if they were still alive. Few men of comfortable circumstances were free of the fever of collecting specimens and describing nature. It was just this passion in France that produced at the end of the century the *Institut d'Egypte*, whose savants are described as being so busy collecting specimens that they were oblivious to the plagues, rebellions, lack of wine and boredom that made life hell for the soldiers.

Geological eras and animal kingdoms were defined and governing principles laid down to explain the formation of earth and life. If Newton could claim to see further than most men because he stood on the shoulders of giants, Darwin could have claimed to enjoy the same elevated vantage point. Four of his six main predecessors whose researches were the ascending steps offering a better view of the distant horizon were French: Georges-Louis de Buffon (d. 1788), Georges Cuvier (d. 1823), Jean-Baptiste Lamarck (d. 1828) and Etienne Geofrey St. Hilaire (d. 1844). The other two giants were the Swede Karl von Linné (d. 1778), known by his Latinized name Linnaeus, and Darwin's compatriot and older contemporary, Charles Lyell (d. 1875). They each produced a magnum opus, the cumulative effect of which was to define and organize geology and biology as modern sciences. Buffon's *Histoire naturelle* was in spite of its incompletion an encyclopedia of all geological and zoological knowledge. The first 22 volumes presented a detailed account of the earth's natural history, making Buffon the first naturalist to recognize that the earth's formation was a process that occurred in stages, geological epochs stretching over vast periods of time. The following nine volumes were on birds, which were meticulously drawn, described, classified and philosophically discussed in terms of their nature. Buffon's natural history brought together, also for the first time, the history of the earth and its animal forms, from birds to fish and everything between, and systematically organized all of this knowledge in a comprehensive and coherent way that was at once a thesaurus of information and scientific observation to the naturalist and easily accessible to the general reader. His implication, however, that the earth's long history was marked by violent upheavals and changes that killed off some species that once existed but no longer did, as he was led to believe by his long and careful observations, was most heatedly opposed, even by naturalists.

Born the same year as Buffon, the botanist Linné was simultaneously working out a structure of classifications, relationships and Latin nomenclature for all organic species. His *Systema Naturae* was another magnum opus of 18th century natural philosophy. It went beyond Buffon's botanical and zoological contribution by distinguishing species and systematizing the plant, animal and mineral kingdoms. In a century of scientific firsts that would lead to the crowning theories of the following century, Linné was the first to map out a comprehensive system that defined species and their relationships. His studies provided the foundation for the continuing bridgework of the great French triumvirate of naturalists, Lamarck, St. Hilaire and Cuvier.

Jean-Baptiste Lamarck, whose career overlapped that of Linné, studied invertebrates, from worms to mollusks. The ascending order of invertebrate life from simple to complex formed a paradigm for his general system of life, a vestige of Aristotelian biology in that he saw natural life to be neatly arranged in a tightly assembled biological progression of one species shading into the one above, as if striving to grow out of its form into the next higher. For Aristotle species were fixed. Forms did not change. Lamarck harbored the revolutionary conviction that species possess the power to change in form over a long period of time. Nature moved slowly and required geological epochs to effect the least noticeable change in any life form. Change was induced by the form itself through repeated use of an organ or the atrophying of one by lack of use. Change could result from change in environmental conditions, but change in a species always meant improvement, as if nature had a built-in mechanism working toward betterment of the species. Lamarck summed it up in a law of nature he called "inheritance of acquired characteristics," that is, any advantageous structural or functional variation in an organ of a life form is passed on to the offspring. How these advantages first come to be acquired Lamarck did not make clear. His was a mind more of daring theoretical expostulation and tidy organization than of painstaking accumulation of great masses of data exhaustively analyzed and explored in miniscule detail. He studied small things but thought big. His approach to science was diametrically opposite the methods of Buffon and Linné, who were only comfortable in the midst of prodigious quantities of specimens and endless comments and sketches filling piles of notebooks that could substantiate a conclusion, which was the accepted method. Fearing that the simple, general truths and coherence of nature would be lost in the forests of disconnected data and overly specialized detail that gave Buffon and Linné a security of conviction, Lamarck put forward his laws of nature, which to his critical peers seemed audacious, given that his ponderous conclusions were supported by what they considered a paucity of research. A complementarity may be seen in this: the painstaking researcher devoted to observing and gathering data, and the bold theoretician who with a minimum of evidence sees how nature should work.

Lamarck's generalizations were not out of the air. His research was reinforced by studies made by Linné and his younger contemporaries, St. Hilaire and Cuvier, particularly by Cuvier's work on invertebrates, which Lamarck incorporated in his own system of classification. Expanded from his 1801 work on the classification of vertebrates, Lamarck's *Histoire naturelle des animaux sans vertebretes*, which appeared in multiple volumes from 1815 to 1822, was the summation of his life's work on natural philosophy and became the standard 19th century reference for the study of invertebrates. Though a quarter century older than St. Hilaire and Cuvier, Lamarck learned as much from them as they from him. The research and hypotheses of the three eminent French scientists fed one into the other in spite of their conflict of philosophical orientation.

Geoffrey St. Hilaire had gained a reputation as one of France's leading naturalists by the time he was 26. A specialist in vertebrates, he was invited to join Bonaparte's expedition to Egypt and did. His equally young colleague, Georges Cuvier, another rising star in the French constellation of pioneering naturalists, declined the invitation. He wanted to remain in Paris to finish his research in progress, a comparative anatomy and system of classification that placed all animals into four distinct groups, replacing the linear system that linked all life in a sequential chain from the simplest and smallest to the most complex. Before the French adventure in Egypt was over, Cuvier had published his study on comparative anatomy, in which he argued that the structural and functional characteristics of organs in the body of an animal are a product of interaction with the environment. Rejecting Lamarckian evolution, he maintained that anatomical study of the different groups of animals proved that species had remained the same since creation. Animal species were so well fitted in their environment that any change would have destroyed them. Certain species of animals whose skeletal remains he himself had dug up, flying reptiles, giant lizards and extinct elephants, were according to him victims of natural catastrophes of tremendous geological change: floods, volcanoes, earthquakes, a theory that became known as catastrophism.

St. Hilaire meanwhile, having returned from his research on the flora and fauna of Egypt and resuming his work in France, adopted elements of Lamarck's theory of evolution. His study of vertebrate embryos led him to his principle of the unity of organic composition, meaning that no vertebrate organ arises or disappears suddenly. Great time is required. Vestigial organs proved as much. Corollary to this was that an organ grows disproportionately only at the expense of another organ. A vestigial organ is evidence of another's growth. Convinced by his embryonic studies of vertebrates that organs could fade away and disappear and others grow under the pressure of changed conditions in the natural environment, he came to champion evolution. This, and his principle that the parts of all vertebrates are positioned in the same relative pattern, were published in his groundbreaking two-volume *Philosophie anatomique*, which joined Lamarck's *Histoire naturelle des animaux sans vertebretes* as a standard reference in the field. When St. Hilaire applied his system to invertebrates, Cuvier, whose specialty was invertebrates, reacted. To suggest that vertebrates and invertebrates fell within the same classification violated his rigid separation of all animals in the four immutable groups in which he had classified them. In addition, St. Hilaire's acceptance of Lamarck's evolution contradicted Cuvier's firm belief that though species had died out from natural cataclysms, never could new ones arise, nor had they ever since creation. Species were fixed. They died out but never evolved.

The controversy between the former friends and collaborators divided the world of naturalists between supporters of one and of the other. Both scholars mustered all the evidence they could in defending their respective positions. The controversy between St. Hilaire and Cuvier energized public interest in the subject to a level higher than anything concerning science had entertained public attention during the previous half century. Theirs was one of the great debates in the history of science, but only a mild prelude of what was to come later in the century. As the debate between evolution and fixed species unfolded, young Darwin was preparing for his five-year voyage. Where he stood on the issue at the time even he did not know, but one of the books on naturalism that Darwin took with him was the first volume of the first edition of Charles Lyell's *Principles of Geology*. A student of life forms who was well-versed in Lyell's book might ask oneself: if earth evolved over eons, why not organic nature?

The geological studies of the Scotsman Charles Lyell were as profound in their implications to young Darwin as were the biological studies of Buffon, Linné, Lamarck, Cuvier and St. Hilaire. Geology and biology had much in common in that both were new fields of study in the modern context of science, both focused on changes that the earth and the forms of life that it supported had undergone and both were informed by principles set down as natural law that ran up against the accepted religious belief that creation occurred as told in the Book of Genesis. Lyell's long studies of rock formations and fossils in Britain and the continent convinced him, as it had Buffon, Lamarck, Cuvier and St. Hilaire, that natural forces had shaped the earth over an inestimably long time. Nature worked slowly but surely, and above all uniformly. Uniformity was most important. Nothing, according to Lyell, happened in sudden bursts of catastrophic destruction and transformation, as Cuvier's theory of catastrophism would have it. The French scientific community, many members of which looked as fondly on the Revolution of 1789 as had Napoleon for its having opened the gates of opportunity to talent and offered possibilities of a life richer than might otherwise have been available to them, was not as averse to theories of upheaval as was its insular counterpart across the channel.

Lyell's concept was clumsily called uniformitarianism and was as much a geological as political philosophy. His conclusions, supported, as was the custom, by mountains of data, were presented to the public in his *Principles of Geology*, published in three volumes from 1830 to 1833. The public was not put off by the tremendous amount of data and detail, nor the biblically unorthodox principles they supported. The public demand for the book repeatedly required that new editions be printed. Darwin took Lyell's first volume with him and received the other two volumes as they came off the press and were shipped to him as he sailed the *Beagle* from port to port in South America. He regarded the work, with its mountains of data and observations, as the naturalist's bible in scientific methodology. When he returned from his journey he began to put together his own mountains of data and observations, from which came his conclusions regarding the biological side of nature's power to change and the hundreds of thousands of generations required to do it.

Darwin's clue to natural selection came from a source quite outside the natural sciences, Thomas Malthus's *Essay on Population*, published in 1798. Darwin read the book the year after he returned to England, his mind filled with the variation of species he had seen on the Galapagos Islands and questions on how they came to be. Malthus's fatalistic thesis, that the discrepancy between population growth and food production condemns the poor to inescapable starvation, was the key. Translating geometric growth and competition for survival into the world of animal life, he struck upon the mechanism that could explain nature's way of producing variant species and of condemning to extinction those forms from which they had come during thousands of generations. Armed with the principle of natural selection, Darwin quietly put his supporting evidence together from the specimens he had collected and notebooks he had filled during his long voyage, and from what he continued to observe at home in England. Darwin knew his ideas would cause trouble. Being a gentle researcher who cherished peace and tranquility, he was in no hurry to have his work leave the quiet environment of rational discourse among fellow naturalists and friends for the stormy passions of public debate and accusations of heresy.

It was 25 years before he published, and only then did he agree to do so because a fellow naturalist, Alfred Russel Wallace, was about to claim the distinction of having discovered the principle of natural selection. The Royal Society arranged a joint presentation of the new theory and recognized Darwin and Wallace as co-discoverers, though Wallace graciously admitted his work was but a modest fraction of what Darwin had accomplished in empirically supporting the principle through his many years of analysis and reflection on the massive data he had collected.

When the *Origin of Species* was published in 1859, a public furor arose, compelling more and more people to read it, but apparently not the ones most vociferously condemning it – as with Copernicus's *de Revolutionibus*, not having read it was hardly a reason for not condemning it. Otherwise intelligent people, totally ignorant of the book's contents, proudly boasted they had not read it and never would, for why expose oneself to the blasphemy and stupidity of anyone who preached man came from a monkey? Darwin refused to engage in his defense. He kept quietly to his work, confident that the evidence would speak for itself once the hot heads had blown their steam and reason was allowed to be heard. Other less trusting naturalists took up the defense of natural selection in Darwin's place, the most vigorous, clever and outspoken of them being Thomas Huxley (d. 1895), his aggressiveness on the attack earning him the title "Darwin's Bulldog," a bulldog whose words were sharp as a knife. During an anti-Darwin lecture in Albert Hall, Bishop Samuel Wilburforce, thinking himself to be humorous, asked those in the audience to raise their right hand if they thought they came from an ape on their father's side, their left if on the mother's. Huxley rose from his seat saying in so many words that he would far prefer an ape for an ancestor than a fool who, instead of using the brains that God had given him, would rather choose to blather on against what he knew nothing about. The audience burst in applause.

In a relatively short time evolution came to be publicly accepted in England and on the continent. Darwin's longtime friend and colleague, the eminent geologist Charles Lyell, had opposed natural selection at first but came to accept it by 1865, Darwin generously remarking that to change ideas and admit error for a man of Lyell's age, social position and prior beliefs must not have been easy. The rest of the scientific community followed Lyell's example, the older generation grudgingly, the younger scientists wondering what the fuss was about. By 1880 the older generation had died out and evolution was no longer a problem of scientific or public concern in western Europe. As for religion in a scientifically mature age, bishops could easily claim God worked through natural selection, for God's ways were mysterious. Even when those ways were understood, there was a good market for theological books on the subject.

Darwin was the first scientist to give birth to a revolutionary principle that upset both religion and man's self-esteem and live to see it accepted. He died in the spring of 1882, by which time, as we have seen, his theory of natural selection and origin of species was in the initial stages of being introduced to Arab society.

Note

1 Wm. Dampier, *A History of Science and Its Relation with Philosophy and Religion*, Cambridge University Press, Cambridge, 1948, p. 296.

7 Shibli Shumayyil's Darwin

A theory for everything progressive

The flap over Copernicus no sooner reached its Fikri treatise milestone than another more volatile confrontation with Darwin broke over the horizon, as witnessed by the Lewis Affair.

Unfortunately the Muslim tradition in biology and comparative anatomy failed to offer a lead to modern evolution theory in any way similar to the way that the long tradition in Muslim astronomy did to the heliocentric theory. Classical Muslim science offered no credible purchase that allowed natural selection to be coaxed from the classical Arabic texts on animals by writers such as Dinawari, Jahiz and Qazwini comparable to the success that 19th century reformers had in coaxing Copernican theory from al-Biruni, Nasir al-Din al-Tusi and Qutb al-Din al-Shirazi. There was not much in the biological sciences that could be used to hook a connection between old and new, or to claim that the new was really the old in new dress, comparable to the powerful strain of creative Muslim astronomy that had existed up to the 16th century. Arab reformers nonetheless showed admirable imagination in this endeavor, finding as they did random remarks in centuries-old texts that they turned on the wheel of evolution in laying claim to priority of discovery. But for a handful of exceptions, mostly Syrian Christians associated with Syrian Protestant College, reformist thinkers in the 19th century tended to avoid evolution.

Not until the late 1880s did a few Muslims dare to consider evolution seriously. Those rare few who did were not well disposed to Darwin, but because of the steadily mounting evidence in support of natural selection, they neither rejected evolution out of hand, nor did they quite accept it. Two windows offered them an out, one opening to tentative acceptance, the other to non-rejection: Intelligent Design and insufficiency of evidence to close the case. Most Muslims (and Christians too) who discussed Darwin were absolutely hostile to his ideas, some of them fanatically hostile, to the point of willfully refusing to understand what Darwin was all about. "Man sprang from a monkey" said it all. The caricaturization was pervasive. Shibli Shumayyil, who studied evolution in France, from the wrong sources unfortunately, was the first to write extensively on it in Arabic. It was precisely this image of man suddenly emerging from the skin of a monkey that summed up everything he had heard about Darwin and evolution right up to the time he graduated from the American College Medical School in 1871.[1] The

Syrian Christian thinkers who made the effort to study and understand Darwin's principle of natural selection introduced the theory in the pseudo-philosophical garb of German materialism and Spencerian social Darwinism, pervasions of the theory that were probably more repugnant to the Muslim and Christian ulema than would have been a faithful translation of the *Origin of Species*.

Before 1916, any Arab who could not read a western language had precious little literature of a serious nature available to him on Darwin: no translations, no faithful commentaries, no analyses of natural selection. Other than the brief articles in *Muqtataf*, Arabic writing on evolution was barren of informed comment. In fact, it would be no exaggeration to say that between the late 1870s and the first decade of the 20th century, *Muqtataf* was the only reliable source. During the first few years of the journal's publication more than a dozen short articles appeared, notices rather, collectively covering about as many pages. The first piece of Arabic literature of any length and detail on evolution, of which there is any record, was published under the auspices of *Muqtataf* in 1879. The treatise was composed by Dr. Bishara Zilzal, the author of *Muqtataf's* earliest brief mentions of evolution. *Tanwir al Adhhan fi 'Ilm Hayat al-Hayawan wa'l Insan wa Tafawut al-Umam fi Madaniyya wa'l Umran* (loosely translated as *Illumination of the Mind Concerning the Biology of Animal and Man and the Successive Passing of Civilizations*) was, as the title suggests, a social and anthropological melding of Darwin and Spencer.

Bishara Zilzal was a Syrian Christian and early graduate of SPC's Medical School. Shortly after finishing his medical studies he settled in Alexandria, sometime during the late 1870s, about the time Shibli Shumayyil did.[2] Bishara Zilzal's book was first published in series by a press in Alexandria. The same press then put out a complete edition of it in 1879. According to its card catalogue, the Egyptian National Library has two copies, both of which appear to be lost. What the Egyptian National Library does have of it is the sixth and final part of the book published in its serial form, pages 313 to 368. The Library of Congress does not have a copy of the book, nor does any library in the West. The British Library has a record that a copy exists in the Jafet Library of the American University of Beirut, but that library has no record of having a copy, even though that was the institute Dr. Zilzal was associated with, back when it was Syrian Protestant College. Nor does the American University at Cairo have a copy. If the final section of the book is in any way representative of the preceding five sections, there can be no wonder about the reasons behind its scarcity.

The first half of Zilzal's book was on evolution, but from the content found toward the end of the sixth fascicule it was not the pure science of Darwin but rather a philosophical German version of it, that of Ernst Haeckel. In Zilzal's words: "And we have already indicated our opinion about those who say that man descended from monkeys, the most prominent of them being Haeckel, the philosopher who divides mankind into 12 basic types and 36 races which began with man-monkey and ended with the Indo–Germanic race." Dr. Zilzal took a favorable view of evolution, but in its Spencerian form, which provided him with a razor-edged scalpel of social criticism he used to lay bare what he thought to be the causes of Muslim weakness and backwardness, though he never refers to his society as Muslim but rather as "eastern."

Zilzal's analysis of his society's weakness centers on family structure and relations, the debased position of women, the absence of love and tenderness between husband and wife because of polygamy and the lack of care for children that results from the parental discord associated with polygamy. Predating by 20 years Qasim Amin's critical work on the Muslim family and the plea for women's liberation, his analysis begins with family relations in the West whose societies have produced the most powerful nations.[3] Germany is the strongest (he is writing only a few years after the Franco–Prussian war and Bismarck's proclamation of the new German Empire) because the German family is tightly bound together and children receive love, tenderness and care (*hubb wa hanan*). Anglo–Saxons come next. The French follow, but their family life is loosened by all kinds of unhealthy modes of behavior and dissipation that will eventually take their toll, taking them down the road of vanished tribes. The eastern family is far beyond the French in looseness and unhealthy practices. Easterners are debased. They have no real family life, no firm structure or bonding. Consequently, their children suffer from lack of care. Polygamy produces families whose children have different mothers. It drains away love and tenderness between man and wife, or man and wives. If husband or wife is afflicted, no care is given by one to the other, for no true bonding has taken place. Families fight and break up easily since divorce is easy. The children are deprived of love and parental care. Eastern society reflects the confused, weak and fragmented nature of the eastern family:

> That is why it is said easterners agree to disagree and unite so not to unite, because their social life is so scattered and fragmented in both its origins and its basis: the structure, or lack of structure, in the family in relation to children. Their decline goes back to the absence of rearing, training and educating children. It is no wonder easterners are in the pitiful condition they are in... Early marriage is another reason for decline, girls marrying even before reaching puberty. Even if marriage is delayed until after puberty, a young man is crushed to the ground with marriage expenses and the woman is worn out with all her pregnancies, which produce weakness of bodily structure and short longevity in children. And wretched poverty may lead to killing unwanted babies.[4]

He further criticizes eastern society by inferring that the position of women in it resembles their position in some primitive societies. Primitive bushmen in Africa, Australia and Tasmania treat their women as slaves, concubines and temporary wives, stripped of all dignity. Having received no affection or care, the women have none to transmit to their children.

It was a damning critique. Nothing like it had been published in modern Arabic literature. It was enough to drive people to cast it in the flames. Not only does the book strike at the very heart of Muslim law regarding marriage, family, women and divorce, but it offers a favorable view on evolution. This is implied in the last sentence of the sixth section where Haeckel is credited with having postulated that man originated from an animal species. It is a "theory much opposed, but the truth remains wandering out there somewhere, a cherished object still to be found by him who searches for it." It would be interesting to know if within the first five sections there is a commentary on natural selection according to Darwin and not to Haeckel or Buchner, and how aware the author was of the earlier works of Buffon, Cuvier, Linné, Lamarck and Lyall leading up to Darwin's theory. Until a copy of Zilzal's book turns up, *Muqtataf* will have to be accepted as taking the lead in presenting evolution to the Arab public as it was understood by Darwin.

Pummeled by the religious opposition coming from the Jesuits and American evangelists ensconced in their respective colleges in Beirut, the editors of *Muqtataf* always claimed to take a neutral position on evolution and, as they repeatedly assured, left it to the reader to decide the theory's veracity based on the evidence, though it was always clear to readers on what side of the issue the journal stood. Sarruf coined the Arabic terms to express the word evolution (*tatawwur*) and the phrase "struggle for existence" (*tanazu' al-baqa*). In light of the available literature, Sarruf and a handful of others writing in *Muqtataf* must take credit for having introduced Darwin's theory of evolution to Arab society without the trappings that social, economic and nationalist critics loved to pin on it.

Shibli Shumayyil was the first and most outspoken Arab proponent of evolution. It was he who wrote the first detailed book on it in Arabic, but his approach to evolution was the same as Bishara Zilzal's progressivist materialism borrowed from Ernst Haeckel. Shibli was not a good spokesman for Darwin. His radical materialism was directed critically more to society and politics than science. His being Christian made him an easy target as an intellectual lackey of European ideas. Arab Christians attacked him; Muslims ignored him. His professed atheism didn't help. His interpretation of Darwin through German materialist philosophy loaded the scales against natural selection being given a fair hearing, far more than they had ever been loaded against Copernicus. What possessed Shumayyil to go that route?

Before entering the Syrian Protestant College Shibli studied at a Jesuit school, St. Joseph College at Ayn Tura. Upon graduating from the SPC Medical School he went to Paris for two years to continue his medical training, but instead of medicine he studied the materialist philosophy of Ludwig Buchner and Ernst Haeckel in French translation. Haeckel's *Entwicklungsgeschichte des Menschen*, which had been published and translated into French just before Shibli's arrival in France, captivated the young scholar. It was this introduction that formed his off-center appreciation of Darwin. Haeckel was an exponent of polygenism: that there were many separate origins and independent lines of human evolution in isolation that accounted for the different races. Haeckel also coined new terms such as ontogeny, ontology and ecology, and he originated the erroneous principle that ontogeny recapitulates phylogeny, later corrected by the early embryologist Karl Ernst von Baer to become the principle of progressive specification and differentiation.

Shibli's captivation by philosophical materialism stamped his intellectual life forever and put an end to his career as a budding scientist. In the obituary Sarruf wrote upon the occasion of Shibli's death in 1917, he blamed SPC President Daniel Bliss for not encouraging and giving support to the College's prize science graduate in his quest to become a scientist.[5] That idea had no place in the American College's academic vision; and if it did, there was little chance of the administration supporting someone toward an advanced degree in science who was smitten by an interest in evolution. In any case, Shumayyil's intellectual and creative preferences tended more to literature, philosophy and social thought than they did to pure science. In this he was similar to Sarruf, who wrote several novels and translated Samuel Smiles's *Self Help*, and to Jurji Zaydan, whose youthful devotion to science changed direction to romantic historical fiction. Rather than a scientist, Shumayyil became a social critic, an intellectual revolutionary and a popularizer of a philosophical evolution that carried natural selection into areas beyond anything Darwin ever intended or would have tolerated. But Shibli's was a wise career choice. If he was going to return to the East, he would have more of a chance making a career for himself as a writer than a wretchedly paid science instructor in Egypt, for he could have expected no door open to him at the American College in Beirut while the evangelists were holding the fort against that satanic figure of Darwin spewing atheism paraded as natural science.

It was not the evangelists of the American College who cut short his career as a scientist. Shumayyil himself quite recognized the reality that no one in his generation would ever have the chance to do science in the Middle East. There was no social context for science. "Hardly anyone in the Arab World," he wrote, "is engaged in real science. Those who have the means to be scientists are lost in trivialities, too busy playing and enjoying themselves. So there can be no clubs, institutes or societies bringing people interested in science together." He hoped his generation's children would be able to take up science. But as for now, all that he and his colleagues could do was prepare the way by writing to revolutionize society and its thinking.[6] His writings were influential, but only with those few who shared his radical social philosophy or read him in their tender youth before their minds had become formed, filled and sealed. By preaching the iron laws of materialist evolution and the inevitability of social, economic and political revolution, he found his place at the extreme margins of Arab intellectual society. Influencing some, he frightened and repulsed the mainstream that he hoped to enlighten and convince.

Boldly original in a bizarre way, Shibli Shumayyil's ideas had always been on the far side. As a 17-year-old entering SPC's Medical School he had decided to take no science courses, only medical, because he was convinced that the way science was taught tyrannized the mind by the emphasis scientists put on the laws of science. Laws fenced off the open frontiers that nurtured creative imagination and discovery. A mind cluttered with scientific laws would not be able to think clearly or freely. One is in a quandary what to make of this. Medicine without science? A mind preserved its freedom to discover by being innocent of science? Knowledge of scientific laws destroyed the mind's possibilities of finding new knowledge? This is what he writes about his regard of science as a student: "My studies in school did not poison my mind. I didn't read a thing about the exact sciences which they say broadens the mind but which I believe shrinks it, and it was this that saved my independence of thought."[7] Was this some unique form of Cartesian genius or just the infantile babble of an undergraduate trying to be original? Shibli believed that it was this freedom of mind he preserved at SPC (by not studying science) that allowed him to embrace Darwin wholeheartedly when he discovered evolution theory in Paris. The problem was, he did study science at SPC, and it was not Darwin he discovered in Paris, it was Haeckel and Buchner in French translation.

What he may have meant by his strange ideas on keeping a clear and open mind is that he avoided the evangelist orientation of science that would have made him dead set against unorthodox ideas. Unfortunately for his clarity of mind, young Shibli had to study science at SPC if he was to be a physician. He studied chemistry, biology and physics, but he may in his own bizarre definition of things have considered these to be medical subjects and not scientific since they were listed in the medical curriculum.

In spite of all this anti-establishment rant that he wrote in his memoirs long after his student days, he was quite keen on science during his four years at SPC, graduating first in his class. His ability in, and passion for, science was expressed in publications. In 1871, the year of his graduation, having just turned 21, he contributed three short articles on electricity in Bustani's *Jinan*.[8] Electricity, he wrote, was one of three physical matters that had no weight: light and heat were the other two. His referring to them as matter rather than energy reveals even at that early period in his life his tendency toward the thorough-going materialism that would infuse his scientific speculations. He traces man's interest in electricity back to Thales, who discovered that rubbing wool on amber produced an attracting force. From the word "amber," "elektra" in Greek and "kahrab" in Persian, came the words for this mysterious force in the western and Islamic languages. He follows the history of electricity through Gilbert, Franklin, Galvani, Volta, Ampere and Faraday.

From his descriptions of Galvani's experiments on frogs and electricity he appears to have accepted a relationship between electricity and life and the material basis of both, although he had not at the time accepted evolution. His medical dissertation, "On the Variations of Animals and Man in Relation to Climate, Nourishment and Education," shows the direction of his scientific and philosophical interests, yet he admits to having had an aversion for the theory of evolution at the time. His claim to an aversion is surprising. Young Shibli was so at odds with received ideas and what everyone else believed that it might be thought the administration's condemnation of evolution, and forbidding of the mere utterance of the name Darwin except in a pejorative sense, would have been enough for him to embrace absolute belief in the theory without his having the faintest clue what it was about. But no, the associations that had accumulated in the Beirut and SPC atmosphere were so powerful and so skewed that when by chance the word "evolution" or Darwin was mentioned the only image it evoked in Shibli's mind was that of a man climbing out of a monkey's skin.[9]

Though he was ignorant of natural selection, materialism was already a fundament of his thinking before he came into contact with Buchner's theories in Paris.

While a medical student, and for some years after, he was a serious believer in spontaneous generation, that life can arise from organic matter, proving that the origin of life occurred, or could occur, without the aid of any supernatural agency. Chemical transformation had the power to give birth to life, like maggots being born from decaying meat or cheese. Here was proof that pure matter, mother of all, was the source and agent in the genesis of life.[10] Shumayyil was still writing in support of the theory when he set off for Paris.

The *Origins of Species* had been in print 16 years when Shibli arrived there. Every year since the publication of Darwin's first book evidence had been coming to light in support of natural selection, which by the mid-1870s was becoming accepted in Europe, not only by the specialists in the scientific community but by educated people in general. Shibli was impressed by the careful and methodical observations and enormous collections of data by a century of Europe's greatest scientists, whose conclusions were supported by the rapidly expanding field of geology. Shibli claimed to have studied Darwin and Huxley during his year in Paris. If so, he interpreted them through Spencer, Buchner and Haeckel, all neatly packaged as an ideal scientific philosophy for an Arab cultural revival. Not science, but mid-19th century progressive philosophy was the focus of his study: Darwin Perverted. No book of Darwin or Huxley did he mention that he read while in Paris, nor in England where he had a short stay visiting his businessman brother, who was residing there at the time. His contact with Darwin's natural selection was through a glass darkly. His mission was not to make himself into a scientist but to culturally transform the Arab East, and for this he propounded a philosophy of non-violent social revolution that would come through an intellectual evolution fed by growing scientific awareness. Shumayyil packed as much wish fulfillment into his materialist speculations as nationalists of another generation would in their philosophy of Arabism, and today's political Islamists in their revolutionary ideology of a Quranic society.

The defining corpus of Shibli's intellectual output was accomplished very early in his career, in the mid-1880s, when he was in his 30s and living in Egypt. When he returned from Paris he founded a journal, no doubt in emulation of Sarruf and Nimr. He called it *al-Mustaqbal* (*The Future*), which the journal failed to have, folding after a year. He set up medical practice in Tanta, then Alexandria, where he founded a medical journal, *al-Shifa*, which did not last long but won him an Ottoman Imperial Medal, Third Class, from Sultan abd al-Hamid for service to science and medicine.[11] In 1884 he published his first book, *Sharh Buchner 'ala Madhhab Darwin* (*Buchner's Commentary on Darwin's Theory*). The book was a paraphrased version made from a French translation of Ludwig Buchner's *Die Darwinische Theorie von der Entstehung und Überwandlung der Lebenwelt*, which was a series of lectures Buchner gave at conferences between 1866 and 1869. Auguste Jacquot's translation was made in 1869 as *Conferences sur la theorie darwinienne de la transmutation des especies et de l'apparition du monde organique*. Shumayyil neglected to specify which book of Buchner's he translated, let alone mentioning that it was a paraphrase of a French translation.

Shumayyil's casual approach to his work has resulted in much confusion. It is popularly believed that the book he translated was the French translation of

Buchner's *Kraft und Stoffe*, published in 1855 and translated into French several years later as *Force et Materie*.[12] The negligence that he showed in failing to mention the title of what he translated, and the language he translated it from, is reflected throughout the book, in omitted dates, names and pages, and in his putting Huxley where he meant Haeckel.[13] Why Shumayyil would bother to translate a second rate derivative philosophical work rather than Darwin's scientific classic is at first puzzling. Bishara Zilzal, who was there in Alexandria with him and who seemed to be more familiar with the German materialist philosopher Ernst Haeckel than with Darwin, could possibly have put him onto the other German materialist; or it could have been that Shumayyil brought the French translation of Buchner's lectures back with him from Paris and decided to translate them in Alexandria, finding in them scalpels of social criticism no less sharp than those Zilzal had put to such cutting effect in his own book. The paucity of collected letters, autobiographies and personal memoirs makes it hard to fill in the blanks.

His translating a derivative work of a German philosopher-naturalist rather than advancing scientific knowledge among Arabic readers by providing them with a translation of Darwin's *Origin of Species* must have been a matter of preference in his priorities for achieving social transformation. Rather than translating a scientific text, he wanted to provide a scientific philosophy for that transformation. Temperament may also have been a factor in his choosing Buchner. A philosophically free-minded student who had a penchant for poetry and valued the great classics of Arabic literature, Shumayyil may have found in Buchner's principles of force, matter and evolution a personally appealing philosophical analysis of universals that was made to order for laying bare the causes of Arab social and intellectual retrogression and for providing a theoretical scaffolding to reverse it.

That Shumayyil was considered a pioneer who for more than a quarter century waged what amounted to a one-man war to bring Darwin's evolution of species into the intellectual mainstream shows how distant Arab thinkers were from the original sources. Not until 1918, a year after Shumayyil's death, was the *Origin of Species* translated, and only the first half of it. A second edition of the Egyptian Ismail Mazhar's translation was made ten years later, and this edition contained four more chapters. Not until 1964, more than a century after the *Origin* first appeared, was a full Arabic translation made.[14] It was not a best seller. A copy is impossible to find in Cairo's leading bookstores, in Arabic or any language, though denunciations of Darwin are readily available in innumerable books. Egypt's National Library has only the last half (chapters 7–15) of Ismail Mazhar's translation of the *Origin of Species*, and no edition of the *Descent of Man*.[15]

Shumayyil's contribution was nonetheless significant, coming as it did only eight years after evolution was first mentioned in Arabic letters. His paraphrase translation and commentary of Buchner's lectures offered the reader a 300-page narrative on science from its ancient and medieval origins to modern evolution theory, from Linné, Lamarck and Lyell to Darwin, Huxley and Tyndall, neatly wrapped in the materialist and social spin-offs of Buchner, Haeckel and Spencer. No more than 500 copies of Shibli's book were printed and sold between 1884 and

1900, but that was more than enough to win him much notoriety. His intention that the book be controversial and shock people into waking up to modern science was half fulfilled. In the small circle of people who read it there was plenty of controversy, but the awakening it caused was not as much to science as to its perversity, if Shumayyil's book was taken to represent science.

As a history of science, the book, the first half of it at least, had its merits. It reviewed all the major discoveries in astronomy; electromagnetism; optics; spectroscopy as a means of measuring stellar distances and detecting the presence of known and unknown elements; atomism from Democrates to Dalton and Wm. Thompson; and the principle of chemical combining in fixed proportions of elemental particles or atoms; as well as the theory of the universal ether, that ethereal ocean of subtle matter that filled the universe and by its swirling currents carried the planets along in their orbits and transmitted light waves through space. It was the second half of the book that caused the controversy. It focused on Darwin's evolutionary theory as interpreted by Buchner, who theorized the unity and interchangeability of matter and energy in all its forms – gravity, heat, light, motion, electromagnetism – a grand unified theory of everything that bundled chemistry, physics, biology, geology and cosmology in a philosophy of materialism that explained absolutely all. Everything in the universe was reduced to matter and energy, while creation and eternal soul were absolutely denied.

Life and its origins were explained as a complex form of energy composed of heat, motion, growth and nourishment. Life and matter were interchangeable and indissociable – proved by the fact that a human head severed from the body could continue to think and see as long as enough blood remained in the head. The proof of this was based on a story reported in a French scientific journal about a French physician in North Africa who witnessed a beheading. According to the physician's account, before a profusion of blood had started flowing from the severed neck, he saw the fluttering eyes of the victim and their profoundly mournful and painful look as they followed those of the physician who was moving to the side. The dying head in the sand was aware of its condition and expressing it by its eyes. Life remained in the severed head as long as it contained sufficient blood to sustain the senses. "And all of this indicates that life is not an essence stripped of matter, and that the interaction of life and matter is very much like a chemical reaction with respect to fixity and exactitude."[16]

The material origin of life, combined with nature's evolutionary impulse, and the cosmic unity of being, produces a dynamic reformulation of the Aristotelian chain of being:

> Consider the world of formation, how it begins with minerals then progresses to plants and then animals by a system of degrees and stages. The last on the horizon of minerals is connected to the first on the horizon of plants, and the last of the plants is connected to the first of animals. The meaning of connection in this forming of beings is that the last of one sphere of being is ready to become the first in the next realm of being and ends with man, possessor of thought and speech.

The source of life was protoplasm, a universal substance that was to biology what the ether was to the mechanical system of physics, and phlogiston to chemistry. Life originated from protoplasm and evolved into its many forms. Species developed one from the other over a long period of evolution. To those who deny evolution because it reduces God's power, the reply is, "If one who creates a watch is great, then the one who makes a watch that makes a watch is even greater."[17] As Laplace had said, the system of nature made God a redundant hypothesis. The riddle of the origin of life could now also rid itself of the hypothesis.

So then, Shibli asks, how did life on earth begin? Possibly from some form of protozoa from a stellar body that crashed into earth. And where did that protozoa come from? From the right combination of elements and physical conditions to produce the initial chemical reaction in a chain of reactions leading to the simplest form of life. It could have occurred on earth. The human species came millions and millions of years after the initial chemical reaction in the heat and sunlight of the primordial swamp and after the work of natural selection. Thousands and thousands of years after the evolution of man, civilization arose. This too was the work of evolution. Its work was never finished. "Men today are in an intermediate state between true man and animal."[18]

Humans have another stage to go in their evolution. Consciousness has yet to be completed in order for national, cultural and linguistic divisions to fall, private property to disappear and unity of being to be achieved in its global socio-political context. "Already the power of science and industry has reduced distances between civilizations, connected the world and made French, English and German the world's languages." The language that first divests itself of the frivolities of literature, humanities, theology and law, and invests itself with the language of science, would be the language of the fittest in the struggle for survival and become the world language.[19] This would be French, Shibli was sure, writing in the 1910 edition of his book. The French had a long way to go, but they were in the lead and would one day rid themselves of the shameless buffoonery of La Fontaine, Rabelais, Racine, Moliere, Voltaire, Condorcet, Rousseau, Dumas and Hugo in order to sober up their language in the pure tonic of science.

The Arabs had yet to begin the process. Shibli lamented the fascination of Egypt's literate youth with French novels. He was distressed over the lack of interest that young Egyptian men and women showed in science.[20] As for older educated Egyptians who had a philosophical turn of mind, these types would anywhere else have been natural recruits for scientific endeavor, but in a country like Egypt the only thing that the intellectual elite did was waste their time and their mental energy in futilities, in useless flights of theological fantasy, where minds were chewed up in scholastic dialectics and nothing was done or determined other than deepening the religious divisions of a society already divided and under foreign occupation.

Shibli felt obliged to hold the mirror of the failings of his Egyptian hosts up to them in a light that most harshly reduced them. Egyptians were too wrapped up in mental fantasies of past heroes, of worshipping rulers and scholars and antiquated ways of thought, for them to have any mind or patience for the work of the present and its demands of mastering science and technology, and getting down to hard physical and mental work. Egyptians preferred to rest, to indulge themselves in pleasure and delights, and to lose their minds in sterile dreams and barren imagination. As for the Arabs in general, he concluded, echoing Tahtawi writing half a century earlier, their thinkers filled many pages with beautiful, complex bombast but said little, as if the object of writing was not meant for clarity and understanding but only to display knowledge of difficult and rare words, clever turns of expressions and juxtapositions of words to effect pleasing sounds and rhythms.

Such was the nature of Shibli Shumayyil's critical additions to his paraphrase with commentary of Buchner's lectures. In a perverse way that the author probably expected, his translation achieved its goal: it shocked most of those who read it, but none more than the pious Christians of Syria who were provoked to such an incandescent furor that Shibli was fortunate to be in Alexandria. A book professing a materialist philosophy that made a point of denying, or rather reducing to irrelevance, God, spirit, soul and creation was not going to have many readers or printings in a religiously oriented society. One might have expected that the bitter criticism the book received from the Catholic and Protestant authorities in Beirut would have sent any Arab who could half read rushing to steal, borrow or buy a copy. But the interest it aroused in science and evolution theory was nugatory. Shibli's biggest accomplishment was to provide the opponents of evolution with a book that gave textual substantiation to their accusation that the theory was immoral and atheistic.

In response to his critics, Shumayyil wrote a smaller work on evolution, *al-Haqiqa* (*The Truth*), an 86-page treatise, 62 of which were taken from the first book.[21] Here he reviews the empirical foundations of natural selection but is still unable to divorce Darwin's theory from progressive materialist philosophy. Answering his Christian critics in Beirut, he accuses them of falling back on religion because of being unable to think for themselves: "We don't act like children and accept the ideas because our fathers accepted them. Those who know little or nothing of the universe are subject to the most radical fantasies of imagination."[22] In answer to his Muslim critics he paraphrases Ghazali: "If this [evolution] makes you doubt your inherited belief, that is good enough, because without doubt there is no sight, and without sight there is no understanding, and without understanding there is only blindness and confusion."[23]

Shibli uncharacteristically tried to deflect religious criticism by including God in a restatement of evolution theory in his little *Haqiqa* treatise. God is given center stage, creating and directing life through its successive stages of evolution. However, matter is still eternal and uncreated: it is still the underlying principle of existence that gives rise to nature through its own innate energy and interactions. God's place in nature's self-sufficient processes is that of a conductor of a self-directing symphony. So then, if not totally redundant, where did God come in? Through mysticism! As if Shibli wasn't sufficiently contradictory, buried underneath flamboyant radical materialism was a crypto-mystical streak that now and then peered out from the crypt. He had a penchant for the 13th century Andalusian mystic ibn 'Arabi,[24] whose poetry he cited and whose pantheist naturalism paralleled his own, minus the divinity part of it – except when Shibli was pressed to defend himself against the religious folk. When that happened, evolution turned out to be not purely materialist: "God, as ibn 'Arabi said, is in everything. The power of existence and adaptation is in the matter of living things, but God is there too, as Creator . . . a God whose true religion of mankind is science."[25]

Who knows what Shibli took for truth inside his own head. He might well have believed with the medieval mystic that the divine essence, insubstantial in itself, gave rise to life through the matter it infused. After all, the Jesuits and Lazarists of Ayn Tura had him for years as a secondary student, and young Shibli couldn't have gotten away from them with a mind totally free of the Almighty. At the center of his and ibn 'Arabi's systems is the absolute unity of existence, *wahdat al-wujud*, the mystic's God expressed in terms of matter, primary qualities, spirit, mind, essence, soul, levels of consciousness, love and reality, all of which in Shibli's mystical unity of being corresponded to energy, matter, heat, magnetism, electricity, light, gravity, desire, life and love: variant forms of universal existence. An argument could possibly be made that Shibli brought God into his system not just as defensive stuffing or to deliver modern science to the believers, but out of his own inner conviction: a closet Sufi whose mysticism was an embarrassment to his materialist science. May Ziadeh, a Lebanese writer and poet living in Paris who was a good friend of Shibli's, accused him of as much, and he didn't deny it. Shibli did not publicly express himself in any depth about personal spiritual beliefs, for this would have gone against his public persona as a philosopher of science and progress, to which anything having to do with theology, mysticism and the spiritual world were impediments, regressions to scholastic medievalism. It is not surprising Shibli should have found in ibn 'Arabi, of all the earlier Arab philosophers, a soul mate. Both were intellectual rebels at the edge of heresy, ibn 'Arabi as far out in his times as Shibli in his, their minds consumed in a transcendent unity of existence.[26]

At the apex of Shibli's chain of being is man, the most complexly structured animal in the hierarchy of organic existence. Man, having evolved, remains in a continuing process of teleological evolution directed toward perfection of his intellectual powers. This stage of evolution brings the human species into harmony with nature, with man and civilization concurrently being refashioned in what could be called an ecological eclecticism of Darwinized Aristotelianism cast in a mystical process of pantheistic unity of being, where man's final goal in existence is his consciousness striving to attain perfection and happiness. By becoming one with the universal whole, man achieves ecstatic fulfillment of purpose, the mystical joy of being, of which the late naturalist Eisley Lauren and Jesuit theologian Jacques Monod wrote so profoundly. As nature evolves by the innate force of matter, human consciousness also evolves, lifting man ever higher toward that blessed joy of cosmic wholeness, with society being perfected along with man, until mankind and cosmos resound with the joy of completion in an earthly paradise: an eclectic cocktail of St. Augustine, ibn 'Arabi, Karl Marx and Greenpeace:

> The melding of matter, selection in plants, comprehension in matter, and human will power come together – under one force, call it what you will – life, heat, electricity, light, movement, gravity, sensation or love. They are all one essence.[27]

In the epilogue of the 1910 edition of his Buchner book Shibli writes that the evolution of species is not a contradiction to belief: "Faith is too large to be opposed by the theory of evolution." He confidently predicts that evolution will be accepted in Arab and Muslim society just as it has been in England, France and Germany. "The opponents of Darwin's theory are diminishing. Perhaps it will take no more than a quarter of a generation before opposition to evolution in Europe and the Middle East will fade away to nothing . . . since the laws of nature governing evolution and the coming-to-be of man, and all the laws of the motions of the universe reveal God in a more majestic and powerful light. Which one is it that glorifies God the most, the system that has God turning the outer sphere of the ancients with a ceiling set in gold nails, or the one of infinite worlds united by a universal law of attraction?" It is "incumbent upon us," he concludes, "that we be not mistaken by believing that if God is close to our hearts he must then be distant from our minds."

God can be known by the mind's grasp of science, the divine mind engraved in nature. As for evolution, what does it have to do with religion? Since it is not known when the soul is imparted to man, whether at conception, at birth or after a month or a year, it makes no difference as far as faith is concerned if man descended from an earlier form of life. "If it is not known when the soul enters man as an individual, why should faith be concerned about when it enters the species?" He credits Darwin for the argument.

As a Lebanese Christian, Shumayyil could live peaceably in Cairo and publicize a philosophy that made of science a religion that abrogated the old scriptural religions of the prophets. But it is doubtful he served science beyond inspiring several young philosophically minded writers, infatuated like himself by the aura of science but not so inspired they would devote themselves to studying it seriously. The publicity he gave evolution produced many times more enemies for it than supporters, but at least his books imparted some commotion to intellectual life regarding science and evolution in the region. Referring to the Edwin Lewis crisis of 1882 in his *al-Haqiqa*, which came out a few years after the incident, Shibli claimed not to be surprised by the irrational hostility of the American College's evangelical president, whose stern character stamped the moral tone of the institution. He described Daniel Bliss as a crusader who exemplified western Christianity's evolution to a religion of unbridled power based on egoism and arrogance in its effort to subdue and dominate the earth and the individual. This was unlike eastern Christianity. Here the religion retained the spirit of Christ since the roots of the eastern Church were deep in the cultural soil of the land that gave birth to Christ and Christianity. Rome and its imperial arrogance transmogrified western Christianity.

But in these modern times there was only one true religion, the religion of modern man: of science and freedom, where religion was secular law and social justice. Any system of government and society that was opposed to science perverted social justice and freedom into theocracy and despotism, two oppressors that arm in arm crushed the human spirit, forbade critical thinking and supported a self-serving system of unjust law. Only when law became a science, that is, an abstraction of universal natural principles, only then would man be able to live in harmony with himself, his fellow men and nature. "Such a system would spring from the same principle as the laws of nature: that all things were in process of differentiation and change . . ."[28] For eastern society to advance, science had to be embraced religiously. For this to happen, the powers of conservatism and tyranny had to be swept away. The state had to be free of the old religions whose leaders divided people and diminished the possibility of a general will that united the people and empowered society to advance. Since religion could never be free of its leaders, religion must be separated from the state and disempowered. The weaker that religion was in the affairs of the state and society, the stronger were the people and their state, and the more prominent would be the place of science as a paradigm shaping social institutions, government and values.[29]

In the cases of historical Islam and medieval Latin Christianity, it was an alliance of the religious leaders and political rulers that weakened their societies. The fault was not religion but, in the case of Islam, the shaykhs who manipulated the mass of Muslims for their own selfish interests. They were the root causes of corruption and weakness. Islam as a religion did not corrupt itself. Structures and principles did not corrupt themselves. Only living things were corruptible. Institutions, belief-systems, organizations: they did not corrupt themselves; the people running them did, people living in a set of social, economic and political conditions, the social environment. The atheist mystic Christian Shumayyil came to the defense of Islam when Lord Cromer, the British pro-consul of Egypt, attacked it as a decayed system of society and government that had utterly failed. Shibli corrected him. It was the ignorant ulema and Azhar shaykhs who had failed, not the religion or scripture. Ideas, systems and institutions did not corrupt. People corrupted.

Not until the humanly corrupted elements associated with religion and political institutions were swept away would society be able to progress. The West was no different. Even with its secularized state and high level of science, the West still had its problems with the excesses of misunderstood religious belief. When Ernst Buchner published his *Kraft und Stoffe* in 1855, the book created such a storm of disapproval because of its denial of God, creation, religion and free will that the author had to resign his post as lecturer in medicine at the University of Tubingen. Political tyranny and corrupted religion went together. One could not exist without the support of the other. They were joined, wedded in the corruption of mutual self-interest.

Shumayyil was himself so passionately wedded to this image of the two-headed tyranny that he composed a long poem dedicated to Sultan abd al-Hamid in 1896, called *Shakwa wa Amal* (*Complaint and Hope*). The poem encouraged the sultan to remove the corruption at the highest levels of government that doomed the empire, for only at the head could reform begin to restore health to the state. Decline could eventually be checked by supporting science education and spreading the spirit of science through the empire, since it was from science that came the health of a society. It was from the spirit and culture of science that came the freedom to think and live in a state secured by justice. Lack of science meant lack of health. A society that was not infused by the scientific spirit was diseased, its roots of justice, freedom and liberty withered, its soul dead. Such a society suffered cultural dementia and was doomed to extinction. At the moment, the corrupt body of the Ottoman state was waiting to be devoured by European scavengers. Writing from the safety of British-ruled Egypt, Shibli felt free to publicly tell the sultan in so many verses he was a rotten tyrant ruling a rotting empire. Sultan abd al-Hamid did not respond.

As much as his materialist evolution turned people off for spiritual reasons, Shibli's revolutionary socialism turned them off for materialist reasons even more. It was inevitable, he preached, that private property would be abolished. The same laws of force and matter that governed biological evolution applied to society. Progressive social change driven by evolutionary laws would make private property a thing of the past. Private property and capitalism would go as surely as the dinosaurs had gone. National borders and cultural barriers would also go as science progressed, as human consciousness expanded, as civilization became global and as religion found salvation not in a Judaic Mt. Sinai or a Christian Mt. Calvary or a Muslim Mt. Arafat, but in a universal science.[30] Shibli perversely enjoyed being a minority of one. Certainly he was the only Arab in Egypt when the Suez Canal concession came up for renewal in 1909, and the fever of nationalism was on the rise, who advised the Egyptian government to extend the concession to the Europeans until 1968 and use the money in receipt of the concession for social welfare, since long before 1968 ever arrived the inevitable advance of science and consciousness would have swept borders, nations and private property into the dustbin of history.[31]

Though Shumayyil probably contributed more to the development of socialist ideas in the Arab world than he did to the advance of scientific interest, he was as much a maverick in his socialism as he was in his materialism. When it came to women in society, his evolutionist radicalism of social progress underwent a surprising reversal. Instead of the role of women being uplifted by the rising tide of progressive socialism and broadening consciousness, as socialist and communist ideologues prophesied, Shibli turned it upside down and pasted onto it a staunchly traditional face. Women were intellectually inferior to men since their brains were lighter, and so they had no need of education. Applying progress to women would be a total economic loss. Social resources would be wasted trying to teach them anything. Sexual equality is found only in primitive societies. Civilization, the work of men, put women where nature meant them to be, in bed or the kitchen, barefoot and pregnant. The more civilization advanced, the more inferior became women's position in it, as it should be. Progressive thinking was possible only with men.[32]

His views on women shrink his whole philosophy into a bizarre caricature of itself: Shumayyil the evolutionist and progressive radical deleting half of mankind out of existence, even as Muslim reformers were beginning to speak of mental equality between the sexes and the vital role that female education played in social revitalization. His position on women was as contradictory to the sources of his intellectual formation as it was in stark contrast to the liberal environment of his friends and professional associates. The example of his friend, May Ziadeh, residing and writing in Paris, should have been enough to disabuse him of his perverse judgment. His dear friends, the editors of *Muqtataf*, were always plugging intellectual equality, publishing articles on women scientists, inventors, doctors and musicians, women who broke with tradition and family, who made successes of themselves and contributed to civilization. Sarruf claimed his wife to be an indispensable helpmate as a science editor. Shumayyil's wife was an educated and talented woman. Did he mean to bring the issue of women out in the open by being as perversely provocative as he was in his writings on evolution, socialism and materialism?

The heat Shibli generated came mainly from Christians in Beirut and was directed as much against *Muqtataf* for publishing him as against what he wrote. No sooner had his Buchner book come out in July 1884, than it was attacked by Dr. Samuel Jessup of the American College, joined by Ibrahim Hourani, editor of the weekly newspaper of the Beirut evangelists, *al-Usbu'iyyah*. Ibrahim Hourani, a powerful religious voice in the Christian community, had initially defended Dr. Edwin Lewis two years earlier during the controversy over the commencement address he had given, but whereas Lewis had said nothing in the address challenging religion, Shumayyil's version of Buchner's book was an all-out lethal assault on it. It changed Reverend Hourani's opinion on Darwin's theory not being in contradiction to religion. Hourani claimed not to have understood the theory until reading Shumayyil's book, but he may have in fact understood it and been misled by the materialist philosophy Shumayyil stuffed into it. In any case, Shumayyil's book converted Shaykh Hourani from a supporter to a harsh critic. It may not have crossed Reverend Hourani's mind to read Darwin and then reach his own conclusion. But where would he have found a copy? Cornelius and William Van Dyck would have had one, but they had left the evangelists and SPC two years before Shibli's book appeared.

Shibli's book marked the point at which Shaykh Hourani and the Arab evangelical community joined the American evangelicals in their adversarial posture toward Shumayyil and the editors of *Muqtataf*. It was an unfortunate loss for the cause of Darwin's ideas being given a fair hearing. Shaykh Ibrahim Hourani's word carried much weight in the Christian community. He was also highly regarded by the Muslim ulema in Syria. A friendly biographer and fellow countryman writes that Ibrahim Hourani had nothing to do with religious zealotry or fundamentalist scripturalism, that it was his knowledge of the sciences, philosophy, theology and language, combined with his character and general erudition, that brought him to the head of the Evangelical Church in Beirut.[33] Hourani was familiar with science. He had studied physics, astronomy and mathematics when a secondary student, and he was said to have enjoyed problems in physics, mathematics and philosophy. He even composed short treatises on modern astronomy, algebra, trigonometry and cubic equations.[34] His could have been the calming voice that called for Darwin to be weighed on the scales of reason. Instead, Ibrahim Hourani answered Shibli's book with one of his own in rejection of evolution.

Hourani was not the only loss. The Muslim ulema in Syria and Egypt did not ignore the stance taken by the Arab Christian religious leadership in regard to science. They assumed that what was unacceptable to one religion was most probably unacceptable to the other. A Damascene Muslim named Ahmad Sa'ati wrote a refutation of Shibli's materialism.[35] And from the Christian side, a Beiruti Maronite priest, Jirjis Faraj, wrote a book attacking Shibli on evolution.[36] More attacks would follow as the debate expanded with the growing number of journals founded in the 1890s and after.

In leading the attack against Shumayyil, Hourani identified evolution as a vicious heresy and denial of God. Writing in the *Evangelical Weekly*'s first issue of August 1884, he launched a harsh attack on Shumayyil in a piece called "The Ways of Wise Men in Rejecting Evolution." It likens the theory of evolution and the men who follow it to "a plague, an army of devils unleashed to spread disbelief and division, whose unsheathed swords drip in blood." With this bit of uncharacteristic polemic from Hourani, the furies of religious passion shattered any possibility for calm discourse, and so it was that two years after the damaging Lewis Affair, the SPC press was once again busily at work printing the views of the antagonists, in this the second round of the Darwin drama.

The editors of *Muqtataf* faithfully continued publishing Shumayyil's rebuttals, all the while insisting on the journal's impartiality as a forum of open discussion on a scientific subject. Ibrahim Hourani's Protestant weekly *Nushrat al-Usbu'iyyah* was joined in the fray by *al-Bashir* (*The Good News Gospel*), the Jesuit journal of St. Joseph College. Now two Christian periodicals, one belonging to American and Arab evangelicals, the other to French-oriented Arab Jesuits, were hurling invectives of heresy and unbelief on Shumayyil and holding the editors of *Muqtataf* responsible for spreading his "infernal doctrine of materialist atheism." The editors took the charges seriously. They could ill afford their journal being branded a purveyor of atheism by both Protestants and Jesuits, and now with even Muslim writers starting to get excited over the issue.

The Jesuits had been attacking *Muqtataf* for years. Their hostility to the editors of *Muqtataf* had a long history going back before Shumayyil's articles and books. The editors of the Jesuit journal *Bashir* and the editors of *Muqtataf* had been quarreling for years over a number of issues, a particularly hot one being over an article in *Muqtataf* that debunked magic. The hyper-sensitive Jesuits took this to be an attack on the miracles of saints by those atheist editors ensconced in the American Protestant College, that den of pernicious reformationist heresy. Shibli Shumayyil's book added high octane to an already on-going Jesuit rage that was now aimed at Satan's unholy trinity: Sarruf, Nimr and Shumayyil. The attacks against them in *al-Bashir* were becoming so vehement in August 1884 that the Ottoman authorities felt obliged to intervene, which they did reluctantly. The Ottomans loathed becoming involved in the arcane squabbles of their religious minorities, but news of the Christian furor over Darwin in Beirut had reached Europe, and the Ottomans wanted to calm things before the episode could be used as a pretext for another European intervention to protect their favored Christian minorities.

A word from Ottoman authority was enough to induce restraint. *Muqtataf* had already reported that an account of the controversy had appeared in the *Abendblatt der Frankfurter Zeitung* under the header "Die Darwinismus in Syrien," which related how the translation of Buchner's book had aroused great anger against Dr. Shumayyil and the editors of *Muqtataf*, who were being called heretics and atheists by the editors of *al-Bashir* and *Nashrat al-Usbu'iyyah*.[37] Upon receiving orders from Istanbul, the Director of Foreign Affairs and Publications in Beirut warned the Jesuit editors to cool the rhetoric before the government did it for them.[38] The word from Ottoman authority reduced the temperature from a boil to a simmer.

Sarruf and Nimr saw the crisis as a replay of the Edwin Lewis Affair, but with the Jesuits and Protestants now aligned with the American evangelists against the editors of *Muqtataf*, who were once again branded as heretical outcasts. *Muqtataf*'s relations with the Christian community had degenerated beyond repair. "Our position with respect to *al-Bashir* is well known," began the defense of the editors of *Muqtataf*. What this meant was that there was nothing that they could say or do to change anything in the poor relationship between the journal and the Jesuits. Regarding the Protestants, however, the situation was different:

> As for *al-Nashrat al Isbu'iyya*, *Muqtataf* has had nothing but good to say about it and never intended it harm, and never will, God willing. Indeed, *Muqtataf* is just as eager as it is in opposing atheistic schools of thought, except that our resistance against the attacks claiming we are propagators of atheistic schools of thought comes through the gate of science rather than religion . . . These are absolutely false charges based either on utter ignorance or intemperate anger, as we never gave support to atheistic schools, neither secretly nor openly; rather, we oppose all such schools . . . and our many writings bear witness to this in the face of every enemy. Some blame us because we have not placed our *Muqtataf* on the side of those who oppose Darwin's theory. But had we done that, then the philosophy would have spread through the country and struck roots in it in less than a year and this is not to be desired. *Al-Nashrat al-Isbu'iyya* strenuously opposed it and its followers, and what was the effect this had? It resulted only in increasing the desire of people to read the books of Darwin, and what a desire indeed. Had Dr. Shumayyil published a hundred advertisements in every local newspaper, they would not have caused his book to circulate as much as the resistance to it increased its circulation, to the extent that some people suspect that the Protestant Weekly and Dr. Shumayyil have conspired to increase sales, in the way some Frankish newspapers manufacture conflicts to increase circulation. We hold *al-Nashrat* innocent of this because we know the owners well; yet this is the unintentional result of their resistance.

The short piece concludes:

> Many have asked us about our opinion on Darwin's theory, and if it opposes religion or not. By religion, we take it to mean the existence of God, may he be praised, and the eternal soul and the collective religious truths of Jews, Christians and Muslims. We answer them by saying we have read much

that has been written that both confines and contradicts the theory. And so for this reason it is not correct that we express an opinion on the matter. Nonetheless, we have recently read the address on this matter given only this year at Oxford University by Dr. Temple, the Bishop of Exeter, in which he states that the theory of evolution is not contrary to the teachings of religion in any way. Bishop Temple is a renowned scholar, theologian and author who as a student won many awards at Oxford where he studied mathematics. He later became a priest in the Church of England. In his address he interprets evolution as the highest and most glorious expression of God's universe, manifesting the greatness of the Creator (praise upon him and may he be extolled), and says that it (the theory of evolution) is a great inspiration which advances and enables religious thinking. Its researchers and supporters are deserving of all honor and dignity. His address shows us that many scholars of the Protestant faith have begun to accept and praise Darwin's theory, just as previously they accepted (the new) astronomy and geology after strong opposition.

And so we advise our brethren, the sons of the country, not to be too concerned with these theories and their likes until scientists have subjected them to the test of fire and established them as accepted truths . . . And to the editors of the Christian newspapers, we advise that they concern themselves more with the sayings of prophets . . . than with scientists and science, about which they know nothing.[39]

It was grand hyperbole for the editors to say that Darwin's theory would have quickly spread through the country and taken root had they taken a stand to oppose it, a thing "that was not to be desired." The reasons behind the claim that people believed whatever *Muqtataf* opposed can only be understood in the critical context of the moment, and the sense of isolation that the editors of *Muqtataf* must have been experiencing in their community. Through the words of Bishop Temple, who reflected their own view but which they dared not boldly state as theirs, they hoped to strike a balance, advancing an Anglican Bishop to check an evangelical shaykh. Their introduction of liberal western religious authorities to address the hostility eastern religious authorities had for evolution, and other scientific ideas that were earlier considered threatening, had been the method employed by *Muqtataf's* editors to reach conciliation since its founding. Muslim concilliators would be doing the same before long.

Bishop Temple's address could not but be reminiscent of the one that Professor Edwin Lewis delivered two summers earlier. Indeed, directly following this defensive essay, *Muqtataf's* editors wrote a review of Lewis's commencement address and the discreditable outcome of the controversy, at the conclusion of which they triumphantly declared that Dr. Lewis had at last been vindicated. The president of the college in America where most of the American missionaries in Syria studied their theology (Union Seminary in New York) had himself read the lecture and declared there to be nothing in it contrary to religion: Lewis's sound ideas supported the highest traditions of religion. The president had written to Lewis apologizing for the trouble he had at the American College in Beirut. *Muqtataf* went on:

> Those on the inside of the problem knew the real reasons for what was going on. Behind the curtain, the pretext of religion was used to destroy someone, which is most despicable, using religion as a weapon of destruction. Arming oneself with religion to appear to be opposing science but in reality using it to achieve vengeance on a man of science is the ugliest of all kinds of calumny . . . Our aim in bringing these painful memories up now is not to lay blame on those who were wrong in the past but to show the truth and innocence of a noble man who was terribly wronged – and the worst punishment for committing it is remorse and pain.[40]

Sarruf and Nimr could now forget their college promotions. The article of January 1885 can be taken as their letter of resignation from SPC. Thoughts of resigning and moving to Cairo must have been occupying their minds for some time. Their careers had been dead-ended at the college since the summer of 1882. Added to the blowout with the Christian community, not to mention the unpleasantness of the growing censorship restrictions and public surveillance imposed by Sultan abd al-Hamid's repressive government, the souring of their careers at the American College must have lightened the burden of their decision to relocate.

This second controversy was but another sad chapter in Sarruf's and Nimr's long struggle to have evolution given a fair hearing. Their conflict this time was not only with the missionary administration of SPC, but with religious leaders of their own Syrian community. In their quest to expand knowledge of science among the Arabs, the editors of *Muqtataf* succeeded in uniting all factions of eastern Christianity against them, including the unlikely duo of Jesuits and American evangelicals, not to mention some like-minded Muslim literalists. The time had come for *Muqtataf* to leave. Within months of the January article's appearance, Sarruf and Nimr were on their way out, thankfully leaving the many-layered oppressive atmosphere of Beirut behind them for the free air of Cairo. They had been educated at SPC, and they had met some fine Americans there: Edwin Lewis, Cornelius and William Van Dyck – especially Cornelius. Without Cornelius, and without SPC and its press, *Muqtataf* would never have seen the light of day.

Theirs must have been a bittersweet departure, hard in some ways, easy in others. The College community was no longer in the 1880s what it had been, or appeared to be, in the 1860s and 1870s. The Lewis Affair had left a repressive cloud hanging over the campus that neither the blue Mediterranean below nor the new Bell Tower piercing the blue sky above could ever disperse. Cornelius Van Dyck had resigned in 1882 over the Lewis Affair, and a year later his friend and colleague of 43 years, Butrus Bustani, was dead. The old man's death had come at the saddest of times. Hamidian repression outside the walls of the SPC campus had its own version within them. Bustani had had a long, rich and fulfilling life with the American evangelists. To Butrus they were men of a new breed from a world he could hardly imagine: scholars, tall and lean pioneers, men of languages and the Bible, independent and determined, strong in their faith, in their civilization and in themselves; men for whom action was as important as words, westerners who had come to the East in peace to plant seeds of their faith and knowledge that liberated, men of science and scripture who mastered Arabic, founded schools, journals, science societies, a medical college – and to have it crumble because of a lecture claiming Darwin's scientific method to be sound. Butrus Butani's death could be seen as a metaphor. The institution founded to proclaim truth had quickly grown to be more important than truth. With Bustani's death, his son Salim, who had been editing *al-Jinan*, the intellectual parent of *Muqtataf*, closed the journal down.

By the middle of 1885 *Muqtataf* was in Cairo and freely publishing on Darwin and his ideas. Shibli Shumayyil had been residing in Egypt since 1873. Following his two years of independent study in the West, he joined his prosperous businessman brother, Amin, in Alexandria. Both Shibli and Amin contributed pieces on evolution to *Muqtataf*. Amin wrote a truly strange one, "Darwin's Thought Among the Ancients."[41] Addressing Muslims and Christians, the essay argued the legitimacy of evolution theory through the pedigree of intellectual lineage. Evolution was just one of those ancient ideas that kept coming and going, not to be taken seriously. He referred to ibn Khaldun's adaptation of Aristotle's chain of being, as if to insinuate it was an early form of evolution theory. He then related several curious stories about ancient beliefs: a mule comes from a donkey mating with a horse, a lion from a jackal with a hyena, lettuce from a man impregnating a female jinn. The combinations of sexual unions are indeed bizarre, men mating with not only female jinn, but angels and demons (*sa'alat*) to produce giants, who by masturbating into crevices produce monkeys. Alexander the Great's parents were both offsprings of a human mating with a jinn of the opposite sex. The point of this weird article (it must be assumed it had one) was that various forms of evolution had been part of man's intellectual heritage for thousands of years and so should not be considered something new or unfamiliar. Darwin and his followers were no more than restorers of old traditions and stories, some of which contained prevailing truths, some superstitious tales. "Only God has knowledge of the truth, and though men differ over the truth, this has no harmful effect on religion or what the prophets have brought." Sultan abd al-Hamid's sharp-eyed censors, always sensitive to possible Christian altercation, must have been shaking their heads over this one.

Shaykh Ibrahim Hourani came out with a book just at that time: *The Precise Truth Concerning the Rejection of Darwin* (*al-Haqq al-Yaqin fi Rafd Darwin*). Hourani painted evolution as nothing more than supposition and conjecture, and the universe with its life forms as things only God could have created, not chance or nature on its own. Mindful of the Ottoman warning the year before, Hourani restrained himself from accusing of heresy those who followed Darwin. With Hourani's book, the battle of 1885, shorn of its scorn, mockery and overheated accusations of atheism, simmered down to a quiet debate of European ideas between Syro–Lebanese Christians in Beirut and their brethren émigrés in Cairo.

In Egypt, *Muqtataf* became more open and daring in its support of evolution, with practically every issue containing something either explaining the theory or reporting on new evidence corroborating it. An article of December 1887, provocatively titled "The Influence of Nature on the Shari'a," written by a Christian, Ibrahim Mikha'il Jamal, is a salient example of this new boldness. It argues that the Shari'a, and the moral judgments that compose it, are related to particular states in man's moral character that evolve with his biological nature. Holy law changes with human nature. Nature, not the will and wisdom of God, is the ultimate determinative. Shari'a varies from society to society in relation to differences in the natural environment. By Shari'a the author means the holy law of any society, not just Islam, but using that precise word was nonetheless quite daring. By conflating biological evolution in nature and a presumed moral evolution in civilization, the author's argument that innovation is always reforming tradition and that religious law is always undergoing modernization is given a presumed scientific foundation. Law is the language of the social condition encoded by environmental factors and deciphered by character and natural disposition. Ultimately, it is nature that dictates laws by its power in shaping physical environment and human disposition. Hippocrates and ibn Khaldun said as much by showing the influence that geography and climate have on character, disposition and ethics. Because of mild climate and favorable living conditions, Asians, unlike Europeans who must endure harsh conditions, are tall, beautiful and mild mannered. Soft living makes them so. Europeans are rough, hardy and warlike, a product of their brutal weather and environment. After much investigation of the subject by modern scientists, the principles of "struggle for existence" and "survival of the fittest" ("jihad" is the word the author uses for this) have come to light. Environmental changes in a certain region or area of the world induce changes in organic life through its adaptations to the new environmental conditions, and also induce changes in ethics and character, and ineluctably, law.

The quality of law in a civilization, the author continues, is a complex product of a people's character, which is in turn an equally complex product of natural conditions. A refined and gentle character would tend toward a law imbued with compassion, fairness and freedom. A cruel and brutal people would produce a society ruled by a law of similar characteristics. In primitive societies, for example, women are treated like slaves and servants. In advanced societies they have rights. In sum, the essence of all law, which is justice, is a function of the natural and social environment, but it is, above all, nature that shapes the social environment. Natural conditions are fundamental to social existence and the laws that give structure and stability to society. As such, law is not a pure and simple absolute of universal status, but a product of multifarious influences operating at different levels and always subject to change and rectification.

As the author was a Christian writing in a journal edited by Christians, whose laws had always been secular and subject to change, the article passed quietly. It was a piece of writing that would have also appealed to Muslim readers in favor of change and a modernist reformulation of the real Shari'a. It would not be long before Muslims were writing the same thing.

Muqtataf kept expanding the envelope. Comparable in boldness to Ibrahim Jamal's essay on nature and holy law was Sarruf's "The Principles of Inheritance and Their History."[42] Based on Gregor Mendel's discoveries of the genetics governing biological inheritance made in the 1860s, the piece was groundbreaking in Arabic literature in that it likened the natural laws governing the biological universe to the natural laws governing the physical universe. Parallel to the laws of universal gravitation, electromagnetism and thermodynamics were the laws of genetic inheritance. These laws were still not clearly understood, but scientists believed the sperm and egg contained a system of bacilli (the word had no Arabic equivalent so Sarruf found one, *jarathim*) that belonged to every organ and member of the respective parents. The fertilized egg then contained its own system of bacilli that came from the parents and that determined the features of the child. The article introduced a new science and a new vocabulary into Arabic: microbe, micro-organism, genes, donors, genetic system, recessive genes, genetic transmission. This was now *Muqtataf's* multiform mission: channeling the West's new discoveries to Arab society, promoting the enriching experience of science and continuing to pitch the theory of natural selection, while answering the journal's attackers, which latter task was taking more and more of the editor's time.

As *Muqtataf* forged on in its effort to keep the Arab public abreast of the rapid advance of the physical and biological sciences in the West, the Jesuits and evangelicals in Beirut, with Ibrahim Hourani still at the head of the pack, kept up the attack. In answer to the steady stream of accusations of their being godless, the people of *Muqtataf*, including Shumayyil, published in the journal's October 1889 issue an essay on the natural sciences and religious truth. It drew on the works of Darwin, Huxley and Tyndall, to the effect that their progressive research into the workings of nature produced discoveries that revealed the amazing simplicity of those general laws that directly explain what at first appeared to be multifarious and awesomely complex. Having grasped this, the scientist could but humbly bow his head in admission to the limitations of his knowledge before the infinite wisdom of the Creator who designed this marvelous world of nature, of which science had discovered but a drop in the ocean of divine wisdom.

Huxley, the scientist most thought of as an atheist, the essay went on, had written that anyone who studied the science of plants and animals knew that their species had not come about by accident, but by a guiding wisdom acting through force and matter. What scientists generally preferred to regard as laws governing the system of nature, others might think of as God, as indeed did many scientists. Tyndall, addressing a congress of scientists in Liverpool in 1870, said that God transcends the truth of the theory of species, and so one should say as did Gamaliel of scripture, that if this is from God, it cannot be rejected or denied, and if any scientific theory or hypothesis is wrong, science itself will prove it wrong and reject it.

Those for whom the essay was intended would have nothing of it. *Muqtataf* was preaching to the converted. In 1890 the Jesuits published a ruthless indictment of Shumayyil, who was always the main target. This was a book written by Jirjis Faraj Sfair al-Maruni, a Jesuit philosophy teacher. *The Origin of Man and Existence: A Refutation of the Philosophy of Evolution and Response to Dr. Shibli Shumayyil* was a scoffing caricaturization of Darwin's theory, which in many ways, as will be seen in the following section, echos the ridicule heaped on evolution theory in the famous tract written around the same time by Jamal al-Din al-Afghani, *Refutation of the Materialists*. Sfair's 250 pages of invective are in the form of a dialogue – dialogues and dreams being favorite devices in the modern Arab literature of intellectual controversy – between "Monkey Man," who represents those who believe in evolution, and "Adam Man," who represents believers in traditional religion and the divine origin of man and the universe. There are now two men in place of one, proclaims the narrator: Monkey Man the new man and Adam the old man. The narrator frequently intervenes in the dialogue to support Adam.

The thesis is that the theory of evolution is a vicious malady that has divided man. Hopefully, this malignant schizophrenia is temporary and will soon disappear, leaving man whole again, the Man of Adam. The reader is led to believe that the theory of evolution means man came from a monkey, but a different form from today's monkeys; and that the struggle for existence means that a cat kills a mouse, a wolf a lamb, a tiger a wolf, though the author does later show himself knowledgeable enough to explain the mechanisms of environmental factors in relation to natural selection. The first half of Sfair's book has Adam Man laying bare the pitfalls and gaps in the theory of evolution as Monkey Man follows along in agreement that there is no evidence of intermediary forms, no new species recorded in 5,000 years of history and no changes in the human anatomy. Thomist theology fills the voids and answers the questions that evolution cannot answer by introducing soul, spirit, chain of being and first cause.

The geological ages of the earth's formation and non-organic evolution are accepted, but not biological evolution. Life in all its forms requires a Creator, and so there will always be questions regarding life and its origins that are beyond science and human understanding.[43] Evolution theory could only be acceptable insofar as it was understood within the framework of God as the Creator of the universe and the internal systems that moved it, including the creation of all species as they exist today: "Does the pen create the writer?"

There are some believers, Adam Man tells Monkey Man, who, wanting to reconcile evolution and religion, have made up a malicious and scandalous tale that says God set it all up so that the species of life evolved from earlier forms and that at a certain point God took a monkey or pre-monkey and blew spirit into it to make man. Monkey Man asks if that might not indeed be the case. It would solve a lot of problems. Adam Man replies that this would be the same as God blowing his spirit into a monkey, giving it an eternal soul and calling the monkey "man." No, God created all souls, man's and animal's, each soul for its particular species. To believe otherwise is to believe souls can also evolve, and that is clearly wrong since souls are from the divine Creator and, like the Creator, eternal in form.

The last half of Sfair's book contains a theological treatise summarizing the Jesuit arguments against evolution, followed by a vicious personal attack on Shumayyil. Because of his unforgivable sin of bringing the European disease of Darwin into Arabic, Shumayyil is insulted, cursed, ridiculed, accused of lying and of deliberately perverting what Darwin believed, and shamed for his having translated such vile nonsense into Arabic and polluting eastern Christianity with European heresy. Like Hourani and the Jesuit editors of *al-Bashir*, Sfair was more opposed to Shumayyil as a philosopher than Darwin as a scientist. The ruckus Shumayyil was blamed for having caused must have made his day. The day never ended. Ibrahim Hourani kept writing against him right into the 20th century. Protestant fire against him had by the end of the first decade died out, but the Jesuits of St. Joseph had Father Louis Chiekho to carry on the attack, which he did for decades more. A feisty critical scholar of Arabic history and literature, Chiekho made his fellow Jesuit Jirjis Sfair look anemic when it came to casting curses at Darwin, but moreso at his Arab disciples of evil, Shumayyil, trailed by Sarruf and Nimr. Jesuit Chiekho's invective raised the incivility to a level that if taken any higher would have exchanged the pen for pistols – and might have, had the disputants not been separated by the Mediterranean, a desert and the Ottoman authorities working overtime to keep the peace.

As the old century was giving way to the new, *Muqtataf* became progressively more outspoken in support of evolution. An article appearing on New Year's Day, 1902, offered a general review of natural selection and went so far as to state that evidence was mounting that man and all animals had evolved over many millions of years from a common origin, but "this is still being contested by researchers . . . and it is not our intention to prolong discussion of the subject."[44] In fact, the editors had been prolonging discussion of the subject for more than two decades. Practically every second issue of *Muqtataf* added something in support of Darwin and evolution. The names Sarruf and Nimr went with Shumayyil to form an Arabic synonym for evolution, and for good reason: it was they who introduced the Arab public to the principles of natural selection and created the technical vocabulary to express them. *Muqtataf's* articles were like seeds whose sprouts rooted themselves into the intellectual soil, waiting to be cultivated further by Muslim reformers, who before the end of the 19th century were following in the steps of their Christian forerunners, using the same arguments about the harmony of natural evolution and holy scripture. The Muslim ulema would protest, but much less vigorously than their Christian counterparts.

By the late 1880s the evolutionist controversy was drawing in Muslim voices, but voices that were, on the religious side, almost unanimously conciliatory compared to the noise put up by the American evangelists and their Syrian brethren. Shaykhs Husayn al-Jisr and Muhammad Abduh in the late 19th century, followed by Shaykh Rashid Rida writing into the 1930s, saw no problem in evolution, so long as the theory was referenced to a divine Creator. Theologians could go no further than that without extinguishing the mystery of religion and losing their jobs. With the singular exception of that protean pan-Islamist fire-brand, Jamal al-Din al-Afghani, whose career seared across Islam's intellectual and political terrain like a fiery comet during the final decades of the 19th century, Muslim commentary avoided the rancor and personal animosity that scarred the debates carried on by the Christian antagonists.

In the 20th century, the Syrian Shaykh Rashid Rida and the Egyptian editor Muhammad Farid Wajdi would carry on in the stead of Muhammad Abduh, while the Egyptians Salama Musa, a Copt, and Ismail Mazhar, a Muslim, would carry on for Shumayyil. The former medical student turned novelist and literary critic, Jurji Zaydan, who had left Lebanon for Cairo and there, in 1898, founded his journal *al-Hilal*, was another literary voice for reform, science education and evolution in the early 20th century.

Zaydan's thought on the interrelationships of science, social morality and public spirit was essentially that of Shaykh Tahtawi's, and after him of Shaykh Abduh's and Shaykh Rida's, but with the important distinction that secular Arabism had by then taken the place of Islam at the heart of the national ethos. As Zaydan saw it, the source of ethics and morals was rooted in natural laws of science, leaving precious little for religion to contribute in the work of civilization. Science should be the first thing taught to children to instill morality, virtue and knowledge, for science was religion stripped of fanciful tales and miracles. This was strong stuff even for the relatively liberal literary temper of Cairo. There were limits to what even Christian émigrés from Syria could say. In accounting for creation in a textbook on geography and history that Zaydan was writing for secondary school students, he bowed to the pressure of popular religious feelings by referring to the creation stories in Genesis rather than, as he would have preferred, referring creation to natural selection as the origin of life's forms.[45]

Salama Musa journeyed to Europe as a young man to educate himself the way Shibli Shumayyil had, and like him returned steeped in materialist philosophy, evolution and socialism. By the time Shumayyil died in 1916, Salama had written several books in emulation of him, and right into the middle of the century would still be muddying the waters of evolution theory with the alien stream of materialist–evolutionist socialism he poured into it.

In the introduction of the 1909 edition of his Buchner book, Shumayyil predicted the Middle East would follow closely behind Europe and along the same pattern in accepting evolution. Darwin's theory, he claimed, had first been taught as an official course in the medical school in Toulouse in 1887. Twenty years later, the theory had been accepted and was now a regular academic course in the biological studies of European universities and medical schools. (Natural selection had in fact been accepted by the European scientific community before Darwin's death in 1882.) Shumayyil was sure that in another decade it would achieve similar status in the Middle East, meaning Cairo, Beirut, Damascus, Istanbul and Salonika (Iraq and Iran being beyond the pale).

By one way of reckoning, his optimistic prediction turned out to be reasonably accurate. In the 1923 publication of the *Egyptian National Encyclopedia* (an updated edition of Butrus Bustani's encyclopedia published in Beirut in the late 1870s), its Egyptian editor, Muhammad Farid Wajdi, wrote in his article on Darwin that evolution theory contained nothing contrary to Muslim belief. Considering that Wajdi was soon to become chief editor of the new journal put out by al-Azhar, *Majallat al-Azhar*, his statement carried some weight and can be considered to reflect the views of at least some of the more authoritative shaykhs of al-Azhar. Evolution was far from being introduced in al-Azhar's curriculum, but the leading shaykhs were not expressly against it. Rashid Rida was one who came out to state forthrightly his views on the subject, that religion and evolution had nothing to do with each other and there was no need to reject the theory as long as the holder of the theory did not reject God and creation.

In search of intellectual landmarks in a society where in modern times such marks are scarce, Abdallah Fikri's 1876 treatise is the best that could stand as one in regard to the religious acceptability of Copernicus. In regard to Darwin, that landmark would have to be Muhammad Farid Wajdi's 1923 Egyptian edition of Bustani's encyclopedia. If Shaykh Rashid Rida's articles are taken as statements reflecting both educated Muslim belief and that of his al-Azhar alma mater, Islam was implicitly at peace with evolution before the end of the first quarter of the new century – in spite of desultory religious voices that would speak out against it; in spite of al-Azhar's passive silence on the subject; and in spite of the torrent of popular books published during the last quarter century purporting to be on religion and science that reject evolution, and continue to do so. Evolution, in its framework of Intelligent Design, was a century ago, as it is now, accepted and rejected in Muslim society, depending on where one looks and who one asks.

Notes

1. Shibli Shumayyil, *Majmu'a Shibli Shumayyil* (Collected Writings), Cairo, 1910, p. 26.
2. Like Shumayyil, Zilzal wrote occasionally for *Muqtataf*. In 1880, a year after his book came out, he founded a journal in Cairo called *al-Bayan* with another Syro–Lebanese Christian, the poet-writer Ibrahim Yaziji. The journal lasted less than a year. Also Marwa Elshakry, *Darwin's Legacies in the Arab East: Science, Religion and Politics, 1870–1914*, Princeton PhD dissertation, 2003, pp. 60–68.
3. Qasim Amin, *Tahrir al-Mar'at* (Liberation of Women), Cairo, 1899.
4. Bishara Zilzal, *Tanwir al-Adhhan*, Alexandria, 1879, pp. 316–317.
5. *Muqtataf*, vol 50, 1917, pp. 105, 225, 231, 266–282.
6. Shibli Shumayyil, *Falsafat al-Nushu' wa'l Irtiqa'*, Cairo, 1910, p. 307.
7. Shumayyil, *Falsafat al-Nushu'*, p. 27.
8. *al-Jinan*, vol 1, pp. 94–97, 161–164; 200–201.
9. Shumayyil, *Falsafat al-Nushu'*, p. 26. See also on this: Jean LeCerf, "Shibli Shumayyil, Metaphysician et Moraliste Contemporaine," *Bulletin d'etudes Orientales*, vol 1, 1931, Damsacus, p. 181.
10. For *Muqtataf's* first issue (April 1876), Shumayyil contributed a brief resume on the life and work of John Tyndall (d. 1893), the British physicist and evolutionist who explained it was the scattering of solar rays by molecules in the air that made the sky blue and who opposed the idea of spontaneous generation.
11. Elshakry, *Darwin's Legacies*, p. 138.
12. Georges Haroun, *Shibli Shumayyil, une penseur evolutioniste Arabe*, Universite Libanaise Press, Beirut, 1985, pp. 89–92.
13. Georges Haroun, *Shibli Shumayyil*, p. 92.
14. Najm Bezirgan, "Darwin in the Arab World," in *Comparative Reception of Darwin*, edited by T. Glick, University of Chicago Press, Chicago, 1974.
15. In 2002, a fine Arabic translation of the *Origin of Species* that was sponsored by the Egyptian government was published, though it is not to be found in any of Cairo's bookstores. The translation was done by Dr. Miliji, professor of dermatology at Ayn Shams University.
16. Shumayyil, *Falsafat al-Nushu'*, pp. 294–295.
17. Shumayyil, *Falsafat al-Nushu'*, p. 306.
18. Shumayyil, *Falsafat al-Nushu'*, p. 361.
19. Shumayyil, *Majmu'a*, pp. 108–109; Adel Ziadet, *Science in the Arab World: The Impact of Darwinism, 1860–1930*, Palgrave Macmillan, London, 1936, p. 32.
20. Shumayyil, *Falsafat al-Nushu'*, p. 364.

21 Haroun, *Shibli Shumayyil*, p. 93. The full title is *al-Haqiqa li-Ithbat Madhhab Darwin fi'l Nushu' wa'l Irtiqa* (The Truth in Establishing Darwin's Theory of Evolution), published by *Muqtataf* press.
22 Shumayyil, *Majmu'a*, p. 237.
23 Shumayyil, *Majmu'a*, p. 247.
24 Ibn Arabi was a famous 13th century Andalusian mystic who resettled in the eastern regions of Islamdom where Sufism was more popularly accepted as being a legitimate practice of one's Muslim faith.
25 *Sharh Buchner* (1910 edition), pp. 28–31. The section on God in his *al-Haqiqa* was included in the 1910 edition of his Buchner commentary.
26 Shumayyil, *Falsafat al-Nushu'*, p. 30; A. Hourani, *Arabic Thought in the Liberal Age*, Cambridge University Press, Cambridge, 1983, p. 249. See also for Shumayyil's radicalism: Susan Ziadeh, *A Radical in His Time: The Thought of Shibli Shumayyil and Arab Intellectual Discourse, 1882–1917*, doctoral dissertation, University of Michigan, 1991.
27 Shumayyil, *Falsafat al-Nushu'*, p. 30; Elshakry, p. 151.
28 A. Hourani, *Arabic Thought*, p. 250.
29 Shumayyil, *Falsafat al-Nushu'*, p. 81; A. Hourani, *Arabic Thought*, p. 251.
30 Shumayyil, *Falsafat al-Nushu'*, p. 361.
31 A. Hourani, *Arabic Thought*, p. 252.
32 Bezirgan, "Darwin in the Arab World" for a succinct account of this.
33 Kemal al-Yaziji, *al-Shaykh Ibrahim al-Hourani (1844–1916)*, Beirut, 1963, p. 47. For Shumayyil's and other Arab writers' socialist ideas see: Donald Reid, "Syrian Christians and Early Socialism in the Arab World," *International Journal of Middle Eastern Studies*, vol 5, issue 2 (1974), pp. 177–193.
34 Yaziji, *Shaykh Ibrahim Hourani*, pp. 242–243.
35 Jean Lecerf, *Bulletin d'estudes Orientales*, Institut Francais de Damas, Damascus, vol I, 1931, p. 159.
36 *Kitab fi Asl al-Insan Dahdan li Madhhab al-Tahawwul* (*On the Origins of Man, in Refutation of the School of Transformation*), Beirut, 1890.
37 *Muqtataf*, January 1885, vol 8, p. 241.
38 Elshakry, *Darwin's Legacies*, p. 207.
39 *Muqtataf* (January 1885), pp. 241–243. The Dr. Fredrick Temple (1821–1902) referred to in the article was present in 1860 at the famous meeting of the British Association held in the museum of Oxford University when Thomas Huxley debated Samuel Wilberforce over evolution. On the occasion, Huxley replied to Bishop Wilberforce's mockery of evolution by saying he would rather have an ape as an ancestor than be related to a man who used the brain God gave him to obscure the truth. A quarter century later Dr. Temple gave a series of eight lectures at Oxford University. In the fourth, he stated that "the doctrine of evolution is in no sense whatever antagonistic to the teachings of religion." The lectures were published in 1884 under the title *The Relations between Religion and Science*.
40 *Muqtataf*, vol 9, January 1885, pp. 243–244.
41 *Muqtataf*, vol 10, December 1885.
42 *Muqtataf*, vol 13, 1888, pp. 521–526.
43 Jirjis Sfair, *Origins of Man*, Beirut, pp. 52–53.
44 *Muqtataf*, January 1, 1902, pp. 31–38.
45 Nazik Yared, *Arab Travelers and Western Civilizations*, trans. S.O. Shahandar, Saqi Books, London, 1996, p. 131. For an account of Jurji's shift from a biblical to an evolutionary belief in natural and human existence: Thomas Phillip, *Jurji Zaydan, His Life and Thought*, Beirut, 1979, p. 57, note 2. Phillip traces the change in the articles Jurji wrote in *Hilal* over the years, but Jurji must certainly have accepted natural selection as a medical student. It was he who led the student strikes at SPC in defense of Dr. Edwin Lewis, who praised Darwin's methods of research and was persecuted by the college's evangelical administration, who accused him of supporting natural selection.

8 Scientific Interpretation
Shaykh Husayn al-Jisr and Darwin

An important response to Darwin in the Islamic world was the attempt to reconcile the Quran to modern science. In 1880 an Egyptian physician produced the first of what was to become a modern literary tradition of Quranic Scientific Interpretation. This was Muhammad ibn Ahmad al-Iskandarani's *Kashf al-Asrar al-Nuraniyya al-Quraniyya* (*Unveiling of the Luminous Quranic Secrets*). Advancing beyond what *Rawdat al-Madaris* had insinuated, that Islam and science were comfortable partners, Iskandarani claimed that not only were there no discrepancies between them, but the Quran in fact contained all known science and useful knowledge. Clear proof of it was revealed in Sura 16, verse 91: "We have sent down to you a book explaining everything." Everything covered it all. According to the gospel of Scientific Interpretation, Muslims had the framework of their grand unified theory of everything early in the search.

The space that Iskandarani's book gives to science compared to that given to religion confirms its author as a secular educated physician who intended to legitimize science through religion rather than exalting the Quran through science. In spite of its title, the three-volume work reads like a general introductory primer in the natural sciences tailored for believers. It must have found an appreciative audience since it was published three years later in Damascus under another title *Tibyan al-Asrar al-Rabbaniyya* (*Explanation of the Divine Secrets*). The first volume is on the natural history of stones, rocks, trees and animals; the second on the formation of the heavens, stars, earth and other planets; and the third on plants. God created the universe with the sun at the center and the earth orbiting it by the force of gravitational attraction. The idea of a moving earth was still novel enough that the author felt obliged to explain how it was that the earth moved without it being sensed.

Iskandarani describes the earth's formation in some detail. The origin of the earth was a fiery mass of gases that cooled and contracted over time to form a spherically shaped molten mass encased in a crusted surface, the whole process of sphericity and formation being governed by the laws of physics. The idea of natural law needed no less explication than did the idea of a moving earth. Iskandarani referred to natural law as *'adah* (custom), harking back to the medieval concept of nature being endowed with a "customary" behavior, which saved God's will from being subjugated to laws of nature, making possible the miraculous, the revelation of the Quran being proof of it.

Iskandarani's exposition is a mix of modern and medieval science with religion, where natural objects are either simple or composed, and endowed with substance, qualities and matter. While thunder is a manifestation of God's fearsome power on the Quranic level, on the natural level it is the sound of lightning propagated in waves through the medium of the atmosphere at a particular frequency, amplitude and wave length. Scientific principles that explain the patterns of nature on the physical level of reality serve to exalt the truth and mystery of God and the Quran on the sublime level of reality. Provision has to be made for those verses of the Quran at variance with science: creation in six days, the Throne of God, the Preserved Tablets, angels and jinn. Here God intended a measure of interpretation to be applied in order to render the message comprehensible. The Quranic references to nature and supernatural beings that are illogical or beyond the scope of science are to be taken metaphorically, though there is always the possibility future scientific discoveries might explain them in a rational light.

Dr. Iskandarani's reading of science into the Quran was to be taken up by shaykhs who, thinking to exalt the holy book, soared into flights of fantasy. Indeed, as a book that confessed itself to explaining everything, everything western science had to offer was read into the Quran. Ulema and non-ulema competed in the fabulous exercise, one outdoing the next in stretches of imagination that in short time produced an abundant literature called "Scientific Interpretation." The genre was not exactly new. Al-Biruni, one of Islam's and the world's greatest scientists, believed that the Quran contained all of nature's secrets. This was purely a metaphoric expression of a scientist's religious devotion in believing the Quran to be an endless treasure of wisdom. He had no intention of implying that epicycles, retrograde motion and the value for the inclination of the ecliptic could be found in any of the verses. In Biruni's day, religion did not need bolstering against science. But in the 19th century, the West's political battering of Islamdom, administered with incessant narcissistic assertions of intellectual superiority over oriental irrationality, produced a palpable need on the part of a number of important religious figures to show the essence of Islam, the true Islam, to be equal to and superior to what made the West great.

In modern times, it was an Azharite-trained shaykh from Syrian Tripoli, Husayn al-Jisr (1849–1909), who produced the first substantial work of Scientific Interpretation. Shaykh Jisr's formulation and intent were quite different in spirit from what al-Biruni had meant. The idea behind modern Scientific Interpretation is two-fold and depends on the interpreter's objective. One is to demonstrate the timelessness, depth and modernity of the Quran and "true Islam" by showing that the Quran and Prophetic Hadith agree with science and in fact contain scientific secrets that are still to be discovered. Here the objective is to extol Islam and the Quran. An optional objective of the genre is to legitimize and promote the study of science by showing how the Quran and Hadith thoroughly encourage and extol science as an essential part of Islam. Works of Scientific Interpretation could have both objectives in mind, but usually it is one or the other, coming from either a secular or a religious point of view. Scientific Interpretation would in the course of the 20th century take a larger and larger place in the apologetic literature of Islam in relation to western knowledge, and in turn would give birth to a retrogressive, introverted offspring called "Islamic Science," which holds that modern science is godless, atheistic and materialistic and should be replaced by the new Islamic Science. This new science was to be created by searching the holy sources for an ethical, morally based and spiritually enriching science of nature.

It is perhaps no coincidence that this negation of western science emerged shortly after the crushing defeat the Arabs suffered at the hands of Israel in 1967. The devolution of Scientific Interpretation to Islamic Science marks the triumph of a contrived reading of Quran and Hadith over what the world normally considers to be natural science and signals a defeatist reversal in the struggle to inculcate a true scientific culture in Muslim civilization. Advocates of Islamic Science believe that western science threatens to undermine "true Islam." Indeed, it is no doubt true that a culture of analytical science would in time undermine the unquestioning, uncritical acceptance of the Quran as an eternal package delivered in full from heaven. This in turn would undermine the medieval Shari'a and with it the structure and content of Muslim belief. Many of the religious authorities who do not subscribe to the preposterous pretensions of Islamic Science nonetheless understand the threat that scientific analysis poses to traditional religion and want as much as those who do subscribe to it to keep the holy sources free of any kind of analysis. They are all too aware of what happened to religion in the West.

Scientific Interpretation, on the other hand, is an argument offered by religious and secular reformers, each with their particular emphasis on the scientific or religious end of it, which aims to give relevance to the Quran in a time when science is so highly regarded. On the religious side, the argument is made in the hope of contributing toward building a scientific culture affiliated with religion in the modern age of secular nationalism, an implied recognition by the ulema of the importance and prestige of science. On the secular side of reform, Scientific Interpretation uses religion in hope of jump starting a scientific culture. In either case, the importance, prestige and necessity of science go without question.

Shaykh Husayn al-Jisr's contribution to Scientific Interpretation is dedicated to ennobling religion in the light of science, but not without emphasizing the necessity of science as something vital in itself in a thriving civilization. His straddling of the two orientations goes back to his intellectual formation, the roots of which offer an intriguing study in the merging of the intellectual currents that originated in Beirut and Cairo. Shaykh al-Jisr's career as educator, religious scholar and reformer grew from the confluence of the Syrian and Egyptian streams. His seminal work on the Quran and science, the *Risalat al-Hamidiyya*, published in Tripoli, Syria, in 1886, is the fount of 20th century Muslim thought in Arabic regarding science and religion compounded into Scientific Interpretation.[1] The book is both an exaltation of the Quran in terms of modern science and a call to jihad for Muslims to take up science because of the power it endows to those who possess it. As Salah al-Din took up the sword in retaking Jerusalem from the Latin

Crusaders, Muslims must now take up science to regain what they have lost to the Crusaders' modern successors.

Shaykh al-Jisr came from a traditional family of respected religious teachers in Tripoli, where the memory of the Latin Crusaders lived on, Tripoli having been one of the main Crusader principalities. Husayn followed in the steps of his well-known shaykhly father. In 1862 he left Tripoli for Cairo to study at al-Azhar. As we learn from a biography written by Husayn al-Jisr's son in tribute to his father's intellectual accomplishments, Shaykh al-Jisr, when on his way from Tripoli to Cairo, met the mufti of Beirut. The mufti, who had been a student of Husayn's father, knew Dr. Cornelius Van Dyck. Knowing also something of the science in the books Van Dyck had composed in Arabic, the mufti encouraged Husayn to study science and rational philosophy at al-Azhar because of their usefulness in strengthening Islam. The chance encounter was apparently Husayn's first stimulus toward science and may account for his studying logic and philosophy under Shaykh Marsafi (1815–1890), al-Azhar's most liberal reformist shaykh at the time.[2]

A blind scholar of Arabic literature, Marsafi had studied under Shaykh Tahtawi, and had taught Arabic linguistics in Ali Mubarak's *Dar al-Ulum*, and had his lectures published in *Rawdat al-Madaris*, all of which ties Marsafi closely to the mixed religio-secular reform group of Ali Mubarak, Shaykh Tahtawi, Ali Fahim and Abdallah Fikri. Like Tahtawi, Marsafi worked toward developing a modern literary form of Arabic that preserved the classical structure of the language in clear, simple expression. As a religious reformer, Shaykh Marsafi stands between his teacher Tahtawi and his students Shaykh al-Jisr and Muhammad Abduh (whose place in the Muslim reform movement is analyzed in the following chapter), upon both of whom Marsafi exerted an influence comparable in strength to that exerted upon him by Tahtawi, who was in fact still alive and actively publishing during al-Jisr's years as a student at al-Azhar, 1862–1867. A great part of the modest success achieved by Ali Mubarak's *Dar al-Ulum* and *Rawdat al-Madaris* is that through them Shaykhs Marsafi, Jisr, Abduh and his student Rashid Rida were brought into contact with science and became ardent promoters of it.

At the end of his studies at al-Azhar, Shaykh Jisr returned to Tripoli and studied chemistry, physics and mathematics on his own from Arabic books and pamphlets, many of which had been written by Cornelius Van Dyck for the students of Syrian Protestant College, which had been founded the year before Shaykh Jisr's return. He taught a short while in a traditional religious school in Tripoli before founding his own school in 1879 with the help of donations by the Muslim community, particularly by a large landowner with westernized ideas, al-Hajj al-Danawi, who wanted to see a Muslim equivalent to the Christian Missionary School in Tripoli. Shaykh Jisr named it the *Madrasat al-Wataniyya* (National School). In reactive emulation of the Christian Missionary School, as well as in response to the reformist impulse imparted to him by Shaykh Marsafi, he introduced courses in French, logic, mathematics and the natural sciences, in addition to the obligatory Arabic and Turkish. His was the first Muslim school in Tripoli to teach science and a foreign language. The scientific subjects were based on the Arabic works of Cornelius Van Dyck.[3]

The school was reported by Arab historians as a huge success, registering 1,000 students the first year. The reformist writer Shaykh Rashid Rida attended the school. As a pioneer effort in private Muslim investment to create schools for modern education, Shaykh Jisr's National School is an indication of the Muslim community's sense of urgency in addressing the widening separation between the secularist and religious worlds that Shaykh Tahtawi had written of decades earlier in Egypt. Its effects were now reaching into provincial cities like Tripoli. But for all the urgency of bridging the divide, the school closed down within a few years of its opening. Driven by their resentment of the school's westernized innovations and their worried envy of its success, traditional Muslim clerics pressured the Ottoman authorities to exclude the school's students from being excused from military service, a dispensation given by the government to all students. Because the Ottoman authorities wanted to keep religious tranquility, the dispensation was withdrawn. Enrollment fell off so severely that Shaykh Jisr had to close the school's doors.[4] As in all unraveling empires, the Ottoman government was beset by insecurity over a myriad of apparently irreconcilable differences within its society at all levels, the most wrenching insecurity of all being how one European power or another would react to whatever attempt was made to resolve any one of the mounting problems. For every local impulse to reform in a modernist direction, a counter impulse sprang to life to preserve the status quo in the name of religion, and covertly, in the interests of one or another of Europe's powers.

With the school's closure, Shaykh Jisr moved to Beirut, where he directed an Ottoman school, *Madrasat al-Sultaniyya*. This was another new school run by reformist Muslim clerics in Syria dedicated to instructing students in "useful knowledge," meaning science, mathematics and geography. One of the leading modernist shaykhs in Syria, abd al-Qadir Qabbani (1847–1935), invited Shaykh Jisr to teach in the *Sultaniyya*. Qabbani and a group of like-minded shaykhs in Damascus had formed a Society of Arts (*Jam'iyyat al-Funun*) for charitable and educational purposes. Shaykh Qabbani also edited the Society's weekly paper, *Thamrat al-Funun* (*Fruits of Arts and Sciences*), which was a lesser version in size and depth of Egypt's *Rawdat al-Madaris* but closely akin to it in purpose.[5] He was close to Shakyh Jisr in religious and intellectual outlook, but his rise to become Ottoman Director of Education in Beirut was not a plus for science education: it was through his office that the conservatives in Tripoli were able to have Shakyh Jisr's *Madrasat al-Wataniyya* closed. Even the reformist *Madrasat al-Sultaniyya* was dogged by conservative opposition to the innovations that accompanied reform and cut short Shaykh Jisr's tenure.

Like the *Madrasat al-Wataniyya*, the *Sultaniyya* was a product of rivalry initiated by the rise of the foreign missionary schools that Muslim clerics and notables saw as an intellectual challenge to their relevancy, quite as the political rulers saw the European powers to be a challenge to theirs. Fear and suspicion bred a sense of self-defeating insecurity in both government and religion. So obsessive was it that Sultan abd al-Hamid ordered the *Sultaniyya* Madrasa and its supporting Islamic *Maqasid* charitable organization to be closed. The Sultan was sure that all of the institutions outside of his control were fomenting opposition against him. Many reform institutions that were not crippled by the contention between insecure traditionalist clerics and their reformist colleagues could be said to have been done in by the toxic insecurity that, starting at the top with Hamidian despotism, ran like a poisonous sap down the institutional levels and through society, withering the fruits of thought and action.

Shaykh Jisr was in Beirut in the summer of 1882 when Dr. Edwin Lewis gave his commencement address on science, knowledge and wisdom. He used to visit the SPC library to study natural science. He most probably was reading *Muqtataf's* articles on evolution, and no doubt was within earshot of all the commotion that followed the commencement address. Muhammad Abduh was also in Beirut that year. He had been exiled there for his support of the military government of Ahmad Urabi, who had challenged French and British control of Egypt's finances. The British invaded in 1882, toppled Colonel Urabi, and the new government that was established and supervised by the British sent Abduh into exile. In Beirut, Abduh gave lectures at the *Madrasat al-Sultaniyya*, which Shaykh Jisr was directing at the time. Abduh's lectures at the *Sultaniyya* would later be published as the *Risalat al-Tawhid* (*Treatise on Divine Oneness*), which would soon become one of modern Islam's most important pieces of literature on religious reform.

Not that Abduh's book led to great changes. The fear of change that haunted the great majority of the ulema derived in large part from a realistic assessment that opening the door to theological reinterpretation in order to accommodate science would do more damage to belief in the Quran's divine eternality than the *Tanzimat* legal reforms had done to the Shari'a, and subsequently to the disruption of the social norm. Reinterpretation of the sources would only accommodate the invasion of western social ideas and values, such as the abolishing of polygamy and the veiling and seclusion of women, of ease of divorce and cutting off of hands for theft, and in their place allowing capitalist interest on loans and secular institutions such as a legislative assembly and the like. With the peeling away of the Shari'a would go the Quran, hollowing out all the more the spiritual, legal and cultural core that bound the community together.

Shaykh Husayn al-Jisr was an exception to this mindset in that he believed the acceptance of science did not have to mean loss of the Shari'a in any of its parts as they presently existed in the *Tanzimat's* compilation of the *Majella*. Female education, communal religious equality, international banking and trade, and parliamentary government – all of these could be embraced by the Shari'a without compromising its essentials. Reform and the Shari'a could coexist as comfortably as science and religion, which were different terms for the same thing. They would have to coexist. Shaykh Jisr agreed with the majority of ulema that once any element of the Shari'a was changed or deleted by reinterpretation of the holy sources, the whole of it would unravel and society would be worse off and more vulnerable than before. He also knew that reforms were necessary for modernization and survival. He had welcomed the *Tanzimat* and its importation of western law codes, since, as he believed, nothing essential of the Shari'a had been lost. The personal status laws of the Shari'a, the heart of holy law that mattered most to Muslims in their everyday lives, had been preserved in the code of the *Majella*. Shaykh Jisr claimed to see no contradiction or problem in an educated woman happily accepting to be veiled and cloistered as one of several wives, or to see any risk to cultural authenticity by adopting western learning, as long as that essential core of the Shari'a was preserved. Change and tradition could live side by side once religion embraced change and preserved what had to be preserved for Islam to be Islam.

It is unlikely he truly believed society could modernize without the essentials of the Shari'a having to make some accommodations to the changes reforming the lives of those whom the Shari'a juristically governed. Jisr gave no guidelines for working out a program to achieve this perfect collaboration between change and preservation, other than stipulating science was part of Islam and the Shari'a should not be touched. What guidelines could he give? He must have known through his religious studies that it was precisely because of the fear that science would diminish the Shari'a and Quran that earlier generations of ulema had resisted and warned against those non-Shari'a sciences that subjected everything to reason. But these were critical times. Islam to survive had to meet the challenge of the West with western weapons, and that meant science. There was no choice. Science there had to be. It was an Islamic Catch 22: reject science to save religion and be taken down by the West; or take science to stave off the West and go down by moral collapse through loss of religion and social cohesion.

The only way out, as Shaykh Jisr saw it, was to reconcile religion and science and hope for the best. Metaphor and allegory would have to be applied to the Quran in making the reconciliation. But it could go no farther than that. In no way could the principle of producing new law from interpretation of the sacred scriptures, the *ijtihad* of classical Islam, be reinstituted. Just as easily as the holy sources of Quran and Hadith could be rendered to justify whatever was required of them regarding science, they could be interpreted to render what was required in formulating a western version of law. Once *ijtihad* was allowed, the ties that bind society would loosen and unravel into schism and factionalism. Holy law was the heart and unifying principle of Muslim community and identity. It had to be preserved.

Theology was something else. Theology could be changed for the sake of science but not the Shari'a for the sake of modernity. Law bound the daily lives of Muslims together, whereas theology was but an ethereal flight of intellect into the distant realm of logical abstracts that touched very few. What mattered to Muslims were the daily prayers, the Friday sermon, reciting the Quran, the fast of Ramadan, the pilgrimage, the charitable institutions, the religious feasts, the law with its regulation of personal, family and social obligations, its promise of multiple wives and easy divorce, its laws of inheritance, custody of children, circumcision and female chastity. Science and scripture could be reconciled in a reformed theology, but law must remain frozen in time. In fact, with all of Jisr's insistence that Islam was a religion of science, a close reading of the concluding section of his *Risalat al-Hamidiyya* shows him holding strongly to the Ash'arite line in opposition to the Mu'tazilite doctrines of divine justice, causality, free will and negation of anthropomorphism. How natural philosophy was going to squeeze into that straitjacket was left to the imagination.

Shaykh Jisr published his *Risalat al-Hamidiyya* (so named because it was dedicated to Sultan abd al-Hamid) several years after returning to Tripoli from Beirut. Three years after its Arabic publication (1886) it was translated into Turkish and published in Istanbul. Such was the popularity of the work among the literate Arabs of the empire that it attracted the attention, then the praise, of Turkish intellectuals of the Young Turk period. The treatise's basic premise is that the Quran and its depiction of nature can in no way disagree with the proven laws of science, since both scripture and nature were God's creation. Any contradiction has to be the consequence of a superficial understanding of the Quran. Questions such as how, or how long, or what route the earth took in the course of its formation are irrelevant to religion and pose no problem to scripture. Jisr claims to have been inspired to write his book when coming across an Arabic translation of a review of a book by an Englishman who showed that the difference between Christian belief and science was inconsequential.[6] If Christian theologians can study and accept science without it questioning or diminishing their faith, Jisr asks, then why should it pose a problem to Muslims? Why should not a Muslim search the Quran to discover what it reveals about nature in the light of modern science, as long as the essentials of the Shari'a are kept out of the exercise? Divine Law was one thing, Natural Law another and never the twain do meet.

Another book that influenced Jisr was one by the Syrian Christian we have already had occasion to refer to, Fransis Marrash's *Religion and Science*. The book brought into Arabic literature French Catholic apologetics framed in the defense of religion against the claims of science to explain everything. Marrash was a medical student in Paris during the time an active Catholic philosophical movement was influential in the medical school there, in the early 1860s. The movement "defended religion by stressing its conformity with science, coupled with a skeptical position about the certainty of science."[7] Taylor's and Marrash's books may have provided the idea and format of Jisr's book, but the immediate purpose for his writing it was to answer what he considered an attack on religion by science, or what was at the time being passed off as science, namely Shibli Shumayyil's translation of Buchner's commentary on Darwin.

Emulating al-Ghazali, Jisr wanted to define what parts of the many fields that passed for science were truly proven science and therefore acceptable; what parts of the not yet fully proven sciences were acceptable and on what basis were they not yet taken to be proven; and what parts of them were unacceptable on both scientific and religious grounds. The chief science that fell under the not yet fully proven category was evolution, much of which was unproven, riddled with contradiction and, as such, absolutely unacceptable and dangerous to belief. What part of evolution was not dangerous to belief and therefore acceptable depended on the Quran and how the relevant verses deciding the issue were understood. A proper understanding of the verses was critical.

Jisr divides the verses into two categories: those that are clear enough and cannot be interpreted beyond their obvious meaning, such as those that contain the laws of marriage, divorce and inheritance; and those that are insufficiently clear, or not rational enough to be understood literally, and so are open to interpretation.

By interpreting certain verses of this latter category he concludes that the theory of Darwin does not contravene anything in Muslim belief, even though there are elements of it that have not yet been conclusively established as fact. Evolution is simply matter and motion in biological action, a causal step up from the realm of dead matter acting according to the laws of pure physics, and no more than just one more example of God's will expressed in the divine *sunna* of nature.[8] The materialists are correct when saying the basis of everything is material, but by stopping short and not explaining where matter came from in the beginning they leave science incomplete. Evolutionists are not wrong; they are just short-sighted. When scientists say nothing comes from nothing they are right. Matter cannot come from nothing. It can only come from God, who created matter and put it in motion, and imparted guidance and direction, since matter and motion could not without God's guiding will direct themselves. Matter and motion devoid of divine will are effects, not causes in themselves.

In a half step toward the middle from either direction of Ash'arite theology and modern science, Jisr claims that the causal power that matter and motion have in the realm of natural relationships emanates from God's eternal and pervasive guiding will. Everything in the realm of nature has a precedent: life comes from water, water from hydrogen and oxygen in proportional parts, and just as hydrogen and oxygen must precede water, which preceded life, something has to precede hydrogen and oxygen and all the other 60 elements, and this is God. As God ordered matter in forming the elements, He ordered matter in the formation of the earth through the geological ages, stage by stage, giving form to species of plants and animals during the millions of years they evolved from earlier to later forms. God's creating and preserving power is ever present. God created the seeds from which the forms evolved over time. Muslims know this and therefore would make superior scientists. Islam endows the believer with a more penetrating vision into nature's operations than do other religions. Muslims are more clear-sighted in the workings of nature than western scientists since Muslims understand the source of power, being and change. As a system of processes of matter in motion, science conforms with Muslim belief. Muslims have a universal understanding of science because they have retained in their belief system the final cause of Aristotle that westerners have eliminated.

The image Jisr evokes is the divine clockmaker whose finger is always on the mainspring and who has created for His clock extra parts, such as the angels and jinn, which have to be accounted for since they are included in the Quran. Western scientists are ignorant of these phenomena, and so their science is incomplete. Muslims on the other hand know of angels and jinn and will eventually find them their place in the system of nature.

Behind Jisr's argument for science looms the dominating shadow of Ash'arite scholasticism. Muslims know that nature's laws and causal relationships are only appearances, that it is God's custom that runs the operations of His creation. In other words, for Shaykh Jisr there was no autonomous system of relations unifying nature and the cosmos. Law and causality were in reality God's will in direct and continuous action on all particles composing the universe. God directly created every cause for every effect. Particles of iron that were loosened from a solid iron bar in an acid bath were not loosened because of the chemical action of the acid but because of God's will.[9] Natural relationships were no more than the appearance of phenomena that human intelligence perceived to be related after repeated observation and experience.[10]

Science is the knowledge of the working of divine creation on the physical level of surface phenomena, empirically derived and in conformity with the Quran, Hadith and Shari'a. Jisr likens the modern scientist to one of those millions of microbes in a drop of water whose realization of existence begins and ends with itself. The difference in consciousness between a microbe and a man is even less than that between man and God. How could a materialist scientist possibly be conscious of anything beyond the physical world without the guidance of revelation?[11]

Some Quranic verses required allegorical interpretation in regard to physical reality, such as those that struck images of a flat earth, or of a sun that when setting sank into a hot spring on the earth's surface. These verses had nothing to do with science. Nor could the "six days of creation" be taken literally, because a day in God's reckoning could mean a millennium in man's reckoning. Since the earth's sphericity and motion were established facts, as were the geological ages of the earth's formation, verses that did not tally with these realities had to be rendered allegorically.

Some of these verses gave evidence of physical phenomena only recently discovered. "The heavens and earth were mended together and God rent them apart," was a Quranic insight to the nebular theory and the splitting off of earth and the other planets from the sun. The secrets of magnetism and electricity were revealed in the verse "We sent down iron in which there is for people both harm and benefit." Science could not by itself answer why it is only iron that could be magnetized or why cutting a magnetic bar in two produces two magnets, each with a power equal to the original. The answers were beyond the physical realm of reality, and only Islam could lead to them. The fact of there being a girl in America who could read minuscule writing blind folded and in the dark bore witness: "This story agrees with what the followers of Muhammad believe, that sight is purely the creation of God, as are all the senses." Science reveals the surface of reality, religion its interior.[12]

Toward the latter part of his book Shaykh Jisr restricts the degree of acceptability of Darwin's theory of evolution of species. The theory becomes qualified as one of those sciences that has not been fully verified and cannot be accepted. Where the Quran describes God's creation of the human species the verses are clear and precise and so cannot be allegorized to make way for the evolution of man.[13] As for the bones of extinct species dug up from the earth by paleontologists, these skeletal remains fail to prove evolution, since God may not have been pleased with his design and ended those forms of life to start over with new designs. The conundrum of worshipping an all-wise divinity whose creative efforts may have had a number of false starts is passed over. The absurdity of Jisr's explanation shows he was obviously unhappy with evolution but knew there was too much evidence to deny it outright. His escape is a compromise: to leave it up to the believer to decide on natural selection on one's own without committing oneself, and to explain away the evidence supporting human evolution in any way one can. Even the problematic descent of man has an escape clause: if the issue of human evolution is ever decided by advances in scientific discovery, the Quran could cover it. In other words, the Quran could meet anything science came up with.

Evolution is a special category of science since it has neither been irrefutably proved nor disproved. The Quran reflects this twilight zone in that some verses on the literal level appear to be opposed to evolution, and others not to be, in which case a Muslim is free to believe or disbelieve as long as one holds firm to one's belief in the Creator who is at every instant directing what physically looks to be the variation of species through long chains of causal relationships. A believer is free to allegorize those verses that are seemingly opposed to evolution if one chooses to believe in the theory. If and when science ever proves evolution with the same binding evidence that has established the earth's sphericity and motion, then a Muslim will be obliged to believe it; and verses of the Quran will be seen to confirm it.[14] In the meantime, evolution is suspended in a limbo, a shadowland of belief and unbelief where the believer is left on one's own. By leaving the choice open and the theory in limbo, Shaykh Jisr left it to other shaykhs to carry the argument further. He had taken it pretty far himself, considering he was a member of the Muslim religious establishment. Compared to the restrictive views held by the evangelist Americans in Beirut at the time, he was radically liberal, and had even bothered to learn something about evolution, presumbably through reading *Muqtataf* and Dr. al-Iskandarani's book of 1880.

Jisr's book was read throughout the Arab region. Muslim intellectuals and religious scholars were much influenced by it and would adopt the author's arguments in reasoning out agreement between science and the Quran. The full name of his book is *Risalat al-Hamidiyya fi Haqiqat al-Diyana al-Islamiyya wa Haqqiyya al-Shari'a al Muhamadiyya*(the *Hamidian Treatise on the Truth of Islam and the Holy Law of Muhammad*). Jisr had added *Hamidiyya* to the title and dedicated it to Sultan abd al-Hamid thinking that the Ottoman censors, who had a reputation for losing manuscripts, would not dare misplace anything that had the Sultan's name in the title – or scrutinize too closely anything dedicated to the Sultan, for Jisr feared he might have gone too far in laying scripture open to natural selection.[15]

His fear turned out to be baseless. The Sultan praised the book, had it translated into Turkish and printed. Twenty thousand Turkish copies were sold in short order, making it the equivalent of a best seller. An Urdu translation was made. The reforming grand vizier, Midhat Pasha, thought it was one of the year's most valuable books published in the whole of the Ottoman Empire. The author was awarded several Ottoman medals and gained the reputation of being the most informed Muslim in the empire on the science of evolution. Abd al-Hamid was so taken with the book he asked Midhat Pasha what he thought about having a new interpretation of the Quran made in the light of evolution and modern science, to which Midhat replied that there were only three people able to accomplish such a task, Shaykh Jisr, himself and Jamal al-Din al-Afghani. His including Afghani is most surprising considering the simple minded and uncritical rejection of evolution Afghani had presented to Muslims. Had abd al-Hamid's suggestion been carried out and a sober reformist interpretation of the Quran been produced with the presumed backing of the empire's high ulema and chief mufti, including the rector of al-Azhar, an immense precedent toward scientific assimilation would have been established. One can hardly imagine the conservative fury that would have met the new interpretation, but religious opposition to such an undertaking would have over time abated as long as reformist determination held strong, even if it took a generation for the old to die out and be replaced by the new.

Shaykh Jisr's efforts at "saving" the Quran from the threat of modern science by scientific exegesis are reminiscent of the tremendous efforts of centuries of Hellenistic and Muslim astronomers who strove to "save the phenomena" of the Ptolemaic heavens from the threat of observations that put into question the heavenly spheres revolving in perfect uniform circular motion around the earth at the center. As the astronomers refigured over and over the geometric machinery of planetary models so that the models approximated observed planetary motions, in like manner did Jisr and a century of imitators refigure the meaning of verses of the Quran to the measure of science in order to save the phenomena of the holy book's eternal infallibility. The more that Muslims perceived themselves to be threatened and reduced by the West, the more forcefully the Quran was held up as their defending shield, emblazoned in the logo of an eternal truth that contained and transcended western science. It was a slippery path. Shaykh Jisr was aware of the tricky dilemma allegorization presented. How far could it be taken? What could and could not be played with in order that the eternal word of the Quran, God's immutable mind at work, would come out on the side of science without bending immutability so out of shape it became meaningless? How could the idea of interpreting verses according to the science of the day, and reinterpreting them the next day as new science laid waste the old, be prevented from laying waste the meaning of the Quran? How could Scientific Interpretation do its work and the sacred meaning of the Quran be preserved? Once the door of interpretation was opened, what might not rush in to modernize and allegorize the Quran out of existence? Shaykh Jisr was fully aware of the Pandora's Box he was opening.

First, he denied he was opening the door of interpretation. It was science, not the law that he was concerned with. He insisted that what he was doing was not *ijtihad*: jurisprudential interpretation; he was simply clarifying what had been unclear. But allegorization was necessary in coming to terms with certain Quranic verses. In his own words:

> The followers of Muhammad believe the literal meaning of Quranic verses unless it goes against what is absolutely known, proven and understood. In such a case the text is allegorized to bring agreement between it and what is known by proof . . . For example, sometimes the text says rain comes from the sky, sometimes from clouds. God can have it both ways, but interpretation is needed to reconcile the text with known science: that rain is formed

by evaporation of moisture from rivers and seas, the moisture then rising to become clouds that, when chilled, condense and fall back to earth as rain. But only those who are experts in religion and interpretation (*tafsir*) are allowed to use allegory, since greater damage could be done to religion by those who defend it ignorantly than by those who are its enemies.[16]

Because of the growing number of educated Muslims who by the late 1880s were becoming aware of science, some guidance was necessary in reading the Quran. The Quran was the mother book; it was the existential core of society. Guidelines had to be set to accommodate change and relevancy without compromising immutability. What part of the Quran could not be touched?

Jisr listed the most important of those verses that, though challenged by reason and science, could not be reduced by allegory or metaphor. Those verses that mentioned God's Throne in the highest of the Seven Heavens could not be allegorized nor the ones describing the Heavenly Preserved Pen and Tablet; the Quranic descriptions of the terrors of hell and the fleshly delights of paradise also had to be literally accepted. Jisr must have been aware of the difficulty that Muslims with some knowledge of science, like himself, were having with such ideas, but the imagery of Pen and Tablet, and the exciting expectations of paradise, and trembling horrors of hell where enemies would go, were too dearly cherished by the great majority to be allegorized away or even put up to choice. Diminishing the belief in the absolute reality of hell's punishment and the promise of heaven's pleasure would have eviscerated God's awesome mystery and the anticipation of a joyous after-life. In addition to the inclination of people bathed in religion to cling to its promises, there were sound economic and political reasons to preserve belief in the terrors of hell and the delicious fantasies that men had of paradise.[17]

Yet, for all that, Jisr did allow for some of those cherished but fantastical elements of the Quran to be allegorized out of literal reality. Angels became rays of light shining between heaven and earth; the jinn became the ethereal fluid filling the universe to carry light waves and the forces of gravitational attraction. "If God can cause planets to go as fast as they do by gravity, it is not beyond Him to have angels travel as fast as light."[18] The Quranic anthropomorphism that Ash'arite theology and tradition held to be literal realities were also brushed aside. God's hearing, speaking, seeing and sitting did not mean the deity had ears, mouth, eyes and a posterior. These divine attributes had to be understood in a metaphorical or analogical sense.[19]

Jisr wanted the miracles of prophets and saints along with the science of natural law all rolled up in one belief system. Islam was a religion of science in which miracles were misinterpreted natural events with a scientific basis. Nothing was surrendered. Nothing was lost. Nor was anything lost on the legal level of ordering society, for Islam was also a religion of law. Ease of divorce, multiplicity of wives, veiling and seclusion of women and their inferior legal status – all were divine laws whose perfection in ordering and running society paralleled the laws of nature. But even here, Jisr's thoughts, however conservative, represent a major step beyond Ghazali's admonition to keep science at arm's length. His theological reflections, tortured as they are, form an Ash'arite foundation for moving from Tahtawi's traditionalist restraint to Abduh's tenuous neo-Mu'tazilite reopening of the gate of *ijtihad*: Quranic and legal interpretation for a modernized Islam.

Science was admittedly a problem; rather, it was the unwarranted claims of science that made the problem. Consequently, knowledgeable religious authorities had to lay down guidelines and keep a sharp eye to restrain any claims of science that went beyond itself and into areas where science had no authority to speak. Science should therefore be taught by men of religion, good Muslims of sound faith, ideally coming from the ulema, those who had the power to loosen and bind (*ahl al-hall wa'l 'aqd*.) Only then could it be assured that science and religion would live together in harmony. He thought one hour of religious training a day would be sufficient to keep students of science firm in their faith, with the teacher attributing the wonders of nature to God and not to nature. Thinking it the only way Muslims would be preserved from usurpation and degradation by the West, Jisr appealed to the Ottoman government to build a system of scientific and technical institutes staffed by devout Muslims and religious scholars learned in science and technology.[20] He could hardly have believed that was going to happen.

The optimistic ideal of an ulema immersed in science and technology at the vanguard of modernization as a defense against the West was beyond fantasy. Even Shaykh Jisr clung to tradition when confronted by modern technology. The Quran, he reasoned, could not be recited over the phone or recorded on the phonograph; and anyone associated with religious study or teaching could not be photographed.[21] Though not to the same degree as it did Shaykh Tahtawi, the grip of tradition held Shaykh Jisr in the twilight zone between the medieval and the modern and never let go. The binding force of tradition was, however, not the same across the Islamic world. Nineteenth century Muslim reformers in India had some degree of success in loosening and escaping that grip.

Notes

1 A second edition of Jisr's *Risalat* was published by Khalid Ziyadah in 1925. For an analysis of Shaykh al-Jisr's work: Johannes Ebert, *Religion and Reform in der Arabischen Provinz: Husayn al-Gisr al-Tarabulsi (1845–1909)* (*Ein Islamiscer Gelehrter zwischen Tradition und Reform*), Peter Lang Publisher, Heidelberg Orientalische Studien, vol 18, Frankfurt, 1991; and Marwa Elshakry, *Darwin's Legacies in the Arab East: Science, Religion and Politics, 1870–1914*, Princeton PhD dissertation, 2003, pp. 201–224.
2 J. Ebert, *Religion und Reform in der Arabischen Provinz*, Husaynal-Gisr at-Tarabulsi (1845–1909), pp. 76–77.
3 Rashid Rida, *al-Manar wa'l Azhar*, al-Manar, Cairo, 1934, p. 142.
4 Elshakry, *Darwin's Legacies*, p. 205; also pp. 206–208 for Muslim clerical opposition to Christian missionary schools and to SPC.
5 Elshakry, *Darwin's Legacies*, p. 201.
6 The book, *Physical Theory of Another Life*, Appleton, New York, 1836, was written by Isaac Taylor (1797–1865) and published in 1836. It is a long exposition on the principles of physical science and the possibility of an after-life based on those principles, the thrust of the argument being that there is nothing in the principles that denies an after-life, and much in them that argues for one, with every indication that future science will bring more evidence supporting the reality of an after-life.

7 Aziz Azmeh, "Muslim Modernism and the Text of the Past," in *Islam and the Challenge of Modernity*, edited by Sharifa Shifa al-Attas, International Institute of Islamic Thought and Civilization, Kuala Lumpur, 1996, p. 427.
8 al-Jisr, *Risalat al-Hamidiyya fi Haqiqat al-Diyana al- Islamiyya wa'l Haqqiyyat al-Shari'a al-Muhammadiyya*, Cairo, 1888, p. 149. Shaykh al-Jisr's *Risalat* has been recently published by Dar al-Kitab, Cairo, 2012; and Dar al Kitab al Lubnaniyya, Beirut, 2012.
9 al-Jisr, *Risalat*, p. 177.
10 al-Jisr, *Risalat*, p. 238.
11 al-Jisr, *Risalat*, p. 226.
12 al-Jisr, *Risalat*, pp. 210–212.
13 al-Jisr, *Risalat*, pp. 242–242.
14 al-Jisr, *Risalat*, pp. 238–240.
15 The Sultan asked Shaykh Jisr to write a second book, this on the rectitude of Islamic principles, which the shaykh did, entitling it *al-Husun al-Hamidiyya li'l Muhafazat al-Aqa'id al Islamiyya* (*Hamidian Strongholds for Defending Islamic Doctrines*), Istanbul, 1905. See Rudolf Peters, "Resurrection, Revelation and Reason: Husayn al-Jisr (d. 1909) and Islamic Eschatology." In J. M. Bremer, P. Peters, & T. P. J. van den Hout (Eds.), *Hidden futures: death and immortality in Ancient Egypt, Anatolia, the Classical, Biblical and Arabic-Islamic World*, Amsterdam, Amsterdam University, 1994, pp. 221-231. Press.
16 al-Jisr, *Risalat*, pp. 283–284.
17 al-Jisr, *Risalat*, p. 261.
18 al-Jisr, *Risalat*, pp. 263–265.
19 al-Jisr, *Risalat*, p. 17.
20 al-Jisr, *Risalat*, pp. 212–214.
21 In relation to this see Rudolf Peters, "Religious Attitudes Toward Modernity," *Die Welt des Islams*, vol 26 (1986), pp. 76–105.

9 Darwin between Sayyid Ahmad Khan's *Natcheriyya* and Jamal al-Din al-Afghani's refutation

Copies of Shaykh Jisr's *Risalat al-Hamidiyya* spread throughout the Arab world. Turkish and Urdu translations made it available in the wider Muslim world, where secular and religious reformist thinkers in the major regions and languages of Islam were just at the time coming into contact with evolution theory. Writing in Urdu, Sayyid Ahmad Khan in India was promoting evolution as the central principle of his philosophy of nature, which he called *Natcheriyya*. Writing in Persian, Jamal al-Din al-Afghani was attacking evolution and particularly Ahmad Khan's *Natcheriyya* version of it. His attacks damaged the Middle Eastern perception of natural selection as much as did Shumayyil's support of it. Distorted by both supporters and opponents, the theory of natural selection was long in being allowed a fair hearing in Muslim societies with the exception of the works of Shaykh al-Jisr and Ahmad Khan, that former offering conditional support, the latter effusive support, and for that reason being castigated and denigrated in the storm that followed, swallowing up the landscape of rational discourse.

Two sets of combatants engaged in the debate that raged – the word is not too strong for the emotional temperature of exchange on the issue – between the supporters and attackers of evolution in the half century between the founding of *Muqtataf* and the publication of Muhammad Farid Wajdi's *National Encyclopedia*. The first to enter the ring were the Christians of Syria and Mt. Lebanon who fought it out in Arabic. Shaykh Jisr introduced Arab Muslims to the fray. With *Muqtataf's* relocation from Beirut, the ring was extended to Egypt, where, a few years after Jisr's book was published, Shaykh Muhammad Abduh began writing sporadically on evolution, but taking a much more cautious approach than had Shaykh Jisr. The second set of combatants, non-Arab Muslims, entered the ring not long after the match had begun, adding Urdu and Persian to the fighting words of Arabic.

At the center of the Muslim debate was Ahmad Khan's philosophy of *Natcheriyya* and al-Afghani's denunciation of it. Traveling the Muslim and Arab world and Europe while being all things to all people with the single vision of advancing pan-Islamic unity, Afghani linked the battle going on among Muslims to the one among Christians. The sharpening of knives began in India when Ahmad Khan, a mild pacifist accountant working in an agency of the British East India Company with little knowledge of science, wrote a conciliatory treatise on science and

Islam. His philosophy of *Natcheriyya* was a plea for Muslim deism, according to which God was manifested by nature and the Quran was a palimpsest upon which divine revelation was written over the fabric of nature's cyclical patterns.

Ahmad Khan and *Natcheriyya* were products of a long period of cultural assimilation of western ideas among Hindus and Muslims in British India, where the transmission of science and its interaction with religion were altogether different from what took place in Cairo, Istanbul and Beirut. In all four regions the interaction was, of course, the result of western influences penetrating the East, but profound significant differences existed in the way these influences were channeled. In Cairo and Istanbul the government initiated and attempted to control the process of modernization through secular schools, translations, student missions, government journals and the hiring of Europeans to direct the new institutions. In Syria, the interaction was initiated and mediated through French Catholic and American evangelical religious missions. In India, the intellectual bridging between Islam and the West came in the form of British occupation and colonization, which went back to the 18th century. By the last decades of the 19th century, the western ideas that came from a western occupier and its institutions had had generations to work their influences.[1]

Indeed, in regard to western occupation, Egypt and the Caucasus also experienced direct foreign control: the brief French occupation of the former that produced the *Institut d'Egypte* and Hasan al-Attar; and the Russian occupation of the latter that produced Qudsi of Baku. Attar and Qudsi were intellectual preludes to the programs of intense modernization undertaken by Muhammad Ali and Sultan Mahmud II. For that matter, the French Jesuits and American evangelicals might also be seen as a form of foreign occupation, of a non-military but nonetheless militant regimen, in which the intent was religio-cultural expansion rather than geo-political hegemony. The forms of occupation and their consequent influences varied immensely. The British occupation of Egypt that came late in the 19th century differed fundamentally from its occupation of India in that Egypt was never an integral part of the British empire in the same sense India was. Whether Indians or British liked it or not, and in spite of the Sepoy Rebellion, British India came to express by the mid-19th century a cultural association and investment of identities that were completely foreign to what was meant by British Egypt, an expression of alien domination and coercion, where rulers and ruled existed in an uneasy condition of continued hostility and resistance. British India was indeed that but also much more.

The British came to India in the 17th century as merchants who easily took to the relaxed ways of Indian culture. The merchants dressed Indian and took Indian wives or concubines. This of course changed as British assimilation gave way to hard-edged colonization, when British ways and wives were transplanted in India. The British came to Egypt in the late 19th century in the form of a naval armada and army of occupation to secure the investments of their financiers and entrepreneurs, and above all, to secure the Suez Canal as Britain's passage to India. Very little intermarriage and cultural assimilation into local life on the part of the British colonials existed in the heat of 19th century imperialism with its theories of national superiority divided the world into whites and wogs. Britain in Egypt was a tenuous affair. Almost every year for two decades the British promised the French and the Egyptians that they would soon depart. The British were sure their presence would be ephemeral. In Egypt, education had no place on the British agenda of financial, administrative and military control. Egypt was only a debt to be paid, a waterway to be controlled and peasants to work the land and be taxed. The British in India were sure they would be there forever. India was British. And with India being British, it was natural that British educators would build schools and colleges, if for no other reason than to prepare Indians to serve in the administration of colonial rule and, when possible, make Christians of them. A member of the Court of Directors of the East India Company proclaimed in 1813 that the "Supreme Disposer" had put India "providentially into our hands . . . not merely to draw an annual profit from them, but that we might diffuse among their inhabitants, long sunk in darkness, vice and misery, the light and the benign influences of Truth, the blessings of well-regulated society, the improvements and the comforts of active industry." "Darkness, vice and misery" covered whatever the colonizers failed to understand in Indian culture or went against their interest.

Regardless of the separation of wogs from whites, and the inhumanity that wiped out the amicable fraternization and assimilation of earlier generations, the wogs came to respect and appreciate certain features of their colonizer's civilization. India presents a unique case of Muslim interaction with, and appropriation of, western knowledge. The process got off the ground with as many false starts, difficulties and tergiversations as did reform in the Ottoman Empire and Egypt. Around the time of Sultan Selim's *Nizam-i Jadid* and Bonaparte's *Institut d'Egypte*, the autonomous provincial Muslim ruler of Awadh, Asaf al-Dawla, had Newton's *Principia* translated into Arabic, which was still the language of science throughout the whole of Islamdom. This was between 1778 and 1792, long before a comprehensive text on Newtonian science became available to Ottomans with Hoja Ishak's *Compendium of Mathematical Sciences* in the mid-1830s, and longer still before it was available in the Arabic-speaking region. The translation would seem to have been the dawn of a brilliant beginning of assimilation, particularly when Asaf al-Dawla began construction in Lucknow of an observatory, which was completed by his successor. Both rulers were avidly interested in science, but as in the case of the silver age of Muslim science in Andalusia, Maragha and Samarqand, lack of sustained continuity of interest and investment precluded the birth of an on-going tradition of significant longevity.

In 1799, an aristocratic Indian Muslim associated with the ruler of Awadh, abu Talib Khan, traveled to Europe on his own and remained there five years. Upon returning, he published his impressions of his European travels and experience in a humorous book, *Masir-i Talib fi Biladi-i Afranji*, translated as *Travels in Asia, Africa and Europe*.[2] The book is in many ways an Indian prequel to Tahtawi's observations of Parisian life a generation later, but has nothing to say about scientific institutions. Abu Talib was impressed with the education and freedom enjoyed by women, and their moral character, which he contrasts favorably to the deviousness of Muslim women, which he understood to come from their being condemned to illiteracy and locked up in seclusion.

Abu Talib Khan was also impressed with Britain's industrial factories. He perceived the regularity and precision of their machines to be the source of British punctuality and unremitting hard work: having built these marvelous machines, they came to act like them. He equally admired their judicial court system, though not the aggressive way barristers attacked defendants and plaintiffs – he likened a debate in the House of Commons to flocks of parakeets squawking at each other from two rows of opposing trees. His interests did not include the Royal Society, Greenwich, the museums, observatories, scientific exhibits, universities and scientific laboratories that were the pride of England. Informative as his book otherwise was, with its many acute observations of British life and institutions, it found no spark of interest in that dimension of Britain's greatest contributions to western might and civilization. Indian interest in western science didn't arise until the 19th century, when schools were founded based on British models.

The first British-influenced colleges in India were established by a group of Hindu merchants, who had grown rich through the British and the East India Company. In 1816, the Calcutta Hindu College was founded. Two years later another was founded in Benares. The British colonial government then founded one in 1821, the Hindu Sanskrit College at Calcutta, which emphasized science and technology.[3] In a way resembling the Syro–Lebanese experience with French and American missionaries, it was the colleges founded in India by British missionaries that provided the incubation chambers from which came the first deep breath of Indian interest in science. Delhi College, founded in 1827, was one of the first of these. Class lectures were in Urdu. School texts were translated from English into Urdu by British and Indian Muslim scholars. British presses using Urdu font printed the translated texts so that students of science, mathematics and medicine had sufficient reading material for their courses. Students were thus spared the worst of the textual and translation problems that hampered education in the new schools that were at the time coming into existence in Cairo. A medical college was founded in Bombay in 1845. Two years later, an engineering school was founded in Roorkee. About the same time, another engineering school went up at Agra in the northwest. A college for science was founded in Benares, giving India three colleges at the time that offered an education in modern science: the Agra College, the Delhi Government College and the Benares College.

The headmaster of the Delhi College, Felix Boutros, an Indian convert to Christianity, founded the Society for the Promotion of Knowledge and translated a total of 30 books on scientific and related subjects from English into Urdu. His successor, Alois Sprenger, founded a scientific journal, *Qiran al- Sa'adayn (Conjunction of the Two Happy Planets: Venus and Jupiter)*, which featured articles on modern science and recent European discoveries. This was in 1845. A dozen years later the Indian humanist and mathematician, Kayasta Ramchandra (1821–1880), founded another scientific periodical in his quest to communicate western science to the Hindu community.

The British-style schools prepared the soil for indigenous scientific interest to take root. By the 1830s, the same time that the schools of engineering and medicine were functioning in Cairo and Istanbul, young Indians, many of them converts to Christianity, were seriously engaged in studying science in English, but unlike the students in Cairo and Istanbul, who were government selected appointees assigned to technological, industrial or medical study in order to serve the state in whatever capacity they were ordered to serve, the students in India were mainly studying science and mathematics as a philosophical approach to learning about the universe as a source of personal fulfillment or preparing themselves for careers of their own choosing in government or civil society. Being a part of the British empire, the state in India already had the power to defend itself and did not need technically trained students to serve the state and the military. It was a different kind of problem that the Indians had with the colleges.

Because of the sense of racial superiority that arose in the 19th century, which the British did little to hide once colonial government had taken over the merchant colonies that had quietly and comfortably gone Indian, it was not easy for Hindu and Muslim Indians to avail themselves of the British schools. When British wives and missionaries had finished God's work of returning the Indianized British merchants back into proper white Englishmen, the impermeable curtain of racist segregation descended, and the Indians only grudgingly accepted the advantages offered by the schools of their imperial masters. Suspicions of British motives exacerbated by the wounded spirit inflicted by white missionaries associated with the East India Company, who were dedicated to the "moral improvement" of the Indian people, made the preparatory schools and colleges appear to them as Christian conversion chambers. In this respect, the British educational offerings presented more of a threat to the self-esteem and religious pride of Indians than did the secular schools to Muslims in Cairo and Istanbul. Hindus and Muslims who came to the British schools came with a large swallow of pride, especially Muslims, proud with memories of Moghul splendor and 11 centuries of Muslim political and cultural dominance. This may help explain why Hindus outnumbered Muslims in the schools 6 to 1 between 1835 and 1870.

More than pride was at work in making Muslims resistant to foreign knowledge. In the 1660s in Moghul India, Shaykh Ahmad Sirhind and other influential religious figures wrote fatwas forbidding Muslims to study science, mathematics and other rational subjects. The mentality that had given rise to that prejudice, reaching back a millennium and typified by Hanbali traditionalism, was still very much alive in the 19th century. It was not until the 1840s that Muslims began following Hindus into the British schools, particularly the British school at Agra, which had been a traditional center of Muslim learning. But when the British turned the school into an Anglican missionary center, the Government School at Agra started to look like the Syrian Protestant College: students at both institutions had to swallow the evangelical host as the value added tax on tuition for their science education.

Of all the British Government colleges, the one at Agra became the most formidable institution of scientific learning. Lieutenant-Governor James Thomason provided special donations for the college's science courses. This meant that classrooms had sufficient chairs, desks and blackboards with chalk, and that the students had textbooks, laboratory equipment, a science library and competent English and science teachers – an educational splendor that Ali Mubarak in Egypt, who was at the time teaching military officers geometry with sticks and strings and figures scratched in the dirt, could have imagined existed only among the houris in paradise. John Herschel's *Outlines of Astronomy* and William Paley's *Natural Theology* (published in 1802 and professing the medieval cosmological precept that "the coordinated structures in natural organisms lead us to infer the existence of an intelligent Designer") were translated into Urdu and taught at the Agra College.[4] The College also sponsored public lectures on scientific topics of the day, given in Urdu, Hindi and English. In return for Lieutenant-Governor Thomason's generosity to the Agra College, a Hindu scholar teaching there dedicated a book to him on the harmony of western science and Hindu philosophy. In sum, a lively scientific culture was growing in Agra by the middle of the 19th century, but one that as yet was without active Muslim participation. In time Muslims would come.

The British Government College at Agra was, as alluded to previously, India's version of the American Syrian Protestant College, with Hindus playing the role of eastern Christians in preparing the way for Muslim participation. In the 1860s, after half a century of slow assimilation and propagation of scientific interest by British educators, seconded by Hindu students and Hindu converts to Christianity, several intellectual leaders in the Muslim community rose to prominence as advocates of reform calling for Muslims to embrace the exact sciences. Foremost among these was Karamat Ali and Ahmad Khan. The former, whose career coincided with Shaykh Tahtawi's, accepted western science unconditionally. In his remarkable book of 1865, *Ma'khidh al- 'Ulum (Source of the Sciences)*, Karamat Ali took up the call for Muslims to embrace science, advancing it to a level of sophisticated argument not reached in the Arab regions until decades later. By extolling the Quran and Islam for their scientific nature, he called for Muslims to take up their religious duty of studying the sciences unconditionally.

Passages in Karamat Ali's book sound very much like what would later be called "Scientific Interpretation" and "Islamic Science" all rolled into one: science was the essence of faith and revelation; science *was* religion; a Muslim could be no truer to the sources of one's religion than by studying science, whatever one thought of its apparent origins. The true origins of science were none other than the sacred Quran and Hadith, in which could be found the secrets of science, some only recently discovered. A careful reading of Quran and Hadith, with special attention to their metaphors, similes, allusions, hidden meanings and express declarations of nature's workings, could be a guide to future discovery: "The whole Koran is full of passages containing information on physical and mathematical sciences. If we would but spend a little reflection over it we would find wondrous meanings in every word it contains. . . . What a strange coincidence exists between the Koran and the Philosophy of modern Europe."[5] What Karamat Ali was saying in so many words was that science, through religion and for the sake of religion, trumped religion. As will be seen, this was an Indian Muslim version of Shaykh Muhammad Abduh's "cutting the head of religion with the sword of religion to save religion" – as to say, to cut the umbilical cord of tradition in birthing modern science from the womb of religious reinterpretation.

First lambasting Muslims for their mental lethargy, Karamat Ali then exhorts them to endeavor in a religious jihad to learn European languages as a key to the sciences. He praises the educational reforms of Muhammad Ali of Egypt and Ottoman Sultan Mahmud and calls them true Muslim rulers doing their duty in following the right path to empower the Muslim community through propagation of science, and sharply criticizes Iran for failing Islam by its incomprehensible disregard of science, considering the grand contribution Iranians made to Muslim thought and science during the pre-Safavid period and then what little they had done after the fall of the Safavids in the early 18th century.

Following Karamat Ali's lead was Sayyid Ahmad Khan (1817–1898), whose fame as a religious reformer in Muslim India came to soar far above the name of his predecessor. Ahmad Khan came from a well-off landed family in the northwest of the country. He was given a traditional religious education devoid of science and modern knowledge. His traditional religious upbringing would seem to have made him an unlikely candidate of reform, but a traditional background and religious education were characteristic of all the early reformers, from Shaykh Tahtawi and Ali Mubarak to Shaykhs Muhammad Abduh and Rashid Rida: there were no other backgrounds and educations to be had. Rather than continue on to advanced religious study, Ahmad Khan took a position through family connections as a clerk in the East India Company.

Around 1840, when he was a young man in his 20s, the company commissioned him to its offices in Agra, where the British Government College was rising to scientific prominence. It was there, in association with British employees of the East India Company, in the shadows of the British Government College, that he learned, to his shock and initial disbelief, that the earth revolved and rotated. Ahmad could not at first fathom that seemingly intelligent and rational people of a nation that dominated world trade could possibly believe such an absurdity; that they believed it to be a scientifically proven fact added shock to absurdity. He declared the idea of a moving earth wrong and openly argued against it in favor of the traditional Ptolomeo-Islamic system. To erase all doubt, he produced a logical proof of the earth's immobility at the center of the heavens in the fashion of medieval Aristotelian dialectics.[6] One can imagine the bemused response of Ahmad Khan's British colleagues in their East India Company offices when he presented his proof to them. This was close to a decade after Hoja Ishak Efendi's *Compendium of the Mathematical Sciences* had been published in Istanbul, which gives an idea of the glacial rate of intellectual communication among the primary linguistic regions of Islamdom.

The failure of the Sepoy Rebellion (1857–1858) was the turning point in Ahmad Khan's intellectual life. Making the connection between British power and science, he realized that changeless tradition was a one-way road to destruction. From that point on, he had no difficulty accepting Copernicus, Galileo, Newton and the new science – including Darwin. The Rebellion proved that violent resistance to the British was futile. If Indian independence was to be won, it would only be through cooperation with the occupying power, by assimilating its science and technology. He believed that Muslims in all the different regions of their world had to learn this painful lesson on their own in defending themselves from the West, and that, in the case of India, the institutions that were required for the people to stand on their own could best be acquired through their acceptance of the British and their remaining loyal to the colonial ruler. Institutional assimilation would lead to the intellectual and economic development that was necessary to create, solidify and guarantee a people's political freedom. As there were no indigenous roots in Muslim or Hindu culture from which these institutions could sprout, the knowledge that was needed to make them one's own would have to be learned from the British. Loyalty to the British was the key to liberation. The progress that India would experience in cooperation with the colonial power would be the "most wonderful phenomenon the world has ever seen."[7] To many Muslims, this policy would look more like treacherous collaboration with the enemy and heresy than the road to liberation.

However aware Ahmad Khan was of the transformative power of science, he failed to avail himself of the scientific education that was readily available to him in Agra. As in Egypt and the Ottoman Empire, few 19th century Muslim reformers bothered to study the science that they extolled and eagerly urged others to learn. Preaching it to the younger generation was easier than practicing it oneself. Toward that purpose, Ahmad Khan founded the Scientific Society of Ghazipur in 1864. The Society sponsored lectures and translated a few secondary level scientific books from English into Urdu. The achievement was enough for the Royal Asiatic Society to make him an honorary member. After three years in Ghazipur, Ahmad Khan moved his Scientific Society to Aligarh, where with British assistance he set up an experimental farm.[8] In 1869, he visited England for a year and, having been knighted, returned much beholden to the British and impressed with what he had seen. By the end of his stay, the British could claim him one of their loyal servants of empire: "Without flattering the English," he wrote, "I can truly say that the natives of India, high and low, merchants and petty shopkeepers, educated and illiterate, when contrasted with the English in education, manners, and uprightness, are like a dirty animal is to an able and handsome man."[9] This did not win him many fans at home.

Wanting to educate Muslims in science and humanist ideas, he solicited funds from the Muslim community, which he used to found the Muhammadan Anglo–Oriental College at Aligarh. His hope was that it would become Muslim India's Cambridge University and lead the Muslims of India to the world of science. In the late 1870s, while he was actively building his Muhammadan College to engage Muslims in science, he devoted himself to develop a philosophy that integrated humanism, science and Islam. His model for that integration was the Indian mathematician Ramchandra, who a generation earlier had accomplished this philosophical integration for the Hindus. Ramchandra, working within the British scientific community, had been able through his own studies and experience to communicate to his students the larger social, philosophical and spiritual ideas that were implied in a creative scientific tradition. Outside academic life and with very little knowledge of science, Ahmad Khan faced more formidable obstacles than had his Hindu counterpart. Ramchandra's task was facilitated by the porosity of Hindu practice and mythology, which rendered the religion more amenable to a modern reading than did Islam with its integrated system of law, scripture, tradition and religious education – and its twin burden of pride and shame: pride of having been for a millennium world leaders in science and civilization, shame of having lost it all. The Hindu community was also unburdened by being free of the 12 centuries of anti-western hostility that conflicted Muslims in their approach to western knowledge.[10]

Ahmad Khan's *Natcheriyya* philosophy was as eclectic in its sources as it was unified in its purpose, which was simply to follow Karamat Ali's lead in reading modern science into the Quran. He borrowed heavily from Karamat Ali's works. In a rare instance of cross-linguistic influence within the Muslim world, he borrowed also from the Tunisian reformer Khayr al-Din Pasha's *Aqwam al-Masalik* (*The Surest Path*), whose message reiterated the reformist staple that nothing in Islam could possibly stand in contradiction to proven science. Based on sources from the liberal West, Ahmad Khan's *Natcheriyya* philosophy interpreted Islam as a moral religion of divine revelation grounded in nature. In order to clear the way for his naturalist interpretation, he adopted the puritanical reforms of Muhammad abd al-Wahhab in the Arabian peninsula of a century earlier. It was a surprising source for a modernist reformer. Wahhabi reform was literalist and looked back to Hanbali traditionalism of the *salaf*, the early Muslims, and presented a vision of Islam diametrically opposed to Ahmad Khan's.

What attracted Ahmad Khan to it was Muhammad abd al-Wahhab's stripping away of the millennial accretion of Sufi saint worship and miracles that was smothering "true Islam." *Natcheriyya* went further. It stripped away even the Quranic miracles. Nothing was spared: neither the *Isra'*, Muhammad's flight from Mecca to Jerusalem on the back of the flying horse, Buraq; nor the *Mi'raj*, the Prophet's midnight journey to the Seven Heavens. They were nothing but dreams. Verses that sounded fantastic or counter to reason or nature were rationalized out of existence. Angels became physical properties; Satan became the dark and irrational passions of human nature; the jinn and earth spirits referred to diseases, bacteria and germs.[11] Quranic verses that had been interpreted to support slavery, polygamy, punishment by mutilation or prohibiting interest on loans were radically reinterpreted to conform to the ideals and values of modern civilization, as defined by western humanism and capitalism. Hadith was cut away until nothing was left that did not support *Natcheriyya*. Anything in the Quran or Hadith smacking of slavery, polygamy or any practice incompatible with science and modernity was explained away as non-Islamic. *Natcheriyya* went beyond science and nature. Reinterpretation meant turning the Quran to conform with ways and ideas embodied in the legal, financial, economic, political, educational and marital institutions of the occupying power. Ahmad Khan's surgical reshaping of Islam made the *Tanzimat* reformers across the way in Istanbul look archaic.

On the British side of this reformist eclecticism was a book by the Anglican Archdeacon of Calcutta, John Pratt, entitled *Scripture and Science Not at Variance*. The book was published in 1856 and translated into both Hindi and Urdu, and Ahmad Khan made liberal use of it in his literary contribution to Muslim religious reform and scriptural interpretation, *Tabyin al-Kalam* (*Clarification of Theology*). The book presented a two-truth universe of spirit and nature, the former unchanging and absolute, the latter changing with time as human comprehension came to understand nature's operations over the course of history and advancing civilization. Existing in their separate realms, the two truths could never be in contradiction. The spiritual depth of the Quran and the often unfathomable mystery of certain verses rendered the Quran as God intended: a universal and never-ending source of unfolding wisdom and truth that embraced all of science. The Quran was spiritual in essence, but because of the physical part of man's nature and the physical world he must live in to survive, multi-layered truths of the spiritual and physical worlds were folded into the holy book. Allegorical interpretation would reveal these hidden layers as the continuing course of scientific discovery laid bare the secrets of nature. Science and Quranic mysteries would unfold together. This did not mean that the holy book was sent down as a revelation of nature; natural truth was only passively imbedded in the Quran. But the application of allegorical interpretation, the same practiced by the earlier Mu'tazilites, opened the deeper or hidden meanings of verses, like buds blossoming in the sunlight of science. Vigorous scrubbing of the theological stables would leave the Quran and Islam rational, natural and scientific.

To fend off the attacks that were sure to come because of his perceived evisceration of cherished beliefs, he claimed that his having made a science out of allegorical interpretation had preserved all of the essentials of God's true religion. In his *Sources of Exegesis* (*Tahrir fi Usul al-Tafsir*, Lahore, 1913), he delineated a set of principles that purported to establish a methodology and a set of limits for applying allegory, metaphor and analogy to the Quran in order to render a verse in the proper sense. The principles of course were nothing more than a veil to conceal the simple and obvious fact that interpretation was going to wrench meanings out of the verses that agreed with established science, whatever the words in the verses were. No one was fooled who did not want to be. An associate of Ahmad Khan's, more truthful than most reformers straining at the bit to equate Islam to science, described *Natcheriyya* as believing that the laws of science were "correct, certain and irrefutable and [Ahamd Khan] has given them precedence over the Quran itself."[12] *Natcheriyya* nonetheless found warm approval among young Muslims at the Agra College who were eager to believe their religion was rational, natural and scientific. The names of several young followers of Ahmad Khan's during the 1870s and 1880s became national icons as modern Pakistan's founding philosophers of progressive reform.

More honest critics regarded *Natcheriyya* as reducing the Quran to a secondhand textbook of western discovery. An equally damning criticism pointed out that *Natcheriyya* on the one hand claimed science and revelation to be one, and on the other hand that they each existed in their own separate places of reality and as such would not require reconciliation, however blatantly some verses in the Quran stood in contradiction to science. The circular reasoning of positing that the Quran is true because natural science agrees with it and then saying that natural science is true because it agrees with the Quran was clear to anyone who cherished the Quran as a divine revelation with its ineffable mysteries, contradictions and majestic irrationalities. *Natcheriyya's* allegorical interpretation was seen as a guise for Ahmad Khan's descripturalization that scoured the holy book of all meaning by making it "almost infinitely interpretable."[13] Those Muslims who were most passionate about arguing science into scripture would appear to be of a lesser depth in faith than their coreligionists who saw no problem between science and religion, leaving no reason for churning out tortured treatises on the subject that convinced no one but those who needed no convincing. Ahmad Khan's *Natcheriyya* was resisted by more restrained scholars who truly believed science had nothing to do with scripture. The prestigious Aligarh Islamic College proscribed it as being too close to a mechanical deism to be considered religion.[14]

In the 20th century, Amir Ali and abu'l Ala Mawdudi adopted Ahmad Khan's *Natcheriyya*. The former has been discredited by Pakistani nationalists as a fawning servant of the British, as had been Ahmad Khan in his day. Mawdudi on the other hand, who has become a kind of Pakistani patron saint of religious modernization and Scientific Interpretation, extended Ahmad Khan's naturalism to claim not only that all science was contained in the Quran but that the Quran by definition was science and all the world was Muslim – in fact, all the universe was Muslim, since the universe followed the laws of creation, and following God's laws meant submission to God, and that defined Islam, exactly submitting to God, the very meaning of the word. "Thus, the sun, the moon and the stars are Muslims," for they followed God's law of universal gravity. Even the fetus in the womb of an atheist was Muslim in that it obeyed the biological and physiological laws that God prescribed for organic matter.[15]

Such extreme claims by Muslim theologians would become common as the 20th century progressed. The abiding failure of Muslim government and society to launch a bonafide scientific culture of Muslim scientists engaged in real science provided fertile ground for turning the Quran, the most precious piece of literature in that society's cultural heritage, into a mirrored repository of discovery by others. Quranic virtual science was to become a popular exercise. In comparison, the ulema's collective passivity to modern science was healthier for Islam and the sanctity of the Quran than the plunge of these would-be reformers into the thickets of theology, indiscriminately wielding their sword of Scientific Interpretation to cut heart and soul from the holy book.

Jamal al-Din al-Afghani

Ahamd Khan and *Natcheriyya* found a fierce critic in a chameleon-like Shi'i Iranian reformer who passed himself off as a Sunni religious authority from Afghanistan. Janus-like, Jamal al-Din of Asadabad showed one face to Muslims, and an opposite one when facing West. The "al-Afghani" he fastened to the end of his name was as deceptive as his real thoughts were illusive.

Jamal al-Din (1838–1897) was a well-born child of a prestigious religious family whose status derived from an ancestry going back to the bloodline of the Prophet, allowing them to put the honorific "sayyid" at the head of their name – a more credible addition than the "al-Afghani" that Jamal al-Din was later to put at the end of it. Following a traditional religious education in Shi'i Islam, he went to India, where, seeing Muslims under British colonial rule, he began to think about the sources of western power. It was the mid-1850s. He was 17 or 18. Another sayyid in India, Ahmad Khan, who was 20 years older than Jamal al-Din, was still to work out his philosophy of *Natcheriyya*. As western-influenced reformers, Jamal al-Din and Ahmad differed little in their ideas about what Muslims had to do to save themselves from the West. They differed on how to go about it. The point of departure was the Sepoy Rebellion. Jamal al-Din was 20 when the Rebellion broke out. Ahmad Khan was 40. Where the older man accepted the reality of superior power and saw that cooperating with Britain was the best path to mastering the sources of power, the younger man rejected cooperation, accepting violent opposition to Britain as the only way to meet the imperialist threat. Twenty years after the rebellion, Jamal al-Din was a recognized religious scholar, a philosopher and reformer passing as a Sunni from Afghanistan, writing harshly against Ahmad Khan and his treacherous collaborationist *Natcheriyya* that threatened to destroy the fundaments of Islam.

His anti-evolutionist tract *The Truth About the Neichari Sect and an Explanation of the Neicharis* was written in Persian in 1880–1881 and translated into Arabic and published as *Refutation of the Materialists* in 1885, a year after the publication of Shumayyil's paraphrased translation of Buchner's materialist commentary on Darwin. Between them, the theory of natural selection couldn't have had more damning advertisement. Compared to Shumayyil's ponderous though flawed work, Afghani's *Refutation* was a feather-weight polemic that deserved anything but the popularity it received in the Arab world as a deeply philosophical reflection on science and religion. Jamal al-Din's profound ignorance of the principles of Darwin expressed in his polemic is at first glance as inexplicable as is the fame and prestige he achieved throughout the Muslim world as a great religious scholar and reformist philosopher. While to a Muslim audience he made Darwin look like a fool, when speaking westwards he revealed a far more informed side. The contraries lose their mystery in light of his pan-Islamist political activism. He was not above feigning ignorance for the sake of debunking evolution before an insecure and scientifically ignorant community of believers. His absurd caricature of Darwin as having propounded a philosophy that claimed men were born from monkeys, and his assertion that, "According to the views of this individual [Darwin] it would be possible that during the passage of centuries a mosquito could become an elephant and an elephant, by degrees, a mosquito," could only have been taken seriously, and given intellectual stature to the author, because of the pervasive ignorance of and hostility to the theory of evolution in Muslim society.[16]

Afghani the philosopher adeptly played the public's ignorance to the hand of the politician in him. When his perverse diatribe came into Arabic through Shaykh Muhammad Abduh's translation of the Persian original and was acclaimed by Muslims who should have known better as a study of merit by a great Islamic thinker who had mastered the science and philosophy of the West as much as he had the theology and philosophy of Islam, those few Arabs who had an idea of the scientific foundations of Darwin's work must have been shocked and depressed. Some were not. Jurji Zaydan incredibly likened Jamal al-Din to Cornelius Van Dyck as a propagator of modern ideas in Muslim society.[17] Other Syrian Christian writers agreed. Upon Jamal al-Din's death, Bishara Zilzal and Ibrahim al-Yaziji extolled him in their short-lived journal of science, medicine and industry, *al-Bayan*, as a great reformer and man of secular and religious knowledge. Equally surprising, educated Ottomans from the more sophisticated ranks of Istanbul's secularists and high ulema also took Jamal al-Din to be a great thinker on religion and modern science. The public's depressed state of scientific knowledge allowed him to pass as a towering, even heroic intellect by brandishing the sword of Islam and hacking away at the intellectual foundations of the West.

Jamal al-Din al-Afghani knew a lot more than he wanted Muslims to know that he knew and believed. His attack on evolution was deceptive. His statements on evolution in his other writings were less hostile; some were in fact receptive, as for example when he writes, "I can see that all living creatures which lived on this earth are from one primitive form, which the Creator gave life to."[18] He could even criticize Shibli Shumayyil for having done harm to Darwin's theory by injecting his materialism and atheism into it. What may appear in Afghani's fiery career to be contradiction, deception and duplicity becomes more nuanced in the context of his overriding goals of bringing political congruence to a fractured Muslim world. Like the good Shi'i he pretended not to be, he lied about his religion, practicing what the Shi'ah sect calls *taqiyya*: deception about one's confessional persuasion permitted to Shi'i Muslims living in Sunni society – a sectarian variation of struggle for survival to preserve the species. He dissimulated to survive not as a Shi'i but as a thinker, reformer and pan-Islamist whose overriding mission was to unite all Muslims: Sunni, Shi'i, Ottomans, Egyptians, Iranians, Central Asians and Indians, under the universal banner of Islam, in order to break the western tsunami of imperialist aggression sweeping over Islamdom.

Afghani's life of dissimulation as a religious reformer, political revolutionary and pan-Islamist made the metal of truth malleable to the occasion, so that he could argue for or against science, depending on to whom he was talking. Shaykh Muhammad Abduh had accurately summed up the dilemma of religious reformers who wanted fundamental change in a society whose traditions and culture had over the centuries of Islamic history, through Hadith and custom, been subsumed into religion and then crystallized as its essential, unchanging core. This was Islam in the public mind, and the ulema affirmed it as being so. But true Islam was hidden inside the centuries of extraneous overgrowth that had to be cut away to reveal the real thing. This is what was behind Shaykh Abduh's thinking when he told Afghani that the sword of religion had to cut the head of religion to save religion.

Was this suicidal self-decapitation or Sunni dissimulation? Abduh had intended it as a reformist virtue but may have been aware of the deeper truth in his remark to Afghani: that real change, once launched, will indeed end up cutting the head of religion. Abduh wanted to cut the head of traditional religion and replace it with a modern version, whatever that was, and he dissimulated enough to keep from being declared a heretic and stripped of his shaykh's robe and turban, as would happen to others coming after him who spoke out in favor of the same things he had advocated.

The direct object of Afghani's scornful attack in his *Refutation of the Materialists* was not Darwin's theory or Shumayyil's Buchnerian version of it, but the Indian reformer Sayyid Ahmad Khan (1817–1898) and his *Natcheriyya* philosophy that, as mentioned, interpreted Islam to be a "natural" religion in harmony with nature and the scientific laws abstracted from natural phenomena, an early version of modern "Scientific Interpretation" – something Afghani himself on occasion argued for. More than his philosophy, it was the person and politics of Ahmad Khan that was the real target of Afghani's tirade.

Afghani learned of Ahmad Khan and his *Natcheriyya* theology when he had returned to India in the early 1880s. Ahmad Khan had been advocating cooperation with the British ever since the failure of the bloody Sepoy Rebellion in 1857: if the foreign rulers could not be forced out by defeat in battle then they might be ousted by Muslims learning the sources of British knowledge and power. To a pan-Islamist revolutionary like Afghani, this was treasonous collaboration with the imperialist enemy that, having taken over India a century earlier, was now taking over Egypt. Cooperation with the British amounted to collusion in perpetuating foreign domination. Ahmad Khan's accepting to be knighted by Queen Victoria and using the title "sir" was proof of it. A Sunni Indian playing a phony Englishman was so much worse than a Shi'i Iranian passing for a Sunni Afghani.

Afghani attempted to destroy the traitor by destroying his credentials as a Muslim, and in doing so did much damage to the work of those who wanted to present Darwin's theory in a fair light. His rejection of evolution was politically motivated and unrelated to religion. Afghani had no problem with science and little to do with religion. In so far as he was a believer, his theological stance was neo-Mu'tazilite, accepting nature as a system of matter in motion undergoing change in accordance to causal relationships and laws under divine dominance. His reformist views were in fact no less liberal than those expressed in Ahmad Khan's *Natcheriyya*. While the latter was being declared a heretic by the ulema in Mecca, Afghani was being booted out of Istanbul for comparing the Prophet Muhammad to a philosopher.[19]

A little more than a year before the publication of his *Refutation*, Afghani had been in Paris, where he met Ernest Renan. Renan had gained fame in France as a philosopher in 1852 with the publication of his doctoral dissertation, *Averroes et Averroisme*, in which he attacked the ulema of Cordova as religious fanatics who forced the Muwahhidun ruler to exile ibn Rushd. Based on that, Renan went on to argue that there was something in the Arab race that informed Islam with an antipathy to reason. Generalizing his racial assumption of Arab unreason, he characterized Islam as a changeless religious monolith irreconcilably hostile to science, philosophy and any form of free thought. Islam, for as long as it existed, would be a willing weapon and ally for political rulers to crush any new strain of creative thought or movement for change. For this reason, Islamic civilization was doomed to extinction, since the West would grow more powerful with science, and Islam ever weaker for being without it. Step by step, the West would push Islam into an ever-diminishing circle until it disappeared, as indeed appeared to be happening.

With Renan's fame based on such ideas, his coming into contact with Afghani would seem to promise a grand display of intellectual fireworks. As it turned out, their debate, though indeed lively, was cordial, even friendly. Having exchanged ideas, the two men discovered they had much in common and came to like each other, with Renan being convinced that Afghani was a fellow rationalist and infidel.[20]

Shortly after their meeting, Renan delivered a lecture at the Sorbonne in which he reviewed his arguments on Islam's intrinsic hostility to science, philosophy and the whole rational spirit of intellectual curiosity and exploration. Afghani responded to the lecture with a long letter that was published in the spring of 1883 in *Journal des Debats*, the same in which Renan's lecture was published. Accepting a number of Renan's points and criticizing others, Afghani objected to Renan's blanket characterization of Islam as being hostile to reason. The charge was unfair to Islam. Why? Afghani's answer to his own question was startlingly frank: because all religions were hostile to reason, not just Islam. In medieval times, Christian religious authorities had acted much more brutally than the Muslim ulema in persecuting scientists and philosophers. In Christendom, philosophers had been accused of heresy and burned at the stake; in Islam only their books were burned.

In his westernized mode, Afghani agreed that all religions persecuted philosophers. That was in the nature of religion. Persecution of thinkers who trespassed beyond the limits of thought set by the religious authorities was as old as organized religion. But as religions went, Islam was at least better than the rest. And if Islam could but be cleansed of its alien accretions it would be better yet. When the day came that Islam would be purified by its equivalent of a Martin Luther, Muslims would be more supportive of science than even Europeans were now, since Islam in its essence was a rational religion that gave free scope to all spiritual and intellectual possibilities. The religion's corruption being scrubbed off and purified by a Martin Luther was not quite the description of Islam Afghani would have given in Cairo, Istanbul or Agra.

Afghani went on to disagree with Renan's belief that it was the Arab race that rejected science in Muslim society. The Arabs, he explained, had contributed greatly to a scientific renaissance in classical Islamic civilization. It was the perverted form of Islam, not the Arab race, that was the obstacle to rational thought. Afghani went even further – he could afford to, he was in Paris, and the Muslims back east would never hear or read his French words: science and religion, he said, were by their very nature inveterate enemies doomed to struggle until one vanquished the other. Historical Islam had destroyed science and creative thought and allowed tyrants to snuff out political life. But so it was with all religions:

> It is permissible, however, to ask oneself why Arab civilization, after having thrown such a live light on the world, suddenly became extinguished; why this torch has not been relit since; and why the Arab world still remains buried in profound darkness?

The answer was religion. Wherever it became established, religion set itself against the sciences and entered the service of despotism. Afghani refers to the 15th century Egyptian historian, al-Suyuti:

> Al-Suyuti tells that the Caliph al-Hadi put to death in Baghdad 5,000 philosophers in order to destroy the sciences in the Muslim countries down to their roots. Admitting that the historian exaggerated the number of victims, it remains nonetheless established that this persecution took place. I could find in the past of the Christian religion analogous facts. Religions, by whatever names they are called, all resemble each other. No agreement and no reconciliation are possible between these religions and philosophy. Religion imposes on man its faith and its belief, whereas philosophy frees him of it totally or in part. How could one therefore hope that they would agree with each other? . . . Whenever religion will have the upper hand, it will eliminate philosophy; and the contrary happens when it is philosophy that reigns as a sovereign mistress. As long as humanity exists, the struggle will not cease between dogma and free investigation, between religion and philosophy; a desperate struggle in which, I fear, the triumph will not be for free thought, because the masses dislike reason, and its teachings are only understood by some intelligences of the elite, and because, also, science, however beautiful it is, does not completely satisfy humanity, which thirsts for the ideal and which likes to exist in dark and distant regions that the philosophers and scholars can neither perceive nor explore.[21]

Afghani's response to Renan was not translated into a Muslim language. Religious criticism was not for home consumption. Learning that his disciple Muhammad Abduh had an Arabic translation made of his letter to Renan and was planning to have it published in Cairo, Afghani hurriedly wrote to him from Paris not to publish it, since this blunt assessment of religion and its repression of thought would do him no good with Muslim religious leaders. Abduh wrote back telling Afghani his letter had come just in time, and at the end of the letter came his famous remark that they would "cut the head of religion with the sword of religion," meaning that stealth and dissimulation were necessary to remove the conservative leadership of Islam in order to make way for the modernization that would save the Muslim world from the corruption and backwardness that the West fed upon. Not exposing Muslims to Afghani's rationalist response to Renan presumably came under the rubric of cutting the head of religion. This equivocation of saying the opposite to different audiences makes Afghani's writings, taken as a whole, inconsistent, contradictory and confusing. His true sentiments regarding Islam, it would seem, would be those expressed in Europe, where he was considered by some to be, if not an atheist, a Muslim deist – unless he was hiding behind his dissimulating Shi'i *taqiyya* again, passing himself off as a European when with them. Shibli Shumayyil, believing that it took one to know one, was convinced that Afghani was a devout atheist.[22]

A year later, when writing his *Refutation* in Persian for home consumption, Afghani inverted the argument he made in Paris and described Islam as the one and only religion that was based on reason and freedom of thought: "Human reason therefore can fulfill itself in Islam alone; the law which the Prophet received from God is the same as the law of nature, which man's mind can discern from a study of the universe."[23] In this and other works he wrote for Muslim readers, Islam was at one with science. He claimed that a close reading of the Quran would reveal the discoveries of modern science as well as technological inventions such as electricity, railways, steamships and also modern political institutions.[24] Verses that were vague would become clear in the light of modern discovery, and those that were not clear to reason had to be understood symbolically.[25] Some years after writing his *Refutation*, Afghani went so far as to claim that it was the Arabs who had discovered evolution, not Darwin, though he nonetheless praised Darwin's perseverance and contribution to natural history, and credited him as a devout man who believed God breathed his spirit into matter to begin life.[26]

Afghani was free to be what he wanted to be in Europe. Travel, translations and communications between the two worlds being what they were at the time, he had little to fear for his reputation among Muslims. This made for a profound difference between Afghani's two personas, so much so that a modern Middle Eastern historian has gone so far as to call him, along with his friend and disciple, Muhammad Abduh, religiously insincere and even heretics because of their freethinking philosophy and their use of religion toward political ends, a charge that would make heretics of a great many in all religions at all times.[27]

Afghani's intellectual life was as full of contradiction as his political life was of turmoil. But viewed through the scope of his political call for Muslim unity in resistance to western subversion, the various sides of his active life can be integrated in terms of bringing purpose to the person and integrity to his works. Political pan-Islamism transcended intellectual and theological consistency. His fear of Muslim society falling into more divisions than it already had fallen into may explain why he never worked out a program of reform. A defined program would be bound to alienate one side or another. In a way, the Janus figure of the Muslim reformer, looking and speaking one way to Europeans and another to Muslims, personifies the split that had by the 1870s riven Islamic society to its core: the secular and the religious inhabited one country but lived in separate, totally different worlds.

When once Afghani had finished playing to the prejudices of the public with his childish caricature of evolution and *Natcheriyya* in his *Refutation*, he then, in a later section of the treatise, states frankly, clearly and sensibly what can be taken as his undissimulating understanding of the problem that so badly confused Muslim religious leadership in the intellectual challenge posed to it by modernization:

> Since the state of these ulema has been demonstrated, we can say that our ulema at this time are like a very narrow wick on top of which is a very small flame that neither lights its surroundings nor gives light to others. A scholar is a true light if he is a scholar . . .
>
> The strangest thing of all is that our ulema these days have divided science into two parts. One they call Muslim science, and one European science.

Because of this they forbid others to teach some of the useful sciences. They have not understood that science is that noble thing that has no connection with any nation, and is not distinguished by anything but itself. Rather, everything that is known is known by science, and every nation that becomes renowned becomes renowned through science. Men must be related to science, not science to men.

How very strange it is that the Muslims study those sciences that are ascribed to Aristotle with the greatest delight, as if Aristotle were one of the pillars of the Muslims. However, if the discussion relates to Galileo, Newton and Kepler, they consider them infidels. The father and mother of science is proof, and proof is neither Aristotle nor Galileo. The truth is where there is proof, and those who forbid science and knowledge in the belief that they are safeguarding the Islamic religion are really the enemies of the religion. The Islamic religion is the closest of religions to science and knowledge, and there is no incompatibility between science and knowledge and the foundation of the Islamic faith.[28]

The criticisms expressed here are the same as the ones he wrote in Paris in his response to Renan, and can be taken to be as close to his true sentiments as the historian is likely to get.

A student of classical Islamic philosophy and author of a philosophical treatise, *The Benefits of Philosophy*, Jamal al-Din al-Afghani was well-versed in the accomplishments of earlier Muslims in science and philosophy. The liberality of his ideas in rethinking the Quran and Hadith fell short of Ahmad Khan's call to abandon Hadith but went beyond the limits set by Shaykh Jisr in interpreting the Quran. Afghani allowed that the Quran in its entirety should be subjected to reason and not understood literally, not even those verses that spoke of Preserved Tablets, heavenly thrones and paradise. The interpreters had to be well-qualified religious scholars with deep knowledge of the Prophetic Traditions, of the Prophet's companions and the *salaf*, those pious ancestors who immediately followed the companions and whose knowledge and practice of religion had to be considered authoritative. Scholars having the sound credentials of high religious scholarship were to be the supreme court of interpretive limits. To them the Gate of Interpretation, of *ijtihad*, closed for a millennium, would now be reopened. Reinterpretation would purify and reinvigorate religion and society, and bring Muslims back to the state of grace their ancestors enjoyed in early Islam, in accordance with God's words in the Quran: "God changes not what is in a people until they change what is in themselves." Since this implies that a people must have the will to change, God has allowed free will. The doctrine of predestination did not belong to early Islam. Afghani declared al-Ash'ari wrong in his denial of free will and causality. False theology was the beginning of the corruption and weakness that destroyed the Muslim creative spirit. If true Islam were to return to itself and Muslims become true Muslims, the civilization of Islam would be the most powerful and creative organization the world had ever seen.

Many of Afghani's ideas were popularized in the Arab world by his more famous follower, Muhammad Abduh.

Notes

1. For a brief account of the British economic and intellectual colonization of India see Muzaffar Iqbal, *Islam and Science*, Ashgate, Farnham, 2002, pp. 213–254.
2. C. Stewart, *Masir-i Talib fi Biladi-i Afranji* (Travels in Asia, Africa and Europe), London, 1814.
3. M. Iqbal, *Islam and Science*, pp. 227–228.
4. Ian Barbour, *Religion and Science*, Harper Collins, San Francisco, 2013, p. 51.
5. Karamat Ali, *Ma'khidh al- Ulum*, trans. Ubaydi and Amir Ali, Calcutta, 1867, pp. 25, 29–42.
6. Christian Troll, *Sayyid Ahmad Khan: A Reinterpretation of Muslim Theology*, Vikas Publishing House, New Delhi, 1978, pp. 148–149.
7. Aziz Ahmad, *Islamic Modernism in India and Pakistan, 1857–1964*, Oxford University Press, London, 1967, pp. 32–33.
8. M. Iqbal, *Islam and Science*, p. 245.
9. M. Iqbal, *Islam and Science*, p. 247.
10. Troll, *Sayyid Ahmad*, pp. 154–170.
11. Aziz Ahmad, *Islamic Modernism*, p. 48.
12. Javed Majeed, "Nature, Hyperbole and the Colonial State," in *Islam and Modernity: Muslim Intellectuals Respond*, edited by John Cooper, Ronald Nettler and Muhammad Mahmoud, I.B. Yauris and Co., London, 2000, p. 20.
13. Javed Majeed, *Nature*, p. 28.
14. Fazlur Rahmen, *Islam and Modernity: Transformation of an Intellectual Tradition*, University of Chicago Press, Chicago, 1982, p. 52.
15. Abu'l Ala Mawdudi, *Understanding Islam*, cited by W. C. Smith, *Modern Islam in India*, London, 1946, pp. 70–71.
16. Nikki Keddi, *An Islamic Response to Imperialism: Political and Religious Writings of Sayyid Jamal al-Din al-Afghani, Including a Translation of the Refutation of the Mateialist From the Original Persian*, 1968, University of California Press, Berkley, CA, pp. 135–136.
17. Thomas Philipp, *Jurji Zaydan, His Life and Thought*, Beirut, 1979, p. 34.
18. Marwa Elshakry, *Darwin's Legacies in the Arab East: Science, Religion and Politics, 1870–1914*, Princeton PhD dissertation, 2003, p. 178.
19. Abdullah al-Omar, *The Reception of Darwinism in The Arab World*, PhD dissertation, Harvard University, Cambridge, 1982, pp. 52–68, 101.
20. Keddi, *An Islamic Response*. For Afghani and Renan see also Iqbal, pp. 256–258, 263–264.
21. Keddie, *An Islamic Response*, pp. 88–89, citing A.M. Goichon, "Reponse de Jamal ad-din al-Afghani a' Renan," in *Refutation des Materialistes*, edited and trans. by A.M. Goichon, Paris, 1942, pp. 176–177.
22. Georges Haroun, *Shibli Shumayyil, une Pensee evolutioniste Arabe*, Beirut, 1985, p. 68.
23. Jamal al-Din al-Afghani, *Refutation des Materialistes*, edited and trans. A. M. Goichan, p. 70.
24. A. Hourani, *Arabic Thought in the Liberal Age*, Cambridge University Press, Cambridge, 1983, pp. 126–127.
25. Muhammad Makhzumi (editor), *Khatirat (Memoires) Jamal-al-Din*, Beirut, 1931, pp. 161 ff.
26. Abdullah al-Omar, *The Reception of Darwinism*, pp. 149–150, and Muhammad Makhzumi, Khatirat, pp. 183–185. See the final paragraphs of Darwin's *Origin of Species* where the Divine Hand is written. Though this could be similar to the protecting shield written as a preface by Andreas Osiander to save Copernicus and and his *de*

Revolutionibus from religious condemnation. Darwin, a gentle, quiet man who avoided controversy, did not want to ruffle Anglican feathers.
27 Majid Kedourie, *Afghani and Abduh: An Essay on Religious Unbelief and Political Activism in Modern Islam*, Frank Cass Publisher, London, 1966. Rather than a historical analysis by a political scientist, Kedourie's curious study reads more like the report of a grand inquisitor.
28 Jamal al-Din al-Afghani, *Refutation of the Materialists*, in *An Islamic Response to Imperialism*, edited by Nikki Keddie, University of California Press, Berkeley, 1968, p. 107.

10 Muhammad Abduh

The theory of evolution was at the center of religious debate in the early 1880s and has been ever since. Subsumed in the long debate was the more general issue of the place of natural science in Muslim society. By the beginning of the 20th century, a host of Christian and Muslim thinkers voicing a broad spectrum of views on science, evolution and religion had joined in the chorus, from Jurji Zaydan, Iskandarani, Hasan Husayn, Ismail Mazhar and Salama Musa writing from a secular, pro-evolutionist viewpoint that was first articulated by Shibli Shumayyil, to Muhammad Abduh, Rashid Rida, Tantawi Jawhar, Imam Isfahani and the Jesuit Louis Chiekho writing from a religious viewpoint that was first articulated by Shaykh Jisr and the later writings of Jamal al-Din al-Afghani. The most famous of the religious commentators was Shaykh Abduh, whose name is until today synonymous with religious modernism.

By the late 1870s, Muslims everywhere who were anxious over their powerlessness against the West were looking for political leadership to defend them and their borders. Devout Muslims were also looking for the religious figure of authority who would thwart the continuing marginalization of Islam. Devout Muslims who were politically aware and knowledgeable of the West were looking for the religious figure of authority who would think out a system that interpreted modern knowledge into the essentials of belief to bridge the separation between the modernizing secular stream of society and the traditional stream: a modern Ghazali who in a convincing dissertation would resolve the contradictions of the day and revive Islam in the light of modern science, economics and political institutions, with religion resuming its central place in a creative society. In the Arab world, the treatise that came closest to such a synthesis was Muhammad Abduh's *Risalat al-Tawhid* (*Treatise on Divine Oneness*), which consisted of the lectures he had given at the Ottoman *Madrasat al-Sultaniyya* in Beirut in 1882–1883.

Owing perhaps to the advanced stage that secularization had reached in urban Egypt by the end of Khedive Ismail's reign, Abduh, steeped in the same religious culture of the countryside as had been Tahtawi, successfully freed himself of those binding roots of traditionalism and tenuously attempted to bridge the chasm by revitalizing religious thought and action.[1] Coming to the same conclusions as the Young Ottomans, who had been appalled by the *Tanzimat's* wholesale borrowing and trade-off of Muslim culture that they saw did nothing but widen and deepen that socio-cultural divide, Abduh realized that revitalization could never come from institutional borrowing or imitation of Europe. It would have to emanate from a transformation of mind, a revolution in values, a new way of thinking about indigenous customs and institutions that had to begin with a rethinking of the sources of religion.

How did this rural Egyptian of traditional background and Azhari education break free from the stultifying effect of Quranic memorization and mental obedience to authoritative texts in order to think outside the existing religious system? Part of the answer may be found in his good fortune of having a maverick uncle. Young Abduh returned to his village after a boring and disappointing first year at al-Azhar determined not to suffer another. His paternal uncle Darwish, a village shaykh who was as much a non-conformist in the narrow life of a small rural village along the Nile as Abduh was to be on a grander scale, took his unhappy nephew under his wing. He introduced him to logic, mathematics and geometry, and encouraged him to enliven his studies at al-Azhar by pursuing these subjects on his own since they were not offered there.[2]

Taking his uncle's advice, Abduh resumed his studies. Back at al-Azhar he met another unusual man who was to stimulate his intellectual growth. This was Shaykh al-Tawil, a liberal scholar at whose house Abduh privately studied classical Islamic philosophy, another rational discipline al-Azhar did not offer at the time. Shaykh Marsafi was another liberal-minded mentor who taught and influenced Abduh in his early years. Shaykhs Mustafa al-Arusi and Muhammad al-Mahdi were other important liberal reformers at al-Azhar in the 1860s and 1870s. In 1865, Khedive Ismail commissioned Shaykh al-Arusi to reform al-Azhar by having him introduce modern studies and bring some organization and structure to the courses and the way they were taught. Arusi tried to introduce geometry, physics and other science courses, but finding shaykhs to teach them was a problem. In any case, his attempts met stiff resistance, and by 1870 the conservative faction was able to have the Khedive reverse himself and withdraw Arusi. In 1872 Shaykh al-Mahdi took his turn in re-introducing the reforms that Arusi had initiated, but this turned out to be just as unsuccessful.[3] Clearly al-Azhar had liberal teachers; their numbers were just never enough to loosen the institution from that hard-cast traditionalist mold that reformers ever since Tahtawi complained of.

Another early influence on young Abduh was Jamal al-Din al-Afghani, whom he met when a student at al-Azhar. Afghani advised him to study the Mu'tazilite theologians, in addition to the logical system of the non-Mu'tazilite theologian Taftazani (d. 1389). Since these subjects were outside al-Azhar's bounds of theological respectability, Abduh studied them on his own. His intellectual non-conformity did not escape notice at al-Azhar. When he graduated and was offered a teaching post there, the rector asked him if he had given up Ash'arite theology for Mu'tazilite. Abduh replied frankly that he had not given up one form of *taqlid* (following traditional authority) to take up another form of it, but had given them both up.[4] To the rector's credit, Abduh was still given the position.

Abduh's education prepared him to think from both sides of the East-West divide. He credits Afghani with directing his study of the sciences, teaching him some mathematics, falsafah and theology, and introducing him to Ahmad Khan's treatise on *Natcheriyya*, which Abduh translated into Arabic, confirming it was Ahmad Khan's politics that gave Afghani a problem, not his naturalist interpretation of Islam. Under Afghani's tutelage, Abduh studied ibn Sina's philosophical works and taught ibn Khaldun's *Muqaddima* (*Introduction to History*) at Ali Mubarak's *Dar al-Ulum*.[5] In the privacy of his home, he taught Miskawayh's ethics, Guizot's *History of Civilization in Europe* and Ghazali's *Revivification of the Religious Sciences*, and familiarized himself on one level or another with western science. In the meantime, he had left al-Azhar and was serving in the Ministry of Education, where he was working when in 1876 the Ministry collaborated with the editors of *Muqtataf* and *Rawdat al-Madaris* to have Abdallah Fikri write his treatise on the agreement between Copernicanism and the Quran. Abduh may have played some part in its composition.

By the time he reached full intellectual maturity he had absorbed the different reformist outlooks spanning the century: Tahtawi, Marsafi, Ali Mubarak, Abdallah Fikri, Afghani, Ahmad Khan, Shumayyil, Shaykh Jisr, the science in *Rawdat al-Madaris* and *Muqtataf*, and perhaps even something from the Young Ottoman thinkers. His great desire was to bring these together as a roadmap to social reunification around a reinterpreted Quranic core and reformed Shari'a. Just as the ulema had accommodated itself to the popular innovations of coffee and tobacco in the 17th century by issuing fatwas legalizing their (by then irreversible) consumption, the same could be done for science and religious reform. For Abduh, as for so many reformers before him, Islam was a religion of reason and tolerance. The problem facing contemporary Islam, as he saw it, was that the application of reason to religion had gone out with the Mu'tazilites. The appeal to reason meant reinvoking the interpretive principles of the Mu'tazilite scholastics. It meant readmission of *ijtihad*, personal endeavor in interpreting scripture to establish law.[6] Abduh showed more courage than Shaykh Jisr in calling for this. Reformist members of the ulema generally feared going so far.

Those religious scholars who saw the situation perilous enough to warrant reinterpretation of the sacred sources feared that if they were openly to call for it, their peers would accuse them of being heretical innovators. Abduh faulted the one for their timidity, and the other for their paralytic dependence on ancient authority. The ulema had all their lives been taught that those who knew Islam best were those who were closest to the Prophet in time. The older the source, the more authoritative it was. Fearing to strike an intellectual course of their own, they called heretics those who did. In his *Treatise on Divine Oneness*, Abduh turned the argument around, claiming Islam condemned uncritical imitation in matters of belief and the mechanical performance of religious duties. The Muslim was not made to be blindly led like a domestic beast with a rope around the neck, but rather to guide oneself by science and knowledge, the science of the universe and the knowledge of things past. The Quran came to liberate man from false authority. Islam came to turn man away from exclusive attachment to the things that came to them from their fathers. Islam was a revolution against paganism and its traditions and showed that the beliefs of any particular generation or century did not constitute proof of infallible knowledge or superiority of mind and intellect that should dominate the minds of the generations that followed. Ancestors and descendants were equal in critical acumen and natural ability. Islam liberated believers from the chains of tradition and wrong belief and delivered to them the power of reason so they could preserve their freedom from that blind imitation of ancestral ways that had enslaved them. Islam endowed Muslims with the power to think for themselves and make their own decisions in accordance with their sound judgment and wisdom. Though reason must humble itself before God and stop at the limits set by faith, within those bounds there was no barrier to its activity and no limit to rational speculation.[7]

The idealized Islam of Abduh's mind was a religion that made science a way of life, rooted in freedom and progress. He had read Tahtawi. When properly married, science and religion fulfilled the conditions for society's highest achievement. They needed each other. Without freedom science could not exist, just as freedom and progress could not exist without justice.[8]

Though Islam was a rational religion embracing science, the Quran was not a book of natural principles but a moral, spiritual and legal guide: "Religion resides in the stirrings of the heart. There is no relation between what is in the heart and what the mind acquires. The divide between reason and religion is complete and there is no way of joining them as one."[9] Even though they exist one from the other in separate self-contained spheres of truth, they nonetheless exist in sympathetic resonance, finding mutual support and reaffirmation, one of the heart, the other of mind, but one in the soul: *'aql wa naql*, reason and tradition, the twin pillars supporting and unifying Muslim religion and society. God speaking through the Quran enjoined man to perfect the human order by uncovering nature's secrets: "God created for you all that is on earth."[10] A glimpse at the heavens where all the moving and fixed bodies are held together by a natural law of forces determining their orbits and positions is proof enough of cosmic order and harmony. Were the planets to go beyond their orbits, the universal order, as known through the science of astronomy, would collapse, all of which bears witness to the knowledge of its Creator and wisdom of its organizer.[11]

Natural law is God's *sunna* or custom in running the affairs of the cosmos, parallel to the way the Prophet's *sunna* informs the holy law or the Shari'a in ordering the laws that govern human affairs. God gave man freedom of will, but to nature and the universe he ordained fixed laws.[12] The Quran confirms it. So resiliently abiding was the millennial opposition of the ulema to natural philosophy that Abduh cites several of the very same verses that ibn Sina cited in his *Risalat al-'Arshiyya* to prove the fixity of nature: "Such has been the custom (*sunnah*) of God with those who lived before them, and no change can you find in the custom of God."[13] "Look they then for aught but God's custom with references to the peoples of old? You shall not find any change in the custom of God – indeed, you shall not find any variation in the custom of God."[14] In his *Risalat al-Tawhid*, Abduh cites another verse to demonstrate fixity and natural law in God's ordained *sunna* of the cosmos: "Verily, We did not create heaven and earth and everything between them as a game to play," a cosmic dictum that would find other words of expression in the West a generation later when Albert Einstein, confronted by the conundrum of uncertainty in quantum theory, made his well-known assertion that God did not play dice with the universe.[15]

God did not create nature as a game to play. He created it for man's benefit and for man to contemplate. But for all the Quran's many references to nature, and its emphasis on directing man to contemplate God's creation, Abduh rejects the claim universally made by all other religious modernists, that science is an essential component of the Quranic message. Though the Quran excites and directs man's attention to natural phenomena, science is not any part of the holy book's intent or what the Quran is about. Broadly interpreting the Sura *al-Baqara*, verses 18–19, which mentions a storm cloud of heaven, big with darkness, thunder and lightning, Abduh writes that the truth about lightning, thunder, the storm cloud and the reasons for their occurrence is not among the subjects investigated by the Quran. These things belong to the science of nature in the atmosphere, knowledge of which does not depend on spiritual inspiration. When the Quran mentions natural events, it is their impact on human senses that is the essential component, the object being to strike awe, to incite consideration and direct man's reason toward a better understanding of God. God did not send revelation in order to clarify facts and explain the appearance of natural events in a scholarly sense.[16] While directing man to strengthen one's understanding of nature, the Quran transcends science by revealing a reality beyond it. The agreement between the Quran and modern science is not essential to either one. Any disagreement between them would be equally irrelevant.

Abduh worked at the margins of composing an Islamic equivalent to a Thomist synthesis but sensed that religious support for this was not there. In a society that was on the defensive and shrinking in every way, the critical condition of his religion and civilization required a radical change that had to come from religious authority, but the authority was not forthcoming. With his *Treatise on Divine Oneness*, he appeared on the verge of taking on the task, but then thought better of it. Shaykh Abduh knew himself to be much alone. Unlike Aquinas, he lacked the support of the institutional equivalent of a Dominican order and a legion of eager scholastics high on reason and natural philosophy and a church hierarchy to stamp his work with its seal of approval and to defend him. What support he had amounted to a miniscule following of young religious and secular reformist well-wishers who would melt away the moment the leaders of al-Azhar unsheathed their pens for the fatwa that condemned anyone who strayed.

One of the leading opponents to the kind of change Abduh sought in religious thinking was the popular head jurist of the Malikite school of law, Shaykh Muhammad 'Ilish (1802–1882). Abduh's conflict with the venerable shaykh went back to his student days when 'Ilish chastised him for deviating from Ash'arite theology to read Mu'tazilite literature. Abduh's brash reply to 'Ilish, who was 80 to Abduh's 30, that he was devoted to neither one nor the other, resulted in his fellow students tearing his turban from his head and insulting him.[17] Abduh's reputation as an irreligious free-thinker sent even reform-minded Azhari students running from him for fear of losing their faith, as if their faith was so fragile it would shatter in the mere presence of an open mind.

The need for radical religious rethinking impelled Abduh to go so far as to embrace even the Mu'tazilite doctrine of the "created Quran," that the Quran was a divinely created revelation at a point in time and not eternal and coterminus with God. Stated in the first edition of his *Treatise on Divine Oneness*, it was a daring if not dangerous assertion for any Muslim to make. The doctrine of the uncreated Quran had been a cherished belief for a thousand years and could not be lightly challenged. Belief in a created Quran would bring the scriptural word of Islam down from the unquestionable heights of divine majesty to that of a text subject to rational understanding through philological analysis. This would open the way to all sorts of debasing pitfalls. How to account for the Quran's changes in style? Would this suggest different hands other than God's were at work here? What of the apparent contradictions between one verse and another in a holy book of 106 chapters and many thousands of verses? And what of the verses inferring anthropomorphic attributes to God? Once the door to metaphorical and allegorical interpretation was opened how would it be closed before the Quran was emptied of all heavenly substance? Where, once begun, would end this soulless explication of the Quran's usage of certain words? Or of its shifting positions on causal relationships, free will and divine justice as understood by reason.[18] In the end, the Quran would be reduced to the status of just another of many holy books, a textual corpse whose innards had been extracted and analyzed to death. Abduh had little support in braving the challenge of the millennial institution of al-Azhar. No one rallied behind him, and rather than chance the possibility of becoming a reformist outcast, he deleted from the second edition the passage about the Quran being created. It did not reappear in any of the succeeding editions in the 20th century.[19]

The deletion was upon the advice of an older shaykh, al-Shanqiti, who was sympathetic to Abduh but who knew the limits of the possible, beyond which awaited professional self-destruction. Abduh's demystification of the Quran by his claiming all the miracles found in it had a natural explanation was an equally radical departure from tradition that few in al-Azhar would share or openly support. To demystify was to disembowel. Where was the beauty, power and majesty in Moses crossing the Red Sea at a shallow point during low tide, as Abduh suggested, or the pharaoh and his army arriving just in time to be swept away by the inrushing high tide? How about the miraculous birds that saved Mecca – picking up stones in their beaks and dropping them from on high upon the invading Ethiopian army and its elephants – being a species of germ-carrying mosquito or fly, and the stones being chunks of desiccated mud infected by insects and blown by the wind, making for airborne microbes?[20] Why make the miraculous Quran into a scientific fairy tale?

Abduh realized that pinning the Quran to the vicissitudes of science was unwise. Shaykh Jisr had practiced Scientific Interpretation within certain limitations, believing he was ennobling the Quran by showing how scientific it was, and Abduh did the same up to a point, but reluctantly, for he knew what it would lead to: one scientific theory being discarded for the next, the Quran cheapened by its repeated reinterpretations in the wake of scientific discovery. His friend, student and biographer, Shaykh Rashid Rida, urged him to go further in reconciling Quran and science, but Abduh resisted the easy, simplistic and, as he saw it, ignoble practice that was to become so popular and excessive in the next century.

Instead of their despoiling the Quran by having it lap up western science, Abduh advised the ulema to encourage Muslims to engage in science and independent thinking. Engagement was the surest way of showing Islam to be in tune with modernity. This was the ulema's duty. The government's was to appropriate funds for modern education and research institutions. The public's was to donate what it could toward establishing private schools, scholarships and scientific societies. Here Abduh meant the well-to-do class. As early as 1881 he was publicly chastising the ruling class of Egypt for its irresponsibility in not contributing anything to raising the level of education and awareness of science. The social class that should have taken the lead was wasting itself in drink, women and self-indulgent pleasure. The intellectuals also failed wretchedly to make their contribution, thinking more of themselves than their mission as educators to lift society to higher levels of consciousness.[21] The ulema were no better, filled as they were with superstitions, and so besotted with heretical beliefs in miracle-performing saints that they were more devoted to watching Sufi spectacles than they were to improving education, with the best of them sinking their minds in the swamp of medieval dialectics, blissfully oblivious to the idea of progress and modern world sailing away into the future.[22]

Abduh's analytical framework for differentiating between medievalism and modernism was taken from Auguste Comte's evolutionist philosophy of civilization. His knowledge of Comte's theory of civilizational progress probably began with Afghani and the writings of Shumayyil. Based on Comte's three-tiered pattern of civilizational "progress" captiously lifted from Darwin's theory of natural selection, Islam had progressed from the mythic to the metaphysical stage of civilization but still had to reach the scientific level. In the struggle to survive, Muslim civilization must either advance to the scientific stage or become extinct like the dinosaurs.[23] Islam was once powerful and had been a threat to other civilizations, but its essential nature was betrayed and the civilization weakened, falling prey to one that had for long been weak but evolved to be strong. Abduh's account of what went wrong in Islamic history that caused Muslims to lose their scientific spirit after centuries of brilliant discovery and then plummet to the wretched condition in which they now found themselves is framed in the same general principles of liberalism that Shaykh Tahtawi, and later Shumayyil and Afghani, learned during their years in Paris. Accordingly, Abduh's is a deeply personal view of history.

The story begins in medieval Islam with the fateful falling out between metaphysics and *kalam* (dialectics), when certain imprudent practitioners of *'aql wa naql* (rational and religious sciences) went beyond their respective spheres of understanding. Because of the close relationship between science and philosophy, the contention spread from metaphysics to the whole of philosophy and the rational sciences. Consequently, religion ended up opposed to science. The confusion caused by the dialectics of *kalam* and conflicting theological interpretations added to the malaise by turning intelligent and spiritually sensitive believers away from the main body of Sunni Islam. As authoritarian tradition took over, the mass of orthodox Muslims got lost in the complex morass of conflicting dialectics, and with them got lost the true principles of Islam, leaving Sufism to fill the spiritual void. By winning the hearts of believers, Sufism turned Muslims all the more away from knowledge of the physical world and science.[24]

Social tolerance for the natural sciences had already been drained by Muslim philosophers when they uncritically accepted Plato and Aristotle. Al-Ghazali's hypercritical overkill in rejecting philosophy and all that went with it was another dagger in the heart of the rational sciences. Philosophers contributed as much as ulema to the transmogrifying desiccation of Muslim thought. Both philosophers and ulema practiced a form of *taqlid*, the unquestioning acceptance of their traditional authorities, the one devoted to Aristotle, the other to Ash'ari. The resultant crippling of intellectual freedom was the death of the sciences. Religious suspicion and hostility continued through the ages to intimidate intelligent minds, making sure science would stay in the grave.[25]

Science was oppressed in subtle ways:

> By "oppression" I don't mean to say that people of science were maltreated in Muslim countries in the violent way they were exterminated and tortured in Christian countries, where various methods of punishment and versatile instruments of destruction were created and inflicted upon those who fell under suspicion, and where merely an accusation was sufficient reason for condemnation and execution. That never happened among Muslims, neither during their days of scientific glory nor their time of ignorance. Rather, by oppression (in Islam) I mean shunning or avoiding knowledge, or ridiculing men of science to their faces and insulting them and keeping a distance from them.[26]

What these methods failed to do in snuffing out the spirit of inquiry was accomplished by corrupt and greedy rulers. Islam then settled into long centuries of stagnation, paralyzed by both religious and political authorities who used each other toward their own selfish ends. But it was fanatical and envious religious leaders who were mostly to blame, such as when ibn Rushd was deposed as chief *qadi* in Cordova and exiled because the *"ulama"* was jealous of the philosopher-physician's position with the Muwahhidun sultan, ending philosophy and science in Muslim Spain. Abduh saw the fanatics of ibn Rushd's day to be the same as those in his own. The fanatics were always there, always working to keep the scientific spirit from being reborn: "Are not the ulema among the Muslims today the enemies of the modern sciences? Are not the people still following them?" Abduh complained of being unable to introduce even geography into al-Azhar's curriculum. When he tried, the other shaykhs publicly denounced him in the newspapers. He described his opponents as so hidebound in authority that they could not see the world around them, nor were they able to come to a decision without poring over their authoritative texts to find an answer from the past for a question in the present. In a society where the present must be addressed by the past, there can be no future. In fact, by their shirking responsibility and hiding behind texts, the *'ulama'* had already despaired of the future:

> If it is said to them: The affairs of society are ruined, corruption has taken over, belief is in error, faith has weakened, evil ways have become the norm and poverty extreme, the *'ulama'* reply that this is not their concern or responsibility, it is that of the rulers, and if they the rulers do not attend to it, it is because it is the end of time; and so the *'ulama'* go about proving it is the end of time by verses of the Quran and *Hadith*, and by so doing cut hope and action from the soul, so nothing is ever done.

He follows this up in a later section of the same piece saying, "Those of the *'ulama'* who deny reason and science know nothing of religion. They are its enemies." He quotes a verse of a poem by the famous mathematician–astronomer Umar Khayyam to the effect that if Muhammad were to return from the grave he wouldn't recognize Islam, so changed for the worse has it become at the hands of those religious thinkers who followed him. But the battle is not yet lost. The religious scholars can still be roused to duty. Fears of the blind forces of ignorant reaction and irresponsibility can be overcome. An intelligent ulema can still take the lead in creating a free and intelligent public. Islam can be great again. In a free atmosphere, with moral character disciplined by religion, Muslims can compete with Europeans and equal them in civilization: "Our first duty is to endeavor with all our might to spread science throughout the country." But he knew it was a duty stripped of hope.

Disgusted with his fellow ulema for their reluctance to change al-Azhar's curriculum, Abduh had resigned his position after only a few years to join Ali Mubarak's *Dar al-Ulum* as a more promising institution of change. Fifteen years later, he returned to al-Azhar, in 1888, only to meet the same old resistance to change. When he tried to have ibn Khaldun's *Muqaddima* accepted in the curriculum, the rector replied that this would be breaking tradition. Abduh then asked in exasperation how was it there were books being studied in al-Azhar that were written by Azharite scholars who had died only a few years ago. Where was the tradition to be found that supported studying those books?[27] Though the rector had no ready answer, he was not about to admit ibn Khaldun into the curriculum. If a recently revived classic like ibn Khaldun's was unacceptable, then what chance did modern science have?

Abduh had in fact the year before asked al-Azhar's rector and his supporting leadership if it was permissible to teach mathematics, science and related subjects if for no other reason than to keep up with the West. After all, he argued, Mother Egypt was weak, laid out supinely in her fifth year under British occupation. How else to get from under the foreign master but by mastering the knowledge and techniques of modern civilization? The leading shaykhs studied the question Abduh had posed. They searched the works of al-Ghazali for an answer, and concluded that the modern disciplines should be studied, but only so that Muslims could acquire their usefulness. But not physics. Physics could only be studied in accordance with the Shari'a and not in the way of medieval Muslim philosophy, and certainly not in the way of modern physics. What this meant was that natural causation and the idea of laws governing physical phenomena could not be held, putting even Aristotle, ibn Sina and ibn Rushd off limits.[28] Abduh was so beside himself with al-Azhar's immobility in regard to getting itself out of the medieval quagmire of Ash'arite theology he went to Egypt's newly founded newspapers to vent his frustrations. Going public did him well with the modernist reformers, who began to see the shaykh as one of their own, but it distanced him all the more from al-Azhar's leadership. His efforts to channel the energy of religion toward intellectual modernization had no support where it counted. The more the shaykh drew closer to the modernizers, the more he was alienated from the councils of al-Azhar.

As Abduh neared the end of his life, having accomplished little of what he had hoped, he came to the same conclusion Tahtawi had come to at the end of his a generation earlier. That is, if Islam was to survive as a religion and a way of life, and Muslim society was to compete in the modern world, then the ulema and their leading shaykhs had to be forced to study science. Otherwise, Islamic civilization would never reach the scientific level, and Muslims would be condemned to remain frozen in the theological-metaphysical realm, an irrelevant residuum of a long ago era, dominated by the West and regarded with disdain and contempt as a useless member of the world community. It would be either that or Islam would wither away and disappear over time as Muslims gave up on their hopelessly outmoded, stagnant religion and left it to join the world on their own.

For an advocate of religious reform whose independence of thought flew in the face of tradition and the conservative temperament of al-Azhar, Abduh managed to go a long way. Though it certainly didn't go down well with his fellow Azharites, the favorable opinion the British rulers of Egypt had for the maverick shaykh did his career no harm. The British administrators and resident scholars liked and favored him for his pro-western ideas. Even Lord Cromer, the arrogant pro-consul of Egypt who was openly contemptuous of so-called educated Egyptians, to him an oxymoron, was impressed by Abduh's reformist ideas, for what could be more endearing to colonial masters than an Azharite shaykh in robe and turban who thought almost like an Englishman? The very model of an imperialist, Lord Cromer could not believe a Muslim could think the way Abduh did and still be a real Muslim. He was convinced the shaykh was an atheist, quite as Renan had suspected the same of Afghani. So deeply ingrained in the western psyche had become the imperialist prejudice that Muslims could not think and act rationally on their own that it had become in the course of the 19th century a generally accepted self-evident truth: a critical rationalist could in no way be a believing Muslim. The shaykh was feigning belief. Going hand in hand with the appearance of Muslim irrationality was the European conviction that Muslims had trouble with truth and honesty.[29]

Lord Cromer's embrace of this singular rational shaykh enhanced Abduh's career. Shortly after the British occupied Egypt, Abduh was appointed editor of the Egyptian National Gazette, *Waqa'i al-Misriyya*, the post that shaykhs Attar and Tahtawi had filled before him. In 1895 he was appointed head of an administrative council created to reform al-Azhar, a position that gave him the chance to make the curriculum changes he had been trying to make for decades. He succeeded to some small extent in having the modern sciences taught, but the victory was trivial. Students were allowed to study them on their own if they wished and stand for final exams administered by the institution. Obviously, very few students took advantage of the offer to do self-study courses without any guidance in something as challenging as science.

However, in 1908, as a result of the momentum Abduh had generated during his decade at the head of the administrative council, al-Azhar at last accepted that mathematics, geography, physics and chemistry be taught as obligatory subjects, though only on the primary and secondary levels. Coming three years after Abduh's death, it was a posthumous victory of sorts, but far too little and a century too late to make a difference in saving Muslims from having to suffer through another bad century. By 1908 relativity theory had been born with quantum theory in gestation, leaving Islamic societies to the rear in terms of two scientific revolutions and going on three in technology. The chance of Muslim society participating in the progressing venture of science was beyond the vanishing point.

Abduh's career culminated a century of reformist thought, bridging Attar, Tahtawi, Marsafi and Mubarak to Afghani, Shumayyil, Ahmad Khan and Jisr. He brought their ideas together and dared to formulate them as a basis for the reinterpretation of the sources of religion. The legacy he left was taken up by his followers and carried on in various forms and directions into the middle of the 20th century. "He, more than any other man, gave Egyptian thought a center of gravity, and created . . . a literature inspired by definite ideals of progress within an Islamic framework."[30] Toward the end of his years he made his own summation of his life as a reformer and what he stood for:

> I spoke out on behalf of two great causes. The first of these was the liberation of thought from chains of imitation and the understanding of religious faith as members of the early Community understood it before dissension arose, and the return of religious learning to its original sources, and consideration of religion in the scale of human intelligence that God created to repel the excesses of faith and diminish its errors and stumbling so that the human social order prescribed by God in His wisdom may be attained. In this way religion may be counted the true friend of science, a stimulus for inquiry into the secrets of the universe, and in cultivating our spirits and reforming our actions. All this I have considered to be a single matter. In appealing on its behalf I found myself in opposition to the views of the two great groups of which the Community is composed: the devotees of the religious sciences and others of their type, and the devotees of modern techniques and their partisans.[31]

His career drew to a close with a succession of personal successes. Appointed chief mufti of Egypt in 1899, then shortly after that becoming a permanent member on the state legislative council, he ascended to Minister of Education.[32] This may not have happened without the influence the British rulers exerted in favor of the non-conformist shaykh. British favor, personal success and non-conformity came with a price.

Abduh's intellectual independence dogged him throughout his life, right from the very beginning of his religious studies at al-Azhar when his dissatisfaction turned him to science and Mu'tazilite theology. His association with the even more radical maverick Jamal al-Din al-Afghani reinforced his independence, giving him the courage to take up western ideas – which as seen by his fellow Azharites expressed a willful non-conformity at the fringe of heretical innovation. As he pursued his career of peaceful reformer during the final quarter century of his life, he retained his independence of mind and was not afraid to express it. He traveled frequently to Europe, lived in Paris and London, studied in the libraries of Oxford and Cambridge, corresponded with Tolstoy and G. B. Shaw, conversed several times with the social evolutionist philosopher Herbert Spencer and greatly enjoyed European life and civilization, so much that he continually returned to it when, as he candidly admitted to his biographer Rashid Rida, "he felt the need to renew his soul . . . I never once went to Europe that there was not renewed within me hope of the change of the present state of Muslims to do something better."

In view of today's dark feelings clouding the relations between Islam and the West, such an admission having come from a leading religious shaykh must sound incredible. Even in the relatively relaxed period of Muslim relations with the West that existed in Abduh's day his ideas were somewhat extreme for a high religious dignitary. They were not easy to take for the shaykhs he was trying to win over. Some of his expressions of admiration for Europe must have sounded like heresy. When reflecting on the long way Muslims had to go to catch up to the West and on al-Azhar's resistance to change, he felt discouraged, but that "whenever I return to Europe and remain there a month or two, these hopes come back to me, and the attainment of that which I had been accounting impossible seems easy to me." Abduh died in Alexandria just as he was about to embark on another tour of Europe for spiritual renewal of his Muslim soul.

The stark deterioration of the relationship between Islam and the West during the last century, beginning with the mandates after World War I and growing worse after World War II and the creation of Israel, and now with what today in the 21st century clearly looks to Muslims to be an American–Israeli-led western alliance to dominate and weaken the Muslim world, has made Abduh something of a curiosity in the anti-western attitudes that predominate in contemporary Muslim society. An Azharite who advocated reinterpretation of the sources of law and religion in order to bring them into tune with modern times, who took a Mu'tazilite position on free will, putting scripture to the test of reason, who even once wrote that the Quran was created and not the eternal mind and language of God, who broke ranks with his fellow Azharites to follow Ahmad Khan's naturalist interpretation of Islam and advocate the study of science and who openly admired western civilization so highly he felt it necessary to go there periodically for spiritual resuscitation – any one of the above would be enough for a fatwa of heresy and death in today's dismal climate.

Abduh had followers from both sides of the secular-religious divide. They took his ideas in divergent directions. His followers within al-Azhar tried to shake the institution from its glacial inertia in order to bring it into the modern world and bridge the epistemological chasm. His secular devotees exerted his ideas in their reformist efforts through literature, journals, newspapers, secular law courts and teaching at Cairo's new university. In the 1920s, as the relations between Islamdom and the West were souring, followers of Abduh from both sides were accused of heresy for their reformist ideas, Ali abd al-Raziq and his brother Mustafa of al-Azhar and Taha Husayn and Nasr Hamid abu Zayd of Cairo University being the most famous cases. Since the last decades of the 20th century, anyone even suggesting a reinterpretation of law and Quran, let alone attempting it, had to run for one's life, literally, as will be seen. Just being declared a heretic was by then no longer considered sufficient punishment.

Running a close parallel to Muhammad Abduh's reformist religious rethinking was the intellectual career of Sa'id Nursi (1877–1960) during the Ottoman and Republican period. Reared in the 1880s at the fringe of western influence in Kurdish eastern Anatolia, he had, like his older Egyptian counterpart, a traditional religious education, which he was eventually able to shake off as his appreciation of reform and modern science matured. Born into a poor rural family of clerical tradition, Nursi grew up as the empire was falling apart bit by bit. Belief that behind the *Tanzimat* reforms was a European-driven conspiracy to accelerate the empire's destruction and divide the pieces among the Armenians and Christian powers seemed to be authenticated when Russia appointed a raft of Armenian officials in northeast Anatolia, following the disastrous Russo–Ottoman war of 1877–1878. This suspicion looked to be confirmed when the Armenian Patriarch in Russia demanded an Armenian state during the Congress of Berlin that formally ended the war. Secret revolutionary organizations of young Armenian nationalists in the towns and villages of Anatolia stoked Muslim suspicions that an Armenian revolt emulating the Greek revolt in the early part of the century was imminent. This was the background to what the West would call decades later the Armenian massacres. "Massacre" would later be upgraded to "genocide."

His fear of a western-driven political apocalypse that colored young Nursi's thinking was likely a good part of the reason behind his rejection of the West and its knowledge. Rather than looking westwards for cultural and religious renewal he turned to the East, to Neoplatonic (Ishraqi) illuminationism and the works of al-Ghazali. He became a member of the Ottoman ulema and came into contact with the reformist ideas of Jamal al-Din al-Afghani and Muhammad Abduh, initiating a new phase in his intellectual maturation, which included becoming familiar with western science through popular publications, but all the while holding fast to his anti-western feelings.[33]

These were all the more strengthened by a comment the British Secretary of Colonies made during the troubles between Muslims and Armenians in Istanbul in 1895, to the effect that the Turks would never be civilized until they abandoned their Quran. Nursi's reaction to it was to write a book in Arabic, the language of the Quran, that combined modern science and Muslim gnostic illuminationism:

Risalat al-Nur (*Treatise on Light*). The book, earning him the sobriquet *Badi' al-Zaman* (Wonder of the Age), was a reformist defense of the Quran, similar to Shaykh Abduh's *Treatise on Divine Oneness*. Nursi's name became known among high Ottoman officials. Invited by them to advise on a Muslim scientific revival, he urged the government to incorporate science courses into the madrasa curriculum and to oblige the ulema to engage in scientific study, for only by government forcing it through the portals of religion could science gain credibility as a legitimate field of study in the minds of Muslims. This was a sentiment unanimous among Muslim thinkers. Neglect of science had led to the decline of Muslim civilization. Other factors had ensured decline: Sufism, theological disputation (*kalam*) and failure to keep in touch with Europe and its sciences. While internal religious reform would address the first two, robustly reaching out to learn science from the West, as the Japanese were doing without losing or compromising their indigenous culture, would complete the process of Muslim revitalization.[34]

Nursi's program of religious reform closely followed Abduh's. As Abduh had been challenged by western materialist thought in the 1880s and 1890s in Egypt, Nursi was concomitantly challenged by those secular reformist ideas that were popular among Ottoman deist intellectuals during the Young Turk period. Imam Nursi interpreted science and its natural laws in the Quran without compromising his Sunni belief of God's absolute power. Nor did he compromise when the Kemalist Republic replaced the Ottoman Sultanate and strictly enforced secularism and Turkish nationalism over religion. The government prohibited publication of Nursi's *Treatise on Light* until 1956. Defying the secularist laws of the republic, Nursi continued to call prayer in Arabic and suffered a year of imprisonment. For the rest of his life he was in and out of jail, under constant surveillance and repeatedly put under house arrest. His courage and strength of belief bore him more than half-way through the 20th century without his bending to the secular authorities or relenting in his mission of rethinking Quranic injunctions in the light of science and the conditions of modernity. Drawing on the century-long heritage of Arabic and Turkish religious reformers, Sa'id Nursi united the overlapping ideas found in the writings of Shaykh Tahtawi, Hoja Tahsin, the Young Ottomans, Husayn al-Jisr, Muhammad Abduh and Rashid Rida, and was a fount of the current rise of religious consciousness and pride of Muslim civilization, striking fear into the securalist hearts of die-hard Kemalist guardians of the republic.[35]

Notes

1. A. Hourani, *Arabic Thought in the Liberal Age*, Cambridge University Press, Cambridge, 1983, p. 136.
2. In his study of Egyptian education Heyworth-Dunne (pp. 61–65) lists a number of texts in logic, geometry (*handasa*) and mathematics (*hisab*) that were there in al-Azhar's library, available to students, but the subjects were not taught for lack of staff to teach them and students interested to study them.
3. Marwa Elshakry, *Darwin's Legacies in the Arab East: Science, Religion and Politics, 1870–1914*, Princeton PhD dissertation, 2003, pp. 281–282.

4 C.C. Adams, *Islam and Modernism in Egypt*, Oxford University Press, London, 1933, pp. 42–43.
5 Abduh, "Sirati," in *al-A'mal al-Kamila li'l Imam Muhammad Abduh*, edited by Muhammad Imara, 7 vols, al-Mu'ssasa al-'Arabiyya li'l Dirasat wa'l Nashr, Beirut, 1972–1974, vol 2, pp. 332–375.
6 Abduh, *al-Islam w'al Nasraniyya* (Islam and Christianity) 5th edition, Cairo, Matba'at Ali Subayh, 1938, p. 202; Hourani, *Arabic Thought*, pp. 143, 148.
7 Abduh, *Risalat al-Tawhid*, Trans. Moustapha abd al-Raziq and B. Michel, Geuthner, Paris, 1925, pp. 107–109; H.A.R. Gibb, *Modern Trends in Islam*, University of Chicago Press, Chicago, 1947, p. 43. See also M. El-Bahay, *Muhammad Abduh: Eine Untersuchung Seiner Erziehungs – Methods Zum National-Bewusstsein*, Hamburg, 1936, p. 45, citing R. Tawhid, Cairo, 1896, pp. 15, 101.
8 Abduh, *al-Ahram*, issue 832, October 1880.
9 Muhammmad Imara, *al-A,mal al-Kamilah li'i Imam Muhammad Abduh* (vol 3 of Imara's serial collections of the works of Tahtawi, Afghani and Abduh), Beirut, 1972 (no name of publisher).
10 Sura al-Baqarah, verse 29; 'Imara, *al-A'mal al Kamila*, vol III, pp. 363–364; Adams, *Islam and Modernism*, pp. 122–123.
11 Abduh, "Risalat al-Tawhid," in 'Imara, *al-A'mal al-Kamila*, vol III, p. 373.
12 M. al-Bahay, *Muhammad Abduh*, p. 53 ff.
13 Quran, *Surah* 33, verse 62.
14 Quran, *Surah* 35, verses 41–43.
15 'Imara, *al-A'mal al-Kamila*, vol III, p. 384.
16 Ignaz Goldziher, *Die Richtungen der Islamischen Koransauslegung*, Brill, Leiden, 1970, citing Abduh, *al-Manar*, vol XII, p. 486.
17 For a brief account of the difficulties that Abduh's call for change caused him with al-Azhar shaykhs and students, and with Shaykh 'Ilish in particular: Elshakry, *Darwin's Legacies*, pp. 297–317. Shaykh 'Ilish was himself a reformist who worked with other reformist shaykhs, such Arusi and Mahdi, but Abduh's ideas of doing away with *taqlid* (intellectual dominance of past authority) were for the elderly 'Ilish beyond the pale.
18 M. al-Bahay, *Muhammad Abduh*, pp. 2–53.
19 R. Caspar, "Le renouveaux Moatazilite," *Melanges d'institut Dominicain en l'orient* (MIDEO), IV, 1957, pp. 141–202; Nasr Hamid abu Zayd, "Divine Attributes of the Quran," in *Islam and Modernity: Muslim Intellectuals Respond*, edited by John Cooper, Ronald Nettler and Muhammad Mahmoud, I.B. Yauris and Co., London, 2000.
20 Aziz Azmeh, "Muslim Modernism and the Text of the Past," in *Islam and the Challenge of Modernity*, edited by Sharifa Shifa al-Attas, International Institute of Islamic Thought and Civilization, Kuala Lumpar, 1996, p. 423; 'Imara *al-A'mal al-Kamila*, vol 5, p. 529.
21 Abduh, "al-Waqa'i al-Misriyya," in 'Imara, *al-A'mal al-Kamila*, vol I, pp. 49–50.
22 Abduh, pp. 55–58.
23 Aziz al-Azmeh, "Muslim Modernities," in *Islam and the Challenge of Modernity*, by Sharifa Shifa al-Attas, International Institute of Islamic Thought and Civilization, Kuala Lumpar, 1996, p. 393.
24 M. el-Bahay, *Muhammad Abduh*, pp. 83–85.
25 Abduh, *Risalat-al-Tawhid*, in *al-A'mal al-Kamila*, vol III, pp. 364–365.
26 Abduh, *Risalat al-Tawhid*, in *al-A'mal al-Kamila*, vol III, pp. 343–344.
27 Abduh, *Risalat al-Tawhid*, in *al-A'mal al-Kamila*, vol III, p. 177. Fazlur Rahman, *Islam and Modernity: Transformation of an Intellectual Tradition*, Publications for the Center of Middle East Studies, University of Chicago, Chicago, 1982, p. 64.
28 F. Rahman, *Islam and Modernity*, p. 68.
29 A. Hourani, *Arabic Thought*, p. 141.
30 H.A.R. Gibb, *Modern Trends*, p. 43.

31 Malcolm Kerr, *Islamic Reform: The Political and Legal Theories of Muhammad Abduh and Rashid Rida*, University of California Press, Berkeley, CA, 1966, p. 108; A. Hourani, *Arabic Thought*, pp. 140–141.
32 Mahir Hasan, "Wafat al-Imam Muhammad Abduh," *Al-Masry al-Youm*, issue 2584 (July 7, 2011), Cairo, p. 2.
33 Sharif Mardin, *Religion and Social Change in Modern Turkey*, New York University Press, New York, 1989, pp. 60–75.
34 Sharif Mardin, *Religion and Social Change*, p. 86.
35 For Nursi's thought on science and religion and his deep and enduring influence in contemporary Turkey see Taner Edis, *An Illusion of Harmony: Science and Religion in Islam*, Prometheus, Amherst, NY, 2007, pp. 86–93.

11 Abduh's legacy

Muhammad Abduh is considered by eastern and western historians of Islamic intellectual reform to have been the seminal figure in initiating a reconciliation between the essentials of religion and the exigencies of modernization. During or after his lifetime, however, no religious consensus was clearly established concerning the on-going argument over the agreement between religion and science, certainly nothing that could stand as a general resolution comparable to the particular one that Abdallah Fikri's treatise established in regard to the question of Copernicanism.

Secular and religious followers of the intellectual lead bequeathed by Abduh continued to argue the same issues of modernization, at the center of which was science, touchstone of modernity, and at the center of that, the question of Darwin. For a century the discourse on science would revolve around evolution and its materialist philosophy, carried on in a number of successful journals and newspapers founded in the 1890s and early 20th century. These new publications presented a broad range of views, from both secular and religious perspectives.

Sarruf and Nimr founded a daily in Cairo, *al-Muqattam*, named after the plateau at the edge of the city (where Salah al-Din and the Ayybid Dynasty he founded, followed by Mamluks, Ottomans and Muhammad Ali, had garrisoned their troops and built their citadels). But it was their *Muqtataf* that continued to maintain its lead position among the secular journals, long after the founders were dead. Another duo of Syrian Christian émigrés, the Takla brothers, founded the daily *al-Ahram* (*The Pyramids* – a leading and highly respected news organ in the Arab world until after the military seized power in 1952). Jurji Zaydan's *al-Hilal* (*The Crescent*), a literary and historical journal, added richly to the body of modern secular literature arising in Egypt, as did Zaydan's historical novels. Farah Antun (1874–1922), another Syrian Christian seeking a literary career in Egypt, followed in Zaydan's footsteps and founded *al-Jami'a*, a periodical that reviewed contemporary western thought and espoused Shumayyil's ideas of socialism. The Egyptian Christian Salama Musa's many books that ardently embraced Shumayyil's evolutionist materialism, with its progressive socialist spin, found their place on the far left of the shelf. A Muslim counterpart to Salama Musa's Shumayyilist radicalism was Ismail Mazhar, author of many provocative books and the first to translate the principal chapters of Darwin's *Origin of Species* into Arabic.

Contributing on the religious side to the growing and contentious literature on science and evolution, Shaykh Rashid Rida, another Syrian émigré from Tripoli and student of both Jisr and Abduh, founded his *al-Manar* in Cairo. A journal of theological, political and historical thought, it expressed reformist Muslim views on science in general and evolution and materialism in particular. Shaykh Rida's biography of Muhammad Abduh, "Our Teacher" (*Ustadhina*), as he refers to him, is, except of course for Abduh's own writings, the leading source for the life and thought of one of Arab Islam's most important religious thinkers in modern times.

Writing caustically on the Catholic side of the issue was the Syro–Lebanese Jesuit historian Louis Chiekho, chief editor of *al-Mashriq*, a literary, historical and religious journal founded by the Jesuits at the French College St. Joseph in Beirut. And still propounding the Protestant view in Beirut was Ibrahim Hourani, that iron horse of moderate evangelism who right into the 20th century continued writing against Shumayyil and the editors of *Muqtataf* in the *Evangelical Weekly* (*al-Usbu'iyyah*), but in a gentler manner than the pugilistic Jesuit of St. Joseph.

In a lively and often acerbic idiom, these disparate organs interacted among themselves in their attacks and responses, bringing the debate on science and religion to a wider public. Ordinarily, to ensure cordial relations and not to give cause for government intervention, the argumentation was kept within the confessional communities, Christian criticizing Christian, Muslim attacking Muslim. The Jesuit Chiekho, fierce defender of Catholic orthodoxy, never attacked Shaykhs Abduh or Rida, not even for their qualified acceptance of evolution, nor even the nominally Muslim Ismail Mazhar, who in addition to being a socialist and suspected atheist was a professed evolutionist and, horror of horrors, translator of Darwin. However, as for the Christians who leaned toward the theory of evolution – Shumayyil, Sarruf, Nimr, Farah Antun, Jurji Zaydan, Salama Musa – these were all fair game for the Jesuit's bludgeoning critiques, which occasionally turned to personal insult. It was the same with Shaykh Rashid Rida. While going gently with Christian evolutionists, he dealt most harshly with Ismail Mazhar and other Muslims of Mazhar's evolutionist persuasion who failed to accept and emphasize God's enactment of evolutionary laws and creation of man.

Rarely did the lines of fire cross the confessional borders. Ideas that were viciously attacked within the community were graciously tolerated when held by those outside of it. Fighting was kept within the family, but even then, once started it could fall out of control and lead to religious strife, with all sorts of unintended consequences. It will be recalled that the Ottoman authorities had to intervene in the 1880s before the scrap between Ibrahim Hourani and Shibli Shumayyil fired up religious passions to the point they became violent. That had been a controversy within the Christian community. Responsible religious and government authorities feared that any dispute crossing the religious lines could become bloody once it got beyond the circle of literary combatants. Communal strife had to be avoided. Syrians and Ottoman government officials remembered the Druze-Maronite massacres of 1845 and 1860, which led to Christians and Muslims killing each other in Damascus and ended with French marines occupying Beirut, and Mt. Lebanon being made into a semi-autonomous administrative district with guarantees of European protection. The Ottomans did not want a return visit.

One community that seems to have remained silent during the controversy was the Jewish. No Jewish writer entered the arena to support or reject evolution, not at least in Arabic. It would be enlightening to learn whether in the 19th and early 20th centuries Jewish writers and scholars carried on among themselves a debate parallel to the one in Arabic involving Christians and Muslims. The Jewish communities were well integrated in the economic and intellectual life of Islamic society, and like Christian Arabs, they contributed to Arabic literature and journalism, at least up until the threatening intrusion of Zionism resulting from the British occupation of Palestine after World War I.[1]

One of the rare exceptions to the rules of engagement regarding this unwritten rule of limiting fire to co-religious miscreants was the exchange between Shaykh Abduh and Farah Antun. Broadly viewed, the point of controversy was a recapitulation in modern dress of the extended argument over reason and revelation carried on in the 11th and 12th centuries by ibn Sina, al-Ghazali and ibn Rushd. But the difference in views between Abduh and Antun was almost non-existent compared to the difference between Ghazali and the philosophers. Because the ideas of the secularist Antun and the religious reformer Abduh were so close – they were arguing for the same thing from different perspectives – Antun was as likely as Abduh to use al-Ghazali and ibn Rushd in buttressing an argument.

That the medieval debate was still being waged in the 20th century shows the ulema's remarkable diligence in preserving a grip on their populist position in face of the century-long whittling away of their wealth and central place in education and society by reformist rulers. There was indeed much in the feelings and attitudes of Muslims to make the anti-western ulema popular: rulers perceived as corrupt, oppressive and overly dependent on the West provided a lot of it; western occupation, military incursions of Arab lands provided more. The assault by state reformers on much of what had been the prerogatives of religion ensured the ulema a strong voice among the less fortunate classes of the splintering society. Some members of the ulema cooperated with the secular state hoping to bridge the divide, and in this Abduh continued the work of Shaykhs Attar, Tahtawi and Marsafi. His debate with Antun was an effort in building the bridge.

Because Abduh and Antun were on friendly terms and were sensitive to the dangers of communal strife, their contretemps was conducted with restraint and polite civility, even amicability. On that score, their contention echoes the debate between al-Afghani and Renan in France 15 years earlier, Antun playing the French philosopher to Abduh's Afghani. Antun had in fact translated Renan's *Vie de Jesus* to demonstrate that Christianity was inherently irrational and anti-scientific. He also followed Renan by writing a book on ibn Rushd, the subject of Renan's doctoral dissertation, publication of which, as *Averroes et Averroisme*, had first brought Renan fame as a philosopher and "orientaliste" in his own right.

Renan's and Antun's books on ibn Rushd were meant to demonstrate Islam's hostility to science, just as Renan's *Vie de Jesus* and Antun's translation of it were meant to show the same for Christianity. In other words, as Afghani had said in

France, religion, whatever name it went by, crippled the rational spirit. For Antun, the one great service religion performed for humanity was when the eastern Christian scholars mediated the transfer of Greek knowledge into Arabic.[2] That was a bit strong for Abduh. He took issue over Antun's regard of Islam as being non-rational, just as Afghani had with Renan in the earlier staging of the debate. Abduh had no problem agreeing with Antun that Christianity was irrational. What could be more irrational, he asks, than belief in raising the dead, changing wine and bread to blood and flesh, fish and bread magically multiplying, three gods in one, God having a son who was also God and having a human mother? Where did that leave poor Joseph, cuckolded by God? Paul was right when he said that reason had no place in Christianity. When the Christians came to power what did they do? Brutally murder the woman philosopher Hypatia in Alexandria. Then they burned Bruno, silenced Galileo and set up the Inquisition. The Protestants were no less harsh. Luther called Aristotle a dirty lying pig, whereas in Islam he was given the honorific title of the First Philosopher.

Antun reminded Abduh that al-Ghazali had claimed Aristotle and other Greek philosophers to be leaders of religious disbelief. Yes, Abduh rejoined, but this was not true Islam.

Abduh was defending an idealized Islam, not the historical Islam of Antun's criticism. From that point on, the argument was between a Muslim Platonic idealist and a Christian Aristotelian. Abduh's true Islam was corrupted in history after it came down from heaven and got mauled in the clouded minds and material hands of men. What passes for Islam is a perverted un-Islamic Islam. It is this form of Islam that needs to be purified back to its original state.

Other than Antun's doubt that the beautiful moment of Abduh's perfect Islam had ever existed and could be reinvented, the two reformers had little to disagree on. They nonetheless made the best of it and debated on as if having some serious differences of opinion. The point of the exercise was to give public airing to a debate on the need for science and socio-religious reform. More agreement than argument, their controversy was a staged performance to direct public attention to serious issues.

Abduh's idealization of Islam abstracted from the first generation of Muslims became a staple in reformist thinking. Taking his lead from Sayyid Afghani, Shaykh Abduh argued that Islam was fundamentally different from Christianity and all religions. Islam was a model of reason. It encouraged rational inquiry and science. Islam tolerated no miracles, no saints, no magic and no superstition. Whereas Europeans had to reject Christianity to gain science, devout Muslims were great scientists and philosophers simply by virtue of their religion. For this reason, an enlightened ulema of a reformed Islam with a modernized Shari'a as the legal foundation of a modern state could be partners with a secular ruler, each side fulfilling its separate responsibility while working harmoniously together in execution of legal, political, financial and economic affairs. Muslims did not need to put materialism in place of God to accept science in a modern state. Any Muslim who rejected reason and science was not truly a believer, for true Islam insisted that science be pursued. There was no religion without science, no science without religion. Rejecting science was to reject religion. Science and religion were independent of each other, but came together as one in a godly society, as they had in the early days of Islam, when Islam was what it was meant to be. Science, the productive work of the rational intellect, dwelt apart from but was akin to that religious conscience residing deep in the spiritual wellsprings of the heart.

For Antun, the intellect proceeded by observation and experiment in a purely material world, while the heart was moved by acceptance of scripture without critical examination or analysis of causes and reasons. The analytic powers of the mind would reduce religion with all its mysteries and absurdities to rational understanding, making it something other than religion. A scientific religion or a religion of science were contradictions in terms. Science and religion had nothing in common, nor should they have. They existed in separate realms. They had no congruence or common ground. They had nothing to do with each other. Otherwise, why have religion if you have science? Science reflected on the objects of this world; religion reflected on virtue and vice, goodness and evil, and heaven and hell. Neither could refute the other. Problems arose where philosophers and theologians failed to recognize their separate realms. The resulting confusion always led to a false conflict of one overcoming the other:

> Ibn Rushd would have allegorized scripture to make religion subservient to reason and science. We do not agree with this, for neither should be subservient, but both totally independent. Ibn Rushd's attempt at creating a harmonious agreement between science and religion was what brought him down.[3]

Or, as Afghani had said in Paris, as soon as science and religion were brought together, one would tear the other down, with the side of darkness and ignorance winning by the sheer numbers in their ranks.

Abduh could not have agreed more with Antun's heart and mind compartmentalization of religion and science. Their disagreement lay in their divergence of perspective with regard to religion and historical development. Abduh dismissed the idea of historical development, seeing Islam to have existed in its pure and true form only during the earliest generation of Muslims, that is, the *salaf*, those who were close to the Prophet and whose hearts were filled with religion and whose minds rationally guided the community, back in that pristine time when Islam was itself and in harmony with science and the rational spirit. Antun, on the other hand, saw Christianity as having become its true self and achieving its highest expression of ethics, ideals and values through history, when the Renaissance, Scientific Revolution and Enlightenment had extirpated the sources of intolerance and oppression that had been inherent in society because of the medieval church's political power. Only when the church had been stripped of its power by the secular state was Christianity able to achieve intellectual freedom and high spirituality. Religious authority had to be separated from political authority; otherwise there could be no "true civilization, no toleration, no justice and equality, no security and friendship, no science, philosophy and progress." Islam would have to follow the same historical pattern in order for Muslim society to reach a comparable level of civilization.[4]

Abduh's historical line of vision toward fulfillment of an Islamic high civilization went in the opposite direction: to the past, not to future movements in emulation of western Christianity. The key to Islam's future greatness was rational reform modeled on the past in order to recapture the greatness that had been lost. Abduh believed that only with an enlightened ulema at the forefront of scientific thought and at the intellectual core of a revitalized society could Islamic civilization take its place as a full partner in the modern world. Antun believed only a secularized society could achieve high civilization. The difference became the front line of their exchange.

Beneath their polite verbiage, the flint that sparked Abduh's reaction to Antun's book on ibn Rushd was not as much the question of secularization as his believing that Antun's intent was to attack Islam. He was only partly right. Like his hero Renan, Antun was attacking all religions as being equally oppressive. In response, Abduh wrote his book on Islam and Christianity in which he argued that once Islam was cleansed of its corruptive elements, science and reason would flow into it, when properly introduced. Islam, truly understood, and practiced, was the key to happiness in this world and the sure path to the next. Unlike Christianity, it did not lead men to renounce the goods of this world, but rather encouraged them to enjoy the material things of life as a blessing, and gave them the eternal delights of paradise at the end. Islam was a religion of balance and moderation. When followed, society flourished; when disobeyed, it decayed. Taking a line from Bonaparte's propaganda to the Cairo shaykhs a century earlier, Abduh blamed the Turks and their ignorant slavery to tradition and authority for bringing Muslim civilization down. All this would change once the true Islam of the Prophet and his companions was made a living reality.

Antun conceded that a reformed Islam cleansed of its scholastic dogmatics and stultifying traditions of imitation, memorization and repression of thought could possibly be amenable to a culture of science, but the pristine Islam of Abduh's mind, a philosophy more than a religion, was a medieval skeleton draped in modern garb that could serve no purpose in modern civilization. It existed as a useless organ of a former species, exactly what religion in western society had become. If Islam was really a religion of reason, Antun argued, then let it be exchanged for the real thing: science.[5]

This was for the sake of argument. Antun recognized that Abduh's aim in rebutting him the way he did, by depicting "true Islam" as an idealized form in an imaginary moment of history, was meant to get Muslims to study science and sharpen their minds by making Islam and science out to share a common spirit. The two thinkers were equally committed to this, Abduh speaking to convince Muslims, Antun to convince Arabs whatever their religion, though he could only regret Abduh's discrediting exaggeration of Islam being a religion created in the image of scientific inquiry, a religion that, if studied by the British people, would, as Abduh had embarrassingly declared, compel them to convert to it in droves.[6] Antun knew that if Islam were so imbued with the religious spirit, its followers would not presently be so backward and science not so feared and ignored. The science that had been created during the classical period of Muslim civilization would not have been rejected and lost.

The exchange offered the public a review of the arguments supporting the amicability or enmity between religion and science as articulated by a leading Muslim shaykh and a Christian secularist. Abduh was too far ahead, or maybe just too outside of the Azharite mainstream to be considered a spokesperson for what was or was not acceptable to the Muslim community. The legion of Europeans fawning over him aside, his arguments appealed mainly to a small circle of religious and secular students who were thrilled to hear that the heart of Islam was synonymous with reason, science, individual liberty and progressive civilization. This was the message received and vigorously advanced in the 20th century by followers who found in Abduh a modernist voice giving religious credibility to their reformist ideas.

Shaykh Rashid Rida vigorously advanced Abduh's arguments for religious reform and science education, but later, shying away from his teacher's Mu'tazilite tendencies and daring stance on reinstituting *ijtihad* for reinterpretation of the Quran and Hadith to formulate a modernized Shari'a, he reverted to a more traditionalist *salafi* position of venerating established religious authority – similar to Shaykh Tahtawi's reversion to traditional ideas a generation earlier. Abduh's secularist followers diverged toward an extreme in the opposite direction, abandoning the balance he tried to achieve between the interpretive demands of modernism and preserving the spiritual and legal essentials of established belief. Their overly eager efforts in continuing Abduh's work reduced the Quran to a revelational repository of science and technology interspersed with morality, duties, mystery and the hereafter, with thermodynamics and chlorophyll substituting for angels and jinn.

Between the religious enthusiasts and the radical secularists, the religious and secular strands that Abduh had drawn together in his reformist thought were torn apart and taken to their extremes. The breech was symptomatic of the widening split in society. Abduh had resided mentally in both worlds. His followers failed to sustain the balance. The promising beginning that Abduh had made in the modernization of his religion failed to become the normative view. As the strands came undone, they diverged further and further from the center he had established. The unraveling can be seen in Rashid Rida's harsh tone in the debate he resumed with his fellow Syrian, Farah Antun. It was during the last year of Abduh's life. In the introduction of the 1904 edition of Antun's treatise on ibn Rushd, the author complained of Rashid Rida's unmannerly fanaticism in attacking him. Antun had been friends with Abduh, and with Rashid Rida as well – they had traveled together by ship from Tripoli to Alexandria when emigrating from Syria, making Antun lament all the more that loss of civility in scholarly discourse he had earlier shared with Shaykh Abduh and Rashid Rida.

While Antun was crossing swords with Rida, a parallel duel was concomitantly being fought out over the same issues. This one was between Louis Chiekho in Beirut and the Jesuit's Syro–Lebanese coreligionists in Egypt. The contretemps was a heated continuation of the Edwin Lewis Affair and the religious frenzy of Protestants and Catholics over Shumayyil's paraphrase translation of Buchner's commentary. Anything Shumayyil wrote after having published that book could not help but make the exchange all the nastier. And as it was all within the Christian family, civility was uncalled for.

For some years in the early 20th century it looked as though a Jesuit-Azharite axis had been established between Beirut and Cairo to counter the Christian evolutionist materialists, whose ranks were ominously being joined by even some Egyptian Muslim writers, particularly Ismail Mazhar, Mustafa Mansuri and Hasan Husayn. While Rashid Rida was taking aim in Cairo on Farah Antun and the Muslim evolutionists, Chiekho was from his Jesuit fortress in Beirut blasting the Christian contingent among the enemy: Shibli Shumayyil, Jurji Zaydan, Salama Musa and also Farah Antun, who was now being attacked from both sides.

Chiekho's ideas regarding science and religion were akin to those of Abduh, Jisr and Rida, though somewhat to the conservative side: the three shaykhs accepted evolution by divine design, while the Jesuit rejected Darwin and evolution out of hand as a grotesque perversion of science. Apart from evolution, the scholarly Chiekho was otherwise on amicable terms with science. He believed it brought men closer to God, and seems to have known a little more about science than the Azharites. He referred to the deep religiosity of Copernicus, Kepler, Galileo, Descartes, Leibnitz, Linné, Cuvier, Ampere and Pasteur. He commended Roger Bacon and Copernicus for having been scientists and monastic priests; Newton was so austere and devoted to biblical study and science that he may as well have been a monk.

Darwin, however, for all his piety, was beyond the pale. In an article entitled "Contradictions Between Religion and Society," Chiekho described him as being as far from science as science was from the heavens.[7] This was in answer to articles supporting Darwin that appeared in *Muqtataf* and Jurji Zaydan's journal. Chiekho criticized the editors for supporting Darwin's hypothesis as a proven theory and vowed that the Jesuit *Mashriq* would remain critical and unaccepting until positive and undeniable proof elevated evolution to a science, which Chiekho was sure would never happen. He advised the editors of *Hilal* and *Muqtataf* to follow the same policy, since the materialist philosophy of evolution that they espoused was irredeemably opposed to religion. Indeed, it was a mortal threat to faith. Evolution's discrediting of the Book of Genesis was to Chiekho the opening wedge that threatened to discredit the whole of scripture and with it the basis of religion.

Religion had to be defended against the materialists and Père Chiekho stood pen in hand at the vanguard. In answer to Jurji Zaydan's accusation that *Mashriq* failed to distinguish between what was science and what was religion, Chiekho wrote that the journal did indeed distinguish between them; it was a religious duty to do so:

> Science and religion are twins bound by an unbreakable bond.... Two eyes of one face, they emanate from the same divine source, and any religion that refutes true science is not true religion.... If religion were opposed to science, then as science grew religion would diminish. But such is not the case. It is men of religion who have built science, from St. Augustine to St. Thomas, Roger Bacon, Copernicus and up to the present. Scientists are

imbued with religion ... Transubstantiation and the Trinity do not contradict science: they are mysteries beyond science and reason and have nothing to do with them. Take them away and nothing is left of religion.

The Christian defenders of religion sounded remarkably like their Muslim counterparts: minus the references to the Trinity and Transubstantiation, Chiekho's sentiments could have been those of Shaykhs Husayn al-Jisr, Muhammad Abduh and Rashid Rida.

The testy exchange between *Mashriq*, *Muqtataf* and *Hilal* went on for decades. On occasion it turned vitriolic. In August 1914, just at the commencement of the World War that was to be such a dark turning point in the region's history, *Muqtataf* questioned *Mashriq's* credentials as a scientific journal. It accused it of being no more than a religious publication dedicated to holding the line against scientific thought that disagreed with Catholic orthodoxy. In rebuttal, Chiekho asked how *Muqtataf* could consider itself a scientific journal when its editors passed off theories that were "more fanciful than factual" as proven science, and who confused speculative philosophy (meaning Darwin) with positive science. "How many times did they publish, in the name of science, fantastic philosophies that were utterly and ridiculously false, devoid of all science? ... If all the foolish things *Muqtataf* took to be science over the past 17 years, that is, since *Mashriq* was founded, were collected and published in a book, the journal's editors and all those who wrote for it would be the laughing stock of genuine scientists." Chiekho proceeded to unload a storehouse of perceived grievances *Mashriq* had accumulated at the hands of *Muqtataf* over the years:

> Where is the science in *Muqtataf*'s claim that holy water in church basins contains typhoid and diphtheria microbes? Or that the manna from heaven that fed the Israelites 40 years was from "*asarat al-turafa*" [tamarisk juice]) when there wasn't enough in the whole of Sinai to feed a quarter of the Israelites for one day, let alone 40 years. Or that man's fear of snakes is an inherited instinct that survived through the generations from primitive man's existence. Or that the nipples on the male breast are a vestigial survival of a prehistoric time when men had breasts like women and breastfed the children, and that when men became devoted to war their breasts withered for lack of use ... But all of these examples diminish to insignificance when compared to *Muqtataf*'s propagation of materialism, its denial of the spiritual mind and the spirit's pure, non-material essence. Ever since the founding of *al-Mashriq*, we have stood against this false philosophy that *Muqtataf*'s editors continue to espouse, including even the claim that man's mind is no more than the cumulative effects of the brain's actions and that thought has weight, as if thinking is something like onions that can be weighed. In their article "Before Birth and After Death" the editors of *Muqtataf* go so far as to deny not only the existence of man's spirit but his eternal soul as well.

Chiekho excoriates the editors for their support of evolution and their claim that primeval life arose from dead matter by self-generation, which they said could explain the origin of life, including human, as primeval species evolved progressively from their origins. The Jesuit's accusation was unfair. *Muqtataf's* Ya'qub Sarruf had claimed the same proviso of Intelligent Design as did Husayn al-Jisr, Abduh and Rida. As close as Sarruf ever came to explicitly endorsing evolution before 1914 was to review the theory of natural selection and state that it in no way opposed religion as long as it was believed God originally bestowed life to matter and laid down the laws of natural selection and generation of species. Whether he actually believed that Darwin believed in God or not, Sarruf repeatedly emphasized Darwin's profound belief. Where natural selection was found wanting, *Muqtataf* was quick to publicize it, happy to undermine the pretensions of those overly heated enthusiasts of evolution, such as the supporters of the theory of spontaneous generation that had been put forth as evidence that life originated in non-living matter.

The editors of *Muqtataf* could in fact be as bruising as Chiekho in their critiques of Shumayyil's materialist philosophy. A few years before Chiekho's 1914 attack on *Muqtataf*, Yusuf Salhat had written in *Muqtataf* a review of the 1909 edition of Shumayyil's annotated paraphrase translation of Buchner's materialist commentary on Darwin. Entitled "Struggle for Existence Among the Sciences," Salhat's review was highly critical of both Buchner and Shumayyil and the whole materialist philosophy they advocated. His criticisms were almost identical to those that Chiekho would publish in 1914. One of the few instances of agreement between *Mashriq* and *Muqtataf* was in regard to the 1909 edition of Shumayyil's book. It is easy to see why.

Shumayyil, a derivative materialist who had parted from critical science a long time previously, added an introduction to the new edition of his Buchner paraphrase in which he foresaw a one-world society emerging as a political parallel to the universal laws that unified nature. One grand unified law would embrace the whole of nature just as one global political body would embrace the world. Einstein was already searching for it. Shumayyil was sure it would soon be found. In this universal society that was surely emerging through the on-going political struggle of nations for survival, religion would fade away along with political borders, as would social customs and all the traditions that divided the people of the world into nations, races and religions. In this coming new world, science, which served equality, democracy and unity, would replace religion, which served servitude, division and autocracy. As the new supplanted the old in the ineluctable onward course of social evolution toward universal unity, it was inevitable that religion, philosophy and metaphysics would wither away and be supplanted by science. Light, the key to relativity, was showing the way.

In a refreshingly perverse turn of historical reinterpretation that was typical of Shumayyil, the burning of the books in the Alexandrine library became a triumph of reason and intellectual liberation: the old must be burned down to make room for the new. (Presumably the ulema-induced burning of philosophical books in the caliphal library in Cordova was another liberating triumph of reason.)

> So too will today's knowledge and its religions become a historical relic, and it will come soon, since in these days of rapid change a year is as a century in

times past. Religion, social philosophy, tradition, customs, all will give way to a society whose system of law, justice, organization and behavioral patterns will be analogs of natural science and drawn as precisely as the mathematics that define its relationships.[8]

To this, Yusuf Salhat responded:

Religion and philosophy have their place with science and come into agreement as they disperse the darkness of ignorance prevailing over people in matters relating to their religion and world outlook. What Dr. Shumayyil fails to realize is the reality of the soul, that spiritual entity which separates materialists from men of philosophy and religion.

Shibli would have none of it. But Père Chiekho must have applauded to see *Muqtataf*, Shumayyil's old ally, going after him. Outwardly, however, Chiekho stayed his course of accusing the journal of immoderation in its support of evolution and the materialists who perverted Darwin's thinking:

Even though Darwin believed in God and put a limit on the power of evolution, those who followed in his footsteps went beyond that limit, such as Haeckel, whom *Muqtataf* supported as it had Darwin.

That was a huge admission on the Jesuit's part: not Darwin, but Shumayyil and his German materialist mentors were the villains. Taken in its most positive sense, the statement seemed to be enough of a conditional acceptance of Darwin's moderation and faith as to bridge an accommodating truce between the editors of *Mashriq* and *Muqtataf*. But combat continued. On the eve of World War I, Chiekho, his Jesuit fury reverberating in a replay of the American evangelists' condemnation of Edwin Lewis and Darwin 32 years earlier, accused *Muqtataf* of falsification, deception and intellectual corruption in its method of reporting on evolution.[9] *Muqtataf's* sin was in giving any space at all to evolution, however critically it reviewed the unscientific spin-offs of Darwinianism. The journal's other sins were just as damning: doubting the literal truth of creation as told in Genesis; doubting the stories of Adam and Eve; doubting Paradise, the snake and the tree of wisdom; doubting all the way through Genesis and Exodus up to St. Bernadette and the miraculous healing powers of the water at Our Lady of Lourdes.

Chiekho could tolerate no questioning of Catholicism's accepted miracles by his fellow Syro–Lebanese Christians. The liberal climate of Egypt, to where they had earlier fled, gave them no protection from the Jesuit's wrath. The cynicism of *Muqtataf's* editors was insufferable, he wrote. They dressed their articles in a thin cloak of pseudo-analysis, beneath which their cynicism, sarcasm and mockery burned through like a poisonous acid. Their unmistakable tone of doubt that had become associated with *Muqtataf* amounted in fact to nothing more than a specious, barely disguised attack on all that was sacred in the church. For Chiekho, the Guns of August had already sounded.

As has been pointed out in reference to Shibli Shumayyil's version of evolution, much of the trouble Darwin's thought had in being accepted in the Middle East, as compared to Copernicanism, was owing to the added baggage that Arab commentators piled on the theory. Shumayyil saddled it with Buchner's materialism and Spencer's social Darwinism, while in *Muqtataf* it was associated by implication with Haeckel. Later, the Egyptians Salama Musa, Mustafa Mansuri, Qasim Amin, Ismail Mazhar and Hasan Husayn would march Marxism and women's liberation into it.

Fashioned into a handy all-purpose tool for anyone advocating change, natural selection was undermined as a legitimate science in the minds of everyone who believed in God, private property, polygamy and easy divorce. So heavily burdened with extraneous ideas that posed threats to the defenders of tradition, religion, marriage, property and social cohesion, Darwin's principles of evolution became a favorite target, drawing fire from every direction and being reduced to an absurdity as risible as Jamal al-Din al-Afghani's caricaturization of it in the previous century. Since there were no scientists as yet in Muslim culture of high enough stature to command attention and correct the record, and also since Darwin's works had not been translated for any fair-minded reader to have a chance to set things right for oneself, Darwin's science continued to be freely overlaid with unrelated social and political theories in the push for reform by one side, while being ridiculed by the other that depicted natural selection as monkeys in high hats and suits smoking cigars.

To take but one of many examples, in his *History of Socialist Schools* (*Tarikh Madhahib al-Ishtirakiyya*, Cairo, 1914), Mustafa Mansuri depicts the relentless forward march of evolution acting in nature and society. Central to his book is the socialist promise to eliminate poverty and polygamy, and to offer a state-supported system of universal education that included females. Mansuri was the first Muslim to accept Darwin fully and openly, without religious conditions; but by pinning natural selection to "scientific socialism" and popularizing it as a political ideology for egalitarian change, he transmogrified it into a threat to social conservatives whose acceptance was vital in preparing the way for an indigenous scientific culture. He also provided more fuel for the caricaturists.

There was no way to shield natural selection as a science from the zealous reach of secular reformers. Like the Quran, there was no science that could not be proved by it. Qasim Amin, a follower of Muhammad Abduh and advocate of women's liberation, wrote at the turn of the century that it was not religion but scientific thought that was the basis of civilization, and that the science of evolution proved the inevitability of social and intellectual progress.

The issue of what precisely Darwin's principles of evolution were, stripped clean of the pseudo-scientific social, economic and political philosophy that had been grafted onto natural selection, became all the more clouded with World War I and the Allied propaganda blaming the war's barbarity and destructiveness on German militarism and quest for power. This got all mixed up with German philosophical materialism. Sarruf, who up to then had been both tolerant and critical of Shumayyil's ideas, now openly rejected his materialism in belief that Germany's aggressive war machine and political ideology came from the philosophical materialism that had been made popular by writers like Buchner.[10] Space was given in *Muqtataf* for Shumayyil to give his rebuttal: Philosophy, he wrote, had nothing to do with the war. Like all wars, this one was being fought for self-interest, one side being no better than the other. The British occupiers of Egypt did not like such talk, and they made it known. The blistering rhetoric that resulted obfuscated Darwin's science all the more in the minds of the literate public.

Compared to their Christian counterparts, secularist Muslim thinkers generally took a more moderate position in reconciling religion with reason and evolution. There were, as always, exceptions. Mustafa al-Mansuri, Ismail Mazhar and Hasan Husayn were no less ardent supporters of science, evolution and social progress than were their Christian counterparts Bishara Zilzal, Shibli Shumayyil, Farah Antun, Jurji Zaydan and Salama Musa. For the most part, Muslim secularist thought was defined by men who followed Abduh's reformist lead in rationalizing the Quran, defending free will and reinterpreting the sources of jurisprudence for a modernized version of Shari'a law within the limits of what Abduh considered the essentials of belief. The reformist literature of Qasim Amin, Muhammad Muwaylihi, Muhammad Farid Wajdi, Muhammad Kurd Ali and Ahmad Lutfi al-Sayyid, whatever their private beliefs may have been, always left room for a divine Creator who dispensed souls and who would judge them at the end of time. The paradise and perdition of Quran and Hadith, and the ethics and morals based on those sacred sources, were paid lip service but little else in return for al-Azhar's seal of silent approval. What the Muslim secularists wanted was modernity through science education and all that would come from it, but in arguing for modernity they could do little more than plow the same soil their 19th century predecessors had.

By the 20th century, Muslim soil had been well seeded with reformist arguments of religion's scientific harmony and conformity wrung from Quranic verses, Prophetic Traditions and early history reinterpreted. However, whatever effects these efforts might have provided in preparing the soil for a scientific culture went unexploited by the state, which remained steadfast in its disinclination to fund science in a serious way. As long as this was the case, efforts to generate a scientific culture in Muslim society remained, and would remain, a barren exercise. This was the case in all Muslim states that up to World War I had maintained their independence. Under the British thumb, the Egyptian state was far from independent, whatever the British-imposed treaty of independence declared, but the government's lack of propensity to fund science prior to Britain's occupation gives no reason to believe it would have been different had Egypt escaped British occupation.

Egypt had long been the Arab world's intellectual center of gravity. Occupation imposed drastic limits on government action, but the Egyptian government was free to build schools and universities and send students to study in Europe – if it chose to do so. The apathy of the Egyptian government in regard to promoting science education remained a target of the more critical reformers. Owing to government lethargy, a new dimension of reformist criticism was opened by one of Abduh's more famous secular followers, Qasim Amin. His *Liberation of*

Women (*Tahrir al-Mar'a*), published in 1899, indicts state and society for Muslim backwardness. According to Amin, the ills began with Islam's tradition of absolute autocracy that separated government from society. His book brings into public discourse many of the criticisms first aired by Bishara Zilzal 20 years earlier. Both authors interpret Muslim decline in medieval times as a case of failed natural selection, in which tyranny over women atrophied their vital role as the moral teachers of children. This was one of the root causes of social stagnation and decay. The tyranny of religious tradition has halted the growth of science and crushed the spirit of women by condemning them to ignorance and servitude. Political and religious tyranny have deprived society of science, creative thinking, and the economic and intellectual potential of half its population.

To show how wrong were those who boasted of Islam as being a higher civilization, Amin contrasted the productive role of women in western society to the depressed condition of women in Muslim society. To Amin it was absurd to think that Islamic civilization, which ceased to grow long before the West made its great scientific discoveries, was superior. He praised western society for its having broken those forces that in Muslim society were responsible for stunting the civilization. The West accomplished what it did only after a long and bloody struggle that took education from the hands of religion and delivered it to science. He admired the West for its having made science into a new religion. What for Tahtawi in the late 1820s was as incomprehensible as it was reprehensible, substituting science for religion, had for Amin at the end of the century become a triumph of civilization and the human spirit: an achievement to be emulated. Science, he wrote, will never become a part of Muslim civilization without people struggling to create the social and political conditions required to support the freedom of mind for scientific inquiry. Muslims had to go back and study the history of their civilization in order to understand what their ancestors accomplished and how the conditions that prevailed then differed from the present conditions. Only then could they go about rectifying or eliminating the defective elements of their society:

> The study of our past history makes us realize that there was no political organization in Islamic society, only the autocratic will of the ruler whose power went unchecked. The fate of society rested on the ruler's and his court's desires. Justice was either upheld or discarded. War and peace were the autocrat's own private decision, as were taxes . . . Strange as it seems, the people of Muslim political society never reached the level of the Greeks or Romans in establishing institutions that fostered stability, public interest, political participation and enjoyment of freedom. These earlier societies had representative assemblies and parliaments that together with the ruler administered affairs and made political decisions. There was no real scientific social thought in Islam, nor political or economic. These are new sciences. Even the great thinker ibn Khaldun in his philosophy of society, economics, justice and the state did not once mention the family, the basis of social organization. Given this political condition of the Muslim past, what is there that we could want from it? Family relations were stripped of all organization. A man could

marry several women and divorce them with the flimsiest of excuses, without respecting the limits imposed by the Quran. This continues until today, as is well known, and no ruler or religious scholar thinks of regulating family life to prevent the damage caused by the lack of family bonds. In Islam family ties are chaotic; they were not in Greece or Rome and they are not in Europe today. This family chaos came early in Islam, right after the death of the Prophet, when the Arabs started tearing at each other's throats and consuming themselves in internal conflicts, tribal hatreds, envy and self interest, even while the Arab empire was at war and expanding. While all this was going on, one of Ali's sons was marrying and divorcing more than 100 women.[11]

In order for Islamic society to enter modern civilization, Amin goes on, not only must science be studied but the conditions of its study must be created, meaning unveiling and giving rights to women, making legal controls for marriage and divorce, providing for female education and carrying out political and social reform to give women an equal place in society with men. The past has to be surrendered:

Holding to the past holds society back. Our feeling of weakness and lack of confidence in our ability to build a state appropriate to our times keep us hanging onto the past. Infatuation with the past is a great weight that weighs on us and makes us feel too defeated in the present. Trapped in the past, we are made victims of ourselves, of our self-inflicted fate of being too dependent on past achievements. Believing we were so great in the past that we can never surpass it, we don't try. We take refuge in the past to soothe our inferiority. We hide from recognizing the West's advance over us and fool ourselves into believing we are superior to the West in literature and spirituality. It is our disease. The only way we can ever cure ourselves of it is to raise our children so they are educated in western civilization.

Qasim Amin's criticism was stronger and more penetrating than had been Bishara Zilzal's and Shibli Shumayyil's criticism of what to Muslims was the sexual core of Shari'a law: women, wives, family, divorce.

Shaykh Rashid Rida's reformist ideas took a different tack from the center that Abduh had outlined. Where the secularist Qasim Amin saw renewal through taking science as the new religion and through the social elevation of women along western lines, Rashid Rida came to see it in the bowels of Islam: a return to the ways of the early Muslims, the *salaf*, a time when women were active in society at the highest level. Muslims did not need to look to the West; their glorious past was the mirror they should look to. Here he differed from his teacher, Abduh, who preferred Mu'tazilite reinterpretation over *salafi* adoration. Nonetheless, whether the road taken was Abduh's Mu'tazilite rationalism or Rida's *salafi* traditionalism, in the minds of their respective beholders both roads were bedded in religion and science. However much Rida diverged from his mentor, he carried on Abduh's portrayal of Islam as a religion of reason and science. An enduring theme in Rida's journal, *al-Manar* (*The Lighthouse*), was Abduh's call for Muslims and Muslim states to take up modern science. It was a Muslim moral imperative. Islam was science translated into religion. Islam was the only religion that was rational and imbued with the scientific spirit. In order for young Muslims to be educated in the true spirit of Islam, religion and science had to be taught together as dimensions of truth originating from a single source.

Manar's introductory issue proclaimed its mission to be the awakening of young minds to true Islam, to the dangers of western political and cultural imperialism, and to the need for education in science and technology in order to address the defects of society. Taking up many of the themes of the Young Ottoman critics of the *Tanzimat* reformers, Rida attributed the fatal flaw of the *Tanzimat* to have been its lack of religion, its failure to promote science and its dog-like lapping up of western institutions. Uncritical imitation had weakened the empire. Muslims must wake up. They must learn the science and technology that the West has used to rule Muslims. Muslims must start building for themselves instead of borrowing and allowing themselves to be subjugated:

> Oh ye Easterner drowned in joyful sleep with its delightful dreams! Take care! Take care! For you have gone beyond the limit of comfort in your sleep and are almost unconscious or dead. Wake up, wipe the sleep from your eyes and look at the new world! . . . Your brothers have seized power of nature. They have put steam and electricity and light to their service. They have pierced mountains . . . know that this is the era of science and action – 'ilm wa 'amal!

Science and action were *Manar*'s equivalent to *Muqtataf*'s logo of quill and adze. Rida had at first cast the editors of *Muqtataf* into the same anti-religious bin as Shumayyil and Antun. Some years later, in the early 20th century, he came to a reappraisal. *Muqtataf*'s articles gradually convinced him that he had misjudged Sarruf and Nimr and the fairness of their journal, whose goals he recognized to be no different in terms of the region's social ills than the ones he expressed in his *Manar*. The all-important difference of course was that secular *Muqtataf* stood for separation of the religion and government, while *Manar* advocated the guiding hand of religion in the affairs of state, public policy and education.

In its early years, as the 19th century rolled into the 20th, *Manar* was a revolutionary call from the minaret. Muslims had to resuscitate themselves or perish in ignorance and lassitude. Resuscitation began with coming to an understanding of authentic Islam through a re-examination of the Quran. This would reveal the values of science and action at the heart of true Islam, the Islam of the Quran: not the Islam of the masses and benighted ulema.[12] Of all the religions of the world, Islam was the one whose scripture and Prophet most clearly advocated the study of science as a way to an expanding consciousness of God as Creator. But where in Islamic society was the science? Where the action? With the foreigners!

Rida shamed Muslims for relying on their government to do everything for them and shamed Muslim governments for relying on Europeans to build everything that was built in Muslim countries. The Muslim people were as weak and corrupt as their government. It was a closed circle of bribery, corruption and concentration of wealth in the hands of a few at the top that left the strong to devour the weak. While the rich devoured the poor and Muslim governments devoured the Muslim people, Europeans devoured both Muslim governments and people. Only the people could break the vicious circle that was eating away at Muslim society. Muslim governments were too corrupt to change, too lazy, too fat, too dependent on Europeans to build their railroads, dams and factories, too dependent on the bribes and payoffs that came with the contracts. Nothing good could come from government. It was too corrupted, too deep in the pockets of western companies and governments. The moral decay of Muslim leaders and notables was a cancer spread through the whole of society. Rida summed it up with a proverb: "The fish begins to stink from the head."

Regeneration had to come from an authentic culture rooted in the common people. The people expected the government to do everything. The Quranic command to action was so alien to the emptied souls of the day's Muslims that they thought it only natural that the government do everything. It was a law of life. People saw themselves existing only through the ruler, regarding him as a kind of divinity, the way the Fatimid Caliph Hakim bi Amr Allah regarded himself.[13] Because of this fawning acceptance of governmental majesty, people divorced themselves from independent action and became inert, irresponsible and alienated from political life. Rulers of weak people were themselves weak compared to rulers who ruled over strong people. The West was occupying Islamic lands and ruling over them through their surrogate Muslim princelings and through the schools and institutions that westerners had established in Muslim countries. Muslim culture was being dissolved in the acid of western education. The young generation, the only generation that could offer hope of change, was being stripped of its own culture. The young were made to feel embarrassed about themselves, to the extent they denied what they really were. Their western education alienated them from their culture and made them into people who were neither eastern nor western. Not knowing who or what they were made them all the more vulnerable to the authorities above them: their fathers, their rulers, their western teachers who represented western interests. In the same measure their weak rulers were subservient to the West, they were subservient to both their rulers and the West.[14]

When Rida wrote this in 1897, he thought that if young educated Muslims were ever to get themselves together and begin acting, 40 years would suffice for a generation of independent men to come into existence who could overcome the inertia of *jahl wa kasl* – ignorance and sloth – and replace it with the *'ilm wa 'amal* that were necessary to create authentic Muslim versions of modern institutions of government, finance, communications and industry based on Islamic law and justice. Moral regeneration had to begin on the personal level. The individual had to assume a moral sense of self-responsibility and act in accord with the principles of religion and science. This would give rise in 40 years to a leadership of intelligent, self-reliant and responsible people molded in the virtue of action.

The figure of 40 years came from Rida's estimation of the process of modern state-building based on Japan's accomplishment. By decisively asserting its national self-will, Japan had committed itself to science and action and within that period of time reversed the inferior position imposed on it by the West. Two years before Japan's crushing defeat of the Russian navy, Rida wrote that the success of Japan's transformation was owing to the united effort of government and religion. The Mikado was the head of the state and the head of religion. Unity of the two made for a powerful and purposeful society. In Japan, religion was a positive force for reform and change. When the Mikado decided Japan should industrialize, all institutional obstacles were swept away. Society moved as one.

Rida contrasted this to the Muslim experience. Religious leaders not only held back from change but fought tooth and nail against those politicians, and those among themselves, who advocated it. The most poignant example of this was the resistance to the ideas of Shaykh Muhammad Abduh, whose reforms were opposed by the Azhari leadership. Rather than taking Abduh's groundbreaking *Treatise on Divine Oneness* (*Risalat al-Tawhid*) as a starting point, the shaykhs, who were mentally incapable of writing a book on the harmony of Islam and science themselves, shunned it as though its words were drops of poison. They accused him of being a Mu'tazilite, as if to declare him a heretic. Their mental lethargy out-competed their incompetence. Only Englishmen and Indian Muslims had the initiative to write on Islam and science. The Azharites knew so little about science, politics and the world that they could offer nothing but sullen rejection in defense of archaic tradition.[15]

As mirrored by *Manar* and *Muqtataf*, the Japanese success was, in Muslim and Middle Eastern minds, a source of both hope and despair: hope that modernization would be possible for them also to achieve; despair in that Muslims were still as far away as ever from achieving it. In the late 19th and early 20th centuries, *Muqtataf* had hoped that Muslim society could follow Japan's lead, since the example of an Asian country would be easier for Muslims to accept and learn from than the aggressive and hostile West that gave Middle Easterners so many psychological problems.[16] But *Muqtataf*'s hope was tempered by shame that the Japanese would now join westerners in looking contemptuously down on backward Middle Easterners.[17]

Japan's success gave *Muqtataf* and *Manar* a mirror to reflect their society's failures. The Japanese people's virtues of social unity and homogeneity, their honesty, leadership and respect for law, and their submission to the state and hard work mirrored the very opposite qualities in Middle East society, which, though blessed with exceptionally gifted individuals, was cursed with too many gods and no leaders, resulting in social disunity. The new national university founded in Cairo in 1908 generated another spark of hope that the country would follow the Japanese success in science and technology. But, this too on occasion became a mirror that revealed flaws causing despair. An American visiting professor of chemistry had during his stay in Egypt discovered the beneficial ingredients in the popular Egyptian drink, karkadeh. For countless centuries Egyptians had been drinking karkadeh, knowing it was healthful, but it took a visiting American chemistry teacher to find out why it was. Karkadeh even! Egypt was standing dumbly by as the caravan of science moved on. "How desperately our country needs a new spirit."[18] Like a double-barreled shotgun, *Muqtataf* and *Manar* blasted out their withering criticism. By 1916, the fragile flame of hope sparked by Japan had turned to ashen despair.[19]

Rida's articles in *Manar* reflect the deepening chasm between the secularist reformers who called for science and modern civilization and the so-called religious traditionalists who opposed science and any change that was tainted by western influence. But how powerful were the latter? Unlike the reformers and their literary supporters, the traditionalists have not left a body of literature sufficiently representing their views that would enable the historian to find from their ranks counterpoints to an Ali Mubarak, a Shaykh Jisr, Abduh or Rida. Could it be that these contrarian traditionalists, so often referred to in the reformist literature, were an imaginary resistance? Did the ulema's putative lethargy in transforming themselves from medieval religious scholars to modern educators serve as a scapegoat set up by the reformers themselves to explain their society's lack of success compared to Japan's, and at the same time excuse their own ineffectiveness as reformers? No doubt these traditionalists existed, but how influential were they? Was their opposition merely passive as they let the wave of westernizing reform wash over them while tending to their traditional duties among the nether levels of society that were hardly touched by the *Tanzimat* and ensuing reforms?

In the absence of strong government pushing for change and funding it, and the lack of a united voice among the rival factions that advocated reform, the sullen obstructionism of the traditionalists could look to be strong. The growing chasm that Tahtawi, Abduh and Rida saw in Egyptian society was the result of a new class advancing itself in the cause of reform, and an underclass continuing on normatively, surviving as people had survived traditionally, succored by an ulema that came from them and thought like them, and who were as resentful as they were of the godless new class of citified French-speaking effendis that fattened on change.

Traditionalists had started calling the secularists unbelievers, *kafir*. Because of their western dress, foreign languages and learning, the secularists looked to have left their religion and traditions to become *kafirs*. The word, according to Shaykh Rida, had gone from simply meaning a non-Muslim to becoming an insult that was laden with contempt and accusation of religious betrayal. Europeans were called *kafirs*. But with the western incursion and the reforms, any Muslim associated with anything western was also now a *kafir*. The traditionalists and the mass of society that was guided by them were becoming successful in equating science to heresy and atheism. Muslims were the heretics, Europeans the atheists. The strength of the traditionalists was not in books and periodicals, but in sermons shaping the attitudes of their followers and hurling pejorative words at their perceived adversaries, and hurling them often enough that they hit home to become the common idiom.

Reinforced by anti-western attitudes based on political grounds, the demeaning association of words was fast becoming a fixture in the Muslim psyche. Before science could find its proper place in society, its stigma of atheism had to be erased, and then a bridge built connecting it to religion. On the one side was a small class of westernized intellectuals and government-supported reformers, effendis, lawyers, physicians and teachers who followed the ways of government ministers and the foreigners who had occupied Egypt. On the other side was the mass of Muslims, mostly rural in outlook, who followed God and Prophetic Tradition and kept on wearing what their fathers and ancestors had worn, studying what they had studied and living the way they had lived. The two societies lived their own lives in their own space within an emotional spectrum that varied from muted disregard at a distance to contempt at close range. In blaming the traditionalists for Egypt's failure to match Japan in the Olympiad of modernization, Shaykh Rida might seem to have conjured a phantom target at which to vent his angry cry of frustration. Government and political leaders were more worthy targets of his poisoned arrows. Placing blame for the divide and the supine weakness it brought may have been a meaningless exercise; how to bridge it was not. Rida analyzed this more sensibly. Before a bridge could be built between the secular and traditional culture, Muslims had to learn that Europeans were believers in their own religion and that they did worship God. For them to learn this, a common system of education, with a unified set of principles, and an emphasis on science, had to be established. Free will and natural law would have to be made fundamentals in Muslim theology. In other words, Ash'arite theology had to be replaced by the Mu'tazilite version. (Shaykh Rida would modify his views in later years, after time had worn down the influence of Shaykh Abduh's calm tenacity in holding the reins of secularism and traditionalism to the center, and before Rida had gone Hanbali-*salafi* in disgust and depression at the fall of the Ottoman Empire and the occupation of the Arab lands by France and Britain, and the apathy of Muslim political leadership.)[20]

Muslims were caught in a tragic condition. Blessed with a religion that above all others encouraged science and action, as Rashid Rida described it, Muslims were saddled with an ignorant ulema and corrupt political leadership that passively watched the idol-worshipping Japanese and polytheistic Indians make great advances to the east of them, even while to the west of them, the Europeans, a people who have for the most part done away with their religion, continued rushing in upon the Muslims from every direction. Did Muslims know no shame? The world was forging ahead. To the west and east of Islamdom, private individuals contributed to educational institutes and gave prizes to students for excelling, while Arabs and Turks, thinking nothing of the common good, wasted their resources on parties and luxuries, letting foreigners profit from what Muslim leaders squandered away. The idea of "science and action" was beyond them. Social and political leadership among Muslims had been stricken by a self-inflicted sickness of perceived inferiority that paralyzed them from undertaking great projects on their own:

> As for the Muslims in general, they have been ruled so long by hated tyrants and oppressive governments, so beaten down by confiscations and arbitrary taxation, that their competitive spirit has been broken, their moral fiber in tatters. Seeing their country plundered and sucked dry by its leaders, the people

of education who should be role models and leaders in society seek refuge in the foreigner. By adopting foreign clothes, manners and lifestyles, they make it easier for foreigners to take over.

Muslims have been so badly governed and religiously misinformed for so long they are Muslims only in name. They have lost the spirit of "science and action" that once made their civilization great. Westerners and Japanese are more Muslim than Muslims.[21]

Rida's criticism was relentless. What Afghani and Abduh had dared express only to Europeans, or in private among their confidants, Rida proclaimed openly, angrily and frequently. "There can be no denial," he writes in 1900. "Muslims are in the most wretched condition. They have failed to join the march of progress in science and civilization." Not only have the idol-worshipping Japanese left the Muslims behind in the dust, but also the Jews of Europe, who have made a huge contribution by their assimilation of European civilization and science. In an allusion to the Dreyfus Affair, he describes the Jews as having risen to the top in science, technology and government, "to the extent that Europeans are now worried about Jewish influence and are oppressing them everywhere."[22] In 1902, he angrily accused the ulema and political leadership of making the Muslim *umma* fodder for the advancing nations. It was only a matter of time before Islam fell under western occupation. Local schools were teaching English more than Arabic. Soon English would be more important than the mother language. The social backbone was so weak that it had reached the state where European teachers who were employed in Egyptian schools were teaching Muslims about Islam. Muslim education was in shambles. Al-Azhar's studies had no relation to the condition of Islam or life in Egypt. Lethargy, passivity, confusion, neglect, incompetence, ignorance and rejection were making Muslims easy meat for the West.

> Grim is the future of Islam when the highest aspiration of a student is to find employment in the government where he can rest secure for life in mediocre physical comfort and mental tranquility. Sacrifice and personal effort to improve society is foreign to the Egyptian mind. Individual responsibility and creativity are extinct. How could Muslims be so apathetic when the Quran, the heart of their spiritual life, calls the faithful to the work of science and civilization? The ethics which the Quran calls for are no different than the ethics of today's modern society and civilization. The Quran also contains the principles of sovereign authority and government. The Islamic principles of government, political law, justice and war agree with what European nations have established. There are still some Islamic principles the Europeans have yet to discover, and if they do discover them, they will come to depend on them. The Quran has a remedy for every poison of civilization and social sickness.

By virtue of European scientific and technological endeavor,

> The hidden words of God have come to them (Europeans), since all of their science approximates what is said of it in the Quran. If Muslims were to ever

discover Islam and become truly Muslims, they would understand the verses of the Quran and accept science the way the Japanese have done and surpass both them and the Europeans; a deep understanding of the Quran would lead Muslims to the highest state of science and civilization.[23]

By emulating the virtue of Europeans and Japanese, Muslims would return to the essence of their religion: "The most worthy people with respect to strength of faith in God are the natural scientists who understand more about the universe than any others."[24]

No other of the reformist ulema had gone so far in advancing the cause of science. What in the 1820s had shocked Shaykh Tahtawi, that the French respected their scientists more than they did their priests, had become 70 years later an ideal to be hoped for. Science was a path to God, and true Muslims were true scientists. Even the Shari'a was not above being reformed in its light. Going way beyond his fellow Syrian from Tripoli and teacher, Shaykh Husayn al-Jisr, Shaykh Rida accepted that anything in the holy law that happened to be askew of God's natural laws would have to be rethought and changed accordingly.

This did not mean that anything in the Quran and the Prophetic Tradition as embodied in the Shari'a was in any way erroneous, but that the power of man's reason over his freedom of choice in interpreting the Quran and Hadith to determine the Shari'a had been flawed at the time that the Shari'a was being formulated. While invoking Abduh's appeal for a revival of *ijtihad* to reject *taqlid* and rethink the law, Rida bypassed the Mu'tazilites for other past authorities. The multitude of past authorities with their differing emphasis on the sources of holy law gave reinterpretation a broad field of possibilities. Writing in *al-Manar* in 1913, Rida based his argument for the legitimacy of rethinking the law on two medieval legists, Najm al-Din al-Tufi (d. 1316) and abu Ishaq al-Shatibi (d. 1388). Al-Tufi was a Hanabali scholar who studied with ibn Taymiyya and who liberally held that public interest (*maslaha*) had priority when a conflict arose between a law and what was considered best for the good of the community, even when the law was supported by holy text. Al-Shatibi was a Malikite legal scholar from Andalusia.

Following in the steps of Muhammad Abduh and several other shaykhs of the reformist ulema who equated natural law to the *sunna* that God established for the biological and physical operations of his creation, Rida made a tenuous foray into the work of theological reconstruction early in his career. It began with troubling questions Muslims were asking themselves after having learned of astronomical discoveries that had recently been made in the West. The heavens were home to myriads of galaxies and heavenly bodies scattered through the universe. What did this have to say about the possibility of intelligent life existing on other planets? Did these discoveries have any bearing on the message sent down by God through a prophet for all mankind for all-time? Rida explained that no matter how many galaxies and star systems existed, they were all bound together in one stable physical system under God's *sunna* of universal gravitation. As for the question of the Prophetic message coming for all the peoples that were possibly scattered throughout the wide universe, there was no indication in science or the authoritative texts of religion to answer this. God was Lord and Creator of all, and only

God knew "the number of soldiers in his army . . . so silence about things not known is safer." In other words, accept science and don't think about unanswerable questions in regard to religion, for there can be no contradiction between the two, and in God all is resolved – a modern analogue of Ash'ari's *bi-la kayf* – "don't ask how, only God knows."[25]

Rida attempted to loosen Sunni theology from its medieval mooring in Ash'ari's denial of a Mu'tazilite doctrine so to permit a less forced modernist interpretation of religious belief and the law that framed it. Accordingly, he posited that all things in God's creation were distinguished by an outer and an intrinsic nature, respectively called *tabi'a* and *fitra*. While the former collectively governed the outward appearance of nature, the latter signified the essence in a thing's creation that subjected it directly to the divine *fitra*, or mind. This preserved the appearance of an autonomously governed system of physical nature within a theological system of divine absolutism wherein all reality was totally and directly dependent on God as the one and only cause in the universe. Rida defensively explained that if Muslims saw this as a departure from established belief, it was because the ideas and terms of earlier religious authorities were understood only vaguely by Muslims who appeared on the scene at a much later time. The many intervening generations had darkened the glass of perception. To clear the glass, terms had to be reviewed and precisely redefined. Earlier philosophers in Islam

> related things to nature, believing nature to be self-creative and autonomously moved by its own causality. Accordingly, Muslims called such people unbelievers and materialists because they denied what was beyond matter and did not believe in God or the next world. In India, these Muslims were called *Nayshari* [*Natcheriyya*]. In general, Arabs only understood the atheistic materialist meaning of the word nature. But the fixed laws of the universe are God's Shari'a written through nature. Such things had to be clarified so people would not attack what they did not understand.[26]

Rida's expectations that the Egyptian and Ottoman ulema would anytime in the near future come to understand the value and necessity of science and join him in making the proper theological emendations were not high. A measure of his despair of the Arab and Ottoman condition was his hope that the Muslims of India, which like Egypt was under British occupation, might follow the Japanese example.[27] The work of Ahmad Khan and his associates in *Natcheriyya* convinced him that Indian Muslims were of a higher intellectual and religious spirit than Arabs and Turks, and of all the people of Islam, the Indian Muslims had the best chance of building a Muslim state that could compete in modern civilization. Upon Ahmad Khan's death in 1899, Rashid Rida praised the Sayyid for his good works as a leader of the Muslim awakening in India. *Natcheriyya*, according to Rida, was a perfectly sound philosophy of God working through nature and was perfectly in harmony with Islamic belief. Sayyid Ahmad Khan embodied the ideal of science and action that Arabs and Turks should follow.[28] If Arabs and Turks could not learn from Europeans and Japanese, then maybe they could learn from their fellow Muslims in India, and with this in view, Rida proposed that Egyptian Muslims begin the learning process by emulating the Indians who were at the time collecting donations to build a new Muslim college.

In later years, Shaykh Rida and his *al-Manar* shifted from Abduh's neo-Mu'tazilite theology of reason and allegorical interpretation to the more conservative posture of neo-Hanbali reliance on the tradition of Muhammad and the earliest Muslims, the *salafi*, a shift reminiscent of Tahtawi's traditionalist metamorphosis in reverting from Copernicus back to Ptolemy a half century earlier. Rida's shift may be accounted for by the strength and independence of the conservative reformist Wahhabis in Arabia compared to the weakness and corruption of the puppet Arab governments set up by the British and French in the divided and mandated Arab homeland. Especially reviled were the Hashimites, whom Rida accused of betraying sultan, caliph and Islam by their siding with the British in World War I against their fellow Arab and Turkish Muslims. The Hashimites betrayed the Islamic *umma* for a desert emirate called Trans Jordan, and a kingdom in Iraq, where they sat powerlessly contented in the sun of British protection. Rashid Rida's contempt and disgust of corrupt, grasping, petty-minded Arab political leadership made the vigorous Wahhabi-Hanbali movement of reform in Arabia, and the Muslim reforms in India, look like the only hope for an Islamic salvation.

With the exception of the Arabian brethren of Muhammad abd al-Wahhab, conservative Islam, though otherwise unorganized and disparate in focus, provided a fortress of resistance to, and refuge from, corrupt, weak and subservient rulers in the early decades of the 20th century, just as political Islam today provides a refuge and defense for the poor, uneducated masses at the bottom and the educated, but unconnected, disillusioned and dissatisfied at the top.

Notes

1 Iraqi Jews writing in Arabic were important contributors to the Iraqi literary scene. For this: Shmuel Moreh, *Arabic Works by Jewish Writers, 1863–1973*, Magnes Press, Jerusalem, 1973; Reuven Snir, "My Heart Beats With Love of the Arabs: Iraqi Jews Writing in Arabic in the 20th Century," *Journal of Modern Jewish Studies*, vol I, issue 2 (November 2002), pp. 182–203.
2 Farah Antun, *ibn Rushd wa Falsafatuhu*, Alexandria and Cairo, 1903, p. 132ff. Antun's whole treatise was published in his journal *al-Jami'a*, Alexandria, 1903.
3 Antun, *ibn Rushd*, pp. 122–126; A. Hourani, *Arabic Thought in the Liberal Age*, Cambridge University Press, Cambridge, p. 254.
4 Antun, *ibn Rushd*, p. 174.
5 Antun, *ibn Rushd*, p. 124.
6 Antun, *ibn Rushd*, p. 209, citing Abduh's "Wafaq al-Inkliz 'ala al-Islamiyya" (Agreement of the English With Islam) in *'Imara, al-A'mal al-Kamila*.
7 *Mashriq*, 1900, issue 9, pp. 303–309.
8 *Muqtataf*, vol 34 (March 1909), p. 284 ff.
9 *Mashriq*, vol 17 (1914), p. 694 ff.
10 *Muqtataf* (April 1916), p. 393.
11 Hasan, Ali's oldest son, had surrendered all claim to the caliphate to Mu'awiyya in return for a life of voluptuary pleasure. He became so infamous for divorcing his many

wives that he was called *al-Tallaq*: the Great Divorcer, though in all fairness his wives numbered little more than a hundred, and he lived long.

12 *Manar* (September 1906), p. 636.
13 *Manar*, vol I (1897), p. 43.
14 *Manar*, vol I (1897), pp. 56–57.
15 *Manar*, vol I, pp. 369–371, 591.
16 *Muqtataf*, vol 32 (July 1907), pp. 577–580.
17 *Muqtataf*, vol 32 (August 1907), pp. 609–616.
18 *Muqtataf*, vol 38 (May 1911), pp. 488–489.
19 *Muqtataf*, vol 49 (July 1916), p. 32; and later, *Muqtataf*, vol 52 (1927), p. 177.
20 Charles Saint-Prot, *L'avenir de la tradition entre revolution et occidentalisation*, Rocher Press, Paris, 2008, pp. 405–408.
21 *Manar*, vol I, pp. 634–636.
22 *Manar*, vol I, p. 810.
23 *Manar*, vol V (1902), pp. 682–693.
24 *Manar*, vol XIII (January 1911), p. 914.
25 *Manar*, vol VI, "Astronomy and the Quran" (1903), pp. 379–380.
26 *Manar*, vol I (1897), pp. 15–16.
27 *Manar*, vol V (March 1904), p. 928.
28 *Manar*, vol I (1897), p. 587.

Part II
Science, society and government in the modern Muslim world

12 Overview of the 20th century

A dozen and more leading writers, mostly Egyptians, shaped the Arab discourse of science, civilization and religion during the first half of the 20th century. Among the Muslim writers it was of course the influence of Muhammad Abduh that prevailed, though his reformist ideas would be carried in ever diverging directions by the two interpretive tendencies taken by his followers: the religious one of Rashid Rida, Tantawi Jawhar, Muhammad Farid Wajdi, Ali abd al-Raziq and Amin Khuli; and the secularist one of Qasim Amin, Ismail Mazhar, Ahmad Lutfi, Taha Husayn, Abbas Aqqad and Muhammad Kurd Ali. The secularist wing was joined by Christian writers and academics, Louis Awad being one of the most renowned. A substantial divergence of thought distinguished individual writers within these two general categories, enough diversity in fact among the secularists to warrant a sub-category, composed of those more radically minded thinkers who followed Shibli Shumayyil in rejecting nationalism and religion for socialism and materialism. This was a miniscule group led by Salama Musa, a Copt, and Ismail Mazhar, a Muslim, both of them Egyptians calling for a humanist socialism. Taha Husayn, another disciple of Abduh and the Arab world's leading essayist, literary critic and educator between 1925 and 1950, was a westernized humanist who could in many ways be considered to inhabit the same intellectual space as Salama Musa and Ismail Mazhar in regard to science, civilization, and the West, but minus the materialist philosophy and socialism. The same could be said for the literary critic and academic Louis Awad, who in cultural philosophy and choice of career followed in Taha Husayn's footsteps.

The dialogue embracing these large subjects – religion, science, socialism, materialism, reform, rejection or acceptance of the West – had in the last decades of the 19th century and up to the end of World War I been carried on in Cairo and Beirut by writers across the intellectual spectrum, from the radical margin set by Shibli Shumayyil, Bishara Zilzal, Mustapha Mansuri and Qasim Amin, to the moderate center set by Louis Chiekho, Husayn al-Jisr, Muhammad Abduh and Rashid Rida, with their counterparts in Istanbul writing in Turkish on the same problems, all of them in search of a meaningful future for their society, their religion and their civilization in face of an expanding West that was rapidly engulfing them.

By the 1920s and 1930s a century of reformist thinkers had come and gone. The body of thought that had come from that century's interaction with the West was sharpened and intensified by a less amicable interaction, namely the deforming crunch of historical events following the Great War. The collapse of the Ottoman Empire, followed by Anglo–French occupation and colonial rule of the Arab lands that the two victors divided as they wanted between them, and the British-backed success of Zionism in colonizing Palestine, made for a bitter history. Secularist and religious feelings hardened against the West. The fund of Arab goodwill toward the West that had risen in the 19th century, and the hope for friendly cooperation in developing the region, dried up. Anti-western sentiment was poisoned all the more by the impassioned mythology of nationalism that arose after the Great War. The religious front saw the West with its science and secular institutions to be a threat more menacing than ever, while the secular front saw the West, in spite of its grasping and threatening inimicability, an inescapable power whose institutions and knowledge had to be learned, modified and adopted, or else.

The Ottoman Empire was replaced by a nationalist republic allied with the West. Its founder, Mustafa Kemal, then did away with the sultanate and caliphate, leaving those who feared the West and believed in Islamic government feeling abandoned, disoriented and defenseless. The more radical reformers were happy enough to see the old swept away. For Salama Musa and Ismail Mazhar (and of course Shibli Shumayyil had he still been alive), Mustafa Kemal's fervently secularized Turkish Republic was a triumph of liberation and independence, a model that all Muslim countries should follow.

The historical setting in which the dialogue over reform and the West first emerged in the Tulip Period was drastically altered in the intervening two centuries, and with it the tone and temper of discourse. What had been a distant, almost unthinkable possibility for a generation in the early 18th century – the loss of Ottoman-ruled Muslim territory – had become a disastrous reality for another generation in the early 20th century. The loss of Hungary had metastasized to the loss of empire. British and French mandates were set up in the very heart of Islamdom. The loss of Palestine was in progress. The heady call of nationalism to unite the Arabs in their struggle against the French and British occupiers drowned out the call from the minaret. Pan-Islamism faded away with the passing of al-Afghani and the Ottomans. Nationalist and secularist movements of change that had arisen in the name of liberal parliamentarianism, socialism, communism and fascism to drive out the occupiers and their puppet governments appeared to have overwhelmed religion as a force of change.

Though always weak, few in numbers and under government surveillance, the secularist movements of many hues pushed the ulema to a more desperate defensive posture. Between the anvil of secular nationalism and the hammer of western occupation, the ulema perceived their enemy to be a devil's brew of heretical reformers in league with atheist western occupiers pulling the strings of puppet tyrants: a grand conspiracy against Islam, whether the participants in the conspiracy recognized it as one or not. These were the same accusations made against the Tulip Period reformers in the early 18th century. The ulema were above all consistent in detecting their devils – those serpents in disguise who would have man pluck clean the tree of knowledge.

In a religiously oriented society crippled by poverty and illiteracy, and torn by secularist nationalism, this did not bode well for the cause of science, whose leading devil was now Charles Darwin. As aggressive as some of the ulema were in opposing Darwin as the distillation of all that was wicked with the West, and opposing the fallen Muslims bewitched by him, the equally aggressive defense of Darwin, whom his Arab champions had cloaked in materialist socialism, ensured that the writings of Shumayyil, Musa and Mazhar would not be best sellers, or even found in the bookstalls of Cairo and other Arab capitals. The mere mention of their names and Darwin's ignited the devil's sulfur.

Academic study, literature and intellectual critique were in the Arab world centered in Cairo. The literary output of a host of westernized Egyptian writers would dominate the intellectual scene of the Arab world until the 1960s, when the effects of a censorious military dictatorship with its secret police, economic stagnation and successive defeats at the hands of Israel and the West undermined every reforming movement that had meant anything – westernization, secularism, nationalism, socialism, everything except religion, or what was presented as religion. The Arab–Israeli war of 1967 laid bare the pretensions, incompetence and wastage of military government that had seized power in 1952. Not too long after the defeat, political Islam would emerge from the shadows, where it had been relegated for more than half a century.

During that period, the dark cloud over Islam's and the Arab nation's future drove some religious writers, and secular ones too, into a defensive mode of mind that called for rejection of the West. For some intellectuals, rejection was coupled with denial: denial of the validity of everything western, even its science. Heretofore considered an unquestionable pillar of power, even by devout shaykhs implacably hostile to the West, science was first diminished by its being subsumed into the Quran. Through "scientific commentary" the Quran was interpreted to have prediscovered all science. The rejectionist fantasy progressed later in the century to a literary movement espousing a supposedly authentic science for Muslims: a moral and ethical science of nature that was to be extracted from the Quran and Hadith. It was a rejection of despair veiled in a deeply wounded pride of a glorious past, a despair in which the spiritual search for truth in scripture transcended scientific research into the workings of the material world.

This blind alley of delegitimizing science was another obstacle confronting those reformers who continued the long effort of generating an indigenous scientific culture. The effort had been going on for well more than a century in Egypt. In the 19th century, reformers had hopes of catching up to the West. Before the end of the century those hopes were dimming. It was becoming apparent that western science was progressing at an accelerating rate. Muslims realized they were falling further behind.

Their long and hard experience of struggle against the West was seen to be a losing match. Recognition of having missed the train was expressed in the journal literature. *Muqtataf* registered an early note of despair in reporting on a glittering Japanese success at an international exhibition of modern industry, arts and crafts held in Paris, in 1888:

> The Japanese who are not forerunners in the field of civilization amazed the world with the precision and excellence of their work, excelling over the Europeans themselves in their engravings, sculpture, photography, silk weaving,

dyeing and artistic design. Japanese products were the most prized and everything they had at the exhibit was sold. The young Japanese men managing the exhibit spoke French and English and were so refined and polite that they could have been taken for young intelligent Parisian gentlemen, were it not for their features. On the other hand, the exhibits of our dear country [Egypt/Syria] offered nothing but drummers, singers, sword dancers and vendors, all of which made people at the exhibit laugh and scoff in ridicule at our backwardness. The only things worth buying were some Syrian and Egyptian textiles and woodwork.[1]

The plaintive pessimism concerning the chances of Egypt, the Arabs, the Ottomans and the world of Islam to close the gap became a familiar refrain in *Muqtataf* from the mid-1880s, to be joined a decade later by Rashid Rida's scathing pessimism in *al-Manar*. The Japanese victory over Russia in 1904 gave the editors of *Muqtataf* another occasion to lament the Middle Eastern failure to advance in science and technology. The Japanese, Sarruf feared, would now join the Europeans in looking down on the peoples of the area. It was a cultural shame. The Middle East was destined to sit alone on the sidelines, passively observing the other societies of the world compete in creativity as civilization marched on. Middle Easterners seemed not to mind their status as perpetual observers. They were more interested in the past than the present. Sarruf, who certainly was not alone in his vexation, vented his disgust with the culture's passive, backward-looking tendency in the responses he wrote in answer to letters that *Muqtataf's* editors received from its readers who boasted of the Arabs having discovered the truths of nature centuries before the Europeans rediscovered them. In the autumn of 1908 a letter arrived from a Muslim, Ali Sayyid Yusuf, dismissing the significance of western science in general and Darwin in particular by extolling earlier Muslim scientists and their discoveries, and claiming ibn Miskawayh had discovered evolution in the 9th century. Rather than ignoring the letter as a product of benighted chauvinism, Sarruf answered it at length. His reply revealed his frustration:

> Did ibn Miskawayh devote himself to years of research examining fossils and living species in the far, uncharted corners of the globe? Did he produce books of analytical scholarship based on mountains of observations, data and facts and years of unremitting reflection? Did he compose a general theory of evolution explaining and unifying the data? No! Darwin did more than spin out an idea in a few pages of mental abstraction from a world of possibilities. He acted, he worked, he devoted his life to this one field of research and the complex of ideas that brought this ocean of research together. Did Miskawayh argue it was nature, not God that provided the force driving evolution? Darwin was not satisfied with words. He spent many years researching, checking, observing, thinking . . . His book is equivalent to 10 issues of *Muqtataf* in size . . . The Ancients said as much as Miskawayh about the evolution of plants and animals, but all these scraps are to Darwin's work what a tiny village rowboat is to an ocean liner of 40,000 horsepower carrying

10,000 passengers, or a donkey cart to a train, or a peasant mud village to cities like Cairo, Paris, London. If glorifying Arab thinkers of the golden age is the object, Darwin is not the field for it.[2]

Sarruf's gloom reappeared a decade later, when toward the end of World War I he published an article in which he surveyed the condition of the Muslim world:

> The Arabs and Ottomans are going down the same way Central Asia fell under the Russians, with Iran now following. While the West and Japan take control of the world, Arabs and Ottomans sit around glumly watching, content to discuss their past glories. After a century of reform there are still no scientific laboratories, no equipment, no research, no scientists, and no support publicly or privately to create them.[3]

A decade after that, the famous Sorbonne-educated humanist and literary critic Taha Husayn wrote in similar terms. He deplores the irresponsibility of government, of rich Muslims who do not contribute to education and science but squander their treasure on amusement, luxury and meaningless trifles, thereby contributing to the widening internal social gap between literate and illiterate, and externally to the civilizational gap between Islam and the West. "In the West almost everyone is educated, or at least literate, while Egypt has no learning. She is a parasite on Europe and America for science, borrowing everything from them."[4] Two decades later, in the late 1940s, Salama Musa is decrying the pitiful state of education in Egypt that paralyzes the country. The West, in spite of having endured a second devastating war, is leaving Egypt and the Arabs ever more to the rear. Not until the mid-1920s did a girl receive a high school diploma in Egypt. Salama's critique of political lethargy and corruption was vitriolic and constant. The government expressed its recognition of the distinguished writer, then in his 60s, by accusing him of firebombing a cinema. His imprisonment deepened all the more the despair and cynicism of the intellectuals calling for reform and intensive investment in science.

Government inactivity in such dire times drove reformist cynicism to even darker depths. In education, the concomitant existence of half-heartedly enforced government innovations that lived alongside medieval traditions that refused to die produced a monstrous psychoschizmatic nightmare. Two parallel and contradictory systems of primary and secondary education, one secular and westernized, the other religious and traditional, each with its own values and methods of learning, produced a two-headed epistemological contradiction leading to cynicism and unbelief in those who, after years of traditional religious education in the mosque and madrasa, went from one system to the other. Many Muslims, hopelessly subjugated by the science and technology held over them like a sword by the West, and despairing of government to address political and economic stagnation and social sterility, anesthetized themselves with great drafts of religious extremism, or if too intellectual for that, escaped into the cold depths of detached cynicism. For the former, what could be more gratifying than surrendering to the belief that God would lead Muslims to triumph over the power, materialism and arrogance of the West and its Arab surrogates propped up as leaders? Some could not contain the fury of the divine calling that burned within them. Political assassination in the name of God was about to become vogue in the jihad of Islamist activism following World War II. Conjoined with the cynicism that soured the intellectual atmosphere, taking up the sword of God made for some feverish ideas. The jihad of Scientific Interpretation and Islamic Science became the writer's equivalent of divine terror and assassination.

In its salad days following World War I, secular nationalism would claim for the Arab genius those same discoveries and inventions that had been appropriated by the scientific interpreters mining the Quran and Hadith. To boost the Arab spirit in its quest for an independent constitutional republic modeled on the democratic West, the Syrian nationalist writer Muhammad Kurd Ali appropriated the printing press and airplane as Arab inventions. An Andalusian Arab had made a set of wings and taken off from a cliff, marking the first flight.[5] The Arab nationalist spirit, not the Islamic, was extolled. Rather than diminishing western science, it was simply appropriated by claim of prior discovery through imaginative reference to classical texts. Not all writers gave in to this seduction of lost pride, just as not all Muslims pandered to the Islamization of science or joined militant Islam.

Secular nationalism had no problem implicitly supporting science over religion: both were taken to be expressions of the greatness of Arab genius. The Egyptians Taha Husayn and Abbas Aqqad, the Lebanese Amin al-Rihani and the Syrian Muhammad Kurd Ali, to name but a few of the secular Arab nationalists who formed the third generation of literary reformers who studied or traveled in the West, understood, as had the Young Ottomans before them, that science was more than its mathematics and the technology spun from it. Science and the basic research that gave life to science were vital in a way that went beyond the material comfort and military power extracted from the practical application of science. Science was a way of thinking and viewing the world and life. Science was a product of intellectual freedom, its work of discovery a source of joy akin to discovering God. This was the Arab voice of 20th century nationalism echoing Sarruf, Nimr, Shumayyil, Zaydan and the Young Ottomans of two generations earlier. The liberal litterateurs between the World Wars were promoting science and democracy for the greater glory not of Islam but of the Arab nation. The same was being proclaimed for the nation of Turks in the new republic, but in vernacular Turkish written in the new script of Latin letters, Mustafa Kemal's ultimate secularist rejection of all religious authority and past tradition being his replacing of Arabic script.

Writers during the relatively liberal period between the World Wars, when nationalism, constitutionalism, westernization and party politics appeared to be defining the future of state and society in Turkey, Iran, Egypt and the defunct Ottoman Empire's former Arab provinces, were telling the expanding number of graduates of the newly founded national universities more or less the same thing *Muqtataf* had been saying since the day it was founded. In the modernized literary Arabic developed between roughly 1840 and 1940, from Tahtawi to

Taha Husayn, young Middle Easterners, beardless men in western suits, starched collars and cravats, were being told by their favorite writers, themselves graduates of European universities or newly founded national universities in Cairo, Damascus and Baghdad, that scientific research was fundamental to the advance of life and civilization.

Their variations on this century-old theme were spruced up with an air brushing of brash slogans and baseless pronouncements in the name of nationalism, social progress and Arab unity that boasted a bright new day dawning. The new day's promises were blared over the radio. A generation or two later it would be television, when the great leader's face could not be escaped. Audiences got to see their leaders ad nauseum. Their benevolent Pharaonic faces were everywhere to be seen: wall posters, bill boards, every other page of every newspaper. Big Brother had arrived. Salvation was at hand. Journals, newspapers and books fulsomely praised the pioneering works of the people's great rulers, whose inspiring visages, smiling with the morning blush of that new day, were wherever one looked. But the flimsily staged political theater hardly hid from public view the disarray and division, the lack of leadership, the illiteracy and poverty, and the festering social problems and intellectual cynicism that darkened the atmosphere of real life.

Up until the early 1960s, the nationalist public very much wanted to believe in the promise of that bright new day, gloriously emblemized by Gamal abd al-Nasser. Many may have actually believed it was dawning. No one dared or wanted to say it wasn't. The heady rush of nationalist fervor had muted the religious voice. The tradition of religious study and the madrasa continued, but not at the center. It survived at the edge, under the growing shadow of the army of secular lawyers, writers, bankers, businessmen, film stars, singers, professors, schoolteachers, students and servants of the blossoming tourist industry with its new hotels, restaurants, boutiques and night clubs. The inhabitants of this new world wore western dress and spoke French, English, German and Italian. The brightest young men saw their future in medicine and engineering, or in academics and journalism, or in the new court system with its laws and procedures modeled on European institutions. They shared public space with the robes and turbans of the traditional sector of society, whose lives the ulema informed and whose galabiyyas filled the streets and coffee houses. The tarbush (or fez), that once-fashionable mark of modernity of the professional and government official, the effendi, had given way to the brimmed hat seen in western films and photographs of Ataturk.

The suits and robes crowded together in public but were worlds apart in thought and life style. By the mid-20th century it seemed that it would be only a few generations before the divide would be settled in favor of the western suit, with the robed ulema accommodated at the edge, seen but not heard, existing in benign neglect. Ramadan, Friday prayer and the holy feasts would of course have their place, just as Christmas and Easter had their place in the West. The shaykhs would continue to write their books for the devout followers of tradition, whose numbers would shrink through education in the school system of the secular state. Kemalist Turkey and Pahlevi Iran previewed the Arab future. Careers in religion were for the benighted.

In the Arab region, each of those two worlds voiced its own understanding of science. The secular nationalist intelligentsia complained that the state wasn't investing enough into it, while the shaykhs, struggling for relevancy, composed scientific commentaries to show that the holy sources not only contained science but completed it by giving it a moral and spiritual context, making it a higher authority than science. Over and above the sound and fury of words, slogans and boastful claims, little was done in the way of laying a basis to appropriate science by action: to effect ownership by marrying into the international family of scientists through the creative act of science. The act of doing science, even preparing the institutional infrastructure that was needed to open the way to do it, was dismally lacking in all Muslim countries midway through the 20th century, and seriously lacking during the second half. Egypt's one Nobel Prize scientist, coming at the end of the century, had to go to Philadelphia to do the graduate training and research in chemistry that it took for him to win it. The story of Pakistan's Nobel physicist is no different.

Though politically independent after World War II, the Arab states were weak and ruled by inexperienced leaders. They lacked any credible military defense, and were consequently poorly prepared for the challenge that faced them in the bitter and self-defeating politics of inter-Arab rivalry, poisoned all the more by the superpower rivalry of the Cold War that divisively imposed itself on an already politically fractured Middle East. In 1948, the promise of Balfour had been fulfilled and Israel was born, reducing Palestine to a state of mind – and a political minefield that blew away many Arab promises, slogans, armies, governments and much of what credibility was left among Muslims and Arabs who believed the West was the way to cultural renewal. The loss of Palestine was followed by a series of military coups d'etat and revolutions taking over civil government, first in Syria, where one coup after another followed in a quick succession, then in Egypt in 1952 ending the Muhammad Ali Dynasty. The Hashemite Kingdom, set up in Iraq by Britain in 1922 in an act of theatrical absurdity that could only make sense in the most extreme form of 19th century imperialism, lasted all of 36 years. The period was punctuated by a series of military coups and revolts before the monarchy met an end as bloodily horrific as its beginning was comically absurd.

The inter-Arab political scene between 1948 and 1967 was a snake pit of autocratic and ruthless military governments, each blaming the other for the loss of Palestine and trumpeting its own brand of party nationalism while plotting to undermine its Arab rivals. Domestic policy of these military governments included confiscation, nationalization and sequestration of the property of its wealthy citizens in the name of Arab nationalist socialism and all its empty slogans. In Egypt, leader of the Arab world, the inefficiency and incompetency of military government, in spite of its early high minded intentions and efforts to alleviate the poverty and misdistribution of wealth, wasted the infrastructure that had been built up since the time of Muhammad Ali and Khedive Ismail. Opening the universities free of charge to all students able to pass the entrance exam, without meeting the challenge by commensurately expanding the faculties and facilities to teach the incoming waves, diminished the quality that had been achieved. New universities and research institutions were opened, but so pitifully underfunded they belied the name. Advances made in land distribution, electrification, irrigation and health were offset by mismanagement, military expenditures, overpopulation and the growth of a parasitic military feudalism, where untrained and inexperienced military officers became a self-serving new elite class of supposedly industrial, commercial and agricultural managers. Burdened with increasing foreign debt because of the military and its ambitious but misdirected programs, Egypt once again found itself teetering on the brink of bankruptcy. Pulling the country over the brink was a bankrupt foreign policy that sucked Egypt into the quagmire of a civil war in Yemen that battered Egypt's military and further drained its resources. When the 1967 war broke out, the heart of Egypt's army was bogged down in the mountains of Yemen. It most likely would not have made much of a difference in that war where the army was. The Israeli victory was so complete and the Arab military so incompetent, it is hard to imagine that another Arab army or two would have made any difference.

Notes

1 *Muqtataf*, vol VIII (1888), pp. 760–761.
2 *Muqtataf* (October 1908), pp. 878–880.
3 *Muqtataf*, vol 50 (March 1917).
4 Nazik Yared, *Arab Travelers and Western Civilization*, Saqi Books, London, 1996, p. 56, citing Taha Husayn's *Min Ba'id* (*From Afar*).
5 M. Kurd Ali, *Ghara'ib al-Gharb* (Strange Things of The West), Maktabat al-ahaliyya, Cairo, 1923, vol II, pp. 141–144; 164–165; 199. Yared, Arab Travelers, p. 59 ff.

13 Darwin at the center of debate

Isfahani

While Shaykh Rashid Rida in Cairo was accommodating Islam to "Intelligent Design" Darwinism in his *al-Manar*, a Shi'i scholar in Karbala on the other side of the Arab world composed a serious study in two volumes on the subject. Published in Baghdad in 1912, Abu Majd al-Isfahani's *A Criticism of Darwin's Philosophy* (*Naqd Falsafat Darwin*) was the first significant piece of literature on modern science to come out of Iraq and the first extensive critical analysis of Darwin's natural selection to appear in Arabic. A book on science and Islam by an Iraqi physician, Hibbat Allah, was published in Baghdad in the mid-1880s, as noted in *Muqtataf*, and though it is nowhere now to be found, the notice is indicative of Iraq's entry into the Arab world of ideas in modern times. Isfahani's work comes as a striking confirmation of it.

Abu Majd al-Isfahani (1870–1935) was a respected shaykh from a scholarly religious family whose origins went back to the Iranian city of his name. The scope and depth of analysis of his work is impressive, considering he had little if any scientific or medical training and only fragmentary source material to work from. None of Darwin's writings existed in Arabic or Turkish before World War I, and articles or commentaries on evolution in European languages, even if Isfahani had been able to read them, would have been fairly rare in Karbala and Baghdad. He writes that he was obliged to work from articles in Arabic journals and some few chapters in no more than a total of 10 books. Among his meager sources would no doubt have been some bits on evolution he found in *Muqtataf* and *Manar*, and perhaps even Bishara Zilzal's book and Shumayyil's paraphrase of Buchner's commentary, in addition to his *al-Haqiqa* follow-up to that. Whatever Isfahani's sources, they had to be a paltry collection of diverse bits and pieces randomly come his way. Upon this fragile, desultory foundation he bravely set out to clear the air of that flurry of false attributions, misconceptions, condemnations and extraneous ideas that claimed to be Darwin's theory.[1]

Isfahani was quite aware that much of what was being attributed to Darwin was not Darwin. Establishing what was authentic Darwin was only the first task; the second was to critique it. As he was a religious scholar, it was of course Islamic belief and scripture that provided his critical framework. Repeating Shaykhs Jisr and Rida, Imam Isfahani finds nothing in the Quran or Prophetic Tradition to be contrary to the evolution of animal species as exposited by Darwin. The creation of man, however, is a special case that Isfahani puts beyond the reach of natural selection. But even this, he believes, could be worked into agreement with the Quranic account, if the hypothesis were one day shown to be true. He admits that possibility later in his work after having initially rejected it, a sign his mind remained critically at work as he wrote this long book.

A Shi'ite counterpart of Shaykhs Jisr, Abduh and Rida, Abu Majd al-Isfahani was one of that small group of religious scholars who knew it was as vital for Muslims to cultivate science for its own sake as it was to guard religion from those who would either deliberately or unwittingly pervert one or the other to the detriment of both. He openly favored western science, regretted the dire lack of Arabic translations of modern scientific works, such as Darwin's, and deplored the miniscule number of Arabs studying science, since ignorance of science meant ignorance of the world and eventual political extinction. The year was 1912. Little did Isfahani know how near that day of political extinction in its Ottoman form he was.

Isfahani reiterates the plea that had been made over and over since Tahtawi's early days almost a century before, that the shaykhs should be at the vanguard of science study to avoid the marginalization of Islam and the fate that religion suffered in the West. Islam could avoid this only if students received a thorough grounding in religion and science.

As a Shi'i, Isfahani believes in the legitimacy of independent reasoning in interpreting the holy texts to establish an Islamic law and set of beliefs that could accommodate the science, ideas and ways of the modern world. Accommodation could be made only through the process of rational thought, and since *ijtihad* remained a religious practice in Shi'i Islam through the institution of the *mujtahids*, the gate of interpretation opened religion to modern knowledge. According to Isfahani, the individual enjoying freedom of thought who errs in judgment is better than the imitator who errs not but whose thought is either non-existent or sterile.[2] He credits the world as being all the richer for the works of religious men like Lamarck, Darwin, Wallace and Spencer. That their theories were wrong in part or were incomplete did not diminish their contribution or piety. Isfahani also includes Thomas Huxley as a believer, generously explaining away his self-professed agnosticism as just Huxley's odd manner of accepting God's mysterious ways of guiding creation through the laws of evolution. Following the path of science could not lead one astray from religion. Every new discovery uncovers a speck of God's creation. "Intelligent Design" proves reason and science as valid paths of understanding the Creator.

Isfahani's book recapitulates the historical development of evolution theory in some detail, from Buffon, Lamarck, Cuvier, Linné and Agasiz to Owen, Darwin, Wallace, Huxley and the philosophical spin-offs of Spencer and the German materialists. At the time of its publication and for decades later, nothing in Arabic or any Muslim language approached his critique in comprehensive analysis and argumentation of religious legitimation. It remains one of the most fully and cogently worked out reconciliations between evolution and religious belief in 20th century Arabic literature. That the work was rarely reviewed or referred to by the dozens of Arab reformist thinkers involved in the debate over Darwin since 1912 is remarkable but understandable. The few copies that were printed had a narrow circulation in the Arab world. The author being a Shi'i undoubtedly limited its readership in the Sunni community. It was precisely to avoid this sectarian diminishment that the Iranian Jamal al-Din of Asadabad passed himself off as a Sunni from Afghanistan.

Dar al-Kutub, the Egyptian National Library, possesses a copy of Isfahani's work, both volumes in mint condition with not a single notation of conservative protest or scribbled outrage in the margins or across any offending passage. (The decades of dust that came with the two volumes when brought from the shelves rivaled even the century-long layer that had collected upon the volumes of *Rawdat al-Madaris*.) No indication was evident that either of the two volumes had ever been checked out or even opened. Yet a Jordanian professor of Arab intellectual history writes that Isfahani's work "is without doubt a milestone in the dissemination of western scientific ideas among the Arab and Muslim readers in the East."[3] It is that indeed, but the milestone would have been all the more significant had the volumes been read and taken as a point of departure rather than left to collect dust. The book's being written and published at the Irano–Arab fringe of the Muslim world may have been a factor in its undeserved lack of attention in the Syro–Egyptian circle of thinkers writing on the subject, since people like Shumayyil, Zaydan, Antun, Salama Musa, Ismail Mazhar, Hasan Husayn and all the other secularists who followed them in the next generation would have welcomed Imam Isfahani, Shi'i or not, as a voice against their religious detractors. As far as concerned the crosscurrents of disputation over Darwin and Islam across the Arab and Muslim world, Isfahani's work passed practically unnoticed.

Of the sources Isfahani vaguely refers to regarding his knowledge of evolution and Darwin – articles in newspapers, journals, selected chapters of ten books, all of them in Arabic – he mentioned only one by name, *al-Irfan*, an ephemeral journal edited by a Shi'i from Tripoli. The most obvious Arabic journal that could have served Isfahani as a source for evolution theory, *Muqtataf*, went unmentioned, as did the *Risala* of Shaykh Jisr, who happened to be from the same Tripoli as the editor of *al-Irfan*. Even Shibli Shumayyil went unmentioned, though it is clear by implication that Isfahani had read, or knew of, Shibli's Buchner book, since he attacks both translator and translation as carriers of the European materialistic heresy into Arabic. To the religious scholar's credit, he had learned enough from his meager and desultory sources to distinguish between what was Darwin and what was Buchner. Aside from some questionable points of detail involving a few apparent contradictions and unproven elements in the science of evolution, Isfahani sees nothing in Darwin's theory as it relates to life forms governed by an instinct to survive that is in principle opposed to religious belief.

However, applying the theory of life above the instinctual level does present some problems when it comes to the reality of soul and reason that elevates man beyond one's instinctual nature. That the human species transcends the principle of natural selection is the central problem between religion and evolution: "The fixity of species is a matter of divine wisdom and does not derive from the ways of natural science."[4] God determined a final state of nature for all forms of life and brought these forms to completion through evolution, making creation an evolutionary process toward a divinely predetermined end that, once reached, put an end to the process. In other words, evolution was God's instrument in creating all species, but the human one became human only when receiving soul and reason, and so was not strictly speaking a product of evolution but of God's immediate creation. Isfahani has it both ways, evolution within divine creation. Natural selection acted in the evolution of what would become humankind up to the point God endowed the species with soul and reason, thus completing the creation of homo-sapiens and the evolutionary process. Having it both ways produces some shifts and hesitations in Isfahani's narrative. His rejection of the social philosophies spun out from the principle of natural selection sometimes sounds as if he's rejecting Darwin, throwing the baby out with bathwater. Given the obfuscations and distortions that muddied the water of Darwin's thought, Isfahani's was not an easy task.

He rejects those followers of Darwin who perverted his philosophy for their own corrupt purposes of denying creation as an evolutionary product of a wise Creator. This is directed against Haeckel, Buchner and, above all, Shumayyil, whom, as noted, he does not mention by name. Isfahani's purpose is not to prove Darwin right or wrong but to cleanse his principles of their materialist interpretations and distortions: "It is not our intention to verify the truth of Darwin's thought but to show, in defense of scientific truth, where Darwin is misunderstood by his followers."[5] Later in the same volume he states another intention: "To defend human nobility over and above the animals from which evolutionists claim man descended."[6] This includes showing that the essentials of Darwin's theory do not oppose Islam. Evolution theory is of no concern to religion and does no harm, as long as natural selection is attributed to the Creator's wisdom.[7] The materialists who went to the extreme of making nature out to be an autonomous, self-directing system of matter and energy, from which, they claim, evolved the forms of life, put an otherwise harmless, and in many ways fruitful, theory beyond the limits of religious belief. Isfahani refers to them as *mu'attila*, one who breaks things, renders them useless. There was nothing these materialist philosophers would not do to undermine religion and belief in a divine Creator who created the universe and all that is in it. He reproduces Haeckel's doctored photographs of the early fetus of different animals as evidence of the lying and deceitful chicanery that these godless people would stoop to in order to advance their false theory that all animals, including man, evolved from a single source. Isfahani also reviews the case of the forged Piltdown man, the supposed missing link, as yet another fraud of the materialists in their godless perversion of Darwin.[8]

Muslims have to be on their guard against those fraudulent claims and theories that pseudo-scientists slap onto western science like so much frosting hoping it will stick. Isfahani likens western knowledge to an island of poisonous and beneficial herbs that live side by side. Easterners themselves, he writes, no doubt with Shumayyil in mind, have indiscriminately brought in the poisonous with the beneficial. By imbibing the evil herbs clinging to the good, Muslims risk losing their religion, their character and their values. Science is vital and has to be taken from the West, but in taking it there is yet another danger just as pernicious as the poisonous weeds, the danger of western power. How to take science from the West without giving an opening to the West to insert itself and dominate? Isfahani reminds his readers that when Muslims took science from the Greeks a thousand years ago, Greek power had vanished. Muslim power had been at its height, leaving little threat of Muslims being spiritually, culturally and politically seduced by drinking from alien sources. Back when Muslims were first learning science, people like Plato, Aristotle, Euclid, Appolonius, Ptolemy, Archimedes, Hippocrates and Galen were looked upon as angels having descended from the heavens bearing treasures of divine knowledge. Had the science Muslims created from their Greek inheritance remained and continued to be pursued by Muslims, the world (here Isfahani means either the Muslim world at its greatest extent or the whole world that would have become Muslim had the devotion to science not been abandoned) would have become a paradise of civilization. But the scientific heritage of Islam had been lost, and now the science of the powerful West enjoyed the position Greek science had a millennium ago. Western power made its science something other than just pure knowledge that could be injected into the bloodstream of Muslim culture. What came with the science could be dangerous. This did not mean science should be rejected. Islam urges men to know:

> And if you find a treasure in the mouth of a pig you don't throw it away. You wash it and use it to benefit the community. . . . But know your religion well before engaging in the science of other people so you don't fall in the trap of following what opposes tradition and sound mind.[9]

The false had to be washed from the pure. Fraudulent scientists such as Haeckel and those like him who fabricated their data, who cheated, lied and forged photos to convince people of their godless materialism, had to be guarded against. The philosophy of evolution was filled with false assumptions that had been cunningly folded into it. Beneath the corruption and falsity there was much that could be accepted, for there was nothing in the simplest and purest form of evolution that opposed religion: "Neither the Quran nor Sunna stipulates in any clear way whether or not life came into existence species by individual species without any variation since the moment the process of creation first began."[10] "There is nothing in scripture that says God cannot change nature and species from head to foot anytime He wishes."[11]

The weighty evidence of science indicates God created evolution out of "choice, intent and purpose." Religious circles, however, regard evolution as a synonym for heresy, "the mother of corruption." This is a grave error. The odium of heresy should not be on Darwin, a pious god-fearing scholar, but on the materialists who perverted his science. Darwin and his colleague Alfred Russel Wallace believed in the oneness of God the Creator, and even Buchner recognized the existence and action of God as Creator of the primeval substance, *al-hayuli*, from which evolved the physical and organic universe.

Isfahani here goes on to say Buchner's materialist theory of evolution does not contradict religion in so far as the divine act of creation is concerned. Only the mode of creation according to Buchner differs from the scriptural account.[12] Isfahani graciously spares Huxley too from the opprobium of atheism: Huxley may have disbelieved in religion and called himself an agnostic, but he believed in God the Creator, a belief that saved him from atheism and presented no contradiction to his being a scientist of evolution, as he understood the theory.

Acceptance of a Creator was Isfahani's hook to reel the fish of evolution into the boat of belief. He emphasizes Darwin's belief in God several times. Isfahani wants to believe Darwin was a believer. It is crucial that he was. Darwin's belief in a Creator saves his theory from religious denial. Darwin cannot be rejected. Reminiscent of al-Ghazali's earlier warning to Muslims who would reject mathematics and astronomy, Isfahani warns that for Muslims to regard Darwin and evolution as enemies of religion would be most harmful to Islam. Those who would reject Darwin were themselves enemies of religion, even if they were members of the ulema. Isfahani here urges the ulema to study the science of evolution so they would know what is involved and lead believers on the right path, teaching them the causes and effects that led to the stages of biological and geological formation. If the common believers themselves attempt this without guidance from an ulema well-instructed in evolution, they could easily fall into error, as have so many scientists themselves, for the complexities of evolution are fraught with dangerous pitfalls and false paths that lead straight to heresy and unbelief.

Isfahani's recurring equivocation over Darwin's *Descent of Man* shows he seriously wrestled with the problem. He writes at various points that the idea is a clear contradiction to the Quran, that the human species is a special case outside of natural selection and that Darwin's application of the principle to man was confused, doubtful and flawed with contradictory speculations and opinions, which Darwin himself admitted to. One of the more serious flaws was that Darwin failed to take into account the laws of heredity, which were not yet known in his time. Darwin was aware of this too and hoped that someday they would be, "and we can only hope with him."[13]

Darwin's failure to emphasize the hand of God at work in evolution was the root cause of his scientific shortcoming – or most likely, as Isfahani wanted to believe, Darwin did, in the secret depths of his soul, see the hand of God at work, but did not admit to it because of his fear of censure from his fellow scientists who would have considered it a breach of principle for him to introduce an agency outside of nature to explain nature, a kind of cheating as they saw it. Peer pressure has kept many scientists quiet in regard to the place of God and has served science poorly. This was the great failing of western science in general, the attempt to explain nature without reference to a wise Creator. "Scientists who base their research on matter only will have the same fate as those who base their astronomy on Ptolemy." Materialism is a shifting sand: it provides no sure ground upon which to base a scientific system. Isfahani gives the example of the ether, that hypothetical invisible airy matter that was supposed to transmit light waves and gravitational forces through the universe. It turns out there is no ether. Waves can travel through a vacuum. All is possible with God. Materialism, Isfahani is sure, will disappear the way of the ether, out the window of advancing science and into thin air.

Since religious truths were eternal and science was always changing, and because true science could not contradict religion, religion had to be the measuring stick in determining what was true and what was false in the science of the day. The religion that served to do this had to be religion as understood by the highest intellects. As for Darwin, though much of what was considered science in his theory still lacked proof, there was, nonetheless, nothing in it against religion as religion is most intelligently understood. Isfahani offered the example of causality and natural law as a case in point of what was at an earlier time considered to be a contradiction between religion and science but in reality was not. Causality and natural law were in fact God's rational will at work in the material world. God could not have willed a world devoid of natural causes and laws. These realities were constructs of the Creator's wisdom that nourished the sinews of a science comprehensible to the rational mind. Religion misunderstood had rejected what was right: "God created causal relations and natural laws and Muslims accept this, just as they accept that the material universe follows laws, but laws that come from God." This general acceptance included evolution:

> If semen evolves first into a baby and then into an old person, facts of evolution that in no way trouble Muslim belief, can there be any problem by believing in the transformation of matter through laws God made for a process of change that transforms matter into sun and earth, as long as the scientific proofs are complete and beyond criticism? . . . The evolution of existence, species by species, is evident when the book of creation is analyzed word by word.[14]

It will be noted that his example of causality and natural law is not a case of science being measured by religious truth but of the theological shift from an Ash'arite to a Mu'tazilite position that had been coming into favor by some of the reformist ulema since the time of Sayyid Ahmad Khan and Shaykh Abduh. His adoption of the Mu'tazilite position, which allows anthropomorphic verses in the Quran to be rendered allegorically and metaphorically, gave Isfahani, who as a Shi'i was free of the Ash'arite theological hang ups with causality, free will and literalism, room for taking figuratively (*majazi*) certain passages in the Quran where creation is described.[15] Muslim, Jewish and Christian scriptural descriptions of creation had to be understood metaphorically or allegorically for two reasons: the growing influence and evidence of evolution theory, which could not be ignored, and the way God was described in scripture as blowing into man's nostrils to create the spirit of life. Since God had no mouth or nose, no hand to mold the clay and no anatomical features at all, scripture here had to be taken figuratively in order to preserve its coherence. The believer had no choice.

If nature had the power to change life forms by principles of heredity, so too could it change man as a species of animal life. Those Muslim and non-Muslim religious opponents who claimed this to be wrong on the basis that no physical or organic change had yet been recorded or observed failed to understand the immense periods of time and number of generations it took for the most miniscule of changes to occur:

> We are overcome by the shock of our human existence being but an instant in the reckoning of the time it took the earth to form over its geological history . . . In order for natural selection to occur and its effect be seen, tens and hundreds of thousands of generations are necessary.[16]

Like every theologian and philosopher since al-Ghazali and ibn Rushd, Imam Isfahani warns that such studies are best not entered into by believers untrained in the religious sciences but left to scholars of the ulema, for the question of man's origins can easily lead one into self-deception, ridicule and, worst of all, heresy. Isfahani must have assumed his readers were well-trained in the religious sciences and could therefore face evolution without their souls being endangered, as there could be no denying of evolution. Support for the theory, he wrote, came from many directions: the similarity between the skeletal structures and intestinal tracts of man and certain primates; the susceptibility of man and certain animals to some of the same diseases; the addiction of man and monkeys to coffee, tea and alcohol; the similarities of the early fetus of fish, dogs, frogs, birds, apes and man; and the fact that human blood mixed with orangutan or chimpanzee blood was not lethal, as it was when mixed with blood of lower levels of the ape family.[17] From what sources Isfahani garnered all this would be interesting to know.

He referred to works of classical Arabic literature that considered the question of man's evolution in a positive sense, such as Damiri's *Book of Animals* and the *Epistles of the Brethren of Purity*, as if to say that if the great writers of the classical past could contemplate human evolution, then it was already a part of the Muslim intellectual heritage and so should be all the easier for modern Muslims to accept. Isfahani cited what Damiri detected in the way of striking similarities between monkeys and man: laughter, playing, singing, speaking, walking on two legs, taking wives, having family relationships and manipulating objects with their hands. The monkey, according to Damiri, was the only species of animal to have eyelashes. The Brethren of Purity went even beyond Darwin in drawing anatomical and behavioral similarities between monkey and man. Isfahani concluded that evolution was just another member of the extended family of scientific ideas initially developed by Muslims and taken over and expanded by Europeans. This was a huge step for an imam to take, and it was not taken without trepidation. Isfahani's thinking on human evolution appears to have developed in fits, starts and restarts. Early in his work he is building a case for human evolution, but after reviewing the argument in his narrative for the descent of man, he takes a step back by concluding that the scientific evidence does not necessarily support the theory that ape and man share a common ancestor.[18] Some 60 pages later he states his doubt more emphatically:

> If scientists were to dig to the center of the earth and fill all the museums of Europe with decayed bones that were assumed to be the remains of animals that lived ages ago, they would not find a thing they could claim as evidence of human evolution, or as evidence of the origin of human existence, and would ultimately have to accept the account given by religion, that the father of all mankind was a man created from clay.[19]

But this does not necessarily preclude the possibility of human evolution, he then adds, reversing himself in a step toward acceptance. Darwin did not say man derived from ape but that man, monkey, horse and all animals derived from a common source, which would have to mean clay, a material substance acted on by God's mind giving rise to the first life forms. In effect, Isfahani is fusing his religious belief of creation to Darwin's theory of evolution in a system of metaphysical materialism. The metaphysics of it replaces the materialist belief of life coming from the blind chance of chemical reactions in primal matter. It was not blind chance. The chemical reaction that transformed primal matter to living organism required a governing catalyst, God's mind.

If the existence of species were the programmed evolutionary product of a divine mind, which implies a perfection of design, how then to explain the implied flaw of vestigial organs that evolutionists claimed were the result of one species evolving to another? What of the human appendix and the human male's atrophied breasts? These traces of an earlier form had to be included in the divine plan of purposeful development.[20] Haeckel's hermaphroditic theory that the male's breasts were atrophied vestiges of an evolutionary transition from male to female was to Isfahani – and here a surprising note of male chauvinism leaps out of his pen – "shameful." But shameful as it appeared, it did not preclude acceptance: "As long as a Muslim believes in a wise creator who did not create things vainly or nugatorily, but with purpose, it is permissible to accept the existence of atrophied organs as vestiges of the evolutionary process."[21]

Isfahani's positional shifts in giving evidence that supports human evolution in one chapter and then denies it in another show how difficult evolution was for him, or how difficult he thought it would be for his readers. If the believer chose to be convinced by the evidence, one was free to do so, as there was nothing in evolution that went against Muslim belief. The believer could decide on one's own.

One of the most vexing questions that human evolution raises for believers, that is, for Isfahani, is: At what point did soul and mind enter the human body? Man's gift of intelligence and speech is proof of his having evolved not from lower animal forms but from the mind of God. Here again Isfahani ascribes spiritual reconciliation to the words of evolutionists themselves. The famous naturalist Richard Owen (referred to as Bernard Owen by Isfahani) explained the great difference in intelligence between man and ape as being simply the way God created things.[22]

Owen, like Darwin, believed in both God the Creator and the natural processes of evolution. If scientists can believe in both, Isfahani asks, why not Muslims? "You are human by soul, not by body. Or as Owen put it, by mind, by that great power of mind that is the distinguishing separation between man and monkey." Man's essence is mind, not body. Isfahani takes this to be anatomically substantiated by folds discovered in the simian brain that are absent in the human. The structure of the human brain is what lifts man to a special realm of creation, endowing man with speech, intellect and a concept of soul: God acting through evolution to fulfill the grand design.

Another vexing problem was natural selection's principle of new species being the result of chance variations that within the complex of environmental conditions made for a natural advantage of one variation over another. Human evolution as the product of genetic blind chance throwing the dice in the casino of environmental change, devoid of plan, purpose or progressive improvement toward a final form, was absurd. Does an architect design a building without an overall plan? There had to be a guiding light. If proof of this light was needed, all one had to do was look at a woman. Women were the ultimate proof of Intelligent Design. In the preface of his section on Darwin's idea of sexual selection as a special form of natural selection, Isfahani asks how nature, acting by pure chance, could have ever fashioned something as bewitching, lovely and desirable as a woman:

> Her dark eyes and bright pupils, her full lips and mouth, the beautifully arched eyebrows, long lashes and hair, her breasts, cleavage, waist and curved hips . . . Only the will of a creator could have designed such beauty. Instead of sexual selection, Darwin should have named it *Tahsin Allahi*: [Divine Beautification].[23]

On the same whimsical note, Isfahani declares that if Samuel Butler's idea was true, that necessity was a determinant in the evolution of advantageous variations, then days after man became man he would have grown wings to fly to the beloved that was so ardently desired and needed.[24] Had Darwin called sexual selection by its proper name, *Tahsin Allahi*, his theory would have been spared the religious opposition it aroused. His omission of God not only obstructed the acceptance of his philosophy but emptied it of scientific meaning and coherence, for scientific discovery is the light of the divine shining in the seeker's mind. Scientists observe the surface of reality, which appears the same to all observers, whether they are believers or not. It is the scientist-believer of the illumined mind who discovers the secrets hidden deep in nature.[25] The illumined mind perceives the Creator's power, wisdom and beauty of craftsmanship, which explains why those who are the most eager to learn nature's secrets are closest to God. Harvey and Pasteur were examples:

> Harvey who discovered the circulation of the blood said he never dissected an animal without seeing the power and wisdom of God at work . . . Pasteur said the more he learned of science, the more profound became his faith in God.[26]

Many other examples of illuminated scientists could be given, Darwin among them. It was because of Darwin's lack of courage and fear of his peers that he omitted the mention of God from his work and refrained from using a term like *Tahsin Allahi* that implied the creative presence of God. That which Darwin called natural selection, thinking it to be triggered by chance occurrences in environmental conditions giving a slight advantage to a variation of a species in the competition for survival, was in reality the action of divine wisdom that drove nature toward a predetermined end. Natural selection was a poor choice of terms. Otherwise, he was a most careful scientist whose thought was guided by the evidence.[27]

Darwin knew there were limits to what could be known by science. The naturalist wisely understood a realm of knowledge existed that offered no answers to experimentation and observation. This was Darwin's pious genius, his awareness that proofs and evidence were related to particulars in the realm of nature, whereas wisdom related to universals in the realm of the divine. Unfortunately, because many of Darwin's followers failed to realize the difference between scientific knowledge and wisdom, the philosophy of evolution, "in which there is much good and no harm, was given a bad name among Muslims who are free to believe in it."[28] Isfahani praises Darwin's freedom from dogmatics and his unwillingness to commit himself to any conclusion concerning questions not answered by sufficient data and observation. Isfahani gives the example of Buchner. This lifted Darwin above other scientists, most of whom were more devoted to theory than evidence. While Buchner dogmatically posited that life had arisen from a single source, from which all the species evolved, Darwin allowed the possibility of multiple sources, and took no firm position.

The question of one source or many was for Isfahani irrelevant to religious belief. The question was a scientific problem relating to mundane physical reality. However many the sources, in the dimension of wisdom they all ultimately derived from God. Accepting this, the believer has no problem with evolution, or with any science, for religion is neutral in matters of science.[29] The supposed problem between science and religion is really between what sometimes passes for religion and science; as for instance, in regard to the theory of spontaneous generation. Hoping to do away with the reality of a divine Creator, some materialists advanced this theory, which invested all force, action and generative power in matter and matter alone. For proof, they pointed to the sprouting of mushrooms, the appearance of maggots in spoiling meat and cheese, and fermentation. "Then Louis Pasteur carefully conceived and executed microscopic experiments and proved fermentation is a chemical transformation which produces a multiplication of organisms, not a case of spontaneous generation." Showing that matter is incapable of generating life by itself, Pasteur's discovery was a triumph of religion as much as science. Only God has the power to create life from unliving matter.[30]

Written a century ago, Isfahani's work stands as the most thorough, fair-minded and balanced endeavor by a religious scholar to open Islamic belief to the science of evolution. The author's equivocation can be disconcerting, but it must be kept in mind he was writing on a subject heavily smeared with accusations of heresy, making equivocation a method of explication. The book could easily have been written in one volume and been all the better for it, but all in all, this work on Darwin by a Muslim religious scholar in Karbala at the beginning of the 20th century is a bulwark of intellectual and religious courage and honesty. Unlike the apologists and scientific interpreters who would follow, Isfahani did not twist and turn Quranic verses to his purpose, but seriously and intelligently subjected Darwin's theory and its materialist offsprings to detailed critical comment and analysis, and concluded that except for its putative divorce from the Creator, natural selection was an accredited science in which discoveries were constantly being made to support it. Isfahani showed how a believer with good conscience could accept the theory.

Considering the author's conservative religious background and the fact he was working from the few scraps of secondary information that had made it into Arabic and then all the way to Shi'i south Iraq, Isfahani's critique is a remarkable accomplishment. That it was ignored is equally remarkable, but understandable in a society where even after a century of reform and western interaction not much headway had been made in implanting a scientific culture. Isfahani would remain a singularity, an imam who, with exceedingly little relevant literature at hand, in a desert where scientific interest was concerned, endeavored and succeeded to verse himself in a science that was not only largely regarded heretical but had been hopelessly entangled with unrelated ideas that were other than scientific.

Hasan Husayn

Any ameliorative effect Isfahani's book could have had on the perception of Darwin and evolution in the Arab world was more than canceled out by the efforts of succeeding writers. Evolution theory did not come into Arabic direct from the language in which Darwin composed his books. In its eastward voyage from England, natural selection took a route that was as unnecessarily bumpy as it was circuitous. Shibli Shumayyil brilliantly managed to get natural selection off to one of the worst starts possible by improperly considering the French translation of a series of lectures that Ernst Buchner had given in German on force and matter to be a commentary on Darwin, then muddied the water all the more by passing off his own careless Arabic paraphrase of its French translation as a faithful rendering of Darwin's principles. Then Jamal al-Din al-Afghani dipped his duplistic oar in the swamp and churned up more muck to obfuscate the issue. Natural selection was so congealed in misconception and Darwin's name so demonized that it would have taken more than Isfahani's book to scatter the poisoned clouds surrounding the science of evolution, even if his volumes had been read.

The confusion was only to get worse. Some 12 years following the appearance of Isfahani's book, an Egyptian writer, Hasan Husayn, made what he claimed to be a partial translation of Darwin's *Origin of Species*. But this was not quite true. As if the waters were not opaque enough, Hasan Husayn based his translation not on the English original but on Ernst Haeckel's *Entwicklungsgeschichte des Menschen*, first published in 1874. Like his Lebanese predecessor Shibli Shumayyil, Hasan Husayn had chosen to translate a German work heavily tinged with materialist philosophy rather than go directly to Darwin's purely scientific *Origin of Species* or *Descent of Man*. This reluctance to go straight to the source is all the more bizarre since Egypt had been ruled by England ever since 1882 (by coincidence the year of Darwin's death). The Victorian upper-crust of Darwin's homeland, who by then had come to accept both natural selection and the descent of man, were in occupation of the country. A copy of Darwin's books in English or French translation would not have been difficult for a determined writer to obtain in Cairo or Beirut between 1882 and 1924, when Hasan Husayn's book was published.

The oddity might perhaps be explained by Arab cultural predilections for philosophy over science, or for books about science rather than science itself. Translating Haeckel's *Entwicklungsgeschichte* was of course a lower level scientific enterprise than translating Darwin's *Origin of Species*, but on the other hand, what would be the motivation to translate books of pure science, being there was as yet hardly any market for Arabic translations of scientific texts, nor even a community of Arab scientists to read them? Anyone with a motivation to read Darwin would most probably have preferred the original English or a French translation, and that wouldn't have amounted to many readers: it was not until the mid 1920s, about the time Hasan Husayn's book was published, that Egypt had a functioning university; and except for tiny Lebanon, the other Arabic-speaking states were at the time in the dark ages compared to Egypt.

Even in Egypt, when it came to science, people read articles, not books. Journals were the main media by which science was transferred. Short articles on science were less daunting than thick, densely compacted tomes, and much less costly, an important consideration for even those 20 percent or less who by the 1920s were literate and had not to fret over the price of bread. An Arabic translation of Darwin was not going to buy many lunches for anyone before mid-century. Science translation, if there was to be any, had to be funded by academic or governmental institutions; there were no private or public ones to fund scientific translation. The Geographical Society of Egypt sponsored some fine translations related to Egypt, but the biological sciences were outside the Society's range of interest. In absence of institutional funding, scientific translation would have to be an undertaking that only an aristocrat in search of a pastime would consider. And this, as will be seen, was in fact the case. Not until one of the idle rich with a rebellious spirit and an inclination for scientific dabbling came around was a major part of Darwin's *Origin of Species* translated. As for Hasan Husayn and his undertaking, he was no more interested in promoting science and evolution or translating Darwin than were a few other religiously oriented Egyptians writing on evolution at the time, namely Tantawi al-Jawhar and Muhammad Farid Wajdi, as will be seen.

Hasan Husayn's stated intention in translating Haeckel's book, like Isfahani's in writing his analytic commentary on Darwin in Ottoman Iraq a decade earlier, was to show there was nothing in science or evolution objectionable to Muslim belief. The title he gave his book, *Fasl al-Maqal fi Falsafat al-Nushu'wa'l Irtiqa'* (*The Decisive Treatise on the Philosophy of Evolution*), is telling in its evocation of ibn Rushd's *Fasl al-Maqal* (*Decisive Treatise*) that seven centuries earlier had argued the harmony between religion and philosophy. Husayn's *Fasl al-Maqal* argued Islam's rationality in a roundabout way by showing that Haeckel's *Entwicklungsgeschichte* was a heretical deviation from both Islamic belief and Darwin's science, and that it was the science imbedded in Islam that conformed to the true theory of evolution, orthodox evolution. Orthodox evolution filled the spiritual vacuum in Haeckel's heretical materialism with the light of God's Quran that illuminated both the mystery of life and the physical universe.

Husayn had much in common with his fellow Egyptian writer on the subject, Muhammad Farid Wajdi. Neither were shaykhs, both had a mix of religious and secular education, and for a period of time both held religious positions in government. Both wrote on science from the religious point of view that science fell short by its neglect or denial of God and revelation; and both liberally agreed that rational interpretation was required where the Quran expressed things that seemed to contradict science. But where Wajdi's knowledge of the science that he wrote about was grievously deficient, Hasan Husayn's was totally lacking, his book a carelessly written and unresearched muddle of error that revealed a monumental miscomprehension and perversion of evolution that approached even the ignorance and willful misrepresentation of al-Afghani's populist version.

Like so many Egyptian apologists who were blooming in the relatively liberal age between the World Wars, Hasan Husayn caricaturized and trivialized science more than reconciling it with his religion. An honest and intelligent work of reconciliation would have at least been something of a contribution by its bringing into relief the concept of natural selection clearly stated. His claiming the Arabs of classical Islam had said everything Darwin did and that the *Origin of Species* was nothing but a "collection of old opinions molded and refined in the light of modern discoveries" served no purpose other than to add to the already formidable confusion and ignorance over evolution and impede its acceptance as a bonafide science. With writers like Afghani, Shumayyil and Hasan Husayn, and no one willing to take on a competent translation of Darwin, it is of little wonder that Imam Isfahani was ignored and evolution failed to find a foothold in the educated public mind. Also not helping were the books and articles relating evolution to progressive socialism that were being published by young Egyptian reformist writers in the 1920s.

In 1914, the same year Chiekho was directing fire against *Muqtataf* over its pro-evolution stance, an Egyptian Muslim, Mustafa Hasanayn al-Mansuri, published a book on socialism that contained a chapter on Darwin and evolution. Mansuri argued that evolution agreed with the Quran, Prophetic Tradition and the scientific precedents of classical Islamic intellectual history.[31] But his fastening a philosophy of social progress and socialism to natural selection did the name of Darwin as much good as had Shumayyil's books. Since there were no scientists in Muslim culture to answer to the perverse use to which Darwin's science was being put, bending natural selection to social and political purposes was totally defeating. Even those who knew something of Darwin's theory made a progressive social program of it – probably an unavoidable distortion given the Arab reformers' zeal for immediate socio-political change in order to join the advancing caravan of civilization in the shortest possible time, before, as they feared, the West advanced so far there would be no catching up. With a passion equal to Shumayyil's, Mansuri depicts the relentless forward march of evolution acting in nature and in its human civil analogue, society and civilization. Central to the book is the socialist promise to eliminate poverty through monogamy, late marriage and a state-supported system of universal education that included females. Mansuri was the first Muslim to accept Darwin in writing, fully and openly, without religious conditions; but by pinning evolution to "scientific socialism" and popularizing it as a political ideology for egalitarian change, he made it a threat to those whose acceptance was vital in preparing the way for an indigenous scientific culture to take root, thereby undermining it as a natural science.

World War I, and the allied propaganda blaming the war's barbarity and destruction on German militarism and quest for power and domination, also had a confusing effect. Sarruf, believing the propaganda, attributed Germany's purported aggressive war machine and political ideology to the philosophical materialism made popular by Buchner and Haeckel, and openly rejected Shumayyil's evolutionary materialism.[32] Up to then, Sarruf had published Shumayyil's articles without voicing support of his ideas. Now, pro-British to the core, Sarruf was attacking him as a supporter of German materialism, militarism and aggression, as if Shumayyil and German philosophy were somehow responsible for the war. Given space in *Muqtataf* to reply, Shumayyil most sensibly wrote that philosophy had nothing to do with the war; that like all wars, the present one was being fought for self-interest, one side being no better than the other. His argument did little in Egypt to disarm the religious and public hostility to Darwin. In the heat of fervent nationalism rising from the fires of the World War, and the burden that the British imposed on Egyptians to help them fight the Ottomans across Sinai, rejecting the science of Darwin the Englishman became enmeshed with the idea of opposing British occupation and imperial arrogance.

In sum, the source of much of the trouble Darwin had in being accepted in the Middle East, as compared with Copernicus, was the added baggage piled onto evolution. So burdened was the simple principle of natural selection with the excess baggage of Marx, Spencer, social revolution, materialism and atheism, it was not until deep into the 20th century that it at last received a fair hearing.

Muhammad Farid Wajdi

Al-Azhar's implied acceptance of evolution as a bonafide science came in the writings of the essayist and encyclopedist Muhammad Farid Wajdi (1875–1954). The pattern of acceptance was similar to the way that religious authorities in Egypt signaled their acceptance of modern astronomy through Abdallah Fikri's 1876 treatise in *Rawdat al-Madaris*. Wajdi, like Fikri, was not a shaykh, nor had he attended al-Azhar as a student. His education, as had been Fikri's, was secular. The little religious instruction he had was from secondary school.

Of a moderately well to do middle-class family, Wajdi was born in Alexandria. He received his early education in a government school in Suez where his father was an official. He excelled in French and religious studies – Quran, Shari'a, jurisprudence – but had very little science or mathematics to prepare him for what would be his greatest contribution to the modernist movement in Egypt, publishing a revised edition of Butrus Bustani's 1870s encyclopedia, *Da'irat al-Ma'arif*. Published in Cairo between 1923 and 1925 as *The 20th Century Encyclopedia*, later to be called *The Egyptian National Encyclopedia*, this reworking of Bustani's half-century-old encyclopedia brought Wajdi to the height of his career as a reformist thinker.[33] He had first gained something of a name as a promising reformer a quarter century earlier when, barely in his 20s and inspired by Shaykh Jisr's work and Muhammad Abduh's foray in rethinking Islam in the light of the modern world, he published a short work of scientific interpretation, *al-Madaniyya wa'l-Islam* (*Civilization and Islam*).

Published a decade after Jisr's *Risala al-Hamidiyya*, Wajdi's treatise carried scientific interpretation of the Quran to more distant frontiers. As implied by its title, the simple theme of his book, by then having become a cliché, is that Islam is the essence of science and civilization: "There is no principle of science affecting the progress of civilization which is not heard in verses of the Quran or in the Hadith, to the point that one might imagine that all the energy and intent of scientists were directed to proving the truth of the religious principles of Islam." The good Muslim modeled one's life on science and reason. Following science and reason was to follow the Quran. Muhammad the Prophet preached the freedom of thought that made science possible. In the Prophet's words, "An hour spent on science is better than 60 years of worship." Islam embodies progress and progressive ideas such as "struggle for existence" and "survival of the fittest" in regard to individuals and civilizations. Because Islam opens the way to science and progress, to be civilized is to be a true Muslim. No other religion can be compared to Islam. As science grows with the continuing discovery of nature's secrets, all the more will the light of knowledge shine on the Quran, illuminating its verses in their deeper meanings. Progress in science reveals the depth of nature, just as it reveals the depth of meaning in the Quran. The Quran and science march in step together. Verses that are vague or poorly interpreted are rendered clear as day by modern science. It is a continuing process.[34]

Wajdi gathered all the arguments that reformers had made since Tahtawi, al-Jisr and Jamal al-Din al-Afghani to show that Islam was the guiding beacon of science, civilization, reason and moderation. Whereas in Christendom, the books and living bodies of scientists and philosophers had been burned by the church, whose authority first had to be crushed before science and civilization could flourish, quite the opposite was true in Islam: when religion flourished, science and civilization flourished; when religion was corrupted, misunderstood or ignored, science and civilization declined. This was because of the balanced nature of Islam, a religion of easy going moderation that combined the exigencies of physical comfort and enjoyment of life in this world with those of a spiritual nature that would lead to everlasting life in the next. Islam offered a harmonious, integrated pattern of life that provided for freedom and balance, physically, psychologically, intellectually and spiritually.

Wajdi's hyperbole would become commonplace. The continuing dearth of scientific interest and activity in Muslim society that was everyday confronted by the West with its accelerating scientific advances and tightening grip on the jugular of Muslim countries through their pliable leaders guaranteed it. Frustrated by the seeming acquiescence of Muslim government in accepting subservience and serving western interests as their countries fell further behind, a great many Muslim intellectuals joined in a contest of ever mounting claims of Quranic scientific precedence to convince themselves of their worth.

Buoyed by his youth and the modest success of his little book of 1897, Wajdi began publication of a journal in Suez, *al-Hayat* (*Life*), which popularized his interpretation of Abduh's ideas on Islam and the modern world. As so many others like it, the journal soon folded for lack of readers in a society that was dogged by continuing illiteracy. This was followed by Wajdi's brief tenure in the Ministry of Awqaf (Pious Endowments). Then, in 1907, returning to publishing, he set up a press in Cairo and put out a daily, *al-Dustur* (*The Constitution*). This survived until 1910. A few years later, with the first glimmer of secular Egyptian nationalism rising on the horizon and inspired by the national call for parliamentary government and independence from the British, he founded yet another journal, this one named after himself, *al-Wajdiyyat*: it consisted mainly of his intellectual musings on politics, nationalism, progress and civilization in the light of world affairs. This too was short-lived. In 1918, with the end of the war and the mounting surge of nationalism being pumped up by a new generation of secular lawyers, journalists and intellectuals demanding independence and constitutional government, Wajdi began writing a three-volume critique of materialist philosophy (*'Ala al-Atlal al-Madhhab al-Maddiyya*: *On the Ruins of Materialism*), which consisted of a "thorough review of naturalism's latest materialistic tendencies and errors," from Lamarck to Spencer.[35]

Published in 1921, the book established Wajdi as a leading intellectual on the conservative side of Muslim reform. At the same time he was writing his work against materialist philosophy he was busy revising Bustani's encyclopedia as a nationalist endeavor of intellectual rebirth. In 1923, using his own press, he started printing the first of what would become ten volumes. In the course of preparing it for publication he read up on cosmology, physics and evolution, not so much to learn science out of intellectual curiosity as to defend Islam against those who accused it of being stagnant, reactionary, irrelevant or backward.[36] Secular in education and outlook, he wrote in defense of Islam being a religion that contained all the buds of modernity, including science. Idealization of Islam as a substitute for science became a psychological defense, answering on one level to western domination and on another to Muslim social and political failure in providing the real thing. The abysmal lack of Muslim interest in science could have been made no clearer than by the fact that here was Wajdi, in the mid-1920s, editing Butrus Bustani's *Da'irat al-Ma'arif*, a modest mid-19th century vintage encyclopedia written by a Lebanese Christian associated with the American evangelical mission and Syrian Protestant College. In the intervening half century neither the Egyptian government nor any private association bringing together the sources of wealth and scholarship that existed in the country produced an encyclopedia that Egypt could truly call its own. Wajdi's edition of the badly outdated work was proclaimed a major intellectual event that made him an important figure in the Egyptian Awakening.

Reworking Bustani's encyclopedia for Muslim consumption, Wajdi expanded at length on entries he thought would give his correligionists problems. The entries he reworked indicates that not a lot of progress had been made in public assimilation of science since the 1870s. In the article on the earth ("*al-Ard*"), he treats the earth's motion as though it were a virgin concept of revolutionary impact that had to be couched in the gentlest of terms and absolutely proved, so as not to overly shock the public.[37] The given impression, assuredly mistaken, is that all the Arab literature that had been written on the subject during the past three generations had had little effect in informing the public, as though Abdallah Fikri's article in *Rawdat al-Madaris* and all the articles in *Muqtataf* over 50 years, all the articles in other journals and books that described earthly physics and motion, and all that Iskandarani, Jisr, Abduh and Rida had written on the subject – all that literature had not moved the idea anywhere near religious or public acceptance.

In fact, like other Arab writers dealing with science, Wajdi dared take nothing for granted. The idea of a moving earth was assumed to be too far beyond the horizon of the public's knowledge of science. Wajdi accordingly felt obliged to inform his readers not only of earthly motion, but even of the earth's sphericity, and then to convince them that believing such things was permissible by stating: "Nothing in the Quran denies sphericity." Then he answers the reader that "When the Book says flat it means that is the way people see it. Everything of that nature found in the Book is a special expression and absolutely does not mean flatness of the earth." He feels compelled to refer to medieval Muslim religious authority for support: "Fakhr al-Din al-Razi said in his *Tafsir* after a long discussion of the matter that the earth is undoubtedly spherical, as is plain to anyone who reflects on the matter."[38] Such was what a reformist thinker composing the *Egyptian National Encyclopedia* in 1924 thought had to be said. It became a pattern. Even into the 21st century, Muslims writing on science and religion would be proving earthly sphericity and motion, and then referring back to past Islamic authorities for the stamp of approval. The enduring power of authoritative tradition and its religious mythology of early Muslim history, combined with the intellectual's equally enduring conviction of public imbecility, compelled 20th and 21st century writers to prove much of what must have been common knowledge, and legitimize believing it by paying respect to the past.

In discussing the end of the earth and its causes – cooling of the earth's crust, cooling of the sun and catastrophic meteoric collisions – Wajdi cites seven Quranic verses that he claims to support cosmic collision. One of them, "And God created the Seven Heavens and like them the Earth," reveals the vastness of space and existence of other earths, in addition to revealing the present endeavor of exploration for intelligent life on other planets in the universe by sending radio signals into space.[39] He then refers to early Muslim authorities who are assumed to have enjoyed the freedom of creative thought that Islam provided when the religion was followed as it was meant to be followed. These authorities, according to Wajdi, reasoned out hundreds of years ago that the creation of the Seven Heavens implied that God created multiple earths, seven being a metaphor for an infinitude. Wajdi assumes that the last part of the verse, "And like them the Earth," refers to earth's geological layers and epochs that have been discovered recently. The astronomical compendium of a 17th century Iranian Shi'i illuminationist theologian, Baha al-Din al-'Amili, a far stretch for a 20th century Egyptian Sunni secular reformer to reach in search of an acceptable authority, is invoked to give legitimacy to the idea of God's having legislated natural law, and to the hypothesis that the earth and its sister planets were originally chunks from the sun.

Darwin's ideas are touched on at some length in the *Egyptian National Encyclopedia*. Wajdi had avoided evolution theory in his *Islam and Civilization*, but by the time he was editing the encyclopedia some 25 years later, the subject was no longer so forbidding. *Muqtataf* had been patiently feeding the Arabic reading public condensed packets of evolution theory in its many dozens of short articles that appeared in the journal's more or less 600 issues published over the previous half century; Shaykh Rida and Imam Isfahani had given believing Muslims a religious version of evolution that made for a more palatable alternative to Shumayyil's hard-edged paraphrase of Buchner's materialism; and the theory of natural selection had been fully introduced in Arabic in the important chapters of Darwin's *Origin of Species* that had been translated in 1918 by Ismail Mazhar. Wajdi could have easily deleted the brief description of Darwin's theory of natural selection that Bustani had written in his *Encyclopedia*, but instead he expanded at length on it. Since the *Egyptian National Encyclopedia* was given al-Azhar's imprimatur, as it were, Wajdi's restatement of Darwin's fundamental theory can be considered to have been given religious approval.

"Suppose Darwin's principles turn out to be correct?" Wajdi asks after reviewing natural selection and Darwin's replies to those scientists and theologians who attacked him. Wajdi's answer is that a true Muslim accepts truth even from one's enemy:

> A Muslim dies searching for truth in the path of God to whom he has surrendered himself. Everybody naturally defends their way, even if by deception and ruse, but in the end, when the storms of doubt become irresistible and defense must be abandoned, surrender is inevitable. Such is the case of contemporary religious leaders before the overwhelming force and authority of science. The Muslim does not fall into despair and defeat, but accepts the truth, however bitter, for the gravest error is to deny what must be accepted. Rather, a Muslim abandons a false belief, even if he has held it 40 years of his life, and does so rejoicing, as in the story of abu Zayd al-Bistami who said "I have studied under 99 Shaykhs and if I die before the hundredth I die short of Islam" . . . No scientific theory that is true can harm a Muslim. I don't say this as a friend of Darwin's theory or to reconcile it with Islam, for the theory is still in doubt and so has yet to reach the status of exact science. But if the many gaps are filled and the theory does reach this level, then it would

become necessary to address the question further, and God will be successful in preparing the way, since there is nothing in Muslim belief that would object to Darwin's philosophy of the origin, evolution and variation of species. Rather, the theory of evolution elaborates on the wisdom of the Creator in begetting from one source the whole chain of life, as Darwin himself said.

"As for the moral aspect," Wajdi knew of "no valid objection to the theory that challenged human virtue." The simplest observation of history and life confirmed much of the theory. History was filled with examples of the struggle for survival. Dynasties and wealthy families were always rising, falling and disappearing. The principle of natural selection was simply the same thing played out in the realm of nature:

> And so there should be no hesitation in its being accepted. As for the law of inheritance, this is intuitively obvious to anyone who knows anything about the resemblance of offspring to their families down the generations and is furthest from any consideration of having an effect on ethics and moral character.

The truths and triumphs of science have nothing to do with religion directly, but can enhance the purity and depth of belief. In Wajdi's words:

> I reckon that if I were to see with my own eyes that scientists in their laboratories had given life to the dead or formed a person from clay . . . my belief in God would only be stronger and I would most likely benefit from it scientifically.

Wajdi then asks the next most important question: Does evolution pose any problem to the Quran's description of God creating man from clay and blowing living spirit into man? Not at all. The ulema has taken many verses in the Quran to be allegorical, among them the description of paradise, the divine command ordering the angels to bow down to man and verses referring to God having anatomical features, not to mention the description of the earth as being flat and stationary. "And so are we not able to do the same for Darwinian theory regarding those verses whose literal meaning contradict the idea of autonomous creation?"

Wajdi's encyclopedic article on Darwin, for all of its reservations and verbal wrestling, is as forward as any statement on the subject made up to that time by a Sunni Muslim who enjoyed a reading public and religious standing in the eyes of the Sunni ulema. It bears with respect to religious acceptance of Darwin's theory of evolution, or better put, to religion's passive toleration of it, the same significance that Abdallah Fikri's treatise had regarding Copernican astronomy. Wajdi was the first of all his Muslim Arab predecessors, all the way back to Tahtawi a century earlier, to state unequivocally that cherished religious beliefs, among them the story of God's creation of man and the pleasures of paradise as depicted in the Quran, had to be rendered allegorically and that a Muslim was obliged to consider science impartially and accept what science had irrefutably proved to be true, whatever it was, however painful the loss of the old and acceptance of the new.

Between his *Islam and Civilization* of 1897, which swept into Islam everything scientific under and beyond the sun, and his *National Encyclopedia* of 1923–1925, which accepted the abandonment of literally understood descriptions in the Quran that were cherished beliefs deeply rooted in Muslim religious culture, Muhammad Farid Wajdi seems to have experienced a transformation of religious thinking in regard to science that was second only to Shaykh Muhammad Abduh's a generation earlier. The difference was that Wajdi had no religious credentials. Yet, ironically, though he was neither a shaykh nor member of the ulema, Wajdi was more of a spokesperson for al-Azhar of his generation than Shaykh Abduh was of his. Abduh was for his time a shaykhly singularity, a horizon event over which the Azharite sun never quite rose, while Wajdi, al-Azhar's secular mouthpiece, was mainstream all the way.

In 1935, by which time Wajdi's fame had been made as the editor and publisher of the *Egyptian National Encyclopedia for the 20th Century*, he was appointed by the Rector of al-Azhar to be the chief editor of its new journal, *Majallat al-Azhar*. Not being a shaykh, Wajdi had no standing to speak for Muslims on what was acceptable and not in religious belief, not even as chief editor of al-Azhar's journal. His position was rather like Ali Mubarak's in his capacity as editor of *Rawdat al-Madaris*. Both journals and their chief editors intended to modernize Islam within moderate parameters by bringing science and religion together. The big difference between them was that in his *Rawdat al-Madaris*, Ali Mubarak seriously wanted to spread scientific knowledge and encourage the youth to study science and was using religion to do it, whereas Wajdi and his Azharite editorial advisors were only interested in science in so far as it could be turned to mirror Islam and the Quran as scientifically compatible and supportive. Scientific Interpretation had no place among the purely scientific and techno-industrial articles of *Rawdat al-Madaris*.

As chief editor of al-Azhar's official journal, Wajdi was more restrained than he had been in editing Bustani's encyclopedia. There was no more about allegorizing angels, anthropomorphism and the sensual pleasures of paradise. As a secularist encyclopedist, he could interpret more or less as he wanted, but as an editor for *Majallat al-Azhar*, he wrote in his own name that which the leading shaykhs considered religiously acceptable but cared not to write in their own names, or could not because of their not knowing enough about science to comment intelligently on the issues. As editor of *Majallat al-Azhar*, Wajdi had always to mind the silently imposed constraints of the shaykhs.

For almost 20 years, up until 1952 and Gamal abd al-Nasser's military takeover of Egypt, Wajdi was al-Azhar's secular point man and protective buffer on the prickly things of science that stung religious sensitivities. Anything he wrote that turned out to be perceived as having transgressed the limits of pious acceptance, as measured by the temperature of populist reaction, transmitted upwards by lower members of the ulema to the leading shaykhs, could be put on him. His articles were reviewed for their adherence to orthodoxy before being published, but the shaykhs had little to fear from the self-professed follower of Abduh, for Wajdi's advocacy of Shaykh Abduh's reformist initiatives in rethinking Islam had taken a turn to the conservative side. Since writing his *Civilization and Islam*, never did Wajdi in any of his writings express the slightest hint that the Shari'a should be modernized or not be the law of modern Muslim society; nor did his adamantine opposition to Qasim Amin's advocacy of women's liberation and education diminish in intensity. He wrote nothing purely in promotion of science, and on occasion he misrepresented science in order to prove a religious point. Like Husayn al-Jisr, he used anything that served his purpose: as, for example, when straining to demonstrate that matter was not the basis of everything but was transcended by spirit, he referred approvingly to spiritualism by accepting that disembodied spirits communicated with the living – an argument that must have sent a shudder of suspected heresy through at least a few of the Azharites. The fact that the force of gravity could act across great empty distances and light waves propagate themselves through a vacuum was to Wajdi yet another proof of spirit transcending matter.[40] The fall of the ether hypothesis was a score for divinity.

Wajdi's writings for al-Azhar, compared to the articles that appeared in *Rawdat al-Madaris*, gives a measure of how little progress had been made in introducing science to the corridors of Sunni orthodoxy from the 1870s to the 1930s. The journal *Rawdat* had been formatted and edited to relate religion to science as a means of promoting science and technology in order for Egypt, or Islam on the larger scale, to catch up and compete with the West: Wajdi, writing in *Majallat al-Azhar*, served the inverse dynamic of science sanctifying religion through Scientific Interpretation. In other words, by the 1930s, the attempt by a growing number of intellectuals to promote the cultivation of science had been traded in for the less taxing exercise of showing Islam to be scientific. Wajdi's Quranic commentary of Scientific Interpretation, *Safwat al-'Irfan* (*The Purity of Knowledge*), is equally symptomatic of this defeatist tendency.

Aware that the Quran, as the unquestioned testimony of divine wisdom and truth, could not escape the pervasive analytical dissection and critical doubt that came with science, Wajdi and his fellow apologists used Scientific Interpretation to extract the tooth and claw of science. Only by eviscerating science could the Quran and Shari'a remain inviolate. The lifeless shell of science, its discoveries and laws, were admissible, but not its inner workings, the explorative freedom of the analytical mind in search of the deepest relationships that brought science to life. This part had to be disavowed. This is what is implied when Wajdi wrote of "that cultured skepticism born of caustic modern knowledge that has found its way into men's hearts," and of the threat of "the materialist school of thought which has spread with the speed of fire in twigs."[41]

Rather than allow the serpent of science in and let it go for the Quranic jugular with its venom of endless questioning that would convulse the foundations of law and belief, the Quran would defang, tame and subsume science, thereby making it its own. The hollowed out husk of science would make religion the thesaurus of modern knowledge. Since the state was doing so little to institutionalize science, which otherwise might have actually given it a quiver of life in Muslim society and produced some scientists who could speak on behalf of their profession, the field was left open to religious apologists to scientifically interpret the Quran, with few who dared refute them.

Wajdi represents an important trend in turning the reformist call for science as a means to transforming society and the Muslim condition into a call, in the name of science, that would cut science short by having it subsumed in religion. According to an Islamist who analyzed Wajdi's contribution to *Majallat al-Azhar*, Scientific Interpretation appealed to doubters and disbelievers whose faith had fallen away but who wanted desperately to be proud of their heritage, and were willing to pay the price of intellectual dishonesty for it: "A great deal of this defensive writing betrays rather pitifully the intellectual insincerity of its writer."[42]

Another feature Wajdi introduced in his religiously oriented version of Scientific Interpretation comes to the surface in his *Majallat* articles, that the incompleteness of science is a basic flaw that undermines its materialist foundation. The spiritual realm of Islam as seen through the Quran presents the fuller picture that is necessary to complete science. By quoting western scientists who critically comment on the gaps, the shaky hypotheses and the unanswered questions in contemporary science, all of which are in fact essential in directing scientific inquiry, Wajdi claims to prove the incompleteness of western science, as if it were an unfinished opera, a flawed project. Rather than science being a process of asking questions and seeking answers to fill the gaps, it should be a completed system worked out in all its details, a finished product, and only Islam can complete the task. Anything else would be a wobbly, disconnected skeleton. Being incomplete and unable to answer all questions, as Aristotle's system had been able to do, today's science can only be completed by Islam. Western scientists were presently too blind to see that Islam was the answer. But once they realized that they must search into things other than material nature for their answers, there would be a fundamental intellectual revolution that would bring scientists and philosophers to the spiritual world.[43]

A great many books conveying Wajdi's brand of Scientific Interpretation would flow from the Arab presses in the last quarter of the 20th century and after. Works with titles like *The Quran, Sources of the Sciences and Wisdom* (*al-Quran, Yanbu' al-'Ulum wa'l 'Irfan*) would be commonplace, one pretty much repeating the ones that had come before it in the stock-in-trade revelations interpreted to reveal science from the Greeks to the present, all typically relying on the same few score of verses, as for example: "And it is He who made for you the stars to be guided by in the darkness of land and sea. . . . Do they not see that God had the rain fall from heaven, by which we produced fruits of many kinds?" – taken to embody all of astronomy, meteorology and agronomy.[44]

The first title mentioned in the previous paragraph is that of a book by Ali Fikri, an Egyptian whose dream world of wish fulfillment was carried to the far shores of fantasy along the current of Scientific Interpretation, a voyage his father Abdallah had sailed before him when writing his treatise reconciling Copernicus and the Quran in *Rawdat al-Madaris* more than a half century earlier. From father to son,

Scientific Interpretation had gone a long way. The treatise of Abdallah the father, a modest dozen or so pages published in a student journal dedicated to fostering scientific interest and encouraging religious support of it, had by the time of his son Ali's two volumes of 775 pages (published in Cairo, 1942, with a preface written by M. F. Wajdi) transmogrified the Quran to include all the general principles of physics, mathematics, geometry, medicine, gynecology, astronomy, astrophysics, geology, chemistry, biology, genetics, dietetics, geography, zoology, agriculture, animal husbandry, mineralogy, electricity, metallurgy, archaeology, swimming, tourism, radio, television, airplanes and military science, to name only a few of the Quran's recently revealed secrets – with rocketry, electronics and space travel to come. Between state apathy and this consequential escapist trend of manipulatively confusing science and religion, a scientific culture had little chance of sinking roots in Egyptian soil, or any soil where Scientific Interpretation became a popular literary genre. With the Quran, who needed science?

According to Wajdi writing in the 1930s and 1940s, the Quran contained everything that natural science, philosophy, medicine and politics did not discover until the 20th century. Early Islam established the world's first democracy; evolution theory, just one of many other theories, was discovered by Muslim scientists many centuries before western scientists thought of it. Quite likely, the consciously constructed mythology of Scientific Interpretation appeals more to educated Muslims whose faith has been seriously damaged, if not destroyed, by westernization than it does to pious Muslims, even those with advanced secular educations who took to heart Abduh's two realms of truth. Though depressed by the malaise of defeat, failed states, sick economics and the wretched leadership that took the place of an all too glorious past of flawless heroes, they find no need for the flimflam of a faith-patching apologetics that scoops up every fish the sea has to offer. The simplest thing in the world for a believer is to accept that all things are possible with God, even evolution, however it works, and go on working, praying and trusting in God. Science only becomes a problem when deliberately stirred into religion by self-promoters: politicians, evangelicals, pseudo-intellectuals, charlatans. Once the populist ulema themselves began preaching and writing on the Quran's last word in science, the way was open to the mainstream. With the continuation of political repression, the worsening of corrupt government and the deepening of social problems, it was only a matter of time before the flood gates burst. Anyone susceptible to Scientific Interpretation would have that much less trouble believing that blowing oneself up in a crowded marketplace or flying a jet into a building would guarantee a ticket to paradise.

Salama Musa

The year 1924 was eventful in Egypt for evolution-related publications. Hasan Husayn's mixed translation and commentary of Ernst Haeckel's *Entwicklungsgeschichte* was published that year; Muhammad Farid Wajdi's ten-volume *Encyclopedia* for the 20th century was being published; Ismail Mazhar, who six years before had translated the first five books of the *Origin of Species*, published his lengthy commentary on evolution, *Malqa al-Sabil*; and Shaykh Tantawi Jawhar's 23-volume scientifically interpreted commentary on the Quran had started coming out. It was also the year a young Coptic writer, Salama Musa (1887–1958), published his *al-Yawm wa'l Mustaqbal* (*Today and the Future*), a book that, in reaction to the mindless carnage of 1914–1918, looked to the evolutionary progress of science, genetics and civilization that would eliminate world hunger, disease, aging, energy shortages and war – in retrospect an optimistic outlook.

Yet oddly enough, in that same year, in spite of this flurry of evolutionist publication, the chief editor of *Melange d'institut Dominicaine des etudes Orientale*, a scholarly journal published in Cairo, expressed amazement at Egypt's and the Arab world's total absence of interest in evolution. Lucien Leclerc, the editor, mentioned the works of two authors who wrote on evolution, Shibli Shumayyil, who had been several years dead, and Salama Musa, who had been writing in his stead for a decade. Ismail Mazhar's name should rightly have been mentioned as an articulate public advocate of evolution theory, and why it wasn't is puzzling. Nonetheless, Leclerc's observation is not a whole lot off the mark. It is not that evolution was not being written about and reflected on by some thoughtful Arabs, but that there were not that many of them; and only a small body of pro-evolutionist literature of a serious nature was available: a few books and some dozens of relatively brief articles in the secular journals.

Evolution was a subject that held little interest for the reading public. Even Isfahani's book was next to non-existent in the public sense. This was not only because of the psychological difficulty presented by the idea that all forms of life, including one's own, evolved from a primitive antecedent, and because of the ridicule that had been heaped on the idea of evolution by popular figures like Afghani and Marrash, predisposing people to scoff and think of evolution as man being born from a monkey, but as much for the extraneous social and economic theories Arab authors had packed into natural selection in order to suit their revolutionary desires. The temptation to insinuate social transformation into a well established science was too attractive to be passed up by progressive minded writers who saw their society frozen in a hopeless condition of weakness, passivity and ignorance. Serious commentators on evolution believed only revolution offered a prayer of a chance to break away from the strangling morass of lethargy, self-satisfaction, corruption and stagnation.

The fusion of socialist ideology and natural science continued long into the 20th century, guaranteeing the public mind would remain closed to Darwin. What Shumayyil had begun in the 1880s, Ismail Mazhar and Salama Musa continued up to the middle of the 20th century, when military dictatorship began taking over Arab governments and military censors decided what was proper reading for the benighted publics they must shepherd.

Shumayyil, Mazhar and Musa were outsiders in Egypt, writers at the margin with a marginal following. The first, a Lebanese Christian, lived as an émigré in Egypt and was thought of as one. The second, an Egyptian Muslim professing a personal God and contending that Islamic civilization at its greatest had never reached rationality, might as well have been a foreigner. Salama Musa, an

Egyptian Copt from the countryside, was a self-professed stranger in his country and was so regarded. Like Shumayyil, a man of independent means who traveled and studied in Europe, Salama Musa spent four years in France and England, only to return a cultural alien, no longer able to live at peace with himself abroad or at home. The more he lived and studied abroad, the more he yearned to return home, and when he did, the more he found his society wanting, to the point he came to detest it.[45] Shumayyil had found his science in Buchner and German materialism, Musa in an eclectic collage of Kant, Darwin, Nietzsche, Bergson, Marx, Engels, Freud, Spencer and Shaw. Musa's earliest education, the part of it that had any meaning to him, was, like the education of so many other budding Arab intellectuals born during the last half of the 19th century, the pages of *Muqtataf*.

Echoing Jurji Zaydan of an earlier generation, Salama Musa tells of devouring *Muqtataf*'s articles on science and philosophy with youthful zeal. This continued even after his years in Europe. He returned from his independent studies abroad convinced that civilization progressed in accordance to a Hegelian rationality, just as surely as the physical and organic forces of nature operated rationally in a system of laws. Socially organized human action also operated in a rational dynamic of progress, subject to its own laws of natural selection and survival.[46]

Musa's uncritical embrace of purely rational and progressive systems of social philosophy was abetted by a pent-up reaction to the chaos and irrationality of his early schooling. Recording his childhood memories in his autobiographical sketch, he recalls the cruelty and ignorance of life in the countryside, the stories of demon spirits that children were brought up on, of terrible *ifrit* that filled them with fear and superstition, and that terrified them of nature. The irrational fears of those days in the village primary school never left him. Nature was a place of terror and evil. There was nothing good or beautiful about it. His recollections of secondary school in Cairo are filled with another kind of terror, personal humiliation. It would seem from his description of the insults and sharp slaps students suffered for giving a wrong answer, or for failing to recite flawlessly from memory long passages of which the students had no understanding, that educational methods had not changed all that much from Muhammad Ali's day. Fear of punishment and humiliation rather than encouragement and the reward of opening young minds to the joy of learning was the enduring mainstay of pedagogy.

Salama was 19 when he left for Europe. France and England were a planet apart from Egypt. The undreamed-of world he discovered enchanted him. The experience turned him from his own culture. He could see no good in it and no bad in European culture. In Europe, his eyes were opened to the cultural stagnation he believed was caused by religion. He later compared the difference between the countryside of Europe and Egypt to that between heaven and hell. In western Europe religion had been put in its place and civilization allowed to progress freely. Egypt and the Arabs had to follow. In England, Salama became a member of the Fabian Society. High on Nietzsche, he joined the Eugenics Society and later wrote a book in Arabic on the future Superman in which he advocated a radical system of social engineering to improve the Egyptian race, claiming a millennium of first-cousin marriages had washed out the nation's mental creativity. For proof he pointed to the dearth of creative genius and the striking similarity of facial features between the ancient Egyptians depicted on funerary walls and those of the modern Coptic community. The tradition of first-cousin marriage, as common among the Muslim community as the Coptic, was a cultural flaw that exacted a punishing price and had to be abolished.

Years later, when the Turkish Republic had arisen, Mustafa Kemal's revolutionary reforms offered a model closer to home than Europe that the Arabs should follow. As it had in the new Turkey, religion had to go. The Arabic script too: everything associated with religion. If the Arabs were ever going to cut away from the past and start moving ahead, the Turkish example of tossing religion and sacred script into the dustbin of history had to be followed. Even the most radical minded reformers would have had trouble with this.

The quintessential outsider, Musa found intellectual companionship with those in the society of the small group of Syrian Christian émigrés of the 1880s and 1890s who were still alive and active in Egypt during the 1920s and 1930s. Shumayyil had died in 1916, but Farah Antun, Sarruf, Nimr and Jurji Zaydan were still around. When Zaydan retired in 1923, Musa took over the job of editing *al-Hilal* and published a number of religiously incendiary articles in it. Being Christian saved him from Muslim attack in Egypt, but made him a target of the Jesuit wrath of Père Louis Chiekho in Beirut. Lambasting Salama as punishingly as he had Shumayyil and the editors of *Muqtataf* decades earlier, the feisty priest initiated a third round of inter Christian journalist invective, this one fought out in the late 1920s and over the same issues. Père Chiekho's critique of Musa's 1927 book *Today and Tomorrow* (*al-Yawm w'al Ghadd*) tears into the author for

> striking the same chord over and over again in all his books. The author's intellectual atheism and unbridled hostility to religion, which he joins to the pseudo science he has picked up here and there from heretical westerners, form a marriage whose bastard children spring up in page after page of his writing that upon close inspection amounts to nothing more than humbug, imbecility, historical error and downright lies, but which mixed with scientific jargon and a certain literary elegance will nonetheless mislead those readers unable to distinguish between poisonous error and simple truth. Examples of the repulsive book's lack of decency, good taste and knowledge abound with statements such as "Christianity is nothing but a fusion of earlier religions"; "Jews worshipped idols before becoming monotheists"; "There is doubt Christ ever existed as a person!" How could hundreds of thousands of intelligent Jews and idolaters have embraced early Christianity and shed their blood for it if they were not sure that Christ the Lord God created the religion and that he was an existing person?[47]

Chiekho was one of the few to confront Musa publicly. The usual treatment was to ignore him, along with Mazhar. Shumayyil was easier to ignore; he was dead. Chiekho would soon join him. His critique of Musa in 1927 was one of the last things he wrote before his death the next year. For 30 years St. Joseph

College's combative Jesuit had fought the fight of religion in Arab Christendom that al-Azhar's Rashid Rida concomitantly fought in Arab Islamdom. By the end of the second decade of the century, the generation of Muhammad Abduh, Ya'qub Sarruf, Faris Nimr, Shibli Shumayyil, Jurji Zaydan, Ibrahim Hourani and Louis Chiekho had given way to younger voices entering the arena – Salama Musa, Ismail Mazhar, Muhammad Farid Wajdi, Hasan Husayn, Taha Husayn, Louis Awad, Abbas Aqqad.

At the end of the 1920s, Musa joined Sarruf, now an elderly man of 80, to found a scientific and cultural society with its own journal in an attempt, once again, to build a popular scientific culture in Egypt. Called the Egyptian Society for Scientific Culture, the enterprise's life of a year is no doubt indicative of the continuing lack of interest in science, but that the founders were Christian and that Salama Musa was a professed atheist did little to commend the society to the broadest circle of the Cairene intelligentsia. One Muslim whom the society did attract was Ismail Mazhar. This certainly must have doomed whatever chance the society might have had for a longer life. Salama Musa's advocacy of a secular society with a system of controlled breeding to prevent first cousins, and the physically and mentally impaired from marrying or having children, must have ranked in mass appeal with Shumayyil's call to abolish nationalism along with national boundaries and let the British keep control of the Suez Canal. If Musa and his intellectual association with the deceased Shumayyil weren't enough to sink the society, Mazhar's lecture at its first annual meeting, "Evolution and Its Impact on the Future of Thought," guaranteed that few Egyptians would be submitting membership applications. Rashid Rida attacked the society as a nest of atheism. Even Mazhar's journals lasted longer than did Sarruf's and Musa's science society. For half a century Mazhar and Musa vied over being Shumayyil's runner up as the Arab world's least popular thinker.

Guaranteed to give Musa a leg up in the competition was his explanation for Egypt's and the Muslim world's cultural sterility: that the Quranic prohibition of sculpture and painting deprived potentially creative minds from analyzing anatomy and natural life, the very thing, he claimed, that impelled 18th century Europe to scientific investigation and comparative analysis of living forms, which in turn had prepared the way for Darwin. Musa argued that the refusal to accept evolution was rooted in a mental block that went back to religion and it was this that kept Arabs and Muslims behind. Muslim society prohibited even the discussion of these questions. Not one book, he said, could be found in Arabic on the development of religion, society and ethics.[48] Arabs understood systems but not processes. They thought life, matter and the universe had come into existence fully fashioned, when in fact it had been an evolutionary process of development from stage to stage, each one being destroyed in the development of the next, the new built on the rubble of the old. Law, ethics, religion and society – everything was transitory, nothing final. Evolution ruled every facet of every level of universal existence.

As long as Arabs and Muslims continued to believe in the myth of the absolute, the wholly finished product, the fully fashioned, complete end-of-the-line perfection of law and social form, their culture was condemned to stagnation.

"Until evolution is accepted as a religion, Arab culture will never grow. . . . The chick is born by breaking the shell." But the Arabs preserve their shell, thinking it a protecting armor, and consequently continue to lose out on life. Their worship of tradition makes them easy prey for the imperialists who devour the weak and backward as surely as the strong in nature triumph over the less advantaged of their kind. Societies blinded by belief in a future happiness in paradise are condemned to servitude on earth. They may as well be dead. History has no place for them. While the Arabs dream of fairy tales of happiness after death, their imperialist masters laugh and suck up their oil.[49] Musa only wished that medical science would develop an inoculation against what he called the "Arab Disease" of forever looking backwards to the great days of religion and conquest, and forwards to death and happiness in paradise.

Even the language with its subjective expressions fettered the people's minds to the past, condemning them to the inescapable ruts of ancient thought patterns in the same way the iron chains of ancient tradition bound their behavioral patterns. Language, history and tradition acted on Arab/Muslim society the way that natural laws of heredity did on living bodies. The only way out of Egypt's cultural impasse was to let go of the past and whole-heartedly accept progress in emulation of the revolutionary action of Mustafa Kemal's secularism and language reform in Republican Turkey. Otherwise, Egypt would remain eternally condemned to live in its fog between yesterday and tomorrow, lost in the meaningless confusion of old and new, where a government with a modern assembly of deputies lived side by side with a medieval ministry of religious endowments and a Shari'a court based on ancient religious law; where a system of higher education in the modern university of Cairo lived side by side with medieval al-Azhar, suits, trousers and ties mingling with galabiyyas, caftans and turbans; where Jews and Christians were still called infidels; and where Muslim notables shared out Circassian girls among themselves to lighten the skin of their progeny so they would look European!

Salama Musa's cutting description of Egypt's condition echoes the analysis of a European scholar commenting on the cultural disorientation and cynicism that characterized Egyptian intellectuals between the two World Wars. According to that analysis, students suffered from a lack of intellectual coherence and unity of knowledge, educated as they were in a confusion of secular western and traditional Islamic systems, where shaykhs educated in al-Azhar taught side by side with those educated either in Egyptian secular schools or in Europe. The content and principles considered valid by the rival schools clashed head on, producing intellectual instability and throwing intellectual life into a stultifying confusion. On the one side was a set of dogmatic religious fundamentals to be blindly obeyed, and on the other a set of intellectual principles based on independent critical inquiry and analysis. The end product was moral skepticism, intellectual cynicism and a debasing relativity of values.[50] The contradictions between Islamic faith and western imports pointed out by Tahtawi in 1830 were a century later Egypt's living reality manifested in education, literature, clothes, marriage, lifestyles, and legal and social institutions.

For Musa, the inevitable contradictions meant subservience to the West. Only by accepting western knowledge and institutional models could Muslims evolve from subservience to independence. There was nothing reprehensible about looking to the West. It was a fact in the pattern of history. Egypt's being tied intellectually to the West was not cultural or religious betrayal but a response to a millennial historical pattern that traced itself from ancient to Islamic times. For more than a thousand years, Musa writes in his *Today and Tomorrow*, Egypt had been tied to the West. Not just in Greek, Roman and Byzantine times, but into the Islamic period. Influences went both ways. Jawhar, the general who had conquered Egypt for the Fatimid Caliphate and founded al-Azhar, was a Sicilian Muslim. Al-Azhar was the paramount model adopted by medieval European universities. The back and forth flow of cultural and institutional exchange made Egypt and Europe partners in civilization.

Today Egypt had a parliament, secular courts, schools, journals and newspapers, all based on European models and giving hope to a better tomorrow. What remained of the old did harm to the new and had to be uprooted by the continuous advance of the new if Egypt was to reach its tomorrow. The choice was clear: either set sail from Asia to Europe or sink further into the abyss of ignorance, squalor and fanaticism: "Egypt is today's yesterday of traditional authoritarianism, Europe is our tomorrow." Salama Musa's overall castigation of all that was old and eastern was not so much an infection contracted from rubbing up against European orientalism as it was the rant of a reformist writer angry at his culture and his own despair. Small wonder Lucien Leclerc failed to find any of Salama Musa's books in the stalls of Cairo.

Not just Egypt was mired in today's yesterday. Today's West also had its yesterdays. Musa saw in the John T. Scopes trial a mentality as medieval as anything in Egypt. The 1925 law passed by the state legislature of Tennessee outlawing the teaching of evolution was America's equivalent to Egypt's religious trial and prosecution that same year of Ali abd al-Raziq, the young shaykh who interpreted the caliphate as a historical evolution produced by the political infighting of early Islam. Abd al-Raziq's case proved that secularist intellectuals could not rely on the institutions of the secular state if they came up against al-Azhar. Published the same year that the trials of Ali abd al-Raziq and John T. Scopes took place, Musa's *Today and Tomorrow* presented Muslims and Americans as people whose lives were so vested in religion they were psychologically unable to accept and understand evolutionary processes in things religious or in actions having to do with nature and society.[51]

In the 1930s and 1940s, evolution theory comprised but a very thin slice of what little scientific discourse existed in Egypt, not including that which occurred in the sterile exercise of Quranic Scientific Interpretation. To the limited extent they were read or discussed, Salama Musa and Ismail Mazhar kept the subject of evolution alive in some small region of public consciousness. In this they were unwittingly assisted by a number of nationalist academicians and popular writers whose liberal ideas and productive literary output during the period between the wars made free discussion, within limits that were never defined, an accepted practice. No official censorship silenced proponents of evolution, but some matters related to the principles of natural selection could have been considered too risky to the established order to be aired publicly, especially after the chill produced by al-Azhar's suppression of Ali abd al-Raziq for his having written his doctoral thesis on the office of caliph being a product of historical evolution, a political contrivance of human invention coming after the death of Muhammad and not a divinely inspired institution whose basis was Quranic. The literary critic Taha Husayn's humiliation for writing a book (*Fi'l Adab al-Jahiliyya*) that appeared at this time (mid-1920s) showing that pre-Islamic Arabic poetry was in fact a creation of Islamic times written for tribal-political purposes put another damper on the freedom that writers thought should be theirs. However, according to Taha Husayn writing in the 1920s, evolution was taught freely in Cairo University and the New College for Teachers. No restraints were put on teaching sciences, unlike Arabic literature and Islam. Critical analysis of the Quran and early Islamic history, as shown by the abd al-Raziq case, were implicitly forbidden: neither the government nor the university wanted to offend al-Azhar.[52]

The limits for free rational inquiry were never set down. Censorship was self-imposed. Every editor and writer had to rely on one's judgment. Since in the popular mind socialism was identified with atheism, Sarruf thought better of publishing a socialist tract Salama Musa had written for *Muqtataf*. At the same time, Muhammad Farid Wajdi could write more or less positively on evolution in the national encyclopedia *Majallat al-Azhar*. This was not in contradiction to the atmosphere of intolerance and intellectual oppression created by al-Azhar's condemnation of Ali abd al-Raziq, Taha Husayn or any of the others whose creative ideas were seen as threatening: accepting the theories of science within the contextual framework of religion, that is, in support of Intelligent Design, was one thing; applying the critical methods of scientific analysis to the sources of religious belief, or to anything associated with sanctified tradition in the way of historical or social investigation that might lead to embarrassing reinterpretations, was something else. One never knew what was within and what without the limits of censorship until the line had been crossed, and one could be sure that the beleaguered government was not about to stand up to al-Azhar on behalf of any secular intellectual, not with the British-created monarchy in one corner, British power in Egypt in another and in the third, the mass of Egyptians who, alienated by corruption of office and governmental disregard of wrenching social crises, were looking more and more to the Muslim Brotherhood. No one was immune to religious prosecution for stepping over the invisible line, however secular the transgressor, for no transgression was secular. The blind writer, scholar and Minister of Education, Taha Husayn, as secular as any Muslim could be, unwittingly stepped over the limit for what he thought was a purely literary study and suffered the same inquisitional process as the deposed al-Azhari shaykh, Ali abd al-Raziq, who thought he was writing a historical analysis of a medieval institution.

Ismail Mazhar

The translation of Darwin's *Origin of Species* was a long time coming. Not until 1918 did it finally begin. In that year Ismail Mazhar (1891–1962) published his translation of the first five chapters, the heart of Darwin's explication of natural selection. Ten years later, Mazhar published the translation of four more chapters, and not until 1964 was the whole of Darwin's book translated, a full century and more after it had first appeared in England. That alone signaled the region's desultory, directionless and lethargic progress in creating a scientific culture that would take seriously the translations of primary texts.

In 2004, a new and much more professional translation of *Origins of Species* was made by Majdi al-Maliji under the auspices of Egypt's Supreme Council for Culture. However, neither Mazhar's nor Maliji's translations are to be found in any of Cairo's bookshops. In fact, hardly anything of a scientific nature concerning evolution is to be found. Darwin's *Descent of Man* has yet to be translated. It might have been expected that after the 1882 Lewis Affair in Beirut a sense of urgency would have set Shibli Shumayyil or Bishara Zilzal, or Cornelius Van Dyck or his son William, both of whom excelled in Arabic and were more than favorably disposed to Darwin, to produce an unadulterated translation of Darwin's books. Jurji Zaydan, a medical student involved in the Syrian Protestant College crisis of 1882, was another who would have been up to the formidable task. As it turned out, it was not until almost two generations after that crisis that the challenge was at last undertaken, by an independently wealthy amateur with minimal medical and scientific training.

Ismail Mazhar came from a well-off Egyptian family of secular outlook and education. His father and paternal grandfather had been engineers, graduates of schools founded by Muhammad Ali and Khedive Ismail. As government engineers, they had acquired wealth, allowing Ismail Mazhar to be raised in luxurious surroundings. He lived in a palace staffed with eunuch slaves, chamber maids, cooks and coachmen, and had no need to earn a living. Like the interests of practically all intelligent young men of this class, his intellectual interests were in law, literature and philosophy. A few courses in Arabic literature at al-Azhar were the extent of his formal higher education. The university had not yet come into operation during his student years. During his short time at al-Azhar he was introduced to Muhammad Abduh's writings and would later consider himself a follower of the shaykh.

Being energetic, intellectually disposed and comfortably spared the necessity of having to work or prepare himself for a specialized career, Ismail read on every subject from all the books he could find in Cairo. It would seem his self-education was as random, unstructured and scattered in purpose and direction as was the scientific literature that haphazardly found its way into Muslim society. The one steady staple in Ismail's intellectual diet was *Muqtataf*. As with so many other potential intellectuals during the last quarter of the 19th century, the journal was his introduction to science. He writes in his memoirs of reading it religiously.

Perhaps it was in emulation of the journalist success of Sarruf and Nimr that he founded his *al-Sha'b* (*The People*). He was 18. The journal was a one-man operation. Ismail was writer, editor, printer and distributor. It lasted a year. Sources accounting for Mazhar's intellectual career are meager. Very few Egyptians and no westerners have written on him, excepting possibly someone who wrote an unpublished doctoral dissertation on him or mentioned him en passant in a publication. His contribution to Arab modern thought has found little attention. Arab writers refer to him but mention little more than his translation of Darwin. Like Shumayyil, he was an outsider with no popular appeal and only a few followers.

In the manner of so many other young Egyptians and Syrians of comfortable circumstances, Ismail traveled to Europe, where through direct cultural contact he became familiar with ideas he had first met through *Muqtataf* and the writings of Shibli Shumayyil. He remembered distinctly many years later the impression Shumayyil's *Falsafat al-Nushu'w'al Irtiqa'* (*Philosophy of Evolution*) made on him: "Upon reading it, a revolution that is beyond description started to take place in my mind."[53] From then on, evolution would become the central idea in his growing understanding of science, philosophy, history and civilization. He did not study science or medicine in Europe, as had the 19th century sojourners who had gone on their own. Rather, in the pattern of other secularly educated young men of his generation – Salama Musa, Muhammad Kurd Ali, Ahmad Lutfi al-Sayyid, Abbas Aqqad, Taha Husayn, Louis Awad, writers who brought western ideas and literary forms into Arabic literature – Ismail Mazhar found his role in writing about science and modernity.

Studying science for the sake of science and obtaining an advanced degree in order to return home and teach it as a building block to modernity, the time for that had not yet come, and like the translation of Darwin into Arabic, was a long time coming. Compensation for the hard work of science in terms of prestige and pay awaiting a young man who returned home after years of hard and expensive study in Europe was reason enough to discourage any bright fellow, and anyone who did invest one's energy and resources to study science abroad would likely not have returned, not for long. Other than government paying a starvation wage for a dead-end job, who would hire a science graduate? Academic opportunities were rare. Cairo University offered only undergraduate courses in the sciences before the 1950s. Medicine was the only faculty related to science that offered advanced training. A locally trained physician might at least be able to survive. The alternative was to write about science. Writing about science as a vital part of modern life offered a more promising career. Some people at least read about it. There was a market for that, meager as it was: no more than around a half of the Egyptian male population, and up to a quarter of the female, were literate by the mid-20th century.

As in the last three decades of the 19th century, the reformist writers of the first half of the 20th century who had studied science abroad and ended up as journalists in Cairo and Beirut found their calling in writing to encourage others to study science, hoping, like Tahtawi, Sarruf, Nimr, Zaydan and Ali Mubarak had before them, that their literary efforts would prepare the way for science and scientists to evolve into a thriving home-grown culture, each generation fertilizing the ground for the next. The problem was that the fertilizing rewards never materialized. The garden failed to blossom.

The science professors at Cairo University were mainly Europeans. There were few exceptions, a notable one being Mustafa Musharrafa (d. 1950).[54] Musharrafa received a doctorate in physics in England, then published cutting edge research articles in leading journals. Having become highly regarded in the European scientific community, he returned to Egypt with a professorship at Cairo University. Another Egyptian became a professor in the Department of Biology and wrote a textbook. These were most remarkable exceptions, but as exceptions bordering on singularities, they were not enough to make an indigenous scientific culture. More than a century of effort had produced by the 1920s and 1930s a popular literature on science and modernity, but little of a scientific culture that Egyptians, Arabs, Iranians or peoples anywhere in Islamdom could find pride in or call their own.

Ismail Mazhar's career throws a light on that reality. In 1927, toward the height of his career, Mazhar had a second go at founding a journal. His first had been called *The People* and lasted a year. This one was called *al-'Usur* (*The Ages*) and lasted longer. Printed at the top of the cover page of each issue were two logos: "Know Yourself" and "Liberate Your Thought." These stood in place of the customary religious invocation that began any piece of writing by a Muslim, the Bismallah, "In the name of God, the Benificient, the Merciful." The full text of *al-'Usur's* second logo read like the preface of a manifesto:

> Liberate your thought from all inherited traditions so that you may, in the event you discover truths that contradict them, find no difficulty in rejecting any idea or school of thought which gives your soul security or your mind tranquility.

If this wasn't enough, his enthusiastic endorsement of Mustafa Kemal's revolutionary reforms, particularly the one separating religion from the state in the secular Republic of Turkey, completed Mazhar's declaration of war against the religious establishment. His avowal of a personal deity over and above the communal one of the Quran, Prophetic Tradition and Shari'a would have in a less liberal period been enough for al-Azhar to charge him with heresy, and al-Azhar would have, had Mazhar gone the extra step and called for a modern investigation of those sacred texts. Bad enough was the middling storm of literary protest he churned up across the Arab world by his singular contention that classical Muslim civilization, for all its grand cities and its science, medicine, literature, architecture and commerce, had been, in the world scale of things, no more than a secondary level civilization. Only the West had achieved the third and highest level: the analytic-scientific. His put down infuriated both the religious authorities and the rising generation of nationalists, Christian as well as Muslim. Mazhar took delight in publishing letters he received accusing him of atheism. Like his early mentor Shibli Shumayyil, he considered anything he wrote a failure if it didn't swamp his office with letters of outrage.

The stated intent of *The Ages* was to foster modern ideas through critical examination of the received ideas of tradition. Living up to this ideal gave the journal a lifetime of four years. The authorities shut the journal down because of Mazhar's sharp criticism of official corruption and the government's lack of social policy. Mazhar's secular jihad for enlightenment, social justice and public interest in science, spearheaded by his demand that the state undertake social reforms to eradicate disease, illiteracy and poverty, and combat the blight of uncritical obedience to tradition, all of which implied that the government was doing nothing, went beyond what the authority in power could tolerate. Mazhar's stinging criticisms of government were stated directly, unlike the style of *Muqtataf* where criticism was obliquely couched within the context of a news report or account of a great scientist or inventor, leaving it to the reader to ask or answer an implied question. Mazhar was less circumspect. He dared decry as criminal the irresponsibility of political leaders in regard to the poor condition of the peasantry, education, health and urban labor. The political leaders were causing the country to rot and die. Their disregard of public health, education, social security and all those institutional services modern government was expected to provide was opening the way for an ultra-conservative, socially conscious, anti-western religious movement to do what the secular government was failing to do. While government leaders shouted nationalist slogans against the British occupiers and filled their pockets, caring not a whit about the stagnating country, retrogressive religion was gaining ground.

Mazhar's fear that the moral vacuum created by the government's negligence, corruption and social irresponsibility was being filled by traditional religion was well-founded, as seen by the swelling membership of Shaykh Hassan al-Banna's conservative Muslim Brotherhood that had begun in the late 1920s. When in an issue of 1929 Mazhar again lambasted the government for its rampant corruption, and demanded action to address the public crises in health, education and social welfare, the political leaders were too fragile and inept to accept the criticism, and the journal was closed down. Mazhar was branded a hot-headed communist agitator (the government forgetting for the moment that he was raised in the lap of luxury and privilege in a palace served by cooks and eunuchs), to which charge the religious authorities would have added atheism. Considering Mazhar's merciless criticism of the leaders from the start, it was a triumph of sorts that *The Ages* lasted as long as it did.

Its scorching criticism of government aside, *The Ages* was a thoughtful journal in the secular tradition of *Muqtataf* and *Hilal*. It offered monthly articles on recent developments in the sciences of evolution, zoology, astronomy, relativity and quantum theory, as well as on history, philosophy, social thought, and Arab and western poetry and literature. The degree of complexity of several of the articles on science would suggest that toward the end of the 1920s something of a rudimentary scientific literacy was beginning to bud in the younger generation of Egyptians. For example, the April issue of 1929 contains a lecture given by professor Ahmad Efendi Khayri Sa'id to the Young Men's Muslim Society in Cairo. Entitled "New Directions in Science," the lecture reviewed discoveries in the electrical composition of matter, which included the Curies' experimental work in radioactivity, Niels Bohr's and Edwin Shroedinger's theoretical work in the new quantum theory and Einstein's relativity uniting space, time and gravity in a four-dimensional universe. With classical Newtonian mechanics having been replaced by quantum theory on the sub-atomic level, scientists were now in the revolutionary stage of searching for a new theory that united the basic paradigms of nature as expressed by electromagnetism, relativity and quantum mechanics, a trinitarian oneness that the lecturer, who was no more able than Shibli Shumayyil and Salama Musa had been in keeping science separate from speculative philosophy, identified with the *wahdat al-wujud*, or unity of existence of ibn Arabi and Sufism. Mazhar's journal gave astronomical discoveries a prominent place. He wrote a long article on evidence indicating the possibility of water on Mars, based on the latest telescopic observations of the Red Planet's valleys, river beds and canals. This aroused speculation concerning the possibility of life on Mars, for where there was water, there likely was life. In deliberate provocation, Mazhar claimed that the discovery showed there could be life whose origins had not been accounted for in scripture.[55]

Evolution was another of his provocations. Arabs, he asserted in one of his books on evolution and civilization, were lacking the freedom and courage to speak out, and for this they hadn't yet broken the chains of tradition to reach that higher level civilization whose creative output was informed by "doubt, criticism and exactitude." Arabs were always moving toward that level but without ever quite getting there because they lacked the leaders and reformers with the courage to speak out critically and freely, and without these, a civilization could never transit from tradition to freedom. Since in regard to the affairs of competing nations and civilizations people do not have the luxury of limitless time, the Arabs, if they did not reach this level very soon, would disappear as a civilization in the way a species disappears in nature by natural selection, by the law of survival of the fittest.[56] It was not that Arabs were unequal to westerners in scientific ability. History proved there were many scientifically gifted Arabs. But it was not simply a matter of so many individual geniuses that counted in a civilization's reaching a competent level of scientific creativity. What counted was the level of development of the whole society with its supporting institutions:

> We must overcome the obstacles in the way of reaching this last stage by allowing the abilities that nature has given us easterners to develop patience and stamina for the toil of thought and research . . . We must shake the dusk of fantasy from our eyes and see the rays of critical thought in this age of transformation and progressive scientific thought . . . The past rules the present when there is no future.[57]

The West speeds forward into the light; the Arabs grope blinking and stumbling toward the light just before them but never quite reach it. Mazhar posits Einstein's theory of relativity to be symbolic of the growing separation between the West and Islamdom. While the West is embarking on a second Scientific Revolution based on the universal constant of light, the Arabs, proclaiming a benighted mind like Jamal al-Din al-Afghani a great thinker, are left to wrestle in the dark with Copernicus and Darwin.

Lost in the dusk between medieval and modern, Arab society was languishing in stagnation and mental turpitude, hamstrung by fragmentation and division. The few scientific thinkers who dared to doubt and question were checked by the forces of religious tradition. Those who came from a mixed education of medieval and modern, of traditional religion and science, of East and West, were children not of creative doubt but of deadening uncertainty and confusion. The rest in the great middle of Arab society were left in moribund sterility. Where to look for hope? Even the reformers had fallen into division. Those on the religious side were speaking of the crisis of religion and the threat of its disappearing at the same time secular reformers railed on about the domination of religion and its frozen grip on the minds of men: the former wanted religion to be the fount of knowledge and center of education, the latter to have religion's acquiescence and support of separating itself from secular knowledge and education. Students who studied in both camps were left in a cloud of contradiction.[58]

In one of the last issues before the government closed *The Ages* down in 1930, Mazhar published his intent to translate Darwin's *Descent of Man*. This he would do as soon as he finished translating the *Origin of Species*.[59] He sees the many obstacles and hardships facing him in this task but insists it has to be done. Not only the translation is required but an account has to be made of the many advances made in evolutionary biology since Darwin's time. This means new words will have to be created to keep Arabic alive as a language capable of expressing science in the modern world. Mazhar proposes to do this. As it turned out, he never started the *Descent of Man* and never completed translating the whole of the *Origin of Species*, another of many great projects well enough begun but never finished.

In spite of the lethargic intellectual ambience regarding evolution, Ismail Mazhar appears from his writings to have done well in keeping up with advances in the field, but like Jisr, Isfahani and Shumayyil, he is silent on how he accomplished his task, on what sources he used, what western books or journals were available to him for making his translation, what assistance he may have had from scientific scholars in Cairo.

Several Muslim writers in particular opposed his translation. There was of course Shaykh Rashid Rida. He was unhappy not for Mazhar's translation of Darwin and popularization of evolution but for his not giving "Intelligent Design" a prominent enough place. Another shaykh who attacked him was the scholarly Amin al-Khuli, followed by a prominent Syrian scholar, Mustafa al-Shihabi, author of a popular treatise *On the Origins of Scientific Thought* (*Hawl 'Usul al-Fikr al-'Ilmi*), a miniscule version of Tantawi Jawhar's 24-volume work of Scientific Interpretation. Their contention was not so much over Mazhar's belief in evolution as it was his claim that Arab classical thought with its large and creative scientific tradition had failed to reach the positivist level of LeBon's three-tiered hierarchy. They also rejected his dismissal of Afghani as a thinker.[60] If Shaykh

Khuli's and Shihabi's attacks were not enough, there were the Jesuits and Protestants of Lebanon accusing him of atheism in their letters of denunciation.

Muhammad Farid Wajdi, a follower of Muhammad Abduh whose reformist ideas fit more comfortably with those of Rashid Rida, added his voice to the anti-Mazhar chorus. In 1930 he wrote a defamatory piece against him, "The Assault of Heresy on Religion." In reply to Wajdi's accusation of heresy, Mazhar turned the argument around and wrote "The Assault of Religion on Freedom of Thought," one of his last pieces on the subject to appear in *The Ages* before the government shut it down. To his attacker's accusations of heresy, Mazhar reviewed religion's persecution of Thales, Socrates, Copernicus (who was not persecuted), Bruno and Galileo, claiming Wajdi had it all wrong: how could heretics or heresy launch an assault on religion when there were no government, court or state institutions that ever empowered heresy to persecute religion? It was state-empowered religion that assaulted people by labeling anyone a heretic or atheist who dared think beyond the strict limits imposed by religion. Religion was most comfortable when in bed with the state to crush freedom. What chance did heresy have attacking that partnership in collusion? The only state free of this collusion was the Soviet Union, and this was simply because it was the one atheistic state that had arisen in history. All the others had religion, and it was the religion in the state that did the assaulting.

The favorite target of religious assault was science, for science above all required freedom of thought. Mazhar shows Wajdi's claim that religion was being attacked to be based on nothing more solid than the undermining of certain scriptural passages by recent scientific discoveries. In order to defend religion against science, Wajdi prescribes the reinterpretation of religion. But, Mazhar asks, what does that mean? Reinterpretation means that the standing interpretation must be flawed, along with the religious beliefs that go with it. It means that out of blind obedience to mindless imitation of a fossilized tradition that had been extracted from ancient authorities, past generations of believers believed in the wrong interpretation and followed the mistaken practice of what was supposed to be the essence of their religion. Reinterpretation meant accepting the way of defeat and deception, for today's interpretation would be reinterpreted tomorrow, making religion a series of generational misinterpretations. In other words, it meant reducing religion to an endless confession of error, where science led the way and religion trailed behind, revising and reworking the words of revelation. To reduce religion to interpretation in the light of scientific discovery was to suck religion dry of its spiritual essence, its sanctity and mystery.

Mazhar explains that what Wajdi really meant by religion being attacked by heresy was the threat of free thought let loose to examine critically the sources of religion. Behind Wajdi's charge of heresy was the fear that the sources, those pillars of authority, if analyzed rationally, would be seen to be as feeble as they were faulty, and the whole contrived edifice of religious thought would come tumbling to the ground. Those who attacked thinkers as heretics were afraid of reason, for once the venerated authorities were shown to be no more than a generation's contrivance for the sake of having a guide for stability and permanence, the structure supporting traditional practices and beliefs would collapse like a house of cards, bringing all of religion into question. The simple truth was that Wajdi and all those who feared rational thought took the very idea of freedom to be heresy.

Mazhar's spirited response to Wajdi's article brought the letters streaming in from several Arab countries. Even the Jesuit Chiekho, who rarely wrote against freethinking Muslims, could not refrain from attacking Mazhar. That *al-'Usur* lasted all of four years and its editor not adjudicated a heretic and condemned might be taken as a measure of religious and political toleration during Egypt's generation-long flirtation with parliamentary democracy, as weak and prone to manipulation as the British designed the Egyptian political system to be. Several other reformers writing between the World Wars were not as fortunate. Mazhar lost only his journal.

In 1930, the same year the authorities of religion and politics combined to sweep Mazhar's *al-'Usur* from the bookstalls of Cairo and confiscate his press, al-Azhar, with government blessing, cut down another reformer for his heretical revisionism. Unlike Ismail Mazhar, the non-conformist was a member of al-Azhar and therefore an easy candidate for heresy. As noted earlier, Shaykh Muhammad abu Zayd published an annotated edition of the Quran (*Interpreting the Quran by the Quran*), criticizing the old commentaries and interpreting the spirits (*ifrit*), devils, jinn, heavenly thrones, Preserved Tablets, angels and other such Quranic supernatural figures to be metaphoric expressions of natural phenomena. Shaykhs Jisr, Abduh, Rida and Jawhar had done this previously, as had Sayyid Ahmad Khan in India, but in abu Zayd's case, as in Ali abd al-Raziq's and Taha Husayn's, the high authorities of al-Azhar decided the shaykh had crossed the invisible line. He was denounced, his book confiscated, and he was forbidden to write, teach, preach or hold any religious meetings or position.[61]

Abu Zayd was not a scientific interpreter. He was a reformer whose intention was not to promote science through religion or show how scientific Islam was, but to strip Islam of the irrational elements that adhered to it. In the mind of the Azharite leadership, scientific interpretation was unquestioningly legitimate: at the time of the abu Zayd case the Egyptian Supreme Council for Islamic Affairs published a Quranic commentary that asserted that modern science was anticipated or preceded by the Quran.[62] Yet, the kind of sober rationalization that explained away the supernatural was somehow considered heretical when not adorned in the glossy veneer of science and modernity that proclaimed Islam a thesaurus of knowledge, past, present and future. Tawdry apologetics were honored, serious religious reformers punished as heretics.

Ismail Mazhar was severely criticized but never officially condemned for heresy, thanks to his having stayed away from theology, the Quran, religious treatises, revisionist interpretations of early Muslim history and anything directly bearing on articles of faith. His criticisms were diffused and aimed at everything in politics and obedience to tradition, like so much buckshot from a double-barreled shotgun; and though many pious butts got stung by the broadside blasts, there was nothing specifically of a religious nature in his writings that could be used to bait him to the hook of heresy. The best the authorities could do was to take his press and journal away. But he still had *Muqtataf*, that bastion of science and free thought that was still going strong, to publish his unpopular ideas. Mazhar had published in *Muqtataf* before founding *al-'Usur*. The present editors, as had their predecessors earlier with Shumayyil's articles, cautiously disavowed *Muqtataf's* support of Mazhar's ideas; but no one was convinced, and so *Muqtataf* and its new set of editors were once again attacked for publishing things that few wanted to hear or have discussed publicly. Sarruf, Nimr, Hourani, Chiekho and Rida were gone, but the same old battles over evolution and other scientific issues raged on in the journals.

In 1945, by which time Sarruf and Nimr were long dead, Mazhar became chief editor of *Muqtataf*, a position he retained until his retirement in 1949. In his second year as chief editor, when political life in Egypt was rapidly unraveling with rampant corruption, assassinations, student strikes and the nationalist Wafd Party sinking into the slime along with the monarchy – as the Muslim Brotherhood's membership continued soaring – Mazhar wrote a critique of the government that surpassed any of Shibli Shumayyil's and Salama Musa's excoriations, outdoing even his own flame-throwing criticisms back in the days he was publishing in *al-'Usur*. First, he faulted the government for allowing Egypt to fall into two separate societies, each with its own dress code and system of education, with the broadening separation threatening to break out in open class warfare. The educational schism allowed no chance for the birth of scientific enterprise that could in time heal the collapsing society. Education was sterile. Cultivating the wonder of nature in a young mind was to be found nowhere in Egyptian schools, religious or secular. The complete absence of instilling curiosity was the only thing the two sides of the educational schism had in common. Both were at a dead end that had brought ruin to the country. Peasant children memorized the Quran, while students of westernized families, cloistered in their own private schools, memorized their lessons as if they were scripture. The two sides shared nothing but their own form of blind imitation, one uncritically following traditional authority, the other just as uncritically following the ways of the West that they hardly understood. The two sides were strangers to each other. Those Egyptians with European educations were no more able to relate to the Egypt of rural tradition than the traditionalists were to the secularized society. Education in Egypt, modern and traditional, was like a monstrous being with two heads but no stomach. The heads ate but digested nothing, stricken by mental constipation from force-fed memorization.

This was Mazhar's summing up of Egypt's condition close to mid-century, after more than a century of so-called reform, in half of which he had actively participated. He had come to the end of his career. Little could he have suspected that as bleak as Egypt's future looked to him in 1947, the time would appear to another generation of Egyptians to have been halcyon days.

He had published 20 books and countless articles on history, literature, politics, science, religion and civilization, rivaling in literary output his contemporary and compatriot Salama Musa. Like their earliest mentor and inspiration, Shibli Shumayyil, neither Mazhar nor Musa enjoyed a large following. Their ideas had little resonance in the Arab intellectual marketplace. Mazhar is not even mentioned in

Albert Hourani's highly regarded study on modern Arab thought in the so-called Liberal Age – liberal only in comparison to the ghastly nightmare that came to smother the region in the last half of the 20th century and on. Although Mazhar's lack of recognition would seem to belie his significance as a merchant of western ideas imported and translated into Arabic literature, his translation of the *Origin of Species*, or most of it, was the first work from the great books of modern primary scientific literature of any length to be put into Arabic, which in itself should be enough to place Mazhar among the leading figures of the Arab intellectual revival. By late 1918 he had translated the first five chapters. The publication was little noticed, possibly because, as has been suggested, public attention was distracted by the end of the World War and the Egyptian nationalist revolt against the British in 1919. Public disinterest in science, and especially in evolution, would count as an even greater distraction.

Mazhar translated four more chapters of the *Origin* in 1928.[63] The work was no trivial matter. Finding or creating the best words and phrases to capture Darwin's meaning was indeed a monumental task, no less in some ways than Hunayn ibn Ishaq's translation of Galen's medical works a thousand years earlier, though the printing press eliminated the horrendous problems posed by the errors and lacunae in the manuscripts of negligent copyists of Hunayn's day. Taxonomy was the big problem. Some of the technical vocabulary of evolution had already been supplied by Sarruf, Shumayyil and others in more than 40 years of science writing in *Muqtataf*. Imam Isfahani's double-barreled critique may also have been available to him.

Though he makes no mention of sources that he used in tackling the problem of nomenclature, technical vocabulary was a problem Mazhar treated seriously: modern science had to begin with a suitable vocabulary. Many terms he had coined himself. He composed a technical dictionary, and wrote a small book on a method of scientifically forming Arabic equivalents of Latin and Greek terms that had become an essential part of western scientific vocabulary, *The Renewal of Arabic to Become Sufficient in the Demands of the Sciences and Technology* (*Tajdid al- 'Arabiyya bi-hayth Tasbihu Wafiyya bi-Matalib al- 'Ulum wa'l Funun*).

Mazhar's translation allowed Arabs to read Darwin's first book in their own language. The reputation he gained from his translation did not extend much beyond the circle of secular writers and reformers associated with the editors and readers of *Muqtataf*, *Hilal* and Mazhar's short-lived *al-'Usur*. Adamantly opposed to his ideas were the editors, writers and followers of *Manar*, *Mashriq* and *Majallat al-Azhar*, edited respectively by Shaykh Rashid Rida, Père Louis Chiekho and Muhammad Farid Wajdi. In the eyes of those three, and the faithful they spoke for, Mazhar was the heretical reincarnation of Shibli Shumayyil, a devil spewing the poison of materialist atheism and evolution into the ears of Arabs. It was a role he seemed to accept as readily as he did the ideas of the former devil-in-chief, but one he had to share with the Coptic community's own satanic representative, Salama Musa. Soon after the appearance of his translation of the *Origin*'s first five chapters, Mazhar began publishing in *Muqtataf* on physics and evolution. It was a fitting statement of his having taken the place of the recently deceased Shibli Shumayyil.

Mazhar's contributions guaranteed that *Muqtataf's* reputation as the Arab world's leading scientific journal would continue. His article on Einstein and relativity in *Muqtataf's* May issue of 1922 explained in simplest terms the temporal relation of events in a four-dimensional space-time continuum. Mazhar reported that the theory the young Einstein revealed in a series of articles in 1905 was as profound, revolutionary and challenging in the domain of material physics as Darwin's theory of evolution had been, and continued to be, in the domain of organic life. Mazhar reminded the reader that it was not that many centuries ago the discovery of the earth's motion around the sun had boggled the public, as well as a good part of the scientific community. Having been at first rejected by scientists and non-scientists, the idea was accepted with time and with verification by advancing research.[64] Mazhar's optimistic implication of evolution being inevitably accepted one day by Arabs, and by Muslims in general, had some basis: Muhammad Farid Wajdi, future editor of al-Azhar's *Majallat*, was at the moment writing up his modernized version of Bustani's encyclopedia, in which Wajdi declared Darwin presented no obstacles to Muslim belief. Wajdi's article on evolution caused no fireworks, nor, as might be expected, did Mazhar's on Einstein and relativity. The latter passed into Muslim acceptance unopposed, if passively, since the fourth dimension and speed of light as a limiting physical constant in the relation between mass and energy were abstracts that, vaguely understood, appeared to have no bearing on anything in religion. If anything, the whole theory seemed nothing but a mathematical form of other worldly Sufi symbolism that was as illusive as the illuminationist alchemy of ibn Arabi.

Not so with evolution. In spite of all the literature that Jisr, Abduh, Rida, Wajdi, Tantawi and Isfahani had put out since the 1880s on the Quran and Islam having no problem with the theory within the framework of what would later be called Intelligent Design, evolution continued to meet intimidating opposition through the 20th century. The principle of natural selection, which took the creation of man from God's caring hands and placed it in an autonomous system of nature, proved as much and more of a stumbling block for believers as did the principle of natural law, which took the whole universe from God's hands. Intelligent Design was not enough to cover the monkey's rear. As late as 1923, *Muqtataf*, still pretending to be the neutral moderator of intellectual exposition and exchange, felt obliged to publish and answer a letter it received from a Muslim attacking Darwin's "struggle for survival" as a denial of all that was good in man: ethics, feelings of amity, peace, brotherhood; and oppositely, an exaltation of all that was destructive: enmity, power, aggression, rivalry, war, extinction. Hewing to the journal's oft-stated principle of presenting scientific ideas from a neutrally objective perspective while encouraging discourse over controversial ideas, Sarruf prefaced the journal's replying article with an apologetic note to the effect that the purpose of *Muqtataf's* opening the subject of evolution "is purely the desire to advance knowledge, interest and understanding, and to sharpen the mind in discussion." This was followed by a restatement of the journal's function of providing a forum for public discussion and intellectual exchange without taking sides on the issue, a claim that was not taken too seriously by anyone, given *Muqtataf's* half a century of running articles on discoveries that supported evolution. This time the editors relied on Ismail Mazhar, a Muslim, at least nominally, to answer the attack. He was the only one around who could write with knowledge and conviction on the merits of Darwin's science. He was the only one who dared to. Other Muslims who wrote or knew anything about it in the early 1920s were concerned principally with how it squared with the Quran or was prediscovered by Arab scientists hundreds of years before Darwin.

Mazhar explained that Darwin's theory and its principles had been so misused, abused and purposely misinterpreted by scientists and non-scientists alike that Darwin had become hopelessly lost in a cloud of confusion and distortion. Nothing, he said, could be more true of this than the confusion and misunderstanding surrounding Darwin's principle of struggle for survival, *tanazu' al baqa'*, a term that had been grossly misinterpreted to mean life at any cost, that nature was one bloody war of aggression, destruction and death, with the strong devouring the weak. The false and repulsive picture caused people to reject Darwin's theory out of hand. Natural selection as survival by adaptation to natural conditions was not being comprehended in its scientific context. Darwin, he explained, had conceived the term to define a complex process and used it only for lack of a better way to capture in words the action of nature. Referring to Darwin's own words, Mazhar writes:

> He himself had problems with it. In the beginning of the third chapter of his *Origins of Species*, Darwin wrote that he took the term in a purely metaphorical sense in order to express the conditions of plant and animal life.[65] The sociologists took it over and coining the phrase "Life At Any Cost" made it the basis of their theoretical constructions and this did much harm to the theory in its scientific context. The same was done by the so-called materialist realists. These people, Nietzsche among them, because of their prolixity and misapplications of a scientific theory, have done and still do a great injustice to a great scientist of the 19th century, the aim of these words here being to do justice to him after all the wrong done.[66]

This was the pot calling the kettle black. Ismail Mazhar indeed performed the long overdue task of translating the *Origin of Species* and contributed to an Arabic taxonomy of evolution, but he was as culpable as Shibli Shumayyil, Bishara Zilzal and Salama Musa in applying Darwin's principle of natural selection to society, civilization and history. With them, he held a most salient corner in their collective formation of modern Arabic literature's golden square of exploitation in interpreting Darwin's theory into their own social and political ideas of reformist wishful thinking and passing it off as scientific. Mazhar as much as Musa most prolifically carried on what Shumayyil had begun, basing social, political and religious analyses on the principle of natural selection cast in an ascending three-tiered Comtean structure of intellectual consciousness and social progress, from mythological to metaphysical to scientific. As reformers, they had priorities that did not conform to the strict disciplines of science or history of science. Science had to be put into the service of reform. But there could be no science without reform. Without reform there could be nothing but more of the same, more humiliation, more foreign domination, and more poverty, illiteracy and ignorance.

Accordingly, the niceties of pure science had to be tailored to suit the greater good of reform. Reform had priority over everything, and everything was put to its service. The lecture Mazhar gave at Sarruf's and Zaydan's science society, "Evolution and Its Impact on the Future of Human Thought," was as much an argument drawing on scientific principles for the progressive reform that Mazhar and his associates knew to be necessary for cultural survival as it was a typical example of the wrongful application of Darwin's principles. A few years after his having blamed non-scientists of perverting Darwin's principles and giving the great scientist a bad name, Mazhar published another essay in *Muqtataf* in which he interpreted the development of Muslim thought in terms of natural selection in a Comtean framework.[67] Mazhar's inconsistency is understandable. He wrote not analytically with close attention to facts, but as a reformer focusing on the social and intellectual condition of Egypt. For this reason he was able to portray Jamal al-Din al-Afghani, whom he had criticized elsewhere for his having ignorantly ridiculed Darwin, as a zealous advocate of intellectual change and a heroic thinker who led Muslims to those analytic sciences that started them on their way to the third and highest stage of civilization. This was Afghani interpreted wearing his European hat.

Mazhar's insight in this article comes more on target when expressing his understanding that it was the scientific and literary periodicals and newspapers founded in the 19th and early 20th centuries, *Muqtataf* being the mother of them all, that made possible the Egyptian intellectual journey toward a civilization based on exact knowledge patterned on the natural sciences. Playing a part similar to the one played by journals and pamphlets in effecting intellectual change in early 18th century England, these Arabic journals, according to Mazhar, prepared the Muslim mind to think of change in terms of progressive development. The literary and scientific journals of Egypt gathered all the isolated elements that had come into the country since the time of Muhammad Ali, and in this way of synthesizing the accumulated bits of knowledge that had come in and continued coming, the periodical literature made a real change by opening the eyes of people to see things together:

> Like the sun's rays clearing the clouds, the journals started us on our way from the second to the third degree of civilization, but those rays of clarity that enable us to see change and unity are still only weakly shedding their light upon us.

In Hegelian fashion, Mazhar predicts that in order to complete the transition of becoming a full civilization, where science and critical examination of life and society lead the way, there has yet to be a final clash between the proponents of progress and the defenders of tradition. Out of the clash of old and new will emerge the highest form of Muslim civilization, where religion is truly at one with the onward march of science in a progressive society.[68]

The best known of Mazhar's works is his *Theory of Evolution at the Crossroads* (*Malqa al-Sabil fi Madhhab al-Nushu' wa'l Irtiqa.'*). The book was published in 1926, more or less midway between the publications of his partial translations of the *Origin of Species*. The book presented a long introduction on evolution, but failed to avoid being drawn into the philosophical materialism and social progressivism that had so deeply colored the thinking of other secular reformers. Mazhar's intent was to render evolution acceptable in its own terms, that is, as it turned out, in the broadest of terms to which the theory had been stretched, from enlightened humanism to the social philosophy of Comte and Spencer, with strong influences from Fichte's and Hegel's philosophy of spirit. The terms were so broad that the essential science of Darwin was lost in a sea of social critique and philosophy. Here again, a work that was meant to be scientific ended up focusing not on science, but on secular reform and formulating a cure for the Arab malaise: to restore society to health and put it on the road to high civilization.

The "*Malqa*," or "Crossroads," in the title Mazhar gave his book was meant to convey the idea that evolution was the central principle from which emanated all paths of elevated human endeavor. Evolution was not just a principle of nature, but of man and all his endeavors in building civilization. Man being an animal product of evolution, everything he put his hand to manifested that principle. It was man's essence, his spirit manifested in literature, music, architecture, art, religion, philosophy, science and history. Man's essence was his mind freeing itself from truth to truth. Anything that obstructed the mind in its struggle to free itself had to be taken down. The positive measure of progress and freedom of mind was scientific advance:

> The enemy of science is religion's monopoly of intellectual authority and discourse, abetted by weak political rulers. Tyranny and religion monopolize power to crush freedom of thought. Freedom to criticize is a sign of a healthy intellectual life, while quiescence and blind imitation of tradition are signs of death and disease . . .
>
> In the struggle for control of the mind, religious leaders in cooperation with political rulers gained the upper hand and all knowledge came under the authority of religion, with the sword of the state its executioner.[69]

Such, Mazhar continues, had been the case in both the medieval West and Islamdom. But in the West, beginning with Francis Bacon and his *Novum Organum*, science was redefined and given a firm and independent basis that was free of the restraints of religion. Without this freedom there could have been no discoveries. Not only authoritarian politics and religion were enemies of science and freedom, but scientific-minded reformers themselves sometimes contributed to the intellectual blockage. This was the case of the theory of evolution as delivered to the Arab world by Shibli Shumayyil. Much harm was done. Shumayyil made a grave error in his exposition of evolution by failing to account for "spirit" in his philosophy, for it is not in pure matter that truth resides but in the spirit or essence that transcends it.[70]

Shibli Shumayyil's great intellectual flaw, Mazhar claims, was his failure to realize that the religious impulse is woven into the fabric of human nature and cannot be ignored or denied, as Shummayil insisted it would be one day. Shibli wanted to replace the religion of prophecy by the religion of materialism, the belief that matter in itself gives rise to the origin, principles and structure of the universe. He was wrong. Religion is an eternal psychological necessity, though it is also true that religious beliefs are at any one point in time a function of intellectual progress to higher understandings of religion that come with the advance of science, philosophy and social norms. Religion itself is a constant, while the individual elements of belief that form the integrated content of religion are variables that come from the conditions of the particular civilization. Religion itself is never a means to advancing the levels of thought or liberating the mind from existing beliefs and patterns of thought. Quite the converse:

> Belief was successively transformed from mythology to theology, then to science, that is, from submission, surrender, fear and obedience to higher levels of freedom, but always within an unchanging religious need to believe.[71]

For all his fault-finding criticism of Shumayyil, Mazhar esteemed him the greatest scientific thinker that the "Awakening," with its shortcomings and unfulfilled aspirations, had so far produced. Flawed as the movement itself, Shumayyil is faulted for not going deeply enough into science to perceive the progression of spirit that integrates belief, evolution and the physical sciences.[72] Mazhar presumes to correct Shumayyil's mistaken approach by reviewing the principles of physics, chemistry, geology, astronomy, mechanics, electromagnetism, gravity, light, atomism and evolution in order to show their interrelationships and underlying unity. The effort took him to a medieval philosophy of soul, spirit and matter to explain how abstract thought was produced in that part of the brain that was referred to as mind. The integration of science and the essence of eternal religion through the action of brain-energizing spirit made for a larger cosmic unity. Toward this end, and in order to score a crucial point against Shumayyil's materialism by showing that science shares with religion a belief in the existence of a physically undetected reality, Mazhar gives the unfortunate example of the ether, a theory that had been negated by the Michelson-Morely experiment in 1877 that proved the speed of light to be the same in every direction, and therefore uninfluenced by the motion of the earth, and Einstein's publication of his papers on relativity in 1905 that showed the speed of light to be a fundamental universal constant. Science no longer needed the weightless, tactile, invisible ether to explain the propagation of light and gravitational forces. Mazhar's earlier article in *Muqtataf* on relativity (1922) makes clear he was aware that the ether had gone the way of phlogiston, into oblivion. But the historical truth of science was of less importance than was making a place for science in a religious society by toning down Shumayyil's radical materialism.

Mazhar defined the essence of religion as the innate need to believe, to grasp the unknown and make sense of life, nature and the universe in bringing them to order. This was also the essence of science. Organic evolution, social development and the history of science, religion and philosophy through the ages were interwoven in an elaborate paradigm. Epistemological bed fellows, science and religion were the warp and woof of civilization's pattern as it progressed from age to age. Mazhar reached the same dichotomy of heart and mind struck by Abduh a generation earlier:

> Religion is an expression of the spirit turned more to viewing life inwardly than outwardly. The outward physical world is the domain of science with its objective judgments of the mind . . . Science and religion each has its own language; neither likes for the other to be spoken of in its language; but since the word *'ilm* is the same for both scientific and religious knowledge, and is so vague, ill-defined and universal in its application, complications and tensions became inevitable during the development of science and religion in classical Islam.

Another culprit who did much damage to the cause of science was Jamal al-Din al-Afghani. Though Mazhar praised Afghani as an analytic thinker in his *Muqtataf* article of 1926, in his book published the same year, he accused Afghani of having made science an enemy of religion by "his confused ideas about Epicureanism and materialism, of which he had not a clue."[73] Afghani was a confused fanatic who equated the philosophy of materialism and its socio-economic expression, socialism, to atheism and moral corruption. His *Refutation of the Materialists* was a gross perversion of Darwin's theory. Mazhar is one of the few Muslim writers in the first half of the 20th century to recognize that Afghani had been a liability for scientific assimilation. Afghani's absurd caricature of natural selection, that a flea could become an elephant and then devolve back into a flea, was not only stupid but damaging to both Islam and the cause of science. His taking refuge in ignorance to escape reality was the kind of denial that kept Islam and the Arabs backward. That the otherwise intelligent Shaykh Abduh chose to translate Afghani's poisonous tract from Persian into Arabic added to the calamity.

Mazhar found it inexplicable how Abduh, a true reformer, could have thought so highly of Afghani, or even how Afghani could even now still be considered a great reformer. The man had been a catastrophe for Muslim reform. He had closed Muslim eyes to the science of evolution with his mindless calumny of labeling it a destroyer of morals and civilization. How could the study of evolution destroy morals and civilization? How could Afghani's flimsy and confused *Refutation* stand as a defense of truth against a century and a half of meticulously detailed study in anatomy, biology, geology and paleontology by a multitude of scientists in Germany, France, Holland, England and Italy?[74] And even though it was true that some western scientists still rejected Darwin, they at least knew the principal of the theory they were rejecting. Muslim religious leaders rejected evolution without having the slightest idea of what they were rejecting. They rejected it because they were told it disagreed with scripture.

Mazhar finds the religious fanatics in the West no different. Communities exist in America that agree with their Muslim counterparts in forbidding evolution from being taught in the schools or discussed openly and fairly on the merits of the paleontological evidence. Some states in America have criminalized the teaching of evolution. Our ulema would do the same if anyone dared teach it. Evolution is not the enemy of civilization; the true enemies are the defenders of "mythic fantasy" in Islam and Christianity, those who place the literalist reading of the scriptural story of creation over science. Afghani's perverted depiction of serious science was an act of intellectual prostitution that pandered to the weak and ignorant who were being badly misled. Shaykh Abduh's calling Afghani's *Refutation* brilliant was an intellectual crime, as destructive to civilization as his translation of it from Persian into Arabic.

Mazhar was sure that the malignant atmosphere Afghani and his acolytes produced had set Muslim chances of experiencing a scientific awakening back a generation or more:

> Just as those great critical thinkers such as ibn Khaldun who appeared periodically in the Islamic past were swallowed up, digested and forgotten . . . leaving no successors and snuffing out any chance for the birth of a critical tradition, so also are they now swallowed up and silenced, as if they had never been.[75]

In fact, Mazhar goes on, the fame ibn Khaldun enjoyed today as a critical philosopher of history was owing to the West's discovery and appreciation of him. As far as the Arabs were concerned, ibn Khaldun could have been Italian. Critical analysis and extensive thematic narrative were not valued in Arabic historiography or literature. History was simply facts strung together in relation to time without any underlying unity of relationships or integrated themes to give them meaning beyond themselves as isolated incidents. Arab histories were not histories but chronicles, good only as sources for history, poetry or literature. The only unity they had were the pages they were written on and the glue and string of the binding that held the pages together.[76] If Arabs were to read ibn Khaldun's philosophy of history seriously they would understand that the source of their weakness is their lack of social solidarity, 'asabiyya. Arabs exist divided in tribes and rival factions. Their weakness makes them irrationally defensive, which becomes self-destructive. One of the sorry manifestations of this is that Arabs go all out to defend their religion in fear it will be blamed for their sorry condition. They do not see that the religion does not need defending. A religion succeeds or fails by the moral excellence or failure of its followers. Muslim backwardness goes back to moral weakness, which leads to social fragmentation. As ibn Khaldun said, a strong moral sense is the tie that binds individuals. In other words, moral character makes the religion, not religion the moral character.

> Neither materialism nor religion can alter the moral strength and civil virtue of a society. It is a civilization's general principles of breeding, character and humanist spirit that plant the seeds of strong morals and character.[77]

Mazhar's jeremiads joined the chorus of reformers lamenting the little progress that had been made in creating a scientific culture and ameliorating the ills of society after a century of trying. The relative optimism of the 1870s had by the 1920s soured to a general pessimism damping the social voice to a cry of despair. Mazhar accuses the Arabs of having failed to manifest their "spirit." They were stuck somewhere between the theological-metaphysical and positivist-scientific stages of civilization, lost in a fog, blankly squinting at the world passing them by. They had been stuck there for a thousand years. The "Awakening" that Arab intellectuals wrote so proudly of was a lie. After a century of reform and education Egypt and the Arabs were still spectators sitting passively on the sidelines of world civilization and political power. In any realistic assessment of the Arab condition, science was non-existent. There were no researchers, no scientific institutes or societies, only scientifically educated people in search of a role:

> With all the fine physicians in Egypt there is not one medical research institute, not one doctor devoted to medical science . . . We never ever consider forming an institute for research. We never ever consider the importance of science and research institutes as foundations of civilization. Egyptians lack the seriousness and gravity of character that scientific work requires. We the Arabs lack the intellectual disposition, the cultural orientation and historical sense for mastering the scientific thinking it takes to comprehend the relationships that make a tradition of science. Hence, Egyptians study science without adding anything to it . . . We don't study the relationships between scientific thought and other fields of thought, nor recognize the effect of science on the history of 18th and 19th century intellectual development which produced the 20th century's intellectual triumphs, a scientific achievement whose roots stretch back over 25 centuries . . .
>
> Orders from above cannot produce science. Nor is it just the wealth or freedom of a society that produces scientific interest and activity, it is the mental attitude of a society in its regard to natural knowledge. Even while being torn apart in the 15th century, Italy continued to be scientifically productive because of the prevailing freedom of mind, or rather of mind in the act of freeing itself, since the struggle for intellectual freedom, like science, is a continuous and endless process.[78]

Writing in 1930, Mazhar saw Muslim society as far away as ever from that hypothetical third and last advance up the ladder to the ultimate triumphant stage of civilization, where critical reason, analysis and scientific advance are enshrined. How could it be reached? For every rung upward, the ladder grew taller: scientists in the West went on advancing, uncovering fossils from across the geological ages, making progress in all fields of science, none of which found much space in the Muslim mind. If the theory of evolution was not rejected, it was frozen out in the same deafening silence that had met his, Mazhar's, belated translation of Darwin's *Origin of Species*.[79] Islam and the Arabs were condemned to dwell in the deadening cave of their dark world. What better proof of this darkness than Shaykh Rashid Rida's condemnation in his *al-Manar* periodical of the "Egyptian

Society for Scientific Culture" that was formed at the end of the 1920s to promote scientific interest. Shaykh Rida's attack was on the basis that some of the society's founders were "heretics and corrupters of religion." What in the world, Mazhar asks in his article answering Rida, did religious belief have to do with members of a scientific society? It was science, not religion, under discussion!

There was cause for despair. Here was Rashid Rida, a reformer calling for science and technology, *'ilm wa 'amal*, holding Japan up as an example, and then as soon as something was done toward that end, out came the call for religious credentials. Mazhar was beside himself. Did the absence of correct religious belief mean that certain inventions of modern technology by non-believers would have to be abandoned? If religious belief, he retorted, were the criteria for true science, then much of science would have to be discarded along with medicine and pharmaceuticals. Edison's light bulb would have to be replaced by lanterns, the printing press by copyists. Since Lister, Pasteur, Edison and Gutenberg were not believers, all their science and inventions would have to be rejected. He tells Shaykh Rida that if he holds religious belief to be the criteria of accepting or rejecting science and technology, then "you had better dress in leaves and animal skins, and throw your turban away since the fabric came from Europe!"

Mazhar was the first Egyptian, if not one of the very first Muslims, to speak with such passion and honesty about the logical absurdities of religious certification of science and technology.

Notes

1 abu al-Majd al Isfahani, *Naqd Falsafat Darwin* (Critique of Darwin's Philosophy), 2 vols, Baghdad, 1914, vol I, p. 120.
2 Isfahani, *Naqd*, vol I, p. 16; Adel Ziyadat, "Muslim Responses to Darwinism," *Western Science in the Arab World: The Impact of Darwinism, 1860–1930*, Palgrave Macmillan, London, 1936, p. 97.
3 Ziydadat, *Muslim Responses*, p. 106.
4 Isfahani, Vol I, p. 136.
5 Vol I, p. 172.
6 Vol I, p. 235.
7 Vol I, pp. 16–21.
8 Vol I, pp. 106–113.
9 Vol I, pp. 8 ff.
10 Vol I, p. 16.
11 Vol I, p. 27.
12 Vol I, p. 21.
13 Vol I, pp. 139–142.
14 Vol I, pp. 40–41.
15 Vol I, p. 43.
16 Vol I, pp. 142–143.
17 Vol I, pp. 81–82.
18 Vol I, pp. 55–59.
19 Vol I, pp. 117–118.
20 Vol I, pp. 59–61.
21 Vol I, pp. 78–80.
22 Richard Owen (1804–1892), a British biologist famous for his work on invertebrates, zoology and comparative anatomy, believed in evolution but for some reason opposed

his friend Darwin's theory of natural selection, though ever respectfully and politely so as not to harm the friendship.
23 Vol I, pp. 149–152. Isfahani's conviction that the female form proved God's guiding hand in evolution received support some 30 years later when the sultan of Morocco asserted that the movie star Rhonda Fleming's body was "tangible evidence of the existence of God."
24 Vol I, p. 163.
25 Vol I, pp. 184–185.
26 Vol I, pp. 188–190.
27 Vol I, p. 193.
28 Vol I, p. 185.
29 Vol I, p. 194.
30 Vol I, p. 199.
31 Mustafa Hasanayn Mansuri, *Tarikh al-Madhahib al-Ishtirakiyyn* (History of Socialist Movements), Cairo, 1914.
32 *Muqtataf*, vol 50 (April 1916), p. 393.
33 Anwar al-Jundi, *Muhammad Farid Wajdi, Ra'id al-Tawfiq Bayn al-'ilm wa'l – Din* (Pioneer in the Agreement Between Science and Religion), al-Hayah al-Misriyya al-'Ammah li'l Kitab, Cairo, 1974.
34 Wajdi, *Madaniyya wa'l Islam*, Cairo, 1899, pp. 30, 40, 41, 64, 68, 69, 86.
35 Marwa Elshakry, *Darwin's Legacies in the Arab East: Science, Religion and Politics, 1870–1914*, Princeton PhD dissertation, 2003, p. 243.
36 Jundi, *Muhammad Farid Wajdi*, p. 28.
37 *Da'irat al-Ma'arif fi qarn al-'Ishrin* (Encyclopedia for the Twentieth Century), edited by M.F. Wajdi, al-Hayat al-Misriyya al-'Ammah li'l Kitab, Cairo, Vol I, pp. 181–196.
38 *Da'irat al Ma'arif*, edited by M.F. Wajdi, Cairo, Vol I, p. 192.
39 *Da'irat al-Ma'arif*, edited by M.F. Wajdi, Cairo, Vol I, p. 191.
40 This in Wajdi's *Fusul min Sirat al-Rusul*, Cairo, 1997, pp. 354–359.
41 W.C. Smith, *Islam in Modern History*, Princeton University Press, Princeton, NJ, 1957, p. 122; *Majallat al-Azhar*, IX, p. 419.
42 W.C. Smith, *Islam in Modern History*, p. 148.
43 "How Do We Preserve Religion in This Age?" *Majallat al-Azhar*, Azhar Press, Cairo, vol XIII (1942), pp. 12–19.
44 Muhammad al-Ghamrawi, "al-'Ilm wa'l Din" (Science and Religion), Majallat al-Azhar, Azhar Press, Cairo, vol VIII (1937), pp. 59–67. This is the first chapter of a book Ghamrawi wrote called *Fi Sunan Allah al-Kawniyya* (*On God's Cosmic Laws*).
45 Adel Ziyadat, *Muslim Responses*, pp. 38–48; Perlman, "The Education of Salama Musa," *Middle East Affairs* (August/September 1951); Yusuf Sarkis, *Dictionnaire de Biographie Arabe*, vol 2, Cairo, 1928, p. 1038.
46 Salama Musa, *Nazariyya al-Tatawur w'al-Asl al-Insan* (The Theory of Development and the Origin of Man), Cairo, 1927.
47 Pere Louis Chiekho, *al-Mashriq*, Beirut, vol 25 (1927), p. 907.
48 Salama Musa, *al-Insan qummat al-tatawwur* (Man, Summit of Evolutionary Development), Cairo, 1961, p. 27.
49 Salama Musa, *al-Insan*, p. 28.
50 H.A.R. Gibb, "Studies in Contemporary Arabic Literature," *Bulletin d'etudes Orientales*, Damascus, vol II, 1931, p. 313.
51 Salama Musa, *al-Yowm wa'l Ghad* (Today and Tomorrow), Cairo, 1927, p. 61.
52 Taha Husayn, *Fi'l Adab al-Jahiliyya* (Dar al-Ma'arif, 17th printing), Cairo, 1927, p. 57. Taha Husayn was condemned by al-Azhar for his analysis of pre-Islamic Arabic poetry to prove that most of the poetry was written during early Islamic times for the political purpose of advancing the position of certain tribes in the expanding enterprise of Arab Islam. Bending to religious authority as always, Egypt's secular government upheld al-Azhar's condemnation and forced the author to remove the offending passages.

53 Isma'il Mazhar, *Malqa al-Sabil fi Madhhab al-Nushu' W'al Irtiqa*, Cairo, 1926, p. 5; Ibrahim A. Ibrahim, "Isma'il Mazhar and Husayn Fawzi: Two Muslim 'Radical' Westernizers," *Middle East Studies*, vol 9, issue 1, 1973, p. 35–41.
54 A child prodigy, he received his baccalaureate at 16 and studied mathematics at the then-recently founded Teacher's College. The Egyptian Ministry of Education sponsored his graduate-education in physics and mathematics at the University of Nottingham. He received his doctorate in 1923 from King's College London in the shortest possible time permissible according to the regulations there. In 1924 Musharrafa was awarded the degree of Doctor of Science, the first Egyptian and the 11th scientist in the entire world to obtain such a degree.
55 Ismail Mazhar, *'Usur*, vol 4 (Cairo, 1929), pp. 419–432.
56 Ismail Mazhar, *Malqa al-Sabil fi Madhhab al-Nushu wa'l Irtiqa'*, Cairo, 1926, p. 128.
57 Ismail Mazhar, *Malqa al-Sabil*, pp. 128–130.
58 Ismail Mazhar, *Malqa al-Sabil*, pp. 130–141.
59 Ismail Mazhar, *Al-'Usur*, vol 7 (1930), pp. 37–41.
60 *Muqtataf*, vol 68 (1926), pp. 140–149; vol 69 (1927), p. 75.
61 H.A.R. Gibb, *Modern Trends in Islam*, p. 54; Muhammad Abduh Jeffrey, "The Suppressed Quran Commentary of Muhammad abu Zaid," *Der Islam*, vol 20, 1932, pp. 301–308.
62 J.J. Jansen, *The Interpretation of the Koran in Modern Egypt*, Brill, Leiden, 1980.
63 Najm Bezirgan, "*Darwin in the Islamic World*," in *The Comparative Reception of Darwinism*, Thomas Glick, (ed.), University of Chicago Press, 1988, p. 380.
64 *Muqtataf*, vol 47 (May 1922), p. 445.
65 "In a largely metaphorical sense," in Darwin's words: *Origins of Species*, Modern Library, New York, 1936, p. 52.
66 *Muqtataf* (July 1923), pp. 60–62.
67 *Muqtataf*, vol 68 (1926), pp. 137–145.
68 *Muqtataf*, vol 68 (1926), pp. 137–145. On a less elevated if more realistic level, there was little reason for a Westernized Egyptian writer living in Cairo or Alexandria between 1925 and 1950 not to believe that his society would inevitably become thoroughly secular, with science becoming increasingly more important and religion finding some accommodating niche in society commensurate to the new conditions, as it was in France and England. Republican Turkey was the model other Muslim countries would follow. So might it have appeared at the end of World War II, but unseen at the time was something that would have been regarded by Arabs as beyond the realm of all possibility: an American-led neo-imperialist resurgence in the Arab and Muslim world that from the early 1950s on would manufacture a Cold War and, after 1967, unleash Islamic political movements with a violence: Before 1950, even up until 1967, secularization defined the future, and there seemed little reason not to believe it.
69 Ismail Mazhar, *Malqa al-Sabil*, pp. 14–18.
70 By spirit Mazhar means the abstract power of mind that discovers relationships in the material universe, a power derived from divine *Hikmah*, wisdom, which he defines as the universal insight that integrates the moral and material realms of reality, an idea formulated in Qusta ibn Luqa's *On the Difference Between the Soul and the Spirit* that goes back to early Muslim philosophy.
71 *Malqa*, pp. 40–48.
72 *Malqa*, pp. 32–33.
73 *Malqa*, p. 110.
74 *Malqa*, p. 95.
75 *Malqa*, pp. 139, 195.
76 *Malqa*, p. 141.
77 *Malqa*, p. 161.
78 Taha Husayn was at the time making the same criticisms: *Fi'l Adab al-Jahiliyya*, pp. 16, 58.
79 *'Usur*, vol 7 (May 1930), pp. 61–67.

14 Inverse appropriation
Science by Quran

Though little in the way of real science was being done in any Muslim society, reformist writers poured out rivers of ink in explanation of why science was necessary and why it should be studied and subsidized. Not only did the Quran and Hadith encourage science, the holy sources demanded it. Science and Islam were a unity. The Quran was scientific, and science was Quranic. Science and Islam were not exactly the same, but they were mutually supportive, or at least they were non-contradictory in their separate realms of spiritual truth and experience. They coexisted in peace and harmony. Where the word of scripture intersected with the fact of science, it was a secure crossing. Yet all the declarations in the world by ulema and secularists in support of these claims, written and oral, in books, articles, newspapers, lectures and sermons, failed to give wings to the bird of knowledge. Words without actions failed to fly. The wings of promise given by all those declarations and proofs of a religion whose ethos was scientific were clipped by the lack of adequate social support. The lack of private and public investment in schools, books and equipment, and of preparing competent teachers and rewarding them sufficiently in pay and prestige for them to maintain a positive attitude in the importance of their professions, made the words of the reformers ring hollow.

Religious scholars remained religious scholars instead of becoming the scientists their holy book purportedly commanded them to be, and secular governments remained governments failing to plan or fund an integrated system of science-based education and research institutes. That no Muslim government bothered to send a delegation to discover the secret of Japan's success is indicative of how disinclined government was to set aside funds to invest in a generation that decades later would have relieved the state of the costly burden of purchasing industrial plants and technological expertise from the West. For government, it was the quick and easy fix of buying off-the-shelf packages from western industries, with no regard to long-term expense or development of an indigenous techno-scientific infrastructure. As the editors of *Muqtataf*, *Manar* and *'Usur* bitterly lamented, Middle Easterners had become accustomed to sitting on the sidelines watching the world pass them by. Reformers were constricted to writing on science in a society without scientists or a scientific tradition. They wrote in a vacuum, pouring out words and arguments that lacked the social energy that would have otherwise been generated had the words come from practicing scientists. Only by creative action could a civilization claim science as its own. Though reformers and apologists constantly argued that western science sprang from Islam and was thus essentially Islamic, science remained an alien body, existing at the margin, unfed, starved of substance. No practice of it emerged to make it Islamic and give substance to the words and arguments of the reformers and apologists who claimed it as their legitimate cultural heritage. Five generations of reform had accomplished little more than some scientific translations, a few popular scientific journals and introductory courses in Cairo's King Fuad University.

The absence of shaykhs with scientific credentials meant that the religious argument that some few of them made for science had to be pitched by men who knew little or nothing of science but much about scholastic theology. Consequently, the shaykhs, who were as divided as their society on the issues of modernization, argued their case for or against science in the manner of medieval dialecticians in search of logical contradictions in a system of knowledge they perceived to be a threat to religion. Those of them who argued for science were just as much spectators as were the government and society they were hoping to convince. There were no participants. Up until the 1930s, when a trickle of Arab students began returning home with doctorates in chemistry and physics from France and England, the closest any Middle Easterners came to an active involvement in science were the handful of Christians and Muslims in Lebanon and Egypt who only wrote about it. They were writers who respected science, but were not students of it. They were non-participating cheerleaders. A living and growing embryo of science failed to be conceived in society because of the lack of learned and respected scientists among the faithful. The Muslim community was without the living examples needed to give substance to argument. Muslims of religious standing armed with the credentials of scientific degrees, publications and international recognition had yet to be born. Such models would come late in the last half of the century, but so rare were they, and so absent since it was only in the West where they could continue their research, that they may as well not have existed as far as their own societies were concerned.

Apropos to this Muslim lack of models, it will be recalled that in the Latin West, from roughly 1100 to 1400, the greatest natural philosophers were men of the church who in the beginning sought Arab texts for medicine, astronomy and most urgently the logic of Aristotle in order to compound a convincing theology. Some of these churchmen pursued science for itself. Grown in the comforting angelic womb of the church, the fetus of science was given a sound religious basis in "Intelligent Design," until which time the baby would be brought to term and delivered into the harsh light of secularism, umbilically severed from its erstwhile nurturing Mother Church. Science in early and medieval Muslim civilization had no such comforting mother giving legitimacy to its, as it were, foreign born offspring. So that in modern times, with no living embodiments of scientific greatness, the dialogue was left mired in the medieval verbiage of dialectics and theological constructs so familiar to al-Ghazali and ibn Rushd, whose arguments were constantly being reiterated by their 20th century would-be counterparts.

A young Azhari shaykh could not have become a scientist without leaving Egypt. Before World War II it would have been nearly impossible for anyone to receive a doctoral-level scientific education anywhere in the Middle East. After years of education abroad, the shaykh would return to find himself no longer commanding religious authority. The two who did go to Europe and preached science at home, Tahtawi and Abduh, were not well regarded by their peers within the halls of al-Azhar.

The possibility of producing home-grown scientists had its modest beginning with the founding of an Egyptian University early in the 20th century. The University employed a fair number of highly qualified European professors, Italian, French, German and British, but the courses in chemistry, physics, astronomy, mathematics and biology were introductory. Graduate research did not exist until after mid-century. Graduate study meant going to Europe. In any case, pure science offered few job opportunities. Law and medicine were the great attractions. The British rulers of Egypt, unlike their counterparts in India, did nothing to encourage the study of science. Egypt was not thought to be a legitimate member of the empire and so not worth investing in. Egypt was a sometime thing, an almost accidental acquisition, an imperial burden necessitated by the Suez Canal and India. To the colonial pro-consuls the only Egyptians worth their salt were peasants. An educated Egyptian could only mean trouble. To educate the natives would only produce anti-British nationalists.

Not until late in the 20th century, when relations between Islam and the West had gravely deteriorated and the internal divide in Muslim society had become egregious, if not unbridgeable, did a handful of Indian Muslims, by then called Pakistanis, reach the highest ranks of scientific research and speak out to establish in the cultural mind the religious connection to science.

A somewhat different situation prevailed among the Turks. During the last decades of the 19th century the Ottomans were producing scientists in medicine, physics, chemistry, biology and botany. Three students received doctoral degrees in chemistry. Joseph Zanni, a Christian who studied in Germany under Robert Bunsen, inventor of the Bunsen Burner, received his doctorate as early as 1876. A decade later, two Muslims received theirs, Khalid Edhem at Berne University, who wrote a book on geology and mineralogy, and Mehmet Arif from Halle University, whose dissertation was published in *Annalen der Chemie*.[1] An Ottoman mathematician, Husayn Tawfiq (Tevfik), published a book on linear algebra in English in 1882, which was considered an original contribution. But these successes had come too late in Ottoman times for them to have been multiplied over the decades in creating a bridge to the technological culture of industrial development, ship building and general economic expansion that was required in order to defend against the West.

The Ottomans disappeared in the political debris left after World War I, but even had they remained neutral and survived the war, there is little in the last decades of Ottoman history or early history of the Turkish Republic to suggest the Turks would have zealously taken up science and technology and amazed the world, as the Japanese did in the 19th century, and gone on to join the scientific club. Still technologically challenged, the Turkish government finds itself forced to sell its water in exchange for imported Israeli technology. Nor are the modern Turks without their secular-religious culture war, with all the same bizarre ramifications that are found among their equally insecure Arab and Pakistani brethren battling over Darwin with the same feverish avowals that Islam is science and more. The world still awaits the first Turkish Nobel winner to join Pakistan's Muhammad Abdus Salam and Egypt's Ahmad Zewail. Though in truth, the two Nobels are less local than western products.

As the gap between Islam and the West has widened in step with the internal separation between the secular and traditional division in society, the claims that Islam is scientific have become more strident. "Scientific Interpretation," and its even more radical spin-off, "Islamic Science," become more and more an exercise in fantasy, where the appropriation of science becomes an "inverse appropriation" in that science is simply claimed to be Islamic and an essential element of the religion. The claim is passed off as an inescapable fact proven by the scientific knowledge found in the Quran. The exercise begins with certain words occurring in the Quran, such as moon, sun, stars, sky, heavens, lightning, thunder, rain, clouds, wind, earthquake, mountains, motion, etc. These are stretched to comprehend the whole of modern physics, astronomy, meteorology, chemistry, geology, paleontology, thermodynamics and electromagnetism. "Eat, drink, but not to excess" (Sura 7, verse 29–31) was a miraculous revelation in the early seventh century of the collective corpus of 20th century medicine. The modernist Pakistani scholar Mawdudi who claimed "Sun, Moon and stars are . . . all Muslims" went beyond the Quran in equating Islam to astronomy and astrophysics.[2] Before the end of the century verses would be found revealing relativity, quantum mechanics, black holes, the Big Bang, high energy physics, DNA, spectroscopy and space travel.

Fathullah Gulen, modern Turkey's evangelist equivalent of Billy Graham, exposits true Islam's rationality and modernity and the Quran's science-based revelations where the jinn, invisible beings in the material world, are likely candidates as the cause of mental diseases such as schizophrenia or epilepsy, or of cancer:

> When science finally accepts the existence of the metaphysical realm and the influence of metaphysical forces, its practitioners will be able to remove many obstructions and to make far greater advances and fewer mistakes.[3]

Gulen and the large public he addresses believe Islam can teach how the jinn can be used as sources of energy, space study and long distance communication. Because the jinn can live a thousand years, they can be a source for establishing historical facts. Gulen became so popular in the 1990s that the Turkish military, praetorian guard of Kemalist secularism, presently having been elbowed to the shadowed margins of power by religionist president Erdogan, had him exiled, but his popular following remained. Gulen, at the moment hibernating in the Pocono Mountains of Pennsylvania, has legions of counterparts across the Muslim world, where governments, rather than exiling, collude in popularizing them and their claims of Islamic Science.

When the leading proponent of Scientific Interpretation in Egypt, Tantawi Jawhar (1862–1940), was criticized by his fellow Azharites for wringing so much out of so little, and thereby misrepresenting the Quran in his grand 26-volume commentary, *al-Jawahir fi Tafsir al-Quran al-Karim* (*Gems of Quranic Interpretation*), and his *al-Quran wa'l Ulum al-'Asriyya* (*The Quran and the Contemporary Sciences*), Jawhar responded, to the anger and embarrassment of his religious critics, that he was doing no more in his Quranic commentary than what legists in the early centuries of Islam did in formulating a comprehensive system of holy Shari'a law from the handful of moral exhortations and legal prescriptions found in the Quran. Why could not the same be done a thousand years later for a system of celestial mechanics? Jawhar's historically credible defense failed to prevent his commentary from being prohibited in the then recently Wahhabi-established Saudi Kingdom in Arabia. Today it is otherwise. Saudi Arabia has become one of the great factories of Scientific Interpretation and funders of books and congresses promoting an "Islamic Science." Tantawi Jawhar has gone from marginal to mainstream.

Tantawi Jawhar

Initiated by the French-educated Syrian Christian Fransis Marrash and the Egyptian physician Iskandarani, and given religious credibility by Shaykhs Jisr, Abduh and Rida, Scientific Interpretation was slipping into mainstream practice by the early 20th century. The works of Shaykh Tantawi Jawhar and his secular contemporary Muhammad Farid Wajdi (1875–1940) led the way. Jawhar's contribution was the most remarkable. Like so many of his Egyptian reformist forerunners in the ulema, he was a poor farm boy whose education began in a primitive village Quranic school. He continued at al-Azhar and then capped his education by years of self-instruction in the modern sciences through reading whatever was available in Arabic.

Jawhar never once left Egypt during his whole life. He was 15 when he began his religious studies at al-Azhar, where he remained 12 years, 1877 to 1889, the last few as a teacher. As a student he was selected to study at Ali Mubarak's *Dar al-Ulum*, a successful case in point for what the school was designed to accomplish: marrying science to religion by producing shaykhs who not only appreciated the importance of science but knew something of it and could counter those shaykhs who were hostile to it out of fear and ignorance. Rather than remaining at al-Azhar or *Dar al-Ulum*, Jawhar chose to teach in a secondary school where he thought he might be effective in arousing young minds to the wonders of nature before they had hardened in the iron mold of tradition's obeisance to unquestioned authority. Years later he was to write that it was while a student and teacher at *Dar al-Ulum* he first conceived of his grand scientific commentary. The purpose of his grand undertaking that took 26 hefty volumes to express was of course to inspire the young generation of Muslims to study science. He saw that very few Egyptian intellectuals knew much about it and that it was almost totally ignored, as important as it was. And so, to inspire students to take on the physical sciences he would shine the divine light of the Quran upon them: the Quran that itself, when read and uderstood correctly, illuminated the truths of the sciences.

The 26-volume modernist interpretation of the Quran is most extraordinary in its passion for science and nature. Jawhar's descriptions of nature are ecstatic. They express a lyrical intoxication for nature and nature's processes. His embrace of nature borders on mystical pantheism. Shaykh Tantawi Jawhar's expansive love of nature and mystical inebriation by it find no antecedents in modern Muslim religious literature. Love of natural beauty, he writes, is a lens through which man's love traverses to focus on the Creator, making of Islam a religion based on a love effulgent with the beauty of nature. Love runs through the universe. It is the cosmic force that drives hydrogen and oxygen to unite to form water, sodium and chlorine to form common salt, and plants and animals to reproduce. "God's greatness fills all existence with love and beauty. The more one understands the beauty of nature, the closer one comes to God."[4] The study of nature is the study of God.[5] The key to the Quran is science, the deeper the understanding of the one, the deeper the understanding of the other.[6] Nature, like the Quran, is a revelation whose complexity of design and elegant simplicity of expression, and above all whose beauty and inherent wisdom, point to God.

Two qiblas define the polar axis of Jawhar's universe: the Ka'ba in Mecca is the moral one toward which the believer faces in prayer; the second is nature, the metaphorical direction the believer faces in one's reflection of the manifold beauty of God's creation, its creatures, its flowers, stars, trees, seas and mountains.[7] Nature is a religious experience, an unceasing prayer. Those whose ears are open hear and understand. Nature more than affirms the existence of a Creator. It transports the contemplative observer to the Creator's mind, the intensity of the divine experience being in measure to one's appreciation and understanding of nature. This comes with study. Nothing is received from what is ignored. The believer who ignores nature ignores as well the Quran's repeated references to nature's beauty, wisdom and power, and the Quran's injunction to observe and study it.[8]

Deviating from Shaykh Abduh's thought, Jawhar claimed that science and divine truth did not exist in separate realms of matter and spirit. Spirit was diffused in matter. He found proof of this in places that should have shocked believing Muslims. Spiritualism and mesmerism proved that the divorce between the physical world and the one beyond was false. However heretical the source, if it served to seal the continuum of physical and spiritual reality, Tantawi snapped it up. Even stories attributed to English officers about holy men in India whose contact with the spiritual world enabled them to write poems and thoughts that were in the minds of those around them, even though the holy men didn't know the language of the person thinking them, were taken as valid evidence. A spiritual force moved the hands of the holy men, conjoining the material and the divine. Jawhar's explanation of this – the minds of the English officers flowing into those of the holy men by the action of enveloping magnetic fields – sounds like science fiction. Encoded in the fields was the information required to move the hands in order to shape the letters of the words that were being thought. Magnetism was proof of the spiritual world. What appeared to be miraculous was really supraphysical scientific action, a twilight zone where the physical world of magnetic fields folded into the realm of the spiritual.

Jawhar's experience with science reaffirmed his belief without fundamentally changing his world outlook. He simply read science into the Quran without questioning or examining the holy sources in the light of modern knowledge and conditions, as Abduh had urged, and so remained as true to tradition and the rural roots of his ancestral faith as had Shaykh Tahtawi a century earlier. Nature was a blessing full of wonder, but it was the gift of the miraculous Quran that was God's special blessing to mankind, since it contained not only the secrets of nature and knowledge of this world but the mysteries of the next as well.

Published at two volumes a year between 1923 and 1935, with references to Shakespeare, Bacon, Voltaire, Rousseau, Tolstoy, Gandhi, Einstein and a legion of other great scientists and thinkers, the commentary is a mélange of scientific history and biography interspersed with fulsome descriptions of the wonders of nature, theological reinterpretations, criticisms of the injustice and oppression of Muslim government and the irresponsible rich who do nothing for Muslim society, the deadening effect of Quranic memorization that passes for primary education and other long digressions that are labeled as such. The work as a whole is 90 percent Scientific Interpretation in which science reveals the wonders of nature and the Quran, and wields the sword of jihad.

Tantawi Jawhar and Rashid Rida were the first speakers for Islam in modern times to interpret jihad as a struggle of believers to achieve science. The holy war was to be fought not by armies with swords but scientists with thoughts. Only when armed with science could Islam complete its mission of bringing true religion to the whole world as God's promised blessing. Tantawi Jawhar claimed success was inevitable: "Islam will be completely triumphant according to God's plan."[9] But God's plan had for the moment taken a bad turn. Mental laziness and lack of interest in science allowed the Franks to leave Muslims in the dust of a past age. Young Muslims had now to be encouraged to study science, first in order for them to reach Europe's level, then to fulfill God's plan through the promise of Islam. Jawhar intended his commentary to open their eyes, influence their minds and get them going.[10] Nothing amazed him more, he writes, speaking for every Muslim who ever reflected on the contemporary condition of Muslim society in regard to science and the West, "than a people whose religion is based on God's wisdom being surpassed by a people like the Franks!"[11]

The love and beauty of nature that Jawhar described in such detail and claimed to be divine qualities running through the universe were meant to be inspirational, leading men to God. All goodness, joy and beauty originated in God and flowed through nature, binding man, God and nature in an indissoluble bond. But then from where did evil, hate and suffering originate? These also originated from God, the Creator of all things, good and bad. But how could God who is all good give birth to evil? The old question of medieval scholasticism was resolved by Jawhar in his own way. Evil coming from good and good from evil were transitional phases. Even evil had a transitional good. World War I with all its evils, ugliness and suffering produced advances in aviation and medicine. The European occupation of Arab lands he likened to a painful surgical operation, evil in every way at the present, "but which will, only God knows how, turn to future good."

A student of Abduh, Jawhar was a thinker who in spite of his adherence to orthodoxy was otherwise free enough of tradition to break with several cherished tenets of Muslim belief, any one of which would carry grave consequences were a shaykh to pronounce it today. The story of the apple of the Tree of Knowledge in the Garden of Eden was all wrong because God could not possibly have willed something that went so directly against Islam as the forbidding of knowledge. Other startling breaks with tradition for a shaykh to make were his stand on the required five daily prayers and the pilgrimage. These, according to Jawhar, were not incumbent on Muslims. Prayers should not be performed in the rigid formalism of tradition since the form had become more important than the substance of prayer. The pilgrimage and certain other prescribed acts should not have to be necessary since the time they required put limits on a believer's productive activity. Such prescriptions were limiting in that the believer came to accept that following them was all that was required and no more. But Muslims can do more for the general interest of the community and should be free to act as they see fit in order to reach their fullest potential. To limit activity by legislating a prescription of social behavior into holy law was not only wrong, it was sinful.[12]

The amount of time and effort Muslim scholars poured into the study of law and jurisprudence was also wrong because of its wastefulness. The subjects were given too much importance and drained away too much mental energy that would be better used in the service of advancing civilization. Instead of getting lost in the trifling details of legal formalism that benefits or enlightens no one, scholars could go into other things that would bring direct benefit to the community. One of these beneficial endeavors would be rethinking the holy law in order to save substance from being sacrificed to form. The law prescribed that before prayer a believer had to wash up to the elbows. Up to the elbows was not enough of a washing. People of civilized societies washed themselves beyond the elbows. Taking a note from Freud, Jawhar put cleanliness and science as the measures of high civilization.

Islam had once been the most advanced of all civilizations in science, until the corrupted ulema caused its decline in middle Abbasid times. Even before that, in fact as early as the assassination of the Caliph Uthman and the subsequent civil wars that fragmented the community, when Islam was still in its bloom of vigorous youth, religious and political leaders were corrupted. Corruption, a sign of greed and ignorance, destroyed the conditions that science needed to survive. The ulema, a timorous child of corruption and ignorance conceived in the bed of small minded self-interest, would have to be re-educated in order to make science once again a part of the faith and the community. Science had to be taught in al-Azhar side by side with religion. Science was a religious discipline and had to be desired "as passionately as people desired children and women lusted for gold." Science education began with the youth. Girls too should be educated. Education had to become imaginative and creative for the minds of children to be opened, rather than closed by drilling obedience and custom into them. Infants should be allowed to play freely to develop their minds. Education should not be negative. Minds should not be stuffed and frozen with commandments against things that are forbidden. Positive education engenders love for the subject.

Jawhar only briefly touched on evolution. He thought Darwin and Huxley had taken science in a reverse direction, yet was non-commital about accepting or rejecting evolution and deplored Darwin's being branded an atheist by those who knew nothing of his ideas. He diminished the importance of Darwin by claiming that the Arabs back in Abbasid times had developed more advanced theories on evolution. This could be seen as a backhanded acceptance of natural selection, but what little Jawhar wrote on the subject shows his knowledge to have been limited to a few erroneous catch phrases. Darwin's "survival of the fittest" extolled aggression and legitimized the domination and extermination of the weak by the strong into a pseudo-scientific principle. It denied the possibility of peaceful coexistence. This was what led to the Great War and the cynical disregard of agreements made between allies at the end of it.[13] Like Afghani, he believed natural selection meant that man was descended from a monkey, though he expressed the misconception without the mindless comic sarcasm of some critics of Darwin. Jawhar's ignorance of the subject would appear to have been willful since Ismail Mazhar had translated the most essential sections of Darwin's *Origin of Species* a few years before Jawhar began his commentary.

The voluminous commentary brought Shaykh Jawhar little fame in Egypt. European scholars showed more interest in it than did his compatriots and coreligionists. The French scholar Carra de Vaux referred to the commentary as an example of modern Scientific Interpretation in his article on *tafsir* in the first edition of *The Encyclopedia of Islam*. Another French scholar, Jomier, who wrote a critique on the commentary, summed up the shaykh's modest place in modern Egyptian religious thought during the early decades following Abduh's death: "If he broke windows of his prison to have a breath of fresh air, he only saw what he was able to see from behind the bars. He opened his eyes, and even that was a lot."[14]

It was only his own eyes he opened. Tantawi's commentary failed to inspire. While the majority of religious scholars feared it sacrificed the divine message on the altar of modern science, secularist scholars were embarrassed by it. Also, the French scholarly attention given him may possibly have poisoned his reputation with the ulema, but there was more than enough questionable theology in his grand commentary to cast him into the shadows of possible heresy. Secular reformers were especially put off by his acceptance of spiritualism and took little interest in him or his ideas. The opening of Egypt's first national university with its faculty of modern science gave the secularists far more to celebrate than an Azharite's commentary interpreting the Quran scientifically.

Undaunted by being neglected, Jawhar harbored an elevated view of himself and his literary output, which, in addition to his monumental commentary, amounted to more than 20 books on science, philosophy and religion, and as many articles. In fact, so highly did he regard his contribution that in 1939 he requested the Minister of Education to support his nomination as a candidate for the Nobel Prize for literature. The minister thought wisely to ignore the request, but with Jawhar's persistent urging the minister at last acted on it. The faculty of the sciences of King Fuad University reviewed seven of Jawhar's works and reluctantly communicated their support to the Nobel Committee. However, the ambitious shaykh died months later, and, with a collective sigh of relief from the minister and the science faculty, the matter was left quietly to follow Jawhar to the grave.

Tantawi Jawhar lacked the influence and following that Abduh and Rida had at the apogee of their careers. He held no high government office and possessed no journal to propagate his ideas. Considered a reformist thinker of no particular stature or originality, he has been ignored by scholars of Arab intellectual history, though he did imaginatively mine the Quran for all it was worth in hidden gems of science. When Scientific Interpretation became popular later in the century, his huge commentary became a handy thesaurus for generations of eager interpreters.

The ambiguity that Tantawi left hanging over the religious acceptability of Darwin was answered by his contemporary, Muhammad Farid Wajdi, who was a less effusive follower of Jawhar's brand of Scientific Interpretation. Though not a shaykh or even a graduate of al-Azhar, in fact having written little on religion and earning no credentials that would confer any pedigree of religious learning upon him, Wajdi enjoyed far more prestige, and won far more respect, among the Azharite leadership as an authority on science and religion than Shaykh Jawhar was ever awarded for all his literary output. The nationalist government during the reign of King Faruk thought highly enough of Wajdi to name a square in Cairo in his honor. In that respect, Tantawi Jawhar's oblivion exceeds even his minimal legacy in the annals of religious reform. But as a master craftsperson in the delusional constructions of "Scientific Interpretation" he made himself his own public square, an architectural embarrassment at the time but to become a half century later a highly regarded treasure.

Islamization of science

A world of difference separates Scientific Interpretation, or the Islamization of science, from its offspring, "Islamic Science." Scientific Interpretation reads science into the Quran either to justify science and promote its study to Muslims as part of a larger program of westernized reforms or else to demonstrate how superior the Quran is to modern knowledge in order to relieve Muslims of the necessity of having to adopt anything from the West, other than its technology, of course. This latter has led to what is called "Islamic Science." Scientific Interpretation accepts what is normally considered to be science. Islamic Science rejects modern science as being western, secular, alien and spiritually destructive, much in the same way self-appointed theologians of the American religious right and their acolytes reject scientific evolution and in its place put Creationism or, going back to Averroes and Aquinas, Intelligent Design.

Islamic Science calls for the rejection of modern secular science in order to reframe a spiritual and ethical science to be extracted from the Quran. Some advocates go so far as to claim western science to be an invidious imperialist conspiracy designed to destroy Muslim belief by spreading atheism. To defend Islamic belief from this subversive attack, they would expunge the western knowledge, values, life styles, entertainments and institutions that secular reformers have imported into, or western colonial powers have imposed upon, Muslim societies over the last two centuries. In their denunciation of western science they echo the more radical brand of traditionalist ulema who a millennium earlier railed against Muslim scientists and philosophers for clinging to the dangerous rational imports that had been translated from Greek into Arabic.

The modern version proclaims to believe that adherence to the holy sources of Islam (Quran, Hadith, Shari'a) can provide the science and the institutions – political, economic, legislative and judicial – that are needed to make Muslims the world masters they once were. It finds its activist counterpart in the political and paramilitary movements committed to overthrowing secular governments and restoring the Shari'a as the law of the land. Born in anger and with a confounding inability to alter the political malaise of weak governments that to save themselves they abjectly followed policies that served western interests, the proponents of Islamic Science arose largely in the 1980s as the rift between the Muslim world and the West deepened. At the top of the lengthening list of grievances were Israel's accelerated colonization of the West Bank and repeated invasions of Lebanon and Gaza, American support of corrupt and oppressive Muslim rulers and the American-led destruction of Iraq beginning in the early 1990s. The list continues. Muslim animosity mounts daily with each instance of collateral damage caused by American drones in Yemen, Afghanistan and Pakistan.

Having begun with a small radical minority wanting to drive out everything western, this hostility has now spread like a raging virus through the ranks of Muslim society, particularly in countries whose governments actively or passively accommodate themselves with western policies.

Though the hostility can be understood psychologically, its effect becomes surreal when reaching certain spheres of activity beyond religion, politics and economics. Science has not escaped it. Hitler's rejection of Einstein's relativity as Jewish physics has its parallel in the idea of an Islamic natural science, as if a number of possible natural sciences exists, each depending on the religion and culture of its scientists. The only rational meaning such an idea could have would be that of religion providing a moral compass and set of ethical principles to guide Muslims in their study and research, a kind of Hippocratic Oath in Quranic dress that would curtail the application of science in order to prevent gross economic inequality, pollution, development of weapons of mass destruction and other technologies that have ravaged the earth and its inhabitants. But this is not the case. According to the principles of Islamic Science Muslims must derive a science rooted in revelation and Prophetic Tradition in order to avoid the West's moral and spiritual corruption. Otherwise, if Muslims persist in absorbing western science, the same corruption and death by materialist-rationalist analysis will happen to Islam that happened to Christianity in the West. If Islam is taken to be a non-analytical, non-critical understanding of the Quran and Muslim belief, this is absolutely right.

An early promoter of an Islamic Science was abu'l Ala Mawdudi (1903–1979), a self-educated Indian Muslim born shortly after the death of the *Natcheriyyist* Sayyid Ahmad Khan, of whose extended family Mawdudi was a member. Intellectually there was no relationship. The modernity to which Ahmad Khan dedicated himself was opposed and driven back by Mawdudi, whose *Jami'at -i Islam* (Islamic Society) was akin in name, ideology and goal to the Egyptian Hassan al-Banna's Muslim Brotherhood. Both al-Banna and Mawdudi acted to replace secular government by one true to the Shari'a and principles of a purified Islam. Society and education were to be cleansed of the secular institutions introduced by state reformers since the 19th century, and the British, in occupation of both Muslim Indian and Egypt at the time, were to be ousted. Mawdudi's *Jami'at -i Islam* was a driving force in the creation of a Muslim state partitioned off from the Hindu population of India. The state was to be for Muslims only.

By the time India was partitioned and Pakistan came into existence, Mawdudi was a middle-aged author whose many books had made him a leading religious figure with a strong social base in his *Jami'at -i Islam*. With his political dream now an internationally recognized state, he dedicated his life to fulfilling the social, political and legal realization of its name: Pak-i Stan, the Abode of Purity, where Islam would reign pure in its new earthly setting. He and his *Jami'at* would guide the new country along the treacherous road of attaining and preserving this state of blessed purity. This meant the new state had first to divest itself of everything western that had come into it through its parturition from an Anglicized India, and then protect itself from all things western threatening to re-enter and sully the religious purity of the state and its people.

All education had to be Islamic. Everything non-Islamic was to be prohibited, including western science. Because it analyzed nature without reference to God and caused believers to stray from the truth, it was dangerous.

Using arguments that went back to conservative opposition to reform in the 18th century Ottoman Empire, Mawdudi explained that the sorry condition of the Muslim world was the result of the secularization of education that had for so long been replacing religious education. Mawdudi's message was forcefully echoed by his younger associates inside Pakistan, and then given a wider audience by his first biographer, Margaret Marcus. She was a young Jewish woman from New York who had traveled to Pakistan, met Mawdudi, converted to Islam and took the name Maryam Jameelah. Under this name she wrote more than a dozen books on Islam and modernism, and on the dehumanization of technology and other evils of the West. Written all in English and published in Lahore during the 1970s and 1980s, Maryam's books gave Mawdudi's name international recognition.

Inside the country, he and his *Jami'at -i Islam* gained popularity because of the promise of hope they gave for a better future in face of the failures of the secular state with its rampant and open corruption, economic stagnation, recurring military dictatorship and ineffective system of education. Widespread illiteracy and mounting poverty provided an eager audience. After his death in 1979, Mawdudi became a saintly legend in Pakistan: a holy man whose learning, wisdom, piety, humility and simplicity of life raised him in the eyes of his followers to a level rarely achieved. Revered as a connection to the divine, his writings have posthumously elevated him almost to being an honorary companion of the Prophet.

By 1991 his *Jami'at -i Islam* had become influential enough to have the Pakistani National Assembly and Senate pass legislation that mandated the state's secular education be replaced by religious education. The "Shari'a Bill," as it is known, is supposed to bring the nation closer to God. Strict guidelines were written by the *Jami'at -i Islam* in association with the Institute for Policy Studies in order to keep the teaching of science within the bounds of religion. During his life and after, the movement that Mawdudi had evoked overturned much of the work accomplished by Sayyid Ahmad Khan and his followers that had previously informed Pakistani society. His anti-western puritanism had hearty supporters throughout the Middle East, including educated people who might have been expected to be among the most vociferous opponents of his educational policies.

In the same manner that American anti-evolutionist Christians preaching Creationism and Intelligent Design can boast of a number of supporting bonafide biologists and other scientists among their ranks, Islamizationists are joined by a surprising number of professional scientists and academicians. They meet at international conferences to discuss the necessity of a natural science valid for Muslims. They formulate principles for such a science. Financed mainly by Saudi Arabia and to a lesser extent the Pakistan government, these conferences bring together scholarly ulema and scientists who have doctorates from ranking western universities. The purpose is for ulema and scientists to brainstorm the idea of a science for Muslims and propound the pious principles that would frame such a science. They do this in all seriousness, at least outwardly. Sometimes they go beyond the framework of general principles to actually concoct abstract mathematical equations that are claimed to relate elemental religious forces to one another, in the same way natural science relates physical forces. Prayer, forgiveness, sin, good deeds and spiritual rank in paradise become spiritual analogues of mass, charge, velocity, distance and magnetic spin. The papers given at the conferences are published as serious science and distributed throughout the Muslim world.

In the pervasive atmosphere of hostility to the West, Muslims who see this for what it is tend to remain silent lest their religion and loyalty be questioned by their appearing to be too pro-western. The few who dare to speak out are those whose prestige and credentials give them some protection. Two of the most vocal opponents of "Islamic Science" are respected atomic physicists, Muhammad Abdus Salam and Pervez Hoodbhoy, both Pakistanis. The former shares a 1979 Nobel Prize with Steven Weinberg and Sheldon Glashow for discovering the fundamental theory uniting two of the four basic forces of nature, the "weak" and "electromagnetic."

Dr. Hoodbhoy's book, *Islam and Science*: *Religious Orthodoxy and the Battle for Rationality*, published in 1991, is a scathing denunciation of Islamic Science and its followers. The bizarre notion that science has to be religiously correct has reached into government policy on education. An exam was instituted to test prospective science teachers on their religious correctness. Those who pass the exam and go on to become science teachers, the author contends, are less committed to science than those who fail, while the ones who get to teach science are those whose true avocation is religion. An example of the pervasive influence of this absurdity is that the weather forecast, determined by precision instruments on satellites, had to be taken off national television because it was seen by the religious authorities to be a heretical invasion into divine territory: only God could know the future.[15]

The state-funded international conferences on Islamic Science that have since the early 1980s been held periodically are now mainstream events, conducted with grave solemnity and pious conviction. Dignified theologians, scholars, scientists and high government officials are the conferees of these conferences and are far from the run-of-the-mill religious fanatics who would ordinarily flock to such meetings. The fantasy of Islamic Science is for them normal intellectual discourse.

Conference publications provide an idea of what passes for substance at these meetings. An International Conference on "Science in Islamic Polity" was held in Islamabad in 1983 under the auspices of nothing less than Pakistan's Ministry of Science and Technology. Its deliberations were published as *Islamic Scientific Thought and Contributions of Muslims* and edited by the Secretary General of Pakistan's Academy of Sciences. In the introduction of the lead article, "Industry, Science and Technology: Profiles of Muslim Countries," co-authored by the Director of Studies of Pakistan's National Science Council and a consultant of the same Council, it is explained why western science has to be rejected and what is to take its place. In a sweeping inversion of the historical record, the sciences of the Muslim period are taken as religiously legitimate since the motivation of the scientists of the time had been spiritual and because "the paradigm universally accepted by the Muslim scientists during the period of their ascendancy was determined by their firm belief in Divine Unity, the unity of the universe and divine law." These new theologians now accept what their ancestors had either rejected or held questionable, which is a step forward for medieval science, but for the modern version it is a canceled entry visa and one-way ticket back to the West where it came from. In the words of Dr. Hoodbhoy:

> Science in the Muslim community is to be "based on the unity of nature, on synthesis and the vision of the whole of being, without which the parts have no meaning. There is no science for the sake of science; all knowledge is confirmation of Divine Unity . . . The Muslim Ummah has to eliminate the mechanistic, hedonistic and deterministic outlook, as well as the amoral attitude of the West which is accompanying the thoughtless and mechanical transfer of science and technology . . . Muslims scholars and scientists must exert themselves to undertake thorough studies in the philosophy of Muslim Science in order to bring out guiding principles, evolved in the best Islamic traditions, and to apply these to the present resources for producing the framework in which the present-day scientists in the Ummah may pursue their future research efforts for the greater glory of Islam and the service of science.

In other words, a modern version of Islamic Science must begin with studies in the philosophy of medieval science, as if al-Kindi, al-Farabi, al-Biruni, ibn al-Haytham, ibn Sina, ibn Tufayl and ibn Rushd had not been ignored or held in disrepute by the ulema of their day. Out of curiosity, Dr. Hoodbhoy attended one of these international scientific conferences. It convened in Islamabad in October 1987. The theme of the meeting was the existence and efficacy of Quranic miracles: "The Scientific Miracles of the Quran and Sunna." The conference, the third to be held on this subject, was jointly organized by the International Islamic University and the Organization of Scientific Miracles based in Mecca, and was hosted by the then president of Pakistan Zia al-Haq and chaired by Dr. Maurice Bucaille, the French convert whose book on science and Islam inspired a legion of Muslims to contribute to the voluminous literature of Scientific Interpretation. Bucaille's brand of interpretation emphasizes religion over science and slips easily from Scientific Interpretation into Islamic Science.

The conference according to Hoodbhoy was an extravagant affair with hundreds of delegates and some 70 papers being delivered in between lavish banquets. The scientists and religious scholars who spoke at the conference established to their satisfaction that not only did the miracles described in the Quran occur, but indeed, all science has its origins in the Quran and *sunna*. Moreover, what is considered to be science in the secular West, where no heed is taken of God or morality, and where deterministic cause and effect and natural law take the place of divine will, and nature is analyzed in isolated bits and pieces rather than regarded as an organic whole, is inappropriate for Muslims. An appropriate science awaits discovery in the holy sources. In fact, by the titles of a number of the papers delivered, it would appear that some of that science-in-waiting was well on its way to being discovered: "The Chemical Composition of Milk in Relation to Verse 66 of The Bee"; "On the Description of Man at High Altitude in the Quran"; "Revelation of Some Modern Oceanographic Phenomena in the Quran."

These subjects were discussed in earnest and occupied the attention of highly placed educators and scientists, among them Bashiruddin Mahmud, a former nuclear engineer in Pakistan's weapons program and expert on plutonium production and uranium enrichment. Bashiruddin Mahmud claims to have made a fundamental discovery in Islamic Science: that the jinn, the earth sprites of the Quran, are in fact physical realities composed of fire, and that careful analysis of the verses in which they are mentioned suggests they could be harnessed. If so, he concludes, they could be converted into an inexpensive source of fuel to ease the energy crisis and save the environment. Responding to Dr. Abdus Salam's criticism of the theory as being typical of the nonsense put out by the advocates of Islamic Science, Bashiruddin asks what could be expected of someone like Abdus Salam who has no religion? And of what significance is the Nobel Prize for physics compared to that?[16]

In addition to the jinn as alternative sources of energy, a few other discoveries have been made in Islamic Science. A Pakistani scientist formulated mathematical equations relating hypocrisy and belief to collective social religiosity. This involved the author's computing indices of corruption and hypocrisy for the societies of different nations, the nations chosen being western. No Muslim country made the list. Another scientist determined the mathematical relationship between heavenly reward and prayer density (the number of individuals packed together in prayer divided by the area they occupy). Dr. Hoodbhoy also describes the curious paper given by a German convert and scholar of Islamic Science. The German had apparently computed "the angle of God," but because no one understood what he was talking about, the blasphemy went undetected by the pious assembly of scientists, mathematicians, engineers and theologians.[17]

Animosity and rejection of the West, conjoined to public gullibility, gave rise to these conferences of Islamic Science, but the ministries of government that participate and the high caliber of many participants raise the suspicion that the whole thing is a sham concocted by government and academic hucksters out to bilk rich oil countries and their religious foundations by playing on their fallen pride to enjoy a moment of past glory, reborn in Islamic Science. How could the idea of rejecting western science not lead to the next logical rejection: western technology and its telephone, radio, radar, airplane, cinema, television, computer, automobile, cassette recorder, video, tank and weapons system?[18]

Abdus Salam and Hoodbhoy are two of the few bonafide Muslim scientists courageous enough to stand up to Islamic Science as a hoax, "a slogan with no meaning," behind which many responsible people hide their failure to compete scientifically with the rest of the world. As for all the ballyhoo of Islamic Science being pure and ethical, Abdus Salam writes, "But Islamic ethics are universal anyway – care for the environment . . . for wholeness and so on. To call this Islamic Science is an absurdity . . . It seems that those who do not want to do real science talk of Islamic Science."[19] Among the proponents of Islamic Science are those who have earned scholarly reputations in the West and who hold high academic positions in leading universities. The Iranian scholar Sayyid Hossein Nasr, an MIT PhD in physics and author of many books and articles on Muslim science, philosophy and mysticism, sees in Islam's lack of zeal in embracing modern science and technology a positive moral strength in that all learning and experience devoid of a unifying religious vision are anathema to Islam. For Professor Nasr the only permissible science for a Muslim is one that flows from religious belief: "A truly Islamic science cannot but derive ultimately from the intellect which is Divine and not human reason." Islam's refusal to embrace science is a moral strength. Western science, rooted as it is in secular humanism, is a faith-destroying cancer.[20] Islamic knowledge, rooted in faith and God, whose oneness embraces everything in the universe, transcends the reason and empiricism of modern science.

This would suggest a devout Muslim could never be a scientist in the accepted sense of the word. It would then deny that the Nobel Prize scientists Muhammad Abdus Salam and Ahmad Zewail could possibly be the believing Muslims they claim to be. And what of the Greek and Indian science that went to make classical science in Muslim civilization? Must that great contribution to the world be rejected as well? No. This science, Nasr argues, is completely different from the modern. Classical science was unified by the Aristotelian principle of a divine purpose and love that everything in the universe strove to reach its perfection through love of the first Cause, God, or Mind. Science and philosophy were the handmaidens of theology. Dr. Nasr accepts the Aristotelian chain of being as a unifying principle in the science that was produced by Muslims in the early period, while ignoring the fact that it was not at all accepted by the ulema of the time and was at least as extraneous to Islamic religious thought then as science in its setting of secular humanism is today.

The question of science and faith is highly subjective. Who is to deny a modern Muslim scientist cannot in one's own mind accept one's specialized knowledge as a part of the divine whole, that nature is God's mind at work and that science, an expression of God being revealed through His creation, is as moral as the morality the individual scientist invests in it? The Muslim scientist's silent awe and recognition of a spiritual higher reality is exemplified by Dr. Abdus Salam, who lives ably in both the modern world of science and the spiritual world of his faith. In a brief address at the Nobel Banquet in 1979 he recited the Quranic verse, "Thou seest not in the creation of the All-merciful any imperfection. Return thy gaze, seest thou any fissure? Then return thy gaze, again and again. Thy gaze comes back to thee dazzled, aweary." He then went on to explain: "This in effect is the faith of all physicists; the deeper we seek, the more is our wonder excited, the more is the dazzlement of our gaze."[21]

Dr. Abdus Salam shows how simply yet eloquently the Quran can be read in resonance to the wonder that has driven scientists since the first human being looked up at the night's sky or down at a budding flower and wondered how things came to be. Nobel winner Abdus Salam is a living example that science and faith form a life-enhancing symbiosis.

The Egyptian Nobel winner in chemistry agrees. Ahmad Zewail's autobiography, *A Journey Through Time*, rings true as the profession of a Muslim scientist's simple faith in his religion, free of the wrenching logic of medieval scholasticism. To Abdus Salam and Zewail could be added the names of all those other believing Muslims who have made science their life professions but who remain anonymous for not having published autobiographies or won Nobel Prizes.

It appears that secular science is being rejected today by those Muslims who share Dr. Nasr's views for the same reason that the ulema ignored or opposed the rational sciences in medieval times: the fear of scientific reasoning penetrating and diminishing what is sacred and cannot be questioned. Regarding Professor Nasr's call for an Islamic Science, the research physicist Dr. Hoodbhoy asks: To whom will the divine intellect be revealed and to whom will be entrusted the task of deriving science from revelation? By what method is science to be done? "The success of Dr. Nasr's new 'Islamic' science is obviously contingent upon finding interpreters of the Divine intellect who are presumably to be chosen from among the holy and the pious."[22] Professor Nasr is vague on the subject because nothing more than pious sounding generalities can be made. For all the sound and fury coming from supporters of an Islamic Science over the past few decades, its realization has not gone beyond comforting generalities.

An equally avid proponent of a science for Muslims is the Pakistani author Osman Bakar. Bakar validates an Islamic Science on the same grounds as Professor

Nasr and has just as little to say about its methodology and substance, other than the new science is to be based on the same principles as the old science. From his book on the subject, *The History and Philosophy of Islamic Science*,[23] one would not learn that those principles had been rejected as heretical by Osman Bakar's ancestral counterparts, from Ahmad ibn Hanbal and al-Ash'ari to al-Ghazali and ibn Taymiyya. Scientific Islamizers have little idea of the rough ride the pious ulema of the medieval period gave their rationalists. Contemporaries tend to see their past, particularly Islam's first few centuries of it, as a sacred garden bathed in a rosy glow of Muslim purity and harmony. Critical analysis of this history is as forbidden as it is of the Quran, as was shown by the case of Ali ibn abd al-Raziq and his book on the origins of the caliphate.

Islamic Science's foremost theorist is Ziauddin Sardar, a prolific Pakistani writer who though making his life in London has successfully inoculated himself against being infected by any germ of liberality of thought floating in the London air. His purity of thought is repulsed by the offense of Muslim scientific interpreters who go so far as to accept from western science that which they mistakenly perceive to be in harmony with or relevant to Islamic principles. Attempts to make Islam relevant to modern knowledge are all wrong and un-Islamic. In his *Future of Muslim Civilization*, Sardar insists it is not Islam that must be made relevant to modern knowledge, but modern knowledge to Islam. Every civilization needs its own science that reflects its values and spiritual essence. Western science reflects the destructive and immoral nature of western civilization, which, because of its science, ended in atheism. But again, the relevant steps in establishing a bonafide Islamic Science are, not surprisingly, left by Sardar in the mist of abstraction.

Though Sardar admires Dr. Hossein Nasr and his principles of creating an Islamic Science (but nonetheless faults these principles for their being based on metaphysics rather than a set of quantitative relationships), Sardar offers no more guidance than does Dr. Nasr in determining the form and substance of the principles, whether metaphysical or mathematical. Sardar goes no further in criticizing Dr. Nasr's metaphysical principles than to say Islamic Science is against "tyrannical" science, presumably referring to Maryam Jameela's critique of the dehumanizing effect of modern technology and the often cruel and violent ends toward which the West's godless science is directed.

He does nonetheless evaluate the "Islamicity" of science and technology on a basis of ten Islamic values he defines as divine unity, religious duty, piety and so on, something like the way investment companies evaluate the solidity of stocks and bonds. In this way, a catalytic cracking unit commonly used in fractionating crude oil could be quantitatively evaluated for its Islamicity. Sardar also produces a modernistic flow chart in seven connecting boxes to outline the organization of a grand project that is to lead society to an Islamic form of modern civilization that he calls UMRAN, a neat acronym that in Arabic means civilization. The first of the seven boxes in the organizational chart represents the Model State of Medina; the last box in the process is labeled PAYOFF, for Plans and Assessment to Yield Options for the Future. In Dr. Hoodbhoy's words, "If cuteness of acronyms were all that was needed to make projects fly, UMRAN would be up in the sky."[24]

The ideas of Mawdudi, Hossein Nasr, Bakar and Sardar are the products of creative minds spinning between opposite poles, namely the noble search for cultural authenticity as a source of revival in a moribund society ruled by unpopular dictators of questionable legitimacy on the one hand, and, on the other, the rejection of an invasive civilization whose compelling intellectual, scientific and technological achievements are compromised by a repelling imperialism that reveals an ever more inimical face to Muslims. As well meaning as these leading scholars of Islamic Science are, they only serve to delegitimize the scientific work of people like Abdus Salam, Pervez Hoodbhoy and Ahmad Zewail, and facilitate the conditions that force other Muslim scientists to live in the West if they wish to keep up with science and continue their research.

By delegitimizing science and accusing it of stripping Islam of its spiritual content, Islamic Science denies scientists their religious belief. It plays the same undermining role as the conservative ulema of a millennium ago who judged science and philosophy as snares of the devil. Doctors, scientists, engineers and skilled professionals – none is immune to its self-defeating seductions, concocted in a culture of fear, weakness and bitterness, of which there is cause enough for such poisonous emotions to fill the hearts and minds of Arabs and Muslims in their regard to the foreign policies of some western nations. The bitter brew is a fermentation of violence and revenge that justifies in the name of God all means toward driving out the imperialist enemy and its godless client regimes.

A review of career profiles and credentials of a number of members in al-Qaida's leadership shows the quality of scientific and technical expertise that can be attracted to fulfilling by violence the implications, or outward religious professions, found in the Islamization of not just science but all knowledge. It is a subject written on constantly in the Middle Eastern press by secular and religious intellectuals, who feel the middle ground they are standing on to be slipping away from under their feet. A highly popular television show in Egypt fascinates its Muslim viewers by demonstrating how all science is revealed in the Quran.[25] A novelty in the 1970s, Islamic Science has made tremendous gains in the past 30 years. Akbar Ahmed, a Cambridge-educated Pakistani anthropologist and former cricket player, and now professor at an American university, returned to Pakistan after many years abroad to discover to his dismay the intensity of anti-American feeling. But more to his dismay were the extreme views that had asserted themselves as being true Islam. So foreign were they to the Islam he knew before leaving for England as a young man that he failed to recognize them as belonging to the religion in which he had been reared. Professor Akbar Ahmed writes in his books, *Islam under Siege* and *Journey into Islam*, that except for the older generation, the modernist view he grew up with has all but collapsed.

Notes

1 Emre Dolen, "Ottoman Scientific Literature During the 18th and 19th Centuries," in *Introduction of Modern Science and Technology to Turkey and Japan*, edited by Feza Gunergun and Kuriyama Shigehisa, International Research Center for Japanese Studies, Istanbul, 1996, p. 177.
2 J. J. Jansen, *The Interpretation of the Koran in Modern Egypt*, Leiden, Brill, 1980, p. 75; W. C. Smith, *Modern Islam in India*, London, 1946, pp. 70–71.

3 Taner Edis, *An Illusion of Harmony: Science and Religion in Islam*, Prometheus, Amherst, NY, 2007, p. 21.
4 Tantawi Jawhar, *al-Jawahir fi Tafsir al-Quran al-Karim*, Matba'ah Mustafa al-Babi al-Halabi, Cairo, 1928, Vol XV, p. 114; J. Jomier "Le Chiekh Tantawi Jawhar (1862–1940) et son commentaire du Quran," *Melange de l'institut Dominicain d'Etudes Orientale du Caire*, vol V (1958), p. 150.
5 Jawhar, Vol XXV, p. 272.
6 Jawhar, Vol VII, pp. 136–137; vol VIII, p. 182; vol XXVI, p. 22; Jomier, pp. 156–157.
7 The orientation of the qibla in a mosque directs the believer to Mecca for prayer.
8 Jomier, *Le Chiekh Tantawi*, pp. 154–155.
9 Jawhar, Vol 5, pp. 87–88; Jomier, p. 172.
10 Jawhar, Vol I, pp. 2–7.
11 Jawhar, Vol I, p. 8.
12 Jawhar, Vol XXIV, p. 137; Jomier, p. 160.
13 Jawhar, Vol XXII, p. 245.
14 Jomier, *Le Chiekh Tantawi*, p. 173.
15 Pervez Hoodbhoy, *Islam And Science: Religious Orthodoxy And The Battle for Rationality*, Zed Books, London, 1991, p. 46.
16 Bashiruddin Mahmud was arrested along with two other pro-Taliban Pakistani nuclear engineers several weeks after the September 11 destruction of the World Trade Center. *New York Times*, November 2, 2001, section B, page 4.
17 Pervez Hoodbhoy, *Islam And Science*, pp. 146–149.
18 On this see Bassam Tibi, *Islam's Predicament With Modernity*, Routledge, London, New York, 2009 pp. 65–94.
19 Muhammad Abdus Salam, "The Failure of Arab Science," *The Middle East*, June, 1986.
20 S.H. Nasr, *Islam and Contemporary Society*, Kegan Paul, London, 1987, p. 179.
21 Muhammad Abdus Salam, Nobel Prize Banquet speech, December 10, 1979. (His speech can be found on line: Nobelprize.org).
22 Pervez Hoodbhoy, *Islam And Science*, p. 73.
23 First published in Malaysia as *Tawhid and Science* (*tawhid* being Arabic for divine unity); then published again in 1999 under the new title by the Islamic Texts Society in Cambridge, England.
24 Pervez Hoodbhoy, *Islam And Science*, p. 76.
25 Hassan Fattah, "Islam's Best, Brightest and (Increasingly) Radical," *International Herald Tribune*, issue 38677 (July 26, 2007).

15 Scientific Interpretation

By the early 20th century Muslim reformist thinkers in Egypt, following in the steps of their counterparts in British India, had reframed the metaphysical underpinning of Ash'arite theology to accommodate religion to science. This had been the work of individual men whose conclusions, based for the large part on Quranic Scientific Interpretation, did not carry the force or authority of an expressed Sunni consensus. No institutional imprimatum made it official. Perceived incongruencies between science and religion made for an unending quarrel in which all participants had vested interests. The only questions that could be said to have been settled were those that were no longer asked, while the questions that continued to bother religious minds opened the gates of Scientific Interpretation ever wider, as revealed in the literature, mainly in the journals of the day, in articles and letters to their editors, and in critiques by Azhari shaykhs in answer to secularist books and articles coming out on the meaning, content and importance of science.

Between the World Wars, the literature relating science and religion expanded from the efforts of a handful of reformers in debate with their conservative opponents to a broad front of divergent perspectives engaging a far wider public than it had during the previous generation. This was a consequence of growing literacy, modest though it was, and the increasing number of journals promoting an interest in science. By the 1920s the subject was being argued across a wide spectrum of viewpoints: the radical materialism of Salama Musa and Ismail Mazhar, who popularized the ideas of Shibli Shumayyil among a small portion of the reading public given to progressive socialism; the more centrist *Al-Muqtataf* and the journal's new editors and science writers continuing the moderate secularist tradition of Sarruf, Nimr and Zaydan; the liberal nationalism of writers, mainly Egyptians, such as Taha Husayn, Muhammad Kurd Ali, Abbas Aqqad and Louis Awad, who carried on glorifying Arabism by extolling Arab racial virtues as underlying the genius of Muslim civilization and the religion that inspired it; the Abduh-inspired religious reformism of Azharite shaykhs such as Rashid Rida and Tantawi Jawhar, who wielded Scientific Interpretation in the style of Husayn al-Jisr to argue the relevancy of religion while pushing for science education – and here could be added Muhammad Farid Wajdi, who as editor of *Majallat al-Azhar* spoke for the moderately conservative, non-institutional Muslim mainstream. The troubling questions manufactured by all this debate, and the various responses to those questions, opened the locks for a rich stream of imaginative interpretation. There was no problem Scientific Interpretation could not resolve. The growing industry of discovering science in the Quran inspired Copts to search the Bible. A Coptic schoolteacher in Mahallat al-Kubra wrote in a letter to *Muqtataf* that Isaiah spoke of a spherical earth and Job of earth being alone in space.[1]

The inanity of passing scripture off as scientific repositories was seen by Ismail Mazhar and others for what it was. Their protests did little good. Even religious scholars who agreed with them saw in Scientific Interpretation a certain attraction. Claiming science to be contained in scripture served to deflect what theologians perceived as science's latently inimical threat to religion: its pervasive questioning and demanding of proofs that would ultimately tear away the spiritual mysteries, the supernatural awe, and with them the fear and passion that made revelation what it was, the heart and soul of religion. On the other hand, rejecting science had consequences just as threatening. Between the unpalatable options of accepting and rejecting, the compromise of Scientific Interpretation offered a way out.

The possible options and their consequences all but paralyzed the shaykhs of al-Azhar in making way for science education. The reformers among them managed to convince the rector of al-Azhar to accept some modest change, but greater changes had to be imposed by the state, as when in 1908 the government mandated that al-Azhar students would take science courses. But those courses were only taught at a secondary school level, as was philosophy when introduced in 1930. The more serious students went to King Fuad University.

The military ruler Gamal abd al-Nasser forced a more serious program of modernization on al-Azhar in the 1960s. Schools of medicine, agriculture, engineering and secular law were introduced. The rector was reduced to a government appointed shaykh, effectively stripping the institution of its autonomy. While for some shaykhs the loss was offset by the modern sciences that were to be taught, for others it was as though the devil had clawed through the walls. Forced to change by the willful rule of military government, the ruling shaykhs put on the best face they could; some of them justified the study of the non-religious sciences by putting forth the argument that a number of reformist shaykhs had been making all along, that modern science presented no threat to religion, and leaving it at that. Other younger shaykhs seized on Scientific Interpretation to show modern science had been revealed in the Quran long before westerners made their discoveries.

At the heart of the issue was evolution. It was a difficult subject for all sides. Reformist shaykhs equivocated, scientific interpreters avoided it, conservative shaykhs declared it against religion and God, while almost everyone else opposed it as unscientific. Those few who conditionally accepted it culled verses from the Quran that they could turn to support the theory as God's hand at work since creation. If this was still giving too much to science, an escape clause stated that the theory was still unproven and only the future would decide the issue. Everything else in modern science was given Quranic substantiation and swept in unconditionally: relativity, quantum theory, wave theory, the Big Bang, black holes, neutrinos, spectroscopy, dark matter, space-time travel, string theory and every other marvel that made sense only in the language of mathematics and the Quran.

In regard to any realistic sense of scientific assimilation, al-Azhar has contributed far less in the 20th century than its shaykhs of the previous century had to the modernizing efforts of Muhammad Ali and Khedive Ismail. Attar, Tahtawi, Marsafi, Jisr and especially Abduh, to name but a few of the leading figures, had set a precedent of Azharites engaged in modernity in the 19th century. But their efforts were left hanging. Rather than Abduh's line of thought being extended, there was in the early decades of the 20th century a turning back. Rashid Rida turned Abduh's initiation of a modernist, neo-Mu'tazilite religious interpretation back to the conservative authority of the pious ancestors of early Islam, the Hanbali *salafiyya* devoted to the Shari'a. The few Azharites who dared carry on further in the spirit of Abduh were declared heretics and forced to recant their modernizing ideas.[2]

While the religious wing that was inspired by the rich possibilities of Abduh's legacy was having its feathers plucked, the secularist wing, whose program of reform focused on social, economic and political modernization, stood back in fear of usurping the theological office of al-Azhar. It was not for secularists to push for a reinterpretation of scripture or religious law. The task of finding religion's place in the modern world was left to the shaykhs. If religion was going to have a place, the shaykhs would have to be the ones to shape it, but those of them who tried were slapped down, along with a couple of trespassing secularists. The condemnations of Ali abd al-Raziq, his brother Mustafa, Taha Husayn and Muhammad abu Zayd were evidence that al-Azhar was in no mood to go modern. Cooperation and marginalization in the 19th century had given rise to obstructionism in the 20th. Correctly in the long run, the leading ulema interpreted modernism to mean the secular state's usurpation of religious authority, and they were no longer willing to contribute in bringing about their own demise. Would-be Abduhs were not allowed to blossom. Opposition, even if passive, was more attractive to the leading Azharites than actively participating any further in their institutional emasculation. In addition, the perennial weakness of internal rivalry paralyzed the institute's leadership when faced with important decisions regarding change. By their abandoning the task of answering to the theological challenge of modern science and secularism, the shaykhs by default left it to thinkers outside of al-Azhar. However, pronouncements on religion regarding the world of modern knowledge made by secularists were considered neither satisfying nor authoritative. Also, the chilling precedents of al-Azhar's heresy charges that had brought down some reformist thinkers, young and old, gave pause.[3]

Consequently, in the absence of a reasoned relationship between science and orthodox Islam being worked out by an established religious scholar and accepted by consensus, Muslims outside the religious establishment, along with a number of those inside, had a field day showing how science was either hopelessly flawed or already revealed in the Quran, and no one was going to call that heresy. A hundred different voices spoke for Islam and science. Scientific Interpretation proliferated in Pakistan and the Arab countries, and also did well in secularist Turkey. Though a democratic republic closely watched over by a military guardianship of uncompromising Kemalist principles designed to keep religion under the secular thumb, Turkey was not immune to what was going on in the Muslim world. The religious scholar Sa'id Nursi (1877–1960), who had been reading science and technology into the Quran during the Young Turk period, inspired a movement named after him that flourishes today in the Turkish realm of Scientific Interpretation. The movement's literary jewel is Nursi's *Treatise on Light* (*Risalat al-Nur*), composed in Arabic and regarded by Nursi's followers as the next thing to sacred scripture.[4]

The *Treatise on Light* parallels what interpreters were proclaiming in the Arab world, that only the Quran can complete wisdom and civilization and bring happiness and progress to humanity. The Quranic names for God are identified to individual fields of science; Quranic verses reveal scientific and technological discoveries. Moses striking a rock to bring forth water prefigures modern drilling and irrigation technology; Solomon flying through prefigures air flight technology; and Jesus healing the ill and raising the dead prefigures modern medicine.

The first Soviet Sputnik produced a conference of religious and secular scholars who assembled in Cairo to study the Quran in the light of space exploration.[5] The conferees consisted of shaykhs from al-Azhar, members of the science and engineering faculties of Cairo University and the chief mufti of Arab Jerusalem, which was at the time under Jordanian control. Space and rockets now opened a new branch of interpretation. Shaykh Muhammad al-Banna', a firm exponent of scientific exegesis in the tradition of Tantawi Jawhar, delighted the audience with the many Quranic verses he claimed related to space travel. For good measure, he found one for the hydrogen bomb. Some discussants at the meeting were openly disturbed that the spiritual, mystical and inexplicable verses of the Quran, the essential core of divine mystery, were being used so bogusly by the shaykhs. They almost spoiled the party, and would have, had the avid scientific interpreters not reached a compromise to calm their protests. The compromise, struck by the assistant dean of Cairo University's faculty of law, Professor abu Zahra, an Azharite-trained shaykh, was based on two Quranic verses. One was, "We have omitted nothing from the Book." This was accepted to allude to space travel and everything else having to do with science and technology, in both their present and future states. The verse met the minimum demands of those in favor of Scientific Interpretation. The second verse was, "We have delivered to you a book so that everything will be clear to you as a blessing and guide for a people who believe." This was accepted as referring to the traditional religious sciences and the spiritual and supernatural elements in the Quran, and met the minimum demands of those who wanted to impose some restraint on interpretation.[6]

The compromise was one that Shaykh al-Banna' could live with. He believed the Quran had something to say about everything in the world. The Quran itself said so: "We have not neglected anything in The Book." To his more restrained opponents who took the verse to mean only religious matters, Shaykh Banna' insisted it meant everything in religion and everything in the world, *din wa dunya*. If not, then what else could the verse "We will show them our signs on the horizons and in their souls" mean? And what else but interplanetary travel could be meant by the verse "Oh you jinn and spirits, if you can penetrate the realms of heaven and earth, then go!"[7] The satellites that were being sent up to orbit the earth were manifestations of God's power and glory, divinely intended to increase faith in God's awesome might among the believers.

To anyone outside the reinforcing pressure of the group's thought, the meeting was a surreal exercise in western scientific and technological triumphs inverted to show the Quran's divine wisdom and truth of Islam, and nothing more than a desperate search for dignity and respect by men of learning in a Muslim world dominated by stagnation, corruption and western power. Another consensus reached at the conference gave a nod to reality: that the Quran covered only the generalities of science and technology, leaving the specifics to man:

> No doubt, those things such as the atomic bomb and space satellite . . . come from man's study of nature's secrets, which study is incumbent on all believers to the extent of each one's capacity. The Quran does not teach us how to smash an atom or build a hydrogen bomb or rocket or satellite, but it makes clear the general bases upon which these are made, as a product of human intelligence informed by the secret laws of the cosmos . . . it is with God's help that those things are accomplished, not by man's intelligence alone . . . In sum, the Quran commands human intelligence to discover the secrets of creation . . . and calls for this knowledge of nature in order that the believer's faith be strengthened.

Since science is always changing, the Quran does not go into details. The purpose of the Quran's references to nature is to show the believer God's greatness and power.[8]

Such were the sober reflections of a conference of leading Muslim dignitaries. In effect, the Soviet Sputnik of 1957 aroused them to search the Quran for space science more than it did their governments to search for funds to join the competition. The absence in Muslim society of active involvement in science and technology found its virtual reality in Quranic interpretation, the lack of one empowering the other. Like the political activists who when confronted by unyielding corrupt dictatorships took up in desperation the call of Islam and the sword, so did intellectual activists escape the humiliation and powerlessness of their society by taking up Scientific Interpretation, and then later its step-sister, Islamic Science.

The Cairo meeting that was convened to find Sputnik in the Quran would be followed by many other of these scientific conventions. With each new advance in space exploration, scholarly reputations were to be made by those who proved themselves most adept at turning verses into predictions of rockets and satellites. Space travel and astrophysics became increasingly popular subjects for the continuing stream of books and articles devoted to Quranic interpretation. One of the first of these is a book by the Egyptian religious scholar abd al-Raziq Naufal that goes to the extreme in its interpretations, bordering on heresy. Science, Nawfal writes, is modern revelation. God is revealed by scientists. Their discoveries create a path to understanding God. Where in the past it was divinely inspired prophets who were chosen for revelation, scientists are now chosen. The Quran, the timeless word of God, bridges the old science and new. Transcending and substantiating science, the Quran reveals a universe of experience and knowledge that is synonymous with science.

Nawfal's book elicited little comment from al-Azhar. What a century earlier had been a heresy to Tahtawi, who it will be recalled had been shocked to learn the French regarded their scientists as modern prophets, was becoming acceptable interpretation. Each chapter of Nawfal's book is headed by a verse intended to make clear that the science discovered since the Copernican revolution is either expressed directly or implied in the Quran. "Have they not looked to the sky above them, how we built and decorated it." "God has the night follow the day and in that is a lesson." "Let man look to what he was created from." In these brief verses and dozens like them are to be found the structure, organization and substantive principles of modern astronomy, physics, chemistry, geology, meteorology, physiology, biology, genetics, embryology, ophthalmology, oceanography, relativity and quantum theory – everything but evolution, which Nawfal rejects as a mistaken theory that was even being rejected by western scientists. Evolution continued to be the one science that even the most rabid scientific interpreters could not stomach. Echoing Afghani, Nawfal claims the subject to be an object of mockery and ridicule: "In all the centuries of recorded history no one has reported seeing one species change into another or an animal approach becoming a man or a plant an animal, not a snake becoming a camel or even a beetle or cockroach."[9]

The burst of enthusiasm Sputnik sparked in the minds of the researchers into the Quran's virtual science elicited at least one public reaction. Many others there must have been, but they passed in silence for fear that criticizing Nawfal would be taken as denigrating the Quran. Accordingly, the views of Egyptian Shaykh Amin al-Khuli (d. 1966) can stand as representing the silent voices opposing the fraught direction that al-Banna', abu Zahra, Nawfal and a host of others were taking the Quran. In both his article on *tafsir* in the Arabic translation of the *Encyclopedia of Islam* and his book *The Paths of Renewal in Language, Grammar and Quran Interpretation* (*Manahij al-Tajdid fi'l Lugha wa'l Nahwa wa'l Tafsir*, Cairo, 1957), Shaykh al-Khuli rejects Scientific Interpretation as not only diluting the spiritual message of the Quran, but washing it out completely. The brand was wholly outside the accepted methods of interpretation as had been established by authority and was to be rejected without question.

The great authority abu Hamd al-Ghazali, Khuli admits, wrote that the Quran contained the sciences of language, medicine, anatomy, magic and sorcery, and also the sciences that had disappeared, as well as those not yet known, but in spite of what the great authority said about it, scientific exegesis was just as wrong in Ghazali's day as it is now, and had been in fact opposed by religious scholars centuries ago.[10] Ibn al-Shatibi (d. 1388), among others, rejected it on the basis that the Shari'a proscribed astrology and augury of all kinds. Shaykh Khuli recapitulates Shatibi's arguments that the Quran is meant for mostly illiterate people and would not include philosophical ideas or scientific principles. The Quran's references to nature are meant to strike wonder, fear and awe of God's power and wisdom into people, not instruct them in natural philosophy.

Khuli laments the reappearance of Scientific Interpretation in the 19th century. The works of Abdallah Fikri, Iskandarani and Shaykh Jisr were meant for the most part to encourage people to study science and government to support it. In the 20th century its intent had come to extol the Quran. The Quran did not need this kind of cheap glorification. Scientific exegesis perverted the Quran by interpreting it beyond the moral, legal and spiritual purpose for which it had been revealed. The most egregious transgressions perpetrated by these interpreters was their playing mathematical games with the Quran by using numerical equivalents of the letters of the Arabic alphabet to show that the verses reveal scientific laws and principles. Rather than showing that all of nature's secrets were locked up in the Quran, this invidious idiocy desecrated the holy book.[11] Shaykh Khuli asks sarcastically if it could be expected that the Arabs of Muhammad's time could possibly have understood anything of science, even if it was expressed in the Quran. And if the sciences were there, then why did the Arabs need a revival in modern times? Why did they not discover these scientific laws themselves, they who read the Quran so religiously? Why were the discoverers Europeans who do not read the Quran? Is it rational to believe a religious book would mention physical principles on a scholarly level? Why would a holy book take up precious space for chemistry, astronomy, physics and hydrology when the principles of these sciences are always being modified toward greater accuracy and precision of expression?

It was clear to Khuli that those who imputed scientific depth in the Quran wanted only to prove its miraculous nature, as if wanting to convince themselves more than anyone else. He suggested that the Muslims who flock to scientific exegesis were those most afraid of science because of its having undermined their own faith; and so they were compelled to eviscerate the source of their diminished faith by making the Quran the mother book of science. "Renewal begins," Khuli writes, "with a devastating inquiry into the past," not by sweeping everything the West discovers into the Quran.

Brave words: "a devastating inquiry into the past." Considering what al-Azhar did to Shaykh abu Zayd, Taha Husayn, Mustafa abd al-Raziq, Ali abd al-Raziq and Nasr Hamid abu Zayd, while the Egyptian government sat by passively acquiescing, there was little chance anyone was going to launch a devastating inquiry into the authoritative version of the Islamic past.[12]

Shaykh Amin al-Khuli's career is in some ways reminiscent of Shaykh Tahtawi's. Like Tahtawi, he was an Azharite shaykh sent by the Egyptian government to Europe, where he spent several years in the 1920s as an official Egyptian consular official in Berlin and Rome, from which vantage points he studied the West, as Tahtawi had from Paris. Based on his experiences in the West, Khuli wrote several books on cultural and national renewal and ended his career in education as vice dean of the arts faculty in Cairo University. Also like Tahtawi, he maintained a balance between his traditional culture and the knowledge he gained from the West. Even in the timing of their deaths a parallel is seen. Tahtawi died in 1873, and was spared the sequential distress of the Khedive's bankruptcy three years later, of European control of Egypt's debts and finances, and finally of British occupation. Amin al-Khuli died in 1966, less than a year before the devastation of the Arab armies by Israel in the Six-Day War that revealed the hollowness of the strutting, vociferous military dictatorships bellowing out the Arab renaissance of secular nationalism and socialism. The humiliation delivered by Israel was a boon to political Islamism and its intellectual cognates, Scientific Interpretation and Islamic Science, while the restrained voice of Shaykh Khuli was drowned out by the cacophony of interpreters and their offspring, those who believed, or wanted to, that Islam was the way, not imitation of the secular West; that there was in the Quran and Hadith an Islamic natural science, pure, complete and wholly divorced from the science of the West, and once that science was discovered and the Shari'a was restored as the law, justice would reign in Muslim society and the Muslim people would rise and take back what had been taken from them.

Preceding the 1967 war, the rise of military dictatorship and the police state in the 1950s and 1960s throttled the relatively lively socio-religious critique that had existed since the turn of the century. Scientific Interpretation had been a part of it, but the purpose had been to embarrass the government into doing something to fulfill the Quranic message of scientific productivity. Between the police state with its severe repression of the press, and the Six-Day War that totally discredited the corrupt and incompetent military dictatorships and all Arab governments, Scientific Interpretation was taken up by those who believed that religious government could not help but be an improvement over the hopelessly ineffectual leaders they had. Believing that the Quran contained all of the science of the West was in addition a balm to the wounded soul.

The steadily building flow of publications in the literature of Scientific Interpretation also signaled an increase in public attention to science. This was the genre's original purpose: convincing Muslims that science and religion went hand in hand and the Quran commended them to study science. More importantly, the genre was intended to convince rulers to invest state resources in developing a scientific culture, for the greatest obstacle blocking the way to scientific literacy was the lack of educational opportunity. The social failure in taking up science was the fault of the government, not the people. As government continued in its irresponsibility and the prestige of science continued to soar owing to manifest success in its technical application to industrial production and war, Scientific Interpretation was transmogrified from its original purpose to showing how scientific and modern the Quran was, where Islam meant progress and modernity was a Quranic invention.

Scientific Interpretation continued to be practiced by some to promote interest in science, but by the last decades of the 20th century, when Muslims saw themselves falling further and further behind the West, and then behind other parts of the world that they had been ahead of earlier in the century, Scientific Interpretation went from being a means to catch up to becoming a mental mechanism to displace the bitter reality of having failed in the world of science and technology. The religious side of the coin of scientific exegesis filled the void. The depressing emptiness of techno-scientific backwardness was for some filled by a shadow science cast by the Quran, a virtual surrogate for the real thing in order to heal the broken spirit. Holding to the holy book as to life itself in face of the stagnation of Muslim government and the overwhelming power of the expansive West whose inspirational source was seen to be science, Scientific Interpretation sought to empower Muslim society's own spiritual source, the Quran, and thereby society itself, by infusing it with that new religion of the West.

How things had changed from the 1920s to the 1980s. Scientific Interpretation had spoken for a small minority of Muslims in the early 20th century. Tantawi Jawhar's exegesis had found little favor among his peers. High Azhari shaykhs considered it a disturbing innovation and denounced it as excessive in its poetic marriage of nature to the Quran. Sober theologians feared the lack of control that Scientific Interpretation introduced to the venerable science of *tafsir*. In Arabia, the Wahhabi ulema banned Tantawi's exegesis.

Eventually, a number of al-Azhar shaykhs came to espouse it. As early as the 1930s it was being promoted by Muhammad Farid Wajdi in al-Azhar's monthly periodical and continued to be for as long as he was the journal's chief editor. The more critical shaykhs found this distressing. They revered the Quran as being self-sufficient and having no need to be in line with science. They saw the Quran's eternal message being traded off for a quick fix in modernity, spiritual reality giving way to exegetical fantasy. Scientific exegesis disregarded the established principles of *tafsir* by forcing verses to accommodate natural science. It diminished the Quran's message of ennobling social and spiritual life.[13]

Such admonitions failed to dim the appeal of Scientific Interpretation. Too many Muslim intellectuals and members of the ulema shared Wajdi's compulsion to defend Islam against the secular knowledge of the West by co-opting it through Quranic pre-discovery. The implication that Wajdi's articles in al-Azhar's periodical signaled a promotion, albeit an oblique one, of western science by al-Azhar was illusory. Although Wajdi had written positively on western science in his 1897 *Science and Religion* and more or less favorably on the acceptability of Darwin's theory in his edition of the *National Encyclopedia*, his appointment as chief editor of *Majallat al-Azhar* did not translate to a liberal shift in the venerable institute's regard of science and evolution, at least not expressly. Al-Azhar's approach in facing the challenge of modernity, unless forced into action by interpretations that openly challenged the sanctity of the Quran, was silence. Where no challenge was recognized, none existed. Muhammad Farid Wajdi was left to speak for al-Azhar on matters of science and religion. What he said could always be denied if challenged on grounds of religious orthodoxy, for ultimately it was the certified theologians and only they, the ulema, who spoke for Islam.

The ulema's distance from science and the currents of modern ideas insulated the religious scholars from the exigencies of having to accommodate their religion to the changing world. No one else dared do it in their stead. Arab laymen did not write on, define or presume to be authorities on religious questions other than as apologists, propagators of Scientific Interpretation or public intellectuals following precisely what the consensus of shaykhs declared religion to be through their books and fatwas.

During the last several decades restraint in Scientific Interpretation has been cast to the winds. The Quran has been used to fill the void of despair born of backwardness, defeat, humiliation and the political ineptness of corrupt, self-serving ruling elites. The despair has deep historical roots. The Six-Day War was a turning point, but the cultural malaise began a half century before: the fall of the Ottoman Empire; the failure to achieve independence; the French and British mandates that divided the Arabs and through pseudo-nationalist surrogates ruled the puppet democracies that they set up to serve their imperial interests; the loss of British-controlled Palestine to Zionist settlers from Europe; the secular military governments that instead of improving the Arab position in the world made it far worse by failing to build viable economies and overcome the regional divisions imposed by the mandates; and the repeated defeats at the hands of Israel. The list goes on.

Continued failure has torn apart the cultural ego. Religion becomes an assuaging poultice. The refusal of Hamas to cave in under Israeli-American terror, the credible performance of Hizb Allah against the American-backed Israeli invasion of Lebanon and the Iranian stand against the U.S., Israel and Europe to develop nuclear technology are praised by Arabs and Muslims in proportion to the depths of their wounded national egos and hunger for a redemptive victory. Their cries of vengeance for what happened to Lebanon, and is presently happening to what is left of Iraq, Syria and Palestine, are directed as much against their own governments for falling silently in line with Israeli-American policies of repression and expanding settlement in the occupied territories as they are against the U.S. and Israel. The American drone-war has deposited another layer of hate.

Scientific Interpretation feeds on these feelings as much as do militant movements. The latter meet violence with violence. The former sublimates the violence, hatred, humiliation and vindictive rejection of the West by producing a fantasy science. What has failed to be mastered through government expenditure and real scientific institutes is mastered through a fantasy that though rejected by most Muslims nonetheless deepens the pit of despair.

A glimpse into the literature reveals the depths.

One of the sources most often quoted by contemporary scientific interpreters for the correlations between science and the Quran is, paradoxically, a book by a French physician, a convert to Islam, Maurice Bucaille. Bucaille was a practicing physician in Pakistan when out of curiosity he picked up a copy of Ali Yusuf's translation of the Quran. He was immediately struck by what he perceived to be the profound congruity between the Quranic version of cosmogeny and the modern theories of cosmic origin as compared to the Bible's grossly primitive and contradictory account in Genesis. Further study convinced him of the Quran's divine origin:

> The existence at an early state of the universe of the "smoke" referred to in the Quran, meaning the predominantly gaseous state of the material that composes it, obviously corresponds to the primary nebula put forward by modern science . . . How would a man living 14 centuries ago have made corrections to the existing description to such an extent that he eliminated scientifically inaccurate material and, on his own initiative [referring to Hadith], made statements that science has been able to verify only in the present day?[14]

His book, *Le Bible, le Quran et Science*, was translated into English in Karachi in 1976 and later into Arabic. Dr. Bucaille, untutored in Arabic and Islamic studies, came into the religion with the convert's unsullied missionary zeal of delivering the truth to both believers and unbelievers. His missionary work was his book. Here was a former infidel, a western doctor, a man of science who saw the truth of Islam, embraced it and opened the door to its infinite wisdom. What more authority for the Quran's scientific content could one want?

The temptation to engage in this delusionary exercise of beating the West at its own game of science by trumping it with religion was too seductive for many otherwise sensible Muslims to dismiss as nonsense. Bucaille gave it a sense of respectability. Muslims who saw their world being taken over, their culture dismissed in contempt and mockery (the Danish cartoons insulting Muhammad and Muslims, for example), could not resist. Instead of fading away with Muhammad Farid Wajdi and Tantawi Jawhar, Scientific Interpretation was given new life. Coincidental with the publication of Bucaille's book in the middle of the 1970s, several non-Muslim Asian countries were sweeping past Muslim countries to join the select club of high technology dominated by the West and Japan, making it all the more painfully obvious that the Muslims were being left further behind. Compensations had to be made for the wounded psyche. Conferences began being periodically held in Pakistan and Saudi Arabia to discuss the Quran as a source of contemporary science and technology. Paid for mainly by Saudi Arabia, these gatherings proved to be a rich source of material and funding for the many books of Scientific Interpretation that sprang up like wild flowers in the desert after a spring rain.

Bucaille's Quranic book became the general pattern that contemporary interpreters followed. More and more writers entered the field. More and more Quranic verses were continually being turned to reveal scientific fact. But there are only 116 Suras in the Quran, a fraction of which alludes to nature. With so many books coming out about a limited set of verses, the frequency of plagiarism asymptotically approaches the axis of inevitability. In the literature of Scientific Interpretation it is not uncommon to find one author following another word for word, over long paragraphs and pages, without quotes or acknowledgement. Their titles tell the story:

> *The Creation of Man: A Scientific Study of the Quran* (*Khalq al-Insan: Dirasat 'Ilmiyya Quraniyya*), by Dr. Muhammad Tira, Cairo, 1988;
> *With the Quran in the Cosmos* (*Ma'a al-Quran bi'l Kawn*), by Dr. Muhammad al-Fandi, Cairo, 1992;
> *Islam in the Scientific Age of Science* (*al-Islam fi'l 'Asr al- 'Ilmi*), by Muhammad al-Ghamrawi, Cairo, 1993;
> *Cosmic Phenomena Through Quranic Signs* (*Mazahir Kawniyya fi Ma'alim Quraniyya*), by Muhammad Mahmud Abdallah, Cairo, 1992;
> *Miraculous Scientific Signs in the Quran and Hadith* (*Min Dala'il al-I'jaz al- 'Ilmi fi'l Quran al-Karim Wa'l Sunna al-Nabawiyya*), by Dr. Musa al-Khatib, Cairo, 1994;

The Glorious Quran and Modern Science (*al-Quran al-Karim wa'l 'Ilm al-Hadith*), by Dr. Mansur al-Nabi, Cairo, 1991;
Miraculous Scientific Verses in the Glorious Quran (*Min Ayat al- 'Ijaz al- 'Ilmi fi'l Quran al-Karim*), by Dr. Zaghloul al-Najjar, Cairo, 2002.

These are a few of the many. They keep coming. Considered reputable scholarly books, they are found on display for purchase in the bookstore of the Egyptian National Library and Cairo's many bookstores. This goes for any Muslim capital city. Having remarkably escaped censure by al-Azhar and other religious authorities in the Muslim world, the literature has gained an aura of respectability, in spite of the Quran's being cast in a fantastic twilight zone where symbolism, metaphor and science fiction devour devotional inspiration. The literature has opened the door to the excesses, for it is not a long leap from the dream world of interpretation to the occult of magic, superstition and astrology.

Two of the favorite verses of the interpreters are Muhammad's miraculous flight to Jerusalem and his Ascension to the heavens, because of their implications of space travel. Another favorite for space travel is, "Lo, were we to open a gate in the heavens for them and they were to ascend and tarry there, they would say 'Our eyes have become intoxicated, we are a people entranced'" (*al-Hajar* verses 14–15).[15] Landing men on the moon is prefigured in, "By the twilight and night, nor the moon, but let them ride level upon level" (*Al-Inshiqaq* verses 18–19), "level upon level" referring to the depth of space, the ionosphere, troposphere, ozonosphere and beyond; or, the stages of a multi-booster rocket as suggested by Dr. Musa al-Khatib.[16]

Muhammad al-Ghamrawi's contribution to the literature is typical of the genre's tone in its assertion that compared to the Quran's universal embrace of natural truth western science is a stagnant pool. "A century ago scientists were sure they knew all there was to be known about the atom and here they are today still drowning in their studies of it."[17] Ghamrawi continues, "If one compares what scientists know today with what is still to be discovered in the Quran, it can be seen that the state of western science is a state of ignorance. For example, analysis of Muhammad's Night Journey from Mecca to Jerusalem and Ascension to heaven proves that light is not the fastest physical motion possible in the universe as western physicists believe. The Quran holds the secret of particles that travel faster than photons." Ghamrawi computes the time it took Muhammad to travel between Mecca and Jerusalem, perform his prayers as he is reported by tradition to have done and then travel back again. Tradition also reports that his favorite wife A'isha testified to the Prophet's bed still being warm when he returned. Taking all of these factors into consideration, Ghamrawi concocts a mathematical proof that Muhammad exceeded the speed of light. What for religious reformers of an earlier generation had been interpreted as a spiritual dream has become for today's scientific interpreters a sterile physical reality disproving a fundamental principle of accepted science.

Dr. Mansur al-Nabi, who describes himself a professor of physics, claims in a footnote on page 230 of his book to have computed the speed of light from two Quranic verses, 5 of *al-Sajdah* and 47 of *al-Hajj*, both of which say that a heavenly day is a thousand years in human reckoning. Dr. Nabi does not explain how he converts the ratio of a day to a thousand years to obtain the speed of light, but he claims his calculation agrees precisely with the accepted value and urges western scientists to study the Quran, for not only would they find answers to their scientific problems, but more importantly they would find answers to their spiritual questions.[18]

Al-Fandi expands on this in his *With the Quran in the Cosmos*: "God's first book is the universe, His second the Quran." The Quran is the gate to science. Quranic truth is like white light: its truths are bound up as in a spectrum, one ray of the spectrum being spiritual, another being physical. Al-Fandi calls the spiritual light "*al-mastur*": the veiled. The physical ray is "*al-manzur*": the visible. This is made evident in verse 53 of Sura *Fasalat*: "And We will show them our signs on the horizons and in themselves so that the truth will be clear to them."[19] According to Dr. Fandi, if western scientists were to take the time to explore these verses of the Quran they would be cured of their blind arrogance in believing that their knowledge is above God's. As proof, Dr. Fandi lists a string of discoveries revealed in the Quran – solar energy, ultraviolet light, relativity, absolute zero on the Kelvin scale, the Van Allen Belt of cosmic radiation, nuclear fission.[20] He takes western scientists to task for their having struggled so long to unravel the mysteries of nature when the answers have been there all the time waiting to be discovered in the Quran's oceanic depths of natural knowledge. But to plumb the depths of the Quran's secrets and discover the scientific wisdom hidden therein, the reader must have proper spiritual insight, since the Quran only opens its secrets to the truth-seeking believer. "Science shines like the sun from the Book wherever the believer may look." Where Muhammad's mystical journey to Jerusalem and heaven was for Ghamrawi proof of Quranic physics transcending accepted physics, for Dr. al-Fandi it is the key to modern rocketry, space travel and artificial satellites. Buraq, the winged creature that transported Muhammad to the heavens, stands as a prefiguration of the spaceship of the future that will exceed the speed of light by a yet-to-be-discovered process of hyperfusion. Scientists investigating the Quran will also by then have unraveled the enigma of the dual nature of light as wave and particle.

From analyses of the verses relating the Night Journey and Ascension (*Mi'raj* and *Isra'*) will come a unified field theory. A clue is to be found in the root of the word *mi'raj*: *a'raja*, meaning curved, which conveys the topological conception of non-Euclidean geometry and the curvature of space.[21] Another verbal form of *a'raja* employed in verses 3 and 4 of *al-Ma'arij* refers to the physics of powerful gravitational fields that bend light, a fact of Quranic science revealed 13 centuries before Einstein.[22]

Knowledge of the organization and mechanics of the solar system, the immensity and expansion of the universe, the physics of comets, meteors, galaxies, nebulae, black holes and all the astronomical knowledge gained through spectroscopy, telemetry and space telescopes is locked up in verse 5 of Sura *al-Malak*: "Verily we have lit the heavens with lanterns and made of them missiles to cast at devils." Pulsars and quasars are revealed in *al-Waqi'a*, verse 75: "Swear not by the positions of the stars" – supposedly referring to stars that do not radiate light.[23] Atomic fission and the physical dualism of light are evident in a verse alluding to the world of the unseen: "Do not swear by what you cannot see."[24] The invisible world where reside angels and jinn is a spiritual world as real as the visible and invisible rays in the light spectrum.[25] Electrons and protons, matter and anti-matter, and gravity and anti-gravity are revealed in the words *izwaj* and *zawjayn* (pairs, couples, mates), where they are found in several verses: "And for everything we created mates" in *al-Dhariyat* (*The Dispersing*), verse 49; and "Praise to who made couples for everything growing on earth" in *al-Rahman* (*The Beneficient*), verse 25.[26]

The earth's geological epochs and their reconciliation with the scriptural account of creation in six days are clearly laid bare in *al-Nahl* (*The Bee*): "And to guide you rightly God threw down on earth the deep rooted mountains and rivers and passes"; and verse 4 of *Ma'arif*, where a day with God is given as equivalent to a thousand years and an "Angelic Year" as 50,000 human years. The vastness of space and number of galaxies make it more than likely that life exists elsewhere in the universe. This is revealed in *al-Shura* (*Consultation*), verse 29: "And among His signs is the creation of the heavens and the earth and the animals He scattered over them."[27] Verse 30 of *al-Anbiya'* (*The Prophets*) proves the Big Bang theory of the universe's origin, where the heavens and earth are described as being cleaved from one another. The Quran also resolves the problem of the universe's end that has puzzled scientists for years: Will the universe continue to expand until reaching a steady state of balance, will it go on expanding forever with the temperature falling until all life is ended or will it reach a point at which the total mass of the universe will be sufficient to reverse the expansion, causing the universe to contract and implode on itself, initiating another Big Bang cycle of expansion and contraction? The answer for this is in verse 4 of *Yunus*, where it states that God originates creation and returns it back to its source; and in verse 104 of *al-Anbiya*: "One day we will fold up the heavens like a written scroll and turn it back as it was before the first creation and then we will return it. This is our promise, and verily we will do it."[28] The future is the end and the beginning.

The word *lawaqih* occurring in *al-Hijr*, verse 22, reveals both the earth's circulatory hydraulic system and the modern method of cloud-seeding to produce rain: "And we sent the seeding wind and from the sky we sent water, and from it we watered you [made you fertile] and you are but its containers."[29] The carbon cycle of life is apparent in *al-Baqar* (*The Cow*), verse 28: "How can you disbelieve in God when you were dead and He made you live again. Then He will make you die again and will raise you again, and to Him will you return."

With all this uncovering of the science imbedded in the Quran, more than one of these scientific interpreters has asked the obvious question of why is it that those scientific-minded Muslims who studied the Quran did not see its treasure of science and make the discoveries that westerners made? Why are not Muslims at the frontier of scientific study? The answer is that they would be, had they not been turned away from the spirit and meaning of the Quran by corrupt leaders who pervert religion and use it against itself.[30] For both militants and interpreters, the corruption and perversion of religion by illegitimate rulers representing no one but themselves and their coddled military are the cause of the prevailing conditions that continue to corrupt and destroy Muslim society. Another question is how is it that the Quran can be so freely, frivolously and fantastically interpreted beyond all interpretive guides and controls while academic scholars who advocate or initiate rationally based analytical reinterpretations of the Quran or Shari'a law can be brought to court, declared heretics and discharged from their positions, and even threatened with execution? Obviously, glorifying the Quran in non-traditional ways is safe as long as traditional meanings remain unchanged and unquestioned. Interpreters who in the light of modern knowledge glorify the Quran as the eternal word of God without questioning the authenticity of Prophetic Tradition that sanctifies the divinity of Shari'a law will have little to worry about from the enforcers of militant political movements parading as pious Muslims or from the established religious authorities and secular state courts that the militants have successfully intimidated. An indication of how far in spirit these contemporary scientific interpreters are from the reformers who originally enlisted Scientific Interpretation in the cause of modernization is their assertion that the Prophet's miraculous medical knowledge was expressed in his prescription of female genital mutilation, which only recently has been discovered by medical science to be hygienic and beneficial.[31]

This literature has a ready market, lucrative enough to have attracted even some shaykhs who haven't minded cashing in on public gullibility. Several leading Egyptian writers have expressed their concern in newspapers about the growing popularity of books that insinuate magical incantations and occult fakery into religion, and above all, about the failure of al-Azhar's shaykhs to take a forceful stand against this growing popularity of necromancy and false religious belief whose books fill the outdoor stalls lining the streets all around al-Azhar.[32] What these critics fail to mention is that the shaykhs do not speak out against the literature precisely because it is so popular.

Al-Azhar's collaboration in Scientific Interpretation's mis-direction of mind, if not squandering of spiritual sustenance, is made apparent by its passive silence, though it is not entirely passive or silent: an instructor of "Quranic Sciences" at al-Azhar, Muhammad Mahmud Abdallah, whose book *Cosmic Phenomena Through Quranic Signs* has been noted previously, was able to write without censure that "It is well known that nothing happened or ever will happen in the universe that is not recorded in the Quran." Even the strictly traditional Wahhabi establishment has given its blessing to this. In the holy city of Mecca an institution was founded called the Organization of Scientific Miracles in the Quran and Sunna. It held its first international conference in 1987 in Pakistan. The Organization of Scientific Miracles has held several other conferences since then for the same purpose of discovering science in the Quran, and a good number of books, several of which have been referred to previously, have resulted from the papers delivered at these meetings. These high level international conferences, lavishly funded by the Saudi government and attended by Muslim scientists, theologians and high dignitaries representing both the state and the religious organization, cannot but serve to popularize and legitimize belief in the Quran as a repository of all scientific truth and technological achievement. Intellectually self-defeating, this extreme but popular form of Scientific Interpretation threatens to fill the minds of Muslims with nonsense and convince them that the exploration of nature begins and ends with the Quran.

It is remarkable that while accepting everything under and over the sun that modern science has produced, these interpreters, with very few exceptions, either scrupulously avoid or totally deny the science of evolution, as if unaware of, or silently rejecting, Muhammad Farid Wajdi's and Shaykh Rashid Rida's acceptance of Darwin within the framework of Intelligent Design, or Shaykh Muhammad Abduh's dualism of heart and mind that separates science and religion.

Notes

1 *Muqtataf*, vol 48 (May 1916), pp. 495–496.
2 Abduh had been very close to Westerners and Western ideas. After World War I and the betrayal of British promises made to Arab leaders who joined the British in the war by rebelling against the Ottomans, it was not easy to show enthusiasm for the West, especially by a member of the ulema. The colonialist grip of the British on Egypt, the insolence of British officials and the Anglo–French mandates imposed on the Arab provinces of the former Ottoman Empire poisoned the reservoir of amicability that a liberal-minded shaykh might otherwise have felt toward Western ways and ideas. For in-depth accounts of the sense of betrayal felt by Arabs see Usama Makdisi, *Faith Misplaced*, PublicAffairs, New York, 2010, and David Fromkin, *The Peace to End All Peace*, Holt, New York, 1989.
3 Dan Crescilius, "Non-Ideological Responses of the Egyptian Ulema to Modernization," in *Scholars, Saints and Sufis: Muslim Religious Institutions in the Middle East Since 1500*, edited by Nikki R. Keddie, University of California Press, University of California Press, Berkeley, CA, 1972, pp. 180–205.
4 Taner Edis, *An Illusion of Harmony: Science and Religion in Islam*, Prometheus Press, Amherst, NY, 2007, pp. 89–91, citing Sukran Vahide, "Said Nursi's Interpretation of Jihad," in *Islam at the Crossroads*, edited by Ibrahim abu Rabi'a, State University of New York Press, New York, 2003, p. 137.
5 A book on Scientific Interpretation had come out in Cairo a decade earlier, just at the end of World War II. Entitled *The Place of Science in the Quran*, it claimed nothing less than that the technology invented during the war was revealed in the Quran. Yahya Ahmed al-Dardiri, *Makan al-'Ilm fi'l Quran*, Cairo, 1945. The book became a model for the next generation, when Scientific Interpretation blossomed.
6 J. Jomier, "L'exegese scientifique du Coran après le Chiekh Amin al-Khouli," *Melanges Institut Dominicain d'Etudes Orientales du Caire*, vol 4 (1957), pp. 269–280; the compromise is reported in the al-Azhar journal *Liwa al-Islam*, vol II, November 1957, pp. 518–523.
7 *Liwa al-Islam*, vol II, November 1957, p. 518.
8 *Liwa al-Islam*, vol II, pp. 520–521.
9 abd al-Raziq Nawfal, *Allah w'al 'Ilm al-Mu'assar* (God and Modern Science), Cairo, 1957, pp. 227–228.
10 abu Hamd al-Ghazali, *Jawahir al-Quran* (Jewels of The Quran), edited by Muhammad al-Qabani, Ihya' al-'Ulum Press, Beirut, 1990, pp. 28–29.
11 Amin al-Khuli, *Manahij Tajdid* (New Paths), Dar al-Ma'rif Press, Cairo, 1995, p. 296.
12 For the last of those writers who were socially martyred for bringing reasoned analysis into religion see "Heaven Which Way?" by Nasr Hamid abu Zayd, Ahram-on-link, September 12–18, 2002.

13 Amin al-Khuli, *Manahij*, pp. 287–296.
14 Maurice Bucaille, *La Bible, le Quran et la Science: Les Ecritures saintes examinees a la lumier des connaissances moderne*, Seghers Press, Paris, 1976, pp. 142–148.
15 Muhammad Jamal al-Din al- Fandi, *Ma'a al-Quran bi'l Kawn* (With the Quran in the Universe), Hay'at al-Misriiya al-'Ammah li'l Kitab, Cairo, 1992, p. 19; Mansur Muhammad Hasb al-Nabi, *al-Quran al-Karim wa'l 'Ilm al-Hadith, al-Hay't al-Misriyya al-'Ammah li'l Kitab*, Cairo, 1991, p. 201.
16 Musa al-Khatib, *Min Dala'il al-I'jaz al-'Ilmi fi'l Quran al-Karim wa'l Hadith* (*Miraculous Scientific Signs in the Quran and Hadith*), Arabian Gulf Establishment, Cairo, 1994, pp. 291–293.
17 Muhammad al-Ghamrawi, *al-Islam fi 'Asr al-'Ilmi* (*Islam in the Scientific Age*), Cairo, 1993, p. 103.
18 Mansur al-Nabi, *al-Quran al-Karim*, p. 311.
19 Muhammad al-Fandi, *Ma'a al-Quran bi'l Kawn*, p. 7.
20 Muhammad al-Fandi, p. 83.
21 Muhammad al-Fandi, pp. 100–101.
22 Mansur al-Nabi, *al-Quran al-Karim*, p. 237.
23 Muhammad al-Fandi, p. 7.
24 Surah *al-Hamah*, vs. 40–43.
25 Mansur al-Nabi, *al-Quran al-Karim*, p. 229.
26 Mansur al-Nabi, pp. 225, 309.
27 Muhammad al-Fandi, p. 45; *Mansur al-Nabi*, pp. 112–113.
28 Mansur al-Nabi, pp. 306–308.
29 Muhammad al-Fandi, p. 14.
30 Muhammad al-Fandi, p. 62.
31 Musa al-Khatib, *Min Dala'il al-'Ijaz al'Ilmi fi'l Quran*, p. 148.
32 *Al-Akhbar*, Cairo, June 11, 2004, p. 5.

16 Scientific Interpretation and evolution

Since the days of Imam Isfahani and Shaykh Rashid Rida in the early 20th century, the reticence of the shaykhs regarding religion and human evolution has left the field open to secular writers. Expressing a broad range of contradictory views on the subject, these writers have done little to diminish the doubt and confusion that has clouded evolution ever since it was first discussed by Shibli Shumayyil and Jamal al-Din al-Afghani in the 1880s. One of the more knowledgeable of these writers is Ali Ahmad Shahhat, a research assistant in Egypt's Ministry of Scientific Research at the time he wrote his book *The Theory of Evolution Between Science and Religion* (*Nazariyya al-Tatawwur bayn al-'Ilm wa'l-Din*, Cairo, n.d.).

Ali Shahhat

Biology professor Ali Shahhat writes that until a resolution is reached on the religious issue of man's descent no progress in science, and consequently none in social growth and strength, can be expected in Muslim society. Rejecting or ignoring evolution blocks the path to intellectual and social progress.

Thinking to make the case for Darwin that Abdallah Fikri Pasha did for Copernicus a century earlier, Shahhat (like Fikri Pasha a secularly educated Muslim without religious credentials and employed in an educational ministry of government) culls 90 Quranic verses that relate to creation, earth, sky, animals, man and the universe, and interprets them as being in accordance with evolution theory, concluding that the Quran has no problem with the theory. The one problem evolution could present to Muslims is the special case of human beings. As for the rest of nature, the Quran's indications of an evolutionary process are too clear to be denied. What makes man special is religious myth. Take that away and man is just another animal that evolved like all the others. The dramatic scriptural narrative of creation with man at the head of the animal kingdom is essential to neither science nor religion. The essence of creation as it relates to man is consciousness of God and divine unity. Man's physical development is governed by the same principles that govern all living things: evolution over time. The Old Testament and Quran make it clear that God created the male and female of the species, some primitive form of them at least. However, after that act of creation, human development came under the same laws of natural selection that govern all living things.

Scripture cannot be doubted; but it must be properly understood. Nor can the theory of evolution be doubted, if it is understood properly. The theory has proved successful for more than a century of intensive research, even with the gaps that remain in the theory. It is precisely this incompleteness that makes any resolution between evolution and the scriptural account of creation only tentative. Science is never complete. Incompletion is the normal condition of human knowledge. Only with God is it complete. In the sense that man's knowledge of nature expands, never reaching completion, one can say all science is theory, tentative, subject to change with advancing knowledge. Nothing is forever in the world of science. And so where the Quran expresses scientific reality in regard to evolution, Darwin's ideas express scientific theory.

By rendering a science-based explanation of Quranic verses that he takes as not having been well interpreted or understood, Shahhat then builds a reconciling bridge between the narrowing but never closed gap of unchanging reality and changing theory. In order for these verses that touch on nature to be meaningful they have to be understood according to man's knowledge of nature at that moment.[1]

In the concluding chapter of Shahhat's book, an odd non-sequitor points to the growing hostility Middle Easterners started feeling against the West after the 1967 war, whose disastrous consequences regrettably prejudiced them against everything western, including science: "The scholar cannot deny the truth because of racial or religious feelings of cultural solidarity. True science and love of truth do not part ways." Unfortunately, nothing in the interactions between the Middle East and the West after 1967 would diminish those dark feelings or keep them from darkening ever more, further complicating Middle Eastern receptivity to the principles and fundamentals of thought underlying the West's achievements.

Muhammad Tira

Another secular interpreter, Dr. Muhammad Tira, a professor at Cairo's College of Medicine, devotes several chapters of his book *Khalq al-Insan: Dirasat al-'Ilmiyya al-Quraniyya* (*The Creation of Man: A Scientific Quranic Study*) to the evolution of species. But coming to human evolution he turns cautious. He accepts that simple microscopic cells growing out of non-living organic matter constituted earth's first life forms, which then developed over millions of years to form more complex forms, whose survival was favored by external conditions. Humans, however, are excluded from the evolutionary pattern.

The closest Dr. Tira comes to discussing the subject is in his analysis of the word *salala*, a type of clay, which occurs in verse 12 of *al-Mu'minun* (*The Believers*): "Verily we made man from a strain of clay." He describes at length the processes of capillary action, osmosis, crystallization and the formation of silicons, silicates, aluminates and crystals of other chemicals existing in that form of clay, but only to end the narrative in a cloud of pseudo-scientific jargon. So why was the clay brought up for discussion? Apparently in order to bring the reader to the point where one could make for oneself the leap from the chemistry of clay to the evolution of humans. His correlation of the words "growth," "plant," "create" and "life" (or any of their synonyms as they occur in the Quran) with biology, from single cell amoeba to DNA and genetic coding, opens the door of human evolution, but Dr. Tira goes no further. He wishes not to commit himself. As far as he goes in his theology of biological exegesis is that God has created a *sunna* upon which is patterned the life sciences, the *sunna* being the laws (*qawanin*) that determine the growth, physical characteristics and behavior of species. The Quranic reality of these unchanging laws in God's biological *sunna*, as well as God's physical *sunna*, is found in verse 43 of *al-Fatir* (*The Breaking*): "Never in the ways of God do you find exchange or transformation."[2] God's ways were fixed at creation, but the evolutionary process is encoded in those unchanging divine ways. By allowing that there are laws governing biological change that must accord to God's *sunna* but that have not yet been discovered, Dr. Tira opens the door to Quranic acceptance of human evolution, but does not step through it. Nonetheless, the implication is there. For those of the faithful who may wish to make the leap to Darwin, he throws two presumably helpful lines, verse 24 of *Muhammad* and verses 17–18 of *Nuh*. Regarding the first, only a believer would be able to perceive the connection between the words and the science: "Do they not dwell on the Quran, or are their hearts sealed with locks." The second verse offers more of a handle: "God made you as plants to grow from the earth; He will then return you to it and bring you forth again."[3]

Mustafa Mahmud

The popular Egyptian writer Mustafa Mahmud is much more forward. One of his many books on science and Islam focuses on the life sciences. It is written in an open and direct manner. Considered in Egypt to be one of the country's leading intellects (and by a council of European academics to have been among the 20th century's 100 leading thinkers on the human condition), Mustafa Mahmud is not a practitioner of Scientific Interpretation in the sense of the literary genre's defining characteristic of equating Quranic verses to natural laws. As the title of his book *The Riddle of Life* would suggest, he does not subvert science to ennoble the Quran.[4]

Mahmud shares Tantawi Jawhar's exaltation of nature with its beauty, economy and astonishing complexity of systematic organic motion, and though his writing is imbued with a spirit of awe that can only be described as transcendently religious, he is sparing in his use of religious reference and terminology. An elaborate, scientifically updated and lyrically framed restatement of Muhammad Farid Wajdi's article on Darwin in his 1923 edition of Butrus Bustani's encyclopedia, where it is asserted Islam has no problem with the theory of human evolution, Mustafa Mahmud's book expresses a more sincere embrace of evolution. The author is not looking to shine up Islam with the polish of science. Mustafa Mahmud's synthesis of biology and his belief in a transcendent power, florid in its descriptive detail, flow safely along the liberal side of contemporary mainstream Muslim thought, between the materialism of Ismail Mazhar and the exegesis of the scientific interpreters.

The popularity of Mustafa Mahmud's books, and of himself as an imaginative and eloquent philosopher of science and religion, signals a measure of broadening Muslim receptivity to evolution since Mazhar's, Jawhar's and Wajdi's time during the first half of the 20th century. The honor given him by Europeans has greatly added to his prestige among secular Egyptians, while gaining him little credit among the shaykhs of al-Azhar's envy towers of learning.

Mustafa Mahmud recognizes the evidence supporting human evolution to be overwhelming. Evolution is seen everywhere: in the appendix that was once an organ for digesting grass, the gills and vestigial tail of the human fetus, the replication of cells and formation of DNA, the regeneration of organs. But the western version of the theory is cold and empty, a lifeless body lacking heart and soul, a mere corpse or fleshless skeleton. It is the criticism that religious Muslims have made of western science since Tahtawi, that the modern version of science leaves no place for God. Science requires a guiding spirit, the Aristotelian divine mind in the machine that imbued medieval science. Without it, the science of evolution falls flat. The entire spectrum of the study of human evolution points to a transcending wisdom that guides evolution to a final end. Mahmud's is not a defense of religion as much as it is a philosophical synthesis, an explication of evolution and genetics governed by a purpose whose plan is a continuous process of coming-to-be progressing toward a final end, a condensed version of Teilhard de Chardin's elaborate synthesis of evolution and Christianity. One might surmise Mahmud aspired to be exactly that, Islam's Teilhard.

Advancing on the ideas of Muhammad Abduh, Mahmud rolls the laws of evolution up into the corpus of universal natural law, which operates apart from but not independently of the spiritual domain, where the law of religion provides the system of public and personal ethics elevating a society to the requisite moral level that makes the practice of science with its attendant blessings achievable. This is Abduh's two orders of law, or *sunna*, going back to ibn Rushd and Aquinas, but now including evolution. The spiritual *sunna* is mirrored in the laws of the material *sunna*, in accordance with which are patterned the design and operations observed in the cosmos. The laws of religion and nature share a common paradigm. The believer's ordained circumambulation of the Ka'ba is for instance patterned upon the motion of the heavenly orbits.[5]

Here the author slips momentarily into Scientific Interpretation: the Quran, a limitless source of knowledge for both religion and science, possesses secrets that, like those deeply buried in nature, can never be fully known.[6] Science illuminates the Quran: the deeper the science, the clearer the Quran. The light of science shines through the layered veils of Quranic meaning, revealing the holy book's profundity. Science for Mahmud has taken the place mysticism enjoyed for a millennium in penetrating the Quran's depth. Unlike the run of the mill scientific interpreters, he does not anchor this in equating verse to discovery. Discovery through illumination seems to be a one-way process. Scientific discovery reveals new levels of meaning in the Quran, but little is said of the Quran as a miraculous oracle from which new science can be gained without recourse to the traditional methods of experimentation and independent mathematical theorization that together capture nature's ways in laws.

Equally open to evolution is a Muslim Lebanese scholar of some renown at Temple University in Philadelphia, Mahmud Ayyoub, who writes on points of concordance between the Muslim and Christian faiths. Buttressing his own openness, he cites two Arab authors, a relatively unknown Syrian, Tal Ghazal, and an Egyptian, 'abd al-Sabur Shahin, who have reinterpreted Darwin upon a Quranic template. Ghazal unquestioningly accepts evolution, taking verse 26 of Sura 15, where God creates man from "hot and putrefying potter's clay" to mean evolution from primal matter. From this, a form of animal man evolved through natural selection. God established natural laws of evolution for all living things, including mankind. Shahin's book *Abi Adami al-Khaliqah bayn al-Usturah wa'l Haqiqah* (*My Father Adam: The Created Universe between Myth and Reality*) is banned in Egypt but is no less elastic in its stretching Quranic verse to evolution than many others of its genre. Perhaps it is his radical proposal to abandon traditional modes of interpretation and render the Quran in a purely modern scientific interpretation that did Shahin's book in. Other writers simply did it without stating it as a general proposition. Shahin argues there can be no contradiction between science, evolution and the Quran, and where there appears to be, it is because science has yet to advance to a Quranic standard. He does not accept a universal theory of one species evolving into an entirely new one; evolution occurs within each species, perfecting it.[7]

One of the curiosities in the history of Muslim society's coming to terms with evolution theory is that no one espousing it has come close to being charged with heresy or even harassed by religious authorities.[8] No Muslim writing in favor of Darwin has faced the chilling trials that Ali abd al-Raziq, his brother Mustafa, Taha Husayn or the two abu Zayds had to endure in Cairo, or Scopes in Kentucky. Quite the contrary. Al-Azhar's muted, studiously passive toleration of evolution was signaled when Muhammad Farid Wajdi was already selected as editor of *Majallat al-Azhar* in the 1930s.

Putting a secular spokesman like Wajdi at the front allowed the shaykhs to present themselves as engaged in scientific questions and at the same time shield themselves from subjects they knew little about, avoiding embarrassment, even implications of heresy hidden somewhere in the complexities of science, of being contaminated by the touch of the West. No shaykh other than Isfahani, the Shi'i of Karbala, bothered to learn enough about evolution to take on the task. None wished to accept the responsibility of speaking out on the subject. Subjects such as a revisionist history of the origins of the office of caliph, pre-Islamic poetry or reinterpreting the Quran to modernize the Shari'a, these the shaykhs knew well enough to know when the line was crossed and take charge on their own. Evolution and scientific questions were better left to a secular front man. It was safer, easier. Many of the high ulema sensibly accept that science has nothing to do with religion, but in the minds of many believers it does, and so silence from above is neither spiritually healthy nor socially responsible.

Yahya Farghal

Decades after Wajdi served the part, the secular front man was Dr. Yahya Farghal, a professor of philosophy and theology and the chairman of the philosophy department of al-Azhar, which had in the 1950s and 1960s been transformed into a university. Dr. Farghal published a book in 1984 on contemporary trends or directions of Islamic thought on science. A large part of Farghal's *Islam and Contemporary Scientific Trends* (*al-Islam wa'l-Ittijahat al- 'Ilmiyya al-Mu'asira*) is on evolution.

As he understands it, once the lowest form of life sprang into existence, biological evolution began its course over the geological ages. There can be no denying evolution of species. The paleontological evidence is irrefutable. But science falls short when it comes to the origin of life and descent of man. This is the sticking point for Farghal, as it was and is for most believing Muslims dealing seriously with the subject. Organic life coming from chemical reactions of nitrogen, hydrogen, oxygen, carbon, ammonia, chlorophyll and the heat of the sun to form protoplasm has no basis in experimental science. All laboratory attempts to produce living cells have failed. Farghal reviews the experimental history of this in some detail. His arguments are comparable to contemporary American scientists who accept some facets of evolution but within a framework of biblical Creationism. Accordingly, Farghal rejects the materialist origin of life. Ismail Mazhar may have said evolution posed no problem to Muslim belief, but for Dr. Farghal he was wrong. There is a problem. Mazhar is more the object of Farghal's criticism than Darwin, but what is telling is that Farghal does not consider Mazhar to have crossed the line from orthodoxy to heresy. His criticism of Mazhar's *Malqat al-Sabil* (1924) and of Shumayyil's translation of Buchner's lectures that was passed off as Darwinian evolution (1884) is also telling in that it reveals the meager advance that the acceptance of evolution theory had made among intellectuals in Arab society up to the mid-1980s. Nothing had been written more critically significant than what Shumayyil and Mazhar had produced since the 100 and 60 years respectively that had intervened between the publication of their works and Dr. Farghal's. Isfahani's two-volume critique is never mentioned by Farghal, or by anyone. Abbas Aqqad, one of the monumental secular figures in 20th century Arab thought, comes in for some of Farghal's heavy criticism because of Aqqad's unquestioning acceptance of Darwin as being wholly within orthodox belief, but Aqqad's contribution to the literature of evolution was insignificant.

Farghal accepts without question that Darwin's theory has brought fruitful natural truths to light and that great biological discoveries have come from his mechanism of natural selection. Darwin's expansion and refinement of the ideas of those naturalists who preceeded him, and the work of those after him who expanded and refined his ideas to produce an abundance of new science, have produced a rich scientific heritage that continues in all fields, just as it was with Galileo's and Newton's discoveries and the advances made on them by succeeding scientists. But there is still much to be learned. The gaps in evolution theory are forever challenging, the flaws too many for the theory to be accepted uncritically – the lack of "connecting links," for example. Excavations have yet to produce the necessary evidence.

Bending modern discoveries to his own argument, Dr. Farghal interprets Richard Leakey's discovery in 1972 of a skull in Kenya as evidence that homo-erectus existed two and a half million years ago, when the ancestor of the ape also existed, and concludes that man could therefore not have descended from the ancestor of the ape. Western critics of human evolution are cited as decisive authorities to establish that much in the theory as it relates to human evolution is conjecture and hypothesis. The gaps, flaws and contradictions can only be explained by the existence of a "creating will," God.[9] According to Dr. Farghal, the Quran allows no room for Darwin's theory of the descent of man, whatever some Muslim writers and scholars might think or say. Those who claim that the Quran neither confirms nor denies it are wrong. There can be no reconciliation between Darwin's descent of man and Islamic belief: "Just as Jesus was miraculously created without a father, so was Adam created by God from clay and water."[10]

He asks how science can be the ultimate arbitrator of natural truth when it admits both its incompleteness and self-doubt. He then goes on to say that some western philosophers and scientists contend that the concept of cause and effect is built into the mind through habitual experience and is not something in itself, a view close to the Muslim concept of nature's customary but not necessary behavior. In quantum mechanics, Heisenberg's Uncertainty Principle has put a question mark on the idea of absolute determinism in nature and natural law. In the world of sub-atomic physics, the basic laws of science are reduced to statistical analyses and averages; the future state of an electron in a given set of conditions is also statistical and cannot be known absolutely. This makes science descriptive in relation to events in the past, while in relation to the future science is belief, belief here being framed by the Quran.

The conundrums of life's origins, human existence, cause and effect, duality of light, quantum uncertainty, expansion of space, dark energy and matter, Einstein's cosmological constant and the grand unified theory – all will be resolved in the future and then seen to be in agreement with Quranic belief – what in the fundamentalist Christian context of America would relate to the "Intelligent Design" of Creationists. This comes at the apex of the human journey.

Employing the symbolism of Teilhard de Chardin, Farghal posits a point Alpha. Alpha is approached as the philosophy of materialism and the scientist's ideas of determinism in nature fall away in recognition of God's active will in the universe: that divine will cannot be conceived in human terms or in reference to what is understood by human will. Point Alpha is when science is subsumed into religion. Scientists will then understand that divine will underlies the universe in both design and action, and is the cause and power in matter, governing and organizing its actions and interactions in the material universe, "as if in nature a hidden eye is wisely watching over and ordering it."[11] Hume, Descartes, Spinoza, Holbach, Wittgenstein, Bertrand Russell, Einstein, Samuel Clark, Eddington, Planck, Bohr and Heisenberg – they each have contributed a piece to the great puzzle, but Islam will provide the key that brings the pieces together and resolves the riddle of unanswered questions. Science does not intimidate and chase Islam from the scene and force it to hide in a corner. On the contrary, Islam confirms and completes science. That is what is meant when God revealed in the Quran that "Never will there be a change in God's *sunna*." God's spiritual and natural *sunna* will be seen to coincide with the advancement of science. Science reconfirms the progressive way of Islam. Whether conscious of it or not, scientists are continuously coming closer to accepting belief in a divine will in order to bring the pieces of the puzzle together and reach point Alpha.[12] As mankind progresses into the future toward the Final Day, Islam will become the prism through which the transcendent verities of eternity, perfection and infinity will be physically perceived. Point Alpha coincides with Resurrection.

By restoring God to evolution, Islam will undo the perverted work of the atheist materialists. As for science in general, "Islam guarantees the continuation of natural law by revealing the presence of a divine will that presides over universal order." To save the requisites of orthodoxy, Farghal marries this divinely ordained universe of natural law to the unlawed universe of medieval Muslim theology: "The harmony between natural law and divine will is clear, and a place is provided for the breaking of the custom of nature [*kharq al-'adah*] which is manifested from time to time as a reminder to people of the source of existence and its laws, namely God, may He be extolled and elevated."[13] Farghal has it both ways: natural law and a power that can abrogate it.

Mahir Khalil and Nabil al-Nashawati

As far on the liberal side of religious acceptance that Mustafa Mahmud's, Tira's and Shahhat's views on human evolution stand from Dr. Yahya Farghal's more or less conservatively centrist position, the views of several recently published authors stand just as far on the rejectionist side of the spectrum. The books of two authors have been chosen from a great many publications to represent the rejectionists. Taken together, the three liberals, the conservative centrist and the two rejectionists fairly represent the public spectrum of contemporary Muslim thought on evolution, which would be to say there is no generally accepted position, at least as expressed in the literature. The academicians who teach biology in the universities are as quiet on the subject as the religious authorities. The Egyptian government did indeed sponsor a modern translation of the *Origin of Species*, but this is not to be found in any of Cairo's bookstores.

The year after the publication of Dr. Farghal's book refuting Darwin's *Descent of Man* root and branch, a book came out entitled *The Fall of Darwin's Theory in the Light of Modern Scientific Discovery* (*Suqut Nazariyya Darwin fi Daw' al-Iktishafat al- Ilmiyya al-Haditha*, Cairo, 1986). Its author, Mahir Khalil, lacks the credentials of Ali Shahhat and Yahya Farghal, and it is not long into his book that this becomes obvious. Lack of knowledge of the subject is most usually the case with the rejectionists, for it is not Darwin but the West that is being rejected. Where the early westernized Darwinists, Shumayyil, Mazhar and Musa, loaded their materialist philosophy and social progressivism into evolution theory, contemporary scientific interpreters have loaded it with their anti-western hostility. Mahir Khalil's book and the many like it are significant only in that they give an idea of what passes for serious comment in science and religion among the popular classes of literate Arab society.

Like Jamal al-Din al-Afghani a century before, Mahir Khalil puts Darwin's theory down as having no supporting experimental or empirical evidence. He in fact refers to Afghani in admiring terms, even ridicules Darwin in the same fashion of Afghani, claiming that evolution means a cow could become a horse, a monkey become a man. If Darwin's theory was right, he argues, then Darwin would have made the geological and paleontological discoveries that were not made until the late 20th century. That it took so long proves Darwin was wrong. By the same bizarre twist of logic, the post Darwin discoveries that emanated from the guiding principle of natural selection also show Darwin's theory to be unscientific. Darwin's inability to explain the huge expansion in the size of the human brain compared to the monkey's brain is another flaw in the theory that man descended, along with the chimpanzee and monkey, from a common ancestor.[14] Leakey's discoveries, and his claim that the original "Eve" came from Africa, are more proofs of Darwin's errors. If more proof is needed, it can be had in the origins of Darwin's theory: materialism, secularism, socialism, communism, capitalism and atheism, the roots of the moral disintegration seen in the West today. Muslims therefore must either reject this unscientific theory or suffer the same decadence.

This nonsense is in some part at least owing to the unpopular public legacy that Shumayyil and his two acolytes, Mazhar and Musa, imparted to Darwin in Arabic. Mahir Khalil holds them personally responsible for injecting the poison of evolution into the Arab intellectual bloodstream. Particularly poisonous was their including homo-sapiens as a product of natural selection, as if humans were just another animal species. Those who try to reconcile religion to human evolution are guilty of perverting religion because there is nothing in the Quran or *sunna* supporting it.[15] Mahir admits that science has proved the evolution of other animals. Some species became extinct as new ones emerged. But this was not the case of man.

Where Shahhat, Mahmud and Tira left acceptance or denial up to the believer, Mahir Khalil puts human evolution down as an incontrovertible heresy that totally denies religion and corrupts morals and civilization. Even Intelligent Design cannot save it. The heresy of human evolution is the avant-garde of the western conspiracy's intellectual front against Islam. It puts into question the veracity of the Quran, the heart of Muslim society and life. Undermining the Quran threatens Muslim civilization with destruction. The leading agents in this conspiracy are the Jews. Darwinism, communism and Zionism are Jewish conspiracies against all religions, but it is especially against Islam that they are aimed.[16] Those well-intentioned scholars such as Dr. Mustafa Mahmud who try to reconcile science and Islam, Khalil writes, risk slipping into heresy. Mustafa Mahmud, for whom Mahir Khalil expresses great respect, errs by bringing science and religion together. According to Khalil, Mustafa Mahmud's rendition of the Quran that makes human evolution acceptable to believers shows only that he fails to understand the true meaning of the Suras. "God could have created man though natural selection over millions of years, based on the verse 'He created you in stages', but did God do it that way? How is it that Mustafa Mahmud and the reconcilers can speak or believe in gradual evolution that requires millions of years when they know at the same time that when God wants to create something all he has to do is say, 'Be!' And it is?"[17]

In other words, why would God need natural selection unless He kept failing in getting the right design and tossed out the rejects to start over? There is no need for reconciliation. Islam stands on its own, independent of science and evolution. Islam is above them. Reconciliation of Islam with alien ideas like democracy, secular law and science is unnecessary and dangerous. Democracy would replace divine with human law. Society would be destroyed by corrupt laws made by corrupt people. The Shari'a, the Quran, the *sunna* and the advisory institution of the *shura*, rooted deep in Islamic origins, are sufficient for the legal and political organization of Islamic society.[18] In Islam there can be no separation of politics and religion, of state and religion, of law and religion, and certainly not of science and religion. Everything opposed to Islam must be rejected. Everything opposed to Islam that has been imported into society must be rooted out. Bonded to materialism, secularism, atheism and Zionism, evolution is the West's multi-pronged war of terrorism against Muslims. Khalil deplores that Egyptian secondary schools teach evolution in their biology and geology courses and expresses hope that one day this misfortune will be rectified.[19]

The last publication of this genre to be considered is Dr. Nabil al-Nashawati's *The Divine Miracle in the Creation of Man: Refutation of Darwin's Theory* (*al-I'jaz al- Ilahi fi Khalq al- Insan: Tanfid Nazariyya Darwin*, Damascus, 2001). Paralleling Mahir Khalil's prejudicial logic, this anti-Darwin polemic is another example of what passes for serious intellectual comment among those who can be considered religiously conservative and concerned with questions raised by science. Dr. Nashawati places Darwin in the 18th century and confuses his theory of natural selection and the descent of man with the Big Bang theory of the universe's origin. Less surprising, he confuses natural selection with Spencer, socialism and German materialism, and considers Jamal al-Din al-Afghani a leading authority on Darwin and the science of evolution. His book follows true to the spirit of its opening statement:

> Atheistic western thought has attacked our people and peoples of the world. It has seduced the breasts of our youth against their Creator and filled their hearts with contempt of the heavenly laws. It has turned them away from their exemplars and stripped them of their divinely inspired and magnanimous inner character.

Western science and the false philosophies it has spawned have seized the place of God and religion and poisoned the minds of believers. These iniquities are reinforced by the conspiratorial alliance of the West's unholy trinity of communism, Zionism and secularism that spearheads a war against Islam. Included in secularism is secular science, the so-called knowledge of the universe that knows not God. But the Quran is more powerful than western science and all the other conspiracies concocted to destroy Islam. Long before western science came into being, the Quran revealed the secrets of neurology, cell structure, DNA, genetic

Scientific Interpretation and evolution 361

inheritance, procreation and all the basics of modern biology. What the West mistakenly takes to be science is dangerous because of its rejection of God. That the science interpreted in the Quran happens to agree with the facts and principles of western discovery is only incidental and not essential. What is essential is that once God is accepted, dangerous conspiratorial sciences become true science, for the false idols of secularism melt away in the light of religious belief. Arrogance dissolves into humility.

In his attempt to expose western biology for the hoax he claims it is, sections of Dr. Nashawati's book elevate surrealism to a new level. The verse, "Everything is created from water," accompanied by diagrams of chemical structures of complex organic compounds and page after page of dense explication of the chemistry of nucleotides and enzymes, proves the divinity of the Quran by its having revealed modern genetics. For all they claim to know about genetics, western biologists cannot create even a fly, not even a leg or wing of one. Watson and Crick discovered the structure of DNA but could not create it, not even a simple cell. Hence, their trivial accomplishments condemn them as scientific failures.[20]

> The materialist naturalists (geneticists, neurologists, biologists, biochemists, etc.) are liars and frauds; they are deceitful and obstinate before the clarity of God's verses which will shake their minds and joints. They ignore God's verses and persist in their error, led on by their devils and passions and philosophies . . . The Great Creator has revealed the story of creation to us in the Quran . . . Hell fire will be the end of Darwinists and heretics, of Marxists, Masons and materialists, comes the Day of Resurrection. . . . How can it be that people embrace Darwin's philosophy even though modern science has refuted it?[21]

Nashawati damns the evidence used to support human evolution as being forged. Neanderthal and pre-Neanderthal forms existed but they were forms of ape, not early forms of man. The fossils called Peking and Java were also evolutionary forms of the ape species. The forged fossils reveal the western conspiracy to destroy Islam and religion in general. Carbon-14 testing has proved that man did not walk the face of the earth more than six or seven thousand years ago. The Quran being the only acceptable source for understanding the science of human origins, Dr. Nashawati, in agreement with Mahir Khalil, would like to see the books teaching human evolution removed from all schools of Muslim countries, high schools as well as universities.[22]

Each passing year finds Scientific Interpretation to be an ever more popular contest in religious glorification at the expense of science. Each year a new crop comes out, one book hardly any different from the other, with each new addition repeating its predecessors and only on occasion exhibiting some originality of contrived interpretation by adducing verses that are supposed to equate to something recently popularized. During the first decade of the 21st century, Madbuli's, a popular chain of bookshops in Cairo, has had on display in its store across the street from the main entrance of al-Azhar more than half a dozen recently published books on the subject bearing titles such as *The Glorious Quran and Modern Science* (by Muhammad Habbal), *Creation of the Universe Between Science and the Quran* (by Muhammad al-Ta'i), *The Creation of Man Between Medical Science and the Quran* (by Muhammad al-Barr), *With God in the Sky* (by Ahmad Zaki) and *The Darwinian Theory of Evolution: Fables in the Name of Science* (by Dr. Talib al-Janabi). Scientific Interpretation has become a literary industry.

Radio has also become a forum of finding science in the Quran. A dialogue between two writers on the subject was broadcast and later transcribed into a book, *Scientific Miracle in the Quran* by Dr. Zaghloul Najjar. The same verses culled by earlier interpreters from Quran and Prophetic Tradition are run through once again for their miraculous revelations, though one does seem to be an original. The circumambulation of the Ka'ba reveals not only the pattern of planetary orbital motion and electrons orbiting the nucleus, but in addition, the left to right direction of circumambulation reveals what science has only recently found: that it is the left side upon which the essential elements of carbon-based life bond to the carbon atom. With this, Najjar and his colloquist are able to sweep everything into the Quran: DNA, genetic coding, chromosomes, star formation, the beginning and ending of the universe. Only human evolution is missing. Like the al-Azhar ulema, the dialogue kept silent on that.

What is not kept silent in the outpouring of Scientific Interpretation is the anti-western hostility that popularizes this self-defeating pseudo-religious self-praise. The preface of Dr. Zaghloul Najjar's book based on the radio dialogue (written by Anwar Jundi, whose book of Scientific Interpretation was mentioned above) is a virulent condemnation of western science as a mind-poisoning conspiracy designed to corrupt Muslim youth by turning them against religion. Western science and Zionism are the twin components of a secret pact with the devil to overthrow Islam. Proof of this is the Protocol of the Elders of Zion. The science of the West, in collaboration with America's support of Israel and Zionism, is aiming to destroy Islam because of its liberating message of humanism, its call to freedom and dignity. Anyone familiar with the George W. Bush regime's fatuous explanation for the attack of September 11, 2001 will recognize in this argument "they hate us for our freedom."

Unfortunately, U.S. support of corrupt and repressive dictators, combined with western actions and policies in Palestine, Lebanon, Iraq, Afghanistan and Pakistan, with threats of war on Iran, reinforce the anti-western hostility that feeds into the psychosis of Scientific Interpretation. Its corrosive message has been at work for some time now and has, along with militant Islamist movements, reached into the educated professional classes of Muslim society.

As mentioned earlier, a considerable number of authors and scholars periodically gather from all over the Muslim world to attend conferences and give papers on Scientific Interpretation. Muslim associations of scientists, engineers, academics and religious scholars hold conferences in England, Pakistan and Saudi Arabia, and the U.S. professional associations, congresses and journals have been founded to spread the message, transforming what in the 1970s and 1980s was considered a lunatic fringe into a common token of religious and intellectual currency. Typical was the joint conference held in the late 1990s between the

Association of Muslim Scientists and Engineers and members of the International Institute of Islamic Thought. The conference, held in Herndon, Virginia, brought Muslim religious scholars together with scientifically and technically educated professionals residing in North America, with the single purpose of giving and discussing scholarly papers on scientific discovery and the Quran. Even the small community of Muslim scientists has not been immune to the virus.

A gullible and eager reading public has done its share in popularizing Scientific Interpretation. One might call the production a sound capitalist venture in a publishing market where everything is fair game in feeding and expanding it. Books on Prophetic Medicine abound where remedies reported to have been used by Muhammad are touted as being superior to modern medicine because of their spirituality and faith-healing powers. Astrology, magic, talismans, augury and casting spells – all the old enemies of the staunch medieval defenders of strict Sunni Islam have been claimed by interpreters to be rooted in Quranic verse. In some cases, the occult sciences, having at no time ever diminished in appeal, are fused with the real and packed into the Quran.

Books on the occult were always being written to satisfy the emotional needs of believers that traditional religion failed to fulfill, quite as Sufism had served the needs for others of the faithful. Recently, a flood of literature on the occult and the Quran has inundated the bookstores and stalls of Cairo. What is read in Cairo is read in Beirut, Damascus, Aleppo, Mosul, Baghdad, Basra, Fez, Rabat, Marrakesh, Tangiers and Algiers. It is a flourishing market.

Some shaykhs have joined the laymen to meet demand. The profit to be made has proved stronger than either pious prudence or respect of al-Ghazali's or ibn Taymiyya's authority. Articles in the religious sections of some of Cairo's newspapers lament al-Azhar's failure to make a stand against what appears to be an alarming rise in the numbers of these books. Prominent scientific interpreters who relate the Quran to legitimate science for reformist reasons are among the most vocal opponents of occultic interpretation and are the most critical of al-Azhar's passivity. During the summer of 2004 the Egyptian daily newspaper *al-Akhbar* ran a series of articles highlighting the wave of occultic books that claim Quranic support, accompanied by critical interviews with secularists and shaykhs who deplored al-Azhar's failure in holding the line.[23] Al-Azhar had the means to do it but lacked the courage to apply the authority it had.

Back in the early 1960s, al-Azhar was given the authority to censor all literature bearing on religion. This was a political trade-off by Gamal abd al-Nasser to co-opt al-Azhar. The law was renewed in 2001 during the Mubarak regime. While the shaykhs have been lax in applying al-Azhar's authority to cut short the torrent of occultic books and cassettes that flood the sidewalk stalls and bookstores, they have energetically used their censorship power to protect religion by banning what could be considered valuable intellectual and literary contributions. As one critic put it, the shaykhs are promoting

> an Islam of bedouins that leads to schizophrenia . . . The authority of censorship is an unsheathed sword over creativity and innovation in that it willfully allows books on magic and evil spirits and the like. How are these shaykhs of

censorship to meet the challenge of the products coming from the information revolution of computers and the web overwhelming today's world while holding up a white flag to irrational books that destroy minds and open the way to fanaticism? Are we Egyptians, at the beginning of the 21st century, still in need of guardian mind-tenders to protect our belief and faith?[24]

People wondered why the secular military government gave such authority to a religious institution. The government's intention was to regimentize religious expression under tight political control through a close working relationship between the military government and the religious leaders. The law made al-Azhar a state partner in thought control, and the partnership worked well. Al-Azhar's power of censorship took up where military censorship left off, one reinforcing the other. Between the censors of military government and the censors of conservative religion, an intimidating prison wall towered over thinkers, writers, artists, would-be religious reformers and the culture as a whole. The state's fear of religion combined with religion's distrust of science hardened the ground too much for any independent thought, let alone science, to take root. The ungiving ground allowed for a solitary bloom or two, now and then, but never a garden.

Dr. Mustafa Mahmud, the same whom the Council of European Academics considered among the world's top 100 20th century intellectuals, writes of the hardship al-Azhar gave him over his book *God and Man*. Al-Azhar had the authority to take him to court, a secret court, which ordered his book to be confiscated. The experience left a scar for all to see, as if al-Azhar branded his forehead as a public chastisement that could not be hidden. He claims this to be the fate of all creative writers that al-Azhar goes after, zealously suppressing books that enrich while promoting all kinds of harmful ones, books on magic and superstition that are spreading like a cancer and destroying creative thought, all with the blessing of government. Dr. Mahmud claims that the government's intent in issuing the original decree giving al-Azhar censorship authority in the early 1960s was to send a message to the Muslim Brotherhood and show Saudi Arabia that Egypt was no less protective of Islam than was the Wahhabi state. "But that intent has been lost. What good is al-Azhar's censorship now that the market is filled with all kinds of videos, tapes and things on the internet that claim to be Islam but go against the tenets of the religion with their magic and trickery etc"[25]

So where does this censorship leave evolution and the biological sciences associated with it? There are no specific laws against teaching evolution in Egypt. The subject is by implication of syllabi included in some university biology courses in Egypt, though how faithfully the principles of evolution are taught would depend not only on the religious orientation of the instructor but perhaps more so on the fear of teaching something that students could use to bring charges of heresy. Public discussion of the subject is not widely tolerated. In some Muslim countries it is dangerous if not forbidden. In 1990, an eminent Sudanese biologist by the name of Faruq Muhammad Ibrahim was arrested in Khartoum and imprisoned for teaching evolution. In a letter smuggled out of his cell after a year in prison he describes his being beaten in the presence of a member of the government Revolutionary Command Council. Liberal-minded Sudanis who were safely out of the country spoke out in condemnation of the government's barbarity. None inside the country did. One leading critic, chairman of the Imams and Mosques Association in Britain and principal of the Muslim College in London, wrote that the Sudanese government might justifiably arrest people for their political views but not their scientific ones.[26] A more recent case of terror in the name of religion inflicted on a Muslim who dared speak on evolution occurred in 2011 in East London, where a prominent imam stated in a lecture in his mosque that there were no conflicts between evolution and Islam. The death threats Usama Hasan received over the furor his statement aroused were so frightening he not only retracted it but resigned his academic position at Middlesex University.[27]

If the Muslim world's entry into the world of science was glacial, its embrace of evolution was practically paralytic. The first university textbook in Arabic on biological inheritance, *The Science of Inheritance* (*Ilm al-Wiratha*), was written as an undergraduate textbook and not published until 1938, the same year that the biology department of Cairo University was founded, back when Egypt was the Arab world's intellectual pioneer. The author, Ahmad Fadil al-Khishin, an Egyptian Muslim and biology teacher in Cairo University, was one of a handful of Muslim science students who had risen to the level of university teacher before World War II. His work was carried on by his son Aziz in the next generation. Dr. Aziz Fadil al-Khishin did his doctoral study at the University of Edinburgh in the 1960s and in 1966 was appointed head of the biology department at the University in Asyut. By then the government of Gamal abd al-Nasser had founded universities in all the cities of Egypt: Asyut, Aswan, Tanta, Hilwan, Mansuriyyia, with the leading ones in Cairo and Alexandria. In 1971, Aziz Khishin updated and expanded his father's book, calling it simply *al-Wiratha* (*Inheritance*), and used it as the university textbook for introductory biology. This would imply that during the intervening 33 years (1938–1971), his father's textbook had not been replaced by a more modern one, another example of a promising start with little follow-up. Aziz's text begins with Mendel's theory of genetic inheritance and goes up to the Franklin, Crick and Watson discovery of DNA's double helix structure. Natural selection is implied: "evolution proceeds by miniscule changes over billions of years and began with a simple cell." Darwin is only briefly mentioned along with Lamarck and a few of the other pre-Darwin pioneers. The intricate mechanics of natural selection were not included.

Dr. Aziz Khishin's book was one of only two books in Arabic to be found in the biological evolution section of the American University of Cairo library in the summer of 2007. The other book was a 2002 translation of Darwin's *Origin of Species*, entitled *Asl al-Anwa'*, a highly professional piece of work written by Majdi Mahmud al-Maliji, a professor of dermatology. The National Library of Egypt, *Dar al-Kutub*, had neither book, though the Maliji translation was commissioned by Egypt's National Project for Translation under the auspices of the Supreme Council for Culture, and so was very much a government undertaking. Nor is the book found in the bookshops.

Al-Maliji, it should be noted, pays his respects to Ismail Mazhar, the man who made the first translation of the *Origin of Species* and who dared oppose the tyranny that refuses free thought: "and for this we are greatly indebted to him and are obliged to complete the way of enlightenment."[28] It took until the 21st century for the work that Ismail Mazhar accomplished in the early 20th century to be recognized by the government and the secular academic community.

Maliji's crowning of Mazhar's labors was one of love, but not without the hurdles that often frustrate love. There was that enduring reluctance in Egypt to deal with evolution that Maliji had to overcome in order to produce the Arab world's first complete translation of Darwin's *Origin of Species*. Professor Maliji said in a recent interview that no one wanted to touch the project. It was too risky. It took him nine years of devoted study to accomplish the translation, nine years of swimming against the current. What else but a labor of love could it have been, given that he knew that few people would know of the book and that fewer yet would buy it, even if it were to be offered free to the bookshops brave enough, or irreligious enough, to put it on their shelves. One looks for the book in vain, especially in Egypt:

> Few in the Arab or Muslim worlds accept Darwin's idea of evolution and natural selection, least of all Egypt – a 2007 study published in *Science* magazine on Muslim views of evolution found that fewer than 10 percent of Egyptians thought the theory was "true or probably true," the lowest rate of acceptance in any Muslim nation in the study.[29]

An international conference sponsored by the British Council in celebration of the 150th anniversary of the publication of Darwin's *Origin of Species* was held in the recently restored Ptolemaic museum-library in Alexandria, the Bibliotheca Alexandrina. This was an unusual conference for a Muslim country where belief in or acceptance of the possibility of evolution is held by perhaps less than a tenth of the population. But the connection between ancient science symbolized by the Ptolemaic library and modern science by Charles Darwin was too tempting to be put off by a low percentage of popular belief. In addition, no one in Egypt objected, not even the Mubarak government, which in such cases usually bowed to religious predilections and prejudices.

The conference, bringing together 150 scholars and scientists, was not a failure. Lectures in support of evolution were given; Egyptians listened, and opinions were voiced. The occasion offered academics of Egyptian universities, including the American University at Cairo, the opportunity to gauge the public intellectual temperature on evolution as it stood for 2009–2010. One reading on the Darwin scale was that it is not religion impeding Egyptian (and Egyptian can stand here for Arab and Muslim in general) acceptance of evolution, but the way it is taught, or rather not taught, and the "regional investment in putting basic scientific knowledge within reach of the Arabic-speaking public" – in other words, government's apathy in funding science.

Another reading came from Madiha el-Safty, a sociology professor at the American University. Her criticism could have come from Sarruf, Shumayyil, Zaydan, Abduh, Rida or Mazhar a century and more ago: "Our culture, the whole

Arab culture, unfortunately, does not encourage free thinking . . . You're not encouraged to think freely, you're supposed to be molded into certain forms and frameworks."[30] Another critique echoing from the 19th century was the emphasis on memorization over critical thinking. Egypt, once the unquestioned intellectual capital of the Arab world, ranks now, according to the World Economic Forum, 124th of 133 countries in the quality of its primary education. A system in which nothing is taught well, not even Arabic, cannot be expected to do justice to evolution, or to science in general.

Yet another reading from the conference was the response of some university students who were surprised to learn that Darwin's evolution did not mean man descended directly from a monkey – reminiscent of how Shibli Shumayyil and Jurji Zaydan regarded it when medical students at the American College a century and a half earlier. This might be contrasted to the plight of Darwin in other Muslim countries, such as the Arabian Peninsula, Pakistan and Turkey.

Quite as the name of Darwin was in a sense victimized by Shumayyil, Mazhar and Salama Musa in the early generations of Middle Eastern contact with the theory of natural selection, Darwin is now, with the increasing influence of conservative Muslim movements, being rejected anew, along with the modus vivendi worked out by Jisr, Isfahani, Rida, Jawhar and Wajdi. A survey by Dr. Nidhal Guessoum, a Muslim professor of physics and astronomy at the American University of Sharjah in the United Arab Emirates, revealed that in countries such as Tunisia, Egypt, Turkey, Pakistan and Malyasia, taken to represent the Muslim world, only 15 percent of the student and teacher population, from high school to university, believed Darwin's theory to be true or probably true. A survey he conducted of 100 academics and an equal number of students in his university in Sharjah indicated that 62 percent of Muslims believed evolution to be an unproven theory. On the other hand, a survey of non-Muslim university students and professors showed that only 10 percent had reservations: "The rate of acceptance of evolution and the idea of teaching evolution was extremely low . . . I wondered, who are all these educated people rejecting evolution? They are even rejecting the fact that it should be taught as scientific knowledge."

Dr. Guessoum himself accepts the theory. He believes, as did Shaykhs Jisr, Abduh, Rida, Jawhar and Isfahani, that evolution does not contradict religion. Only if scripture is read in a strictly literalist way is there a problem. Dr. Guessoum believes that Muslim doubts on evolution are being heightened by scientific-sounding conservative Christian literature that supports the Creationist theses being spread on the internet.[31]

In Pakistan the resistance to Darwin has a legacy that long precedes the internet and American Creationism. It precedes even the existence of Pakistan. Muhammad Iqbal, the leading religious reformer in India during the early decades of the 20th century, refused to comment on evolution out of fear that it would be lethal to simple religious belief:

> Although Iqbal sought to challenge the traditional interpretation of religious beliefs and to understand religious principles in light of modern scientific thought, he avoided any direct mention of evolution or natural selection in his

Urdu and Farsi writings. This was not because he was unaware of Darwin's works, but probably because he realized his audience was not yet ready to appreciate the significance of these ideas. Given their background of widespread illiteracy and poverty, deep-rooted social and religious conservatism, and colonial rule, religion was these people's last hope – and it was not the time to take that hope away.[32]

Out of such fears, invented or not, did patriarchal religious leaders, since al-Ghazali and before, allow the ignorance that they assumed to benight the lower classes to make cowards of them, and ensure that Muslims would continue to be kept in the dark. According to Ahmed Kayani of Islamabad University's Department of Sciences and Technology, a chapter on evolution was not included in a school textbook until the government's educational reforms of 2002.

In Turkey there is little effective opposition to Adnan Oktar's attack on evolution. Two leading opponents are the Turkish scientists Umit Sayin[33] and Aykut Kence.[34] Turkish scientific institutions indeed protest the pseudo-scientific literature turned out in abundance by the Creationists' Science Research Foundation (*Bilim Arastirma Vakfi*), but the rising popularity of Islam during the last two decades, which is energized by what appears to Muslims to be an American–Israeli-led war of the West against Islam as a religion of terrorists, provides an accepting audience for Creationism. In 2008, Adnan Oktar (Harun Yahya) succeeded in having the website of the anti-Creationist and public atheist Richard Dawkins banned in Turkey. Kenyan-born Dawkins, author of best seller *The Selfish Gene* (1976), and one of the most influential zoologists of his time doing battle to discredit Creationism, was a prime target of Adnan Oktar. In a theatrical show of absurd self-promotion, Oktar offered 6.6 trillion dollars to anyone who could produce a single fossil that proved evolution.[35] Creationists would presumably be the judges.[36]

Turkey's relatively recent engagement in the effort to reduce evolution to an Islamic creationism seems to be pretty much a very well-funded one-man operation. The books that the operation pours out are written under the name of Harun Yahya. This is the pen name of Adnan Oktar. Oktar is the leader of a religious order and has been reported to receive funding from Saudi Arabia and American conservative Christian organizations. This would explain the existence of so many glossy, expensive looking books on Creationism bearing Oktar's pseudonym. So copious are his publications, with full color photographs and illustrations, not counting the articles, videos and web pages (www.hyahya.com), it is hard to believe that this is the work of one man and not the industry of an organization or several of them joined in Creationist belief, Christian and Muslim.[37] The richly adorned books, printed and translated at considerable expense, are sold cheaply or given away. In Turkey they are found wherever books are sold. Much of the material follows the pattern found in the American Institute for Creation Research: so intricate, complex, inter-dependent and purposeful are the workings of nature that only a Creator of miraculous genius could have designed such a magnificent cosmos, from the sub-atomic to the astro-physical.

Notes

1 Ali Shahhat, p. 141.
2 Muhammad Tira, *Khalk al-Insan*, Cairo, p. 187.
3 M. Tira, *Khalq al-Insan*, pp. 191–193.
4 Mustafa Mahmoud, *Lughz al-Hayat* (The Riddle of Life), Cairo, 1989.
5 M. Mahmoud, *Lughz al-Hayat*, pp. 56–57.
6 M. Mahmoud, *Lughz al-Hayat*, p. 103.
7 Mahmoud Ayyoub, "Creation or Evolution? The Reception of Darwinism in Modern Arab Thought," in *Science and Religion in a Post-Colonial World*, edited by Zainal Abidin Bagir, Adelaide, Australia, 2005, pp.173–235; see pp. 185–188. Also, Taner Edis, *An Illusion of Harmony: Science and Religion in Islam*, Prometheus, Amherst, NY, 2007, p. 142; and Raymond W. Baker, *Islam Without Fear: Egypt and the New Islamists*, Harvard University Press, Cambridge, MA, 2003, pp. 262–264. Arguing that Adam was preceded by other pre-human creatures who had evolved to become human, Shahin caused enough of a public outcry to get his book banned and himself accused of heresy.
8 An exception to this is an Egyptian writer, 'abd al-Sabur Shahin, who was harassed and threatened by accusations, but no more than that.
9 Yahya Farghal, *al-Islam wa'l ittijahatal-'ilmiyya al-mu'asira*, Cairo, 1984, p. 50.
10 Yahya Farghal, p. 62.
11 Yahya Farghal, p. 128.
12 Yahya Farghal, p. 135.
13 Yahya Farghal, pp. 136 ff.
14 Mahir Khalil, *Suqut al-Nazariyya Darwin fi Dhaw' al-Iktishafat al-'Ilmiyya al-Haditha* (The Fall of Darwin's Theory in the Light of Modern Scientific Discoveries), Cairo, 1986, p. 86.
15 Mahir Khalil, *Suqut*, p. 169.
16 Mahir Khalil, *Suqut*, p. 117.
17 Mahir Khalil, *Suqut*, p. 185–189.
18 Mahir Khalil, *Suqut*, p. 170.
19 Mahir Khalil, *Suqut*, p. 253. Evolution's being included in secondary school science courses would represent a significant step in its assimiliative progress, but it would be a much watered-down version of evolution that is taught in secondary schools, if it is in fact taught, which is doubtful. I have found no evidence of it.
20 Muhammad Nabil al-Nashawati, *al-I'jaz Allahiyy fi Khalq al-Insan wa Tanfid Nazariyya Darwin*, Cairo, p. 123.
21 Muhammad Nashawati, p. 303.
22 Muhammad Nashawati, p. 307.
23 Mustafa Mahmoud, "Intellectuals Speak Out," *Akhbar al-Yawm*, June 11, 2004; and June 12, 2004.
24 M. Mahmoud, "Intellectuals Speak Out."
25 M. Mahmoud, "Intellectuals Speak Out."
26 Pervez Hoodbhoy, *Religious Orthodoxy and the Battle for Rationality*, Zed Books, London, 1991, p. 48.
27 Steve Paulson, "Does Islam Stand Against Science," *The Chronicle Review of Higher Education*, July 18, 2011.
28 *Asl al-Anwa*, Majdi al-Maliji's translation of Darwin's *Origin of Species*, published by al-Majlis al-A'la li'l Thaqafa (Supreme Council for Culture), Cairo, 2002, p. 51. Dr. Maliji's work is superb for its thoroughness. The translation is precise and easily understandable, with all Western and Latin terms rendered in Latin script and highlighted in bold letters, saving the reader the often troublesome task of figuring out what the Arabic transliteration refers to in the way of plants, animals, people, institutions, books, chemicals, compounds and scientific terms, be they bugle, bagel or beagle.

29 Sarah Mishkin, "Origin of a Translation," *Egypt Today*, vol 31, issue 6 (June 2010), www.egypttoday.com/article.
30 Reported by Michael Slackman, *New York Times*, Thursday, November 26, 2009, p. A-10.
31 Ruth Gledhill, "Muslim Academics and Students Are Turning Against Darwin's Theory," *The Times*, London, November 17, 2009.
32 *Nature*, vol 462 (December 24–31, 2009), p. 984.
33 Department of Neurology, School of Medicine, University of Wisconsin, Madison.
34 Department of Biology, Middle East Technical University, Ankara.
35 Gledhill, November 17, 2009.
36 On Adnan Oktar and his influence see Taner Edis, *An Illusion of Harmony*, pp. 115–163.
37 Umit Sayin and Aykut Kence, "Islamic Scientific Creationism: A New Challenge in Turkey," *Reports of the National Center for Science Education*, 1980, vol 19, issue 6, pp. 18–20, 25–29.

17 The place of Al-Azhar and the ulema

Where stood the institutional custodians of religious discourse in this consuming controversy? They stood firmly in place, unbudged. Those of them within the hallowed walls of al-Azhar who wished to budge found themselves standing alone or on the outside.

The modernism initiated by Shaykh Muhammad Abduh failed to influence sufficient numbers of his peers to continue his lead. His many followers outside the religious institution generated much commentary but no change. Those within the walls of al-Azhar who wanted change and publicly followed Abduh's lead found those walls as insurmountable as the shaykhs were unforgiving to those who broke ranks.

In 1925, Ali abd al-Raziq, a young Azharite shaykh and follower of Abduh, submitted his dissertation for a doctoral degree in theology. Based on his critical re-reading of the early historical sources, Ali argued that the classical caliphate of early Islam was a coercive political institution that was not rooted in the Quran, Prophetic Tradition or anything known about Muhammad's life. The caliphate was in fact an ad hoc institution concocted by a power elite led by abu Bakr and Omar, the first and second caliphs, and forced on the Muslim community. The young shaykh claimed there was nothing religious about it, that it was an office cooked up after the Quranic revelation had been completed and Muhammad had died, a case of religion being used for a purely political end.

Those who succeeded abu Bakr and Omar to the caliphate extended the claims of the office's divine origins, to the extent that the caliph became not just the successor of the Prophet but of even God, whose shadow on earth the caliph was claimed to be, a ruler appointed by God as protector of the true religion and the community of the faithful. The theory of the office became a religious discipline to be studied alongside the Quran, Hadith and Shari'a. Originating as a political expedient, the office assumed a majesty inherited from Byzantine and Sassanian precedents, making religion a tool in the hands of rulers who in its name perpetuated the most brutal political excesses. With the institutionalization of the caliphate, religion was delivered to the hands of tyrants as a weapon of coercion. Religiously instructed that the caliphate originated in the Quran and the life of the Prophet, Muslims were reduced to docile subjects obedient to traditional authority they believed to be legitimized by the highest authority, God.

From this "crime" resulted misrule, corruption, political oppression and the end of the creative period of Islamic science and civilization. What ended the creative period of Islamic civilization was religiously cloaked tyranny, a lethal collusion of political rulers and ulema engendering an obedience to authority for the sake of social quiescence. It was easily justified by the ulema – better tyranny than civil upheaval. One of the examples Ali abd al-Raziq provides is the remarkable career of ibn abi Amir, known as al-Mansur, usurper of Umayyad power in Andalusia. Mansur covered the illegitimacy of his rule by winning support of the ulema of Cordova, in return for which he publicly burned all the philosophical books in the marvelous library of the Caliph Hakam II, unwittingly but effectively undermining the Umayyad caliphate.

Strongly implied in Ali abd al-Raziq's thesis was an argument for the separation of religion and state to end the political pretensions of Islam and free the mind through reinterpretation of the holy sources.[1] Separation of state and religion had been more or less an accomplished fact since the time of Muhammad Ali a century earlier, but no ruler after him could afford not to feign an accordance with the leadership of al-Azhar. Ali abd al-Raziq's questioning of authority posed a threat to both the political and religious leadership. To the authorities of al-Azhar his dissertation was equivalent to Luther's 95 Theses and the beginning of an Islamic Reformation that would have ended up critically analyzing even the Quran. In his call for reform Ali abd al-Raziq was more daring than had been Muhammad Abduh, and more of a failure. He was found guilty of heresy by al-Azhar's council of inquisition, dismissed from his position, expelled from al-Azhar and banned from ever teaching again or writing on religion. Timorously peeking from behind the façade that was supposed to separate state and religion, the Egyptian government forbade the de-turbaned shaykh from holding any office.

It was not simply the leadership of al-Azhar that resisted modern reform. It was the combined bulk of the medieval institution freighted with a thousand years of tradition and the society that followed it religiously, with the secular state marching insecurely along.

In 1945, some 20 years after Ali abd al-Raziq's dismissal, his younger brother Mustafa, a graduate of al-Azhar and doctor of philosophy from the Sorbonne, became rector of al-Azhar. He too tried to introduce the institution to new ways of thinking and met the same opposition that his brother, and before him Muhammad Abduh and Tahtawi, had faced. Mustafa's Sorbonne dissertation, *Tamhid li-Tarikh al-Falsafat al-Islamiyya* (*Introduction to the History of Islamic Philosophy*), was a critical analysis of Islamic jurisprudence that set out to prove that the Prophet Muhammad had used reason in coming to conclusions, as had the early legal thinkers in formulating the holy Shari'a. But even the rector proved helpless against the great weight of a millennium's accumulated tradition and resistance to change.

Five years after Shaykh Ali abd al-Raziq's condemnation, al-Azhar condemned another of its own for transgressing the boundaries of religion. This was when a middle-aged scholar published an annotated version of the Quran that explained away supernatural verses and that criticized the traditional authoritative commentaries on the basis of their having lost the meaning of the Quran by their narrow focus on jurisprudence and theology. Shaykh Muhammad abu Zayd of Damanhur called his treatise on Quranic interpretation *Guidance and Instruction in Interpreting the Quran by the Quran* (*Hidaya wa'l – 'Irfan fi Tafsir al-Quran bi'l – Quran*), meaning the Quran should explain itself without external considerations being brought in and words being taken out of their Quranic context. Shaykh abu Zayd had a traditional religious education in his village before going to al-Azhar. He never traveled to the West. His inspiration to interpret the Quran through itself seems to have come from Muhammad Abduh, whom he admired. Abu Zayd interpreted the verses rationally in accordance to modern ideas in science, law and liberal political philosophy, but did not indulge in equating verses to electromagnetism, microbiology and the sort. His book was more serious than that in its consideration of a complete overhaul of the religio-legal foundations of Islam. In an interview abu Zayd had with the newspaper *al-Ahram* following al-Azhar's condemnation of him, he claimed that he had shared his ideas about Quranic interpretation with the rector of al-Azhar and his fellow shaykhs and they had been inspired by his ideas. Ali abd al-Raziq had claimed the same. But al-Azhar's support vanished in both cases the moment the books aroused a storm of protest. To prove al-Azhar was a staunch defender of tradition and orthodoxy, the rector banned the books, sending Shaykh abu Zayd to a form of exile in Asyut as added proof.

Rashid Rida attacked him as an atheist and spreader of atheism. Rida's earlier apostleship of Abduh's rationalist approach to the Quran had by then completed its reversion to a more traditionalist outlook in visceral reaction to the Anglo–French mandates after World War I and Britain's policy in transforming Palestine into a Jewish state, disestablishing the indigenous population. Long-held intellectual positions are not always invulnerable to untoward political events. Rashid Rida's conversion was suffused in anger and confusion: one moment he was accusing Shaykh abu Zayd of atheism and the next fulminating that abu Zayd got his ideas from him.[2] Al-Azhar's protests were threatening enough for the government to have the police confiscate copies of abu Zayd's book and order him never to preach or hold office again. If this was not enough, the ulema in his hometown of Damanhur attempted to have him declared a heretic and separated from his wife.[3]

A more famous Egyptian reformist thinker to suffer the wrath of al-Azhar was the blind literary critic Taha Husayn, an unabashed westernizer and doctoral graduate of the Sorbonne. His secularist interpretation of Egyptian civilization portrays Egypt as a unique synthesis of Pharaonic, Greco–Roman and Mediterranean traditions. Islamic Egypt is subsumed into the country's Mediterranean orientation, a 20th century version of Khedive Ismail's vision of Egypt as a southern extension of Europe. Taha Husayn's minimalizing the role of Islam won him no friends among the ulema.

What aroused the religious temper against him was his critical philological analysis of words, literary style and usage found in pre-Islamic poetry. His research convinced him that most if not all pre-Islamic poetry was composed during Islamic times and passed off as an earlier creation in order to promote particular tribes along with certain political and religious ideas and local traditions. His thesis undermined much of the careful linguistic structure upon which the interpretation of the Quran had been based. It was an explosive issue. This kind of critical philological analysis threatened to invade the Quran if left unchecked. Al-Azhar declared his work heretical. When the Egyptian civil government backed up al-Azhar's position Taha Husayn was forced to abjure or face condemnation as an unbeliever and threatened with dismissal from his academic post at the University of Cairo. As the Arab world's foremost man of letters went down in the humiliation of having to renounce his meticulous scholarly work, the small secularist society of writers, professionals and academicians sensed themselves besieged by both religious conservatives and a frightened government. By agreeing to excise the offensive parts of his thesis Taha Husayn eliminated what was creative in it. The copies on sale today are censored versions. Rightly fearing that if critical textual and philogical analysis was left free to be applied to pre-Islamic poetry and overturn traditional historical interpretations and that the Quran would be next on the list to be infected by the corruptive amorality of rational analysis, the Azhar shaykhs nipped the bud of Taha Husayn's revision of early Arabic poetry before it could blossom. Nipped along with it was Taha Husayn's grand ambition to reorganize Cairo University on the model of the Sorbonne. He had aspirations of incorporating classical Greek and Latin into the Cairo University curriculum, giving greater importance to the exact sciences and cultivating the critical thinking required to engage in them. His years of doctoral study in Paris had determined him to free Egyptian education from the tradition of memorization that predominated even in the university.

Mirroring Taha Husayn's projected reformation of education was his book on the philosophy of Egyptian culture and its future development: Egypt's culture was a product of its history: Pharaonic, Greek and Roman, fundaments upon which had been built Egypt's centuries-long Byzantine culture. Egypt did not lose these cultural fundaments with the coming of the Arabs and Islam. As in classical times, Egypt was always intellectually, culturally and commercially tied to a Mediterranean culture that bound it to the southern shores of the West. Intellectually binding the West and Islam in a common cultural heritage was the Greek foundation of Islamic science and philosophy that gave rise to modern science. To reject western science was to reject Islam. Egypt was at the geographical heart of this cultural Mediterranean family. The West's secular humanism was Egypt's cultural destiny.[4]

Taha Husayn was no more successful in the reforms he wanted to make in the university than Abduh had been in reforming al-Azhar. His philosophy of Egyptian culture and destiny, which did not put Islam at the front, added to the many enemies he had made at al-Azhar over his revisionist interpretation of pre-Islamic poetry. His criticism of Arab governments and politicians, whom he described as lazy, ignorant and hopelessly incompetent, and whom he blamed for Arab cultural backwardness rather than blaming the usual culprits, the Turks, made him many enemies in government. Nonetheless, overcoming all the enemies his scholarship and frankness had brought against him, he was appointed Minister of Education in 1950, following in the steps of Ali Mubarak and Muhammad Abduh. Like his reformist predecessors, Taha Husayn hoped that his new position in government would allow him to transform education by introducing new courses and changing the traditional way students learned and thought. Rather than mastering written texts through memorization they would analytically take them apart, reinterpret them and with maturing critical ability create original ones of their own. Two years after his appointment, the military seized power in Egypt, aborting his program and bringing his government service to an end.

In his last interview in 1974, given just before he died, he recalls the overwhelming resistance against him because of his two most famous works, *The Future of Culture in Egypt* and *Pre-Islamic Poetry* (*al-Shi'r al – Jahiliyya*). Everyone stood against him: al-Azhar, the government, the public, even the secularists, including the leading nationalist Wafd Party. No support came to him from any corner. Looking back almost half a century, he sees his condemnation as a closing of the Egyptian mind to new ideas and science. In his own mind, reminiscing in the 1970s on the intellectual scene of the 1920s and 1930s, the Egyptian mind had been open and creative. But after 1940, secular politicians divorced culture from politics, eliminating state responsibility for cultural life. Consequently, the cultural mind contracted and the level fell, as shown by the name given his few supporters, "aristocrats." The Wafd Party debased the national culture in the 1940s, and the military dictatorship finished it off in the following decades, reducing political and intellectual life to clichés and empty slogans.[5]

The cases of Ali and Mustafa abd al-Raziq, and of abu Zayd and Taha Husayn, reveal the fears of the shaykhs regarding modernization as it relates to the reinterpretation of history and literature. Taha Husayn's book challenging the authenticity of pre-Islamic poetry (a thesis not overwhelmingly supported by contemporary scholarship) threatened, if his philological analysis was taken any further, to demythologize the eternal divinity of the Quran. The ulema realized that once unleashed, the analytic method of science would reach into the structural foundations of religious belief. There would be others following Taha Husayn, abu Zayd and the brothers abd al-Raziq, right up to the present time – scholars who would be tried by al-Azhar, declared heretics and condemned for advocating reinterpretation of the sources of Muslim law and religious belief, as the secular government stood by nodding in legal confirmation of religion's judgment.

Pre-Islamic poetry, early Islamic history, reinterpretation of the Quran and reformulation of the Shari'a are off limits for modernizers. But not science. No one has been hailed to appear before the inquisitorial court for claiming the Quran supports Copernican astronomy, Newtonian mechanics, Darwinian evolution, modern genetics or astrophysics. Islam has no Bruno or Galileo, and al-Azhar no problem with science as long as proponents of its methodology mind their own business and refrain from intruding their critical analysis into other disciplines that closely touch on religion. In other words, an emasculated science, the semblance or shell of it, is permissible, quite as in medieval times logic, mathematics and natural studies were allowed, though not condoned, as long as the transcendent metaphysics that gave them philosophical and spiritual unity and purpose was excised from the body – as long as the head was cut off, as it were.

Jisr, Abduh, Rida, Wajdi, Isfahani, Tantawi Jawhar, Hasan Husayn and dozens of other modern writers could profess that religion had no quarrel with science or evolution, but their efforts served only to elevate and reinforce religion and its holy sources. None dared question the sources. The interpretation of scientific commentary was the opposite of critical exegesis. Jisr, Tantawi and Wajdi merely reaffirmed the truth of orthodoxy in the name of modern science. Secularists who advocated science and evolution kept their distance from religion. No one writing in the cause of science was accused of heresy, for none tried or even suggested putting the scalpel of scientific analysis to the holy sources.

Writing in 1932, the leading British scholar of Islam at the time, H.A.R. Gibb, observed that evolution was a subject "still very gingerly handled in ultra-conservative circles," by which he meant the avoidance of public discussion of the subject by the shaykhs.[6] Pre-Islamic poetry, the caliphate and early Islamic history had their martyrs. Not science. Nor evolution. Not even the radical gauntlets thrown down by suspected atheist and proponent of Darwin, Ismail Mazhar, were thought threatening enough to warrant a charge of heresy from al-Azhar. While poetry, history, caliphate and religious reinterpretation were off-limits to critical analysis, the corpse of a neutered and disemboweled science was safe enough.

In point of comparison, it was not many years ago, 1997, that Pope John Paul II, speaking officially for the Catholic Church, pronounced Darwin as having no injurious effect on religion. Seventy years before that, Muhammad Farid Wajdi writing as chief editor in the *Egyptian National Encyclopedia* and later in *Majallat al-Azhar*, and Shaykh Rashid Rida in *al-Manar*, had said the same, though not many religious thinkers were to follow them. In fairness to the ulema and the shaykhs of al-Azhar, it must be emphasized that Shibli Shumayyil, Salama Musa and Ismail Mazhar were not natural selection's best ambassadors. The revolutionary socialist materialism they poured into evolution, with a strong splash of atheism to complete the cocktail, was seen to be more lethal to religion than all of the other sciences put together.

The subject of evolution was shied away from in the small body of literature devoted to science and religion between the World Wars. It was totally avoided in a book on science and Islam by Ahmad Dardiri, published at the end of World War II. The author urges young Muslims to take up science in order to save themselves from western domination, though by then it was pretty late for that. Dardiri knew what he was talking about. He had been exiled from Palestine by the British for resisting Zionist colonization of his own land. Thoroughly westernized, an advocate of reform and a religious official in the Young Men's Muslim Association, Dardiri had a strongly positive feeling for science, but could not bring himself to deal with evolution.

With few exceptions (Mazhar, Musa, Mahfuz, *Muqtataf*), in the half century following World War I, writers, reformers and scientific interpreters have taken their cue from the shaykhs and remained silent on evolution. One of the exceptions, the popular Egyptian story teller and Nobel Prize winner Nagib Mahfuz, has risen to the occasion and, through characters in his novels, brought the question of evolution from the subliminal depths of the great silence to the surface. In

Mahfuz's *Palace of Desire* (*Qasr al-Shawq*), published in 1957, one of the main characters, a young man of lower middle-class conservative background and a student at Cairo University in the early 1940s, is studying philosophy. This takes him to science. All is well until Darwin comes into the picture. The evidence for evolution is convincing but troublesome. Being intellectually honest and determined, the young man stretches his religious concepts to reach an interpretation that enables him to live at peace with his inherited beliefs. One day he discusses evolution with his traditional-minded father, who treats his family with iron-fisted tyranny. Hardly able to believe his ears as his son is going on about Darwin, he bursts out in anger that his son is learning heresy and denial of religion and that this man Darwin should be kicked out of the university and sent packing back to England where he came from. He curses the English and commands his son to drop philosophy.

Mahfuz uses the encounter to help lay out the two worlds Egypt is living in (the father wears a galabiyya, the son a suit and tie) and resuscitate and sharpen the intellectual conflict between them that had lain dormant, leaving the son to reach the fragile reconciliation he had come to on his own. The son promises his father to obey; he has no choice under his father's absolute rule that allows no room for discussion. But he knows he cannot obey. His studies are too important. They have become his life. His traditional beliefs have melted away in the heat and light of science and philosophy, banishing the old forever. There is no bringing it back. A new faith must be recast that resonates positively with modern knowledge. Abduh's *Treatise on Divine Oneness* can be heard echoing in the student's head. This new reconciliation that the young man makes for himself is not without periods of agonizing doubt and shifting back and forth between the distant poles of his two worlds, one being love, family, warmth, familiarity, comfort and security, and the other being learning, individuality, expanding consciousness and adventure of discovery. Finally the poles converge: "True religion is science, the key to the secrets of the existence and its magnificence." The young man concludes that, "If prophets were to be sent today, they would choose science as their message. The ignorance of yesterday will perish in the light of tomorrow. The way to God is open and clear. It is the way of science, goodness and beauty." And with this, Mahfuz has his narrator conclude the episode on the student's struggle between traditional religion and modern science, "he bade farewell to the past with its deceptive dreams and false hopes."[7]

But the conflict is not over. It is merely transformed to the generational conflict of father and son. Drawing on the real world of Cairene life, Mahfuz's fiction, or a part of it, weaves young and upwardly mobile characters of urban but traditional background who have imbibed the mélange of western ideas popularized in the articles of *Muqtataf*, the books of Shumayyil, Musa and Mazhar, who have been taught science and philosophy at Cairo University, and who must resolve this side of their mental life with the reality of their traditional families and upbringing.

The image is drawn again in another Mahfuz novel, this in the character of a socialist-minded chief editor of a student magazine who in trying to sever the bonds of his traditional background proclaims that scientists are the prophets of the 20th century.[8] The young characters represent an urban Egypt in transition to becoming what Mahfuz hoped Egypt would become, the same future Egypt that Taha Husayn hoped for and expressed in his historical interpretation of culture, a westernized secular society at ease with science and buffered by the protecting traditions of family and religion, galabiyyas and suits living in an evolved harmony that has by generational change transcended the prevailing disruptive tension between the old that refuses to die and the new that can neither accept nor abandon the old.

That harmony has failed to evolve. During the last half century the division has grown wider, giving wider acceptance to violence, by the state, by the West, by the true believers. Violence has for all contestants become the order of the day. It has empowered and given safe harbor to terror in the name of religion. People like Nagib Mahfuz become vulnerable: he was stabbed by a young man acting in the name of God on a street corner in Cairo as he sat in his chauffeured car. The hunted author of the *Satanic Verses*, Salman Rushdie, was in a way more fortunate, having outlived the fatwa that in the feverish minds of fanatic Muslims legalized his assassination.

What a turnaround from the time between Muhammad Ali and Gamal abd al-Nasser. From the early 19th century on, for a century and a half, every indication was that Egypt would continue the process of secularization as modernity pushed traditional society more and more to the margins. The Arab states in North Africa and the Fertile Crescent, it was assumed by western observers and secular Arabs, would develop in a mildly Turkish fashion as they emerged from imperialist domination and took hold of their destiny as independent states shortly after World War II. The Pahlevi regime had been taking Iran in a parallel direction since the 1920s. There was little to suggest that the development of these states would not follow the path marked out by the Turkish Republic of Mustafa Kemal, at their own pace and to a perhaps somewhat less radical degree of secularist westernization, but westernizing nonetheless.

Nasser's military takeover of Egypt, and the triumphant surge of Arab nationalism in the 1950s with Nasser's disbandment of the Muslim Brotherhood, followed by his nationalization of the Suez Canal and subsequent triumph over the Anglo–French–Israeli invasion to unseat him, seemed to seal the secular nationalist destiny of the modern Arab states. Nasser's call to Arab nationalist socialism appeared to put the final nail in the coffin of the Shari'a-ruled state called for by the defunct Brotherhood. The ascendancy of the nationalist Ba'th (Renaissance) Party in Syria and Iraq was a step along the widely expected way. Religion was firmly under the thumb of the ruthless dictatorial rulers of the nationalist secular states.

Three events within 12 years, 1967–1979, radically altered the landscape: Israel's victory in the Six-Day War; the fall of the Pahlevi dynasty in Iran and its replacement by a religious government under the guidance of Ayatallah Khomeini; and Anwar Sadat's Camp David peace accord with Israel. The first destroyed Arab nationalism and made a sham of modern Arab leaders and their secular socialist states; the second showed the power of religion in overthrowing a supposedly powerful monarchy and humiliating its American supporter; the third withdrew the leading power from Arab ranks, abandoning Jordan, Syria, Lebanon and the Palestinians to Israel's expansionist Likud government. Egypt's withdrawal from the Arab struggle against Israel to regain the territories lost in the 1967 war was in regional terms analogous to the fall of the Soviet Union in the global Cold War. Both events left the field open to the willful power of one player. In their attempt to shape the Middle East to their liking, the local and the global powers joined forces. The close U.S.-Israeli alliance was to cost much Arab and Israeli blood in trying to reach what Israeli expansionists and their U.S. backers regarded to be an acceptable Middle East peace. Egypt could be bought and Iraq invaded by the remaining global power; Lebanon could be invaded and the West Bank absorbed by the remaining regional power, and together they could remake the Muslim world according to design, guaranteeing a secure source of oil for one, land for expansion for the other.

Such is the way Arabs and the great majority of Muslims see themselves being subjected to a new world order of imperial control. Those three events mentioned at the beginning of the previous paragraph have combined to turn the Arab–Muslim world upside down and have deeply wounded the secular society, fatally it would seem in the long run now that the predicted clash of civilizations, as it is popularly, or rather shallowly, called, is becoming every day more of a reality, thanks to the extremists in Washington, London and the Middle East. But the clash is not of civilizations. It is of skewed ideologies of small minorities, one deluded by power and the arrogant surety that all is possible, meaning that the weak must do what the powerful command; the other enraged by defeat, weakness, humiliation and a sense of betrayal by their state dictators, but fortified by the certitude of being God's warriors. The clash is ideology-driven, minority-led, wrong-headed visions pitting the madness of global domination against the madness of divine vengeance.

Signaled in larger than life style by two commercial jets pulverizing the towers of American capitalist power, the clash has sown doubt and confusion in the peoples on both sides – that is, except for the most extreme proponents of violence who welcome and brought on the clash. They are clear-sighted in their goals. In the United States where little if anything is known about the outside world, let alone the Middle East, the question is "Why do they hate us?" – a question fostered by political leaders for it saves having to do a lot of explaining about costly foreign policies. In the Middle East the clash has torn asunder familiar secular orientations cherished by the westernized section of society. As if all direction has been lost, they see the work of a century and more undone.

Who could have believed before 1979 that a westernized quasi-Muslim Pakistani novelist living in England and writing in English would be victimized and threatened with death by a religious opinion issued in a town called Qum by an octogenarian obscurantist who hadn't even read the literary fantasy about a Pakistani dreaming of falling out of an airplane over England, or that Nagib Mahfuz would be stabbed in an assassination attempt because of a fable he wrote depicting Moses, Christ and Muhammad in friendly conversation?

As the whirlwind of violence following the 1967 war swept across the region – militant movements of Palestinian refugees taking over in Jordan and south Lebanon (1968–1970), the Jordanian army fighting and expelling PLO fighters (1970–1971), the murder of Israeli Olympic athletes in Munich (1972), a PLO-Lebanese war (1973), assassination and counter assassination, the civil war in Lebanon (1975–1990), the Israeli invasion of Lebanon in 1978, Israel's bombing of Beirut with U.S. made warplanes and occupation of south Lebanon (1982–2000) and expropriation of swaths of the West Bank, the two Palestinian Intifadas (1987, 2000) against the continuing military occupation and theft of Palestinian land, the brutal Israeli repression – as the bombs dropped, the buildings collapsed and the fires burned, the Arab states watched in helpless paralysis from the sidelines. Adding to the poisonous passions was the United States's response to Iraq's invasion of Kuwait, the American military campaign code named Desert Shield, which put 400,000 U.S. troops in Saudi Arabia, and Desert Storm, which freed Kuwait of the Iraqis, initiating more than a decade of American and British bombing of Iraq, worsened by U.S. and U.N. restrictions on imports to the country, causing tremendous suffering and hundreds of thousands of child-deaths from malnutrition and lack of medical supplies. In the eyes of Arabs and all Muslims over the world, the Iraqi episode further discredited the West, particularly the U.S., whose action against Iraq for occupying Kuwait was a contradiction in policy when contrasted to its quarter century toleration of Israeli occupation and illegal appropriation of Palestinian territory. The double standard was perfectly clear to Arabs and other Muslims, if not to U.S. leaders.

The American-backed Israeli savagery unleashed on Lebanon, Gaza and the West Bank in the summer of 2006, on Gaza again in 2008 with Operation Cast Lead, has spread and deepened already festering hatreds to the point that the popularity of Hamas and Hizb Allah are becoming mainstream. Hizb Allah arose in Shi'i south Lebanon in opposition to Israeli occupation and was responsible for driving the Israelis out and then fighting them to a standstill in 2006. Hamas, its Sunni counterpart, arose in Gaza also in response to long Israeli military occupation and brutality, and was democratically elected to power by a free election that was pushed by Bush II and the Israeli occupiers and then petulantly rejected by them when the wrong people won.

The events referred to previously had also gone to discredit the Arab states, especially Egypt, Jordan and Saudi Arabia, which appeared to be in collusion with Israel and America. The rise of Iran and the touted threat of a Shi'i Crescent, thanks to Bush II's invasion of Iraq, brought the Sunni leaders clinging all the tighter to their imperial protector, thickening the toxic atmosphere that revolutionary political Islam needed to thrive.

What does this all have to do with science? The more that Islam becomes the answer as the way out of the dilemma on the political level, the more threatened are governments, the more repressive is the political atmosphere and the more necessary is funding for the military in defense of government against its people. The repressive effects are communicated everywhere in society. Censorship chokes off creativity in art, literature, film and theater. Scientific creativity does not exist in a cultural vacuum. If but one form of creativity goes, the others wither in fear of being next.

The only show in town that made for some creativity were the comical contortions of political leaders whose puppet performance of party politics produced painful laughter; but laughs came at a high price. Behind the puppeteers stood, and still stands, the military, their only support, and the military, above all, had to be kept happy. Once the military officers left the feeding trough there was not much left. Education and scientific research suffered. Nor was there any payoff for science and technology in the government's cosseting of the military, as all the planes, tanks, missiles and radar systems are made, delivered, assembled and often operated by the providing industrial power. Science scholarships, competitive institutes of technology and research foundations were along with everything else secondary to the military, for that was the only institution enabling the political rulers to hang onto not just their power but their lives.

The lack of productive scientific activity makes for an intellectual void readily filled by Scientific Interpretation. There is no end to the academic charlatans who have rushed in, pens at the ready to pervert religion, while claiming to their shallow followers that they are saving it through science.

The freedom of mind and society that Sarruf, Nimr, Shumayyil, Zaydan, Antun, Abduh, Jawhar, Musa, Mazhar, Lutfi al-Sayyid, Taha Husayn and Mahfuz claimed to be the source of science has given way to Quranic exegesis and adherence to the unreformed Shari'a. Accordingly, as the Shari'a is supposed to map the way to the best governed society, the Quran maps the way to the secrets of nature. This supposition leads to nothing but deeper social and intellectual stagnation, breeding an army of evermore angry young people thirsting to take vengeance on their governments for their faltering society and dead-end lives, and on the American–Israeli axis for the violence that they perceive the deadly duo continually inflicting on them.

From Algeria to Pakistan, the intellectual front of the Islamists struggling in the name of jihad for a republic of the Shari'a has avidly taken up Scientific Interpretation. Many of the interpretive strugglers have advanced degrees. They consider themselves scientists and believe they serve both science and religion by showing how the latter transcends and prefigures the former. Ironically, it is these men, dedicated to sweeping away secularist government and western influences, who of all Muslims have most aggressively appropriated western science as Islam's own.

This mind-fix, considered extreme during the first half of the 20th century by practicing Muslims but now practically mainstream, does not speak for all of Muslim society. Those who have not succumbed to it are by force of circumstances constrained to silence. Open debate has been shown to be perilous. A brave few still dare to speak out now and then, but the liberal ground that at one time commonly supported Muslims and Christian Arabs who voiced their critical ideas in agreement and debate has been swept from beneath them. They see their world under siege. They see their repressive governments as being bought off by American money and power, and in a tacit alliance with a smothering religious absolutism. Recent events, however, beginning with the overthrow of the long-ruling dictators of Tunis and Egypt, are volcanic in their possibilities of fundamentally changing the landscape, but the ground is still shifting, and how it will look in several years remains to be seen. Already in Egypt the military has regained power after crushing the democratically elected but abusive government of Muhammad al-Mursi of the Muslim Brotherhood.

The liberal, westernized, or semi-westernized, section of Muslim society, the professional and intellectual avant-garde of western science, education and democratic reform, has been cut adrift and left hanging in the wind, frightened and helpless. They see their religion usurped by political activists claiming to act in the name of Islam, their political leaders frozen to inaction except when acting to help themselves or tighten the screws of censorship. Crushed by government from one side and accused of heresy from the other, the westernized humanist liberals who had been slowly informing Muslim society since the 19th century, the Christian community well-represented among them, are already in flight from what they see as a hopeless situation.

Political extremism, acting in the name of an Islam conceived in the image of violence, has not been aggressively denounced by the accredited authorities of Islam. In Egypt, the relative silence of al-Azhar, whose ulema have not by any means escaped the extremism swirling outside its gates, has left extremism to its own in its emphasis on holy war over and above the many other dimensions of Islam's rich and complex belief system. Holy war in the hands of non-state actors becomes terrorism. The question of terrorism has put the shaykhs between a rock and a hard place. The leading shaykhs speak out in condemnation of terrorism when the pressure is on, as it was from the West after the London subway bombings in July 2005. On such occasions western leaders and media accordingly applaud the good sense of these good Muslims. But when a year later they speak out in condemnation of the terrorism inflicted by Israel in Palestine and its invasion and destruction of Lebanon, the West cries foul, declaiming their fanatical lack of balance.

Between tyranny of the state from above and populist anger from the streets, the religious institution, infected by that very anger of the people that the ulema supposedly represent, finds itself gripped in a paralyzing set of opposites, polarized as it is between Islamic activism and subservience to the state, as if resolving the polarity of Prophetic Tradition and modernity was not burden enough on al-Azhar. Each thinking to use the other to its own advantage, the state and institutional religion have fallen into an uneasy alliance of convenience based on mutual fear of an Iranian-style Islamic revolution, and of mutual contempt of democracy, parliamentary law and human (women's) rights. The all too holy alliance, reminiscent of the one modern reformers claim ended the creative period of Muslim civilization, has undermined the judicial autonomy of the secular state by the state's appeasement of a newly self-asserting, radically tinged ulema bent on stripping down the modern state and reversing a century and a half of secularism to impose Shari'a law, Sunni Islam's answer to Iran's Shi'i ayatollahs. In using religion to disempower the movement of political reform and secular democracy, the state has unwittingly tripped into a self-defeating policy of religious appeasement that redounds to the benefit of radical Islamic movements operating within an intimidated state. It is a price the state has paid with high interest for its willful stagnation. How this sequence of alliance, appeasement and intimidation came about has a half-century history.

The present-day political power of activist Islamist movements, inside and outside of al-Azhar, as opposed to the quiescent members of the ulema of al-Azhar who prefer to remain non-political and not to oppose the secular state on religious grounds, has produced a critically conflicted condition in popular religion's relation to the lethargic but brutal military state of Egypt, a condition brought on by decisions made by the military government itself at the beginning of the 1960s, and now all the more conflicted and brutal with the military's ousting of the elected president. The modernization forced on al-Azhar in 1961 by President Gamal abd al-Nasser opened the medieval institution to new ideas and new horizons of political and social involvement, but what in fact was a ploy to bring the ulema into the bureaucratic corpus of the modernizing state as a prop of legitimacy to the troubled military regime turned out a few decades later to be an uncontrollable challenge, owing much to the continuing ineptness of government.

Energized by the humiliating defeat of 1967 and discontent with an economy unable to keep pace with population growth, demands for affordable housing, inflation and the demand for professional jobs by the thousands of graduates pouring each year out of the universities that Nasser had opened tuition-free to everyone who had the entry qualifications, populist religion arose to offer a hopeful way out of the malaise. Islamist ranks swelled; opposition to the state grew even among the al-Azhar ulema considered to have submitted to it. Opposition then grew lethal with the unfulfilled expectations excited by President Sadat's promises of prosperity following the 1973 war and his abandonment of Nasserist socialism for the new economic policy of *Infitah* – the capitalist consumer "Opening" to the West – and especially by his Camp David peace accord with Israel, which Egyptians and Arabs everywhere saw to be a surrender to Israel and America, and a betrayal to other Arab states by Sadat's sacrificing the cause of Palestinian justice to get Sinai back.

The liberal policies Sadat introduced during the few years he enjoyed in self-deluding glory following the partially successful 1973 war served to expand al-Azhar's activism. The new policies also activated secular democrats who demanded even more liberal policies. When the pro-western economic policy failed to produce anything more than lucrative supply and construction contracts that the government showered on the well-connected, producing pricey western hotels, luxury apartment buildings and up-scale boutiques for the nouveaux riches, and making for inflation and a glaring gap between the new miniscule class of super-rich and the mass of wretched poor, with a moribund middle class struggling for air between them, open opposition to Sadat's regime spread now to the secular part of the population, whose leaders, from the ranks of lawyers, writers, journalists, small businessmen and manufacturers, began vociferously campaigning for free elections, the right to form political parties and democratic government. In self-preservation Sadat dropped his liberal policies and restored

Nasserist censorship, surveillance, arrest and repression. To create a force opposing the secularist liberal democrats he turned to the Shari'a-based al-Azhar ulema and their Islamist correlatives outside of the institution, which itself was in part radicalized by the rise of the political Islamists whose charities and social activism were challenging its legitimacy as the chief authority in the world of Sunni Islam.

Religious radicalism fed on the deepening social and political malaise. From its ranks came Sadat's assassins. What Nasser had unwittingly started in order to bring religious authority to heel as a buttress of the state he created, Sadat unleashed, and within a few years was devoured by it. But not the state of the military regime. The state continued under the harsh despotism of the third Ramses of the military dynasty. Pharaonic Mubarak played the same game of setting Islamists against those popular leaders left standing who were calling for democratic reform. Thanks to his special police, armed body guards and intelligence agencies he was able to survive a number of close calls by the same or affiliated movement that spawned the assassins of his predecessor. Less guarded targets were not so fortunate. In 1992, Farag Fuda, an outspoken and popular journalist who openly campaigned for separation of state and religion and attacked those who would impose Shari'a law and strip away women's rights, was shot dead in the street.[9] Farag Fuda's murder is widely believed to have been sanctioned by a leading Islamist group in al-Azhar.[10] His elimination rid politicized Islam of a popular secularist and rid the state of a democrat calling for reform. While leaders of the state escaped the vengeful wrath that went in the name of Islam, secular democrats whose calls for political reform were embarrassing the state before its American supporters were left to be crushed between the anvil of state tyranny and the hammer of radical Islam, with barely a peep from their putative American supporters.

Tacit cooperation between al-Azhar and the regime appears to have been sealed in an agreement that the former would condemn radical and violent Islamists, and on the side take care of the regime's other opponents, in return for greater influence in the judiciary and freedom of religious expression in the secular state. "The more violent the conflict between the state and radical Islamists grew, the more leverage al-Azhar gained on the regime, and the more diverse and powerful al-Azhar appeared on the political scene."[11] In other words, narrow-minded religious organizations opened the way to religious authority in a supposedly secular state. A milestone of Azharite influence was reached in 1994 when the state court (*Majlis al-Dawla*), ruling on issues of jurisdiction, "acknowledged the overarching authority of al-Azhar over censorship and made the Ministry of Culture subservient to it."[12]

Intimidated by the numerous political movements that in recent decades have arisen wrapped in banners proclaiming their true Islam, the Islam of jihad, of the Sword and Prophet, and that gained popularity by adding to their words the action of charitable works and social services, that is, by doing what the inert and inept state was failing to do, the leadership of al-Azhar and the secular judicial of the state came together in support of bizarre cases of supposed religious transgression submitted to the courts by the extremists. Al-Azhar, the state and Islamic radicals colluded in supporting censorship and suppressing freedom of speech and open discussion of ideas as threats to both religion and the state. The bearded menace intimidated the whole structure of state and religion; and though the secular rulers knew there was nothing these politico-religious revivalist revolutionaries would have loved more than seeing their heads rolling in the public squares, they were still happy to work with them in the cause of nipping in the bud anything that might encourage freedom of thought and action.

A group of conservative Muslim students at the American University in Cairo who appealed to al-Azhar and the government were able to force the university to pull the French scholar Maxime Rodinson's book *Muhammad* from its shelves and strike it from the syllabus of required reading in one of the university's courses. The offense was that the book treated the Quran not as the eternal word of God but a literary creation of Muhammad. In its turn, the government banned the book. This in turn led government censors to review 500 books used in courses at the American University, a fifth of which were banned. Following this, a considerable number of books were banned over the years, among them Nabakov's *Lolita*, Khalil Jibran's *The Prophet* and Egypt's own Nobel Prize winner Nagib Mahfuz's *Children of Our Neighborhood* (*Awlad Haritna*), along with books on comparative religion and almost all translations of the Quran. Many of the library's banned books are now in a special area and can by arrangement be consulted for a two-hour period in a special room. They can never be checked out or photocopied.

An insecure and unpopular military government, in cooperation with an equally insecure religious institution, confronted by an army of devout men and women seeing religion as the only relief from their neglected and impoverished lives, has choked off criticism and open thought. The 1990s and the first decade of the new millennium have their equivalents to Ali abd al-Raziq, Taha Husayn and Muhammad abu Zayd. A highly respected American-trained Egyptian professor in the American University's Political Science Department, Sa'd al-Din Ibrahim, was arrested, imprisoned and physically mistreated for attempting an analysis of Egyptian elections and criticizing the government's undemocratic nature. His prestigious and internationally funded ibn Khaldun Center for Studies in Political Science was shut down. After years of effort, Professor Ibrahim's American wife was able to have him released. He was then re-arrested, imprisoned for years and again finally released. He has since died.

Professor Nasr Hamid abu Zayd, a literature scholar in Cairo University's prestigious Department of Arabic, author of a dozen books and recognized public intellectual, was accused in 1995 of heresy for his having suggested in one of his books, *A Critique of Religious Discourse*, that the Quran be reinterpreted in the light of modern knowledge – something Shaykh Muhammad Abduh in more liberal times not only suggested but proceeded to do. Shaykh Muhammad abu Zayd (no relation to Professor Nasr Hamid abu Zayd) had gone further in 1930 in his *Guidance and Instruction in Interpreting the Quran by the Quran*. It will be recalled that his book was banned and he was sent to Asyut in a form of exile. The fist of conservatism has tightened considerably since then. It was not conservative shaykhs but radical student militants who in 1993 brought the suit in civil court against Professor Nasr abu Zayd, claiming his book was heretical and should be banned. Flush with victory after winning their case, the students then brought a charge of heresy against him. They won this too. The scholar was legally declared a heretic by a government secular court. The militant radicals then went a step further and demanded that the court issue an order forcing the professor's wife, a literature professor, to divorce him on the basis that no Muslim woman could remain married to a heretic. The court issued the divorce order. This was a civil court of the secular state passing a judgment and issuing an order based on an extreme interpretation of Shari'a law by religious extremists. To call it insecurity would be an understatement of considerable magnitude. The government's weakness was easily sensed. Publicly armed with the declaration of heresy and the state mandated order for the divorce, members of the Egyptian branch of Islamic jihad now called for professor abu Zayd to be put to death for his apostasy. The threat of professor abu Zayd's execution was just another form of violence that saturated the atmosphere.

A few years earlier, the liberal Egyptian journalist and writer Farag Fuda, to whom reference already has been made, was assassinated for writing against the growing power and tyranny of the radical movements of political Islam. As also mentioned, Nobel Prize winner Nagib Mahufz was stabbed in an attempted assassination for his novel in which Moses, Jesus and Muhammad have a seminar on what is true religion. Threatened, harassed and victimized by Muslim militants from one side and the secular state from the other, Professor abu Zayd and his wife fled their country for Holland, where they were offered political asylum and academic positions. In Holland, they fought the divorce order. In December 1996, they won a permanent stay of the order in the Egyptian court of appeals. However, the lethal declaration of apostasy still remained. In December 2009 Kuwaiti authorities prohibited him from entering the country to give a lecture on religious reform and women in Islam. Asked to comment on his being denied entry into Kuwait he said, "The politicians in our countries have become a faint reflection of extremism in the name of religion. It's a major cultural crime that some intellectuals ally with politicians in their so-called war against extremism and terrorism . . . We, the nation, including intellectuals, are their victims."[13] Professor abu Zayd has since died.

The cooperation between al-Azhar and Egypt's insecure regime has progressed so far in its judicial fusion that it is difficult to see any separation between religion and state. In May 2007, five Quranists – scholars wanting to reform religion by interpreting it solely through the broadly interpretable holy book – were put under political arrest in the middle of the night by order of a warrant issued by the Minister of Interior and charged with "contempt for religion" under Article 98 of the penal code, which warrants a five-year prison sentence. The five, put behind bars, had publicized their reformist ideas through a website called *Ahl al-Quran* (People of the Quran).[14] A modernized interpretation of the Quran is the last thing conservative Azharites or zealous Islamists want, and the state acts according to their wishes.

Political Muslim movements in Egypt have been growing in influence in the legal, judicial and educational systems ever since President Anwar Sadat's popularity began falling away in the mid-1970s. He tried using them to check the chorus of criticism rising up against him from all sides: journalists, lawyers, doctors, academics, writers, religious authorities. A broad alliance of secular liberals and religious figures came together to protest the rampant corruption of his government, the nepotism, the cronyism, the economic failure, the rotting infrastructure of municipal facilities and the highly inflammatory peace treaty that he signed with Israeli Prime Minster Manachem Begin, with its implicit surrender of the Palestinian West Bank and Gaza to Israel's fundamentalist settlers and annexationists that supported Begin's Likud party. The very people Sadat was bringing in to counter those mounting critics of his inept government policies were plotting to kill him, which they did in 1981. This has not changed under President Mubarak. He has had his share of close calls but knows better than to stand in review of a military parade without a thick bullet proof glass in front of him. Such leaders are delighted to have American protection, and American leaders are pleased to arm and protect them. The price is popular disgust, contempt and hatred for both leaders and America. The noxious atmosphere gives credence to those who harangue against the West with its materialist values and "de-spiritualized" science.

The strength of the religious radicals clamoring for Shari'a and its promise of clean government, social justice and national regeneration has institutionally intimidated the moderately conservative and relatively liberal shaykhs. None of them prescribe a scriptural interpretation that could adapt religion and religious law to the contours of modern conditions. Ali and Mustafa abd al-Raziq and the two abu Zayds are potent lessons. Fear pervades. The entry of members of ultra-conservative Muslim organizations into the organs of the secular state makes for more fear and confusion among the secularized and moderate Muslim majority of the population, and all the more deprives science of institutional support and mental oxygen, while making possible the onslaught of Scientific Interpretation, the interpreters now as radical as their militant counterparts in the movement of political Islam, with whom they have much in common.

Notes

1 Ali abd al-Raziq, *al-Islam wa Usul al-Hukam* (Islam and the Sources of Political Authority), Mayba'at Misr, Cairo, 1925.
2 It is altogether plausible abu Zayd did receive some ideas from Rida if the latter was referring to what he had written in the early years of *al-Manar*, and from what he was in fact at the time writing on Muhammad Abduh. A. Jeffrey, "The Suppressed Quran Commentary of Muhammad abu Zaid," *Der Islam*, vol 20, 1932, pp. 301–308.
3 H.A.R. Gibb, *Modern Trends in Islam*, University of Chicago Press, Chicago, 1947, note 13 of "Principles of Modernism."
4 Taha Husayn, *Mustaqbil al-Thaqafa fi Misr* (The Future of Culture in Egypt), Matba'at al-Ma'arif, Cairo, 1938, pp. 55–59.
5 *al-Sharq al-Awsat*, London, June 14, 2006, p. 13.
6 H.A.R. Gibb, "Studies in Contemporary Arabic Literature," *Bulletin of the School of Oriental and African Studies*, vol V (1930), p. 464.
7 Najib Mahfouz, *Qasr al-Shawq*, Matba'ah Maktabah Misriyyah, Cairo, 1957, p. 350.
8 Najib Mahfouz, *Sukariyya*, Matba'ah Makabah Misriyyah, Cairo, 1957, p. 91.
9 For a detailed account of radical Islam, al-Azhar and the Egyptian regime see Maliku Zeghal, "Religion and Politics in Egypt: The Ulema of Al-Azhar Radical

Islam, and the State (1952–1954)," *Journal of Middle East Studies*, vol 31 (1999), pp. 371–399.
10 An Islamist newspaper, *al-Nur*, put out a statement submitted by 24 professors, half from al-Azhar and half from Cairo University, calling for President Mubarak to close down Fuda's political party. A few days later he was assassinated by two Islamist militants. Maliku Zeghal, *Religion and Politics in Egypt*, p. 389.
11 Maliku Zeghal, *Religion and Politics in Egypt*, p. 389.
12 Maliku Zeghal, *Religion and Politics in Egypt*, p. 390.
13 *Daily News* (English language daily), Cairo, Egypt, July 6, 2010, p. 1.
14 "Ahmed Mansour, a former professor at al-Azhar University who is currently a refugee in the United States, was the first to adopt the ideas of the movement in the 1980s, but no legal procedure was taken against him." Ethar Shalaby, "Administrative Court Cancels Detainment Decision, Quranists Still Behind Bars," *Daily News*, *Egypt*, August 3, 2007, p. 1.

18 Science and the contemporary state

The Japanese victory over Russia in 1905 came as a bright star for those Middle Eastern optimists who thought their societies might be up to emulating the Japanese in confronting the West. For more critical observers, the Japanese victory came as depressing evidence of their governments' failure to reform. Japanese success was for them a bitter and dispiriting comparison since it made clear that change was possible, the West could be matched, but Muslim governments weren't up to it. The Japanese hadn't initiated reforms until the 1850s, while the Ottomans and Egyptians had by then been trying to reform for generations. Compared to the Japanese, Muslims had failed dismally to meet the challenge. A century and more of reform had from all outward appearances changed substantially nothing in social attitudes and dedication to learning, when measured in terms of science, industry and military performance. What had to be done?

Rashid Rida, who took Japan's success as a Muslim humiliation, preached "science and work" in emulation of the Japanese but in a religious framework. A small group of radicalized secularist Egyptian writers, Salama Musa, Ismail Mazhar, Hasan Husayn and Taha Husayn, collectively inspired by Muhammad Abduh, whose death occurred the same year as Japan's victory, joined the literary elite of Lebanese Christian immigrants in preaching secularism and science: if Arabs and Turks were ever to emulate the Japanese and hold back the West, radical solutions to their many social and economic problems had to be found and unflinchingly applied.

In the heated atmosphere of rising nationalisms, with Britain firming its grip on Egypt and the Young Turk government in control of the faltering Ottomans in the years before the outbreak of World War I, a heightened urgency inflected the call for reform. But then the cataclysm of war changed everything. The Ottoman Empire disintegrated in defeat. Its former Arab provinces succumbed to a divisive Anglo–French colonialist occupation that the peace treaty euphemistically renamed "mandates," once the territorial horse trading and geographical surgery were over. Anatolia, however, was reintegrated as the independent secular Republic of Turkey, saving the Turks from the divisions and humiliation that would otherwise have been imposed on them by colonialist rule. The respective paths of development and historical experience of the Arab and Turkish regions of the former empire would from then on become ever more divergent. Surveying the present-day political and economic condition of the Arab region, almost a century after the fall of the Ottoman Empire, a sympathetic historian might mourn the loss of the protective shield that the Ottomans had provided the Arabs, however feeble that shield was toward the end. As for modern Turkey, the extinction of the empire could be interpreted as much as a failure of Ottoman reform as a success.

Though dissolution of the sultanate and caliphate and abandonment of Arabic script would have been inconceivable at any time in the 19th century, many of the principles of Mustafa Kemal's Turkish Republic were kindred in spirit to those that guided the *Tanzimat*, the Young Ottoman Constitutionalists and the Young Turk reformers of the Committee of Union and Progress, with which Mustafa Kemal had been associated as a young military officer. From these movements of reform came the dynamics that cracked the foundations of empire. But to any Young Ottoman reformers who had been around to witness events, the secularist republic with its revolutionary excisions that divorced the Turks from their proud Islamic past, including even their poetry and historical literature, would have been the worst of all possible catastrophes, a society whose heart and soul had been ripped out.

The pompous slogans of Turkish nationalism, pumped down from the top, buried Islam and the Ottoman legacy. So also did the barrage of slogans touting nationalism, awakening and liberation that filled the air in the newly manufactured Arab states that the allied victors had tailored geographically and demographically to the measure of their colonial interests. The calls were as strident as the Arab governments were ineffectual. Dependent, unpopular, unpracticed in the parliamentary systems created for them by their imperial overlords, Arab governments were a parody of party politics in which contests between communal elites substituted for national issues. The concept of nation was embryonic in these Anglo–French creations freshly carved from the Ottoman corpse. The exercise of power by the surrogate governments was severely restricted by the dictates coming from Paris and London. In those circumstances government and national politics amounted to a theater of personal warfare among local elites whose cultural and political world was that of latter day Ottomans with their clan and tribal traditions of patronage, and the traditional political conviction that government existed to serve and enrich those who were in it. The provincial elites who in Ottoman times had mediated between the local populace and imperial government in Istanbul now did the same as kings, presidents and prime ministers, Paris and London substituting for Istanbul. The old school political culture was alive and well: graft, nepotism, cronyism and fiduciary irresponsibility flourished. In the event the political puppets started showing signs of life, French and British enforcers were there to intervene, by violence if necessary, in the name of political stability, otherwise known as imperial self-interest.

In Palestine, where the British ruled directly, the Palestinian voice went unheard in its opposition to open immigration of Jews from Europe, to Jewish freedom to purchase land and develop state institutions exclusively for Jews. Regardless how eloquently or violently the indigenous population protested against what they correctly saw to be their eventual displacement, Britain, though wavering at times, remained faithful to Lord Balfour's pledge of 1917, dictated by Chaim Weizmann, head of the World Zionist Organization, to make Palestine a Jewish homeland. Except perhaps in the case of Iraq, the mandates were a bitter experience.

When after World War II the Arab states at last gained independence, they lacked experienced rulers. Their government and state institutions were weak and poorly funded and their military wholly unprepared for the challenge that faced them in the raw and bitter politics of inter-Arab rivalry that was all the more poisoned by the Cold War's divisive policies of superpower rivalry over global dominance. In 1948 the promise of Balfour had been fulfilled and Israel born, reducing Palestine to a state of mind – and a political minefield that blew away many Arab promises, pretensions, armies and governments. The loss of Palestine was followed by a series of military coups and revolutions, first in Syria, where one coup after another followed in quick succession, giving an idea of how well the French policy of divide and rule did its work of producing an unstable and politically immature Syria; then in Egypt in 1952, ending the Muhammad Ali Dynasty. The fall of British-created Hashemite monarchy in Iraq followed a few years later. Hashemite Jordan survived, but barely, with timely assistance from Britain and America.

The inter-Arab political scene between 1948 and 1967 was a snake pit of autocratic and ruthless military governments vying and allying with a set of equally nasty kingly despots, the bunch of them blaming the other for the loss of Palestine, each shrilly trumpeting its own brand of nationalism and crying for Arab unity while plotting to undermine its Arab rivals, and this as the military governments confiscated, nationalized and sequestered the property of its citizens in the name of Arab nationalist socialism.

Egypt, still leader of the Arab world at the time, suffered a malaise of inefficiency and incompetency under its military government, in spite of the high minded intentions of its young officers in the early years of the revolution and their efforts to alleviate poverty and the maldistribution of land ownership. Advances made in land distribution, electrification, irrigation and health were offset by mismanagement, military expenditure, overpopulation and the growth of a parasitic military feudalism whose high officers fattened up in spite of the sinking economy. Opening the universities free of charge to all students able to pass the entrance exam, a fine idea in itself but debilitating when the swelling student population was not matched by a commensurate expansion in university facilities and teaching staff, turned out to be the death knell of quality education in Egypt. The level of academic quality that had been achieved at the University of Cairo between the World Wars began to diminish from the 1960s on. The slope of the downward trend grew steeper with each new graduating class. New universities and research institutions were opened, but in the sciences they were so pitifully underfunded they belied the name. The academic malaise was part of a pattern that embraced the whole of Egypt.

Burdened with increasing foreign debt because of the military and its ambitious but misdirected programs, and its untrained and inexperienced military officers having become a self-serving, parasitic elite of incompetent industrial, commercial and agricultural managers, Egypt once again found itself on the brink of bankruptcy. A myopic, over-reaching foreign policy and an overly ambitious military president feigning to preside over the Arab world, the African world and the third world of the Cold War, sucked the country into the quagmire of a Yemeni civil war that further drained its finances and battered its military. When the 1967 war broke out with Israel, the heart of Egypt's army was bogged down in the mountains of Yemen. But regardless of whatever part of the world the heart of the Egyptian army happened to be bogged down in, the outcome of the war could not have been much different. Over in the few hours it took the Israelis to destroy hundreds of Egyptian jet fighters and bombers sitting idly on the runways of the air force, the lightning war gave Israel a victory so complete over an enemy so incompetent, it is hard to imagine that an additional 70,000 troops, 300 tanks and 100 jet bombers would have altered the outcome more than to postpone surrender a day or so beyond the six it took the Egyptians to raise the white flag.

The Israeli attack should not have been a surprise. The Israeli government had given fair warning when President Nasser claimed to have mined the straits of Tiran, which effectively cut off Israel's Red Sea trade. The Arabs, however, up to their necks in fraternal rivalry, were totally unprepared for what came, as if the weeks of escalating Israeli threats, Egyptian counter threats and last minute Arab alliances had been rehearsals for a play designed to amuse the Arab audience and outside world – because they did indeed look to be taken by surprise. Preparations for war, the only ones, as it seemed, took the form of thundering speeches, as if Arab leaders were staging a replay of the 1948 military encounter with Israel.[1]

The monumental collapse of the most powerful and secularized of the Arab countries at the hands of Israel ripped the heart out of Arab nationalism, and with it its secularist aspirations. Twelve years later, the fall of the pro-western Pahlevi monarchy to an Islamic Republic of Iran also diminished the secular culture that had been built up during the century, though it would take some years for the discredited constructions of nationalism and secularism to drain away before the tide of rediscovered religion had risen. Formerly accepted without question by political rulers, reformers and their supporting intelligentsia as the one-way highway to the future, secular nationalism was terminally stricken, and in the minds and hearts of many passed away unmourned. Its legacy of shame, defeat and failure opened the way to long repressed alternatives, not the least being the aggressive rise of political Islam everywhere in the Arab and Islamic world.

Given an adrenaline shot by the revolutionary Islamic Republic of Iran that supplanted the American-supported Pahlevi monarchy, political Islam reversed the eclipse of religion as a political force that had begun in the early 19th century. By the 1980s, secular republics and pro-western monarchies no longer appeared to be the destined direction to the future. The religious leaders of Iran are still firmly in power, though challenged by a youthful population that would like to see an eclipse of the present government's uncompromising enforcement of Shari'a law. Thanks to former President Bush's invasion of Iraq, the country has dissolved into a Sunni–Shi'i civil war, with a section of Iraq's Shi'i population struggling to midwife an Islamic Republic in the image of their Iranian brethren, at least in the southern half of the country. Whatever the 21st century brings, one thing is certain: the role of Islam in Middle East and Muslim politics, and therefore education, will not be as marginalized as it was in the century and a half before 1967, from Muhammad Ali's first student missions to the Six-Day War. The failures of secular regimes to embrace their people by addressing the problems of squalor, sickness, poverty, illiteracy, corruption, misrule and all the ills spawned by the arbitrary and irresponsible rule of elites have made this certain. What follows in this narrative is an attempt to give some measure of this failure within the analytical framework of state funding for science education and research during the last 50 years.

In the golden age of science and Muslim civilization it was the Abbasid Caliph who initiated and supported the translations of scientific and medical texts to Arabic. Wealthy viziers in the caliph's court emulated and on occasion outdid the ruler in this enterprise, and when the unity of the vast empire gave way to a congeries of autonomous and semi-independent provinces, where governors became rulers, it was they who then supported scientific study in emulation of the ruling style in Baghdad. Science spread through the lands of Islam, east and west, capital to capital: Damascus, Mosul, Cairo, Nishapur, Shiraz, Merv, Tus, Bukhara, Maragha, Samarqand, Palermo, Cordova, Seville, Toledo, Marrakesh, where for six centuries and with varying degrees of creativity the intellectual traditions survived and advanced, withering in one city, flowering in another. What made this possible was, on the one hand, the abiding interest in science among a relatively small slice of urban society across the lands of Islam, and on the other hand, a ruler's patronage. Talent always seemed to be around for patronage to cultivate. What might be lacking was the ruler's propensity or the conditions of political stability that would allow patronage of disciplines not altogether welcomed by the ulema. Creative scientific activity had little chance of surviving for long without the ruler's means and willingness of support. Muslim society had no counterpart to the medieval Latin church and its monasteries that preserved and nourished a tradition of science and philosophy independent of the monarchies. Church scholars in the colleges of theology and arts and sciences were the spinal cord of the rational sciences in the Latin West right up to the Reformation. On the other hand, in the Muslim world, the ulema, with not too many exceptions, would have shown little regret had the philosophical and scientific manuscripts turned to dust and vanished from the face of the earth.

Today the place of royal patronage has been taken over by the state. But state budgets for science have continued to be less than royal. The present dilemma of scientific and technological backwardness in the Muslim world is far worse than it was when the Ottomans first awoke to the challenge of the West's technical superiority in the early 18th century. Back in the days of the Tulip Period the Ottoman state had a fair chance to close the gap in science and technology, when modern science was still an infant and technology no more complex than the mechanical clock and refracting telescope. The Tulip Period's bloody end showed that it was going to be no easy task for a Muslim state to adopt the advances of the West. Western science and technology thereafter became steadily more complex, expensive and larger in scale. England's steam engines had been busily revolutionizing economic production for several decades before Selim III's New Order broke against the same shoals of tradition and vested interests that had taken down the reforms and reformers of the Tulip Period. Aborted attempts at reform left Muslims that much further behind the gathering power of the West and out of the running in the global game of nations. Science and the instruments of technology related to war and economic production had by the time of the reforms of Muhammad Ali and Sultan Mahmud II been transformed. Ships were steam-driven, and even then steam was giving way to electricity in powering the engines of industry.

By the mid-19th century the investment required to catch up was rapidly increasing. Making the challenge even worse for Muslim states, their reformist rulers were attracted more by the frills than the substance of modernity and so drove their countries into bankruptcy by their misdirected attempts to close the gap. Muslim dynasts failed to invest enough in their reforms to educate students to a level of competence, and to make pursuit of the new knowledge and practice of the modern professions and crafts attractive enough in prestige and remuneration as to instill the spirit and energy that would make long years of hard study worth the effort. Education reforms were not applied long enough for results to become apparent, except for a few minor instances in the late Ottoman Empire. Cutting expenditures in older ministries of government to finance new ones proved to be too unappealing considering the sacrifices it would have imposed on the well-placed classes of Muslim society. Success on the Japanese model would have meant endowing scientific and technical education with the promise of professional prestige and monetary reward for it to be worth the endeavor. It would have meant buying off the religious students with generous stipends to enter new institutions where science and religion were studied side by side, and providing attractive and decently paid positions in education for those who were sent abroad or who went on their own to gain advanced degrees in science, engineering and industrial management. It would have meant extending secular education to provincial cities, towns and villages to wipe out illiteracy.

Success meant more than annihilating Mamluks and Janissaries. That part, the violent part, came easy, since the old military corps cut into the ruler's power and so had to go in the name of autocracy and the centralized state. The more peaceful part – focus, funding, organization, continuity of investment – was wanting.

The lack of funding and the flawed organization that undermined reforms from within had an external ally: Europe's insistence on preserving the humiliating capitulations, and European intervention in Ottoman affairs in order to preserve them as key components of Europe's economic self-interests. But the essential cause of failure was internal. Not enough young men were sent abroad to study long enough to master science and technology. Not enough European science teachers and technical experts were brought to Cairo and Istanbul to teach the youth long enough so that they could replace the foreign teachers and technical experts and obviate the necessity of sending more students abroad for education. Unlike the Japanese, whose success in modernization stands as the shining example, Egyptian, Ottoman and Iranian rulers failed to provide adequate schools, language programs, translations, equipment, teachers, books and buildings. The example of Ali Mubarak, who made a joke of his having to find a shady place out of the heat of the sun to teach geometry and trigonometry to officers without benefit of chalk, blackboard, books or paper, of being reduced to using sticks to draw lines in the sand, says it all.

Muslims fretted over the Japanese success, contrasting it to the difficulties Muslim societies were encountering in reforming themselves. In all fairness, Japanese reformers were less handicapped than their Muslim counterparts. Tokyo, or Edo as it was called at the time, was as early as the 18th century a relatively secular city free of religious influences that could have impeded progress. Nor did it suffer the rate of illiteracy that dragged Muslim cities down. The male population of the city of Kyoto in the 18th century was close to 80 percent literate, while the whole of the Japanese population reached around 40 percent literacy. Japanese and Ottomans were introduced to western science at the same time, both initially through the Dutch, their merchants in Japan playing the role of their ambassadors in Istanbul. In 1724, when the Tulip Period and Ibrahim's printing press were bringing in a bit of European science and technology, Dutch merchants in Japan were given imperial permission to import European texts on science and technology that Jesuit missionaries in China had translated to Chinese. The Jesuits there had translated ancient, medieval and Renaissance science into Chinese, from Euclid to Copernicus, Tycho Brahe, Kepler and Galileo. Japanese scholars, who had been assimilating Chinese astronomy and mathematics in the 17th and 18th centuries, began assimilating modern western science in the 18th and 19th centuries, the Chinese translations of the Jesuits being the bridge between medieval and modern for the Japanese.[2]

The challenge was taken up by both the government and private individuals acting on their own. In 1745, just as Ibrahim Muteferrika's printing press was being shut down, two Japanese scholars were ordered by the government to learn Dutch and translate scientific and technical texts to Japanese. Their translations laid the basis for "Western Learning," or *Yogaku* as it was called. During the last half of the 18th century two scholars in Osaka, independent of the government, were studying the works of Brahe and Kepler. By the end of the 18th century several private schools teaching Dutch medicine to a hundred students had been established. Newton's mechanics and calculus were brought into Japanese by Shizuko Tadao's (1760–1806) translation of English works on physics and astronomy. An abridged version of Lalande's four-volume *Astronomie* was translated in the very early 19th century and soon became a subject of serious study by a small elite of Japanese scholars interested in science. In terms of modern science in translation, this put the Japanese already ahead of the Ottomans: not until the 1830s did Hoja Ishak's four-volume *Compendium of the Mathematical Sciences* appear in print in Istanbul.

Japan was fortunate not to have its assimilation of science and technology opposed by recalcitrant religious and military institutions, and to be far enough away from the western powers not to have its islands and economy taken over. The example of western expansion in China in the mid-19th century was a lesson to the Japanese. The so-called Opium War, which on the Chinese side was no more than a hopeless bare-fisted resistance against the mercenary armies of British merchant narco-companies forcing the Chinese to purchase Indian opium in order to keep up the lucrative trade in the drug, convinced the Japanese they must prepare to defend themselves against the West or suffer the same humiliation.

The Japanese government expanded its Dutch language training program to include German, French and English, and translated books of science and technology into those languages. The government also set up institutions specializing in military and navigational technology. Ottoman reformers, and later reformers in Egypt, had done the same, and for the same reasons, but in Japan individuals acting independently made scientific assimilation a social enterprise outside of government control. Individuals set up private schools, one of the most important being Doctor Ogata Koan's school in Osaka, which produced politicians, military officers, engineers and academicians. Japanese private initiative had a negligible counterpart in the Arab and Turkish spheres of reform. Muhammad Ali and Mahmud were able to break down the traditional military institutions of Mamluks and Janissaries, and reduce to destitution the religious institution, but the ill-funded institutions that replaced them failed to break down traditional thought patterns.

The Japanese government employed more or less the same methods and procedures as their Ottoman and Egyptian predecessors in assimilating the new knowledge and technical expertise, namely in the translation and language institutes, and the presses to print the technical and scientific books that had been translated. Students were sent to western universities, foreign teachers and industrial experts were invited from the West, and medical and military engineering schools were founded. The desired end product of reform was also the same: a strong military, supplied and armed by domestic industry to defend against the West. There the parallel ends.

As many as 4,000 western experts entered Japan between 1868 and 1900. In the Egyptian and Ottoman experience a few hundred students were sent abroad to master science and technology. With the Japanese it was thousands. It is estimated that by the end of the 1860s, after a decade of reform, almost 2,000 Japanese scholars were engaged in Western Learning, privately and under government auspices. Before the end of the first generation of reform, Japanese teachers and technical experts were taking over the positions westerners held as university department heads, hospital directors and industrial managers, thereby enabling the Japanese to create a technical and academic infrastructure fairly independent of the West.

Except for a few low-tech industries in agriculture and manufacturing, this never quite happened in the modern Muslim states, whose reliance on foreigners for technical support, maintenance, academic expertise, and the planning and construction of large hydrological and industrial projects endures.

The great divergence between the Japanese and Muslim experience began with the first step toward modernization: education. The Japanese government made translation and education top priority projects. The new schools had the books, facilities, equipment and teaching aids to accomplish what they were designed to do. In the Japanese example, an integrated multi-level educational system prepared students to move upward through the levels, from primary to secondary to university to doctoral, the process beginning in the village schools. Where ten-year-old Egyptians were memorizing the Quran, their Japanese counterparts in the 19th century were studying arithmetic and the equivalent of pre-geometry. Where Egyptian and Ottoman reformers were stymied by policy shifts, halts and reversals that came with changes in rulers, the Japanese were able to remain focused and persevere decade after decade, grinding down traditionalist resistance. What Egyptians and Ottomans saw to be secular orders to reform from a secular government, the Japanese took as a sacred duty to their emperor-god. While Egyptian students were terrified at being drafted into one of Muhammad Ali's schools because of the harsh treatment and miserable conditions, Japanese students took to education voluntarily as a personal mission to fulfill their duty in serving god, emperor and country. They traveled to the West of their own volition and expense to enter a university and master one of the new skills that were now in demand. The resistance of some cultural conservatives aside, the Japanese attitude was overwhelmingly positive toward learning science, once the order came down from above. Government orders tended to inspire rather than restrict individual enterprise. Though starting a half century after Egypt's first student missions to the West and almost a century and a half after Yirmisekiz's Ottoman mission to France, the Japanese were by the early 1870s surpassing the achievement made by reforms in the Muslim countries.

Japanese reformers were spared the consuming problems of a medieval theology that jealously defended a God that transcended natural law. The heliocentric theory gave them no problem. Shintoism informed the Japanese that their divine ruler was descended from the sun god. Copernican theory would put them at the center of the universe, where they believed they properly belonged. Darwin, who should have given them a problem given their belief of a celestial origin, was calmly accepted as a fact of life. A visiting American zoologist, Edward Morse, was giving lectures on Darwin in the 1870s. His gifted student Ishikawa Chiyomatsu translated his lectures as *The Theory of Evolution in Animals*, which appeared in 1883, the year before Edwin Lewis's commencement address had almost caused the American College in Beirut to shut down.

Around the same time (mid-1870s) that Sarruf coined the word in Arabic for natural selection, a Japanese compound word was found to express it. Four years before Chiyomatsu's translation of Morse's lectures, Izawa Shuji had translated Thomas Huxley's *Lectures on the Origin of Species*. Darwin's book was not translated until 1896, though between the translations of Huxley's work and Morse's lectures, the essential Darwin was made available in Japanese by 1883, more than 30 years before Ismail Mazhar's partial translation of the *Origin*. A Japanese translation of the *Descent of Man*, which has still to find its way into Arabic, soon followed. Darwin elicited little protest from any quarter of the Japanese public. Evolution was accepted on the basis of the scientific research that supported it.

The Japanese approach to science went directly to the heart of the subject. Young Japanese men studied science at home or abroad and became science teachers. By the 1880s and 1890s their offspring were becoming scientists. Though Herbert

Spencer had been a subject of intense study in Japan ten years before Morse's introduction of Darwin, the philosophical interlude of social and economic theory did not substitute for the study of hard science. Translations were made from the scientific works of scientists, first Morse, then Huxley, finally Darwin. Japanese reformers in the 19th century studied western philosophy, literature, history and economics, and founded journals to propagate their ideas, while others studied to be science teachers and mathematicians, all without having to forge tortured arguments of legitimacy to appease the guardians of scripture.

The order from the divine ruler that his people master western knowledge and technique was equivalent in Muslim terms to the Quranic injunctions to study nature, but what made this work less difficult for the Japanese and sustained it was that at the end of years of arduous study there awaited the student a worthy prize: an equitably paid position that carried status. Without the prize, the will and enthusiasm would not have had the same drive.

The Japanese began their great venture of modernization by setting up the Bansho Shirabesho (Institute for Study of Barbarian Books). Like the language and translation schools of Muhammad Ali Pasha and Sultan Mahmud, this focused on "useful things" for military strength. Books on military science were translated for students to master the technique of fortification, artillery, navigation, machinery, warships, military drill and discipline. From this beginning of translation and concentrated study of "useful things" to master the knowledge and technique of the West (called *rangaku*, "Dutch learning," since for centuries, up until the mid-19th century, the Dutch were the only westerners allowed into Japan to do business) the Bansho Shirabesho evolved into the Institute for Development of technology and industry. This began the second stage of Japan's modernization process. Similar institutes for development were established in other cities. In order to prepare the experts who would staff them, student missions were sent to the West. Seeing the Muslim countries falling under European financial control in the mid-1870s as a result of their going into bankruptcy from the mountains of debt they incurred in trying to modernize, the Japanese may have been convinced that there was nothing positive to be learned about modernization from that part of the world.

The first Japanese student mission was in the form of an embassy composed of 77 men of varying ages sent to sign a treaty with the U.S. in 1860, an event that might mark the organized start of Japanese modernization. The impressions American society made on these first voyagers were not too unlike those made by Paris and Vienna on some of the first Ottoman delegates to visit them in the 18th century. Much like the Ottomans, the Japanese were too proud and confident in the superiority of their own civilization, in spite of its military weakness compared to the West, to express interest in the new technology or curiosity in anything they saw – except for what negatively struck them. The report written by the chief ambassador recorded his shock at the sight of women in public. On the other hand, several of the young men serving as interpreters in the lower ranks of the embassy were keenly interested in what they saw and went on to become some of Japan's most important intellectuals in the 19th century.

Several more missions followed in the 1860s. The first purely student mission came in 1862. It was composed of 11 students who sailed to Holland via Java on a Dutch ship to study navigation, medicine and law. Among them was an excptional young man named Nishi Amane. Nishi wanted to study philosophy and science to discover the pattern of thinking that underlay western civilization. This he believed would be the key to determining the sources that gave rise to the science, technology and socio-political principles that sustained western power. Similar to several of the Young Ottoman exiles in the 1860s, Amane realized that a particular structure of thought had produced not only the medical, scientific and mechanical wonders of the West, but also its system of legislation and laws.

Contradicting Japan's reputation of being a regimented culture (the nail that stands up gets hammered down), many independent-minded young men traveled on their own to the West to study "useful things" for their emperor and themselves, though the large majority went with government assistance and studied what they were ordered. There were also those who were sent by the government but disobeyed orders and studied what they wanted once they reached the West. One such young rebel had been sent to Holland to study the Dutch language and navigation. Soon after arriving he realized Holland was no longer the leading naval power it had been back when Peter the Great went there to study ship building and so made his way as a cabin boy on a steamer to America, where he studied for ten years. Upon returning to Japan he joined up with other western-educated Japanese to found a university in Kyoto. In another case of individual enterprise, five Japanese students assisted by a wealthy English merchant went to England in 1863 to study on their own. Two of them became leaders in the Meiji government. Another who independently gained his education in the West, Yamao Yozo, went to Scotland in the early 1860s, where he worked in a naval yard while studying at a technical college. When he returned home in 1870 the Meiji government appointed him head of the emperor's new technological college, which at the time employed 47 foreign teachers in six departments.

Between 1868 and 1900, more than 900 students went to the U.S. on their own or at their family's expense. Only in India was there anything approximating a Muslim parallel to this intellectual enterprise by individuals. But as we have seen in the case of Sayyid Ahmad Khan, such enterprise excited from other Muslims as much hostility as it did support. The metaphor of the nail being hammered down was perhaps more aptly applied at the time to Muslim than Japanese society. There did indeed exist in Japan conservative resistance against the western imports being brought in by the modernizers, but it was in time ground down and overcome by the zeal of Japan's youth to meet the challenge to which they were called.

One of the most remarkable examples of individual initiative, and the Meiji government's support of it, is the career of Fukuzawa Yukichi (1835–1901). His story brings into sharp relief the difference between the Japanese and Muslim experience. Younger son of an impoverished, low ranking samurai, Yukichi studied "Dutch learning" in a government school in Nagasaki, then went on his own to Nagasaki to learn Dutch, the language with "strange letters written sideways." It was while studying Dutch that he discovered science. He writes of his joy in learning western knowledge, the secrets of science, of electricity and chemistry, this at a time when not a single steam engine or piece of chemical apparatus existed in Japan. "If anyone had looked into our hearts, he would have found there an untold pleasure . . . we students are the sole possessors of the key to knowledge of the great European civilization." Having served in the Institute for Study of Barbarian Books, Yukichi was appointed as an interpreter in different Japanese embassies in the West, where he read extensively and collected a large number of books he brought back with him to Japan. Based on his years abroad in the early 1860s, he published his *Conditions in the West* in 1866. Written in simple style and clearing up many misconceptions the Japanese had of the West, his book met with immediate success, 150,000 copies being sold in the first few months. Bolstered by the popularity and money the book brought him, and thinking it more important to continue working toward spreading western knowledge, Yukichi refused the attractive offer of a high position in the Meiji government. In pursuit of his goal of spreading knowledge he wrote more than 100 books and used the profits to found Japan's first private university, accomplishing what Ali Mubarak would have liked in Egypt but could not.[3] He writes in his autobiography of how proud Japan should be that five years after navigation began to be studied from the Dutch in Nagasaki in 1855, and seven years after the first steamship was seen in Japan (1853), the Japanese were independently able to navigate a steamship to San Francisco with but a 100-horsepower engine. In so short a time did the Japanese master navigation and steamship technology. "No other people in the orient could have accomplished such a feat in just five years. I am willing to admit my pride in this accomplishment for Japan."

By 1872 the Meiji government had laid the basis of a revolutionizing program of educational reform and modernization that became official with the Fundamental Code of Education issued that year. As it was by then accepted by practically all politically relevant sectors of society that Japan's survival depended on rapid change, the Code met with little or no resistance, conservative opposition having by then gone to the grave. If anyone had to be convinced that rapid change was necessary, all they needed to do to think otherwise was look westward and see what was happening in China and the Muslim countries.

Rapid change was taken by the reformist Japanese government to mean exactly that. Reforms would be applied at both the highest and lowest levels of society, working their way from the top down and the bottom up, until the entire society had been transformed: command, direction and leadership from above, universal education from below, with the goal that no community would have an illiterate family and no family an illiterate member. Kido Takayoshi, one of the leaders of the reforms, coined the credo of the Fundamental Code: "Our people are no different from Americans and Europeans of today; it is all a matter of education." The words could just as well have stood for the reformers struggling at the time in Cairo and Istanbul.

The Fundamental Code was continuously and effectively administered. It achieved its goal of making Japan technically, administratively, industrially and educationally free of foreign experts. Within a generation of the Code's issuance, all school age boys and girls could read and write. Once in motion, Japanese modernization became a speeding train. Having attained 100 percent literacy by 1900, Japan took only 13 more years before it was publishing more books than Britain and twice as many as the U.S.

Muslim reformers were keen observers of Japan's progress. From its very first year of publication, *Muqtataf* was noting Japan's success and critically comparing it to the limited progress made in the Middle East. The journal attributed Japan's success to its system of universal education, to its having no government censorship and to the great number of books it published. The implied criticism was that Muslim countries were crippled by government censorship and their lack of a competent system of universal education. The continuing high rate of illiteracy accounted for the meager number of books published compared to the Japanese, a figure that the editor Sarruf said should make Middle Easterners hide their heads in shame. He reported that Japan published 3,792 books in 1880, 4,910 the following year. Among the 8,702 books published during those two years, 500 were on medicine, 350 on geography, 1,410 on education and learning, 230 on mathematics, 45 on chemistry, 32 on natural philosophy and 16 on astronomy. These were books written by Japanese and did not include the scientific books translated from western languages.[4]

Where some writers in Egypt and the Ottoman Empire saw Japan's industrial success and military defeat of Russia as a sign of hope for other eastern peoples, more critical observers like Sarruf, Nimr, Zaydan and Shaykh Rashid Rida, men who had spent their lives writing for reform and measuring its progress against the West and Japan, were humiliated and depressed by the prospect of there now being an Asian nation joining the West in looking down on Arabs and Muslim society. In anger and frustration the editors of *Muqtataf* and *Manar* blamed the sorry condition of the Middle East on the people's mental laziness; other times they put the blame on government irresponsibility in failing to do what the Japanese government was doing. They may not have appreciated the advantages Japan had in being free of capitulations and being so far from Europe and America, whose imperialist compulsion of economic control was attenuated by distance. *Muqtataf* did recognize that Japan had an advantage in possessing a ruler who was considered a divinity, obedience to whom was a religious principle.[5] Orders from the emperor were orders from God, quite unlike the Muslim experience where reformist orders from the ruler and his government were taken not as coming from God but from the sultan's godless reformers and their European masters.

This oceanic difference between Japanese and Muslim religio-political orientations may help to some extent in explaining the success of one and the tribulations of the other, but any comparison must be qualified. Japan was an *umma* free of *millets*. The Japanese were essentially one people, one nation tightly bound in a sense of being uniquely Japanese. They were a nation free of capitulations and unhampered by religious and ethnic minorities with tangential allegiances siphoning off social energy and cohesion into channels other than those set by the reformers. The sentiment expressed by the "heartfelt bonds of patriotism" proclaimed in the *Tanzimat's* Gulhane decree of 1856 legalizing religious equality was not embraced by Muslims in Ottoman lands with anything near the breadth and intensity that comparable words seized the hearts and minds of the Japanese.[6] Japanese reformers were fortunate to have the embers of an already existing "heartfelt bond of patriotism" that they could stoke in order to bring forth the flames of latent energy. Social solidarity was crumbling in the multi-ethnic

Ottoman Empire between the hammer of nationalism and the anvil of European intervention on behalf of the minorities. The passions of many nationalisms – Greek, Serbian, Bulgarian, Romanian, Armenian, Arab – gave no chance to the changes being constructed by the *Tanzimat* and Young Ottoman reformers.

The legacy of 19th century passivity in regard to government action in support of science and technological development did not disappear in the 20th century. A leading authority on science policy in the Arab states wrote in dismay that as late as the 1940s science was a foreign import, with painfully few Arabs knowing anything about it in a professional sense. The great majority of those in the Middle East involved in science and technology were foreigners. Not until years after World War II did scientific research begin, and even then it was on a most modest level and, regarding the Arab region of the Muslim world, limited to Egypt, from where "the rumblings of scientific knowledge were spreading throughout the region."[7] The rumblings fell far from becoming a roar. By the time the military took over in 1952, Egypt still had not entered the international fraternity of scientific enterprise, nor did the military regime bring the country any closer to the threshold of competence.

Muslim societies looked to be the same old spectators sitting on the sidelines watching the world go by that the editors of *Muqtataf* and *Manar* had castigated several generations earlier. In spite of all the ink used glorifying Islam's historical achievement in science, mathematics and medicine, and emphatically headlining the Quran's and Hadith's demands that Muslims study nature, even if they had to go to China to do it, Muslim governments and societies made little progress.

Data collected by researchers in the science policies of Muslim states depict a depressing picture. The bulk of state revenues, whatever of it is left after bureaucratic waste, mismanagement and corruption, is spent abroad for arms purchases, leaving little for education, social services and internal economic investment. Since western technological advances soon render obsolete the costly arms manufactured in the West, new ones must be purchased. The cycle starves education and the domestic economy while fattening the armament industries of the supplying nations. Eighty percent of the almost two billion dollars the U.S. government gives yearly to Egypt goes to pay for U.S. made weapons. Education becomes a low line item. Advanced study in the hard sciences becomes a superfluous pursuit where dictatorships are obliged to placate their only pillars of internal support, the military, state police and intelligence agencies.

Based on data collected in the late 1970s, in all of the 20 some odd countries in the Arab world, comprising a population of more than two hundred million, a grand total of no more than 2,000 of its citizens had been granted doctorate degrees in the exact sciences. Scientific and technical publications were commensurately low. The situation has not changed significantly during the last several decades. Scientific literature in Arabic continues to be miniscule. The number of Middle Easterners who earn doctorates in science and who publish has increased since the 1970s, but the best of them prefer to publish in western journals and often find themselves compelled to leave for the West if for no other reason than to continue their research to remain competitive.

Burdened as they are by crushing military budgets, the economies of Muslim governments find the expense of research too high for the benefits that are most often too long-term to be given priority in the short-term plans of dictators whose policies are narrowly focused on maintaining power. In that inhospitable atmosphere of minimal research facilities and political repression, the only way for scientists to be productive is to integrate themselves into the society of western-based scientific institutions and their scientists through attending conferences, joining professional societies, obtaining visiting professorships and research grants, and keeping in close contact by telephone, e-mail and exchange programs. This "invisible college" provides a network to keep Third World scientists connected and competitive. At the same time, however, it orients their research more to western projects than to what they might be interested in since their research is funded by western institutions. Dr. Zahlan, former physics professor at the American University of Beirut and critical analyst of science funding and the record of Arab governments, sums up the historical process by which Middle Easterners have reached this impasse:

> During the nineteenth century the Ottomans and the Viceroys of Egypt turned to Europeans for technical assistance in the agricultural, engineering and military domains. And this dependence has grown with time. The alternative would have been to look inward and to transform the social, cultural, economic and exploitative structures of both the agricultural and military establishments with a view to releasing the latent aptitudes of the population. Instead, the policies that were pursued further complicated the issue. Whereas the population of the region had had an unrealistic view of Ottoman power before the Napoleonic invasion, they soon developed a feeling of inferiority towards the West. This sense of helplessness and dependence continues to grow the more individual Arab states seek modernity and the deeper the military and economic failures. For whether it is jet fighters, petrochemical complexes, sports arenas, hospitals or harbours, Arab governments today know of only one way to get them: through turnkey projects with foreign international firms . . . Officials appear to assume that those in the know are the best experts to contract for the job. Science and learning are too slow and appear to be marginal processes totally divorced from the task at hand. In some Arab bureaucracies one repeatedly hears that they are tired of studies and plans; they want turnkey projects, they want results.[8]

The Arab world's pattern of buying technology from the advanced nations has over the last several generations gone from habit to addiction, and has not come anywhere near to resolving the blights of poverty, disease, malnutrition and illiteracy, nor to building up its own bank of technical and scientific expertise to break the easy but expensive addiction to turnkey projects that bring no scientific or technical transfer to the buyer. Again, Dr. Zahlan:

> It is interesting to note that from the days when Muhammad Ali embarked on the development of his army, navy, industry and agriculture by utilizing

mostly French officers and engineers to the present, the Arab states have after every major setback only varied the supplier of the "expertise" but not the approach. Some have displaced one European supplier with another, others have substituted East for West, the US for Europe, and the more adventurous have diversified the suppliers. However, and this is most surprising, no Arab state has sought to test new approaches . . .

In the Arab world today development is synonymous with projects and the importation of foreign equipment . . . The absence of adequate historical consciousness, focusing on economic, technological and scientific activity, and the neglect of the analytical study of past experiences have contributed immeasurably to the persistent complacency that pervades the Arab planning and decision-making circles. This neglect of a rich and enormous experience may account not only for the persistence and growth of counterproductive patterns of behaviour but also for the stunted growth of institutions and the sluggishness with which science and technology have grown into the lives of the Arab people. Numerous institutions (inclusive of bureaucracies) are concerned with science and technology in the Arab world. But their activities are circumscribed to a narrow sphere; they persist as impotent instruments kept at a distance from the serious work of planning, designing, evaluating and constructing.

What then is the record on the achievement of the modern Muslim states in promoting science during their half century and more of political independence from western control? Initially, some small steps were made, particularly in the foundation of research institutions, impressive in name but in reality little more than empty shells with grandiose goals and miniscule budgets.

In 1939, Egypt's young King Faruq founded a National Research Council (NRC), the Arab world's first. Because Egypt was the pace-setting country, the NRC became the model of all the other research centers that eventually followed: Conseil Universitaire de la Recherche Scientifique founded in Morocco in 1959; Supreme Council for Scientific Research founded in Iraq in 1963; Jordan Research Council founded in 1964; Conseil de la Recherche Scientifique founded in Algeria in 1965. Research and development in these institutes existed only in name. In comparison to the collective accomplishments of all the science departments and research institutes in all the other Arab countries, Egypt's NRC, even with its paltry annual budget, was a powerhouse of research and development, thanks to the long head start the country had going back to Muhammad Ali.

At the time of Nasser's military takeover in 1952, Egypt had around 2,000 scientists, roughly half of whom held doctorates. Of these, about 200 were in the physical sciences, the remaining 800 being in medicine, agriculture and engineering. Half of the thousand PhDs had been earned abroad, mainly in France and England. In 1956 the young military officers in Nasser's government, still imbued with revolutionary fervor to rapidly modernize the country, set up a Supreme Science Council to advise President Nasser on research and development and to supply enough scientists and technical experts to bring Egypt up to the level of the

West. As an encouragement to study science, the Council awarded prizes to the most promising research students. Periodicals were established in English to publish their articles.[9] However, when it came to the critical stage of funding to get the project up and going, government attention strayed. All of seven million Egyptian pounds over a five-year period (less than two million dollars a year) was budgeted for the Supreme Science Council. And this was to cover expenses for salaries of professional and clerical staff, for assistants, books, paper, typewriters, advertising, student prizes, editing and printing articles, maintenance, janitors, copy machines and all other technical equipment. Established with the purpose of bringing Egypt up to the level of the West, the Supreme Science Council was the military government's version of Ali Mubarak sitting in the shade of a tree drawing geometric figures in the sand for his officer–students a century earlier. The same year that the Supreme Science Council was established, the National Research Council was renamed the National Research Center, which by 1976 employed more than a thousand researchers, of whom only around half held doctorates. Funded on a level comparable to that of the Supreme Science Council, the Center supported research that was understandably modest, limited to local problems such as agriculture, soils, water purification, eye diseases and bilharzia (a debilitating illness caused by worms that flourish in stagnant water and are carried by snails).

Egyptian and other Arab governments have been far more productive in establishing research councils and scientific advisory agencies than the councils and agencies themselves have been in producing what their names suggest they should be producing, to the point where it would seem that Arab government had reduced science education and research to an absurd game of names. In 1962, as if to proclaim its true appreciation of the importance of research, Egypt's military leaders created a Ministry of Scientific Research to fund and coordinate research with the other national research bodies. The ministry was revealed for the empty gesture it was when hardly any funding was provided for it. Little more than a name, the Ministry of Scientific Research was abolished after a stillborn existence of three years. Sixty years of military government has left Egypt no more committed to science education and research than the civil government it replaced.

National undertakings to elevate the level of scientific research in the Middle East have continued right to the present, but true to pattern, they have taken the form of grandly named science policy-making bodies that create little more than an unconvincing illusion of scientific activity. The science councils and research centers most often consist of no more than a single building whose unprepossessing structure and modest library are meant not for research but an assembly hall for local graduates in the sciences to meet UNESCO representatives and hear visiting lecturers. Standing as an emblem of modernity, the research center has become a necessary accoutrement for every newly developing, self-proclaimed progressive state. They have in some small way extended the circle of scientific awareness in Arab society through the intellectual interaction with western scholars and institutions that they provide, but they conduct no significant research, and for lack of equipment could not.

Egypt's Academy of Scientific Research and Technology is typical of this. Founded in 1971 by Nasser's military successor, Anwar Sadat, the Academy was to oversee, coordinate and encourage study and research in science and technology throughout the country, with the focus on applying modern technology to alleviate the country's most pressing problems: water purification and supply, nutrition, health and ecology. The focus was wisely centered, but translated to the reality of entrenched habits of governmental behavior, this meant business as usual, that is, the continuation of the government's buying technology and expertise from the West, as Egypt's new Academy more or less stood by watching. As for its doing research, this stage was presumably to come when Egypt had resolved the worst of its problems, meaning the Academy was just another one of those ill-equipped buildings with an exalted name where some low paid bureaucrats along with a few engineering and science graduates received government orders and, if lucky, got to participate with their western counterparts who had been contracted by the government to do what the Academy had been set up to do.

Understandably, the morale of the young scientists and engineers continues to be low, if not for the unchallenging level of their work, then the level of their pay. The monthly remuneration for a beginning scientist with a PhD in chemistry from a leading American university in 1967 was 25 Egyptian pounds, equivalent to $25 in black market hard currency. The black market disappeared when Nasser's successor, Anwar Sadat, opened the country to the West and a free market economy in hope that a deluge of foreign investment would become the rising tide that lifted Egypt to modernity. Unfortunately, the monumental obstacles of Egyptian bureaucracy with its endless payoffs held back any chance of a deluge. As far as science was concerned, Sadat's opening to the West was no better than Nasser's socialism. Thirty years of stagnation under Sadat's successor, Husni Mubarak, has snuffed out all hope that anything of a positive nature could come from a repressive military regime that for 60 years gripped Egypt in an iron fist.

Foreigners continue to do the work scientists and engineers have been trained to do. Some Egyptians do their graduate studies in Europe and America only to return to unproductive careers at a monthly salary that makes survival even more of a challenge than it had been under the state controlled economy of Nasser. Engineering and science graduates take menial jobs to survive because not enough positions exist to employ them in the professions. University graduates far outnumber the positions that the feeble economy can provide. The crisis is not peculiar to Egypt.

Up to 50 universities serving more than a million students had been established in the Arab world by 1979. Many of these universities have graduate science, engineering and medical programs that look as good on paper as do the pompously named research councils, centers and academies. Like them, the universities support little that could be called research, not for deficiency of student ability but because funding facilities are so inadequate that classes contain four to five times as many students as the classrooms and buildings were designed for. The same overloading goes for laboratories and equipment.

In addition to the severe lack of facilities that only money can buy, scientific training on the graduate and undergraduate levels in Arab universities is debilitated by age-old pedagogical techniques that refuse to go away. Fahim Qubain, a researcher writing in 1966 on science education in the Arab world, found that graduates of Egyptian secondary schools received more instruction in theoretical science than American high school graduates, but that Arab graduates relied on memorization and were less inclined to think independently and put their knowledge to further use in thinking out problems.[10] Memorization remains the preferred method of learning. Beginning with the Quran through mind-numbing repetition during the student's earliest school experience, memorization becomes so deeply rooted it stays with the student throughout the university years. Students simply write down everything they can catch from the lecture and memorize it without delving into the underlying concepts to reach a clear understanding of what is going on. A lesser but nonetheless important problem is that science texts are Arabic translations of western textbooks, and as the translations take so much time to make and science advances so rapidly, the subject material is out of date by the time the books become available to the students.

Science teaching in universities focuses on practical science in order to train students for overseeing industrial machinery and managing factories, but laboratory and training facilities are so deficient that graduates enter their industrial positions with little or no practical experience. The science programs, especially in physics and chemistry, have reduced the theoretical part of a student's research to the level of courses taught in technical colleges and engineering schools, which is fine for serving immediate industrial needs but fails to contribute to building a scientific culture.

Doctoral programs have been functioning in many of Egypt's universities since the 1930s. They are now staffed by professors who by law must have doctorates. As most of these doctorates have been earned at prestigious western universities, somewhere along the trajectory of their education the members of this doctoral elite were able to shake off the memorization habit. Or more likely, they integrated it into the critical thinking and questioning that they assimilated through years of graduate course work and research. Their memorization ability became a readily available tool for storing and retrieving information. Having put their power of memorization in the service of critical analysis and research, their work would now be to pass those skills on to their undergraduate and graduate students. However, because of understaffed departments, heavy teaching loads, crowded classrooms, insufficient support staff and lack of equipment, it is just as difficult for the doctoral elite to impart these skills to their students as it is for them to carry on research. Except for the fortunate few who obtain research appointments and grants from abroad, government failure to invest in science education means the end of a research career for the large majority of PhDs, thereby withering the roots of a creative scientific community.

Scientists who wish to pursue their research are obliged to do it in the West. This removes the highest caliber talent from the national universities for extended periods, if not for good. Nobel Prize winners Muhammad Abdus Salam of Pakistan and Ahmad Zewail of Egypt are prime examples. A Nobel winner for research in chemistry, biology or physics may give prestige to one's country of origin, but it transfers nothing to education or research in the universities of the country. The benefit remains in the West, where the research is done. Pakistani and Egyptian presidents can bestow medals of honor on their winners, but scientifically, as a product of the West, the winner is a western asset. For the creative scientist who wants to contribute one's talents to building up science in one's native country, the price is professional suicide:

> In Third World countries, despite numerous short and long-range plans, educational and manpower policies are disjointed. It is possible, for example, to dispatch thousands, even tens of thousands, of young people to pursue higher education abroad without making suitable provision for their return. When national universities are established they are often shallow reflections of the institutions being copied. Institutions are set up without those conditions most essential for intellectual and scientific activity: a faculty that is socially, economically and intellectually secure; library and laboratory facilities; academic standards for both faculty and students; and tolerance for opinions, findings and criticisms emanating from research and academic institutions. The absence of such conditions in most of the Arab countries is reflected in both the massive brain drain (probably approaching 50 per cent of Arab doctorate holders) and the extremely poor productivity of scientific manpower employed in the Arab world.[11]

A 1960 study by an American group of scientific academics from Pennsylvania State University found that equipment being used in the labs of the science departments of Cairo University dated from the time when the university was founded in 1925. The Pennsylvania report stated that when new equipment was purchased it was the government that decided what would be bought on the recommendation of a bureaucrat who found the cheapest manufacturer, usually one in eastern Europe or China. Whatever the piece of equipment was, it was fairly certain it would not be something manufactured in the Middle East or Muslim world. The lack of spare parts and maintenance meant a "failure of a single circuit element will lay up a whole rack of equipment for months or even permanently."[12] According to the Penn State report, the University of Cairo's chemistry department had a good reputation. It possessed a fine faculty of Egyptian, German and British professors. But, the report went on, the Egyptian government failed to recognize the rising cost of chemicals and equipment. Consequently, the necessities that made for good instruction went wanting. Government deficiency in budgeting undermined the department's educational mission in every direction, the most direct one being the deleterious effect it had on the chemistry professors who saw themselves, on the one hand, left outside the mainstream of their fields of specialization, and on the other, limited in providing their students with a quality education in chemistry. Even when new equipment was ordered, the report continued, the lag between time of request and time of arrival was so great, often a year or two, that the researcher had by then given the project up.

Such was the state of affairs in the leading science department of Cairo University eight years after the military seized power. Conditions were more dire at the

College of Science in Alexandria. Here it was the physics faculty that struck the visiting critics from Penn State as being the College's most active research department. But again, it was a department crippled by a lack of equipment that severely limited research possibilities. There were other limitations, such as professorial positions that were left unfilled because of retirement or other reasons. The physics library was seriously lacking in books and journals. Even the most vital journal of physics, *The Physical Review*, was not to be found.

If physics was the best department in the Alexandria College of Science, what of the other departments? It was in one of those others that Egypt was to gain its first, and so far only, Nobel Prize winner in science. Three years after the Penn State delegation submitted its report, Ahmad Zewail began his undergraduate education in Alexandria University's department of chemistry. His success proved that in spite of all the drawbacks in the Egyptian system, a budding scientist could still emerge, provided there was a way to continue graduate work outside of the country.

Dr. Ahmad Zewail's career highlights the challenges faced by bright young Middle Eastern students who wish to pursue a life in science, in spite of all the frustrations that come with that choice. Ahmad's frustrations began early in his undergraduate career in the mid-1960s. To begin with, as he relates in his autobiography, *A Voyage Through Time*, neither of the two teachers who helped and inspired him in his last two years of undergraduate work in chemical spectroscopy at the University of Alexandria had offices.[13] Both teachers were relatively young, one with a PhD from an American university, the other with one from a German university. Being the most recent members of the chemistry department, they were ranked as lecturers. Lecturer was a lowly level that offered no offices, not even a common room for all the department's lecturers to share. That his two principal chemistry teachers were without offices was a problem Zewail did not fully appreciate as an undergraduate student. But, graduating at the top of his class in science and continuing at the University of Alexandria for a master's in chemistry, he realized how crippling it was to the educational process for a teacher not to have something as basic as an office, even a small corner of one, or at least a table somewhere to write on. In plaintive but cheerfully good natured tones reminiscent of Ali Mubarak's description of his lack of resources as a teacher a century earlier, Ahmad Zewail describes a dark, dirty, cluttered, rat infested corner of a storage room in a derelict building next to the cafeteria that his thesis advisor had discovered and improvised as an office. The place was filled with old papers and odd bits of broken furniture and refuse covered in ages of dust. Debris-ridden and lightless, this was where the future Nobel Prize winner and his advisor, sitting on rickety crates at an improvised table, spoke of the marvels of chemical spectroscopy.

On the brighter side, the chemistry department had just received a new spectrophotometer for measuring different parts of the spectrum, perhaps the result of Penn State's critical review of Alexandria's chemistry department that had been submitted the year before. In 1968 Ahmad Zewail received his master's degree and was awarded a fellowship at the University of Pennsylvania to study for a PhD. It covered tuition and gave him $3,600 a year for expenses, a princely sum for the son of a middle-class family from a small town in the countryside who as a student in Alexandria could not afford to join a modest sporting club. There was one problem. It was the policy of Alexandria University to decide which of their students should go abroad to study. Accordingly, the University of Pennsylvania in Philadelphia was requested to send a letter offering the fellowship to an unnamed student so that the chemistry department could decide which of their students to send. The fellowship would as a matter of course be given to the student with the best contacts, not grades or research ability. The procedure was in line with the Egyptian system of *intisab* (contacts, relationships, cronyism, nepotism), but it revealed how out of touch Egyptian universities were with the system of advanced education in the West. Penn of course refused to send such a letter. After a lengthy exchange of letters, a compromise was eventually reached whereby Penn sent the open letter Alexandria required, it being privately understood the offer would not be honored if Zewail was not the student selected. To cover the niceties of official policy, Zewail was obliged to obtain letters from all the other students in the chemistry department who had earned their master's degree that year stating they were not interested in the University of Pennsylvania fellowship.

There was still the bureaucratic paperwork to complete before being allowed to leave the country. Zewail's is a long and horrendous saga that can be appreciated by anyone who has lived in Egypt and been involved with its devouring labyrinth of bureaucracy that reduces life to a seemingly endless process of going from office to office, building to building, ministry to ministry, in pursuit of forms, stamps and signatures. Once or twice a week for months Ahmad had to take the train from Alexandria to Cairo to get permission from the Ministry of Higher Education to leave the country. He also needed permission from the President of Alexandria University, who happened to be out of the country. Rather than being applauded for being so hardworking and smart for getting a prestigious University of Pennsylvania fellowship, Ahmad was sent from office to office, forced to wait long hours for bureaucrats who were absent from their offices or too busy chatting to notice him. It was not until the summer of 1969, after many train trips, that Zewail obtained all the signatures on all the paperwork required by the Ministry of Education and the university. The final indignity was his being required to pay the university for the tuition grant it had given him during the year he was a graduate assistant: a form of sadistic punishment for his being fortunate enough to have won a fellowship abroad and getting to leave the country.

Zewail's autobiography reveals another problem, one faced by all students from Muslim countries headed for advanced training in the West: lack of preparedness. Ahmad had a master's degree but was unaware of modern developments in chemistry and physics. He had never heard of certain principles that doctoral candidates in chemistry would have been expected to know, such as quantum theory, lasers and large biological molecules. He was equally unaware of large and intricate research equipment, such as superconducting magnets and electron microscopes. He had to learn as a doctoral researcher what he should have learned as an undergraduate and master's degree student. Also, with his English being a little weak at the time, he had trouble following lectures – an echo of the same problem that had haunted the medical and engineering students who had been sent to Europe to study 150 years before Ahmad Zewail landed in Philadelphia.

The main problem for Ahmad was not so much his unfamiliarity with the language as his lack of up-to-date research equipment. In so many gentle words, he warns that the government that puts research and development on a back burner accepts eternal night for its people, and if anything proves that Muslim rulers have accepted eternal night it is the portion of the national budget they have given to scientific research and technical development.

While the dozen or so Egyptian universities that offer an undergraduate and master's level scientific education are competent enough to make it possible for serious students to continue on for doctorates in the West's leading graduate schools, the research facilities in those universities are next to useless or non-existent. The so-called research institutes (mining, geology, astronomy, space science) are no better. They are more like contact centers, conduits that keep at least the idea of research alive by providing a means for Egyptians to maintain contact with their international peers and the expanding world of science. Nonetheless, thanks to these modest assets, a handful of the world's greatest scientists have come from Egypt, Pakistan and Iran to make their contributions in the West. Those unwilling to leave home and family, or who refuse to leave in hope of nurturing a scientific community in their native country, are only with great expenditure of effort and time able to keep abreast of their fields through journals, international conferences and a network of communications. The internet has been a boon to everyone but to no one more than hopeful researchers in Muslim countries. Their greatest hope of success is to gain a research grant or visiting professorship in a western university that would allow the researcher to remain at the cutting edge of his or her field without having to abandon the effort of contributing to the development of a national scientific culture.

Egypt's record in scientific publications reflects the poor condition of research possibilities described in the Pennsylvania State University report. The hope that the Egyptian military revolution would bring a change for the better in the Arab region's record of scientific research drained away during the early 1960s and was once and for all dashed with Israel's crushing defeat of secular nationalist military government with its empty slogans of revolution and progress. Egypt and China were about par in scientific output in the 1950s, but within a generation China became an atomic power and an exporter of technology, leaving Egypt where it had been, a technological cripple dependent as much as ever on foreign expertise and imports.[14] In 1955, with expectations of rapid change for a better Egypt still vibrant from the takeover by the young military officers and their abolition of the lethargic monarchy, a grand total of no more than 29 papers were published in the basic sciences and mathematics.[15] Conditions have not improved over the decades. Measured by the progress of other countries, retrogression would better characterize Egypt's condition.

The record of other Arab countries is even less promising than Egypt's, with one exception: Lebanon. In spite of the country's small population and the fact it had been under French occupation until 1946, Lebanon was the only Arab country with anything near a respectable research record – particularly in medicine, owing to the Medical School of the American University of Beirut. In the decades following World War II, professors at the American University published papers in chemistry and physics, though these were not in pure science but, as to be expected, of practical concerns related to local problems, as in other Arab countries.

Before the 1967 war the total Arab scientific output, as measured by numbers of publications in reputable journals, was less than half of Israel's, 41 percent to be exact. It was hoped by some Arabs, whose optimism had somehow survived the catastrophe of the Six-Day War and the humiliating spectacle of Israel's vast technological superiority, that the defeat would at last do what the shock of 1948, when newly born Israel had trounced the Arab states the first time, had not done: stir the discredited regimes into developing science and technology as the road to re-vindication. As events would show, Arab military dictators and monarchs proved themselves shockproof.[16]

During the five years following the Six-Day War, 13 Arab countries had a total of 750 scientific publications, less than 12 per country per year, with Egypt weighing in at much more than half of them. In that same period, Israel had 1,739 to its credit, four times the number of Egypt's. In terms of publication and population ratios the discrepancy was 52 times in Israel's favor. Measured against all the Arab countries, or the whole Muslim world, the discrepancy reaches well more than a hundred fold in Israel's favor.

The same sorry record continued under President Nasser's successors in Egypt. Anwar Sadat's Academy of Scientific Research and Technology, founded in 1971, turned out to be just another empty façade lacking office space, supplies, technical equipment, scientific books, journals, experimental laboratories, and professional and secretarial staff, but with an imposing name. Poorly supported from the beginning, it was ignored after the ceremonial fanfare of cutting ribbons and snapping photos. It was never intended to be anything but a name. The Academy's research committee that presided over projects in chemistry, biology, physics and geology met rarely, and not once in 1976 or 1977. A research project to find a simple design for the most efficient solar heating units of a prescribed capacity, a sensible undertaking in a sunny country like Egypt, was budgeted $3,000 for one year. This came to little more than $60 a month for each of the four scientists on the research team. This was to cover the expenses of experimental equipment, office supplies, technical support and clerical staff. To add insult to injury, after the researchers had designed, constructed and tested their heating unit and submitted the design and final report to the Academy's research committee, the government ignored the report and imported the units from Europe.[17] Like his Academy, Sadat's Atomic Energy Research Center enjoyed its only moment of achievement when it was given a name. Officialdom's contempt and neglect of home-born expertise withers the soul of a young techno-scientific culture in the making. In addition to heads of ministries ignoring the advice, experimentation and design work of the very scientific bodies they created, decisions in science, technology and industry are made by government chiefs who have no experience or knowledge of the scientific and technological projects they control. They do not bother to solicit the opinions of experts in or out of government service, unless they are foreigners. Such blatant demonstrations of government confidence in foreigners sours the spirit of the young professionals, and with it the small but hopeful blossoms of creativity that the government research centers were supposedly set up to nurture.

Ten years after the 1967 war that was hoped to shock Arab governments into action, Egypt's share of total world output in scientific articles was 0.21 percent, just more than a fifth of 1 percent.[18] Turkey's record was little better.[19] At the end of the 20th century Turkey ranked 45th in the world's scientific output in terms of papers published in peer journals. Turkey's record in the early years of the 21st century (one paper per academic scientist per decade published in an international journal) remains unpromising, though the country's economic rise during the last several years gives some indication of future improvement in Turkey's technology-driven scientific output. Other Muslim countries present an even more dire profile.[20] Measured against the scientific output of the whole Muslim world, Israel's publishing record was almost double, 6,100 to 3,300 papers. According to figures compiled by *Science Watch*, Egypt, continuing by far to remain the Arab world's scientific leader, produced 39,404 scientific papers between 1981 and 2002, as compared to Israel's 157,379, amounting to the same one to four ratio of the previous two decades. In measuring and comparing the relative scientific output and impact of Middle Eastern countries, *Science Watch* excluded Israel since the relatively large size of its scientific enterprise tends to preclude any meaningful comparison with its geographic neighbors.[21] In other words, Israel and the Arab world exist in separate universes.

All the countries of the Muslim world combined barely accounted for a third of 1 percent of the world's scientific papers. This is seven times less than India's output at 2.26 percent. In light of this, it should be no surprise that the Arab world's total manufactured exports amounted in 1989 to less than those of Finland. The comparison should be no less humiliating to Muslim governments than was Japan's industrial and educational success a century earlier to the editors of *Muqtataf* and *Manar*. The simple relationship between science, industry and exports on the one hand and world respect on the other was quite clear to the editors.

Sixty-five years of independent government have not freed the Arabs from a paralysis of will that began with the collapse of the protective cocoon of the Ottoman Empire with all its familiar emblems and institutions of caliphate and sultanate. The imperialist straitjacket of the mandates that followed reinforced the paralysis. An Arab secular nationalist intelligentsia tried to construct a way into the new and threatening world, but their efforts were obstructed by a pseudo political leadership of self-interested, traditional elites from the last generation of Arab Ottomans. The appointed leaders pitifully attempted to conceal their impotence as servants to the real rulers, the French and British high commissioners above them, whose interests they served while acting out their appointed roles as leaders of nationalist liberation in the service of their people, who, far from being hoodwinked, mocked their overheated blather of struggle and heroism.

Independent government, when finally it came, proved no less weaker, nor less self-interested, hypocritical, corrupt and oppressive than had been the parliamentarian surrogates propped up by the mandatory authorities. The willingness of Arab and Muslim leadership to sacrifice their peoples' futures by guaranteeing their continued subservience is no more glaringly advertised than in the absurdly low funding given for research. Examples reflecting this abound.

The same pattern of nationalist bombast and meaningless research centers that has crippled Egypt has been replicated across the Arab and Muslim world. Only Iran, Pakistan and, for a while in the very early 1980s, Iraq have advanced beyond the level of giving names to empty research institutes, but even here, abd al-Qadir Khan, the father of Pakistan's atomic bomb, had to lift the design of the gaseous uranium hexafluoride enrichment centrifuges from the Dutch, with the Iranians relying on Russian and North Korean expertise. Nonetheless, a beginning has to be made somewhere and how else but by relying on the achievements of others. Yet even when a beginning is made, if it is not run aground from within, it is bombed to the ground from outside, such as when in the summer of 1981 the Israelis, with President Reagan's blessing, bombed Iraq's French-built Osirac reactor that was to develop the country's expertise in atomic technology. Not wishing to see its monopoly on atomic weapons in the region compromised, Israel now threatens to do the same to Iran. That Iran was aiming for nuclear weaponry before the Obama-driven nuclear agreement whereby Iran gave up enriching uranium in exchange for the U.N.-imposed economic sanctions has been shown to be false. Iran's advancing from the 3 percent uranium enrichment that Iran has achieved for electrification to the 20 percent it wishes for radioactive isotopes used in medical technology was feverishly, and falsely, claimed by Israel's prime minister Netanyahu to prove that Iran was a step or two from manufacturing a nuclear bomb. What was manufactured was the crisis. Israel and the U.S., both nuclear powers, used every scare tactic there was short of dropping bombs to coerce Iran into surrendering its nuclear program. The pumped-up crisis that held the world of television news enthralled was, in the words of an award-winning investigative journalist, exactly that, a manufactured crisis (Gareth Porter, *Manufactured Crisis: The Untold Story of The Iran Nuclear Scare*, Just World Books, Charlottesville, Virginia, 2014). Israel and the U.S., with the E.U. loyally following behind, hold to the policy that Muslim countries should be allowed to defend themselves but only up to a point. Pakistan was by stealth able to slip out of the choke hold and build atomic weapons in order to counter India's. But the line is being held with Iran. To any objective observer it is absurd that Iran, even if it were to succeed in acquiring nuclear weaponry, is being cast as a threat to Israel and the West, with all their nuclear bombs. What kind of a threat is an oil-rich Third World country that is heavily sanctioned and cut off from international banking and trade, that cannot sell its oil and that even at this late date has not trained its own engineers and scientists to build, operate and maintain refineries and is obliged to import 43 percent of its gasoline, a century after Britain first began drilling, pumping and refining Iranian oil?[22] The fear in Israel and the U.S. is that if Iran became nuclear their power to intimidate and dictate terms to the country would be diminished. The U.S. follows the Israeli lead, and Israel uses Iran to divert international attention from its continuing colonization of Palestinian land.

Far from the realm of particle physics and reactors, the only research that might pass as such in the Arab world's national research centers is limited to soil stabilization, agriculture, desalinization and health – areas that would bring greater social benefits than would be gained in achieving atomic weaponry, if only everyone in the neighborhood were guided by the same reason.

Muslim society has been at war with itself ever since the collapse of the Ottoman Empire. The strife in fact pre-dates the fall: it is an inheritance from Ottoman times. Civil strife threatened the empire the moment that westernized reform was introduced, as early as the Tulip Period and the bloody reaction that ended its reforms. It wasn't just reform that produced the turmoil. Reform presented the occasion, the pretext, the nexus that drew together the socio-economic strands of anger, discontent and desperation that festered just below the surface. Reformist innovation based on western models served as the devil that seduced all that was good. The struggle brought together for a moment rich and poor, social strata that had nothing in common other than defense of religion and empire against the invading evil. The alliance was ephemeral. Each territorial loss to European powers, countered by another round of even more profound reform to survive, generated greater levels of centrifugal force that generation by generation tore away the sense of commonality that bonded the elements of Muslim society.[23]

As for the Arab lands that were stripped away from the empire that had shielded them against European imperialism, they became for the first half of the 20th century the chessboard of old-fashioned Anglo–French colonialism and for the second half the playing fields of the lords of the Cold War. This has not made a congenial stage for scientific enterprise.

Never presenting a promising picture when even a semblance of peace, stability and free expression existed in Middle Eastern society, the picture of science education and research dimmed considerably during the last several decades, coming practically to a standstill during the long maelstrom since 1967. Except for the brief reprise of the Arab Spring with its overthrow of dictators, Arab governments and citizens have lived in fear of each other. To stay in power, the dictators thought more about appeasing their military and intelligence agencies than patronizing education and scientific institutions. Those of them who have chosen to be U.S. clients as a way to hold on to power were obliged to restrain criticism of Israeli and American actions in the region, rendering them all the more illegitimate in the eyes of the people. The governmental order of the day was survival by any means, even if it meant following orders from the U.S. and holding hands with Israel to make life as miserable as possible for the Palestinians of Gaza. To complement Israel's iron-fisted siege of impoverished Gaza and its hammering of the Hamas government into submission, Egypt went so far as to build an underground steel wall to seal off the tunnels used to bring everything imaginable into Gaza. Sadat's assassination by Muslim revolutionaries in the military establishment terrified other Arab dictators. Sadat's successor, Husni Mubarak, had several narrow escapes. Haunted by fear and suspicion of the assassin's machine gun or bomb, those who held the reins of power had little mind for the frivolities of academic institutions and scientific research.

Though less lethal than military dictatorship, state bureaucracy has endured just as long and has been just as effective as the military in crushing any sign of scientific enterprise. Egypt's labyrinthine bureaucracy is legendary, but reflective of others in the region. Reference has been made to Penn State's 1960 report on Egyptian universities that describes how it takes a year or more for research equipment to arrive from abroad, by which time the project has been sucked into the memory hole and the researchers long gone. The contemporary narrative inside Egypt shows that the bureaucracy thrives and remains as resilient as ever. The July 22, 2007 issue of *al-Ahram* describes the government's grand intention to establish (or rather "resuscitate the skeleton of") a Supreme Council for Science and Technology. In association with this new Supreme Council, another Fund for Scientific and Technological Growth is to be established. The Council is to plan a strategy for scientific research in support of the technological development of major projects, three in particular: water, power and nanotechnology. (Nanotechnology seems oddly placed next to water and power and is no doubt there because it was the application of nanotechnology to chemistry that gave Egypt's Ahmad Zewail his Nobel Prize.) The author of the piece in *Ahram* calls the government's intention noble, as the government itself recognized in self-congratulation. But intentions are one thing and past experience something else, so the government's self-applause should be tempered by reality, the author goes on, warning his readers of the "destructive torpor of bureaucracy" with its "obstructionist attitudes" and "temper of negligence, intransigence and destructive tyranny" that retard and bury the noblest of projects:

> It is expected that for approval of the final plans before actual construction begins it will take two to three years and more for the plans and accounting to go through the bureaucratic channels of national and local councils, assemblies, advisory councils, the industrial union etc., more than enough time for bureaucracy to do both the Council and the Fund in and bury them many times over, as has been experienced again and again, no matter how high up in government the supporters of the project reach. This was seen not long ago in the success by University of Cairo's School of Agriculture producing strains of rice and wheat irrigated with water of relatively high salinity in reclaimed sandy soil, that gave rates of productivity higher than even the highest grown in soil of normal clay content.

The author goes on to list other scientific successes that the bureaucracy stymied and likens bureaucracy to a computer virus that must be either exterminated or surrounded by a "fire wall" in order to keep it from destroying all development projects.

The second half of the article criticizes the government's policy of importing everything instead of producing what can be produced inside the country. Even the lanterns for celebrating the holy month of Ramadan are imported from China. This pattern of taking the quick and easy route has cost Egypt the industrial and technological base it had developed during the 20th century, modest though it may have been. "Those who once produced now import, and this has been going on so long that the cost of updating machines discourages anyone from returning to manufacturing. By importing, would-be manufacturers are spared the bother of providing for safety in the factory, paying for workers' insurance, keeping up with technological advances, training technicians, payrolls, etc. Importing the finished product is clean, simple and profitable. The consumer pays the price in the short run and in the long run it is the country and everyone in it who pays."[24] Between the anvil of the dictator's fear of all social activity that is not under state control and the hammer of bureaucracy, not to mention the defeatist culture of importing every product whose manufacture requires a machine, little opportunity exists for productive scientific research and developing technological expertise, not even when the ministries of government might actually favor seeing a home-grown product developed all the way through, from beginning to end.

The portrait of Arab government in relation to science has not been a total eclipse. To the credit of at least a few rulers, some state revenues have been directed to science education. In the early 1950s, university science education on the undergraduate level was expanded. Science graduates in the Arab world began doubling every 5.3 years. In 1975 there were a total of 760,000 science graduates. By 2000 the number was heading to ten million. But few of these graduates were able to find rewarding positions in private industry or government. Graduates with top grades and a commitment to advanced study and research, and fortunate enough to receive a grant or have family financial support, would leave for the West. A miniscule number of Arab science and engineering graduates are able to find managerial positions in the foreign built industries of their own countries, usually through family or government connections. Their highest professional challenge is operation and maintenance, meaning they need only master the factory-supplied operator's manual, translated from Japanese, French or German, to do what is expected of them.

A modern nation's survivability is a function of its qualitative and quantitative scientific and technological expertise. Without research there can be no creative science. Without science there can be no modern technology, and without that it is back to donkeys, pulleys and men carrying baskets of bricks and mortar. A country is either research oriented or destined to have its neck under the boot of one that is. A rough measure of a country's research status based on studies of advanced industrial nations is that a thousand active research scientists per million inhabitants, or one in a thousand, is needed in order to maintain a modest level of research activity. This equates to about 0.7 percent of GNP being devoted to research, and to half of all researchers being university professors in order to train the next generation, and to the research community doubling every decade. In order to support real institutions of technological research and development, the numbers increase to 3,000 engineering researchers per million inhabitants, 30 percent of whom should be university teachers of applied science and engineering. For cutting edge scientific research, the required funding rises to 2.8 percent of GNP.[25]

As of 1980 not one Arab state had contributed as much as 0.5 percent of its GNP to science and technology. Arab countries in the 1960s and 1970s were spending on the average less than $50 million a year on research out of a combined GNP of $34 billion, or 20 cents per person per year. Figures provided by Dr. Abdus Salam relating to the 1980s show that economically active manpower engaged in higher scientific, medical and technical work in the Muslim world was at the time a tenth of the world norm.[26] Twenty years later it was little different. According to figures related to the early years of the current century, the oil-rich Arab monarchies of the Gulf set world records for their lack of investment in science education and research. Saudi Arabia, Qatar and Kuwait spent about 0.2 percent of GNP on science. Developed nations spend more than ten times that, around 2.3 percent. The Islamic Republic of Iran spent only a fourth of that of the developed nations (0.6 percent), but still three times more than the Gulf Arab states. In 2007, Saudi Arabia and Kuwait were each investing about $2 billion in higher education institutes and research centers, still a humble fraction of GNP. Their stated goal was to invest 1.6 percent of the GNP to research and development, that is, eight times the amount they were giving during the first decade of the current century, but this goal was met with some skepticism and for good reason. According to World Bank Development Indicators for 1996 to 2003, Muslim countries on average spent less than 0.4 percent of their GNP on research, six times less than the world average of 2.36 percent. In 2002, the Organization of Islamic Countries (OIC) Standing Committee on Scientific and Technological Cooperation (COMSTECH) proposed that at least one million dollars be provided annually by the Islamic Development Bank for the purpose of upgrading research institutions in the Muslim world. Even that relatively paltry sum for scientific research was not met. About the same time, representatives of 22 Arab nations met at an Arab league summit in Khartoum and agreed to collaborate more closely to increase science funding and encourage public-private research partnerships: "Omar Hassan al-Bashir, president of Sudan, opened the summit with a call to put science at the heart of the nations' strategic plans. He suggested that the increasing revenues from oil production should be used to fund science and technology development. To date, none of these statements has led to the concrete actions hoped for."[27]

Inaction on the part of government has created an endemic skepticism. For some time now the malaise has been draining Arab countries of their scientists, engineers and intellectuals. A 2004 report by the Gulf Center for Strategic Studies in Cairo figures that each year the Arab countries lose half of their newly qualified physicians, almost a quarter of their engineers and 15 percent of their scientists. The drain has been mainly to Britain, Canada and the U.S. In addition, some 45 percent of Arab students studying abroad do not return home after graduating."[28]

The result is that little Israel has been able to out-produce many times over all of the Arab countries combined. With respect to advanced agricultural technology, Israel out-produced the sum product of all the Arab countries by a ratio of ten to one, even before the turmoil besetting Arab countries in the 21st century. The ratio jumps to 16 to one when comparing Arab per capita output to that of the U.S. and western Europe. Technologically crippled, the Arabs produce nothing in the way of electrical or electronic components. Most efforts to produce anything of a technological nature end in atrophy. In the 1960s Egypt initiated programs to build short range rockets, airplane frames and engines but scrapped them for lack of scientific expertise. The foreigners Egypt then hired to do the job were either too expensive to keep for long or were being assassinated by the Israelis.

Writing some 45 years ago, Dr. Zahlan reported that in spite of all the oil money that had for decades been pouring into several Arab countries, there was not among them a single research institute or university science department related to any phase of the oil industry that enjoyed international recognition.[29] The situation has not essentially changed. The reasons for this have nothing to do with intellectual or technological incompetence. The reason has all to do with political leadership. This is clear. Muslim governments have better things to do with state revenues than put them into science and technology. They think it safer to go the more expensive route and buy expertise for industry and weaponry rather than eradicating illiteracy and developing the capabilities of their people to do it themselves. This route, they fear, might lead to a more open society and their demise. To the extent that Twitter, blogging, YouTube and electronic texting represent the fruits of modern science and technology, the dictators were right: these tools of communication did lead to the demise of four or five of them. But the gadgets were bought off the shelf from other countries of the world. The expertise that produced them was not home-grown.

As far back as 1971 the head of Israel's Weizmann Institute and former chairman of the Israeli Atomic Energy Commission observed that

> The gap between us and the Arab states is widening. I had thought for some time that the gap in the technological levels and performance was equivalent to a lag of 50 years. However, today I believe that the Arabs are lagging by 100 years relative to Israel. This fact is evident in all fields of science and technology. It appears that the fossilization of scientific thought over hundreds of years has rendered the Arabs incapable of ever catching up with the developments of our era.[30]

If back in 1971 the gap was perceived to be one century, it certainly could not be any less today.

Gamal abd al-Nasser tried a half century ago to address the imbalance, but even without the assassinations of his rocket engineers and scientists, the effort would most likely have had only limited success. The assassinations, however, raise an important point. If the day comes when Arabs and Muslims have representative political leaders instead of frightened dictators, would Israel and the West permit them to modernize to the extent that they could challenge the West economically, or Israel militarily, any more than Britain in the 19th century tolerated competition from Muhammad Ali's textile industry or Europe tolerated Egypt's growing military power, accepted Ottoman attempts to be free of the capitulatory privileges that favored European residents in the empire, or more recently, allowed the democratic government of Iran to nationalize its oil in 1953, when Iran suffered an Anglo–American coup d'etat that restored a dictatorial shah? It was not long after Iran's loss of democracy that Britain and France joined with Israel to attack Egypt after Nasser made an arms deal with the Soviets and nationalized the canal; and Israel bombed Iraq's French-built Osirac reactor with America's blessing. U.S.-Israeli resistance to Iran's nuclear program is the latest confrontation in a long history of western efforts to keep Middle Eastern countries under "moderate" governments that serve western interests.

Turkey, the most advanced of the Muslim nations, has been trying to close the technology gap ever since the Tulip Period, almost three centuries ago, and has for 80 years existed as a republic pledged to the Kemalist principles of secularism, revolution, democracy and progress, and still Turkey was reduced to contracting Israel to refurbish 170 of its American made M-60 tanks and a fleet of its western warplanes for a total cost of $1,670,000,000. Rather than learning to do it themselves, Turkey had the Israelis do it for them. As part of the agreement, Turkey was to sell 50 to 75 million dollars' worth of water to Israel.[31] After three centuries of catching up, the Turks are reduced to trading their natural resources for Israeli expertise to maintain weaponry purchased from the West. Unlike their Ottoman predecessors, the Turks seemed unembarrassed by it. Scientific and technological subservience has been easily accepted. It has become second nature, part of the order of the universe. In the 18th and 19th centuries, cultural pride caused humiliation by having to accept western superiority. The Nobel Prize physicist Dr. Abdus Salam shows that he is one who feels the humiliation that was expressed by earlier reformers:

> I can still recall a Nobel Prize Winner in Physics from a European country say this to me some years ago: "Salam, do you really think we have an obligation to succour, aid, feed and keep alive those nations who have never created or added an iota to man's stock of knowledge?" And even if he had not said this, my own self-respect suffers a shattering hurt whenever I enter a hospital and reflect that almost every potent life-saving medicament of today, from penicillin upwards, has been created without our share of input from any of us from the Muslim world.[32]

Pakistan has built a small atomic arsenal. It had to be done secretly, but once done there was nothing the West could do about it. Pakistan is now an unfriendly ally of the U.S., but an ally nonetheless. Iran, on the other hand, because of its opposition to Israel's colonization of the West Bank, is labeled a supporter of terrorism, if not a terrorist state for refining uranium to 20 percent. What Iran says is for medical research is for the West proof of an atomic weapons program. As in the case of Iraq before the U.S. invasion, the International Atomic Energy Commission has found no evidence to substantiate any such program. Western policy has become obvious in this regard: perpetual under-development is the silent but not so secret pact that the rulers of Middle East states must accept in return for western certification of their being mentally sane and reasonably moderate, if they want to avoid being called "Hitler" and demonized as evil incarnate and subjected to economic sanctions, cyber-attacks, special operations and other forms of covert subversion, ending in direct military attack.

Of all the Muslim countries, Pakistan was the most scientifically advanced country during the last decades of the 20th century. Its having made an atomic arsenal adds to its technical prestige. But in all of the 19 universities in Pakistan, there were a total of only 13 physics professors: no more than the number that would be expected in one respectable physics department in a middle ranking western university. Out of a population of 80 million, the 19 universities had by the mid-1980s produced a total of only 42 physics PhDs, a reflection of the miniscule fraction of Pakistan's GNP given to science education and research, and the failure of government to generate an interest in science in the student population.

To promote advanced-level research, Abdus Salam urged the Pakistani government to build a politically neutral, billion dollar-endowed scientific foundation patterned on the Ford Foundation, which he hoped to be the seed from which would sprout a scientific culture that would spread east and west through the Muslim world. The government took up Abdus Salam's idea in 1981 but allotted an endowment of only $50 million. The amount was useless given the foundation's far-reaching purpose. The project never got off the ground. Worse than that, a decade later the Pakistani National Assembly and Senate passed the "Shari'a Bill," bringing education in the country all the closer to being under complete religious control, where God rather than cause and effect became the direct originator of human and natural action.

Giving up on Pakistan, Abdus Salam set up his own research center, the International Centre for Physics in Trieste. Its purpose was to assist Muslim physicists in keeping up in their fields and continuing their research. Financial support for his Trieste institute came mainly from Italy, Sweden and the U.N. Not a single Muslim country, including his own, contributed to it, not even one from the oil-rich Arab states.[33]

Abdus Salam was sorely disappointed. He saw a kind of cultural death wish in this paralysis of will of Muslim countries to generate interest in science and fund research. It was not anything so twisted as a cultural death wish that imposed this punishing limbo on Muslim societies. Quite the opposite. What motivated the rulers was their survival, though the price meant cultural death. In the perverse logic inherent in the politics of illegitimate rule, the leaders who tolerate no criticism or freedom of expression pursue patterns of government that ensure their survival, which requires suffocating the social power that comes with the free exercise of scientific inquiry. There could be little doubt in the minds of the rulers as to what would happen to them were they to lose their power and fall into the hands of their people. The desirability of the fall of their regimes was one thing the Arab peoples could agree on, as the uprisings of 2011 and 2012 have demonstrated.

The irresponsibility of Arab regimes in not funding science was a reflex of this fear of failing to survive. The rulers intuit that building a creative culture imbued in science and its life support system of analytical and critical thought, and all that that implies in the way of social and political change, would bring a speedier end to one-man military rule and dictatorial monarchy than would any radical Muslim revolution. This fear of the liberating forces of science makes for an odd alliance. Religious authorities have similar reasons for repressing free scientific inquiry, namely their institutional self-preservation and its fundaments: traditional theology, Prophetic Tradition and belief in the eternal Quran. An embryonic culture of science (as well as its political analogue, free expression guaranteed by representative government) struggles for air beneath a suffocating collusion of political and religious authority, underwritten by western power protecting its regional interests and client states. It is a hard nut to crack.

Scientists in developed countries have often made the argument that Third World countries should limit themselves to technology aimed at solving their basic problems of illiteracy, poverty and disease, and developing agriculture to feed their people, before going into the expense of scientific research. Compelling as the argument may be in regard to Muslim countries, it opens the way to postponing research to some imaginary moment that may never come. The argument parallels those of Arab rulers who for decades argued that democratization cannot begin until the Arab–Israeli dispute has been resolved. But it has been resolved. Egypt, Jordan and the PLO have recognized Israel and signed peace treaties with it. Saudi Arabia, an American client state forced to a complicit alliance with Israel, produces a peace plan every few years, and though it is rejected by Israel and the U.S. because it calls for Israeli withdrawal from the West Bank, the American–Saudi alliance holds firm, as the tensions inherent in the relationship are vented now and then by some Saudi foreign minister's expression of frustration that a peace has not been forthcoming after so many years and so many attempts.

The reluctance of Arab and other Muslim countries to invest in science would appear to be because of the fear, ignorance and hostility that religiously oriented societies have of science, and also, obviously, because of governmental miserliness. The two are mutually reinforcing. Where education and literacy are wanting, the basest forms of religion prevail, which makes for a useful bastion of dictatorship. The general impression this gives to outside observers is that, except for the occasional individual genius, the mass of Arabs and Muslims are passive if not hostile to science, the same as were their ancestors a millennium earlier when the great classical tradition of scientific renaissance was brought to its sputtering end. There is more to it than that. There is the charged emotion against modern science by referencing it to the West. As the West is regarded with mounting hostility because of its imperialist policies, invasions and general anti-Muslim attitudes, the reputation of science suffers by association. To do science is to sleep with the enemy. This perverse mindset, reinforced by certain strains of religious extremism, undermines the active and potential scientific talent in Muslim societies and thereby unwittingly serves the interest of political dictatorship by further narrowing the freedom of thought. Political Islam narrows it from one side, authoritarian government from the other. Lack of funding finishes the job.

As for governmental miserliness of the Arab and Muslim regimes, Abdus Salam's view on this agrees with Dr. Zahlan's earlier analysis of the statistics of stagnation: the regimes saw no payoff in spending on projects or institutions whose results were projected to be decades in the future, after the rulers would have left the scene. Investing in the technological future was alien to those Muslim governments in power the last half century. Through the skewed spectacles by which the region's rulers viewed the world, it appeared cheaper and quicker to buy off the shelf. Industry took time and much investment to build, scientists and engineers to train. It was simpler and more immediate to buy technology. As for the science behind it, this could not be bought and so did not come into the picture. In the long run, the quick and easy route was the most expensive, because of both the onerous cost of purchase and the political and economic problems incurred by a country starved of scientific productivity by not having developed and employed its own pool of scientific talent.

During the 30 years between their independence and 1978, Arab countries had paid more than $400 billion to western companies for turnkey projects, including even those in the oil industry. Thirty years later the figure had risen to the trillions. Oil-rich states, Iran included, continue to rely on foreign companies for building refineries and other installations in the oil industry. Japan, with no oil deposits of its own, set out to manufacture refinery technology and before two decades was exporting it to oil-rich Muslim countries.[34] Muslim dependency on western expertise gave the oil-driven Bush administration the chance to dictate legislation to Iraqi politicians on the exploitation of Iraq's oil that would greatly benefit the Bush people and their friends in U.S. oil companies, to the detriment of Iraqi interests. Part of the problem is that the Iraqis, after almost a century of their oil being pumped up, are still technologically dependent on foreigners.

Overcoming scientific and technological dependency looks impossible even when Muslim governments move to do something about it. In the summer of 1982 the Arab world was traumatized by its helplessness as it watched on television the Israeli invasion of Lebanon and the bombing of Beirut. Up to 20,000 civilians were killed. Arab leaders would do little more than make empty pronouncements of outrage and use their telephones to plead with Ronald Reagan to restrain Israel. Expressions of outrage and long distance telephone calls shown on television news were their only weapons. Public anger brought the lesion home: the Arab states would have to catch up to Israel to defend themselves. Arab leaders decided to hold a conference in Kuwait to consider the immediate adoption of western science and technology.

The conference brought together the rectors of 17 leading Arab universities, but rather than applying themselves to the matter at hand, the conference members were side-tracked by the question whether or not science was "Islamic." The question ended up dominating the conference. The task of designing a master plan to assimilate science was smothered in theological debate. Some conferees, the Saudi members in particular, beholden as ever to Wahhabi puritanism, were sure that science was against Islam. Their fear was that if political authorities embraced the study of science it would not be long before Muslim youth took on the old Mu'tazilite heresy, which would be the end of true Islam. The conference ended with the consensus that even if science was religiously questionable, modern technology was still permissible to Muslims. Otherwise, as Ismail Mazhar would have gladly reminded the participants had he been alive and there to speak, the Arabs would have to surrender their telephones, radios, televisions, computers, cars, jets, pleasure yachts, modern weapons, refrigerators and air conditioning, even their traditional robes and headware because of their foreign-made fabric. Anything run by or made through steam, batteries, fossil fuels, electricity, electronics and every other source of power other than that driven by water, wind, man and animal would have to be condemned as un-Islamic. The fruits of technology were permissible to consume, but cultivation of the tree that bore the fruit was forbidden.

Conservative orthodoxy and unpopular autocracy have made compatible bed fellows. This has been no less true in recent times than when ibn abi Amir al-Mansur usurped the Umayyad Caliphate in Cordova a thousand years ago and, in gratitude of the ulema's support of his illegitimate rule, burned the books of reason in the grand caliphal library. His continued usurpation of power doomed the flourishing state. Within a generation the caliphate was brought to an end; the political unity of Muslim Spain gave way to dozens of petty principalities at war with themselves, as the Christian conquistadors to the north picked them off.

The established leaders of contemporary Muslim religion and government, the former afraid of the critical thought of science that leads to change, the latter of its people who crave change, have dug themselves into a deep hole. The dismal picture that has been drawn by Muslim analysts since the early 1970s, little different in substance from the plaintive comments on the state's lack of scientific initiative found in the monthly issues of secular *al-Muqtataf* and religious *al-Manar* almost a century earlier, continues to endure into the 21st century.[35] The picture may in fact be worse than the available contemporary sources depict. The oppressive, fear-breeding political climate silences scientists about their work. They fear that anything they say could be interpreted by the authorities as criticism of the government and its leaders. Hence, little of a critical nature comes out. Fear has fostered a culture of self-censorship so strictly adhered to that whatever information individual scientists might supply becomes suspect. A researcher in the contemporary scene of worldwide scientific productivity reports a U.N. official as saying that in some Arab countries what is reported has nothing to do with reality. Numbers regarding research, development and expenditure are simply guessed at, jotted down on a form, sent on and from there on taken as fact.

In spite of repeated pronouncements and meetings of Muslim and Arab leaders and scientists to fund and build scientific institutions, the record of productivity remains at the bottom of the ladder. In the mid-1980s, not long after the Israeli invasion of Lebanon, Dr. Zahlan was commissioned by the Arab league to draw up a strategic plan for scientific development. Similar to Abdus Salam's ill-fated project for a research center proposed to the Pakistani government a few years earlier, Zahlan's plan called for the member states of the league "to invest at least 1% of their GDP in research. Few governments implemented any of its recommendations." A meeting of some 500 Arab scientists in 2002 in the Gulf Emirate of Sharjah was "to set the agenda for a foundation that plans to award peer-reviewed grants to the region's researchers. There was also talk of establishing a fund to build scientific capacity across the entire family of Muslim nations."[36] This fared as badly as Abdus Salam's and Zahlan's strategic plans.

This governmental miserliness that harms science reaches into everything that contributes to a strong society. Funds for public health are just as starved. In combating the upsurge of polio in Muslim countries, officials in the World Health Organization express anger and frustration that wealthy Muslim nations contribute so little, despite repeated requests for them to join the battle. Of the four billion dollars expended in attempting to eradicate polio between 1985 and 2005, the oil-rich Gulf states contributed less than three million, less than a tenth of a percent. The half million dollar pledge by Saudi Arabia in the spring of 2005 was undiplomatically but deservedly called "peanuts" by the U.N. Foundation's chief of polio eradication. Kuwait went one better by contributing nothing. "Several calls over two days seeking comment from the Saudi and Kuwait Embassies in Washington went unreturned," leaving the burden of support in fighting polio to governments, private foundations and institutions in the West, including Russia, Japan and Australia, countries, unlike those in the Muslim world, not seriously afflicted with the disease.[37]

The repressive squeeze between autocratic rulers and conservative elements of the established ulema has taken the life out of the creative impulses of Muslim societies. The uncontrolled radical movements of political Islam and their affiliate advocates of an "Islamic Science" put their own squeeze on critical and creative thought. The liberal intelligentsia has been frozen out, and with it the quest for a home-grown scientific tradition. The crisis has deep historical origins. Movements such as the Wahhabi, founded in Central Arabia in the mid-18th century and dedicated to rooting out mysticism and its folk worship of Sufi saints, along with dancing, singing, entertainment and all enjoyment of life in order to follow Prophetic Tradition and the Shari'a to the letter, have spread over the Muslim world. Religion is to be cleansed of its foreign influences and the holy Shari'a restored to its ordained place of rule over the community. The community is to be protected as well from certain ideas in science. Evolution, that lethal virus of secularism, materialism and imperialism, the satanic trinity that threw the West into the pit of atheism, embodied all that was evil in science. In the narrowed vision of this repressive interpretation of religion, what is often called Muslim liberal humanism, with its conciliation of Islam and western science made popular among the Muslim intelligentsia by Muhammad Abduh, has, with Darwin, been pushed to the margins of heresy and beyond.

Political Islam found its greatest success in the Iranian revolution. Ayatallah Khomeini and the Shi'ite clergy co-opted the forces of revolution and sent the pro-American shah packing along with all his American military advisers. The ending of the monarchy was an inspiration to all Arabs and Muslims who dreamed of being rid of their own rulers, though few admired the oppressive religious dictatorship that replaced the oppressive monarchical dictatorship. In some ways conditions became as bad or worse than those that had existed under the shah. Many Iranians fled, many were imprisoned and many were executed. The revolution became a nightmare. Those Arabs who dreamed of their own revolution were horrified at the prospect of exchanging one monster for another. Political Islam was kept at the margins. However, as U.S. policy in the Middle East became increasingly tailored to an expansionist Israeli position in Lebanon and the occupied Palestinian territories, those heretofore marginal adherents of Islamist movements moved from the sidelines toward the social mainstream. The interrelated pressures of revolutionary Muslim movements, repressive governments and U.S. policies have over the last three decades squeezed out the secularized liberal class, from whose children came those most likely to take an interest in science and be supported in it by their families. Those who supported democracy were the same people being squeezed out by the pincer of U.S. supported dictatorship in coincidental collusion with revolutionary political Islam.

Dictatorial governments and their revolutionary opposition ideologically grounded in ultra-conservative religion did battle for dominance; while between these absolutist forces the feeble movements representing democracy and liberal humanism were being ground down to impotence and silence, perhaps similar to the faint-hearted liberal democrats in Weimar Germany who saw themselves overwhelmed by the violent forces of fascism and communism.

Until the "Arab Spring," the call for democracy in Egypt and the rest of the Arab world had long been muted. The choice was voluntary exile or silence. As it was for science, the voice for democracy was a stranger in the land. The few who dared raise a voice suffered as object lessons. Restriction of speech and dismissal of science went hand in hand, condemning society to stagnation.

In the 18th century the widening techno-scientific gap between the West and the Muslim world could be measured in decades. When Bonaparte invaded Egypt and Sultan Selim embarked on his New Order Reforms, the gap had been a matter of superior gunpowder, artillery, muskets, military tactics, wind-driven wooden ships, telescope technology, Newtonian mechanics and steam-driven machines. The spinning jenny, water frame, cotton gin and steam engine were clever but not confounding. In the 19th century the gap in the levels of expertise could be measured in multiples of a decade. By the middle of that century, with the building of steam-driven ships, railways, telegraphs and ever more powerful and sophisticated optical telescopes, as well as the development of electrical power, the burgeoning organic and electrochemical industry, revolutionary methods of steel production and western scientific and technological advance made the gap practically oceanic. Every decade of that century left the Muslims more and more to the rear. In spite of all their reforms, the gap was ever widening. The half century or so between the wars of Napoleon and Bismarck produced a technology so large-scale, complex and expensive that by the 1880s Muslims were beginning to wonder if they were ever going to catch up.

In the 20th century, with relativity, quantum theory, space exploration, genetics, Hadron Colliders and the revolution in Information Technology, the gap has soared into another dimension. The iron cage of technological and scientific dependence that Muslim countries have been locked in for three centuries looks to be as inescapable as ever. The fall of several Arab dictators and the cry for democracy that swept the region between 2011 and 2012 made it look as though the bars of the cage were loosening, but that breath of fresh air in the sunlight called the Arab Spring appears now to have been an ephemeral thing.

Notes

1 In his book *Six Days of War: June 1967 and the Making of the Modern Middle East*, Presidio Press, New York, 2002, the Israeli historian-diplomat Michael Oren makes much of a supposedly well thought out Egyptian plan of attack on Israel, code named "Dawn." But no evidence, documentary or otherwise, of Dawn has been found, certainly not on the scale, depth and seriousness reported by Oren. Like so many plans in Egypt, the military plan, if it existed, had a grand name and little else.

2 Yamada Keiji, "Modern Science and Technology in 18th and 19th Century Japan," in *The Introduction of Modern Science and Technology in Turkey and Japan*, edited by Feza Gunergun and Kuriyama Shigehisa, International Research Center for Japanese Studies, Tokyo, 1996.
3 *Fukuzawa and Jordan*, edited by Yasunosuki Fukukita, Hokuseida Press, Tokyo, 1940, p. 31.
4 *Muqtataf*, vol 61 (1927), p. 177.
5 In a brief account of a Japanese reformer, Jurji Zaydan mentions the various advisory councils guiding the absolutist god-emperor and poses the reformer as a model he only wishes Middle Eastern leaders would emulate. *Mashahir al-Sharq fil Qarn al-Tasi' 'Ashar*, 3rd edition, 1970, Beirut, vol 1, pp. 361–365.
6 Carter Vaughn Findley, "The Tanzimat," in *Cambridge History of Turkey*, vol 4, edited by Resat Kasaba, Cambridge University Press, Cambridge, p. 28.
7 Anthony Zahlan, *Science and Science Policy in the Arab World*, St. Martin's Press, New York, 1980, pp. 99–101.
8 A. Zahlan, *Science and Science Policy*, pp. 13–15.
9 Fahim Qubain, *Science Education and the Arab World*, Johns Hopkins Press, Baltimore, 1966, chapter 6.
10 F. Qubain, *Science Education*, pp. 106–108.
11 A. Zahlan, *Science and Science Policy*, p. 74.
12 F. Qubain, *Science Education*, p. 106.
13 Ahmad Zewail, *A Voyage through Time*, American University at Cairo Press, Cairo, 2002.
14 A. Zahlan, *Science and Science Policy*, p. 35.
15 The papers in basic science were modest projects on such things as the elasticity of glass, electromagnetic induction, hysteresis and polygraphics of antibiotics. Anything more sophisticated than that was beyond the equipment and support available to the researcher. A. Zahlan, *Science and Science Policy*, p. 26.
16 A. Zahlan, "The Science and Technology Gap in the Arab–Israeli Conflict," *Journal of Palestine Studies*, vol I (1972), pp. 21–24.
17 A. Zahlan, *Science and Science Policy*, p. 178.
18 The 1975 issue of UNESCO's Arab Science Abstracts could not cite a single publication from Syria, or even Lebanon, which at the time had the Arab world's only experimental lab for cryogenic physics. That same year, Lebanon's 15-year civil war broke out, destroying the country and paralyzing graduate level education and professional research for a generation. Instability and the destructive forces of war certainly account for much of Arab political failure to invest in the future through science, but the sorry lack of investment existed long before the 1967 war opened the gates of hell.
19 Taner Edis, *An Illusion of Harmony: Science and Religion in Islam*, Prometheus, Amherst, NY, 2007, p. 19.
20 Pakistan's output was but a quarter of Egypt's, Iran's a fifth at 0.043 percent of total world output; Iraq's output (0.022 percent) was almost ten times less than Egypt's. Syria's 0.001 percent was more than 200 times less. Total Arab output amounted to only 40 percent of Israel's. *The Royal Society: The Atlas of The Islamic World, Science and Innovation: A New Golden Age? The Prospects for Science and Innovation in The Islamic World*, London, 2010, pp. 24–29.
21 www.ScienceWatch.com (November–December 2003).
22 Helen Cooper and Steven Weisman, citing the Institute for the Analysis of Global Security, *New York Times*, January 2, 2007.
23 The Turkish Republic has inherited the irresolution in various forms, one of them being the present legal crisis of accepting female adultery as a secular freedom and not a religious crime.
24 Sam Khashba, *Al-Bahth al-Ilmi: Amal wa Awan al-Muhasiba* (Scientific Research: Hopes and the Moment of Reckoning) *al-Ahram*, Cairo, July 22, 2007, p. 12.
25 A. Zahlan, *Science and Technology Gap*, p. 26.
26 Abdus Salam, "The Failings of Arab Sciences," *The Middle East Journal*, June 1986.

27 Jim Giles, "Oil Rich, Science Poor," *Nature*, vol 444 (November 2, 2006); and Declan Butler, "Islam and Science: The Data Gap," *Nature*, vol 444 (November 2, 2006), pp. 26–27.
28 Herwig Schopper (former director-general of CERN) "Where Are the New Patrons of Science?" *Nature*, vol 444, (November 2, 2006), pp.35–36.
29 A. Zahlan, *Science and Technology Gap*, p. 26.
30 A. Zahlan, *Science and Technology Gap*, p. 30, citing *Davar*, April 11, 1971.
31 *New York Times*, April 19, 2002.
32 www.alislam.org/Pakistan/salam-2htm, and D. Abdus Salam home page. Abdus Salam credits Kuwait and Jordan as the only Arab countries showing any interest in science, but they are countries too small to make a difference. Saudi Arabia with its great oil wealth and Egypt with its potential scientific base are the greatest disappointments.
33 Muhammad Abdus Salam "The Failings of Arab Science," *The Middle East* (June 1985).
34 Muhammad Abdus Salam, *Renaissance of Science in Muslim Countries* (collected works of Muhamad Abdus Salam, ed. H.R. Dalafi and M. Hassan) Pub. World Scientific, London, 1994, p. 24.
35 The scientific infrastructure of the region at the end of the first decade of the 21st century is hardly different from what it was in the 1970s. The Arab nations collectively spend 0.15 percent of their combined gross domestic product on research and development. This is ten times lower than the world average of 1.4 percent. The disparity is close to what it was during the past two generations. What funds do get allocated for research and make it through the devouring maws of bureaucracy are eaten up by salaries and administrative costs.
36 Ehsan Masood, "Blooms in the Desert," *Nature*, vol 416, March 2002, p. 120.
37 Donald G. McNeil, "Health Officials Say Gulf Nations Shuold Give More to Polio," *New York Times*, Health Section, May 7, 2005.

Epilogue

Islam is its own unique culture. It cannot be expected to follow in the West's footprints to modernization. If Muslims are ever to experience historical transformations equivalent to those that westerners experienced with the Renaissance, Reformation, Enlightenment and democratic revolutions, they will be achieved in Muslim fashion, in states governed by leaders supported by the people they represent. Social regeneration must begin with legitimate rulers who do not fear the release of the pent-up energies and creativity of the people. Only with legitimate rulers can imperialism, which plays on fracturing societies and setting states against each other, on creating and deepening regional divisions in the traditional policy of divide and rule, be deflected. Legitimate rule must be the beginning in order for the political and intellectual reformation to proceed.

Muhammad Abduh's tentative try to induce enlightenment through a rational reformation of religion and tradition was suspect because of his closeness to the West, which was in either direct or indirect control of too many Muslim countries for any Muslim friend of the West not to become an object of suspicion. Because of imperialism, the rug has been pulled from under those who openly admire western achievements. Westernized Muslims and Arab Christians feel betrayed by the West. The persistence of imperialism with all its hypocrisy, double-dealing and greed has made a mockery of western values and institutions in the Middle East and the wider world of Islam, which has put westernized, secular Middle Easterners in a precarious position, their being seen as sleeping with the enemy. This, but even more the discomforting economic and political climates in their home countries, has resulted in something like half of all newly qualified physicians, almost a quarter of engineers and a sixth of scientists either emigrating to western countries or not returning after having completed their studies and research abroad, according to a study by Herwig Schopper, a renowned scientist himself (Herwig Schopper, *Nature*, vol 442, November 2, 2006, pp. 35–36).

Imperialism has complicated an already complicated problem in regard to change and modernity. Even before the advent of 18th and 19th century empire-building by the European maritime powers, Muslim reformers faced a challenge that was hard enough without having to be accused of importing ideas and institutions from the enemy. Reformers faced a mindset formed by a millennium of history that stood like a mountain before them, defying passage. On the far side was the promised land of modernity displayed by the West. To breach the mountain and reach it would require a cultural revolution in religio-historical outlook. Muslims tend to look back to that moment in history when God's guiding hand gave them a Prophet and a book from which would come a law and way of life that would be pleasing to both man and God, perceived as the perfect way, the only way. Recapturing the spirit and values of that marvelous moment became in time the only hope for salvation from present afflictions. The cultural momentum of that historical outlook has become a defensive reflex more powerful than the logic of any social or economic program promising a future state of bliss.

Modernization looks forward to higher levels of efficiency and productivity through science, technology and social organization, while westernization carries with it the Enlightenment ideals of constitutional government by the people whose elected assemblies make the governing laws, with secularism common to both. One idealizes efficiency, the other freedom, tolerance, equality, rule by law and humanism. But both are forward looking. When contemplating the sorry conditions of the present, the Muslim reflexively thinks of the greatness of one's civilization that started with a poor orphan in pagan Mecca, of Islam's unpromising origins and the small band of believers who sought refuge in Medina and triumphed over Mecca against all odds, then over tribal Arabia and the great civilized empires to the north, and of the conquerors, merchants and missionaries who went on to spread Islam from China to Andalusia. For any Muslim steeped in the glories of religion, and the angelic language of prophecy in the Quran, the historical accounts of the almost miraculous triumphs of the first Muslims, the past is a powerful narcotic. The past is perfect. Reflection on perfection bewitches the mind. The past idealizes the vision of a future that can approximate but never reach that perfection. It is an ideal that can only be captured in mind but must nonetheless be strived for. The past set the pattern for present action striving to reach the future as it converges back on itself, toward the beginning.

But the past can be what it is interpreted to be. It can take many forms and be described in different ways, using many different ideals and models imputed to faithfully represent the past. Sunni Muslims find that magical movement of the past in the Rashidun, the first four so-called Orthodox, that is, Rightly Guided, caliphs who followed the Prophet Muhammad in leading the believers. Shi'i Muslims find that divine moment in the brief caliphate of Ali and the martyrdom of his son Husayn in the seventh century, when the spirit of God dwelled in the hearts of those God had chosen, and evil in the hearts of those usurpers the devil had snared. Mystics find it in the love that resides in the heart as it shines on Quranic verses, revealing an inner truth that brings joy to the soul in its embrace of the oceanic oneness that is the Creator, or existence in pure consciousness. Some young jihadists find it in this world, in blood, bombs, battle, vengeance and martyrdom. Islam, from its origins to its many interpretations through 14 centuries of history, mirrors what is in the beholder.

The past can be molded and remolded for present consumptions, as historians have been doing since the beginning of history. As early as the 18th and 19th centuries Middle Eastern reformers set their sights on emulating the West without saying so. The innovations they advocated were disingenuously argued as being really Islamic in origin. No one was convinced. The reformers and their apologists were seen by their opponents to be front men for the imperialist powers, or for the Muslim governments they served, lackeys and puppets of the West, as they are still called. The reformers from the ulema who saw some good in western institutions and knowledge and interpreted them in Islamic form were just as vulnerable: they were slandered, accused of poisoning religion by embracing western ways and by serving a government that served the imperialist interests of the West. Reform was too heavily burdened by the West's dominating presence and its immodest demonstrations of cultural superiority, its forceful insistence on special commercial and legal privileges in Muslim lands.

The critical literature of those 19th century writers who were by later generations credited with having created a *Nahda*, a Renaissance, makes it clear that they themselves saw their day as one of failed attempts. They merely had to look at the brutality that went with Muhammad Ali's reforms, the fiscal irresponsibility of Khedive Ismail, the cultural dislocation produced by the *Tanzimat*, the misguided militarism of 'Urabi Pasha in Egypt, the reluctance of al-Azhar to reformulate a viable theology for the contemporary condition of society and the impossibly crippled patchwork job of state education that went for a system. The 20th century was no better for reform. Between, on the one hand, pretentious, overblown and incompetent civil leaders who discredited and debased party politics, parliamentary government and democracy, and on the other, military leaders who performed the same job of wreckage on nationalism, socialism and secular government, the reformers had the cards stacked against them. Military failure, technological defeat, political repression and economic retrogression have thrown Muslims back on themselves in search of a culturally authentic way out of their defeatist malaise.

Political Islam, by default, has become the answer to increasing numbers. The call for religious government has been made appealing by many failures, not least among them wretched governments and economies, with serial military defeats abetted by antagonistic western policies making bad conditions all the more intolerable. Given 19th and 20th century history, and the visceral reaction of looking back to the long-gone days of glory, Islam as the way out became almost a logical necessity. What path was left to take? Islam was the answer. What else was there other than submissive surrender to the gallery of mummified autocrats and their western supporters?

Islamic government would appear to be anything but a proper environment for the reforms that would bring democracy and scientific research to a living reality. Though the free process of the country's democratic elections has been shown to be questionable, Iran presents some surprises in science. Seventy percent of all science and engineering students are women. In some quarters of Iranian religious discourse it was being considered that future theology students be required to have degrees in other fields such as computer technology, sociology or science and engineering before going on to advanced religious study to enter the ulema – a more energetic version of Ali Mubarak's *Dar al-Ulum* and the ideas of the Young Ottomans, that scientific assimilation and constitutional government should evolve from the sinews of Muslim society and its own institutions, free of the West's delegitimizing shadow.

Several years ago, the internationally respected Thomson International Science Indicators (ISI) described Iran's rate of scientific publications as soaring. Between 1996 and 2002 Iran's publications increased from around 550 to 1,830 papers in accredited scientific journals, a jump of almost 350 percent.[1] Iran was the first and only Muslim country to rank among the top 31 science-producing nations in the world in 2002. Iranian scientists are presently performing embryonic stem cell research and are at the cutting edge of the field. Ayatallah Ali Khomeini issued a fatwa that stem cell research was in conformity with Muslim religious and legal principles and that modern science posed no problem to Islam's high regard for natural knowledge, as is revealed in innumerable verses in the Quran.[2] Iranian engineers have developed a space program that put a satellite in orbit and are approaching nuclear capability. This has all come a generation after the revolutionary paroxysms that transformed Pahlevi Iran into an Islamic Republic, giving Iranians a sense of pride and self-worth for their having shed themselves of an American-supported dictator. Even if what replaced the dictatorship was another form of the same thing, it was their own. One of the most surprising things about Iran's scientific leap, other than that it happened at all, is that it happened in spite of the Iranian government's paltry allowance for research and development of less than 0.5 percent of GDP: a third of the world average and a quarter of the European Union's, but still considerably more than any other Muslim country.

Iran's present authoritarian government does not mix well with creative science. It arrested two brothers, HIV researchers, for going to foreign conferences and associating with foreign scientists.[3] Given the arbitrary conduct of political power and the government's less than generous percentage of GDP budgeted for research and development, the scientific progress Iran has made in the last decade is paradoxical but demands respect. Its infant nuclear program is a statement of independence and national self-determination in the face of Israeli and western opposition. It is one issue upon which all Iranians can agree.

The essential element in all of this, whatever form the accommodation of politics, religion and secular knowledge takes in Iran, and whatever the political system, is confidence in the nation's cultural authenticity and political legitimacy. The Iranians have at least achieved a foothold in this endeavor. Their sense that the government, though repressive and electorally manipulative, is at least their own and not a dependent client of the U.S. adds to their national self-esteem. Without that and a sense of authenticity, a society, like so many in the Middle East, is unhealthy, undirected and unmotivated. Reflecting Thomson ISI's report, *Science Watch* records Iran's scientific output to be "rocketing." This is not altogether a baseless exaggeration. Between 1993 and 1997, Iranian scientists researching in Iran published 2,152 research papers that ranked among the top 1 percent of the world's most frequently cited scientific literature. In the following five-year period, 1997–2001, the figure for Iran more than doubled, reaching 4,813 papers. Iran was the only Muslim country to be included in a graph made in mid-2004 measuring the number of very frequently cited scientific papers that a nation publishes annually against its per capita gross domestic product. Thirty-one countries, accounting for 98 percent of the world's highly accredited literature of scientific research, made it within the graph's parameters.[4]

The upward momentum of Iran's 350 percent increase in published research papers between 1996 and 2002 was sustained over the next decade. Between 2000 and 2009, Iran's scientific advance in terms of papers published went from a lowly 1,300 to 15,000 (numbers rounded off), with a GDP per capita of $4,071. Iran's was not a long track record, but one might surmise that after Muhammad Abdus Salam of Pakistan and Ahmad Zewail of Egypt, the next Muslim to win a Nobel Prize in science will be from Iran. In a way, an Iranian did win it. There is no Nobel Prize in mathematics. The Fields Medal is the Nobel equivalent, and an Iranian woman, Maryam Mirzakhani, won it in 2014.

Over the recent decades, Iran's number of published articles has increased significantly in the basic and applied sciences including medicine. The January 2009 update of Essential Science Indicators (ESI) accords Iran "Rising Star" status in clinical medicine, microbiology, biology and biochemistry, based on the total citations increase from June to August 2008.[5] The Science Citation Index of 2005 lists three world class scientific journals for Iran. Turkey has three, and Israel has ten. No other Middle Eastern country has one, not even Egypt, which fails even to register in the international scientific indices.[6]

Of all Muslim countries, Iran offers a surprisingly productive record in science research and publication during the last two decades, surprisingly because Iran was so late in developing its scientific potential compared to Egypt and the Ottoman Empire, whose efforts in science and modernity were inherited by modern Turkey. Even with this spurt in productivity, maybe because of it, Iranian writers and scientists are boggled as to how they ended up so far behind the West, given Iran's proud achievement as outstanding contributors, in numbers of scientists and quality of work, to the great period of Muslim accomplishment.

What happened? Iranian thinkers have offered explanations. One is that it took inordinately long (1800–1990) for Iranians to unbind natural 'ilm from its religious counterpart, and then to work their way through the medieval concept that knowledge was discursive and confined to books, which meant knowledge was gained by reading and committing to memory what had been done and recorded in ages past. It took almost two centuries into the period of western contact and modernization for the "book and memorization culture" to break down and give way to the understanding that there was such a thing as new knowledge, discoverable through not passive reading but active experimentation that reworked or discarded inherited knowledge to create new, deeper truths in nature, and that would also in time be refined or discarded for yet more profound understandings.

Also helping to explain Iran's late entry in the global theater of scientific creativity was the long and costly Iraq–Iran war, 1980–1988, during which the country was isolated and friendless, so that in the decade of the 1990s the government placed strong emphasis on science and technology, especially in the nuclear sphere. As a result, Iran's technical and scientific progress has been described as phenomenal. Compared to the country's record from 1800 to the mid-1990s, the claim stands without argument. What compels analytic historians, scientists and the accountants of scientific output indices to go so far in their appraisal of Iran's performance during the period 1995–2015 is its record in not only outpacing by far all other Muslim countries, though perhaps excluding Turkey, its closest regional competitor.

In 2010, a Science-Metrix discussion paper reported Iran as having "one of the fastest build-up of scientific capabilities the world witnessed during the last two decades, and the evidence on growth and emphasis on specific, strategic subfields suggests that this may be the result of Iran's controversial nuclear technology development program." Iranians have come to excel in nanotechnology and stem cell research, which was declared by fatwa to be religiously legitimate, signaling the larger issue of Islam being science-friendly.[7]

According to the Thomson Reuters Web of Knowledge, Iran may be the world's 12th leading research nation in nanotechnology, owing to the output of Sharif University's Research Center for Nanostructural and Advanced Materials.[8] It was the first country to institute a public program in nanotechnology education for schoolchildren.

The Science-Metrix global study of 2010 concluded that Iran's science-technical research output, as measured by its publications, and number of times that the publications were cited in other international journals, increased beyond that of all other countries in the world over the period 2000–2010.[9]

Other indicators of Iran having been launched into the prized circle of global scientific leadership are the country's 58 universities, 25 of which have master's degree programs in physics and engineering, and ten doctoral programs; the two million students that in 2006 were enrolled in Iranian universities, a 20-fold increase since the fall of the shah in 1979.

In the two decades between 1990 and 2009, the world's rate of increase in publication productivity in nuclear chemistry, nuclear technology and particle physics was 34 percent, while Iran's was two and a half times greater at 84 percent. A comparable increase was measured in Iran's publications in medicine, health and animal science. Seventy percent of Iran's science and engineering students are women. Iran is the ninth country to have built its own launcher to put its own Iranian-built satellite into orbit, and sixth to send animals into space.

In the Science-Metrix study of 2010, Iran was given an index growth factor of 14.4, significantly more than South Korea's 9.8, which was ranked the next country below Iran. More than surprising is the previous year's ranking of Iran, whose scientific growth rate was given as 11 times above the average world growth rate, surpassing the Scandanavian countries, including Finland, in addition to Switzerland, Austria and Israel. The National Science Foundation's report of 2012 placed Iran first in the world in science-engineering output as measured in peer evaluated articles, with an annualized publication growth rate of 25 percent. The Institute of Scientific Information (ISI) measured Iran to have increased its scientific publications ten-fold from 1996 to 2004 and predicted that the country would reach the level of Canada by 2017. It wasn't for non-existing nuclear programs or weapons that Benjamin Netanyahu wanted to destroy Iran's scientific infrastructure.

Iran and now Turkey, whose scientific output shot up between 2005 and 2015, offer the only glimmer of scientific light in the otherwise depressing darkness that enshrouds a Muslim world whose statistics have remained constantly gloomy over the decades. Turkey's output between 2005 and 2009 was 81,800 scientific papers, of which 36,800 were in medicine. By 2009, Turkey was producing nearly 22,000 papers a year, tripling the country's share of world output: 0.7 percent to 1.9 percent in a decade, with a 2009 GDP per capita of $6,511, compared to Iran in 2009 with 1.3 percent of world output and a GDP per capita of $4,071. In 2011 it turned out to be Turkey, not Iran, that made the Thomson Reuters ISI list of the top 20 countries in scientific productivity. Turkey came in at 19. Iran, though publishing almost 24,000 papers in 2012 (compared to Turkey's 22,000 in 2009), just missed making it. As of the second decade into the new century, Turkey and Iran are running neck and neck as leaders of science in the Middle Eastern/North African region. The turmoil in Turkey under the Islamist president Erdogan does not bode well for the advancement of science there for the remaining years of the second decade of the century (see note 9 for these statistics).

The Arab part of the region has for the most part been left out of the running. The gross expenditure on research and development for the Arab world, 21 countries with tens of billions of dollars pouring annually into the oil-rich ones, was collectively 0.2 percent of GDP for the period 1981–2002: seven times below the world average and three times and more below the averages for Turkey and Iran. The Arab world, ranking below even sub-Saharan Africa, exists in a state of suspended animation, between treading water and sinking. Egypt gained only minimally in the decade 2000–2009. The Arab Spring of 2011 and its unhhappy aftermath took Egypt and Syria out of competition. Tunis, Yemen and the other Arab countries were hardly ever in it, Lebanon and Jordan barely. The northern countries of the Arab region have had a dismal time of it, with a century and a half of colonialism and western occupation followed by almost 70 years of military dictatorship that, for all the efforts and loss of lives on the part of the people, refuses to die off. The collusion of neo-imperialism and illegitimate dictatorship that paralyzed Arab society for so long has made religiously oriented movements of political opposition a viable option for change and to be rid of the do-nothing governments the people have been groaning under for generations. Honest Islamic government dispensing religious law, justice and punishment is for a large portion of society, especially the majority poor but now also for middle class professionals, preferable to the western-backed thieves ruling them. What else could explain the popularity of the Muslim Brotherhood, mother of all the many Islamist groups born since the U.S.'s demented invasion of Iraq. By acting in the name of Islam and political legitimacy, these movements have usurped the role of defining Islam and turned the religion into a sword and shield of resistance to tyranny, with the radical extreme fringe making suicide bombing an act of worship. The al-Azhar shaykhs, who would speak for a moderate and peaceful way of religion's contending with the horrid burdens shouldered by the people because of their rulers, speak out only when forced to, and when they do their voices bend to the powers that be.

This oppressive, suffocating malaise is the product of many factors: enduring poverty and illiteracy, corrupt dictators supported by foreign powers, economic stagnation and crony capitalism that blights young lives. Hamas and Hizb Allah were born of that malaise: the former after 20 years of U.S.-backed and financed Israeli occupation and settlement of Arab lands, the latter after the U.S.-backed Israeli invasion of Lebanon in 1982 and subsequent occupation of the Lebanese south. The silence of Arab governments adds to the rage and contempt the people have for their rulers, and for Israel and the U.S. Yet for all this almost universal disgust that alienates the people from their rulers, the future, glimpsed through the prism of science education, lightens up somewhat for three Gulf states, and this only because of the riches produced by oil. Saudi Arabia, Qatar and Kuwait are investing more of their GDPs into science education. Saudi Arabia leads the way with a $20 billion endowment in the new university being built along its Red Sea coast, King Abdallah University for Science and Technology (KAUST). This gives all the evidence in the world that it is something more than the empty buildings with bombastic names of the 1970s, 1980s and 1990s. The buildings are up, a faculty of several hundred has been hired and an international body of students, graduate and undergraduate, are attending and have been for the past five years. It has a doctoral degree program and boasts to have one of the world's ten super computers. All it takes is money. The rest is up to time's test of perseverence, which up to now has been in short supply in the Arab world's engagement with science. KAUST promises to break that pattern.

To conclude, it is not the lack of Arab, Turkish or Iranian scientific potential or creativity that holds the region back. The science departments of western universities have their share of world class professors and researchers of Middle Eastern origins. Islamdom has produced two Nobel Prize scientists and a Fields Medal winner, all now national heroes in their respective countries of origin. The raw genius waiting to be directed and shaped is there in the minds of the young students. The depressing fact is that this genius has received little help or encouragement in the home countries and universities. In the case of Ahmad Zewail, Egypt commemorated his achievement with a national stamp bearing his image and a street named after him. Former President Mubarak personally honored him and promised to have a research institute built in his honor. In a grand ceremony in Zewail's presence, Mubarak broke ground for the institute, and an existing building was set aside to be its first home at October 6 University (initial day of the 1973 war). But like so many other research institutes and promises for a brighter scientific future, the building was taken back, and a decade later there was still no research institute. The Egyptian state continues to withhold funding, which closely parallels Muhammad Abdus Salam's experience with the Pakistani government over his own proposed research institute.

Lack of legitimate government, confident in itself, secure in its position, honest in its finances, trusting in its citizenry, and not afraid to fund science education and research, is the rock that sinks science in Islamic society. And with it sinks everything else bound to meaningful life.

Until the Arabs see the day that they are ruled by rulers whom they deem legitimate, who are able to dispense with censorship and the wasteful fortifications of the police state, not fearing the people and their creative energies, or the frontiers of mind to which their pursuit of science will take them – until then no modern-day Kindi, Farabi, Haytham, Razi, ibn Sina, Tusi or ibn Rushd will come to brighten the horizon that will end their long night. This goes as well for government in Turkey, Iran and Pakistan. Until the sun rises in the east, the doctorate degrees and groundbreaking research of Middle Eastern Nobel winners will have been done in the West.

But how to be rid of self-perpetuating dynasts who have such powerful sources of support in this symbiotic relationship of despotism and superpower politics? One of the most repeated Quranic references cited by reformers is that God helps those who help themselves. If one thing is certain, the sword that cuts the Gordian Knot of government that strains to hold its people in a state of paralysis will most certainly have to be unsheathed within Muslim society itself. The brave young Egyptians who fought for democracy in Liberation Square during February 2011 may have been pushed aside, but there is hope they will in time come back to represent a viable party more representative of the Egyptian people than Shari'a-minded Islamists with their truncated visions of religion they would impose upon the people or a clique of military men with their terrorizing security police, their mind-numbing use of the media and their own private crony economics cut off from the larger sovereign state.

Notes

1 Egypt produced 670 more scientific papers than did Iran in 2002 (2,500 to 1,830), but a comparison of the rate of increase of papers published per year between 2000 and 2002 was clearly in Iran's favor, 530 to 200. "Middle Eastern Nations Making Their Mark," www.ScienceWatch.com, 2002.
2 *Washington Times*, April 5, 2009, based on a joint study by Harvard University and MIT; and Aneesh Ramen, "Iran in Front When It Comes to Stem Cell Research," November 17, 2006, CNN.com. Ayatallah Ali Khomeini's fatwa was issued in 2002, and ever since then Iran's stem cell research, as well as its research in many other critical fields of science, have been steadily gaining in productivity, as reflected in Iran's 70 journals in specialized scientific fields and its more than tripling of the counry's GDP devoted to science education and research (from 0.2 percent in 1990 to 0.65 percent in 2005, though still considerably below the gdp world average of 1.4 percent). For stem cell study a special facility was established in the northern outskirts of Tehran called the Royan Institute. By 2009 Iran had advanced to be ranked among the top ten countries in stem cell research, joining Sweden, Japan, Britain, the U.S. and several other western countries. The 0.65 percent GDP for 2005 cited earlier parenthetically may be an exaggeration: Thomson Reuters ISI put it at 0.5 percent for 2012: see S. Kharbaf, *Science Growth in Iran*, Thomson Reuters ISI Web of Science, 2012.
3 The two brothers were sentenced to prison, one for three years, the other for six, for plotting with an enemy government to overthrow the state. *Nature*, vols 457, 517 (January 29, 2009), www.nature/news/2009.
4 Not even the democratic and secular 80-year-old Turkish Republic ranked among the 31. Switzerland, with an index of 0.67 (number of highly cited papers divided by per capita GDP), was at the top, followed by Sweden and Israel. The U.S. was in the middle of the pack with a modest index of 0.25, with Iran at the bottom, a wisker below India and China and two below Brazil and South Africa. David A. King, "The Scientific Impact of Nations," *Nature*, vol 430 (July 15, 2004), pp. 311–316.

5 Farzana Aminpour and Payan Kabin, "Science Production in Iran: The Scenario of Iranian Medical Journals," *Journal of Research in Medical Sciences*, vol 14 (September–October, 2009), pp. 313–322.
6 For a scathing commentary by an Egyptian chemistry professor on science research in Egypt: Declan Butler, "Egypt's Researchers Hungry for Reform," *Nature* (online), February 8, 2011. When asked what his assessment was of the Mubarak regime's record in research, Dr. Hassan Azzazy, associate dean for graduate studies and research at the American University in Cairo, had this to say:

> What record? I am not sure that a government that uses plain-clothes police and thugs to crush protests and kill peaceful protestors would even understand what scientific research means. The current outdated government simply lacks the mindset and vision to strategically support scientific research and lead an innovation-based economy that can compete globally. This is manifested by the lack of necessary infrastructure and national policies and mechanisms to support scientific research and provide effective higher education.

When the streets of Cairo filled with protesters in January and February 2011 to bring down the military dictator Husni Mubarak and his corrupt government, Egyptian scientists joined in, hoping for the freedom that creative science needs to breathe and stay alive and thrive. Michael Harms and Quirin Schiermeier, "Deep Fury of Egyptian Scientists," *Nature* (online), February 3, 2011.
7 The Iranian Council of Stem Cell Research (ICSCR) was founded in 2009. See Reza Mansouri, "The History of Science in Iran from a Physicist's Perspective," chapter 1, pp.15–38 in Abdel Soofi and Sepehr Ghazinoory (editors), *Science and Innovation in Iran*, Palgrave and Macmillan, New York, 2013. In 2003, Iran became the tenth country in the world to generate human embryonic stem cell lines, fifth to reprogram human skin cells to embryonic state and third in the world for total bone marrow transplants.
8 Julian Taub, "Science and Sanctions: Nanotechnology in Iran," *Scientific American*, January 13, 2012.
9 Science-Metrix, *Thirty Years in Science: Secular Movements in Knowledge Creation*, Science-Metrix, Montreal, 2010, p. 5; and Deborah MacKenzie, "Iran Showing Fastest Scientific Growth of Any Country," *New Scientist*, February 18, 2010. See also: The Royal Society, *The Atlas of Islamic-World Science and Innovation: A New Golden Age? The Prospects for Science And Innovation in The Islamic World*, London, 2010; and related to this: "Global Research Report: Middle East," Thomson Reuters Web of Science, Clarivate Analysis: Science Watch, online, 2011. And for Iran, Gareth Porter, *Manufactured Crisis: The Untold Story of The Iran Nuclear Scare*, Just Worlds Books, Charlottesville, Virginia, 2014, p. 84.

Index

Abbas I 36–37, 42, 102
Abdallah, Muhammad Mahmud 348
Abdallah Fikri 92–94, 98, 100, 133
Abduh, Muhammad 48, 99, 171, 178, 202, 377, 385, 429; accomplishments of 219–223, 429; at al-Azhar 211–212; challenge to al-Azhar 215, 217–222; Christianity and 228–232; on Comte and natural selection 216; criticisms of religious scholars 212–213; education of 211–212; efforts at reforming Islam 214–219; idealization of Islam 230–231; influence on Rida 240–241, 243, 247; leadership of 371; legacy of 226–249; Mahmud on 354
Abdus Salam, Muhammad 324, 326, 330, 407, 418, 421–423, 433
Abendblatt der Frankfurter Zeitung 163
Abi Adami al-Khaliqah bayn al-Usturah wa'l Haqiqah 355
Academy of Scientific Research and Technology, Egypt 406, 412
Age of Science in Western Civilization 133–134
Ahl al-Quran 386
Ahmad Khan, Sayyid 190–200, 201, 207; influence on Abduh 212; philosophy of *Natcheriyya* 190–191, 198, 199–200, 201; refutation of 201–207
Ahmed, Akbar 332
al-Ahram 42, 226
al-Akhbar 363
Ali, Muhammad 4, 11, 25, 43–44, 52, 60, 67, 101–103, 334, 393–394, 419; death of 36; desire for modern economy and military power 38; restrictions on education 40; schools under 37, 61, 93; slowdown of reforms after death of 37–38

Ali, Muhammad Kurd 253
Aligarh Islamic College 200
Ali Mubarak 52
al-Alousi, Shaykh 106
American College in Beirut 61, 65–67, 74, 101, 125, 128–129; Edwin Lewis and 120–131; Shibli Shumayyil and 151
American evangelicals 115–120
Amin, Qasim 149, 238–240, 253
Annalen der Chemie 316
Antun, Farah 226, 228–233
Aqqad, Abbas 253, 334
Aqwam al-Masalik 198
Arab–Israeli war of 1967 255, 341, 343, 378, 393, 412
Arab Learned Society 63–64
Arab Spring 426
Arif Hikmat, Shaykh al-Islam 17
Aristotle 217, 230
Ash'arite theology 183–184, 188, 217
Asl al-Anwa' 365
al-Athir, ibn 75
Austria 29
Averroes et Averroisme 228
Avrupa Risalesi 7
Awad, Louis 253, 334
Ayyoub, Mahmud 355
al-Azhar 9, 51, 57, 137, 186, 214, 238, 246, 290, 316; Abbas and 37; Abduh and 211–212, 215, 217–222; Ali abd al-Raziq and 371–372; censorship by 291–292, 340, 364; cooperation between Egypt and 382–387; domination of intellectual life in Egypt 44; eventual support for Scientific Interpretation 342; expulsion of al-Raziq 371–372; Fikri at 93–94; founding of 291; Hamdi and 42; influence on *Dar al-Ulum* 46–48; Jawhar at 318; Jisr at

178; Mazhar and 293, 295, 300; modest changes in science courses accepted by 335–336; Muhammad Ali and 46; Munif at 21; Mustafa al-Raziq and 372–373; rejection of Fikri's treatise 99–100; on Taha Husayn 373–375; teachers at 46; Wajdi and 172–173, 276, 280, 282–284, 303, 323
al-Aziz, Sultan abd 22, 25, 27

al-Badraw, Shaykh abd al-Rahman 47
Bahjat al-Matalib fi 'Ilm al-Kawakib 56
Bakar, Osman 330–332
Balkans, the 27, 29
al-Banna, Muhammad 337
al-Baqli, Ali 40
Barbiri, Rizq Allah 115
al-Bashir 163–164, 170
Bashir, Amir 60
Begin, Manachem 387
Beirut 227; American College in 61, 65–67, 74, 101; Arab Learned Society in 63–64; British YMCA in 64; Butrus Bustani and 50, 62–66, 74–78; Cornelius Van Dyck and 62–67, 73, 78; Fransis Marrash and 70–71; Israel's bombing of 380; Jisr in 180; Salim Bustani and 68–75; scientific journals in 65, 68–74; Western schools in 59–63; *see also* Lebanon
Benefits of Philosophy, The 207
Beshiktash Scientific Society 10–11, 21, 22
Bessemer, Henry 141
Bey, Ali Fahmi 51
Bey, Arif Himet 11
Bey, Salih Zaki 34
Bible, the 74–75, 91, 117, 335
Bismarck, Otto von 29, 149
Bliss, Daniel 61, 65–67, 121–124, 127–129, 131; Shumayyil on 151, 159
Bonaparte, Napoleon 41–42, 46, 48, 50, 93, 192, 426
Book of Animals 269
Bosnia and Herzegovina 27, 29
Boyle, Robert 139
Brahe, Tycho 76
Britain 31, 64, 102–103; India and 191–197; Suez Canal and 39–40, 49, 102–103, 140, 191–192
Bruno, Giordano 76
Bucaille, Maurice 343–344
Buchner, Ernst 232, 237, 273; Isfahani on 266–267; Shumayyil on 153–155, 157, 159, 164, 172

Buffon, Georges-Louis Leclerc 23, 142, 144, 145
Bulaq Engineering School 36, 42, 43
Bulaq Muhandishane 41
Bulgaria 29
Bunsen, Robert 316
Bush, George W. 362, 392
Bustani, Butrus 50, 62–66, 74–78, 84, 152, 172, 353; death of 166–167; encyclopedia 114–115, 117, 277; on natural selection 114–115
Bustani, Salim 68–75
Butler, Samuel 271

Cairo University 290, 294–295, 337, 374, 377, 385, 408–409
Catholic Church 81, 123, *376*; French Jesuits and 59–60, 67, 106, 150, 163, 169–171
Cavendish, Henry 137, 139
Chardin, Teilhard de 357
Chiekho, Louis 171, 227, 232–236; critique of Musa 288–289
China 395–396
Chiyomatsu, Ishikawa 397
Christianity: Abduh and 228–232; in Beirut 59–60, 162, 227; Chiekho on 171, 227, 232–236; Coptic 287, 288, 335; promotion of Creationism and Intelligent Design 326; Shumyayyil on 159–160; transfer of Greek knowledge into Arabic 229
Citadel Engineering School 42
Clot Bey (Clot, Antoine Barthelemy) 37, 40–41, 67
Cold War, the 260, 391, 392
Compendium of the Mathematical Sciences 53, 55, 192, 395
Comte, Auguste 216
contemporary Islamic science 389–426
Copernican theory 48, 55–57, 71, *86*, 226, 397
Copernicus 48, 76, 92, 114, 123, 146, 147, 173
Coptic Christians 287, 288, 335
Cosmic Phenomena Through Quranic Signs 348
Creation of Man Between Medical Science and the Quran, The 362
Creation of the Universe Between Science and the Quran 362
Crimean War 17
critical journalism in the Ottoman Empire 22–26
Criticism of Darwin's Philosophy, A 262

Critique of Religious Discourse, A 385
Curie, Marie 81
Cuvier, Georges 142, 143, 144, 145
Cyprus 27

Da 'irat al-Ma'arif 114–115, 117, 277
Dalton, John 134, 139–140
Damiri, Mohammad 269
Dampier, William 137
Dardiri, Ahmad 376
Dar al-Funun 12–13
Dar al-Kutub 45, 94, 264
Dar al-Ulum 45–49, 91, 178, 212, 318, 431; influence of al-Azhar on 46–48; Mohammad Abduh and 218
Darwin, Charles 23, 48, 71, 74, 78, 104–108, 121–122, 126, 226; accepted in the West 133, 134; Ahmad Khan and 190–200; Alfred Russel Wallace and 145–146; American evangelical community and 115–120; earliest mention in Arabic print 114, 148; growth of Arabic journals dedicated exploration of evolution and 226–227; *HMS Beagle* and 141; influence of Lyell on 144–145; opposition to 146, 159, 254–255; reconciled to Islam by Scientific Interpretation 183; research by 141–142; Shumayyil's translation of 154; *see also* evolution and Scientific Interpretation; Intelligent Design; natural selection
Darwinian Theory of Evolution: Fables in the Name of Science, The 362
Darwinische Theorie von der Entstehung und Uberwandlung der Lebenwelt 153
al-Dawla, Asaf 192
Dawran al-Ard 73
Declaration of the Rights of Man 4
de Revolutionibus 146
Descartes, Rene 123
Descent of Man, The 114, 154, 267, 274, 298, 358, 397
al-Din, Khayr 198, 351
al-Din, Salah 177
al-Din al-Afghani, Jamal 13, 171, 221–222, 237, 360; Abduh and 211–212, 228–229; on Mazhar 308; *Refutation of the Materialists* 200–207, 308–309
Din ve Devlet 25
Disraeli, Benjamin 29
Divine Miracle in the Creation of Man: Refutation of Darwin's Theory, The 360
Diwan al-Madaris 45

Dodge, David 66, 121–124, 128, 131
Dreyfus Affair 246
Druze-Maronite massacres 227

Edhem, Khalid 316
Edison, Thomas 134
Efendi, Ahmad Mansur 46
Efendi, Hoja Ishak 7, 94
Efendi, Kamil 10, 11
Egypt 60, 102–103, 243–244, 316, 378, 436; Academy of Scientific Research and Technology 406, 412; acceptance of European models in 291; Ali Mubarak and 11, 36, 41, 43–45; as Arab world's intellectual center 238–239; book censorship in 385; borrowing by 39; Bulaq Engineering School 36, 42, 43; Cairo University in 290, 294–295, 337, 374, 377, 385, 408–409; censorship in mid-20th century 291–292; Copernican theory and 48, 55–57; Coptic Christians in 287, 288, 335; *Dar al-Ulum* 45–49; defeat of Ottomans, 1839 3–4; doctoral education in 404–407; Egyptian Awakening 44, 310; European tourists in 39–40; Geographical Society 41; under Ismail 38–42, 43–44, 49; Jurji Zaydan and 130–131; lack of funding, planning and continuity in scientific cmmunity of 43–44; medicine in 37, 40–41; under Mubarak 387, 406, 415; under Muhammad Ali 4, 11, 25, 36–37, 43–44; under Nasser 259, 335, 363–364, 378, 383–384, 392, 404–405; nationalism in 161; National Research Council 404–405; non-governmental newspaper in 42; relocation of *Muqtataf* to 106–108; under Sadat 378, 383–384, 386–387, 406, 412–413; schools under Muhammad Ali in 39, 41–42, 61, 93; scientific publishing in modern 411; Shumayyi on 156–157; since the 1960s 378–379, 391–392; slowdown in reforms after Muhammad Ali 37–38; ulema 9; Wafd Party 375; Za'bal Medical School 37; *see also Rawdat al-Madaris*
Egyptian National Encyclopedia 172, 277, 280, 282, *376*
Einstein, Albert 135, 137, 214, 324, 357
electricity 137–138
Encyclopedia of Islam, The 322, 339
Enlightenment, the 3, 20
Entwicklungsgeschichte des Menschen 150, 273, 275, 285

Epistles of the Brethren of Purity 269
Esad, Mulla Mehmad 10
Esas-i Ilm-i Heyet Mir'at as-Sima 12
Essay on Population 145
Essential Science Indicators (ESI) 433
Evangelical Weekly 125–126, 163, 227
evolution and Scientific Interpretation: Farghal on 355–358; Khalil and al-Nashawati on 358–368; Mahmud on 353–355; Shahhat on 351–352; Tira on 352–353; *see also* Darwin, Charles; natural selection

Fahim, Ali 94
Fahmi, Ali 52, 53
Falaki, Ishamil 53
Falaki, Mahmud 53
al-Falaki, Ismail Bey 47, 56
al-Falaki, Mahmud Hamdi 42, 56
Fall of Darwin's Theory, in the Light of Modern Scientific Discovery, The 358
Falsafat al-Nushu 'w'al Irtiqa' 294
al-Fandi 346
Faraday, Michael 133, 138
Farghal, Yahya 355–358
Farouk, King 40
Faruq, King 404
Fasl al-Maqal 274–275
Fasl al-Maqal fi Falsafat al-Nushu' wa'l Irtiqa' 274
Fazil, Mustafa 22, 24, 25
Fikri, Abdallah 93, 172–173, 212, 226, 351
Fikri treatise 92–103, 114, 147
Foucault, Jean 136
France: Jesuits 59–60, 67, 106, 150, 163, 169–171; schools set up in Beirut 59–62; during World War I 31
Franklin, Benjamin 137
French Revolution 3; Declaration of the Rights of Man 4
Fresnel, Augustin 135
Fuad 28
Fuda, Farag 384, 386
Future of Culture in Egypt and *Pre-Islamic Poetry, The* 375
Future of Muslim Civilization 331

Galata Saray Lyceum 28, 34
Galileo 71, 76, 104, 123
Galvani, Luigi 133, 152
Gauss, Carl 136
Gay-Lussac, Joseph 140
Germany 31, 324, 328

al-Ghamrawi, Muhammad 345
Ghazal, Tal 355
al-Ghazali, abu Hamd 97, 217, 222, 228, 230, 339, 363
Ghaziri, Mikha 'il 60
Gibb, H. A. R. 376
Glashow, Sheldon 326
Glorious Quran and Modern Science, The 362
God and Man 364
Gokalp, Ziya 30
Graham, Billy 317
Greenpeace 158
Guidance and Instruction in Interpreting the Quran by the Quran 373, 385
Gulen, Fathullah 317

Hadiqat al-Akhbar 64
Hadith 15, 105, 177, 181, 314
Haeckel, Ernst 148, 150, 153, 154, 273, 275, 285
Hakki, Bereketzade Ismail 10
Hakki, Ibrahim 48
Hamas 343, 380, 436
Hamdi, Mahmud 42, 43
al-Hamid, Sultan abd 74
al-Hamid II, Sultan Abd 27, 29–31, 67, 74, 129–130; Jisr and 185–186; Shumayyil on 160–161
al-Haqiqa 157, 262
Hatti Sharif-i Gulhane 4
Hayek, Yusuf 122
Hayy ibn Yaqzan 50, 105
heliocentrism 147; acceptance of 133
Helmholtz, Hermann von 138–139
Herschel, John 136
Hilal, al- 131, 171, 226, 234, 288
Hindus 191–198
Histoire Naturelle 23, 142
Histoire naturelle des animaux san vertebretes 143, 144
History and Philosophy of Islamic Science, The 331
History of Socialist Schools 237
Hitler, Adolf 324
Hitti, Philip 60
Hizb Allah 343, 380, 436
Hoodbhoy, Pervez 326–329, 332
Hourani, Shaykh Ibrahim al- 125–126, 162–163, 167, 169–171
Hungary 254
Hurriyet: Freedom 25
Husayn, Hasan 273–276

Husayn, Taha 253, 257, 292, 334, 385; al-Azhar and 373–375
Huxley, Thomas 118, 146, 154, 263, 322; Japanese study of 397–398

Ibrahim 3–4, 36, 60, 73
'Ilish, Muhammad 214
Ilm al-Din 44
imperialism 429–430
India 191–199
Institut d'Egypte 41–42, 46, 48, 50, 93, 192
Intelligent Design 315, 326, 357; acceptance in Muslim society 173, 349; Hourani and 129; Isfahani on 263; Marrash's dismissal of 71; Mazhar and 298; as opening for Muslims to accept natural selection 147; Rida on 262; Sarruf on 235; translations of books on 195; *see also* natural selection
International Atomic Energy Commission 420
Iqbal, Muhammad 367–368
Iran 343, 378, 382, 392–393; loss of democracy 419–420; opposition to Israel 420; scientific output of 432, 433–435
Iraq 107–108, 260, 380, 392
al-Irfan 264
Isfahani, Abu Majd al- 351; advocacy religious exploration of science 263; on Buchner 266–267; education of 262; extensive critical analysis of natural selection 262, 263–264; on natural selection 263–273; as religious scholar 262–263
Ishak, Hoja 53, 55, 192, 395
Iskandarani, Muhammad ibn Ahmad al- 175–176, 185
Islam and Civilization 282
Islam and Contemporary Scientific Trends 356
Islam and Science: Religious Orthodoxy and the Battle for Rationality 326–327
Islamic science, modern 315–318, 389–426; accomplishments of 327–328; conference publications 327–328; early promoters of 325–328; government spending on 417–418, 432; Islamization of science 323–332; Jawhar and 318–323; place of al-Azhar and the ulema in 371–387; research done in the West 407–408; suffering under bad governments 436–437; *see also* evolution and Scientific Interpretation; Scientific Interpretation; 20th century Muslim society
Islamic Scientific Thought and Contributions of Muslims 327
Islam under Siege 332
Ismail, Khedive 38–44, 74, 92, 101–102, 101–103, 431; *Dar al-Ulum* and 49
Ismail Falaki 46
Israel 254, 255, 261, 341, 343, 362, 378, 387, 392, 414; invasion of Lebanon 423, 436; Iran's opposition to 420; scientific output 418–419; Six-Day War, 1967 255, 341, 343, 378, 393, 412

Jabbara, Gabriel 90–91
Jacquot, Auguste 153
Jamal, Ibrahim Mikh'il 168
Jami'at -i Islam 325–326
Japan 103, 255–256, 395; Fundamental Code 400; Mikado of 68–69, 243, 311; modernization of education in 396–398; Opium War 395–396; social solidarity in 401–402; student missions 398–399; victory over Russia in 1905 389; Yukichi in 399–400
al-Jawahir fi Tafsir al-Quran al-Karim 318
Jawhar, Tantawi 253, 286, 298, 318–323; Scientific Interpretation and 334
Jeha, Shafiq 124
Jessup, Samuel 162
Jesuits, French 59–60, 67, 106, 150, 163; refutation of Shumayyil 169–171
Jevdet 15
Jews/Judaism 227, 324, 390–391; Zionism and 254, 343, 362, 376, 390–391
Jibran, Fransis Augustin 106
Jibran, al-Shammas Fransis Augustin 105–108
Jinan 57, 65, 68–71, 73, 81, 115; Shumayyil's articles in 152
Jisr, Shaykh Husayn al- 171, 190, 227; Ash'arite theology and 183–184, 188; contribution to Scientific Interpretation 177–178; education of 178–179; influence of *Religion and Science* on 182; influence on Abduh 212; success of 185–186
John Paul II, Pope *376*
Jordan 380
Journal of Science, The 22
Journey in Islam 332

444 *Index*

Kashf al-Asrar al-Nuraniyya al-Quraniyya 175
Kashf al-Buhar 57, 70
Kemal, Mustafa 31–32, 254, 288, 336, 378, 390
Kemal, Namik 19, 22–25
Kepler, Johannes 81
Khaldun, ibn 218, 309
Khalil, Mahir 358–368
Khalq al-Insan: Dirasat al-'Ilmiyya al-Quraniyya 352
Khan, Ahmad 190–200, 325–326, 399; Rida's praise for 248
Khedival Observatory 56
Khishin, Aziz 365
al-Khishin, Ahmad Fadil 365
Khitat al-Tawfiqiyya 50
Khomeini, Ayatallah 378, 425
al-Khouri, Khalid 64
Khuli, Amin 253, 339–341
al-Khuli, Amin 339
Kitab al 'Arus al-Badi'a 109
Koan, Ogata 396
Kraft und Stoffe 154, 160
Kuwait 380, 418, 423, 436

al-Lali'al-Saniyya fi Qawa'id al-Kimawiyya 54
Lamarck, Jean-Baptiste 142–144, 145
Lauren, Eisley 158
Lavoisier, Antoine 134, 139
Lebanon 343, 380; Israeli invasion of 423, 436; scientific output of modern 411–412; *see also* Beirut
Le Bible, le Quran et Science 344
Leclerc, Lucien 286, 291
Lectures on the Origin of Species 397
Lewis, Edwin 110, 111, 120–131, 147, 232, 293; Jisr and 180; Sarruf and Nimr on 165–166; Shumayyil and 159, 162–164
Liberation of Women 238–239
Linne, Carl 116, 142
Locke, John 20, 24
Loi Naturelle 12
Louis XIV 60
Lufti, Ahmad 253
Luther, Martin 204
Lyell, Charles 121–123, 144–145

Madrasat al-Funun wa'l Sina'a 41
Madrasat al-Muhandishane 41, 42
Madrasat al-Sultaniyya 179–180, 210
Madrasat al-Wataniyya 178–179
Mahfuz, Nagib 376–378
Mahmud, Mustafa 353–355, 364
Mahmud II, Sultan 3–4, 5, 9, 10–12, 32, 60, 394; absolutist depotism under 17; death of 37
Mahufz, Nagib 386
Majalla 6
Majallat al-Azhar 172, 334
Majdi, Salih 55
al-Majid, Sultan abd 4, 14
Malqat al-Sabil 286, 356
Malthus, Thomas 145
Manar 241–249, 256, 262
al-Manar 227
Mansur, Ahmad 54, 56
Mansur, ibn abi Amir al- 424
Marcus, Margaret 325
Maronites 59–61
Marrash, Fransis 70–71, 73, 182
Marsafi, Shaykh 178, 212
al-Marsafi, Shaykh Husayn 47
Marvels of Creation 75
Marx, Karl 158
Mashriq 227, 233–234
Masir-i Talib fi Biladi-i Afranji 192
materialism 353; Barbiri on 115; Muslim acceptance of 229, 234; Sarruf on 237–238; Shumayyil on 119, 150, 152, 157, 161–163, 202, 226–227, 253, 287; Syrian Christians on 148; Western understanding of 134, 155; Zilzal's progressive 150
Mawdudi, abu'l ala 325–326
Maxwell, James 135, 138
Mazhar, Ismail 154, 171, 227, 253, 254, 286, 293–311, 334, 353, 423; as chief editor of *Muqtataf* 301, 303; education of 293–295; on essence of religion 307–308; frustration at lack of progress in Arab world 310–311; journals founded by 294, 295–297; lack of recognition for 301–302; on need for Muslim acceptance of evolution 297–298, 303–305; opposition to 298–300; on Shumayyil 307; *Theory of Evolution at the Crossroads* as most significant work of 306; translation of *Origin of Species* 285, 293, 298, 302, 366, 397; on Western religious fanatics 291, 308–309
Mebahis-i Ilmiyye 33–34

Mejmua-i Funun 26
Melange d'institut Dominicaine des etudes Orientale 286
Michelson, A. A. 135
Midhat Pasha 185–186
Mikado of Japan 68–69, 243, 311
Mirzakhani, Maryam 433
Missionary Herald 60
Monod, Jacques 158
Montenegro 27
Montesquieu 24
Morley, Edward 135
Morse, Edward 397–398
Morse, Samuel 14
Mubarak, Ali 11, 36, 41, 43–45, 92, 94, 103, 178; *Dar al-Ulum* and 45–49, 318, 431; influence on Abduh 212; *Rawdat al-Madaris* and 45, 50–55
Mubarak, Husni 387, 406, 415, 436
Muhammad 385
Muhbir 24, 25, 26
al-Muhit 65
Munif 21–22
Muqaddima 212, 218
al-Muqattam 226
Muqtataf 57, 74, 79–92, 100–101, 162–166, 262; Abduh and 212, 233–235; American evangelicals and 115–120; articles on Darwin in 104–108; boldness of 168–169, 171; commercial and intellectual success of 79, 226; Cornelius Van Dyk and 79–80; Darwin's ideas featured in 114, 148; Edwin Lewis in 126; Fikri treatise and 92–103; first astronomical article 81, *82–83*; influence on Jurji Zaydan 108–111; on Japan's success 243, 255–256, 401; Mazhar as chief editor of 301, 303; protest letters to 84, 90–91; relocation to Egypt 106–108, 167; Rida on 241; Sarruf's response to critics of 87, 90; on Shibli Shumayyil 164–165; unity of science and religion in 80–81
Murad V, Sultan 27, 30
Musa, Salama 171, 172, 226, 253, 254, 285–292, 334; Sarruf and 289
Musharrafa, Mustafa 295
Muslim Brotherhood 325, 378, 382, 435
Muslim society: Abduh's efforts to reform 214–219; acceptance of Intelligent Design in 173, 349; Afghani as deceptive reformer of 200–207; Amin's criticisms of 238–240; anti-Darwinism in 254–255; Arab contribution to scientific renaissance in 204–205; Arab Spring and 426; Ash'arite theology and 183–184, 188, 217; crushing military budgets of countries in 403; cultural assimilation of western ideas in 191; desire for political leadership to defend against the West 210–211; dialogue of 253–254; early 20th century 253–261; government inactivity towards reform in 257–259; Husayn on 273–276; increasing diversity in Arab countries and 401–402; in India 191–198; Isfahani on 262–273; Islamic science in the early 20th century 314–318; Islamization of science in 323–332; major influencers in 253; Mazhar on 293–311; medieval decline attributed to natural selection 239; Musa on 285–292; nationalism and 254–255; natural law 213–214; political Islam and 425–426, 431; post-World War I 253–260; post-World War II 260–261; public health in 424–425; as revolution against paganism 212–213; Rida's criticisms of 240–249; Sarruf's writings on state of 256–257; science during height of power of 266; secularist 238, 244–245, 253, 290; secular nationalist intelligentsia in 260; Shari'a law 6, 16, 18–19, 28, 53, 99, 168, 180–181; slow and eventual acceptance of evolution 172–173, 187, 297–298, 376–377; socialism and 161, 227; unique culture different from the West 429; Wadji on dearth of scientific interest and activity in 277–279; Wajdi on 276–285; Zilzal's criticisms of 148–150; *see also* Islamic science, modern; Quran, the
Mustafa, Ibrahim 43
Mustafa, Ismail 42
Mustafa Rashid 11, 12–13
al-Mustaqbal 153
Muteferrika, Ibrahim 395

al-Nabi, Mansur 345–346
Naddah, Ahmad 53
Nahda 431
Najib, Ahmad 55
Najjar, Zaghloul 362
Nashawati, Nabil al- 358–368
Nashrat al-Usbu'iyyah 125, 163–164
Nasr, Sayyid Hossein 329–332

Nasser, Gamal abd al- 259, 335, 363–364, 378, 383–384, 392, 404–405; arms deal with the Soviet Union 420
Natcheriyya 190–191, 198, 199–200, 201, 206, 325
nationalism: after World War I 254–255, 258–259; after World War II 260–261; in contemporary Arab countries 414; in Egypt 161; in Europe 27; Scientific Interpretation and 177; in Turkey 290, 390; Turkish 223; Young Ottomans advocacy of 30–32; Zaydan and 131
National Research Council 404–405
National Science Foundation 434
natural law 213–214
natural selection 108; Abduh on 210–223; acceptance in the European scientific community 172; Amin on 239; Bustani on 114–115; Chieckho on 233–236; al-Din on 190, 200–207, 237; Hourani on 126; Husayn on 273–276; Isfahani on 263–273; Jisr on 185; al-Jisr on 176–188; Mazhar on Arab acceptance of 297–298, 303–305; Musa on 285–292; principle of new species as result of chance 271; Sarruf and Nimr's promotion of 120, 122, 169–171, 235; Shumayyil and 118–119, 150–157, 201; Syrian Christians and 147–148; Wajdi on 280–281; William Van Dyck on 124; Zaydan on 172; *see also* Darwin, Charles; Intelligent Design
Natural Theology 71
Nature's Testimony to the Existence of God and Divine Law 70
Netanyahu, Benjamin 434
Newton, Isaac 56, 71, 81, 84, 121, 134–136, 139, 192
Nicolas of Cusa 76
Nimr, Faris 57, 64, 67, 81, 87, 104, 117, 130, 226; Shibli Shumayyil and 164–165
Nizam-i Jadid 192
Nobel Prize 323, 326, 329, 433, 436
Nubar 36
Nursi, Sa'id 222–223, 337
Nushrat al-Usbu 'iyyah 163

Oktar, Adnan 368
On the Characteristics of Numbers 50
On the Orgranization of Egypt's Nile 50
On the Origins of Scientific Thought 298
Operation Cast Lead 380
Operation Desert Shield 380

Organization of Scientific Miracles 348
Origin of Man and Existence: A Refutation of the Philosophy of Evolution and Response to Dr. Shibli Shumayyil, The 169
Origin of Species 23, 108, 114–115, 117, 146, 148, 153; Husayn's translation of 273–275; Khisin's translation of 365; Mazhar's translation of 285, 293, 298, 302, 366, 397; Shumayyil's translation of 154, 226
Ottoman Empire, the 60; Ali Suvai and 15–21, 27–28, 30; Beshiktash Scientific Society 10–11, 21, 22; borrowing by 26–27; collapse of 254, 390; Committee of Union and Progress 31; critical journalism in 22–26; *Dar al-Funun* 12–13; *Hatti Sharif-i Gulhane* 4; Hoja Tashin influence on science and education in 11–14; loss of social solidarity in 401–402; loss of territory 28–29, 29–30; Munif as philosopher of 21–22; Mustafa Sami and Sadik Rifat as reform leaders in 7–9, 12; nationalism in 30–31; religious scholars as advocates of reform in 9–11; Rose Chamber Proclamation 4; secularization of education in secondary schools 14; under Sultan Mahmud II 3–4, 9, 10–12, 17, 32, 37; *Tanzimat* program reforms 4–6, 9, 11, 12, 14, 16–21, 84, 390, 431; Tulip Period 3, 21, 32, 254, 393–394, 395, 420; views on Western science and museums 7–8, 430–431; World War I and 31–32; Young Ottoman Society 6–8, 11, 16–21, 22, 30–31
Ottoman Scientific Society 22

Pakistan 327–328, 367, 407–408; atomic weapons 420; scientific output 421
Palace of Desire 377
Palestine 254, 260–261, 343, 362, 380, 387, 414–415
Paley, William 71
Paths of Renewal in Language, Grammar and Quran Interpretation, The 339
Philosophie anatomique 144
Physical Review, The 409
Plato 217
political Islam 425–426, 431
Pratt, John 198
Precise Truth Concerning the Rejection of Darwin, The 167
Priestly, Joseph 137, 139

Principles of Geology 144, 145
Ptolemy 92, 97
public health 424–425

Qabbani, abd al-Qadir 179
Qatar 418, 436
Qazwini 75
Qubain, Fahim 407
Quran, the 95–97, 105, 255; Ahmad Khan and 198–199; Beirut and 75; Bucaille on divine origin of 343–344; on creation of humans 184–185, 351–352; Egypt and 31, 32, 45, 48; encouragement of science 314, 332; Islamization of science and 323–332; Jisr's interepretations of 182–183, 186–187; as liberating for man 212–213; Mohammad Abduh and 214–219; as moral, spiritual and legal guide 213–214; Ottomans and 15, 24; science contained in (*see* Scientific Interpretation); on space exploration 337–339, 346–348; *see also* evolution and Scientific Interpretation; Islam
al-Quran wa'l Ulum al-'Asriyya 318

Rawdat al-Madaris 45, 50–56, 68, 70, 91–92, 106, 178, 264; as academic journal 79; Fikri treatise 92–103; Fikri treatise and 92–103; influence on Abduh 212; on the Solar System 84; *see also* Egypt
al-Raziq, Ali abd 253, 291–292, 371–372, 385
al-Raziq, Mustafa 372–373
Reagan, Ronald 423
Recent Truths on the Description of the Seas 50
Refutation of the Materialists 201–207, 308–309
Religion and Science 182
Reminiscences 67
Renan, Ernest 203–205, 228
Rida, Rashid 171–172, 173, 179, 253, 349, 351; Abduh and 215–216, 221, 232, 243, 247; estimation of the time needed to modernize 242–243; on Intelligent Design 262; Jawhar and 320; *al-Manar* 227; opposition to Mazhar 298, 299; praise for Ahmad Khan 248; on al-Raziq 373; reformist ideas of 240–249; Scientific Interpretation and 334; study of Japan's MIkado 243, 311, 389
Riddle of Life, The 353

Riemann, George 136
Rifat, Sadik 8–9, 12
Risalat al-Hamidiyya 177, 181–182, 185, 190
Risalat al-Nur 223
Risalat al-Tawhid 210
Riyad 92
Rodinson, Maxime 385
Roemer, Ole 87, *88*
Romania 29
Rose Chamber Proclamation 4
Rousseau, Jean-Jacques 24
Rushd, ibn 228, 230
Rushdie, Salman 378
Russia 27, 29–30, 31, 222, 389

Sa'ati, Ahmad 163
Sadat, Answar 378, 383–384, 386–387, 406
Sadik, Rifat 37
Sa'id 37, 42, 102
Sa'id, Ahmad Efendi Khayri 296–297
Salhat, Yusuf 236
Sam'ani, Yusuf 59–60
Sami, Amin 43, 50
Sami, Mustafa 7–9, 37
Sardar, Ziauddin 331–332
Sarruf, Ya'qub 57, 64, 67, 81, 84, 87–88, 104, 117, 226; boldness of writings by 168–169; Jurji Zaydan and 109; Musa and 289; on the Muslim world after World War I 256–257; promoted by SPC 130; rejection of Shumayyil's ideas during World War I 276; Shibli Shumayyil and 164–165
Satanic Verses 378
Saudi Arabia 380, 418, 436
al-Sayyid, Mikhail abd 54
Sayyid al-Makhluqat 105
Science-Metrix 434
Science of Inheritance, The 365
Science of Religion, The 50, 92
Sciences and Religion, The 108
Scientific Interpretation 175–188, 318, 334–349, 381; contemporary interpretations of 344–345; continuance into the last decades of the 20th century 341–342; Darwin's theory and 183; debate over 334–335; evolution and 351–368; giving relevance to the Quran 177; Islamization of science and 323–332; Jisr and 177–178, 181; objectives of 176–177; proliferation of

336–337; Wajdi on 277–278, 284–285; see also Islamic science, modern
Scientific Miracle in the Quran 362
Scientific Revolution 134
Scopes, John T. 291
Scripture and Science Not at Variance 198–199
secular nationalism *see* nationalism
Self Help 151
Selfish Gene, The 368
Selim III 32, 394, 426
Sepoy Rebellion 201, 203
Serbia 27
sexual selection 271
Sfair al-Maruni, Jirjis Faraj 169–170
al-Sha'b 294
Shahhat, Ali 351–352
Shahin, 'abd al-Sabur 355
al-Shahrastani, Hibbat al-Din 108
Shakwa wa Amal 160
Shams al-Barr 64
Shanizade 10–11, 37
Sharh Buchner 'ala Madhhab Darwin 153
al-Shifa 153
Shinasi 22–25
Shuji, Izawa 397
Shumayyil, Shibli 118–119, 286–287, 334, 351; books by 153–157; contributions to socialist ideas in the Arab world 161; education of 147–148, 150–152; on Egypt's youth and Arabic society 156–157, 167; on evolution of man and civilization 158–159; on God and Christianity 159–160; Ibrahim Hourani and 162–163; influence on Abduh 212, 232–233; interest in philosophical materialism 150–151, 152–153, 161, 235; Jesuit refutation of 169–171, 235–237; journals founded by 153; on materialism 119, 150, 152, 157, 161–163, 202, 226–227, 253, 287; Mazhar on 307; on opposition to Darwin 159; on origins of life 155–158; refutations of 163–164, 169–171; translation of *Origin of Species* 154, 226; views on women 161–162
Six-Day War, 1967 255, 341, 343, 378, 393, 412
Smiles, Samuel 151
Smith, Eli 60–61, 63, 67
socialism 161, 227
Sources of Exegesis 199
South Korea 434

space exploration 337–339, 346–348
Spencer, Herbert 148, 237, 263, 397–398
Sputnik 338
St. Hilaire, Etienne Geofrey St. 142, 143–144, 145
Suavi, Ali 15–21, 22, 24, 27, 37; critical writings by 24–25; nationalism of 30; petition to return from Paris 27–28; writings from London and Paris 25–26
Suez Canal 39–40, 49, 102–103, 140, 191–192
Sufism 217
Syria 36, 70, 74, 90, 343; Christians and materialism 148; Christians and natural selection 147–148; post-World War II 260
Syrian Bugle, The 64
Syrian Protestant College 61, 62, 67, 109, 125–128, 147, 148, 178; Shumayyil at 150–152
Systema Naturae 142

Tabyin al-Kalam 199
Tadao, Shizuko 395
Tahir 33
Tahsin, Hoja 37
Tahtawi, Shaykh 7–8, 37, 44, 45, 56, 70, 93, 99; influence on Abduh 212, 213; influence on Zaydan 172; Marsafi and 178; *Rawdat al-Madaris* and 51–53
Talib Khan, Abu 192–193
Tamhid li-Tarikh al-Falsafat al-Islamiyya 372
Tanwir al Adhhan fi 'Ilm Hayat al-Hayawan wa'l Insan wa Tafawut al-Umam fi Madaniyya wa'l Umran 148
Tanzimat program 4–6, 9, 11, 12, 34, 37, 84, 390, 431; borrowing for 26–27; critical journalism under 23–26; Jisr and 180–181; secularization of secondary schools under 14; Young Ottomans and 16–21
Taqwim al-Nil 42, 50
Tashin, Hoja 11–14, 26
Tasvir-i Efkar 23
al-Tawil, Hasan 48
Theory of Evolution at the Crossroads 306
Theory of Evolution Between Science and Religion, The 351
Theory of Evolution in Animals, The 397
theory of the ether 135
Thomson International Science Indicators (ISI) 432

Thomson Reuters Web of Knowledge 434, 435
Tira, Muhammad 352–353
Today and Tomorrow 288, 291
Treatise on Divine Oneness 212, 215, 223, 243, 377
Treatise on Light 223, 337
Treaty of Berlin 29
Treaty of Versailles 29
Truth About the Neichari Sect and an Explanation of the Neicharis, The 201
Tuhfa al-Aja'ib 75
Tulip Period 3, 21, 32, 254, 393–394, 395, 420
Turkey 368, 378; attempts to close the technology gap 420; under Kemal 31–32, 254, 288, 336, 378, 390; post-World War I 254, 258–259, 288; scientific output in modern 413–414, 435; secularism in 290, 317; *see also* Ottoman Empire, the 20th century Muslim society: anti-Darwinism in 254–255; dialogue of 253–254; government inactivity towards reform in 257–259; Husayn on 273–276; Isfahani on 262–273; Islamization of science in 323–332; major influencers in 253; Mazhar on 293–311; Musa on 285–292; post-World War I 253–260; post-World War II 260–261; Sarruf's writings on state of 256–257; secular nationalist intelligentsia in 260; Wajdi on 276–285; *see also* Islamic science, modern
Tyndall, John 118

ulema 9, 17, 176, 216, 218; early 20th century 254
Ulum Gazetisi, Journal of The Sciences 26
uniformitarianism 145
United States, the 291, 326, 343, 362–363, 414; Operation Desert Shield 380
Urabi, Ahmad 102, 180
al-Usbu 'iyyah 162
Useful Knowledge 15
Usul 'Ilm al-Hay'a 73
al-'Usur 295–297, 300–301

Van Dyck, Cornelius 50, 62–68, 73, 78, 178; Edwin Lewis and 120, 124–129; *Muqtataf* and 79–80, 166
Van Dyck, William 78, 124, 126–129, 131, 162, 166

Vidinli Husayn Tawfik 33
Vie de Jesus 228
Voyage Through Time, A 409

Wadi al-Nil 91, 98
Wafd Party 375
Wahhabism 198
Wajdi, Muhammad Farid 171, 172, 173, 253, 276–285, 349, 376; al-Azhar and 172–173, 276, 280, 282–284, 303, 323; on the end of the earth 279–280; Jawhar and 323; opposition to Mazhar 299–300; on Scientific Interpretation 277–278, 284–285; Scientific Interpretation and 334; writing for al-Azhar 282–283
Wallace, Alfred Russel 145–146, 263
Waqa'i al-Misriyya 219–220
al-Wataniyya 64
Weinberg, Steven 326
Weizmann, Chaim 391
Weizmann Institute 419
West, the: acceptance of natural selection in 172; Age of Science in 133–146; Copernican theory and 48, 55–57; early 20th century Muslim society and 253–254; imperialism of 429–430; Intelligent Design promotion in 326; opposition to evolution in 291; Ottoman recognition of relationship between science and advance in civilization and power of 7–8, 430–431; Rida's criticisms of Muslim rule by 240–249; Scientific Revolution 134, 137; tourists in Egypt from 39–40; understanding of materialism in 134, 155
Wilburforce, Samuel 146
al-Wiratha 365
With God in the Sky 362
With the Quran in the Cosmos 346
World Bank Development Indicators 418
World Health Organization 424–425
World War I 31–32, 62, 105, 108, 237, 238, 249, 376; nationalism after 254, 258–259
World War II 260, 365, 376

al-Yawm wa'l Mustaqbal 286
Yaziji, Ibrahim 64, 67
Yaziji, Nasif 64
al-Yaziji, Shaykh Nasif *85*
Yemen 261, 392
Young, Thomas 135

Young Ottoman Society 6–8, 11, 16, 37; Ali Suavi and 16–21, 24; critical journalism 22–26; World War I and 31–32
Yukichi, Fukuzawa 399–400
Yusuf, Ali Sayyid 256
Yusu' al-Tibb 40–41

Za'bal Medical School 37, 40
Zahlan, Antoine 403–404, 419, 424
Zahra, abu 337
Zanni, Joseph 316
Zayd, Muhammad abu 373, 385–386
Zaydan, Jurji 67, 108–111, 127–128, 130–131, 151, 171–172, 226
Ziadeh, May 158, 161–162
Zilzal, Bishara 116–117, 148–150, 154, 262
Zionism 254, 343, 362, 376, 390–391
Ziya 19, 22, 24–25
Zewail, Ahmad 329, 332, 407, 409–411, 433, 436